THE PENGUIN CLASSICS BOOK

UK | USA | Canada | Ireland | Australia
India | New Zealand | South Africa

Penguin Books is part of the Penguin Random
House group of companies whose addresses can
be found at global.penguinrandomhouse.com.

First published by Particular Books 2018
003

Book design by Matthew Young
with help from Francisca Monteiro, Theo Inglis,
Claire Mason, Richard Marston, Richard Carr,
Mónica Oliveira, Tom Etherington and Mathieu Triay

Set in Baskerville 10, Mr Eaves and Futura EF
Printed and bound in Italy by Printer Trento Srl

A CIP catalogue record for this book is available
from the British Library

ISBN: 978-0-241-32085-3

THE
PENGUIN
CLASSICS
BOOK

HENRY ELIOT

Henry Eliot is one of the editors of the Penguin Classics series. Before joining Penguin he organized various literary tours, including a mass public pilgrimage for the National Trust (inspired by William Morris, p.226), a recreation of Chaucer's *Canterbury Tales* (p.89) which raised money for the National Literacy Trust, a Lake Poets (p.191) tour of Cumbria and a quest for the Holy Grail based on Malory's *Morte D'Arthur* (p.90). He is the author of *Follow This Thread* and *Curiocity* (with Matt Lloyd-Rose).

THE PENGUIN CLASSICS

A series of
new translations for a new generation,
edited by E. V. Rieu

It is the design of this Library to provide
English-speaking readers with new versions
of the finest and most enduring of the foreign
classics, ancient, medieval and modern. It
was felt that many opportunities for enjoy-
ment were denied to those unfamiliar with
the languages concerned, by the stilted, old-
fashioned and otherwise un-English style
which has too often been adopted by translators. The work was therefore entrusted in
each case to a practised writer who could be
relied on both to satisfy his fellow-scholars
and to present the original in a palatable form.
The great success of the first volumes has fully
justified the enterprise.

*

Contents

Preface

Samuel Taylor Coleridge (p.195) was said
to have been the last person to have read
everything. Nowadays most of us need to be
more selective. The 500 authors in this volume
span 4,000 years of literary history, and their
1,200 books comprise over 500,000 pages of
text. That means that if you found time to read
50 pages a day, every day of the week, it would
take you 27 years to read them all, by which
time the list would most likely have expanded
further still.

This book is intended as a reader's
companion to the best books ever written. It is
a book of suggestions and recommendations,
drawing connections across the history of
world literature, which will hopefully reac-
quaint you with old friends, introduce you to
new titles and suggest ways to map your future
reading. It is also a celebration of an abiding
series of books, which began more than
seventy years ago and has grown incrementally
and idiosyncratically ever since.

Geographically and chronologically the
Penguin Classics form the largest library of
classic literature in the world today, and more
titles join the list every year. In the 1950s, the
editors were concerned they would run out:
'How many more titles in the classical literature of the world are there?' asked Penguin
editor-in-chief William Emrys Williams appre-
hensively, after 60 Penguin Classics had been

published. He needn't have worried. As times have changed, so has this extraordinary list: the definition of 'classic' evolves and expands to embrace new languages, formats and audiences. The titles in this volume do share three key qualities — literary merit, historical significance and an enduring reputation — but within those elastic parameters scholars are adopting new areas of study, translators are broadening their interests and the 'general reader' remains hungry for new books, so the list continues to expand.

This flourishing is not always even-handed, however. A quick flick will demonstrate what a partial list it still is in places: there's a preponderance of 19th-century British fiction (p.190), for example, and many great works of Latin American (p.432), Swedish (p.365) and Japanese (p.389) literature are still missing. Also, only an eighth of the authors in this book are women, which may be because historically fewer women have written works of literature, but is more probably because many works of women's literature have been undeservedly overlooked. Publishing Penguin Classics has always been, and will continue to be, a Sisyphean task of identifying blind spots and filling the gaps.

> A classic [...] survives because it is a
> source of pleasure and because the
> passionate few can no more neglect it
> than the bee can neglect the flower.
>
> ARNOLD BENNETT (p.280)

This volume covers the history of literature from its origins in Mesopotamia to the end of the First World War (p.433), and beyond in a few places. The main body of this book includes every pre-1919 Penguin Classic title that is in print and available at the time of going to press, whereas 'The Vaults' (p.440) display a selection of Classics that have dropped out of the series over the last seven decades. Authors' works are collected together, and where applicable they are all placed within the genre for which that author is best known. Each title is illustrated by its first Penguin cover. Parallel and previous Penguin Classics editions are also listed, and red dots indicate those that are out-of-print. These historical covers visualize the incremental way in which the list has accreted over time, like coral: it is the collective work of generations of editors, translators, typesetters, designers and picture researchers, all of whom have expressed preferences, eccentricities and enthusiasms to shape this living reef of world literature.

In his essay 'On Books', Montaigne (p.126) declares that all he seeks from his library is

> to give myself pleasure by an honourable pastime: or if I do study, I seek only that branch of learning which deals with knowing myself and which teaches me how to live and die well.

I hope this book brings you some of that same pleasure and introduces you to many more years of living well with the best books in the world.

Henry Eliot
Editor, Penguin Classics
2018

The Penguin Classics

Peter and Percival lived in a place
Where the cold is too bitter for People to face,
But Peter and Percival both had contrived
To be Penguins, not People – and so they survived.

On chilly nights, amidst the wail of air raid sirens and the whine of doodlebugs, a man stood on the roof of Birkbeck College in central London, scanning the skyline for fires. Emile Victor Rieu (17) passed the time on these long, lonely shifts translating and re-translating Homer's *Odyssey* (17): 'I went back to Homer,' he recalled, 'the supreme realist, [...] by way of escape from the unrealities that surrounded us.'

Towards the end of the Second World War, with his wife's encouragement, Rieu submitted his translation to Allen Lane, the founder of Penguin Books. It was not a promising proposal on the face of it: eight versions of the *Odyssey* had been published between the wars, including five new translations, of which only two had sold more than 3,000 copies. Moreover, Rieu was not an established academic. He was a retired publisher of educational textbooks; his one previous publication was a 1932 collection of whimsical children's verse called *Cuckoo Calling*. In a characteristically impulsive and ultimately shrewd move, however, Lane not only accepted Rieu's translation of the *Odyssey*, he appointed him general editor of a new Penguin series, a 'Translation Series from the Greek, Roman and other classics'.

'Something important has happened,' reported *Reynolds' News* in January 1946. '[...] There is a new translation of *The Odyssey*, a very contemporary translation, and it costs only one shilling. This is revolutionary.' Rieu's *Odyssey* sold over three million copies. In fact, it was the bestselling of all Penguin books until it was finally overtaken by *Lady Chatterley's Lover* (291) in 1960. 'The King is already familiar with your admirable translation of *The Odyssey*,' read a treasured note from Buckingham Palace, 'and looks forward to reading *The Iliad* (16).'

HOMER

THE
ODYSSEY

A NEW TRANSLATION BY
E. V. RIEU

1946
trans. E. V. Rieu
(see p.17)

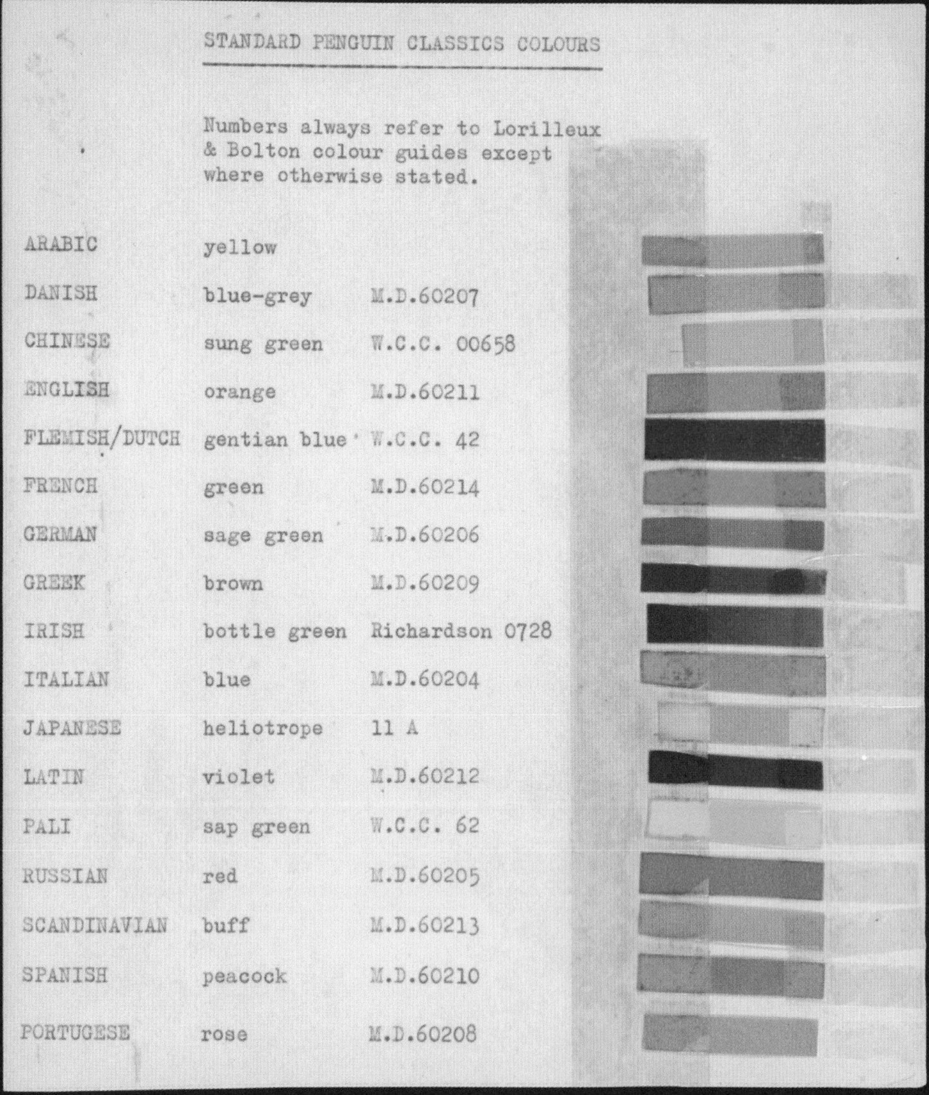

STANDARD PENGUIN CLASSICS COLOURS

Numbers always refer to Lorilleux
& Bolton colour guides except
where otherwise stated.

ARABIC	yellow	
DANISH	blue-grey	M.D.60207
CHINESE	sung green	W.C.C. 00658
ENGLISH	orange	M.D.60211
FLEMISH/DUTCH	gentian blue	W.C.C. 42
FRENCH	green	M.D.60214
GERMAN	sage green	M.D.60206
GREEK	brown	M.D.60209
IRISH	bottle green	Richardson 0728
ITALIAN	blue	M.D.60204
JAPANESE	heliotrope	11 A
LATIN	violet	M.D.60212
PALI	sap green	W.C.C. 62
RUSSIAN	red	M.D.60205
SCANDINAVIAN	buff	M.D.60213
SPANISH	peacock	M.D.60210
PORTUGESE	rose	M.D.60208

The first Classics colour palette,
applied between 1946 and 1963.

John Overton designed the first Penguin Classics covers, which each featured a unique, illustrative 'roundel'. Overton chose Eric Gill's typeface Perpetua, named after the Christian martyr Vibia Perpetua (62), who was attacked by a ferocious cow before being beheaded. The covers were colour-coded according to language: brown for Greek, green for French, violet for Latin, and so on. In 1949, after seven titles, the German-Swiss designer Jan Tschichold made some refinements to Overton's grid and then the design remained unchanged for sixteen years.

E. V. Rieu had a meeting with Allen Lane every few months, but otherwise operated from his home in Highgate, with complete editorial independence, commissioning translators, issuing contracts and fixing royalties as he saw fit. His vision for Penguin Classics was to present 'the general reader with readable and attractive versions of the great writers' books in modern English, shorn of the unnecessary difficulties and erudition, the archaic flavour and the foreign idiom that renders so many existing translations repellent to modern taste'. The second title in the series was H. N. P. Sloman's translation of Maupassant's *Boule de Suif and Other Stories* (318); the third was *The Theban Plays* (21) by Sophocles, translated by E. F. Watling.

'There are three prerequisites for a good translation,' Rieu believed: 'I give them in order of importance. The translator must know his own language; he must fall in love with his work; and he must understand the language of the original.' He began by inviting academics to submit translations for the series, but quickly found many of them unable to write good English; he preferred to commission professional writers and novelists, such as Robert Graves (439), Rex Warner (32) and Dorothy L. Sayers (85). He developed what he called 'the lodestar of the translator's art', his principle of 'equivalent effect': a translator should aim to provide his or her readers with the same *experience* that the work's contemporary readers enjoyed.

In 1946, the schoolteacher and Russophile J. M. Cohen (154) was commissioned to translate *Don Quixote* (153) and on the strength of his translation he was invited to assist in overseeing the modern-language classics, a task he performed from 1950 until 1964, making several further translations himself.

'This extensive and increasing library of Penguin Classics is, by common consent, the best of its kind in English,' declared William Emrys Williams in 1956.

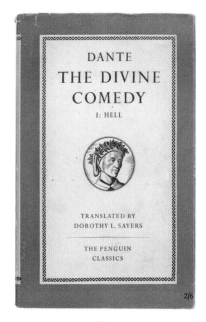

1949
trans. Dorothy L. Sayers
(see p.84)
—
Sayers's translation of Dante's *Inferno* was the first Penguin Classic to be published with Jan Tschichold's revised cover template.

Now Perce was a poet, a moulder of metre,
While prose was the medium chosen by Peter;
Yet Peter delighted in Percival's verse
And the prose of his Pete was as music to Perce.

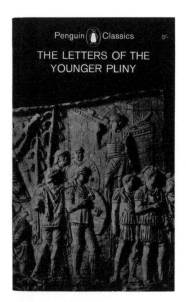

1963
trans. Betty Radice
(see p.51)
—
Radice's translation was one of five
Penguin Classics published in May
1963, the first to have covers designed
by Germano Facetti.

1987 Penguin Books
● ed. William Radice & Barbara
Reynolds
—
When she died in 1985, Radice had
stewarded the series for 21 years,
editing 150 titles. Her son William
and Barbara Reynolds co-edited
this commemorative collection of
essays in her honour.

Betty Radice (51), a classics tutor, had submitted a proposal to Rieu for an edition of the letters of Pliny the Younger (51). Rieu accepted and, as she was a neighbour in Highgate, they developed a warm friendship over morning coffee. Their relationship was formalized in 1959 when Rieu invited Radice to become the assistant editor of Penguin Classics.

But Penguin was changing. In 1960, maverick bookseller Tony Godwin became the fiction editor, later editor-in-chief, and he and Rieu immediately fell out. Radice found herself struggling to keep the peace between 'the Edwardian old fogey' and 'the half educated young upstart' as they termed each other. When Godwin made the executive decision to redesign Penguin Classics, Rieu was incensed. He wrote to Allen Lane: 'I find it hard to believe that you would allow a newcomer to the firm, without discussion with me, its editor, to mutilate a series that you and I had created in 1944 and have since made world famous.'

The Italian designer Germano Facetti was commissioned to overhaul the covers in 1963. He introduced uniform black spines and photographed artworks. 'In designing for the Classics,' he wrote, 'it was assumed that the majority of the great works of literature have inspired works of art, or that works of art have been created with a bearing to literature.' Artworks were selected to be roughly contemporary with each text, a policy that continues today.

The redesign precipitated Rieu's retirement the following year, at the age of 77. When he left, there were over 130 Penguin Classics titles on the list, selling nearly a million copies a year, translated from Greek, Latin, French, Russian, Italian, Spanish, Arabic, Pali, Sanskrit and Chinese. Radice succeeded him as the editor, initially splitting the role with Robert Baldick (320) and then C. A. Jones.

Radice had to adapt to an evolving audience: increasingly the books were being used by students and teachers, especially in the United States. She needed to produce volumes that were both appealing to the general reader and sufficiently scholarly for the academic market. It was a tricky balance to strike, and it laid the series open to criticism from academics on one side and aesthetes on the other. 'I can't please everyone,' she wrote in 1984, 'and sometimes wonder if I may end up by pleasing nobody but myself.' Her major innovations were to begin commissioning verse translations, overturning Rieu's rigid preference for prose, and to introduce indexes, notes and bibliographies for the first time.

In 1985, control of the series was brought in-house, and the list absorbed the Penguin English Library and several other series (xvi). Penguin Classics was no longer a 'translation series': it had become the most comprehensive library of world literature available from any paperback publisher. To mark the event, a third design was launched in August 1985. Steve Kent, the new art director, retained the now famous black spines but added a small colour-coded band: red for British and American works, yellow for European, purple for classical and green for Asian. The front cover featured a cream border and a black text panel, with centred white text. The typeface, Sabon, was a reference to Penguin's design history as it had been created by Jan Tschichold (xiii). Penguin Classics has had one major redesign since, in 2003: now the image fills the space above a black text panel, separated by a white strip with the series title.

For the last thirty years the list has been managed as a whole or in part by a variety of editorial directors. The underlying spirit, however, remains true to its founding principles. 'These texts help us,' said Rieu, '[…] to appreciate and understand the essential differences that divide us, as much as the universal truths that bind us together […] Their value is incalculable, and their loss or destruction would diminish us all.'

When Rieu retired, the invitation to his party included a quotation from his poem 'Peter and Percival, or The Penguin's Revolt', which I have quoted here.

> *So they tripped in their glee through the star-spangled night,*
> *Penguins in harmony, utterly right;*
> *While the silent Aurora went flickering forth*
> *And shivered the sky from the South to the North.*

1985
trans. B. A. Windeatt
(see p.72)

2003
ed. Gregg A. Hecimovich
(see p.224)

The Other Penguins

'Penguin Books has become a vertebrate animal,' wrote William Emrys Williams in 1956. 'The spinal structure, so to speak, is Penguins proper, fiction and crime, which account for over a half of the production and sales; to this backbone are attached the ribs, consisting of several integrated series and sub-series.' Many titles from these diverse series have been incorporated into Penguin Classics over the years, and are referred to throughout this book. Here are a few to look out for.

LETTERS AND NUMBERS

All Penguin books were once numbered at the base of the spine. The Penguin main list began in July 1935 with *Ariel* by André Maurois (196), number '1'. *A Farewell to Arms* by Ernest Hemingway was number '2' and *Poet's Pub* by Eric Linklater was number '3'. The numbering for Pelican Books started again at 1, but the series was given the prefix 'A': the first title, 'A1', was *The Intelligent Woman's Guide to Socialism, Capitalism, Sovietism and Fascism* by George Bernard Shaw (294). Thereafter, each series was assigned a different alphabetical prefix: The Penguin Shakespeare (134) was 'B'; Illustrated Classics was 'C'; and Penguin Classics was 'L'. In 1970, the lettering system was superseded by a new nationwide system of Standard Book Numbers, but most of the Penguin series retained their identities through numerical codes (446).

1937 Pelican Books
● —
The first two Pelican volumes were by George Bernard Shaw (294), who modestly suggested that an expanded sixpenny edition of his book 'would be the salvation of mankind.'

PELICANS 1937
A, 020

In 1936, Allen Lane was in St Pancras railway station, waiting to discuss sales with the manager of the bookstall, when the woman ahead of him asked: 'Have you got any Pelican Books?' 'I knew there wasn't such a series,' he explained – 'she really meant Penguins. But I knew if somebody else started the word Pelican they'd be stealing some of my thunder.' So the next year Lane instigated Pelican Books, a list of original non-fiction titles, designed to 'provide the serious general reader with authoritative books on a wide range of intellectual interests'. This hugely successful series ran for over fifty years and has recently been revived.

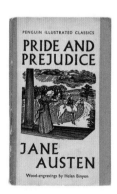

1938 Illustrated Classics
● ill. Helen Binyon (see p.201)

ILLUSTRATED CLASSICS 1938
C

Penguin's first Classics series was short-lived. The Illustrated Classics were launched in May 1938, with ten titles illustrated by wood engravers. More were meant to follow, but low sales, high production costs and the threat of a world war meant the nascent series was swiftly abandoned.

PENGUIN POETS 1941
D, 042

Penguin first published poetry in the Pelican series: the first was *A Book of English Poetry* (87), edited by G. B. Harrison in 1937. In June 1941, a new Penguin Poets series was inaugurated with a selection of Tennyson (263), followed by an edition of Wordsworth (194) and then Burns (193), which was the first to be given the prefix 'D'. Penguin Poets has encompassed various subsets, including Penguin Modern Poets, Penguin Modern European Poets and Penguin English Poets. From D25 *Matthew Arnold* in 1954, the poetry books had colourful, patterned covers.

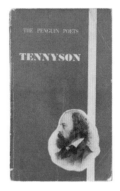

1941 Penguin Poets
● ed. W. E. Williams
(see p.263)

PUFFINS 1941
PS, 030

In 1940, Penguin began publishing Puffin children's books. First came Puffin Picture Books (PP), large, full-colour books of 32 pages. The next year, Puffin Story Books were introduced, designed for older children between nine and thirteen. The first title was *Worzel Gummidge* by Barbara Euphan Todd. Their design mirrored the standard Penguin tri-band format until illustrated covers were introduced in 1944, for PS9 *The Puffin Puzzle Book*.

1941 Puffin Books
● —

1946 Penguin Books
1959 Penguin Plays
● —
(see p.296)

PENGUIN PLAYS 1959
PL, 048

Penguin first published plays in its main list; the first was *Famous One Act Plays* (1937, Penguin 117). In 1959, Penguin Plays was introduced as an independent series. PL1 was *The Doctor's Dilemma* by George Bernard Shaw (294), originally published as Penguin 564. This series also included subsets, notably the New English Dramatists.

1961 Modern Classics
● —
—
The first four Modern Classics were published in April 1961, including *The Heart is a Lonely Hunter* by Carson McCullers.

PENGUIN MODERN CLASSICS 1961
018, 118

Modern Classics were introduced by Tony Godwin as a subset of the Penguin main list in 1961, intended 'to bring the very best of modern literature to the reading public'. It was not until 1989, when the series was temporarily renamed Twentieth-Century Classics, that it was given its own numerical code, '018'.

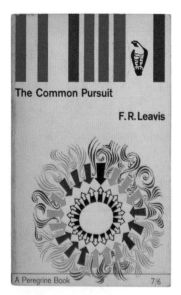

1962 Peregrine Books
●—

PEREGRINES 1962
Y, 055

Peregrines were 'academic books' pitched above Pelicans, intended for serious students. They were larger and more expensive than other Penguin books, printed on better quality paper, with stiffer covers and stitched binding. The first Peregrine was Y1, *The Common Pursuit* by F. R. Leavis.

PEACOCKS 1962
PK, 047

Peacocks were aimed at young adults, in an attempt to bridge the gap between Puffin and Penguin Books. The series launched in October 1962 with *National Velvet* by Enid Bagnold, originally Penguin 232. The series ended in 1979 after about 150 titles.

1940 Penguin Books
1962 Peacock Books
●—

PENGUIN ENGLISH LIBRARY 1965
EL, 043, 143

In September 1965, an English-language 'sister series' was introduced alongside Penguin Classics, edited by David Daiches of the University of Sussex. 'The format, appearance, and price will be similar,' wrote Daiches, in his note to contributors. '[…] The audience to aim at is the intelligent general reader who has always meant to read the English Classics, but has either never got round to all of these or at least not looked at them since his school days.' The first title was *Wuthering Heights* by Emily Brontë (217), with an illustrative cover and an orange spine. 'It seems certain that the Penguin English Library will continue to offer the best supply of well-edited literary texts for academic and general use in paperback form,' wrote John Sutherland, in *Fiction and the Fiction Industry* (1978). The series was amalgamated into Penguin Classics in 1985, but the name has recently been revived for colourful editions of English-language classics, with covers designed by Coralie Bickford-Smith.

1965 Penguin English Library
● ed. David Daiches
(see p.217)

1967 Penguin Education

PENGUIN EDUCATION 1967
X, 080

The results of a private report, commissioned by Allen Lane in 1965, prompted the Penguin Education series, which began in May 1967. This was a list of radical textbooks, with subseries including Connexions, covering topics such as work, marriage, violence and drugs, and Voices, a poetry series for secondary schools. Penguin's budgets were severely affected by the international oil crisis of 1973, however, and one of the chief casualties was this expensive, short-lived series.

PELICAN CLASSICS 1968
AC, 040

Betty Radice (51) was deeply uncomfortable about the establishment of the Pelican Classics series, edited by Moses Finlay. The boundary between Pelican Classics and Penguin Classics was contentious and she foresaw tussles over titles, as was the case with *City of God* by St Augustine (62), the translation of which had been commissioned for Penguin Classics but which was co-opted into Pelican Classics. The definition of 'Penguin Classics as classics of literature and Pelican Classics as classics of non-literature would make a clear demarcation between the two series', noted a memo of a tense editorial meeting, 'provided that a proper liaison is maintained between the editors'. Unfortunately the editors did not liaise properly. 'How nasty your letters can be,' wrote Radice to Finlay in 1970. Radice won the day and Pelican Classics were gradually abandoned after just 30 titles and most of them were absorbed into Penguin Classics.

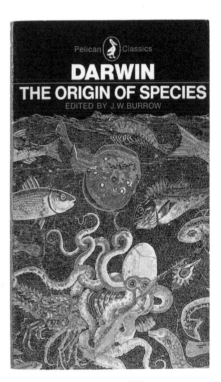

1968 Pelican Classics
ed. J. W. Burrow
(see p.270)

PENGUIN AMERICAN LIBRARY 1981
039

The Penguin American Library was introduced to match the Penguin English Library. It was almost identical in design, except it had pink instead of orange spines. It coincided with the first Penguin Classics originating in America (395). This fruitful transatlantic cooperation has introduced a number of American scholars and translators to Penguin Classics over the years, including Robert Fagles (16) and Mark Musa (84).

1981 Penguin American Library
ed. Andrew Sinclair
intro. James Dickey
(see p.426)

The Ancient World

The Fertile Crescent

THE EPIC OF GILGAMESH

L 100

Writings from Ancient Egypt

The Egyptian Book of the Dead

THE PENGUIN BOOK OF
HEBREW VERSE

EDITED AND TRANSLATED
BY T CARMI

ISBN 0 14
042.197 1

The Bible

The Book of Magic: From Antiquity to the Enlightenment

PENGUIN CLASSICS

At some point in the 36th century BCE, a blunt, triangular reed was pressed into soft clay to create wedge-shaped or 'cuneiform' marks. These began as a simple tally system but gradually evolved into illustrative pictographs, like primitive hieroglyphics.

Then a breakthrough occurred, in the 27th century BCE: cuneiform script was adapted to represent syllables of spoken Sumerian, the language of southern Mesopotamia. For the first time, 'writing' was revealed as a versatile tool that could record and transmit the complexities of human speech, in a medium that would endure across time and space. Writing was adopted by other neighbouring languages, including Akkadian, Elamite, Hattian and Hittite, and it also spread to Egypt. Before long, the earliest written literature began to emerge.

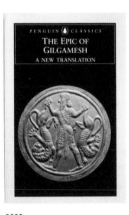

THE EPIC OF GILGAMESH
c. 2100 BCE

The world's oldest work of literature survives on twelve fragmented, biscuit-brown clay tablets. This 4,000-year-old story tells how King Gilgamesh of Uruk-the-Sheepfold achieved wisdom through wrestling monsters and embarking on a quest for immortality. The epic was discovered in 1853, among the ruins of the Royal Library of Ashurbanipal at Nineveh, and the tablets now nestle among 130,000 others in the Arched Room of the British Museum in London.

1960
trans. N. K. Sandars
—
Nancy Sandars translated *Gilgamesh* in 1960, and her prose retelling has remained in print ever since. New fragments and supplementary tablets continue to be deciphered, however, and in 1999 the Assyriologist Andrew George published an award-winning verse translation.

2000
trans. Andrew George

WRITINGS FROM ANCIENT EGYPT
24th – 4th centuries BCE

The pre-literate Egyptians adopted writing soon after the Mesopotamians and developed this new tool over the course of millennia to serve an increasingly wide variety of purposes, from economic management and law-making to religious spells, historiography, songs and lyric poetry.

2016
trans. Toby Wilkinson

2008
trans. E. A. Wallis Budge, 1899
intro. John Romer, 2008
—
Sir Ernest Alfred Thompson Wallis Budge was a Cornish child prodigy who became Keeper of Egyptian and Assyrian Antiquities at the British Museum.

THE EGYPTIAN BOOK OF THE DEAD
15th – 4th centuries BCE

Wealthy Egyptians were entombed with written spells to guide them through the underworld. These had advice on cuisine, shape-shifting and sharing ferries with gods. Above all they contained instructions for the moment of judgement, when the heart was weighed against an ostrich feather. Budge's synthesis of multiple tomb papyri, *The Book of the Dead*, has influenced many writers, including James George Frazer (275), W. B. Yeats (267), and James Joyce, who smuggled Budge's phrase 'the great cackler' into *Finnegans Wake*.

THE PENGUIN BOOK OF HEBREW VERSE

12th century BCE – 20th century CE

This extraordinary anthology spans more than 3,000 years of Hebrew verse, from the 'Song of Deborah', a religious victory song in the Book of Judges, to the work of modern poets such as Dalia Ravikovitch, a peace activist, who began publishing poems while serving in the Israeli army. It includes liturgical verse, love poems, wine songs and rhyming stories.

1981 Penguin Poets
2006 Penguin Classics
ed. T. Carmi
—
The original Hebrew is presented with parallel English translations.

1952 *The Four Gospels*
● trans. E. V. Rieu (17)
1957 *The Acts of the Apostles*
● trans. C. H. Rieu
1964 *The New English Bible: New Testament*
● trans. The Joint Churches Committee, 1961

2006 ed. David Norton
—
Before embarking on his translation of the Gospels, Rieu was broadly atheist; afterwards he joined the Anglican Church and was invited to sit on the Joint Churches Committee, which produced *The New English Bible*. 'It will be very interesting to see what father makes of the Gospels,' said C. H. Rieu, his son. 'It will be still more interesting to see what the Gospels make of father!'

THE BIBLE
King James Version
with The Apocrypha

8th century BCE – 1st century CE

The earliest sections of the Hebrew Bible emerged in the Kingdom of Israel, during the reign of Jeroboam II (788 – 747 BCE); the last portions of the Greek New Testament were written in the 1st century CE. At the Synod of Hippo, 393 CE, which St Augustine (62) attended, a council of North African bishops sifted the Hebrew and Greek scriptures and selected an approved Christian canon, known simply as the 'books' or *biblia*. Soon afterwards St Jerome finished translating the Bible into Latin, and his Vulgate ('common') Bible became the definitive translation for the next millennium. A number of English-language Bibles began to emerge in the Early Modern era (116), including Wycliffe's Bible, the Great Bible and the Bishops' Bible, but most enduring was the King James Bible, which was commissioned by James VI and I at the Hampton Court Conference of 1604, created by a team of 47 scholars and completed in 1611. More copies of the King James Bible have been printed than any other book in history: it soon became the standard Bible in Britain and it is still widely used in church services today.

THE BOOK OF MAGIC
from Antiquity to the Enlightenment

8th century BCE – 18th century CE

If you wish to conjure spirits, simply 'go outside the village and bring with you a brightly shining sword and a hoopoe bird and use the sword to make circles in some remote place'. After you have copied a diagram and made a magic incantation you will suddenly behold sixteen spectral knights, who will swear allegiance to you. 'The hoopoe has great power for necromantic rites and invoking demons.' This advice from a 15th-century necromancer's manual is among more than 150 pieces of magical lore in this anthology, drawn from the Bible, classical philosophy (25), medieval grimoires and early works of science.

2016 ed. Brian Copenhaver

THE PENGUIN BOOK OF THE UNDEAD
Fifteen Hundred Years of Supernatural Encounters
8th century BCE – 16th century CE

From hordes of dead warriors to limping corpses, moaning phantoms and zombies with bad breath, we have always been horrified and fascinated by the idea that the dead might return to the land of the living. This anthology gathers accounts from Homer (16), the Bible (4), Icelandic sagas (91), the Venerable Bede (67) and Shakespeare (134), spanning more than fifteen hundred years of supernatural encounters.

2016 ed. Scott G. Bruce

THE COMPLETE DEAD SEA SCROLLS IN ENGLISH
2nd century BCE – 1st century CE

In February 1947, a Bedouin shepherd fell into a cave in the Judean Desert, a mile from the Dead Sea, and discovered seven ancient scrolls preserved in earthenware jars. Over the next ten years, ten further cave sites were discovered in the cliffs above the ruined settlement of Qumran. In total, 972 manuscripts were recovered, hidden by a Jewish religious community 2,000 years ago. They demonstrate the diversity of religious thought that existed before and after the birth of Christ. In February 2017, a twelfth cave was discovered, but sadly it had already been looted. 'The findings indicate beyond any doubt that the cave contained scrolls that were stolen,' stated Dr Oren Gutfeld, one of the lead researchers.

1962 Pelican Books
The Dead Sea Scrolls in English
1995 Penguin Books
The Complete Dead Sea Scrolls in English
2004 Penguin Classics
trans. Geza Vermes
—
Geza Vermes was a Hungarian scholar who dedicated his life to documenting and translating the Dead Sea Scrolls. He revised seven Penguin editions of this text. His edition was originally published to complement a previous Pelican Book about the scrolls, by John Allegro.

1956 Pelican Books
● —

THE TALMUD
A Selection
3rd – 5th centuries CE

'Talmud' is Hebrew for 'instruction'. This ancient code of rabbinical law includes tractates covering festivals, sisters-in-law, leprosy, and hand washing; it is second only to the Hebrew Bible in its importance to Judaism. Since 1923, tens of thousands of Orthodox Jews around the world have participated in the *Daf Yumi*, a schedule by which they study one page of the Talmud every day. It takes seven and a half years to cover all 2,711 pages.

2009
trans. Norman Solomon

Ancient India

THE RIG VEDA

HINDU MYTHS

Roots of Yoga

The Mahābhārata

ABRIDGED AND TRANSLATED BY JOHN D. SMITH

THE UPANISHADS

KĀLIDĀSA *The Loom of Time*

Rāma the Steadfast

R.K. Narayan The Ramayana

VIṢṆU ŚARMA • THE PAÑCATANTRA

THE BHAGAVAD GITA

ISBN 0 14
044.402 5

L306
ISBN 0 14
044.306 1

PENGUIN CLASSICS

PENGUIN CLASSICS

L163

PENGUIN CLASSICS

PENGUIN CLASSICS

ISBN 0 14
00.4428 0

ISBN 014
04.4596 X

L
121

Sanskrit, *saṃskṛta*, means 'refined'. It was the written language for religious texts in ancient India, as distinguished from *prākṛta*, the common tongue. It originated in the Indus valley in the 2nd millennium BCE and is still in use today in the formal liturgies of Hinduism and Buddhism.

Like all ancient literature, the earliest Indian texts derive from oral traditions. The epic *Mahābhārata* and *Rāmāyana* (9) are full of entertaining stories, intimate spiritual conversations and sweeping cosmic battles. Gods meet mortals, the spiritual meets the sensual and the surreal blends into the sublime.

HINDU MYTHS

12th century BCE – 16th century CE

This sourcebook of Hindu myths, drawn from the *Rig Veda*, the *Mahābhārata* and many other Sanskrit texts, covers the history of the universe from the primordial act of incest to the final battle for immortality, with the many avatars of Vishnu in between.

1975
trans. Wendy Doniger

ROOTS OF YOGA

12th century BCE – 19th century CE

This anthology collects, for the first time, all the core teachings on yoga from a vast range of original sources, covering Hindu, Tantric, Buddhist and Jain traditions. It is organized under headings such as 'posture', 'breath-control' and 'Yogic Powers'.

2017
trans. James Mallinson
& Mark Singleton

THE RIG VEDA
An Anthology

12th – 10th centuries BCE

The 'authorless' Vedas are collections of the oldest Hindu scriptures: anthologies of Sanskrit hymns, mantras and rituals. The *Rig Veda* is the first of the Vedas and the earliest extensive composition to survive in any Indo-European language. It contains over a thousand hymns on themes of wisdom, death, women and the sacred psychedelic soma plant; this volume presents a selection of 108 hymns.

1981
trans. Wendy Doniger
—
'This austerity in commentary may often puzzle the reader,' writes Doniger. 'Good. The hymns are meant to puzzle, to surprise, to trouble the mind; they are often just as puzzling in Sanskrit as they are in English.'

THE MAHĀBHĀRATA

9th century BCE – 4th century CE

The *Mahābhārata* is the longest poem in existence, ten times as long as the *Iliad* (16) and the *Odyssey* (17) combined. It dramatizes a cosmic war between gods and demons, with battles, heavenly cities and the pursuit of *dharma*, the good life. It includes the celebrated spiritual discussion between Lord Krishna and Prince Arjuna, which forms the *Bhagavad Gita* (9).

2001
trans. R. K. Narayan, 1978
—

2009
trans. John D. Smith

Narayan's dramatic abridgement includes decorations by R. K. Laxman; Smith's huge but still abridged selection appends a glossary and genealogical tables.

2004
trans. Valerie J.
Roebuck, 2000

1965
trans. Juan Mascaró
—
Juan Mascaró was a Mallorcan linguist
who dabbled in occultism before
developing a passion for Sanskrit and
Pali. He lived at various times in Sri
Lanka, Barcelona and the hills above
Tintern Abbey.

THE UPANIṢADS
8th–5th centuries BCE

'Upaniṣad' means 'sitting down near'.
Each Upaniṣad presents a philosophical discourse with a seated guru,
who imparts his esoteric knowledge
about the meaning of the world. The
first thirteen or 'principal' Upaniṣads
form one of the foundational texts of
Hinduism. Schopenhauer (348) called
them 'the production of the highest
human wisdom'. The translator Juan
Mascaró describes their spirit as
'comparable with that of the New
Testament'.

Kālidāsa
5th century BCE

**The greatest writer of classical
Sanskrit lived and wrote in
Ujjain, Madhya Pradesh. We
know very little about his life,
but he may have been born in
Kashmir.**

The Loom of Time
A Selection of His Plays and Poems

Rtusamhāram ('The Gathering of the
Seasons') is thought to be Kālidāsa's
earliest work, in which a pair of lovers
react sensuously to the six seasons;
Meghadūtam ('The Cloud Messenger')
is a lyric monody, written during a
long separation from his wife; and
Abhijnānaśākuntalam ('The Recognition of Śankuntalā') is Kālidāsa's
masterpiece, a play that dramatizes
the Śankuntalā episode from the
Mahābhārata (7): a king falls in
love with a beautiful girl, abandoned
at birth, and the plot involves a
magical ring, an angry hermit and a
cosmic journey.

RĀMA THE STEADFAST
An Early Form of
the Rāmāyaṇa
5th century BCE

This early version of the
Rāmāyaṇa (9) tells how the
warrior-prince Rāma joined
forces with Hanumān,
captain of the monkeys, to
rescue a beautiful princess
from a ten-headed warlord.

2006
trans. John & Mary Brockington

1991
trans. Chandra
Rajan, 1989

1977 Penguin Books
1993 Twentieth-Century Classics
2006 Penguin Classics
trans. R. K. Narayan, 1972
intro. Pankaj Mishra, 2006
—
Narayan's abridged translation
is based on the 11th-century Tamil
version by the poet Kamban.

1995
trans.
Chandra
Rajan,
1993

1962
trans. Juan Mascaró, 1962
intro. Simon Brodbeck, 2003

Valmiki

A legendary robber called Ratnakara met a great sage, who advised him to perform a penance. Ratnakara sat down and began chanting the word 'ma-ra' ('kill'), over and over again for several years, during which time he was slowly enveloped by a huge anthill. Eventually the word changed to 'ra-ma' or Rama, one of the names of Vishnu, whereupon Ratnakara broke free and became a sage in his own right. He wrote The *Rāmāyana* and was known thereafter as Valmiki, which means 'anthill'.

The Rāmāyana

5th – 2nd centuries BCE

The *Rāmāyana* tells the magical tale of Prince Rama, an incarnation of Vishnu, who chose to take human form in order to battle the demon Ravana, who could only be slain by a mortal. The epic tale features vultures, monkey gods, love, loss and jealousy.

Viṣṇu Śarma

We know nothing about Viṣṇu Śarma other than his appearance in the frame story of the *Pańćatantra*; he may be no more than a literary invention.

The Pańćatantra

3rd century BCE

Once upon a time, a powerful king had three idiot sons. He offered a hundred grants of land to the 80 year-old Viṣṇu Śarma, if he could instruct these princes in practical wisdom. Viṣṇu Śarma agreed to educate the boys for no remuneration, which he did by writing five books of fables, which make up the body of the *Pańćatantra*. These marvellous fables include 'The Maiden Wedded To A Snake', 'The Mice That Freed The Elephants', 'The Bird Who Dropped Golden Turd' and 'The Three-Breasted Princess'. La Fontaine (155) borrowed some of Viṣṇu Śarma's tales for his own book of fables.

THE BHAGAVAD GITA

2nd century BCE

Known as the 'Upaniṣad of the Upaniṣads'(8), this excerpt from the *Mahāb-hārata* (7) is one of the core texts of Hinduism. It recounts a conversation between Prince Arjuna and his charioteer, Krishna, on the eve of a mighty battle. Lord Krishna, the Supreme Being, reveals himself as a god and instructs Arjuna on his sacred duty as both a warrior and a man.

2009
Clothbound
Classics
trans. Arshia
Sattar, 1996

2008
trans. Laurie L.
Patton

THE DHAMMAPADA
The Path of Perfection
3rd century BCE

Siddhārtha Gautama was an ascetic sage from northern India, living in the 5th or 6th century BCE. After a meal of rice pudding and two months meditating under a fig tree, he attained Enlightenment and became 'the Awakened One', 'the Buddha'. His aphoristic sayings were posthumously arranged under headings such as 'The Mind', 'The Path' and 'The Elephant', to form a lyrical collection of verses that express the Buddhist *dhamma*, the 'path of perfection'.

1973
trans. Juan Mascaró
—
Juan Mascaró compares the spirit of the Dhammapada to Keats's *Ode on a Grecian Urn* (197).

2010
trans. Valerie J. Roebuck

THE LAWS OF MANU
2nd century BCE – 3rd century CE

This ancient legal text presents an encyclopaedic and practical philosophy for living well. Its moral code is universal, covering women's rights, social welfare, self-knowledge and ways of facing the prospect of death. It was translated into English in 1794 and used as a basis for British colonial rule in India (387).

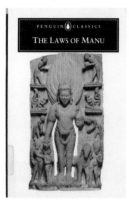

1991
trans. Wendy Doniger with Brian K. Smith

KAMA SUTRA
A Guide to the Art of Pleasure
2nd century CE

Kama, or pleasure, is one of four principle goals of Hindu life. This manual contains advice on the pursuit of pleasure in all its aspects, though it has always been most famous for its sex tips, which include details of the 'tomcat's frolic', 'sucking the mango' and practical hints on enlarging the penis using an emollient of insect bristles.

2012
trans. A. N. D. Haksar

BUDDHIST SCRIPTURES
3rd century BCE – 14th century CE

Buddhism has no central text. Its teachings are dispersed across a broad geographical and chronological spectrum of Pali, Sanskrit, Tibetan, Chinese and Japanese scriptures, many of which are collected in these anthologies.

1959
• trans. Edward Conze

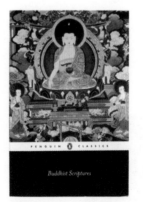

2004
ed. Donald S. Lopez, Jr.

For Medieval India, turn to p.103

Ancient China

TRANSLATED BY **JOHN MINFORD**

I · CHING

PENGUIN CLASSICS DELUXE EDITION

SUN-TZU *The Art of War*

CONFUCIUS **THE ANALECTS**

CONFUCIUS *The Most Venerable Book (Shang Shu)*

MENCIUS

Ta Hsüeh and Chung Yung

LAO TZU TAO TE CHING

The Book of Chuang Tzu

MO ZI *The Book of Master Mo*

QU YUAN AND OTHERS · THE SONGS OF THE SOUTH

PENGUIN CLASSICS

PENGUIN CLASSICS ISBN 0 14 044.348 7

PENGUIN CLASSICS

PENGUIN CLASSICS 140442286

PENGUIN CLASSICS ISBN 0 14 044.1131 X

PENGUIN CLASSICS

ISBN 0 14 04.4376.4

The first emperor of all China, Qin Shi Huangdi, ordered a mass burning of books in 213 BCE. All works of poetry, history and philosophy were condemned to the furnace in an attempt to destroy every belief and story that existed before the emperor seized power. With all contrary views obliterated, he believed, his dynasty would thrive for a thousand years.

It lasted fifteen. The first emperor died in 210 BCE, while seeking the elixir of life on a magical eastern island, and his inept heirs were quickly defeated by the Han dynasty. In the meantime, unfortunately, he did succeed in burning a huge number of fragile, flammable bamboo slips. Some works survived, however, either physically or in the collective memory. In particular, the Han reconstructed the 'Five Classics', ancient works of wisdom that were said to have inspired Confucius (13), and the 'Four Books' of Confucianism, works by the great sage himself and his followers.

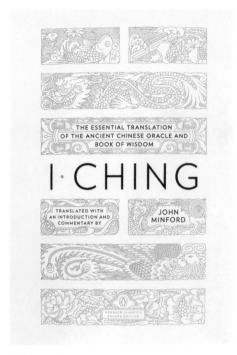

2015 Deluxe Edition
trans. John Minford
—
The earliest exposition of the meanings behind the *I Ching* hexagrams is attributed to the legendary King Wen of Zhou in the 12th century BCE.

I CHING
The Book of Change
9th – 2nd centuries BCE

The *I Ching* is the oldest of the 'Five Classics'. It is an ancient divinatory system consisting of 64 hexagrams, permutations of six horizontal lines, each of which is either broken (*yin*) or complete (*yang*). Consult the *I Ching* by ritually dividing dried yarrow stalks, or tossing a set of three coins. The unique properties of each randomly generated hexagram reveal intimations of future events.

Sun Tzu
544 – 496 BCE

We know little about Sun Tzu. He is said to have travelled from his home state of Qi to become an advisor to the king of Wu.

The Art of War
5th century BCE

Sun Tzu's iconic military treatise has been adopted and deployed over the last 2,500 years by commanders and corporate strategists around the world. Its effective philosophies of deception, indirect confrontation and firm leadership have been applied to a variety of fields: the Brazilian football squad read *The Art of War*, for example, before winning the World Cup in 2002.

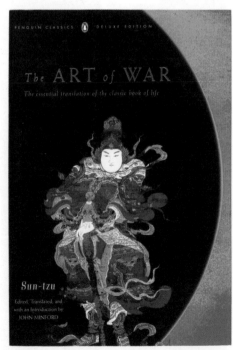

2003 Deluxe Edition
2009 Penguin Classics
trans. John Minford

Confucius

5th century BCE

Master Kong, 'Kong Fuzi', was raised by his impoverished mother in the state of Lu. He spent much of his life in self-exile, discoursing with politicians, rulers and his own disciples while wandering around China. During the Han dynasty (206 BCE–220 CE), his humanist teachings were adopted as official ideology; in the Ming and Qing periods, the 'Four Books' of Confucianism formed the core curriculum of China's legendary civil service examinations.

1979
trans. D. C. Lau

2014
trans. Annping Chin
—
After Din Cheuk Lau's retirement in 1989 he led a project to digitize every extant ancient Chinese work, producing a series of 60 concordances. His obituary described him as 'a bit of a hermit'.

The Analects

(**Lunyu**) 5th–3rd centuries BCE

The fragmentary sayings of Confucius, compiled by his disciples after his death, encourage pursuit of 'the Way': individuals cultivate a benevolent attitude towards others; rulers lead by example; we all seek continued education. This worldly philosophy is expressed in what has become one of the most influential books in human history, the foremost of the 'Four Books' of Confucianism.

The Most Venerable Book

(**Shang Shu**)

4th–3rd centuries BCE

This chronicle of the best and worst rulers in China's ancient history functions as a manual for good governance. It is one of the 'Five Classics', and is said to have been written, or perhaps compiled, by Confucius.

2014
trans. Martin Palmer with Jay Ramsay & Victoria Finlay

MENCIUS

4th century BCE

Mencius is said to have been the pupil of Tzu Ssu, Confucius's grandson. He expanded the aphoristic sayings of Confucius into extended dialogues with kings, generals and philosophers on the subjects of *jen* (goodness) and *yi* (righteousness). This is another of the 'Four Books'.

1970
2004 Revised and reissued trans. D. C. Lau
—
D. C. Lau revised his 1970 edition for the Chinese University Press in 2003.

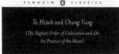

TA HSÜEH *and* CHUNG YUNG

(**The Highest Order of Cultivation** *and* **On the Practice of the Mean**)

2nd–1st centuries BCE

Ta Hsüeh and *Chung Yung* are two of the 'Four Books'. *Ta Hsüeh* is traditionally attributed to Tseng Tzu, a close disciple of Confucius, and Chung Yung to his grandson, Tzu Ssu, who later taught Mencius. In truth, these texts reached their final form in the 2nd or 1st century BCE, long after Mencius died. They focus on practical Confucianism, the observance of ritual and the maintenance of social order.

2003
trans. Andrew Plaks pref. Xinzhong Yao

Lao Tzu

Lao Tzu was the legendary founder of Taoism. Some say he was a contemporary of Confucius in the 5th century BCE, others think he lived during the 5th- to 3rd-century 'Warring States' period. Those with the surname 'Li' claim him as their ancestor.

Tao Te Ching

4th century BCE

Taoism sits alongside Buddhism and Confucianism as one of the three great religions of China. It is based on the concept of the *Tao*, the 'Way', the universal source, pattern and substance of everything. Taoism differs from Confucianism in that it avoids rituals and hierarchy. The *Tao Te Ching* provides practical advice for embracing the *Tao* through self-restraint and modesty.

1963
trans. D. C. Lau

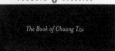

THE BOOK OF CHUANG TZU

4th century BCE

The second text of Taoism is the *Book of Chuang Tzu*. Chuang Tzu was a follower of Lao Tzu. His book consists of original, humorous and frequently fantastical stories, featuring unusual characters such as Wild-and-Surly, Uncle Legless and a man who imagines his buttocks may turn into cartwheels. Chuang Tzu famously recalls a dream in which he is a butterfly, and wonders whether he is in fact a butterfly, dreaming that he is Chuang Tzu.

2006
trans. Martin Palmer, 1996 with Elizabeth Breuilly, Chang Wai Ming & Jay Ramsay
—
Palmer is the religious advisor to the World Wide Fund for Nature (WWF), the Secretary General of the Alliance of Religions and Conservation (ARC), and a UN Special Advisor on Climate Change, the Environment and the Faiths. He has worked with the China Taoist Association to protect the Four Sacred Mountains of Taoism and is a regular contributor to the BBC on religious and ethical issues.

Mo Zi

470–c. 391 BCE

Master Mo was an itinerant philosopher. He was a pacifist with a special interest in defensive warfare. He wandered from state to state during the 'Warring States' period, seeking a ruler who would implement his peaceful philosophies. He is said to have been saddened by the sight of dyed silk.

The Book of Master Mo

5th century BCE

Mo Zi argues against both the rituals of Confucianism and the detachment of Taoism, encouraging self-reflection and authenticity, which he defines as the accumulation of self-knowledge through personal experience and adversity.

2013
trans. Ian Johnston, 2010

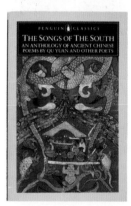

1985
trans. David Hawkes

THE SONGS OF THE SOUTH

An Ancient Chinese Anthology of Poems by Qu Yuan and Other Poets

4th century BCE – 2nd century CE

Chu Ci (*The Songs of the South*) and its northern counterpart *Shi Jing* (*The Book of Songs*) contain all the ancient Chinese poetry that has survived. *The Songs of the South* anthologizes poems about love, regret and growing old. Over half the poems are by Qu Yuan, a minister at the court of King Huai of Chu in the 4th century BCE. Qu Yuan wrote the protest poem *Li sao*, the first in this anthology, after being banished from court and before drowning himself in the Miluo River.

For Medieval China, turn to p.106

Ancient Greece

HOMER · THE ILIAD

HOMER · THE ODYSSEY

The Homeric Hymns

HESIOD AND THEOGNIS

SAPPHO · Stung with Love: Poems and Fragments

AESOP · FABLES

THE ODES OF PINDAR

Greek Tragedy

AESCHYLUS · THE ORESTEIAN TRILOGY

AESCHYLUS · PROMETHEUS & OTHER PLAYS

SOPHOCLES · THE THEBAN PLAYS

SOPHOCLES · ELECTRA AND OTHER PLAYS

EURIPIDES · ALCESTIS AND OTHER PLAYS

EURIPIDES · MEDEA AND OTHER PLAYS

Archaic Greece

As written Greek gradually evolved out of the Phoenician alphabet in the 8th century BCE, the dispersed islands, valleys and city-states around the Aegean began to coalesce into a single civilization. Greek coinage appeared in the 6th century BCE and four prominent cities began to assert their power: Athens, Sparta, Corinth and Thebes.

There were three main literary dialects of Ancient Greek: Aeolic, Ionic and Doric. Homer's works were written in Ionic, with a smattering of Aeolic. The language of Athens was Attic, a sub-dialect of Ionic.

Greek literature begins with the epic poetry of Homer and the works of Hesiod (18). The other early form was lyric poetry, designed to be sung to the musical accompaniment of a lyre. The greatest exponents of these shorter verses were subsequently canonized as the 'nine lyric poets', of whom Sappho (18) and Pindar (19) were considered the greatest.

No work has had more Penguin Classics translations than the *Iliad*. Robert Graves's (439) 1959 retelling combines darkly humorous prose with lyric poetry, evoking the *Iliad*'s roots in the bardic tradition and Martin Hammond's prose translation was acclaimed as 'the best and most accurate there has ever been'. The poet Paul Muldoon praised Robert Fagles's 'Homeric swagger' and compared his epic vision of the *Iliad* to 'that of film directors like Sergio Leone and Sam Peckinpah.' Alexander Pope's (152) 18th-century translation is no longer in print.

Homer

c. 750 – 700 BCE

Homer's identity is mysterious. He may have been a blind minstrel from Ionia, or a Babylonian hostage, or a Sicilian princess (as Robert Graves (439) imagines her in his novel *Homer's Daughter*), or 'Homer' may be a collective term for an oral storytelling tradition. Whatever the truth, the epic poems attributed to Homer, the *Iliad* and the *Odyssey*, have had an unparalleled influence on western literature. From Aristotle (29) to Arnold (272), Homer is the yardstick against which all subsequent literature has been measured.

The Iliad

The archetypal martial epic revolves around ten critical days in the tenth and final year of the Trojan War. The death of his companion Patroclus persuades the (almost) invincible Achilles to rejoin the fight and, carving his chariot through the Trojan forces, he kills Hector, King Priam's son, in what proves to be the turning point of the war. The *Iliad* is vast in scope and universal in its themes of vengeance, compassion and courage under adversity. It is the greatest literary achievement of Ancient Greece and the cornerstone of western culture.

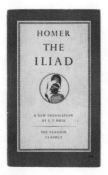

1950
trans. E. V. Rieu
rev. Peter Jones with
D. C. H. Rieu, 2003

1987
trans. Martin Hammond

1992
trans. Robert Fagles
intro. Bernard Knox

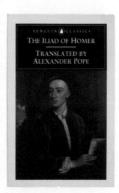

1996
● trans. Alexander Pope, 1715–20
ed. Steven Shankman

2009 *The Anger of Achilles*
trans. Robert Graves, 1959

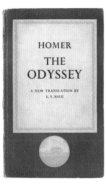

2006
trans. Robert Fagles, 1996
intro. Bernard Knox, 1996

1946
trans. E. V. Rieu
rev. D. C. H. Rieu, 1991
intro. Peter Jones, 1991
—
Rieu's translation of the *Odyssey* was the very first Penguin Classic, published in January 1946 (x). Rieu was unhappy about the illogical roundel, which shows a ship under full sail with its oars in use; the roundel was replaced, but oddly the problem was uncorrected and in fact exacerbated as the sails were now billowing over a calm sea:

The Odyssey

The second poem attributed to Homer follows the fortunes of Odysseus, king of Ithaca, on his journey home from the Trojan War. Odysseus's epic voyage takes him and his crew as far as the western edge of the world. On the way they encounter Circe the Sorceress, the mellifluous, carnivorous Sirens, the monsters Scylla and Charybdis, Calypso the nymph and the lovely Nausicaa. At one point they are within sight of Ithaca, but a bag of winds blows them far away again. It takes Odysseus ten years to get home to his wife Penelope. Perhaps the most memorable episode involves Polyphemus the Cyclops: Odysseus and his crew narrowly escape this fearsome giant by blinding his single eye and smuggling themselves out of his cave suspended beneath sheep. It's been suggested that the myth of the Cyclopes originated with the discovery of fossilised dwarf elephants, which have large central nasal cavities that might have been mistaken for eye sockets. Similar stories are shared by cultures across Europe and the Middle East, and there are several parallels with the Humbaba episode in the *Epic of Gilgamesh* (3).

The Homeric Hymns
7th–6th centuries BCE

These 33 hymns to gods and goddesses were attributed to Homer and are written in the same dactylic hexameter as the *Iliad* and the *Odyssey*. The whole Olympian pantheon is represented, from Zeus to Aphrodite, revealing fascinating insights into the attributes of the Greek deities and the rituals of antiquity.

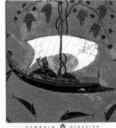

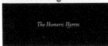

2003
trans. Jules Cashford
intro. Nicholas Richardson

E. V. RIEU

In 1951, the poet Patrick Kavanagh wrote 'On Looking into E. V. Rieu's Homer', echoing Keats (197), and included these lines, addressed to Rieu:

> Like Achilles you had a
>   goddess for mother,
> For only the half-god can see
> The immortal in things mortal

Rieu grew up next to the British Museum, where his father, fluent in 20 languages, was Keeper of the Oriental Manuscripts. He worked for Oxford University Press in India, establishing branch offices in Bombay, Calcutta and Madras, for Methuen as educational manager and managing director, and for Penguin as the editor of Penguin Classics (x). His private hobbies included carpentry, mountains and petrology, the study of rocks, and his 'delight in verbal wit and paradox was matched by a relish for a schoolboy pun or joke', as Betty Radice (51) recalled.

'The Penguin Classics, though I designed them to give pleasure even more than instruction, have been hailed as the greatest educative force of the twentieth century,' said Rieu at his retirement party in 1964. 'And far be it for me to quarrel with that encomium, for there is no one whom they have educated more than myself.'

Hesiod

c.750–c.650 BCE

Hesiod lived in the village of Ascara, in Boeotia, which he described as 'harsh in winter, miserable in summertime, not really good at any time of year'. He had a fraught, litigious relationship with his brother Perses. Ascara lies at the foot of Mount Helicon, one of the mythical homes of the muses. Hesiod describes meeting the muses on the mountain slopes, where they presented him with a poet's laurel staff and breathed a sacred voice into his mouth.

Works and Days

Works and Days, Hesiod's masterpiece, presents a pessimistic view of the five ages of man. He explains that ever since Pandora opened her jar, mankind has been doomed to endless drudgery. This salutary message is conveyed in a majestic yet earthy poem that blends cosmic myths with practical, homely advice.

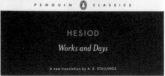

2018
trans. A. E. Stallings

1973
trans. Dorothea Wender

Hesiod and Theognis

Hesiod, *Theogeny and Works and Days*; Theognis, *Elegies*

Hesiod's *Theogeny* describes the origins of the cosmos and genealogy of the gods, from the primordial Chaos to the ascendancy of Zeus.

Theognis was a 6th-century poet, possibly from the town of Megara, which may have been in Sicily. Little else is known about him. His *Elegies* are gnomic, suspicious poems about changes within aristocratic society. They touch on politics, friendship, human nature, wine, wealth and love.

Sappho

c.630–c.570 BCE

The first female poet whose name we know was born on the island of Lesbos. Very little is known about her life, although she seems to have gathered a school or cult of adolescent girls around her, who became the subjects of her lyrical love poems. The term 'lesbian' derives from Sappho's birthplace. **Plato** (26) called her 'the tenth muse', and in the Hellenistic period (34) she was canonized as one of the 'nine lyric poets'.

2009
trans. Aaron Poochigan
fwd. Carol Ann Duffy

—

Aaron Poochigan is a poet from Minnesota; his first poetry collection, *The Cosmic Purr*, was published in 2012.

Stung with Love
Poems and Fragments

Sappho's songs range from women's perspectives on the Trojan War to intensely intimate love lyrics. She writes about goddesses and girls, unrequited love and sexual gratification. Only a tenth of her work survives, including fragments that were discovered 'as scrunched ingredients in papier mâché coffins', as Carol Ann Duffy puts it in her foreword, but even her shortest remnants are striking and evocative.

Aesop

*c.*630–564 BCE

If Aesop existed, he was a slave on the island of Samos; some say he was born in Ethiopia. He was legendarily ugly, but his cleverness earned him his freedom, and he went on to advise kings and dine with the Seven Sages of Greece. His fables supposedly angered the people of Delphi, however, who forced him to leap off a cliff.

The Complete Fables

Aesop is said to have donated his fables to the royal library of Croesus, king of Lydia. It is unclear, however, whether the 358 fables that accumulated under his name are indeed the work of a single author. This is the first English translation of all the fables attributed to Aesop, including well-known stories such as 'The Tortoise and the Hare' and 'The Field Mouse and the Town Mouse' alongside less familiar vignettes such as 'The Bat and the House-Ferrets', 'The Stomach and the Feet' and the rather touching 'Mole and His Mother'.

Handford's translation included illustrations by Brian Robb, the illustrator, cartoonist and Second World War camoufleur.

1954
● trans. S. A. Handford

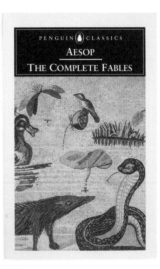

1998
trans. Olivia & Robert Temple

Pindar

*c.*518–428 BCE

Pindar was one of the 'nine lyric poets'. He composed victory songs in praise of the victors at the ancient Olympic, Pythian, Nemean and Isthmian Games. When Alexander the Great (34) razed Thebes in 335 BCE, the only house he spared was Pindar's, out of respect for an ode Pindar had written in praise of Alexander I of Macedon, Alexander's ancestor.

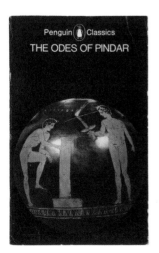

1969
trans. C. M. Bowra
—
W. Jackson Knight was initially commissioned to translate Pindar's odes, but he died before he could make substantial headway. 'The death of Jackson Knight cancelled his contract for Pindar,' writes Betty Radice (51) in a memo, 'and Sir Maurice Bowra has said he will do this for us. [...] I should think the series honoured by the addition of his name.'

The Odes

As well as extolling skill in ancient sports including sprinting, chariot racing and wrestling, these spectacular, linguistically innovative odes also make fascinating comparisons with Greek heroes, myths and gods.

Classical Greece

In 508 BCE, following a period of tyranny, the Athenian aristocrat Cleisthenes made a radical proposal: he suggested that Athens form an *isonomia*, a *polis* or city state in which all citizens would be 'equal under the law'. This profound idea was embraced enthusiastically by the Athenians, who established the world's first democracy and heralded the golden age of Classical Greece. Literature flourished in this period in three main areas: drama, philosophy and history.

DRAMA

Classical Greek verse drama developed in the late 6th century out of the choral songs performed at the 'City Dionysia', a festival of the god Dionysus. Five days each year were devoted to performances, which were staged in the huge, open-air Theatre of Dionysus, the remains of which still exist. Performances were competitive: playwrights presented a set of plays, usually a themed trilogy of tragedies followed by a 'satyr play', and the winning writer would be wreathed with ivy leaves. An early prize winner is said to have been the playwright and actor Thespis, from whom the word 'thespian' derives. His prize was a goat. This might explain the origin of the word 'tragedy', which means 'goat-song'. Comedies were introduced to the festival in c. 486 BCE, in a separate competition.

Aeschylus
c. 525–c. 455 BCE

Aeschylus was an aristocrat who fought at the Battle of Marathon. He wrote over 70 plays, of which seven have survived. He was the first to introduce a second character to the stage, according to Aristotle (29), thereby inventing dramatic conflict. All the surviving tragedies of Aeschylus, with the exception of *Prometheus Bound*, won first prize in the City Dionysia competition. He is said to have been killed by a flying tortoise, dropped by a myopic eagle who mistook his bald head for a rock.

The Oresteia 458 BCE
Agamemnon; *The Libation Bearers*; *The Eumenides*

The *Oresteia* follows the fortunes of the House of Atreus, from the murder of King Agamemnon, on his return from the Trojan War, to the vengeful murder of his queen, Clytemnestra, by their son Orestes, and Orestes' subsequent flight from the wrathful Furies, the 'Eumenides', the winged deities of vengeance. It is the only complete trilogy of plays to have survived from antiquity.

1956 *The Oresteian Trilogy* trans. Philip Vellacott

1977 trans. Robert Fagles, 1975 intro. Robert Fagles & W. B. Stanford, 1975

The Persians
and Other Plays
The Persians; *Seven Against Thebes*; *The Suppliants*; *Prometheus Bound* 472–c. 431 BCE

The Persians tells the story of the naval battle of Salamis, in which Aeschylus probably participated himself. It is unique among the surviving Greek tragedies in describing a contemporary historical event. *Seven Against Thebes* was the third instalment in an Oedipus trilogy, focusing on the brutal fate of his sons; *The Suppliants* has the fifty daughters of Danaus fleeing arranged marriages in Egypt; and the Titan Prometheus is chained to a rock throughout *Prometheus Bound* for having stolen fire from the gods. This last play is now thought to be the work of Aeschylus's son, Euphorion.

1961 *Prometheus Bound and Other Plays* trans. Philip Vellacott

2009 trans. Alan H. Sommerstein

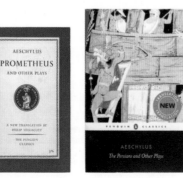

Sophocles
c. 497 – c. 405 BCE

Sophocles lived for 90 years in Athens, and wrote over 120 plays, of which only seven survive. He competed in 30 City Dionysia competitions, winning eighteen times and never coming lower than second place. This success may be because he was the first dramatist to introduce a third character to the stage, reducing the role of the chorus and increasing the complexity of the on-stage relationships. Aristotle (29) also credits him with the first use of painted scenery. Sophocles is said to have died from the strain of reciting an overlong line from *Antigone* without pausing for breath.

1947
trans. E. F. Watling
—
Edward Fairchild Watling was a crossword compiler and a schoolmaster in Sheffield. He was a keen amateur dramatist, directing his own translation of *Oedipus Rex* at the school, and he occasionally graced the boards himself. 'With his tall and slim figure, his splendidly resonant voice, his mobile and expressive features, and an impeccable sense of timing his every performance was stylish and memorable,' read his obituary, 'not least his vignettes as Fairy Queen and short-trousered schoolboy in staff pantomime and revue.'

1984
The Three Theban Plays
trans. Robert Fagles, 1982
intro. Bernard Knox, 1982

The Theban Plays
King Oedipus; Oedipus at Colonus; Antigone
c. 441 – c. 406 BCE

The 'Theban Plays' focus on separate elements of the Oedipus story, but they are not a trilogy: each play was originally part of a different tetralogy, the rest of which has been lost. Aristotle (30) considered *King Oedipus*, or *Oedipus Rex*, to be the highest achievement in tragedy and Sigmund Freud (353) revealed the subconscious 'Oedipal' desires in us all. *Oedipus at Colonus* has the blind king, led by his daughter Antigone, meeting Theseus of Athens at Colonus, the small, rural community where Sophocles himself was born. In *Antigone*, Oedipus's daughter must decide whether to abandon her brother's corpse to the ravages of wild animals, or bury him and face the death penalty herself.

Electra
and Other Plays
Women of Trachis; Ajax; Electra; Philoctetes
c. 441 – c. 409 BCE

1953
• trans.
E. F. Watling

2008
trans. David
Raeburn
intro. Pat
Easterling

In *Women of Trachis*, Heracles is accidentally murdered by his wife after completing his twelve labours; in *Ajax*, the proud hero of the Trojan War succumbs to jealousy, treachery and eventually suicide; *Electra* retells the story of *The Libation Bearers* by Aeschylus (20); and *Philoctetes* is the tale of an archer with a foul-smelling wound on his foot, whose charmed bow could decide the outcome of the Trojan War.

Euripides
c. 480–c. 406 BCE

Euripides was a recluse: he is said to have written his plays in a cave by the sea. His work is innovative and controversial, portraying mythical heroes as psychologically developed human beings, plunged into desperate circumstances. He wrote more than 90 plays, of which eighteen tragedies and one satyr play survive. Towards the end of his life, he left Athens for Macedon, where he was attacked by a pack of Molossian hounds and died.

Alcestis
and Other Plays
Alcestis; *Hippolytus*; *Iphigenia in Tauris*
438–c. 414 BCE

1953
trans. Philip Vellacott

In these three plays, men and women are forced apart and united, in an amoral world manipulated by the Fates: Heracles wrestles with Death and brings a wife back to life in *Alcestis*; in *Hippolytus*, Phaedra's inappropriate advances towards her stepson have fatal consequences; and *Iphigenia in Tauris* sees the ill-fated children of Agamemnon unexpectedly reunited.

Medea
and Other Plays
Alcestis; *Medea*; *The Children of Heracles*; *Hippolytus*
438–428 BCE

1996 *Alcestis and Other Plays*
2003 Reissued as *Medea and Other Plays*
trans. John Davie
intro. Richard Rutherford

Awesome figures are depicted as fallible human beings in these plays: Medea takes revenge on her husband by killing her own children and his new wife; and in *The Children of Heracles*, the sons and daughters of the famous hero flee an old enemy of their father.

Medea
and Other Plays
Medea; *Hecabe*; *Electra*; *Heracles*
431–c. 416 BCE

Powerful central characters are betrayed by their own violent emotions: in *Hecabe*, the defeated queen of Troy avenges the murder of her last surviving son; in *Electra*, Agamemnon's children slaughter their murderous mother; and in *Heracles*, the demigod unintentionally kills his own wife and children in a mad frenzy.

1963
trans. Philip Vellacott
—
'I have just opened a parcel containing two copies of V's *Euripides* Vol. III — *Medea, Hecabe, Electra, Heracles*,' wrote E. V. Rieu in April 1963, evidently concerned about the new Classics cover designs (xiv): 'new cover with a nice reproduction of a vase showing — Medea? Oh no, what an idea! *She* will no doubt be kept in reserve — to go on the Bacchae volume. This one shows a *maenad* — the one holding up a spotted dog — and they say so on the back cover! Oh my poor series, of which I used to be so proud!'

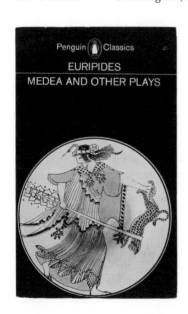

1998
trans. John Davie
intro. Richard Rutherford

Electra
and Other Plays
Andromache; *Hecabe*; *Suppliant Women*; *Electra*; *Trojan Women*
c. 425–415 BCE

Written during the Peloponnesian War (32), these plays describe the aftermath of the legendary Trojan War (16): in *Andromache*, Hector's noble widow becomes a war trophy; grieving mothers mourn their sons in *Suppliant Women*; and the fallen city's womenfolk suffer at the hands of the Greeks in *Trojan Women*.

Orestes
and Other Plays

The Children of Heracles; *Andromache*;
The Suppliant Women; *The Phoenician
Women*; *Orestes*; *Iphigenia in Aulis*
c. 430–405 BCE

These plays express the futility of
war and violence: in *The Phoenician
Women*, the sons of Oedipus murder
each other; in *Orestes*, a son is wracked
with guilt after murdering his mother;
in *Iphigenia in Aulis*, one of Euripides'
last plays, the Greeks decide to sacrifice a princess in order to ensure military
success in the Trojan War.

1972
trans. Philip Vellacott

The Bacchae
and Other Plays

Ion; *The Women of Troy*;
Helen; *The Bacchae*
c. 414–405 BCE

The *Bacchae* is Euripides'
greatest tragedy. King
Pentheus of Thebes mistreats
a stranger, who turns out
to be the god Dionysus
himself. Dionysus' revenge
is catastrophic: Pentheus
is pursued by a crowd of
ecstatic, frenzied women, led by his own mother
Agave. They rip him to shreds
and return with his head. Appropriately, the *Bacchae* won the
City Dionysia competition in the
theatre dedicated to Dionysus.

1954
trans. Philip Vellacott

Heracles
and Other Plays

Heracles; *Iphigenia Among the
Taurians*; *Ion*; *Helen*; *Cyclops*
c. 416–412 BCE

These tragicomedies have fabulous plots: an orphan discovers his
royal parentage in *Ion*; *Helen* involves phantom doppelgängers and
a faked sea burial. *Cyclops* is Euripides' only surviving satyr play, in
which Odysseus blinds the drunken Cyclops and liberates a chorus
of satyrs. Satyrs were short, goat-like creatures with permanent
erections, who traditionally attended Dionysus; satyr plays were
humorous, pastoral dramas about their antics, an antidote to the
preceding tragedies.

1957 *Two Satyr Plays*
• trans. Roger Lancelyn Green
—
Green's translation of *Cyclops*
was published with the
Ichneutae of Sophocles (21),
'The Trackers', a fragmentary
satyr play about a bungled
mission to recover Apollo's
cattle from the infant Hermes,
an episode borrowed from the
Homeric hymn to Hermes (17).

2002
trans. John Davie
intro. Richard Rutherford

The Bacchae
and Other Plays

Phoenician Women; *Orestes*;
Bacchae; *Iphigenia at Aulis*;
Rhesus
c. 410–405 BCE

The authorship of *Rhesus* has
been disputed since antiquity.
In this tale of espionage, King
Rhesus of Thrace is murdered
in his sleep during the Trojan
War, but he returns from the
dead and lives as an immortal
in an underground cave. The
murder features in Book 10 of
the *Iliad* (16).

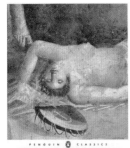

2005
trans. John Davie
intro. Richard Rutherford

GREEK TRAGEDY 458–c. 335 BCE

Aeschylus, *Agamemnon*; Sophocles, *Oedipus Rex*;
Euripides, *Medea*; Aristophanes, *Frogs*; Aristotle, *Poetics*

This anthology collects masterpieces of the three great
tragedians, accompanied
by extracts from Aris-
totle's *Poetics* (30) and
satirical passages from
Aristophanes' *Frogs* (24).

2004
ed. Shomit Dutta
intro. Simon Goldhill
—
Agamemnon (trans. Vellacott, 1956);
Oedipus Rex (trans. Watling, 1947);
Medea (trans. Vellacott, 1963);
Frogs (trans. Dutta, 2004);
Poetics (trans. Heath, 1996)

Aristophanes

c.446 – c.386 BCE

Aristophanes wrote about 40 comedies, of which eleven survive. He combined slapstick antics, lewd humour and verbal dexterity to satirize contemporary Athenian politics and philosophy. He was twice prosecuted for thinly disguised portrayals of the pro-war politician Cleon.

Lysistrata
and Other Plays

The Acharnians; *The Clouds*; *Lysistrata*
425 – 411 BCE

Lysistrata and *The Acharnians* are both ribald, anti-war satires. In *Lysistrata*, a band of women withhold sexual privileges until the men agree to end the Peloponnesian War (32). In *The Archanians*, a lone peasant manages to obtain a private peace treaty with Sparta. *The Clouds* satirizes Athenian philosophers. In fact, Plato (26) believed that Aristophanes' caricature of Socrates was responsible for the latter's trial and subsequent death sentence (26).

1973
trans. Alan H. Sommerstein
—
The decisive event of Sommerstein's career, he says, was the 'purchase in October 1969, for five shillings (25p), of David Barrett's Penguin translation of three plays by Aristophanes'. This volume inspired him to try his own hand at translating.

The Frogs
and Other Plays

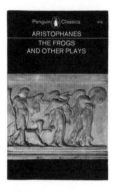

1964
trans. David Barrett
—
David Barrett spent much of his career teaching English at Helsinki University and translating works from Finnish. His obituary describes how he loved to invite his friends to the family home in Wembley, where they would be entertained by his mother, 'a lady with a comprehensive knowledge of the history of London'.

The Wasps; *The Poet and the Women*; *The Frogs*
422 – 405 BCE

A crotchety father and his louche son fall out disastrously in *The Wasps*, winding up in court, and *The Poet and the Women* is a cross-dressing comedy caper in which Euripides (22) persuades a fellow tragedian to infiltrate an all-female festival. In *The Frogs*, the god Dionysus descends to the underworld to bring Euripides back from the dead. While down there, he chairs a debate between the traditional wisdom of Aeschylus (22) and the modern innovations of Euripides, and ends up changing his mind and rescuing Aeschylus instead.

The Birds
and Other Plays

The Knights; *Peace*; *The Birds*; *Wealth*; *The Assemblywomen*
424 – 388 BCE

The Knights is a biting satire aimed squarely at the populist politician Cleon; *Peace* celebrates the imminent peace negotiations that suspended the Peloponnesian War; in *The Birds*, two disenchanted Athenians join forces with a group of

1978
trans. David Barrett
& Alan H. Sommerstein

anthropomorphic birds to build a utopian city called 'Much Cuckoo in the Clouds'; *Wealth* satirizes the economic depression that hit Athens after the war and features the god of riches as a ragged, blind old man; and in *The Assemblywomen*, the women of Athens smuggle themselves into the all-male popular Assembly in disguise.

2006
ed. Erich Segal
—
The Birds
(trans. Sommerstein, 1978);
The Girl from Samos
(trans. Miller, 1987);
The Brothers Menaechmus
(trans. Segal, 1996);
The Eunuch
(trans. Parker, 1975)

CLASSICAL COMEDY

Aristophanes, *The Birds*; Menander, *The Girl from Samos*; Plautus, *The Brothers Menaechmus*; Terence, *The Eunuch*
414 – 161 BCE

The Ancient Greeks seem to have enjoyed fart jokes: in *The Frogs*, by Aristophanes, there is a Greek chorus of parping amphibians and the god Dionysus craps his pants. Some of the grosser classical gags may have lost their piquancy after more than 2,000 years, but this anthology showcases Greek and Roman comedies at their best, with tales of mistaken identity, farcical flights of fancy and bawdy high jinks.

PHILOSOPHY

Philosophy means 'love of wisdom'. According to Aristotle (29), philosophy began on 28 May 585 BCE, when Thales of Miletus correctly predicted an eclipse of the sun: he was the first person to ask the question, 'Why?'

The most important classical philosophers were Socrates, the Athenian stonemason, his pupil Plato (26), and Plato's pupil Aristotle. If Socrates wrote anything it has not survived, but he is preserved as a character in Plato's extensive dialogues, which have survived almost entirely. Aristotle also wrote dialogues, most of which have been lost, but thankfully his wide-ranging ideas are preserved through his lecture notes.

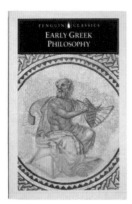

1987
trans. Jonathan Barnes

EARLY GREEK PHILOSOPHY
585–c. 420 BCE

Socrates is known as the 'Father of Philosophy', but he stood on the shoulders of earlier thinkers, known as the Pre-Socratics. This volume collects all the surviving fragments of Pre-Socratic philosophy, from the mind-bending paradoxes of Zeno, to the maths of Pythagoras and the atomic theories of Democritus.

THE GREEK SOPHISTS
c. 485–c. 375 BCE

The sophists were itinerant purveyors of wisdom, who taught young, wealthy Greeks the art of rhetoric and effective reasoning. In particular they claimed to impart the secrets of *arête*, 'skill'. Socrates vehemently denounced the sophists' over-elaborate arguments and costly tuition fees and the term 'sophistry' has come to describe philosophy that is clever but nonetheless false. This anthology includes biographical fragments about — and original writing by — Protagoras of Abdera (27), Gorgias of Leontini (26), Critias of Athens (28) and Alcidamas of Elaea, drawing on Plato (26) and many other sources.

2003
trans. John Dillon
& Tania Gergel

THE CYNIC PHILOSOPHERS
from Diogenes to Julian
4th century BCE

Diogenes lived in a barrel and masturbated in public. He urinated on people he disliked and became famous for being *cynicos*, 'dog-like'. This epithet was subsequently applied to an entire school of philosophy that encouraged simple living and personal freedom through poverty and self-sufficiency. This collection includes writings by Lucian (57), Epictetus (56) and the vegetarian Roman emperor, Julian the Apostate, who defends Diogenes for having eaten a live octopus.

HIPPOCRATIC WRITINGS c. 430–c. 330 BCE

Hippocrates was born on Kos in 460 BCE. He founded the Hippocratic School of Medicine and a vast number of writings were collected under his name, although it is unclear how many of them he actually wrote himself. This selection includes his famous oath, as well as treatises on epidemics, dream diagnoses and heart surgery.

2012
trans. Robert Dobbin

1978 Pelican Classics
1983 Penguin Classics
trans. E. T. Withington, 1928
trans. J. Chadwick & W. N. Mann, 1950
trans. I. M. Lonie, 1978
intro. G. E. R. Lloyd, 1978

Plato

c.427 – c.347 BCE

Plato was born into an influential political family in Athens, but he disowned politics after his mentor Socrates was executed in 399 BCE, and devoted his life to philosophy instead. He founded the Academy, one of the first higher education institutions in the world. Plato's philosophy is discursive: he wrote dialogues, in which the character of Socrates engages one or more interlocutors. These conversations cover a vast range of subjects from maths and science to law, politics, art, ethics and religion. The entire history of western thought has been described by the philosopher Alfred Whitehead as 'a series of footnotes to Plato'. He is said to have died in his sleep, to the sound of flute music.

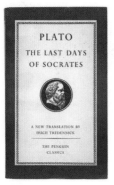

1954
trans. Hugh Tredennick
rev. Harold Tarrant, 1993
—
Tredennick suggested a portrait of Socrates for the cover of his translation and recommended a likeness in the British Museum. 'If, as I assume, you employ an artist to make a line drawing for reproduction,' he wrote, 'he would probably do best to sketch from the statuette itself, which is in Bay VI of the King Edward Gallery.' The bust of Socrates is currently on display in Room 22 of the British Museum, 'The World of Alexander'.

2010
trans. Christopher Rowe

The Last Days of Socrates

Euthyphro; *Apology*; *Crito*; *Phaedo*
c.399 – c.380 BCE

Socrates was accused of corrupting the young minds of Athens. In these four dialogues, Plato narrates the events that led to his teacher's execution by drinking hemlock: in *Euthyphro*, Socrates is outside the courthouse debating the nature of piety; the *Apology* is Socrates' defence of the philosopher's life; in *Crito*, he refuses the opportunity to escape prison; and in the *Phaedo*, the day before his death, he argues confidently for the existence of the afterlife and the immortality of the soul.

Early Socratic Dialogues

Ion; *Laches*; *Lysis*; *Charmides*; *Hippias Major*; *Hippias Minor*; *Euthydemus*
c.399 – c.389 BCE

Plato's earliest dialogues were written in memory of Socrates. In *Ion*, Socrates dissects poetic inspiration with a Homeric rhapsodist; in *Laches*, he attempts to define bravery; *Lysis* considers friendship; *Charmides*, self-control. He engages Hippias, an arrogant literary critic, on the subjects of beauty and lying, and in *Euthydemus*, he exposes the logical fallacies of three sophists.

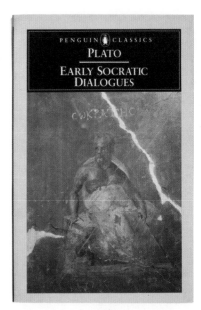

1987
ed. Trevor J. Saunders
trans. Trevor J. Saunders, Iain Lane, Donald Watt & Robin Waterfield

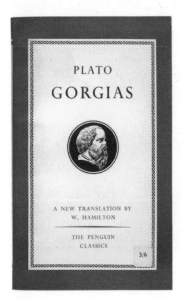

1960
trans. Walter Hamilton
rev. Chris Emlyn-Jones, 2004

Gorgias

c.380 BCE

This dialogue contrasts the rhetorician's art of persuasion with the intellectual rigour of philosophy. The sophist Gorgias thinks good government relies on winning hearts and minds; the aspiring politician Callicles believes that power lies in strength; but Socrates argues that a politician's first duty should be to the welfare of his citizens, at one point taking both sides of an argument to make his point.

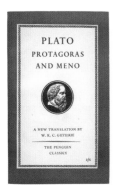

1956
● trans. W. K. C. Guthrie

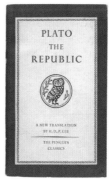

2005
trans. Adam Beresford
intro. Lesley Brown

Protagoras
and Meno

c. 385 – *c.* 380 BCE

These dialogues ask what it means to be 'good'. In *Protagoras*, a youthful Socrates spars with an intelligent and amusing sophist; in *Meno*, a more elderly Socrates silences a young aristocrat, as they discuss the nature of *arête,* 'skill'.

The Republic

c. 375 BCE

Plato's masterwork, *The Republic*, is a cornerstone of western philosophy. Socrates and three interlocutors debate the characteristics of a perfect community and the role of the ideal citizen. The wide-ranging discussion encompasses the nature of reality, the substance of knowledge and the purpose of education. Their imaginary state is to be governed with wisdom and justice: poets are banished, children are raised collectively and rules are enforced by a superior class of men and women known as 'guardians'.

The Symposium

c. 375 BCE

Seven men at a drinking party hosted by the tragedian Agathon expound on the nature of love. They discuss beauty, sacrifice, the difference between sexual gratification and long-term relationships, love as a force of nature and the idea of soul mates. The playwright Aristophanes (24) is among the company. Socrates asserts that the highest form of love is to transcend the physical and emotional, to become a lover of wisdom, a philosopher. *The Symposium* is where the concept of 'Platonic love' originates.

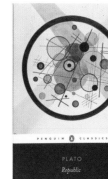

1955
trans. Desmond Lee
rev. Melissa Lane, 2002
further reading Rachana
Kamtekar, 2002

2012 *Republic*
trans. Christopher Rowe

1951
● trans. W. Hamilton

1999
trans. Christopher Gill

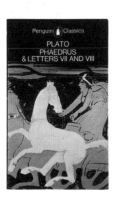

1973
● trans.
W. Hamilton
—
2005
trans. Christopher
Rowe
—
Hamilton's
edition included
two letters by
Plato addressed
to the followers
of Dion (54), the
assassinated
tyrant of Syracuse.

Phaedrus

c. 375 BCE

Set in the countryside outside Athens, Socrates and the young Phaedrus have a flirtatious and wide-ranging discussion about the virtues of romantic love and the pursuit of beauty, touching on the immortality of the soul and the art of rhetoric.

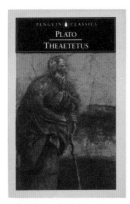

1987
trans. Robin Waterfield
—
Robin Waterfield was a copy
editor and a commissioning
editor for Penguin Books.
He is now a freelance writer,
living with his wife on a small
olive farm in southern Greece
producing organic olive oil.

Theaetetus

c. 375 BCE

A founding text of epistemology, the study
of knowledge itself, this dialogue is a debate
between Socrates and the mathematicians
Theaetetus and Theodorus. The questions they
raise continue to intrigue philosophers. Is
knowledge always subjective? Does it rely on
personal judgement? Do our beliefs require
evidence? Socrates concludes that knowing
what we don't know about knowledge is
valuable knowledge in itself, and departs for
his trial (26).

Timaeus
and Critias

c. 365–*c.* 55 BCE

Timaeus presents a history of the cosmos,
and the physical, metaphysical and religious
laws that govern it, including the concepts
of the four elements, the Platonic solids, the
golden ratio and the World Soul. It laid the
foundation for 2,000 years of western scientific
thought. The preamble to *Timaeus* includes an
account of the lost continent of Atlantis, which
is expanded in the fragmentary *Critias*.

1965 *Timaeus*
1971 Reissued as *Timaeus
and Critias*
trans. Desmond Lee

1982
trans. Robin Waterfield

Philebus

c. 360 BCE

Socrates and Philebus debate the good life:
initially the hedonist Philebus advocates the
pursuit of pleasure, but Socrates dismisses this
as the life of a jellyfish. After discussion, they
conclude that fulfilment is only achievable
through the pursuit of truth and knowledge.

The Laws

c. 355–*c.* 350 BCE

In his last dialogue, Plato imagines a small agricultural community called Magnesia. He lays out an
intricate and authoritarian system of legislation,
overseen by an administrative council, which governs
all aspects of life in the community, from crime and
punishment to education, sport, sex and drinking
parties. *The Laws* is Plato's only dialogue not to
feature Socrates.

1970
trans. Trevor J. Saunders
pref. R. F. Stalley, 2004

'For five years I lived the
Laws,' wrote Trevor J.
Saunders; 'but it is the
only way: the translator
must be pickled in what he
translates.' Saunders was
a 'demon croquet player'
who had a passion for
films and railway history.

Aristotle

384–322 BCE

Aristotle's father was a physician at the court of King Amyntas of Macedon. At the age of seventeen, Aristotle travelled to Athens to enrol at Plato's Academy (26) and he studied there for 20 years until his master's death, after which he returned to Macedonia to tutor the young Alexander the Great. When Alexander succeeded to the Macedonian throne, Aristotle came back to Athens and founded his own school, the Lyceum. Like Plato, Aristotle wrote dialogues, of which only fragments survive, but fortunately the bulk of his work is preserved in the form of lecture notes. These consitute a highly innovative, systematic and comprehensive worldview – a 'river of gold' in the words of Cicero (39) – encompassing subjects as diverse as zoology, ethics, poetry and politics. After Alexander's death in 323 BCE, anti-Macedonian ill-feeling drove Aristotle out of Athens, to Chalcis on the island of Euboea, where he died a year later. He was buried beside his wife Pythias. Medieval Muslim scholars called him 'The First Teacher'.

1986
trans. Hugh Lawson-Tancred
—
Lawson-Tancred is the Ethics Coordinator of the Society for Data Miners, working on an ethical code for data analysts. He has translated widely from Slavonic and Scandinavian languages, as well as Ancient Greek.

De Anima
(On the Soul)

Aristotle imagined three souls: plants have vegetative souls, capable of growth and nourishment; animals have vegetative and sensitive souls, capable of sensation and movement; but humans have vegetative, sensitive and rational souls, with a unique capacity for critical intelligence. Rather than the brain, Aristotle located the rational soul in the heart.

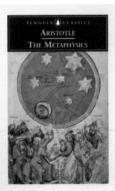

1998
trans. Hugh Lawson-Tancred

The Metaphysics

Metaphysics, the study of the essence of reality, is the 'first philosophy' according to Aristotle. He defined this fundamental branch of western thought, rejecting Plato's (26) theory of abstract forms in favour of a tangible model, in which the true substance of a thing lies in its concrete form.

The Politics

Where the *Ethics* concerns individuals, the *Politics* examines the good of the whole community. 'Man is by nature a political animal,' writes Aristotle: we gather ourselves into social groups that require systems of governance. In the *Politics*, Aristotle analyses a range of city constitutions, exploring how best to order society to ensure the happiness of the individual.

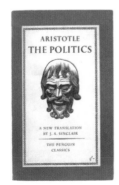

1962
trans. T. A. Sinclair
rev. Trevor J. Saunders, 1981
—
T. A. Sinclair's first initial was initially misprinted as 'J' on the first edition.

1955 *The Ethics*
1976 Reissued as *The Nicomachean Ethics*
trans. J. A. K. Thomson, 1953
rev. Hugh Tredennick, 1976
intro. Jonathan Barnes, 1976

The Nichomachean Ethics

Aristotle wrote three ethical treatises, of which *The Nichomachean Ethics* is the longest and the best known. It discusses how to live one's life, seeking happiness by living 'in accordance with virtue'. Aristotle dedicated the work to his son, Nichomachus, after whom it is named. *The Ethics* was highly influential in the Middle Ages: many scholars, including St Thomas Aquinas (70), sought to synthesize Aristotle's ethics with Christian theology.

The Art of Rhetoric

Rhetoric was an essential skill in ancient Athens, where power lay in one's ability to influence assemblies and councils with persuasive oratory. Aristotle's *Art of Rhetoric* is more than a manual of techniques, however: he analyses the logic behind effective lines of reasoning.

1991
trans. Hugh Lawson-Tancred

Poetics

Aristotle's hugely influential work of literary criticism dissects the tragedies of Aeschylus (20), Sophocles (21) and Euripides (22), identifying the ways in which they approach 'complication and resolution', character development and 'imitation of reality' (*mimesis*). Most intriguing is his concept of *catharsis*, through which an audience's emotions are 'purified' by the experience of tragic art. His companion volume on comedy has been lost.

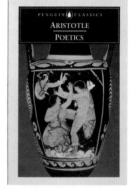

1996
trans. Michael Heath

The Athenian Constitution

This history and analysis of the politics and politicians of Athens was probably written by a student of Aristotle, under his guidance. It provides an invaluable source of information about the Athenian city-state between the 7th and 4th centuries BCE, with accounts of the reformer Solon, the tyrant Pisistratus, the democracy of Cleisthenes and the legendary statesman Pericles (54).

1984
trans. P. J. Rhodes

CLASSICAL LITERARY CRITICISM
Plato, *Ion & Republic 2, 3 and 10*; Aristotle, *Poetics*; Horace, *The Art of Poetry*; Longinus, *On the Sublime*
4th century BCE – 1st century CE

Plato (27) banishes poets from his ideal republic, whereas Aristotle (29) believes tragedies perform an essential societal function. The Latin author Horace (45) advocates poetry rooted in practical ethics whereas Longinus praises pure inspiration. The works in this volume form the foundation of literary criticism in the western world, introducing terms and formulating an enduring conversation about the nature and function of literature.

1965
trans. T. S. Dorsch
rev. Penelope
Murray, 2000

ANCIENT RHETORIC
from Aristotle to Philostratus
4th century BCE –
3rd century CE

A successful orator in the ancient world could sway a courtroom or affect legislation, gain fame at ceremonial competitions or fortune as a politician. This

2017
trans. Thomas Habinek

anthology provides a classical how-to guide for rhetoricians, with advice on strengthening memory, optimizing persuasiveness and finessing one's delivery, with tips from Aristotle (29), Cicero (39), and famous orators and teachers such as Quintilian and Philostratus.

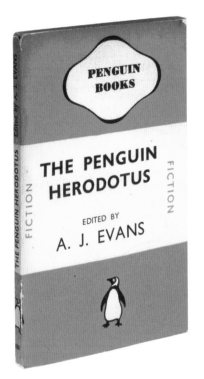

HISTORY

Herodotus wrote what is traditionally considered the first work of history and one of the oldest surviving works of prose literature. Soon afterwards, Thucydides wrote the highly influential *History of the Peloponnesian War* (32), a narrative that was continued by Xenophon in his *A History of My Times* (33). This began a tradition, inherited by the Romans, of extending and maintaining a continuous chronicle of notable events, one writer picking up where his literary predecessor broke off. The first historians were staking out new territory, exploring what it means to write about the past.

Herodotus c. 490–c. 425 BCE

Little is known about Herodotus's life. He was born in Halicarnassus in Asia Minor, and he travelled widely throughout the Mediterranean world. He lived in Athens for a while and was friends with Sophocles (21). He was the first writer to investigate historical subjects critically, and has been known as the 'Father of History' since Cicero (39) described him as such.

The Histories c. 400 BCE

Herodotus wrote his his 'inquiries' into the origins of the Greco-Persian wars 'so that human achievements may not become forgotten in time'. *The Histories* covers a huge variety of topics, from dolphin rides and cannibalism to a grand tour of Egypt, a tribe of dog-headed men and legendary gold-digging ants. He is careful, however, to distinguish between what he has seen with his own eyes and what he was merely told.

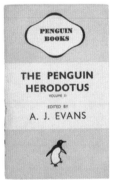

1941, 1943 *The Penguin Herodotus*
• trans. A. J. Evans
Published in two volumes
—
Herodotus was the only classical author published by Penguin Books before the Penguin Classics series was founded: A. J. Evans's two volumes appeared during the Second World War. The first volume appeared in the orange livery of general fiction, though it should really have been blue for history. As Herodotus is also known as the 'Father of Lies', perhaps this confusion is not infelicitous.

1954
trans. Aubrey de Sélincourt
rev. John Marincola, 1996

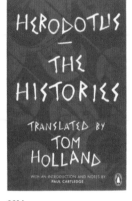

2014
trans. Tom Holland
intro. Paul Cartledge
—
In 2007, Tom Holland won the Classical Association Prize, awarded to 'the individual who has done most to promote the study of the language, literature and civilization of Ancient Greece and Rome'.

2017
trans. John Marincola

ON WRITING HISTORY
from Herodotus to Herodian
5th century BCE–4th century CE

What is the purpose of history? Is it to record great deeds or illuminate local customs, glorify your country or convey the stark realities of war, portray mighty heroes or promulgate ethnographic data? This anthology gathers complete essays by Dionysius of Halicarnassus, Plutarch (54) and Lucian (57) and shorter pieces and extracts by many other classical writers who have grappled with the question of what history is and how it should be written.

Thucydides c. 460–c. 400 BCE

Thucydides participated in the early stages of the Peloponnesian War between Athens and Sparta. After barely surviving the Plague of Athens in 430 BCE, which killed Pericles, he led a squadron of ships to save the Athenian colony of Amphipolis, but he arrived too late: the colony had already been seized by the Spartans. As a result of this embarrassment he was exiled. For the next 20 years he travelled around the Peloponnesian peninsula and further afield as the world's first war reporter, observing both sides of the conflict first-hand. The first translator of Thucydides into English was the philosopher Thomas Hobbes (171), who described him as 'the most Politick Historiographer that ever writ'.

History of the Peloponnesian War c. 431–c. 400 BCE

Thucydides' *History* attempts to present an unbiased account of the war to end all wars. He was more scrupulous with his evidence than Herodotus (31) and never relies on divine intervention to explain events. The narrative covers military engagements, political decisions, reconstructed speeches and details of war machines. It ends abruptly in the 21st year of the war, and it seems likely Thucydides died unexpectedly while writing; some say he was murdered.

1954
trans. Rex Warner
intro. M. I. Finley, 1972

'I found myself listening to a broadcast on the third programme of Rex Warner's translation of Pericles's speech,' wrote the Penguin general editor, A. S. B. Glover, to E. V. Rieu (17) in November 1950. 'It struck me as a remarkably good version. I don't know whether it has ever been published, but it did seem to me on the strength of it that if we could get Rex Warner to do Thucydides for the Classics he would make a very nice job of it'.

Xenophon c. 430–c. 354 BCE

Xenophon was an exact contemporary of Plato (26) and a fellow student of Socrates. Like Thucydides, he was exiled from Athens and spent much of his life under Spartan protection, living in the countryside with his wife and two sons. He is most famous for his involvement in the failed campaign of Cyrus the Younger to claim the Persian throne from his brother Artaxerxes II, which Xenophon recounts in *The Persian Expedition*.

Rex Warner was a novelist and a friend of W. H. Auden, Cecil Day-Lewis and Stephen Spender. He wrote *The Wild Goose Chase*, a Kafkaesque dystopian fantasy; *The Professor*, about a compromised academic under a fascist regime; and his most accomplished work, *The Aerodrome*, an allegory of the choice between earthy reality and airy abstraction. V. S. Pritchett called him 'the only outstanding novelist of ideas whom the decade of ideas produced.'

1949
trans. Rex Warner
intro. George Cawkwell, 1972

The Persian Expedition c. 370 BCE

In 401 BCE, Cyrus the Younger gathered a mercenary army of Persians and Greeks marched into Mesopotamia to overthrow his brother Artaxerxes, king of Persia. The army achieved a tactical draw at the Battle of Cunaxa, but Cyrus himself was killed, rendering the entire campaign a failure, and the Greek hoplites stranded. Xenophon was among the swiftly elected leaders who led this ragtag army, known as 'the Ten Thousand', out of enemy territory, up the River Tigris and beyond, to the shore of the Black Sea, the sight of which was greeted with the famous cry 'Thálatta, thálatta!', 'The sea, the sea!', which James Joyce quotes at the start of *Ulysses*.

1966
trans. Rex Warner
intro. George Cawkwell, 1979

A History of My Times

(Hellenica) *c.* 362 – *c.* 345 BCE

This work is a continuation of Thucydides' *History of the Peloponnesian War* (32). It picks up directly where Thucydides left off in 411 BCE, with the words 'Some days later'. It then proceeds to narrate the next fifty years of Greek warfare, from the end of the Peloponnesian War to the struggle to restrain Theban hegemony, the conflict that ultimately led to the decline of classical Greece.

Conversations of Socrates *c.* 394 – *c.* 354 BCE

Socrates' Defence; *Memoirs of Socrates*; *The Dinner-Party*; *The Estate-Manager*

Along with Plato (26), Xenophon is one of our chief sources of information about the philosopher Socrates. *Socrates' Defence* is Xenophon's account of Socrates' defence at his trial. At one time, it seems to have formed the epilogue to *Memoirs of Socrates*, which is Xenophon's own defence of his teacher and also includes stories about Socrates' life and conversations. In *The Dinner-Party*, various drinkers, including Socrates and Xenophon, discuss which personal qualities they are most proud of, and *The Estate-Manager* is a dialogue about good household and farm management.

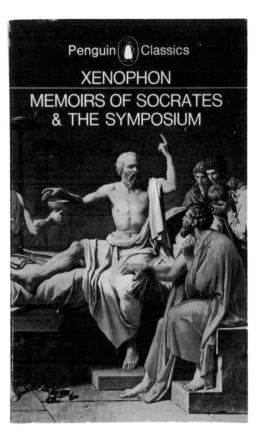

1970 *Memoirs of Socrates and The Symposium*
1990 Reissued as *Conversations of Socrates*
trans. Hugh Tredennick, 1970
rev. Robin Waterfield, 1990

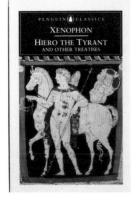

1997
trans. Robin Waterfield
intro. Paul Cartledge

Hiero the Tyrant

and Other Treatises *c.* 367 – *c.* 54 BCE

These essays explore the qualities of good leadership. *Hiero the Tyrant* is a dialogue between an absolute dictator and the poet Simonides; *Agesilaus* is a eulogistic biography of Xenophon's patron, the Spartan king (54); the next three treatises deal with the skills required of a contemporary cavalry commander; and *Ways and Means* is a response to the collapse of the Athenian Empire, suggesting radical economic reforms.

Hellenistic Greece

Alexander the Great expanded the Greek-speaking world east beyond Syria and south into Egypt. After his death in 323 BCE, these new territories were divided among his generals and the original Greek city-states formed confederations known as 'leagues'. This period is known as 'Hellenistic Greece' when Greek language and culture dispersed and formed a supranational identity, the *Koine*. As Greeks emigrated south and east, the centre of Greek culture shifted from Athens to Alexandria, the city founded by Alexander on the coast of Egypt. At the heart of this city was the spectacular Musaeum, the 'Shrine to the Muses', which contained the legendary Library of Alexandria, which held a copy of every work of classical Greek literature.

Menander c. 341 – c. 290 BCE

Menander was an Athenian and the leading proponent of Greek New Comedy, a comedy of manners with domestic settings and complicated love tangles. He wrote over 100 plays, although only one survives intact. They were extremely popular and he had many Roman imitators including Plautus (37) and Terence (38). He is said to have drowned while bathing.

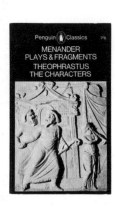
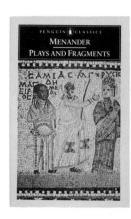

1967
● trans. Philip Vellacott
—
1987
trans. Norma Miller
—
Vellacott's edition included *The Characters*, a survey of character stereotypes by Theophrastus, Aristotle's (29) successor as head of the Lyceum.

Plays and Fragments

Old Cantankerous (*Dyskalos*) is Menander's only play that survives intact; it was discovered on an Egyptian papyrus in 1958. The other fragments in this collection include sections from *The Rape of the Locks*, *The Arbitration*, *The Girl from Samos* and *The Toady*.

Epicurus 341–270 BCE

Born to Athenian parents on the island of Samos, Epicurus served in the same class of ephebes as Menander, a form of Athenian national service. He founded a philosophical community near Athens known as 'the Garden', which was the first to admit women as a matter of course. The inscription above the gate read: 'Stranger, here you will do well to tarry; here our highest good is pleasure.' Epicurus was a vegetarian and died from kidney stones at the age of 72, sitting in a warm bath with a glass of wine in his hand.

The Art of Happiness

Epicurus wrote over 40 major works, almost all of which have been lost; a few fragments and three letters are all that survive. His philosophy advocates a happy, self-sufficient life, free from pain and fear, surrounded by friends. He believed that death should not be feared, that gods are uninterested in humans and that the universe is infinite.

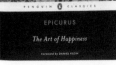

2012
trans. George K. Strodach, 1963
fwd. Daniel Klein, 2012

Apollonius of Rhodes

3rd century BCE

Despite his name, Apollonius of Rhodes
was born in Alexandria. We know little
about his life. At one time he was the
director of the Library of Alexandria.

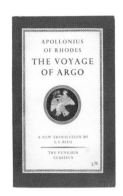

1959
The Voyage of Argo
trans. E. V. Rieu

2014
Jason and the Argonauts
trans. Aaron Poochigan
intro. Benjamin Acosta-Hughes

The Argonautica

The only full account of Jason and the Argonauts' quest for the Golden
Fleece sees the crew of the *Argo* survive enchanting sirens, clashing rocks
and an army of dragon's-teeth, with the help of the witch-princess Medea
(22). Apollonius combines the spirit of Homeric epic with the emerging
genre of romance.

THE GREEK ALEXANDER ROMANCE

3rd–2nd centuries BCE

Alexander the Great died in 323 BCE and almost immediately his life became
the stuff of legend. In this anonymous fantastical biography, Alexander is the
illegitimate son of a seductive sorcerer. He flies in a basket borne by eagles and
descends into the ocean in a diving bell. His daughter turns into a mermaid.
The Alexander Romance was hugely popular in Europe and beyond. It was
rewritten and expanded several times in antiquity and translated into Syriac,
Ethiopic, Armenian and Pahlavi. Some of its stories appear in the Koran (97).

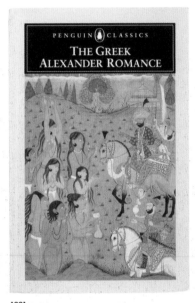

1991
trans. Richard Stoneman

Polybius *c.*200–*c.*118 BCE

Polybius was a Greek politician until he was taken hostage during
the Third Macedonian war and removed to Rome for 17 years.
Whilst there he made prominent connections and following the
sack of both Carthage and Corinth in
146 BCE, when Greece finally came under
Roman control, Polybius was appointed to
arrange the relations between city-states in
the new Roman province of Achaea.

1979
trans. Ian Scott-Kilvert
intro. F. W. Walbank

The Rise of the Roman Empire

Polybius describes how the Roman Republic
came to dominate the Mediterranean, focusing on the period between the start of the
First Punic War in 264 BCE and the Sack of
Carthage in 146 BCE. He was writing to help
his Greek countrymen come to terms with
foreign rule, drawing on a variety of documentary sources and first-hand interviews with
Roman veterans. He provides the most reliable
account of Hannibal's trans-alpine campaign,
as he knew the family of Scipio Africanus, the
general who finally defeated Hannibal in 201
BCE. Livy's account (46)
follows Polybius closely.

*For Greece under
the Roman Empire,
turn to p.54*

Ancient Rome

A 393

Edited by Michael Grant

Roman Readings

A 393

PLAUTUS THE POT OF GOLD AND OTHER PLAYS

L149

PLAUTUS THE ROPE AND OTHER PLAYS

L136

TERENCE THE BROTHERS AND OTHER PLAYS

L156

THE NATURE OF THE UNIVERSE

LUCRETIUS

L18

CICERO SELECTED WORKS

L99

CICERO MURDER TRIALS

L288
ISBN 0 14
044.288 X

CICERO In Defence of the Republic

PENGUIN CLASSICS

CICERO SELECTED POLITICAL SPEECHES

L214

CICERO'S LETTERS TO ATTICUS

ISBN 0 14
044.309 6

The Republic

Rome was founded on 21 April 753 BCE, according to tradition, by Romulus and Remus (45), twin descendants of Aeneas the Trojan (44). The city grew up around the Palatine Hill, where the River Tiber was shallow enough to ford. Following the reign of King Romulus, the Roman monarchy lasted 200 years until the despot Tarquin the Proud was overthrown in 509 BCE. At that point, the government of Rome became a 'communal matter', a *res publica*. The newly founded Republic was governed by two consuls, elected by the citizens for a year at a time, each of whom had the power of veto over the other, and these consuls were advised by a Senate.

Before long, rigorously drilled legions bearing the initials SPQR (*Senatus Populusque Romanus*, 'The Senate and People of Rome'), began expanding the Republic's power base. First they came to dominate the Italian peninsula and then they gained control of lands in North Africa, the Iberian peninsula and southern Gaul. The Republic of Rome gradually took control of the entire Mediterranean seaboard. The surviving literature of this period begins with the comedies of Plautus and Terence (38). The last years of the Republic were dominated by the prose of Cicero (39), the histories of Caesar (41) and the lyric poetry of Catullus (42).

Plautus c. 254–184 BCE

Titus Maccius Plautus began his career as a stage carpenter. He became a comic actor, adopting the stage names Maccius ('buffoon') and Plautus ('flat-footed'), before eventually turning his hand to writing popular plays, inspired by Menander (34). His plays are the earliest works of Latin literature that survive intact. His epitaph read: 'Since Plautus is dead, Comedy mourns'.

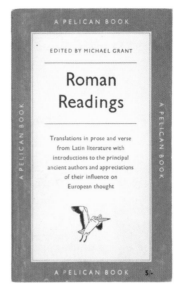

1958 *Roman Readings*
1979 Reissued in Penguin Classics as *Latin Literature*
ed. Michael Grant
—
Professor Michael Grant was a prolific writer and translator. He served alongside David Niven in the Second World War and shared rooms with Bertrand Russell at Trinity College, Cambridge. He was at various times President of the Royal Numismatic Society and Principal of University College, Khartoum, and he retired to Italy in 1966, where he lived with his wife in a 16th-century house near Lucca. Grant's *Roman Readings* originally formed a pair with his Pelican 'description' of Roman Literature.

LATIN LITERATURE
An Anthology
3rd century BCE – 5th century CE

From the orations of Cicero (39) and the poetry of Virgil (44) to the expansive Christian worldview of St Augustine (62), this anthology represents the best of seven centuries of Latin literature, from the height of the Republic to the fall of the Empire and the rise of Christianity. Michael Grant gathers a range of modern and historical translations, from writers including Milton (150), Pope (152), Swift (159), Byron (195), Housman (268) and Graves (439).

1958
• Pelican Books

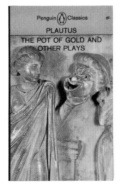

1965
trans. E. F. Watling

The Pot of Gold
and Other Plays c. 205 – c. 184 BCE
The Pot of Gold; *The Prisoners*; *The Brothers Menaechmus*; *The Swaggering Soldier*; *Pseudolus*

The Pot of Gold revolves around buried treasure in a miser's house; *The Prisoners* addresses serious themes of freedom and slavery; *The Brothers Menaechmus* involves a succession of mistaken identities, and formed the basis for Shakespeare's *Comedy of Errors* (136); *The Swaggering Soldier* is a bedroom farce masterminded by a slave; and the lovesick Calidorus attempts to liberate a mute prostitute in *Pseudolus*.

The Rope
and Other Plays c. 205 – c. 184 BCE

The Ghost; *The Rope*; *A Three-Dollar Day*; *Amphitryo*

In *The Ghost*, a fun-loving son persuades his father that a riotous house party is the manifestation of a poltergeist; in *The Rope*, a girl stolen by pirates is reunited with her family after a storm shipwrecks her pimp; *A Three-Dollar Day* features a fake promissory note conveyed for a minimal fee; and in *Amphitryo*, Jupiter assumes the semblance of Alcmena's husband in order to sleep with her in secret, thereby fathering Hercules.

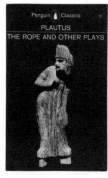

1964
trans. E. F. Watling

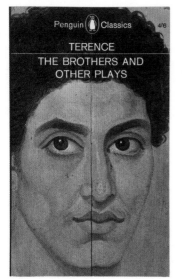

Terence c. 185 – c. 159 BCE

Publius Terentius Afer was a slave from Carthage, named after his master, the Roman senator Terentius Lucanus. He earned his freedom and subsequently wrote six plays, all of which survive and which were much studied by medieval scholars. He died on a journey to Greece at the age of just 25.

The Comedies 166–160 BCE

The Girl from Andros; *The Self-Tormentor*; *The Eunuch*; *Phormio*; *The Mother-in-Law*; *The Brothers*

1965 *The Brothers and Other Plays*
1967 Reissued as *Phormio and Other Plays*
1976 Reissued as *The Comedies*
trans. Betty Radice

The Girl from Andros is the story of an on-off engagement; a father regrets persuading his son to go to war in *The Self-Tormentor*; in *The Eunuch*, which St Augustine quotes in *City of God* (62), a eunuch turns out to be more virile than his mistress imagines; *Phormio* is a romantic farce, untangled by a quick-witted slave; *The Mother-in-Law* features rape, prostitution and shotgun marriages — an early performance was abandoned when rowdy gladiator fans stormed the stage; and *The Brothers* contrasts two radically different parenting styles.

Lucretius c. 99 – c. 55 BCE

Almost nothing is known about the life of Titus Lucretius Carus. We know that Cicero (39) admired his poetry. He is said to have gone mad after drinking a toxic aphrodisiac potion and taken his own life. Ovid wrote in his *Amores* (46) that 'the verses of the sublime Lucretius will perish only when a day will bring the end of the world.'

The Nature of Things

Lucretius's cosmic, philosophical poem expounds ideas of Epicureanism (34), including concepts such as atomism, the survival of the fittest, free will and a universe governed by chance. It is a profound and elegiac exploration of man's position on earth, which informed Virgil's *Georgics* (44) a generation later and profoundly influenced Machiavelli (120), Montaigne (126) and Molière (167).

1951 *The Nature of the Universe*
• trans. Ronald E. Latham

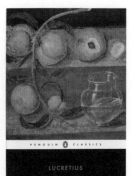

2007
trans. A. E. Stallings
intro. Richard Jenkyns

Cicero 106–43 BCE

Marcus Tullius was an invalid child. His surname, Cicero, means 'chickpea'. He studied Greek philosophy and trained as a barrister, developing a spectacular talent for oratory, on the strength of which he became a highly success-ful politician, ascending the *cursus honorum* **(the hie-rarchy of public offices) in the shortest term possible: he was elected consul at the age of just 43. His philosophy and oratory have been vastly influential, particu-larly on the** Renaissance **(118) and the 18th-century** Enlightenment **(147).** *On Duties* **was one of the very first classical texts to be printed, in 1465. John Adams, the second President of the United States, wrote wrote in 1787 that 'all the ages of the world have not produced a greater statesman and philosopher united in the same character'.**

1960
trans. Michael Grant

Selected Works

70–44 BCE

This anthology provides a survey of Cicero's astonishing career, from the legal prosecution that established his oratorical skills to a pair of philosophical treatises from the end of his eventful life. It also includes a selection of his personal letters and his famous denunciation of Mark Antony (55) after the murder of Julius Caesar (55).

Murder Trials

80–45 BCE

Cicero took his first major legal case at the age of 26: the defence of Sextus Roscius, a farmer's son, on the charge of patricide. The case was a risk: patricide was considered an abomination and Cicero was attributing the murder to a freedman of Sulla (55), the dangerous Roman dictator. His ingenious, persuasive speeches led to Roscius's acquittal, however, and Cicero's fame as a barrister spread throughout Rome. This selection presents four of Cicero's early cases, all for defendants accused of murder.

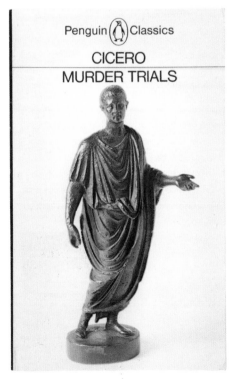

1975
trans. Michael Grant

In Defence of the Republic

70–44 BCE

Throughout his career, Cicero was a staunch defender of the Republic. He strove against corruption and dict-ators, such as Sulla (55), whom he saw as undermining Rome's political stability. This volume showcases all his greatest patriotic speeches, including the successful prosecution of Gaius Verres, an exploitative governor of Sicily, which cemented his reputation.

2011
trans. Siobhán McElduff

Selected Political Speeches 66–44 BCE

During Cicero's consulship in 63 BCE, he suppressed a conspiracy against the Republic, led by the senator Lucius Sergius Catilina: the four vehement orations he delivered drove Catilina and his followers out of Rome, an episode described memorably by Sallust (42). This selection of speeches and legal defences demonstrates the particular eloquence and efficacy of Cicero's orations.

1969
trans. Michael Grant

1978 *Cicero's Letters to Atticus*
● trans. D. R. Shackleton Bailey
1978 *Cicero's Letters to His Friends*
● trans. D. R. Shackleton Bailey
Published in two volumes

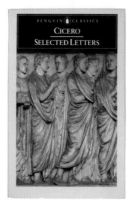

1986
trans. D. R. Shackleton Bailey
—
For his 1986 edition, Bailey made a selection from his three earlier volumes. Bailey was a cat lover. He dedicated the first volume of his 1965 Cambridge edition of Cicero's letters to his white cat Donum, who was 'more intelligent than most people I have encountered'.

Selected Letters
68–43 BCE

Nine hundred letters by Cicero were published after his death. As well as fascinating insights into his private life, they include virtuosic passages of moral and political philosophy, and together they provide a window on to the end of the Roman Republic, as it gave way to tyranny. Many of Cicero's letters were written to his close friend Atticus, to whom he complained despondently from exile, 'I hope I may see the day when I shall thank you for making me go on living. So far I am heartily sorry you did.'

On Government 70–43 BCE

Cicero was not involved in the assassination of Julius Caesar (41), but he later wrote to the conspirator Trebonius: 'How I could wish that you had invited me to that most glorious banquet on the Ides of March.' Immediately afterwards he emerged as the popular spokesman for the Senate, making fourteen impassioned attacks on the consul Mark Antony (55), leader of the Caesarean faction. He called these speeches his *Philippics*, after the Greek orator Demosthenes' denunciations of Philip II of Macedon. They are the brilliant culmination of his political opposition to tyranny.

1993
trans. Michael Grant

On the Good Life 55–44 BCE

Combining his deep knowledge of the Greek philosophers (25) with extensive worldly experience, Cicero formulated a view of the good life that balanced personal contentment with moral virtue. This collection sets out his practical thoughts on the pursuit of happiness, the importance of friendship and the individual's duty to state and family. *The Dream of Scipio* includes a psychedelic tour of the universe, which inspired several of Chaucer's dream poems (89).

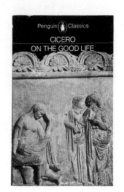

1971
trans. Michael Grant

The Nature of the Gods 44 BCE

In this late work, Cicero presents a three-part dialogue that raises theological questions about the existence of god, the efficacy of prayer and the

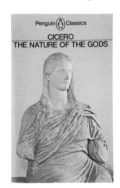

purpose of religion. It was a highly influential work for St Augustine (62) and St Thomas Aquinas (70). In his *Treatise on Toleration*, Voltaire (176) called it 'perhaps the best book of all antiquity'.

1972
trans. Horace C. P. McGregor
intro. J. M. Ross

On Living and Dying Well
45–43 BCE

When Mark Antony (55) formed the Second Triumvirate with Caesar's adopted son, Octavian (43), Cicero was listed as an enemy of the state. He was hunted down and murdered outside his villa in Formiae, and his severed head and hands were nailed to a platform in the Roman forum. Mark Antony's wife Fulvia is said to have pinched his dead tongue and jabbed it repeatedly with her hairpin in revenge for his skills as an orator. This volume collects Cicero's works on living well and dying with dignity.

2012
trans. Thomas Habinek

Caesar 100–44 BCE

Gaius Julius Caesar claimed descent from Aeneas (44), and specifically his son Ascanius, known as Iulus or Julus, 'catkin'. 'Caesar', he believed, meant 'elephant' and he is said to have taken an elephant with him on his invasion of Britain. Caesar was high priest of Jupiter in Rome and was once captured by Aegean pirates, with whom he haggled to bump up his ransom. He was a supremely talented politician and military commander, conquering all Gaul, bridging the Rhine and leading invasions across the Channel. When the Senate ordered him to disband his army in 50 BCE, he refused, crossing the River Rubicon and marching on Rome, where he was appointed Dictator. He continued to execute impressive military victories in the course of a gruelling civil war and conducted an extravagant affair with Cleopatra, the last pharaoh of Egypt. In February 44 BCE, his dictatorship was declared perpetual and one month later he was assassinated, on 15 March. After his death, he was officially proclaimed a god.

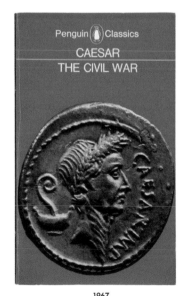

The Conquest of Gaul
58–49 BCE

Caesar conquered most of what is now Belgium, France and Switzerland, and he invaded Britain twice. His account of his campaign details his military strategies and includes portraits of the lands and the people he met including the Gallic chieftain, Vercingetorix, whom he captured and later executed by strangulation.

1951
trans. S. A. Handford
rev. Jane F. Gardner, 1982

The Civil War c. 40 BCE

When Caesar crossed the Rubicon, he instigated a civil war with Pompey the Great, which shook the entire Roman world, from Gaul to Africa and Asia Minor. The latter campaign prompted his famous claim, *veni, vidi, vici*. His own account of the struggle ends in 48 BCE, when Pompey (55) was murdered, but his lieutenants continued the narrative, and their accounts of *The Alexandrian War*, *The African War* and *The Spanish War* are also included in this volume.

1967
trans. Jane F. Gardner

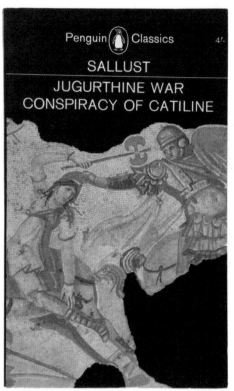

1963 *Jugurthine War* and *Conspiracy of Catiline*
● trans. S. A. Handford

Sallust 86–c. 35 BCE

Gaius Sallustius Crispus was a Roman politician and supporter of Julius Caesar (41). He served Caesar during the Civil War and was appointed governor of the former kingdom of Numidia (northern Algeria), where he amassed a huge personal fortune through exploitation and extortion. With these ill-gotten gains he purchased Caesar's luxurious mansion and parkland in Rome and retired there to write history books

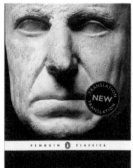

2007
trans. A. J. Woodman

Catiline's War
The Jugurthine War
Histories

Catiline's War is an account of the conspiracy of 63 BCE, led by Lucius Sergius Catilina, which was thwarted by Cicero (39). It portrays Rome in terminal moral decline, headed by a degenerate old aristocracy. *The Jugurthine War* is a record of the war against Jugurtha, king of Numidia, from 111 to 105 BCE; and the fragmentary *Histories* describe the events following the death of the dictator Sulla (55) in 78 BCE.

Catullus c. 84–c. 54 BCE

Gaius Valerius Catullus was born into a wealthy family living on the shores of Lake Garda, and was greatly influenced by the poetry of Sappho (18). In 57–56 BCE he travelled to Bithynia in Turkey and visited his brother's grave in the Troad, a neighbouring province. Little else is known about his life.

The Poems

Catullus's poems are erotic and poignant, full of psychological insight. Many are dedicated to 'Lesbia', who is usually identified as the infamous Clodia Metelli, the aristocratic, nymphomaniac and possibly murderous wife of a Roman proconsul, with whom Catullus seems to have had an ill-fated love affair. One of his more famous poems is just two lines long:

> I hate and I love. And if you ask me how,
> I do not know: I only feel it, and I'm torn in two.

1966
trans. Peter Whigham
—
Peter Whigham's translation is dedicated to William Carlos Williams.

The Augustans

In 27 BCE, the Senate granted Octavian, Julius Caesar's adopted son, extraordinary powers: he changed his name to Augustus and took the titles 'princeps' and 'Imperator Caesar', thereby becoming the first Roman emperor. His reign instigated the *Pax Romana*, two centuries of relative peace and prosperity for Rome. Augustus took a particular interest in literature during his 40-year rule. He encouraged Virgil to produce the *Aeneid* (44), Rome's national epic, and new literary forms were developed and perfected by Horace (45) and Ovid (46).

Vitruvius

c. 90–*c.* 20 BCE

Marcus Vitruvius Pollio served as a military engineer with Caesar during the conquest of Gaul (41). He specialized in constructing war machines including the *ballista*, a bolt thrower, and the *scorpio*, a deadly 'triggerfish' catapult. He was also an architect. The one building he is known to have designed was the basilica at Fanum Fortunae on the east coast of Italy, the remains of which have been incorporated into Fano cathedral. We know little else about his life.

On Architecture

c. 30–20 BCE

Vitruvius's treatise on architecture is dedicated to the Emperor Augustus. All buildings should be solid, useful and beautiful, he writes, and temples should mirror the proportions of an idealized human figure, a concept that Leonardo da Vinci would later illustrate as the 'Vitruvian Man'. Vitruvius's work was a major influence on Leon Battista Alberti (119) in the 15th century.

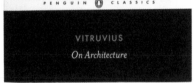

2009
trans. Richard Schofield,
intro. Robert Tavernor

Virgil 70–19 BCE

Publius Vergilius Maro lived most of his life in an Epicurean (34) colony on the Gulf of Naples. He was a shy, sickly man, who abandoned studies in medicine, rhetoric and astronomy to become a philosopher poet. After writing the *Eclogues*, he was recruited into Augustus's literary circle, where he met Horace (45) and the influential Maecena. He secured his reputation as the greatest poet of Ancient Rome with the *Georgics* and the *Aeneid*. In the Middle Ages, he was thought to be a magician and an alchemist. In fact, the Welsh word for pharmacist, *fferyllydd*, derives from his name. Dante chose him as his guide through Hell and Purgatory in the *Divine Comedy* (84).

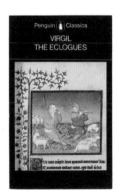

1949 *The Pastoral Poems*
● trans. E. V. Rieu

1984
trans. Guy Lee, 1980

The Eclogues 42–38 BCE

Virgil borrowed a Greek form of pastoral poetry for these ten vignettes of country life. They contain allusions to contemporary politics, including references to Augustus's expropriation of lands in northern Italy. *Eclogue 10* presents Arcadia, a bleak and rocky region of Greece, as the idyllic origin of pastoral verse, an unlikely tradition which nonetheless resonated for many centuries afterwards (131).

The Georgics 37–29 BCE

The *Georgics* is both a practical handbook for farmers and a fabulous celebration of the land. Virgil combines ancient agricultural wisdom with expositions on philosophy, history and mythology, interpreting the cyclical rhythms of the countryside to reveal insights into life, death and the beauty of nature. Dryden (151) considered it the greatest of all classical poems.

The Aeneid 29–19 BCE

Modelled on Homer's *Iliad* and *Odyssey* (16), the national epic of ancient Rome was commissioned by the emperor Augustus to rival the literature of Greece. It tells the story of the refugee Aeneas, fleeing the ashes of war-torn Troy and making the difficult sea voyage from North Africa and on to Italy, where his descendants Romulus and Remus (45) would one day found the city of Rome. On the way, he falls in love with Queen Dido of Carthage, ventures to the underworld and survives the stormy torments of Juno, queen of the gods. It is a staggering portrait of love, war and courage in the face of exile; Tennyson (263) called it 'the stateliest measure ever moulded by the lips of man'. Virgil wanted the manuscript burned after his death, but Augustus intervened and saved the masterpiece.

1982
trans. L. P. Wilkinson

2010
trans. Kimberly Johnson, 2009

1956
trans. W. F. Jackson Knight

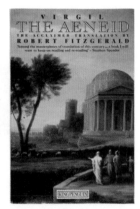

1990 King Penguin
• trans. Robert Fitzgerald, 1985

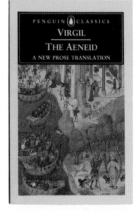

1991
trans. David West

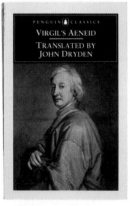

1997
trans. John Dryden (151), 1697
ed. Frederick M. Keener, 1997

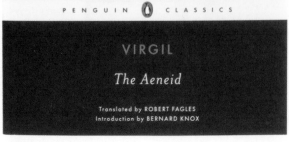

2012
trans. Robert Fagles, 2006
intro. Bernard Knox, 2006

Horace 65–8 BCE

Quintus Horatius Flaccus was the son of an auctioneer. After studying at Plato's Academy (26) in Athens, he fought with the Republican army against Octavian, until they were defeated at Philippi in 42 BCE. Returning to Rome, Horace found his father dead and all his goods confiscated. His lyric poetry was admired by Virgil (43), however, who introduced him to the patron Maecenas, who set Horace up with an income and access to the literary circles of Rome. He became the greatest lyric poet of the Augustan age.

The Satires of Horace and Persius

Horace, *Satires*, *Epistles*, *Ars Poetica*; Persius, *Satires*
c. 35 BCE–c. 62 CE

Horace used his *Satires* to promote Epicurean philosophy (34) and comment on mankind's obsessions with money, power and sex. His *Epistles* were addressed to friends and provide advice on living a happy life, as well as an overview of the history of Latin poetry. Persius (34–62 CE) was a later satirist, whose unusual verses attack contemporary poets and the morals of the aristocracy, including the Emperor Nero (52).

1973
trans. Niall Rudd

1967
• trans. James Michie

1983
trans. W. G. Shepherd
intro. Betty Radice

The Complete Odes and Epodes
with the Centennial Hymn

30–c. 11 BCE

An ode was a Greek lyrical composition, the third part of which was known as the 'epode'. Horace adopted the term and wrote a number of standalone 'epodes': truculent, satirical complaint poems. His odes are more moderate in comparison. They imitate the lyrics of Pindar (19) and Sappho (18), treating subjects such as love, wine, patriotism and the 'golden mean'.

Livy c. 64 BCE–17 CE

Little is known about Titus Livius Patavinus. He seems to have come from an affluent family and was a personal acquaintance of the Emperor Augustus (43). He spent most of his life writing a vast history of Rome in 142 books: *Ab Urbe Condita Libri*, 'Books from the Foundation of the City', covered everything from Rome's legendary origins right up to the Augustan Age. Sadly, only 35 of the books survive.

The Early History of Rome
Books 1–5

The first five books trace four centuries, from the foundation of the city by Romulus and Remus, traditionally dated to 753 BCE, to the invasion of the Gauls in 386 BCE and the Sack of Rome. It covers the reigns of seven kings and the establishment of the Republic, and includes the tragic story of Coriolanus, later dramatized by Shakespeare (143).

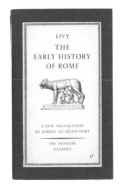

1960
trans. Aubrey de Sélincourt
intro. R. M. Ogilvie, 1971
pref. S. P. Oakley, 2002

Aubrey de Sélincourt was a 'schoolmaster of genius' for twenty-six years, during which time he wrote novels and children's stories. In 1947, he retired to the Isle of Wight: he was a keen yachtsman and wrote several books on sailing. His sister Dorothy married A. A. Milne.

1982
trans. Betty Radice
intro. R. M. Ogilvie

Rome and Italy
Books 6–10

After an almost catastrophic rout by the Gauls, Rome began its rise to power within Italy. The victory that cemented the city's fortunes was the defeat of the neighbouring Samnites in 293 BCE.

Books 11–20 have been lost; they covered the First Punic War (35) between Rome and Carthage, which began in 264 BCE.

The War with Hannibal
Books 21–30

Book 21 opens with the Second Punic War in 218 BCE. Livy describes the epic journey of the Carthaginian general Hannibal, as he crossed the Alps with war elephants and marched on Rome, destroying the Roman army at Cannae and Lake Trasimene. Book 30 concludes with Hannibal's defeat at the Battle of Zama in 202 BCE.

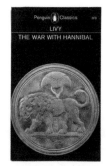

1965
trans. Aubrey de Sélincourt
rev. Betty Radice, 1972
—
E. V. Rieu (17) commemorated 'poor Aubrey de Sélincourt' in 1964, 'whose pen dropped from his hand as he was translating a sentence nineteen pages from the end of Livy's *War with Hannibal*'.

1976
trans. Henry Bettenson
intro. A. H. McDonald

Rome and the Mediterranean
Books 31–45

In the decades following the defeat of Carthage in 146 BCE, Rome began expanding its power base into Greece, Macedon and Asia and Mediterranean supremacy passed decisively from the Hellenistic world (34) to Rome. This episode concludes with the dramatic capture of King Perseus of Macedon in 167 BCE.

Sadly, the remaining 97 books of Livy's *History* have been lost.

Ovid *c.* 43 BCE – *c.* 18 CE

Initially Publius Ovidius Naso trained as a lawyer, but he gave up his studies to travel and write poetry. He married three times before he was 30. His poetry was extremely popular during his lifetime and he had many friends among the Roman literary elite. In 8 CE, however, Augustus banished him to the city of Tomis on the Black Sea, in modern Romania. Ovid said the reason for his exile was *carmen et error*, 'a poem and a mistake', but which poem and whose mistake are the subject of debate. He died ten years later. Ovid ranks alongside Virgil (43) and Horace (45) in a triumvirate of the greatest and most influential of Roman poets.

Heroides *c.* 25 – *c.* 16 BCE

The *Heroides* ('heroines') are epistles from mythical heroines to their absent lovers. They variously express constancy, forgiveness, reproach, frustration and anger: Penelope begins to grow suspicious of Ulysses' lengthy odyssey (17) and Dido rebukes Aeneas (44) for abandoning her to follow his destiny.

1990
trans. Harold Isbell

'It is still hard for me to accept the fact of Betty Radice's (51) death,' wrote Peter Green in 1987, 'to realize that in my work, now, on Ovid I can no longer draw on her immense experience of translation and translators; that never again will I be encouraged, argued with, gently bullied, briskly cajoled, or tactfully steered away from the shoals of procrastination, *Angst*, and unseasonable polemic by her diplomatic ministrations; that henceforth there will be no still small voice of civilized common sense (too long taken for granted) to which I can appeal in moments of need. Like Ovid himself in his exile, I have lost a vital contact with reality as well as a much-loved friend.'

1982
trans. Peter Green

The Erotic Poems
c. 16 BCE – *c.* 8 CE
The Amores; *The Art of Love*; *Cures for Love*; *On Facial Treatment for Ladies*

In *The Amores*, Ovid attempts to persuade his elusive mistress Corinna to sleep with him, through a sequence of tremulous elegies. In contrast, *The Art of Love* is a self-assured step-by-step seduction guide with 'guaranteed' results, and *Cures for Love* is the sequel, explaining how best to terminate love affairs expediently. *On Facial Treatment for Ladies* is an unfinished treatise on the art of cosmetics.

Metamorphoses 8 CE

Ovid's witty masterpiece anthologizes a dizzying array of mytho-logical figures, all of whom go through some form of magical trans-formation: humans turn into trees, rocks, animals and constellations, Pygmalion's beloved statue becomes human and Medusa's hair turns into snakes. Ovid draws thematic connections between each episode and employs multiple literary styles to match the shifting content. This playful epic opens with the creation of the cosmos and concludes with the transformation of Julius Caesar (41) into a god.

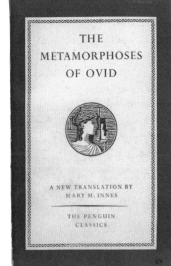

1955
trans. Mary M. Innes

2002
trans. Arthur Golding, 1567
intro. Madeleine Forey, 2002
—
The first major English transla-tion of the epic was published in 1567 by Arthur Golding; this was the text used by Spenser (130) and Shakespeare (134).

2004
trans. David Raeburn
intro. Denis Feeney

Fasti 8–18 CE

2000
trans. A. J. Boyle &
R. D. Woodard

Written during his years of exile, Ovid's unfinished *Fasti* ('Festivals') is an elegiac calendar of holidays and daily rituals, drawing on Roman history, mythology and astron-omy. It is humorous and satirically subversive, pointing out the absurdity of Augustus's (43) self-deification. The six extant books cover the months January to June.

Imperial Rome

The first 200 years of the Roman Empire are known as the 'Silver Age' of classical Latin. New literary forms emerged in this period, from the philosophical letters of Seneca (48) to the first prose novels: the *Satyricon* of Petronius (48) and the *Golden Ass* by Apuleius (53). The period is otherwise dominated by historical writing, and concludes with Marcus Aure-lius (53), the philosopher emperor, whose death traditionally marks the beginning of Rome's gradual decline.

Quintus Curtius Rufus

1st century CE

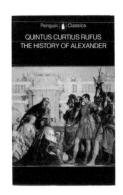

1984
trans. John Yardley
intro. Waldemar Heckel

We know almost nothing about Quintus Curtius Rufus. No other writer mentions him or his one surviving work. He might have been a protégé of the Emperor Tiberius and may have lived in Africa during the reign of the Emperor Claudius, where he might have had the opportunity to consult the Library of Alexandria.

The History of Alexander

The first two books of Curtius Rufus's ten-volume life of Alexander the Great have been lost, but this psychologically plausible portrait of a successful conqueror, ruined by his own good fortune, has still been highly influential. It provided the main source for subsequent Alexander Romances (35). It is the only life of Alexander written in Latin.

Seneca c. 4 BCE–65 CE

Lucius Annaeus Seneca was a Stoic philosopher, politician and dramatist from Cordoba in Spain. He rose to fame in Rome as an eloquent wordsmith and was appointed tutor to Nero (32), the adoptive son of the Emperor Claudius. He remained a close advisor when Nero became emperor. As the matricidal despot became increasingly deranged Seneca attempted to distance himself, but in 65 CE he was erroneously implicated in a treasonous plot and Nero ordered him to take his own life. He opened his veins and died in the bath. The phrase *errare humanum est*, 'to err is human', has been attributed to him.

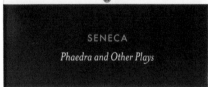

Phaedra

and Other Plays

Hercules Insane; *Thyestes*; *Phaedra*;
The Trojan Women; *Oedipus*; *Octavia*

Seneca's tragedies are *fabula crepidata*, Roman plays based on Greek originals. *Oedipus* is a version of Sophocles (21) and *Phaedra, The Trojan Women* and *Hercules Insane* are adaptations of Euripides (22), as is *Thyestes*, although the Greek original has been lost. *Thyestes* tells the gruesome story of a man who eats his own children, roasted and served up by his brother Atreus. In all his tragedies, Seneca wrings irony out of the twists of fate and the extremes of human brutality, and they were a major influence on Elizabethan and Jacobean revenge dramas (132). By contrast, *Octavia* is a contemporary satire about Nero's divorce from his wife (and stepsister) Claudia Octavia, featuring the ghost of Agrippina, Nero's murdered mother, and Seneca himself, as an ineffective counsellor. Its authorship is disputed as it may have been written after Seneca's death.

1966 *Four Tragedies and Octavia*
trans. E. F. Watling

2011
trans. R. Scott Smith

Letters

Seneca was a master of Latin prose and his letters reveal a humorous, self-critical personality, whether he is comforting his mother, praising the value of friendship or criticizing the cruelty of the gladiatorial arena. Throughout, he advocates the philosophy of Stoicism and the wisdom of mastering one's emotions in the face of life's setbacks.

1969 *Letters From a Stoic*
trans. Robin Campbell

1997 *Dialogues and Letters*
trans. C. D. N. Costa

–

C. D. N. Costa's edition includes dialogues on tranquillity of mind and the shortness of life, as well as extracts from Seneca's *Natural Questions*, on the cause of earthquakes and the location of the cataracts of the Nile.

Petronius *c. 27–66 CE*

Petronius was the Emperor Nero's stylist, his '*arbiter elegentarum*'. According to Tacitus (50), his entire life was devoted to pleasure, sleeping during the day and perfecting the 'science of luxurious living' at night. He was eventually accused of treason and took his own life, although he did so gradually, using his last hours to dictate a comprehensive catalogue of Nero's male and female sexual partners, with details of their particular 'novelties in debauchery'. This sealed list was dispatched to the emperor before Petronius died.

The Satyricon *c. 63–c. 65 CE*

1965
trans. J. P. Sullivan
intro. Helen Morales, 2011
—
The 1977 edition of Sullivan's translation also included Seneca's (48) *Apocolocyntosis*, which means 'gourdification' or 'transformation into a vegetable'. This satire describes the Emperor Claudius's attempt at deification, and his rejection from Mount Olympus.

The outrageous, fragmentary narrative of the *Satyricon* follows the misadventures of Encolpius, a teacher of rhetoric, and his strapping sixteen-year-old lover Giton, as they travel around Italy having their affections tested in a series of orgies, banquets, shipwrecks and erotic scrapes with sacred geese. It has been called the world's first novel, although another contender is *Callirhoe* by Chariton (56). The centrepiece is 'Trimalchio's Feast', an unforgettable banquet hosted by a hilariously vulgar, nouveau riche millionaire.

Pliny the Elder 23–79 CE

There is a statue of Gaius Plinius Secundus on the Duomo at Como, the town where he was born. He was a lawyer and a soldier, but he turned to writing after an inspiring dream. His first work was a *History of the German Wars*. Emperor Vespasian appointed Pliny to a series of senior provincial posts, which gave him first-hand knowledge of many different regions of the empire. He returned to Rome in 75 CE, where he completed his vast masterwork, his *Natural History*. He died four years later, attempting to rescue a friend from the same eruption of Mount Vesuvius that buried Pompeii.

Natural History
A Selection
c. 77–79 CE

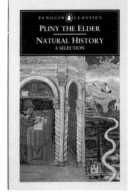

1991
trans. John F. Healy

Pliny's extraordinary, encyclopaedic work collates over 20,000 facts across hundreds of different disciplines, from architecture and astronomy to geography, technology and zoology. It provides a comprehensive view of the classical world in the first century CE, with useful information on how to dive for sponges, build a water clock and remove unwanted wrinkles using asses' milk. There is an entire volume devoted to methods for launching a spear while on horseback. Pliny's nephew, Pliny the Younger (51), described the *Natural History* as being 'as full of variety as nature itself'.

Josephus born 37 CE

Yosef ben Matityahu was born in Jerusalem. He was a rebel leader during the Jewish Revolt, but Vespasian captured him in 67 CE after the six-week siege of Jotapata and brought him back to Rome. There he swapped allegiances and was eventually freed, renaming himself Titus Flavius Josephus. In 70 CE, he accompanied Vespasian's son Titus to Judea, and advised him on the siege of Jerusalem, in which his parents and first wife were killed.

1959
trans.
G. A. Williamson
rev. E. Mary
Smallwood, 1981

The Jewish War 78 CE

Josephus traces the history of Jewish conflict from the revolt of the Maccabees against the Seleucids in 166 BCE through the ensuing Hasmonean dynasty to the fall of Jerusalem in 70 CE. He describes the atrocities of Herod the Great, the arrival of the Roman general Vespasian, the horrors of the siege of Jerusalem and the mass suicides at Masada, the last Jewish stronghold during the Revolt. His account provides the most extensive history of Judaism under Roman rule that survives.

Martial

c. 38–c. 104 CE

Marcus Valerius Martialis was born and educated in Spain, but he came to Rome and lived a bohemian life in a garret room. He avoided regular work and relied instead on generous patronage, accepting gifts of money, food and clothes while he skewered society's foibles in pithy epigrams.

The Epigrams

80–c. 102 CE

May I present myself – the man
You read, admire and long to meet,
Known the world over for his neat
And witty epigrams? The name
Is Martial. Thank you, earnest fan,
For having granted me the fame
Seldom enjoyed by a dead poet
While I'm alive and here to know it.

This is the first of Martial's epigrams; he wrote 1,560 more. James Michie's selection represents about a tenth of Martial's total output.

1978
trans. James Michie, 1973
intro. Peter Howell, 1973
—
Michie's translation includes the original Latin text on facing pages.

Tacitus

c. 56–c. 120 CE

Publius Cornelius Tacitus was an energetic, outdoorsy lawyer and politician with a talent for oratory, despite his name, which means 'silent'. He married the daughter of a celebrated general, and climbed quickly through the ranks of the *cursus honorum*, becoming consul in 97 CE. Thereafter he appears to have largely absented himself from public life, devoting himself to writing. He was a close friend of Pliny the Younger (51).

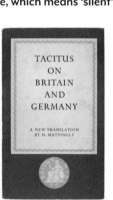

1948 *On Britain and Germany*
1970 Reissued as *Agricola and Germania*
trans. Harold Mattingly, 1948
rev. S. A. Handford, 1970
rev. J. B. Rives, 2009

Agricola *and* Germania

c. 105–c. 110 CE

Agricola is a biography of Tacitus's father-in-law, Gnaeus Julius Agricola, the governor of Roman Britain responsible for much of the conquest of Wales, northern England and Scotland. Tacitus's account includes descriptions of the geography, climate and native inhabitants of the island.

Germania is an ethnographic study of the Teutonic tribes living outside the Roman Empire in northern Europe. It frequently contrasts the 'barbarians' favourably with the decadence of imperial Rome.

The Histories

105 CE

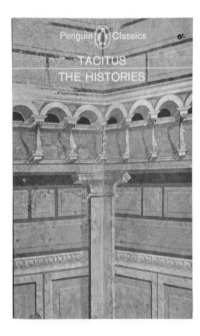

1964
trans. Kenneth Wellesley
rev. Rhiannon Ash, 2009

Tacitus's historical chronicle begins with Nero's suicide in 68 CE and describes the ensuing civil war and the 'year of the four emperors', Galba, Otho, Vitellius and Vespasian. Originally *The Histories* concluded with the assassination of Vespasian's son Domitian in 96 CE, but only the first four and a bit books have survived; the narrative breaks off in early 70 CE.

Annals

early 2nd century CE

The *Annals* form a prequel to *The Histories*: Tacitus returns to the death of Augustus in 14 CE and describes the tyranny of Tiberius, the treachery of the Empress Messalina and the crimes of Nero, exposing the corruption, conspir-

1956 *On Imperial Rome*
1959 Reissued as *The Annals of Imperial Rome*
trans. Michael Grant

2012
trans. Cynthia Damon

acies and scandal at the heart of the imperial city. The *Annals* contain the first secular reference to Christ, in relation to Nero's persecution of early Christians after the Great Fire of Rome in 64 CE.

Pliny the Younger c. 61–c. 113 CE

Gaius Plinius Caecilius Secundus was adopted by his uncle, Pliny the Elder (49), and inherited the latter's wealth and estates when he was seventeen. He married three times and held a number of official positions in the Roman Treasury. He owned a great number of villas, including two on Lake Como, which he called 'Tragedy' and 'Comedy' because one was high in the hills and one was low on the shoreline. Towards the end of his life he represented the Emperor Trajan as the imperial governor of Bithynia-Pontus, where he died.

The Letters of the Younger Pliny

c. 97–c. 113 CE

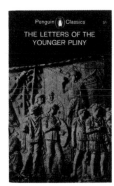

1963
trans. Betty Radice
—
Radice dedicates her first Penguin Classics translation to E. V. Rieu (17), '*magistro discipula*'. 'Her translation of Pliny's letters was undoubtedly the most heartfelt of all Betty's many books and other writing,' says Bryan Platt, a member of the Penguin Collectors Society. 'She believed that Pliny had been sadly neglected and that he had waited 1,900 years for her to bring him and the history of the times into the mainstream of classical literature.'

'You have often urged me to collect and publish any letters of mine which were composed with some care,' wrote Pliny, who prepared nine volumes of his letters for publication, at the request of his friend, Septicius Clarus. They reveal an account of the eruption of Vesuvius, descriptions of early Christians ('a degenerate sort of cult'), a portrait of his celebrated uncle and evidence of friendships with many of the leading literary figures of the day, such as Tacitus (50) and Suetonius (52). In the 15th century, a new manuscript was discovered containing Pliny's official correspondence with the Emperor Trajan, which forms a tenth and final volume.

BETTY RADICE

From childhood, Betty Dawson had a shock of whiter than flaxen hair, which she wore in a braid around her head. Born on the Yorkshire coast, she won a scholarship to Oxford where she met her future husband, the Italian Italo de Lisle Radice. After the birth of their third child, her doctor found her reading the *Odyssey* (17) in Greek. 'I put it down as soon as the baby whimpers,' she explained placidly. She became E. V. Rieu's (17) assistant in 1959, before taking joint editorship of Penguin Classics in 1964 (xiv). 'She was learned without seeming learned,' wrote her son, William Radice. 'She could be reserved, even brusque, on the surface, but anyone who got to know her found warmth and sympathy. She was not frivolously feminine, but she was profoundly feminine for all that. She was never content to be only a housewife but she excelled at household arts. She was an agnostic but she had truly spiritual qualities. She became famous, but was never a public figure. She was both extraordinary and ordinary.' After her sudden death in February 1985 at the age of 73, a scrap of paper was found in her desk, on which she had written Walter de la Mare's poem 'Epitaph' with one additional verse of her own:

Say no more: 'twould be a pity
To o'erpraise her or to flout her.
She was wild and sweet and witty –
Let's not say dull things about her.

Suetonius

c. 70 – c. 122 CE

Gaius Suetonius Tranquillus was born soon after 69 CE, the 'year of the four emperors'. He was a friend of Pliny the Younger (51) and he was the Emperor Hadrian's private secretary, although he was dismissed in 122 CE for some rude behaviour towards the Empress Sabina, the details of which are unknown. Most of his prolific written output has been lost, including titles such as *Greek Games*, *Methods of Reckoning Time* and *Lives of Famous Whores*; the only book that survives intact is his *Twelve Caesars*.

The Twelve Caesars

early 2nd century CE

Suetonius had access to the imperial archives and combined these official records with anecdotes and eyewitness accounts to paint vivid, characterful portraits of the flawed men behind twelve famous names: Julius Caesar (41) and the first eleven Roman emperors, Augustus, Tiberius, Caligula, Claudius, Nero, Galba, Otho, Vitellius, Vespasian, Titus and Domitian. He produced what Robert Graves calls 'the most fascinating and colourful of all Latin histories'.

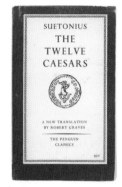

1957
trans. Robert Graves
rev. Michael Grant, 1979
rev. James Rives, 2007
—
When Graves translated this edition, he had already used Suetonius as a source for his own fictional version of the life of Claudius.

1967
trans. Peter Green
—
Green was commissioned to translate Juvenal in 1957. He recalls E. V. Rieu (17) asking him, 'in a discreetly lowered voice, after a good lunch at the Athenaeum: "Now, my boy, *what are we going to do about the smut?*" ("Translate it," I answered, and, since my progress was small enough to catch the revolution of the Sixties, I not only did that, but got it published without trouble.)'

Juvenal *c. 1st – 2nd centuries CE*

We know almost nothing about the life of Decimus Junius Juvenalis. One key biographical source, a dedicatory inscription, is now thought to refer to someone else. He was probably born in Aquinum, central Italy, and he may have been exiled to Egypt.

The Sixteen Satires *c. 110 – c. 130 CE*

'All human endeavours, men's prayers, fears, angers, pleasures, joys and pursuits, make up the mixed mash of my book,' writes Juvenal. His satires cover the range of the human condition: he describes a world of fortune-tellers, whores, lawyers, flirts and teachers, decadent aristocrats who sleep with gladiators and upstart sons of former slaves. All the corruption and profligacy of Roman society is exposed in his satirical poetry.

Beauty and the Beast
Classic Tales About Animal Brides and Grooms from Around the World 3rd century BCE – 19th century CE

It's a tale as old as time: almost every culture in the world has a version of the 'Beauty and the Beast' story, in which a human partners with an animal. Beginning with Hindu and Greek legends, and the tale of 'Cupid and Psyche' from *The Golden Ass*, by Apuleius (53), this anthology collects stories from across the centuries, from strapping Alaskan muskrats, Chilean parrots, Greek crabs and South African pigeons to enchanting Ghanaian tortoises, Indian dogs, Japanese cranes and Swedish swans. As the fairy-tale scholar Maria Tatar observes, each bestial coupling involves 'a high coefficient of weirdness'.

2017
ed. Maria Tatar

APULEIUS
THE
GOLDEN ASS

A NEW TRANSLATION BY
ROBERT GRAVES

THE PENGUIN
CLASSICS

1/6

1950
● trans. Robert Graves
—
E. V. Rieu (17) wrote to Robert Graves in 1944 and invited him to choose a title to translate. 'Will you secure the *Golden Ass* for me?' Graves replied. 'Or is that too barbarous for your public? [...] What is the Penguin policy about classical obscenity?' 'We are not writing for schools,' responded Rieu, 'and I should put my trust in your confidence and skill. The "Pasiphaë" passage in Book X is a bit of a pill.' 'What you call the Pasiphaë bit,' Graves returned, 'is most interesting to me as anti-Christian mockery: apparently Jesus was secretly worshipped as an ass-god by some of his near-Eastern devotees and the *graffiti* which are generally regarded as libels are nothing of the sort'.

1998
trans. E. J. Kenney

Apuleius
c. 120–*c.* 174 CE

Apuleius was born at Madaurus in Numidia, a Roman colony in North Africa, where St Augustine (62) would later go to school. He studied in Athens and Rome and was initiated into several Greco-Roman 'mystery' cults. In Oea, modern Tripoli, he was accused of seducing a rich widow with love magic. He was an excellent public speaker and was given responsibility for staging gladiatorial contests and wild beast shows in Carthage.

The Golden Ass
or, Metamorphoses

This rollicking, raunchy story describes a well-endowed young man called Lucius who accidentally turns himself into a donkey while experimenting with magic. As an ass, he passes from owner to owner and becomes tangled in a series of picaresque scrapes, including dog fights, a gang of storytelling robbers and a carnival sex show. This is the only Roman novel to survive in its entirety: Apuleius's title was *Metamorphoses*; it was St Augustine (62) who called it *The Golden Ass*, the title by which it is best known today.

Marcus Aurelius
121–180 CE

Marcus Annius Verus was the son of a Roman politician. After his father's untimely death, however, he was adopted by Aurelius Antoninus, his uncle by marriage, and heir to the Emperor Hadrian. Marcus changed his name to Marcus Aurelius Antoninus, and when his uncle died in 161 CE, he became emperor himself and ruled jointly with his adoptive brother Lucius Verus. He was the last of the 'Five Good Emperors'. During his reign, the empire was beset by famine, floods and plague and Marcus spent much of it attempting to restore control and fend off barbarian incursions in the Danube region. He died in Vindobona, modern Vienna, and was immediately deified.

Meditations *c.* 170–*c.* 180 CE

During his military campaigns, Marcus set down a series of self-improving reflections in Greek, which he entitled *To Myself*. Known collectively as his *Meditations*, they form a profound work of Stoic philosophy, with nuggets of sage advice, such as 'A bitter cucumber? Throw it away' and 'The best revenge is not to be like your enemy'. His work has influenced many thinkers, including J. S. Mill (273), Arnold (272) and Goethe (335).

1964
● trans. Maxwell Staniforth

2006
trans. Martin Hammond
intro. Diskin Clay

Roman Greece

Greece became part of the Roman Empire in 146 BCE, after the Romans destroyed the city of Corinth. Greek culture continued to flourish during occupation, however, and the Greek language remained current in many of the eastern territories of the Roman Empire.

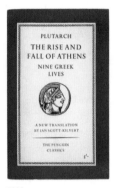

1960
trans. Ian Scott-Kilvert
—
Ian Scott-Kilvert OBE was the Director of English Literature at the British Council and the Chairman of the Byron Society. He was the General Editor of 'Writers and their Work', a series of pamphlet supplements to *British Book News*, which ran to hundreds of editions, including contributions by Scott-Kilvert himself on A. E. Housman (268) and John Webster (146).

The Rise and Fall of Athens
Nine Greek Lives

Theseus; *Solon*; *Themistocles*; *Aristides*; *Cimon*; *Pericles*; *Nicias*; *Alcibiades*; *Lysander*

These nine lives trace the fortunes of the city of Athens over eight centuries, from its foundation by the legendary King Theseus through its heyday under Pericles, who was responsible for building the Parthenon and the other structures of the Acropolis, to its conquest by the Spartan admiral Lysander during the Peloponnesian War, in 404 BCE.

On Sparta

Lycurgus; *Agesilaus*; *Agis*; *Cleomenes*; *Sayings of Spartans, Sayings of Spartan Women*

The lives in this volume cover the rise and fall of Greece's second great city-state, Sparta, from Lycurgus who established Sparta's tripartite ideals of equality, military prowess and austerity, to Cleomenes III, under whom Sparta was defeated by the Achaean League. Plutarch reveals a frugal society that disposed of weakling babies in crevasses and underwent a gruelling regime of physical training.

The Age of Alexander

Artaxerxes; *Pelopidas*; *Dion*; *Timoleon*; *Demosthenes*; *Phocion*; *Alexander*; *Eumenes*; *Demetrius*; *Pyrrhus*

Covering the fourth century BCE and the early third, these ten lives include portraits of some of the most important figures in Greek history, including Demosthenes, the Athenian statesman and orator, and Pyrrhus who was one of the most notable opponents of early Rome. This was the period that saw the collapse of Sparta, the rise of Macedon and the spectacular conquests of the incomparable Alexander the Great.

Plutarch c. 46–c. 120 CE

Plutarch was born into a prominent Greek family from Boeotia. After studying maths and philosophy at Plato's Academy (26) in Athens, he took Roman citizenship and a new name, Lucius Mestrius Plutarchus. His reputation as a distinguished man of letters spread throughout the empire, despite living most of his life near the small town of Chaeronea where he was born. He received many guests at his country estate and is said to have conducted intellectual debates from a marble chair. He is best remembered for his *Lives*, in which he paired biographies of corresponding figures from Greek and Roman history.

Since 2005, the Penguin volumes of Plutarch's *Lives* have been series edited by Christopher Pelling, President of the Hellenic Society.

1988
● trans. Richard J. A. Talbert
—
Spartan Society by Xenophon (32) is included as an appendix. *Agesilaus*, translated by Ian Scott-Kilvert, originally appeared in the 1973 edition of *The Age of Alexander*.

1973
trans. Ian Scott-Kilvert
rev. Timothy E. Duff, 2011
—
In the revised edition, Ian Scott-Kilvert's translation of *Agesilaus* has been removed (it is included in *On Sparta* above) and two new translations by Timothy Duff have been added: *Artaxerxes II*, the Persian king, and *Eumenes of Cardia*, one of Alexander's officers.

2013
trans. Ian Scott-Kilvert, 1965
trans. Christopher Pelling, 1997
rev. Jeffrey Tatum, 2013
—
Scott-Kilvert's translations of the lives of *Coriolanus*, *Fabius Maximus*, *Marcellus* and *Cato the Elder* are revised from *The Makers of Rome* (see right). Previous translations by Christopher Pelling of *Philopoemen* and *Titus Flamininus* are used and the other lives in this volume are translated by Jeffrey Tatum.

Fall of the Roman Republic

Marius; *Sulla*; *Crassus*; *Pompey*; *Caesar*; *Cicero*

In these lives, Plutarch chronicles the decline of the Roman Republic between 120 and 43 BCE.
He describes the struggle for power between Marius and Sulla, the battle between Crassus and Spartacus, the bloody campaigns of Julius Caesar (41) and the dazzling rhetoric of Cicero (39), who defended the Republic even as it was collapsing.

The Rise of Rome

Romulus; *Numa*; *Publicola*; *Coriolanus*; *Camillus*; *Fabius Maximus*; *Marcellus*; *Aratus*; *Philopoemen*; *Titus Flamininus*; *Cato the Elder*; *Aemilius Paullus*

These twelve lives describe the beginnings of Rome, from Romulus, suckled by a wolf, to the establishment of the Republic and the life of the consul Aemilius Paullus, who finally defeated the kingdom of Macedon in 168 BCE.

1958
trans. Rex Warner
rev. Robin Seager, 1972, 2005
—
The 1958 edition of *Fall of the Roman Republic* was mistakenly coloured purple for Latin, instead of brown for Greek. The mistake was corrected in the 1962 reprint.

1965
trans. Ian Scott-Kilvert

The Makers of Rome

Coriolanus; *Fabius Maximus*; *Marcellus*; *Cato the Elder*; *Tiberius Gracchus*; *Gaius Gracchus*; *Sertorius*; *Brutus*; *Mark Antony*

This selection provides an overview of Rome's iconic statesmen, from the hot-headed Coriolanus, the exiled general who led an attack on the city in the 5th century BCE, to the eloquent rhetorician Cato and the principled conspirator Brutus. Together they cover the history of Rome from the early days of the Republic to the eve of the Empire.

Rome in Crisis

Tiberius Gracchus; *Gaius Gracchus*; *Sertorius*; *Lucullus*; *Cato the Younger*; *Brutus*; *Antony*; *Galba*; *Otho*

Rome suffered frequent periods of political instability. This selection covers some of the key crises, from the assassination of the public-spirited brothers Tiberius and Gaius Gracchus to the civil war that gave birth to the empire and 69 CE, the 'year of the four emperors' following the death of Nero, of which Galba and Otho were the first.

2010
trans. Ian Scott-Kilvert, 1965
rev. Christopher Pelling, 2010
—
Tiberius Gracchus, *Gaius Gracchus*, *Sertorius*, *Brutus* and *Antony* are revisions of Ian Scott-Kilvert's translations in *The Makers of Rome*. The remaining lives are translated by Christopher Pelling.

Essays

As well as writing his *Lives*, Plutarch was perhaps the greatest essayist of the Greco-Roman world. This selection includes essays on the benefits of listening, the nature of contentment and the intelligence of animals. It also features a moving letter to his wife, consoling her after the death of their two-year-old daughter Timoxena.

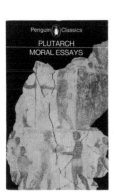

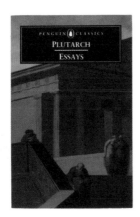

1971
• trans.
Rex Warner

1992
trans. Robin Waterfield
intro. Ian Kidd

Epictetus *c. 50–c. 135 CE*

Epictetus was a Greek-speaking Phrygian slave who belonged to the Emperor Nero's secretary Epaphroditos. His mercurial master allowed Epictetus to pursue his passion for philosophy, but may also have broken his leg. After Nero's death in 68 CE, Epictetus gained his freedom and taught philosophy in Rome until the Emperor Domitian banished all philosophers from the city in 93 CE, at which he point he moved to Nicopolis on the Adriatic coast of Greece, and founded his own philosophical school. The Emperor Hadrian is said to have heard him speak there.

2008
trans. Robert Dobbin

Discourses and Selected Writings

The teachings of Epictetus were summarized in the *Enchiridion*, or 'handbook', by his pupil Arrian, who also transcribed his informal lectures, or 'discourses'. Epictetus was a Stoic; he believed that happiness lies in embracing what is within our power to change and accepting what is not.

Arrian *c. 86–c. 160 CE*

Arrian was taught by the philosopher Epictetus and became known as 'the second Xenophon' (32), another historian taught by a philosopher. He was born in Nicomedia, the capital of Bithynia, northern Turkey. Though Greek, he became a Roman citizen and rose quickly through the *cursus honorum*, becoming consul in 129 or 130 CE. Hadrian appointed him governor of Cappadocia and he led successful military campaigns as the leader of two Roman legions, before retiring to Athens to write.

1958 *Arrian's Life of Alexander the Great*
1971 Reissued as *The Campaigns of Alexander*
trans. Aubrey de Sélincourt, 1958
rev. J. R. Hamilton, 1971

The Campaigns of Alexander

Written over four centuries after the events it describes, Arrian's *Anabasis* is still the most reliable account that survives of Alexander the Great's military campaigns. Emulating Xenophon's *Persian Expedition* (32), Arrian uses his seven books to focus on Alexander's conquest of the Persian Empire.

Pausanias
c. 110–c. 180 CE

Pausanias was a doctor from Magnesia, in Asia Minor, who spent two decades travelling around mainland Greece during and after the reign of Hadrian. He used his first-hand knowledge to produce one of the world's earliest travel guides, written for Roman sight-seers and armchair travellers.

Guide to Greece

Pausanius's gazetteer describes local myths and references a wide range of classical literature. The first volume covers the cities of Athens, Corinth and Thebes and the oracle at Delphi; the second volume covers Sparta, Arcadia, Bassae and the Olympic Games. His guide has inspired many subsequent travellers, including Byron (195) and Shelley (196).

GREEK FICTION
Callirhoe, Daphnis and Chloe, Letters of Chion
1st–4th centuries CE

Callirhoe by Chariton vies with the *Satyricon* by Petronius (49) for the title of the first 'novel'. It is a tale of supernatural beauty and pirates. *Daphnis and Chloe* by Longus (57) is the story of a pair of naïve lovers on the island of Lesbos; and *Letters of Chion* is a 4th-century thriller about the dramatic assassination of the tyrant Clearchus.

2011
trans. Rosanna Omitowoju, Phiroze Vasunia & John Penwill
intro. Helen Morales
—
The cover shows a screen-print illustration of Daphnis and Chloe by the 20th-century Scottish artist Sidney Horne Shepherd.

1971
trans. Peter Levi; ill. John Newberry & Jeffrey Lacey
Published in two volumes

Lucian

c. 125 – c. 180 CE

Born in Samosata on the Euphrates, in the Roman province of Syria, Lucian was initially a sculptor's apprentice, before he decided to learn Greek and study philosophy. He travelled widely in Greece, Italy and Gaul before finally settling in Egypt. He describes his writing career as falling into two parts: the first, 'condemning tyrants and praising princes'; the second, after his 40th birthday, writing witty dialogues.

1961 *Satirical Sketches*
• trans. Paul Turner

2004
trans. Keith Sidwell

The woodcut on the front of Turner's translation is by Cecil Keeling; it shows a group of skeletons being ferried across the River Styx.

Chattering Courtesans
and Other Sardonic Sketches

This anthology of Lucian's work includes bilious diatribes, an imaginary journey to Hades and a eulogy in praise of a fly. 'Chattering Courtesans' is a series of saucy, gossipy dialogues that touch on themes of love, sex and marriage.

Appian *c. 95 – c. 165 CE*

Appian of Alexandria was an ambitious statesman. He moved to Rome where he became an advocate, pleading cases in front of the Emperors Hadrian and Antoninus Pius. Appian wrote in Greek; his only surviving work is a *History of Rome* in 24 books.

The Civil Wars *c. 145 – c. 165 CE*

The most valuable sections of Appian's *History of Rome* are the five books that provide an account of the era of civil wars between 133 and 35 BCE. This period proved critical to the fall of the Republic and the emergence of the Roman Empire, and Appian provides the only continuous description to cover the Catiline conspiracy (42), the First Triumvirate and the assassination of Julius Caesar (41).

1996
trans. John Carter

Longus *2nd – 3rd centuries CE*

Nothing is known about Longus; even his name is uncertain.

Daphnis and Chloe

2nd – 3rd centuries CE

In this tenderly romantic novel, set on the island of Lesbos, a goatherd (Daphnis) and a shepherdess (Chloe) discover that they are powerfully attracted to each other: they eventually overcome total inexperience, unhelpful relationship advice and pirate raids in order to consummate their fledgling love. The lovers' comic naïvety has inspired musicians and writers from Henry Fielding (161) to Maurice Ravel and William Goldman, author of *The Princess Bride* (1987).

1956
trans. Paul Turner
—
The 1968 reprint of Turner's translation carried a notice: 'Former Penguin editions of this third-century Greek novel, the prototype for all Arcadian love-stories, were, we regret to say, bowdlerised. Paul Turner has added the missing passages for this new edition, in which the text is unexpurgated.' A new 2011 translation, by Phiroze Vasunia, is also available in the *Greek Fiction* anthology (56).

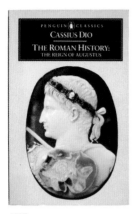

1987
trans. Ian Scott-Kilvert
intro. John Carter

The Roman History
The Reign of Augustus early 3rd century

Cassius Dio *c.*163–*c.*235 CE

Cassius Dio was a Greek historian, born in Bithynia. He travelled to Rome as a young man, entered the Senate and became consul during the reign of Septimius Severus. After stepping down temporarily from public office in order to write a biography of Arrian (56), and his vast *Roman History*, he returned to hold the proconsulship of Africa and a second consulship in Rome, before retiring home to Bithynia.

Dio chronicled over a thousand years of Roman history in eighty books, from the arrival of Aeneas (44) in Italy to his own second consulship in 229 CE. Imitating Thucydides (32) in his objective clarity, Dio provides the fullest account we have of the rise and reign of Augustus Caesar (43), the first emperor of Rome. His biography is the subject of this selection.

For Modern Greece, turn to p.359

The Later Roman Empire

After the reign of Marcus Aurelius (53), Rome entered a period characterized by tyrannical emperors, warring factions and backstabbing politics known as the 'Crisis of the Third Century'. The last ruler of a united empire was Theodosius I. After his death in 395 CE, the Empire was divided between his sons. In 410 CE, the Visigoths sacked Rome, and after sustained barbarian attacks by the Vandals, the Suebi and the Huns (led by Attila) the Western Empire fell in 476 CE. The Eastern Empire survived for another 1,000 years: the Emperor Justinian the Great temporarily reclaimed parts of western Europe during the 6th century, but these were subsequently lost, along with Syria, Armenia and Egypt. When Mehmed the Conqueror seized Constantinople on 29 May 1453, the Eastern Empire, or the last remnant of Ancient Rome as Edward Gibbon (186) viewed it, finally collapsed.

Plotinus *c.*204–270 CE

Plotinus was the last great philosopher of antiquity. He travelled to Persia to learn eastern philosophy and attempted unsuccessfully to persuade the Roman Emperor Gallienus to build a 'City of Philosophers' in Campania, which would have been a commune governed by Plato's *Laws* (28) called Platonopolis.

The Enneads *c.*253–70 CE

In the essays and lecture notes that form the *Enneads*, Plotinus synthesizes Plato (26), Aristotle (29) and religious mysticism to describe a hierarchy of perfect forms of existence: the Soul, the Intellect and the One. Plotinus had a great influence on Christian and Islamic theology, and on later writers including Coleridge (195) and Yeats (267).

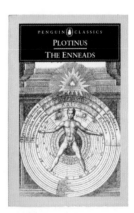

1991
trans. Stephen MacKenna, 1917–30
intro. John Dillon, 1991

—

Stephen MacKenna dedicated his life to translating the *Enneads*, after discovering Plotinus while working as a journalist in St Petersburg during the 1905 Russian Revolution (384). His translation is abridged and introduced by John Dillon.

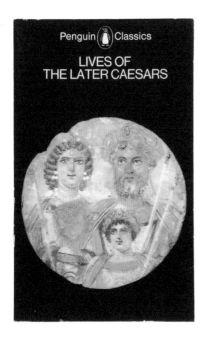

LIVES OF THE LATER CAESARS
**The first part of the Augustan History,
with newly compiled Lives of Nerva and Trajan**
4th century CE

The mysterious *Augustan History* compiles the biographies of Roman emperors between 117 and 284 CE (with an unexplained gap from 244 to 253 CE). It purports to be the work of six biographers working under the Emperors Diocletian and Constantine, but it is more likely to be the work of a single, anonymous author in the 4th century CE, who embroidered the lives of his subjects with liberal additions from a playful imagination, creating one of the earliest works of historical fiction. This volume presents the first half of the *Augustan History*, from Hadrian to Heliogabalus, prefaced with newly compiled lives of Nerva and Trajan, thereby bridging the gap between the beginning of the *Augustan History* and the end of its prototype, Suetonius's *Twelve Caesars* (52).

1976
trans. Anthony Birley

Ammianus Marcellinus
c. 325–*c.* 400 CE

Ammianus was the last great Latin historian of the Roman Empire. He was an army officer from Antioch who wrote a history of his times, picking up where Tacitus (50) left off in 96 CE and finishing with the death of the Emperor Valens at the Battle of Adrianople in 378 CE.

The Later Roman Empire
c. 380–*c.* 391 CE

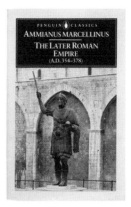

1986
trans. Walter Hamilton
intro. Andrew Wallace-Hadrill

The first thirteen of Ammianus's 31 books are lost: the others cover 25 years and the reigns of Constantius, Julian, Jovian, Valentinian and Valens. Despite being a pagan and an admirer of Julian the Apostate, whom he accompanied on several military campaigns, Ammianus presents a reasonably even-handed portrait of early Christianity. Gibbon (186) calls him 'an accurate and faithful guide, who composed the history of his own times without indulging the prejudices and passions which usually affect the mind of a contemporary'.

Justinian
c. 482–565 CE

Justinian the Great was Emperor of the East and he energetically expanded the borders of the Byzantine Empire, attempting to recover the rest of Europe. His general Belisarius restored Roman control over the western Mediterranean and massively increased the empire's revenue, facilitating a lavish building programme, including the church of Hagia Sophia in Constantinople. In the end, however, Justinian's overreaching campaigns led to the irreversible decline of the western territories and eventually the end of Rome's domination of the Mediterranean Sea.

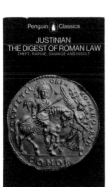

1979
trans. C. F. Kolbert

The Digest of Roman Law
Theft, Rapine, Damage and Insult
533 CE

Justinian's most enduring achievement was his codification of Roman law, a project he commissioned after becoming emperor in 527 CE. *The Digest* still forms the basis for many legal systems in Europe, and provides a fascinating window on everyday life in the 6th century, with advice on tricky cases of runaway slaves, fraudulent tutors and the defamation of married women.

Procopius born c.500 CE

Procopius was the private secretary to Belisarius, Justinian's general, accompanying him on campaigns to Persia, Africa and Italy. He was a trusted member of the Byzantine establishment and the principal historian of the 6th century, writing official accounts of *The Wars of Justinian* and the *Buildings of Justinian*.

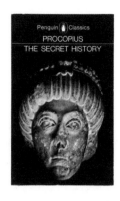

Penguin Classics
PROCOPIUS
THE SECRET HISTORY

1966
trans. G. A. Williamson
rev. Peter Sarris, 2007

The Secret History

In secret, however, Procopius wrote an alternative history, a vitriolic exposé of the tyranny and corruption at the heart of Byzantium. He paints Justinian (59) as a monstrous autocrat, his wife, the Empress Theodora, as a depraved, lustful harpy, and Belisarius as a hen-pecked idiot. The existence of *The Secret History* had been rumoured, but it was not discovered until the 17th century, when a copy turned up in the Vatican Library.

Michael Psellus c.1018–c.1096

Michael Psellus was a polymath child prodigy who rose quickly through the ranks of the Byzantine government service. After a brief flirtation with monasticism, he became chief minister of the empire under Michael VII Doukas. He was an influential Platonist (26) philosopher and the leading professor at Constantinople's great seat of learning, the Pandidakterion.

Fourteen Byzantine Rulers
(The Chronographia)

In his *Chronographia*, Psellus arranges biographies of fourteen emperors and empresses, from the 50-year reign of Basil II, the 'Bulgar-Slayer', to the reign of Michael VII Doukas, with vivid descriptions of the spineless Constantine VIII, the epileptic Michael IV and the brutal Romanus IV. Through evocative character sketches, he traces the rapid decline of Byzantium from its zenith in 1025 to the disarray that helped trigger the Crusades (75) two generations later.

Penguin Classics
MICHAEL PSELLUS
FOURTEEN
BYZANTINE RULERS

1966
trans. E. R. A. Sewter, 1953

Anna Komnene 1083–1153

Princess Anna Komnene was the eldest daughter of the Emperor Alexios I Komnenos. She was born into the purple Porphyra Chamber of the imperial palace and proved to be an intelligent and practical child. She was tutored in astronomy, medicine, philosophy and maths, and read the forbidden, pagan *Odyssey* (17) in secret. She became a prominent figure at her father's court and administered an enormous hospital in Constantinople, which had 10,000 beds for patients and orphans. She taught medicine there and became famous as an expert on gout.

Penguin Classics
THE ALEXIAD
OF ANNA COMNENA

1969
trans. E. R. A. Sewter
rev. Peter Frankopan, 2009
—
Robert Graves had been mooted to translate Komnene as early as 1956, but 'I have these big children who have to get educated,' he wrote, 'and Spain is no good and they have to go to France or somewhere; so I'm going to be very busy making money for that purpose, and can't consider binding myself for an uneconomic job like *Anna Comnene* at present.' Eventually, in 1968, Robert Sewter was commissioned to translate it instead.

The Alexiad c.1143–c.1153 CE

After the death of her father, Alexios I Komnenos, Anna wrote his biography. His reign was a turning point for the Byzantine Empire: it coincided with the First Crusade (75) and the deepening schism between the Catholic and Orthodox churches. Anna modelled her text on the objective histories of classical antiquity, but frequently breaks her narrative to inject personal opinions. Hers is the earliest surviving work of history that we know to be written by a woman.

Christianity

In the space of a few hundred years, Christianity transformed from a small-scale Jewish cult into the dominant religion of the Greco-Roman world. Christians were routinely persecuted by the Romans in the early years, yet somehow the religion blossomed. The reasons for Christianity's early success are unclear. In *The Decline and Fall of the Roman Empire*, Gibbon (186) suggests that the faith's welcoming attitude, the appealing promise of life after death and its beguiling stories of marvellous miracles may have been what made it so attractive.

On the night of 27 October 312 CE, the Roman Emperor Constantine dreamt of a crucifix, and in the morning he ordered his troops to paint crosses on their shields before the Battle of Milvian Bridge. Having won the battle, Constantine gratefully issued the Edict of Milan in 313, officially legalizing Christian worship. A few decades later, in 380 CE, Theodosius I issued the Edict of Thessalonica, under which Christianity was officially adopted as the state religion of the empire.

Freed from persecution and sanctioned by the state, Christianity began to consolidate itself. The books of the Bible (4) were agreed and St Jerome translated them into Latin. Above all, the writings of St Augustine (62) laid the foundations for the ascendancy of Christianity in the Middle Ages (67).

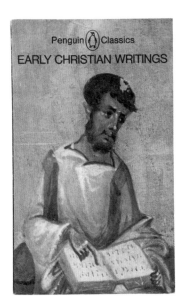

1968
trans. Maxwell Staniforth
rev. Andrew Louth, 1987
—
Staniforth served as an infantry officer in the First World War (433) and as a railwayman on the British Railways in Argentina, before taking holy orders and becoming a parish priest in Dorset, where he worked on this translation.

EARLY CHRISTIAN WRITINGS

1st–2nd centuries CE

This is a volume of letters, treatises and other scraps from the very earliest days of the Christian Church. The authors range from Bishop Clement of Rome to Bishop Ignatius of Antioch, who coined the term 'catholic church'. Maxwell Staniforth calls them Apostolic Fathers: 'those who had known the Apostles and were faithful to their teachings'.

Eusebius

c. 260 – c. 340 CE

Eusebius was born in Caesarea, Herod the Great's city on the Palestinian coast, named after the Emperor Augustus Caesar (63). He studied under Pamphilus, a Christian theologian who had inherited a great ecclesiastical library and was named Bishop of Caesarea soon after 313 CE. He has become known as the 'Father of Ecclesiastical History'.

The History of the Church
from Christ to Constantine

Eusebius set down the only surviving record of the first 300 years of the Christian Church, from the time of Christ to the conversion of the Emperor Constantine on his deathbed in 337 CE. It describes the fierce debates over the date of Easter, a range of conflicting historical heresies and the savage persecution of Christians in the early 4th century.

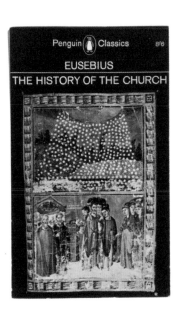

1965
trans. G. A. Williamson
rev. Andrew Louth, 1989

LIVES OF ROMAN CHRISTIAN WOMEN
3rd–5th centuries CE

These letters and documents reveal a diverse group of Roman women who dedicated their lives to Christ, in a period in which Christianity transformed from a persecuted cult into the official religion of the Empire. These women embraced poverty, chastity and even martyrdom: Perpetua and Felicitas, for example, refusing to renounce Christ, were stripped naked and trapped under nets in an amphitheatre, to be gored by savage animals.

2010
trans. Carolinne White

THE DESERT FATHERS 4th century CE
Sayings of the Early Christian Monks

The Desert Fathers and Mothers were ascetic monks of the 3rd and 4th centuries CE who sought isolation in the deserts of Egypt. Most famous were St Antony (63) and Paul the Hermit (63). *De Vitis Patrum* is an encyclopaedic anthology of writings about them, compiled and edited by the 17th-century Dutch Jesuit, Heribert Rosweyde. This is a translation of Book 5, a collection of Words of Wisdom (*Verba Seniorum*), originally anthologised by Pelagius, a 4th-century Breton ascetic, and John, his subdeacon. It organizes the sayings thematically, under titles such as 'Lust', 'Quiet' and 'Possessing Nothing'.

2003
trans. Benedicta Ward
—
Benedicta Ward is a member of the Anglican religious community of the Sisters of the Love of God, in Oxford.

St Augustine
354–430 CE

St Augustine was born at Thagaste, in modern Algeria, to a Christian mother and a pagan father. He studied law at Carthage, where he read Cicero (39) and became increasingly fascinated by philosophy. He led a hedonistic lifestyle in his twenties and conducted a long love affair with a young mistress. He converted to Manichaeism, a dualist sect, and moved to Italy in 383 CE where he came into contact with the Neo-Platonism of Plotinus (58) and the teachings of St Ambrose of Milan. In 387 CE, he heard a child's voice instruct him *tolle, lege* ('take up and read'), upon which he converted to Christianity. He returned to Africa to form an independent religious community and was ordained a priest, against his wishes, in 391. He became Bishop of Hippo five years later and lived in the cathedral community at Hippo for the next 34 years, producing a vast body of highly influential work: it was Augustine who formulated the concepts of original sin, 'holy war' and the celestial city. He died during a siege of Hippo, with the city surrounded by hordes of Vandals. He is the patron saint of brewers, printers and the alleviation of sore eyes.

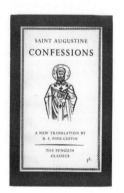

Confessions 397–400 CE

Written in Augustine's forties, the *Confessions* form his candid spiritual autobiography, describing how he grew up, put away childish things and ultimately found his faith. He recalls stealing a pear as a child and believing in astrology, and he describes his son, Adeodatus, whom he had by his unnamed mistress.

1961
trans. R. S. Pine-Coffin

1972 Pelican Classics
1984 Penguin Classics
trans. Henry Bettenson
intro. John O'Meara, 1984
rev. G. R. Evans, 2003

Betty Radice (51) commissioned Canon Henry Bettenson to translate Augustine's *City of God*, but initially the translation was 'press-ganged' into the new Pelican Classics series (xix) edited by Professor Moses Finlay. Pelican Classics was not a success and Radice eventually wrestled *City of God* back to Penguin Classics in 1984.

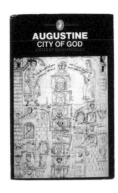

Concerning the
City of God
against the Pagans
c. 413–426 CE

Augustine's vast foundational work of Christian philosophy imagines human history as a cosmic battle between the spiritual 'City of God', the Church, and the 'Earthly City', the non-spiritual world, ruled by the Devil. Augustine wrote the book, in part, to refute the suggestion that Christianity had been responsible for the Sack of Rome by the Visigoths in 410 CE. He argues instead that Rome, the embodiment of the Earthly City, had always been destined to fall. Instead we should put our trust in the ultimately victorious City of God.

EARLY CHRISTIAN LIVES
4th–6th centuries CE

These biographies of early Christian saints depict six extraordinary men: Antony, who resisted the temptations of the Devil in the Egyptian desert; Paul and Hilarion, who were hermits in the wilderness; Malchus, who was sold into slavery and forced to marry a female slave; Martin, a pioneering monk and missionary; and Benedict, who formulated a code that would become the standard template for monastic life.

1998
trans. Carolinne White

THE RULE OF BENEDICT
6th century CE

St Benedict (480–c. 547 CE) founded the monastery at Monte Cassino, between Rome and Naples, and formulated a rule for monastic life, which has provided guidance for western monasticism for the last fifteen centuries. It has advice on the value of silence, communal eating, providing hospitality, travelling safely and caring for the sick, among many other practical aspects of life as a monk.

2008
trans. Carolinne White

For Medieval Christianity, turn to p.67

Boethius
c. 480–524 CE

Anicius Manlius Severinus Boethius was a Roman philosopher. He was a senior public official and an advisor to Theodoric, king of the Ostrogoths, until he was eventually implicated in a failed conspiracy against him. He wrote his masterpiece, *The Consolation of Philosophy*, while in prison in Pavia, waiting to be clubbed to death. He is considered the last representative of the classical world.

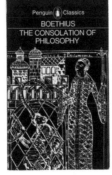

1969
trans. Victor Watts

The Consolation
of Philosophy 523–4 CE

An ailing prisoner converses with Lady Philosophy, whose words of wisdom restore him to health. She points out the transitory nature of fame and wealth and demonstrates that true happiness derives from inner virtue. Boethius discusses free will, human nature and justice, synthesizing Christian philosophy with Neo-Platonism. *The Consolation of Philosophy* was translated into Old English by Alfred the Great (74) and into Middle English by Geoffrey Chaucer (89).

The Middle Ages

Medieval Europe

ADOMNÁN OF IONA · LIFE OF ST COLUMBA

ISBN 0 14
04.4462 9

BEDE: A HISTORY OF THE ⦿ ENGLISH CHURCH AND PEOPLE

LIVES OF THE SAINTS

THE PRAYERS AND MEDITATIONS OF SAINT ANSELM

ISBN 0 14
044.153 0

ISBN 0 14
044.278

HILDEGARD OF BINGEN · SELECTED WRITINGS

THE CISTERCIAN WORLD: MONASTIC WRITINGS OF THE TWELFTH CENTURY

ISBN 0 14
04.3356 2

THOMAS OF MONMOUTH
The Life and Passion of William of Norwich

The Kabbalistic Tradition

Edited by ALAN UNTERMAN

PENGUIN CLASSICS

PENGUIN CLASSICS

AQUINAS · SELECTED WRITINGS

PENGUIN CLASSICS

Christianity

The slow collapse of the Roman Empire coincided with missionary expeditions to the barbarian lands that lay beyond its western borders: St Patrick travelled to Ireland and St Columba set about proselytizing Scotland. When the pagan Anglo-Saxons finally ousted the Romans from southern Britain, St Augustine of Canterbury arrived and converted them to Christianity, and Canterbury became a centre for further evangelical missions to the rest of western Europe. Once King Clovis of the Franks converted in 496, Christianity had become firmly established in the west.

Monasteries multiplied. The wealthy abbey of Cluny led reforms of the monastic code; in response, the Cistercians (69) established a rival order at the abbey of Cîteaux, reverting to strict observance of the Rule of St Benedict (63). Various mendicant, wandering orders also appeared, including the Franciscans, founded by St Francis of Assisi, and the Dominicans, founded by St Dominic. These monks, known as 'friars', took vows of poverty and concentrated their efforts on preaching and missionary work. From the west coast of Ireland, to the shores of the Caspian Sea, and all around the Mediterranean, a cohesive, spiritual identity emerged, known as 'Christendom'.

Adomnán of Iona *c. 628–704*

Adomnán was the ninth abbot of Iona and a distant cousin of St Columba. He instituted 'Adomnán's Law' at the Synod of Birr, which protected women, children and clerics during times of war.

Life of St Columba *697–700*

St Columba was an Irish monk who brought Christianity to Scotland. He founded the influential monastery of Iona in 563, off the Isle of Mull. According to Adomnán, Columba was capable of turning water into wine, quelling sea tempests, raising the dead and repelling the Loch Ness Monster.

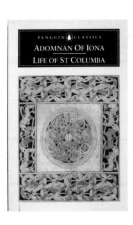

1995
trans. Richard Sharpe
—
Sharpe visited Iona several times while working on this translation: 'Iona has a powerful sense of place, which permeates much of Adomnán's *Life*,' he writes; 'while through the *Life* one can recapture the atmosphere of Adomnán's and Columba's Iona.'

Bede *c. 673–735*

The Venerable Bede met Adomnán of Iona when he was seventeen. He was a Northumbrian monk and a prolific scholar, producing volumes of work on subjects as diverse as the Acts of the Apostles and the age of the universe: he calculated the date of creation at 3952 BCE. Miraculously, angels added the word *Venerabilis* to the epitaph on his grave, and he has been known as the 'Venerable' Bede ever since.

The Ecclesiastical History of the English People *c. 731*

Bede's greatest work was his *Ecclesiastical History*, the earliest surviving account of Anglo-Saxon England. It begins with a geographical description of Britain and the invasion of Julius Caesar (41) in 55 BCE and ends with contemporary debates over the date of Easter.

1955
trans. Leo Sherley-Price
rev. R. E. Latham, 1968
rev. D. H. Farmer, 1990
—
Farmer's revised edition includes translations of Bede's letter to Egbert, his pupil, and Cuthbert's letter 'On the Illness and Death of the Venerable Bede'. Bede is said to have been singing as he died.

THE AGE OF BEDE 6th–7th centuries

Bede, *Life of Cuthbert, Lives of the Abbots of Wearmouth and Jarrow*; Eddius Stephanus, *Life of Wilfrid*; *History of the Abbot Ceolfrith*; *The Voyage of St Brendan*

A pair of friendly otters warmed St Cuthbert's feet after he finished praying in the North Sea, according to <u>Bede</u>'s *Life of Cuthbert* (67). Bede lived in the Monkwearmouth-Jarrow Abbey and wrote a history of its abbots. Also included in this anthology are the history of the Abbot Ceolfrith, Bede's guardian; a life of Wilfrid, Bishop of Hexham, who oversaw a hearing at which Bede was accused of heresy; and *The Voyage of St Brendan*, a fantastical quest for the earthly paradise, in which Brendan and his shipmates encounter devils, a gryphon, an unexpected whale and Paul the Hermit, who lived alone for 60 years, wrapped in his own hair.

1965 *Lives of the Saints*
1983 Revised and reissued as
The Age of Bede
trans. J. F. Webb, 1965
rev. D. H. Farmer, 1983

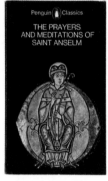

1973
trans. Benedicta Ward
fwd. R. W. Southern
—
In *The Translator's Art* (xiv),
Benedicta Ward quotes
Christopher Smart's *Jubilate
Agno*: 'For I have translated
in the charity, which makes
things better, and so I trust
that I shall be translated
myself at the last.'

St Anselm c. 1033–1109

Anselm was born in Aosta in the western Alps, and as a child he had a vision of God from the summit of Becca di Nona. Abandoned by his father, Gundolf, he wandered around France and considered becoming a hermit, before eventually joining the monastery at Rouen and beginning a distinguished clerical career that saw him appointed Bishop of Bec and finally Archbishop of Canterbury.

The Prayers and Meditations of Saint Anselm
with the Proslogion
c. 1070–1080

St Anselm wrote most of his prayers in the years before he arrived at Canterbury. Benedicta Ward's selection includes the deeply personal 'Prayer to Christ', 'A Letter to Gundolf', and a 'Prayer for Enemies'. She also includes the *Proslogion*, a work of theological philosophy that formulates the 'ontological argument' for the existence of God: he exists in the mind, so he must exist in reality, because being real would be greater than being imagined, and God is 'that than which nothing greater can be thought'. It is a circular but logical and enduring argument, which was not refuted conclusively until Kant's *Critique of Pure Reason* (180).

Hildegard of Bingen 1098–1179

When Hildegard was three years old, she had a vision of the 'Shade of the Living Light'. At eight she was adopted by Jutta of Spanheim, a religious noblewoman, who took her to become a recluse in the monastery of Disibodenberg. When Jutta died in 1136, Hildegard was nearly 40. She was elected Abbess of Disibodenberg and went on to establish her own religious community at Rupertsberg, near Bingen. She wrote on a wide variety of topics including music, science and medicine. She was also a prolific poet and composer, she invented a private language and earned a reputation as a prophetess, conducting popular preaching tours throughout Germany.

Selected Writings

Hildegard's extensive writings display her multitudinous talents as a visionary, a scientist, a songwriter and a nun. This selection includes songs for St Disibod, a treatise on the cosmic egg, an allegory of the Iron Mountain and a poem written in *Lingua Ignota*, Hildegard's invented language.

2001
trans. Mark Atherton

THE CISTERCIAN WORLD
Monastic Writings of the Twelfth Century

The Cistercian monks take their name from the abbey of Cîteaux, south of Dijon, founded in 1098 by Robert of Molesmes. Among Robert's followers was Alberic, a former hermit, who succeeded Robert as abbot: he changed the order's habits from black to white and oversaw construction of their first church, which was consecrated in 1106. Over the centuries the Cistercians have grown into an international monastic order, famous for simple living and brewing excellent ale. This anthology collects the order's early writings, from the historical 'Little Exord' and the rule of Stephen Harding, the abbot after Alberic, to the writings of the influential Bernard of Clairvaux and the spiritual essays of Aelred of Rievaulx.

1993
trans. Pauline Matarasso
—
Matarasso dedicates her translation to 'the community of Mount Saint Bernard, who have made me welcome over the years and provided a living witness to the continuing vitality of their tradition'.

Thomas of Monmouth 12th century

A 12-year-old boy called William was murdered outside Norwich, a few years before Thomas of Monmouth became a monk at the cathedral. Thomas set about promoting William's claims to sainthood, and succeeded in establishing a cult around his memory, thereby propagating the earliest version of the Jewish 'blood libel' and fuelling anti-Semitism in England and throughout Christian Europe.

The Life and Passion of William of Norwich 1150–72

William of Norwich was an apprentice tanner who died under mysterious circumstances in 1144. According to Thomas, William was crucified by the Jews of Norwich, obeying an order from a shadowy international council, which hoped to reclaim the Holy Land if they killed a Christian child every Easter. Thomas's account stoked anti-Semitic sentiment, which culminated in Edward I's expulsion of all Jews from England in 1290. The only surviving manuscript of Thomas's work was discovered by M. R. James (283) and first published in 1896.

2014
trans. Miri Rubin
—
This translation was begun in the 1990s by the scholar Willis Johnson. When he realized he would be unable to undertake the project, for health reasons, he passed it to Miri Rubin, 'with his microfilm, transcription and encouragement'.

2008
trans. Alan Unterman

THE KABBALISTIC TRADITION
An Anthology of Jewish Mysticism
13th – 20th centuries

'Kabbalah' means 'received wisdom' and refers to a set of mystical teachings that originate in Judaism. This anthology, which covers more than seven centuries of Kabbalistic thought, focuses on three phases of the tradition: the *Zohar*, the Kabbalistic foundational text, which emerged in Spain in the 13th century; the Lurianic corpus, Rabbi Isaac Luria's development in the 16th century; and the Hasidic tradition, which originated in 18th-century Ukraine. It includes sections on invoking angels, the alphabet, how to create a Golem, being 'nice to lice', sex, silence and coping with Demon Children.

St Thomas Aquinas c. 1225–1274

Thomas Aquinas became a Dominican friar while studying at the University of Naples. His wealthy mercantile family kidnapped him and held him against his will for a year, hoping to shake him out of this religious phase. His house arrest only confirmed his convictions, however, and he embarked on a lifetime of Christian teaching and writing, and he was canonised as a saint in 1323. He ranks alongside St Augustine (62) as one of the two most influential philosophers and theologians of the Middle Ages.

Selected Writings

This anthology collects sermons and commentaries across Aquinas's career, as well as extracts from his two principal works: the *Summa Theologiae*, an ambitious, unfinished synthesis of medieval theology and the rediscovered philosophy of Aristotle (29); and *Summa contra Gentiles*, an examination of the points of difference between Christianity, Judaism and Islam. Topics include 'Definitions of Soul', 'How Words Mean' and 'The Logic of the Incarnation'.

1998
trans. Ralph McInerny
—
'There is an old maxim, passed on by Pico della Mirandola,' writes McInerny: *'Sine Thomas, Aristoteles mutus esset*: without Thomas, Aristotle (29) would be silent.'

Jacobus de Voragine c. 1229–1298

Jacobus de Voragine joined the Dominican order and was prior in several northern Italian convents before being elected Archbishop of Genoa in 1292. He spent much of his time in office struggling to pacify the fractious Guelphs and Ghibellines.

The Golden Legend
Selections c. 1260

1998
trans. Christopher Stace
intro. Richard Hamer

Voragine's compilation of popular saints' lives was one of the most widely copied texts in the later Middle Ages: over a thousand manuscripts survive and it was translated into almost every European language. The lively stories are a treasury of images and references that proliferated in medieval poetry, painting and stained-glass windows, from St Thais, a beautiful prostitute who was sealed into a lead-lined cell, to St James the Mutilated, whose fingers were cut off one by one by Persian torturers. It was among the earliest works to be printed in English: William Caxton published a copy in 1483.

Meister Eckhart c. 1260–c. 1328

Johannes Eckhart was a Dominican friar from eastern Germany, who held teaching posts in Saxony, Bohemia, Paris, Strasbourg and Cologne. He was a speculative mystic, combining Christian theology with the transcendental metaphysics of Neo-Platonism (58).

1994 trans. Oliver Davies

Selected Writings

The Talks of Instruction; *The Book of Divine Consolation*; *On the Noble Man*; *Selected German Sermons*; *Selected Latin Sermons*

In these brilliant but esoteric works, Eckhart fuses elegant philosophy with deeply felt religion to present arguments that have inspired philosophers from Hegel (345) to Heidegger.

1961
• trans. Clifton Wolters

2001
trans. A. C. Spearing

THE CLOUD OF UNKNOWING
and Other Works
14th century

The Cloud of Unknowing is a masterpiece of medieval English mysticism, a spiritual guide to contemplative prayer: God is revealed as an abstract, transcendent deity, beyond human understanding; we can only hope to comprehend him by abandoning the intellect and surrendering ourselves to 'unknowing'. The author remains anonymous, although he was probably a Carthusian monk. He is also thought to have written *The Book of Privy Counselling*, included in this volume, which clarifies some of the themes in *The Cloud of Unknowing*.

Julian of Norwich
c. 1342 – c. 1416

On 8 May 1373, Julian of Norwich experienced a series of visions, or 'showings', from her sickbed, and she spent the rest of her life interpreting them. She became an anchoress in a simple cell at St Julian's Church in Norwich and developed a reputation as a spiritual advisor. She is the first writer in English who we know to be a woman.

ENGLISH MYSTERY PLAYS
A Selection   14th–15th centuries

The lively, boisterous Mystery Play cycles were performed annually in cities across England at the Feast of Corpus Christi, on the first Thursday after Trinity Sunday: the local craft guilds would join forces to stage a rolling sequence of religious plays around the town, performed in English and covering the entire span of scriptural history, from the 'Fall of Lucifer' to 'Judgement Day'. Four cycles survive, more or less in full: the Chester, Coventry, Wakefield and York plays. For this volume, Peter Happé selects the best of all four to create a composite cycle of 38 plays.

1975 Penguin English Library
1985 Penguin Classics
ed. Peter Happé

Revelations of Divine Love
(Short Text and Long Text) c. 1375, c. 1395

Julian of Norwich wrote two accounts of her 'showings', 20 years apart: an earlier, shorter version and a longer one. Her mystical visions include seeing a figure of Christ bleeding, and holding 'all that is made' in the palm of her hand. She compares divine love to motherly love and pictures a domestic triangle formed by God the Father, Christ the Mother and the grace of the Holy Ghost in between.

1966
• trans. Clifton Wolters

1998
trans. Elizabeth Spearing
intro. A. C. Spearing

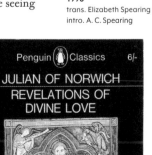

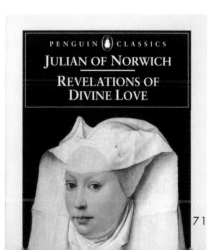

71

1985
trans. B. A. Windeatt
—
Barry Windeatt takes his epigraph from Julian of Norwich (71): 'Botte for I am a woman, schulde I therfore leve that I schulde nought telle yowe the goodenes of God?'

Margery Kempe c. 1373 – c. 1440

Margery Kempe was a merchant's wife who suffered from post-natal depression. She experienced visions of violent demons with flaming mouths, urging her to renounce Christianity and take her own life, until the handsome figure of Christ appeared, sitting on the edge of her bed. Years later, after bearing fourteen children, she persuaded her husband to join her in a mutual vow of chastity and she set off on an adventurous life of pilgrimage, visiting clerics, mystics and recluses around England, Europe and the Holy Land.

The Book of Margery Kempe 1438

Margery's book is the first autobiography in the English language. It describes her extensive travels and extraordinary, time-travelling visions: she was present at both the Nativity and the Crucifixion, for example. Her devotions took the form of loud public wailing with copious tears, and she was tried several times on charges of heresy. At one point she visited Julian of Norwich (71), who confirmed that her tears were evidence of the Holy Spirit in her soul. Margery could not read or write; she dictated her book in the third person, towards the end of her life. The manuscript was discovered in 1934, in a house in Lancashire.

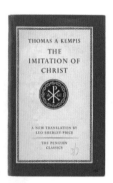

1952
• trans. Leo Sherley-Price

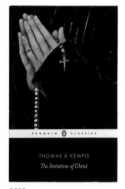

2013
trans. Robert Jeffery
intro. Max von Habsburg

Thomas à Kempis c. 1380 – 1471

Thomas was born in the Rhineland, the son of a blacksmith and a schoolmistress. After finishing school, he entered the monastery of Mount St Agnes, which followed the reformist teachings of the Dutch preacher Geert Groote. Thomas became a prolific writer and copyist: he copied the Bible (4) four times.

The Imitation of Christ c. 1418 – 1427

As subprior at Mount St Agnes, Thomas was responsible for instructing novices. He wrote four step-by-step guides to the spiritual life, which were collected and named after the first chapter of the first booklet: 'The Imitation of Christ'. Other than the Bible (4), no book has been translated into more languages. Thomas More (121) said it was one of three books that everyone should own; the other two were *The Mirror of the Blessed Life of Jesus Christ* and *The Ladder of Perfection* by Walter Hilton, which was published in Penguin Classics in 1957.

St Ignatius of Loyola 1491 – 1556

As a child in Spain, Ignatius longed to be a famous knight, imagining himself as The Cid (80). While recovering from wounds sustained at the Battle of Pamplona in 1521, however, he experienced a religious conversion. He gathered a group of like-minded students and founded the 'Society of Jesus', a new religious order that served as special emissaries for the Pope. They became better known as 'Jesuits' and Ignatius spent the rest of his life as Superior General of the Jesuits, coordinating their international activities from the Vatican.

Personal Writings
Reminiscences; *Spiritual Diary*; *Select Letters*; *The Spiritual Exercises*

The *Reminiscences* describe Ignatius's early life and conversion. His *Spiritual Diary* is a record of his daily communications with God and the *Spiritual Exercises* were written during a year-long period of solitary contemplation and include details of various meditation methods. The *Letters* reveal insights into his direction of the Jesuit order.

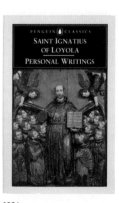

1996
trans. Joseph A. Munitiz
& Philip Endean

St Teresa of Ávila 1515–1582

When Teresa developed an immoderate love of fiction as an adolescent, her family sent her to become a Carmelite nun. Initially she doubted her vocation, but she began to experience regular visions and fits of religious ecstasy, during which she was pierced by a painful yet pleasurable 'spear of divine love'. In 1562 she founded the convent of St Joseph in Ávila, and spent the rest of her life travelling around Spain, founding more convents. She died at midnight on 4 October 1582, the very moment the Julian calendar switched to the Gregorian calendar in Spain, when ten days (5–14 October) were 'lost'. There is therefore some confusion about the date of her death.

The Life of Saint Teresa of Ávila by Herself c. 1567

Teresa was persuaded to write her *Life* by her confessor, Father Pedro Ibáñez. It is an account of her spiritual enlightenment, from taking the habit to the foundation of St Joseph's. After *Don Quixote* (153), it is the most popular prose classic in Spain.

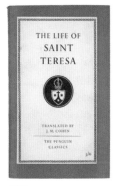

1957
trans. J. M. Cohen
—
The design on the first Classics cover is based on the badge of the Discalced Carmelite Order founded by St Teresa. The crest was provided by the Very Reverend Father Prior of the Carmelite Priory in Kensington Church Street in London.

History

Christendom flourished in the 8th and 9th centuries. Charlemagne united western Europe under the Holy Roman Empire, Christianizing the last pagan Saxons and leading campaigns against the Muslims of Spain. In 1095, Pope Urban II appealed to all Europeans at the Council of Clermont, proposing a religious war to recover the Holy Land from Muslim rule. His call to arms was enthusiastically adopted and the resulting campaign has become known as the First Crusade (75). Initially successful, the crusaders captured Jerusalem and established states in the east, but eight crusades and two centuries later, Jerusalem had been lost again and the last Catholic outposts in the Holy Land fell in 1291. Despite their ultimate failure, the Crusades had a profound effect on Europe. They galvanised commerce and travel in the Mediterranean, allowing coastal cities like Genoa and Venice to thrive; they consolidated a collective, international identity for the Catholic Church; and they provided a fount of heroic, chivalric and saintly stories which were translated directly into the emerging literature of the Middle Ages.

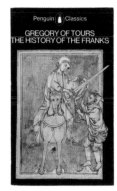

1974
trans. Lewis Thorpe

Gregory of Tours c.538–594

Gregory was a Gallo-Roman who became Bishop of Tours in 573, the most senior prelate in Gaul. He remained in office until his death in 594.

The History of the Franks c.575–94

The Franks were a collection of Germanic tribes from the Rhine region, who took advantage of the power vacuum left after the Sack of Rome and occupied the lands to the west of the Rhine. Gregory begins his chronicle with the Creation and traces the entire history of the world, but most of his book is an eyewitness account of the bloodthirsty politics of 6th-century Gaul and the reigns of four Frankish kings: Sigibert, Chilperic, Childebert II and Guntram.

Einhard
c. 775–840

Einhard was a friend and courtier of Charlemagne. One legend describes how he fell in love with Emma, one of Charlemagne's daughters, and eloped with her.

Notker the Stammerer
c. 840–912

Notker Balbulus was a poet and composer who taught at the Swiss monastery of St Gall. He was commissioned to write his biography of Charlemagne by the Emperor Charles the Fat.

Two Lives of Charlemagne
c. 826–c. 887

1969
• trans. Lewis Thorpe

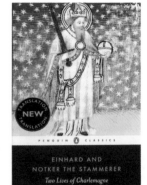

2008
trans. David Ganz

Charlemagne (742–814), son of Pepin the Short, was king of the Franks and protector of the papacy. On Christmas Day 800, he was crowned 'emperor of the Romans' by Pope Leo III, in an attempt to revive the Western Roman Empire. Charlemagne was a great lover of books, particularly the works of St Augustine (62), and he sponsored a large number of spiritual and secular literary projects during his reign. Einhard takes Suetonius (52) as a model for his biography; Notker collates posthumous anecdotes and presents a fragmentary portrait of the first Holy Roman Emperor.

ALFRED THE GREAT
Asser's *Life of King Alfred* and Other Contemporary Sources
888–99

Alfred the Great (849–899) was king of Wessex, famous for repelling Viking invasions, introducing legal reforms and burning cakes. In 893, Asser, the Bishop of Sherborne, wrote his biography, drawing inspiration from Virgil (43), the Venerable Bede (67) and Einhard. He describes Alfred as 'more comely in appearance than his other brothers', perhaps aware that the king would be among his readers. This edition also includes relevant passages from the *Anglo-Saxon Chronicle* and extracts from Alfred's laws, will and own translations, including a section of *The Consolation of Philosophy* (63).

1983
trans. Simon Keynes
intro. Michael Lapidge

—

'The Penguin Classics series of translations is one of which King Alfred the Great would have heartily approved,' write Keynes and Lapidge. 'Amid great difficulties, and among many other undertakings, he initiated a programme for the translation into English of "certain books which are the most necessary for all men to know", and he made arrangements to ensure that they received wide circulation.'

2011
trans. Patricia Skinner
& Elisabeth van Houts

MEDIEVAL WRITINGS ON SECULAR WOMEN
9th–15th centuries

The diverse writings assembled in this anthology cover seven centuries and are taken from locations ranging from Britain to Baghdad. They are arranged according to the stages of a medieval woman's life, from infancy and girlhood to marriage, motherhood, old age and death, with entries including the 'Fear of Giving Birth to the Antichrist', a 'Heroic Struggle against Marriage', a 'Widow in Business as a Miller' and the epitaph of a sweet-voiced rabbi's daughter called 'Urania of Worms'.

DOMESDAY BOOK
A Complete Translation 1086

The *Domesday Book* is one of the most famous documents in English history. It was compiled towards the end of William the Conqueror's life, after the Norman Conquest of England, when he commissioned surveyors to travel the length and breadth of the country, itemizing the 'possessions of each of the magnates, their lands, their habitations, their men'. No other country has an equivalent historical resource. Its official name was the 'Book of Winchester', after the city where it was stored, but it soon acquired the nickname 'Doomsday', the Day of Judgement, because the accounts it contained were considered absolute and indisputable.

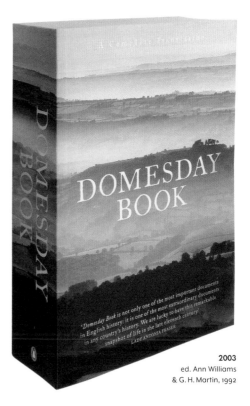

2003
ed. Ann Williams
& G. H. Martin, 1992

2012
ed. Christopher Tyerman,
2004

CHRONICLES OF
THE FIRST CRUSADE 1096–9

This anthology collects contemporary accounts of the First Crusade, from medieval Latin, Old French, Provençal, Greek, Armenian, Syriac, Arabic and Hebrew sources.
The volume opens with Pope Urban II's call to arms in 1095, and includes the writings of priests, knights, pilgrims, noblewomen, an Iraqi poet called Abu Muzaffar Muhammad al-Abiwardi and Princess Anna Komnene (60), all of whom were swept up in the holy war. It concludes with the fall of Jerusalem in 1099.

Peter Abelard 1079–1142

Peter Abelard was the greatest logician of the 12th century. He taught in Paris, attracting students from all over the world. In later life, his unorthodox views clashed with those of Bernard of Clairvaux (69).

The Letters of Abelard and Heloise 1132–42

The letters exchanged between Abelard and Héloïse narrate the story of their passionate but doomed love affair, from its reckless inception, through the ensuing public scandal, the birth of their son (whom they named Astrolabe) and their enforced marriage. Eventually Abelard smuggled Héloïse to the secluded convent of Argenteuil, where she became a nun, but he continued to visit and sleep with her. Outraged, Héloïse's uncle had Abelard forcibly castrated.

Héloïse d'Argenteuil c. 1090–1164

Héloïse was Abelard's pupil and lover. An accomplished scholar, poet and musician in her own right, Héloïse eventually became Abbess of the Oratory of the Paraclete in Champagne.

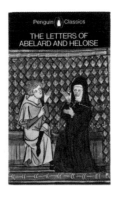

1974
trans. Betty Radice
rev. M. T. Clanchy, 2003

Geoffrey of Monmouth c. 1095–c. 1155

We know little about Geoffrey of Monmouth. He was fascinated by Merlin and wrote a biography of the mythical wizard while living in Oxford, and later collected the 'Prophecies of Merlin', which became a central section of his *History of the Kings of Britain*. In 1152 he was consecrated as Bishop of St Asaph in North Wales, but died a few years later.

The History of the Kings of Britain c. 1136

Geoffrey's *History* provided Britain with a national myth: he traces the foundation of the realm to Brutus, the great-grandson of <u>Aeneas</u> (44), who landed at Totnes, rid the land of giants and named the country after himself. He describes <u>King Lear</u> (142), <u>King Cymbeline</u> (144) and <u>King Arthur</u> (90) and traces the monarchy all the way down to the historical King Cadwallader, who renounced the throne for a life of pilgrimage in 688. His spurious but highly popular chronicle influenced writers from <u>Malory</u> (90) to <u>Dryden</u> (151) and <u>Tennyson</u> (263).

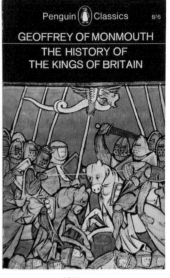

1966
trans. Lewis Thorpe
—
Lewis Thorpe was introduced by his wife, Barbara Reynolds, to E. V. Rieu (17) while Reynolds was completing Dorothy L. Sayers's translation of Dante's *Paradiso* (85). 'My greatest inspiration,' he writes, 'was to have been present at the reception given in honour of Dr Rieu on 22 January 1964 on the occasion of his retirement from the editorship of the Penguin Classics, to have talked there with him and Sir Allen Lane and to have inspected with some awe all the volumes in the series which had been published up to that date, spread out on the grand piano in the Great Drawing Room of the Arts Council building.'

Gerald of Wales c. 1146–c. 1223

Gerald of Wales was a member of the formidable 'Geraldine' dynasty, which still holds hereditary titles in Ireland. He was the grandson of the first castellan of Pembroke Castle, the Norman Gerald de Windsor, who married a Welsh prin-

cess called Nest. Gerald was an influential cleric who dreamt of becoming Bishop of St David's, breaking with Canterbury and persuading the Pope to appoint him Archbishop of Wales. In the end, he died in obscurity.

The History and Topography of Ireland 1188

Gerald first visited Ireland in 1183, during the Norman invasions. His book is an outsider's description of the Irish countryside and the island's early history. He describes magical springs, deadly whirlpools, barbaric customs, bearded ladies and mysterious sprites.

1982
trans. John O'Meara, 1951

The Journey through Wales *and* The Description of Wales 1191–4

The Journey is the whimsical travel diary of a preaching tour that Gerald undertook with the Archbishop of Canterbury in 1188 to gain Welsh support for the Third Crusade. *The Description* covers the geography of Wales, as well as its social and economic conditions.

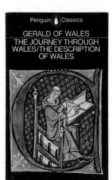

1978
trans. Lewis Thorpe
—
Barbara Reynolds adds a prefatory note to this volume: 'My husband's first book, *La France guerrière*, was published by Penguins in 1945. As he was then in Italy on active service, I had the privilege of correcting the proofs in his absence. The proofs of this, his last book, arrived a few days after his death. Once again I have performed the same service.'

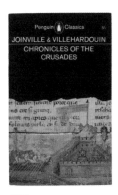

1963

2008
trans. Caroline Smith

Geoffrey of Villehardouin *c.* 1150–*c.* 1212

Geoffrey was born in Champagne. He 'took the cross' in 1199 and was immediately involved in the planning of the Fourth Crusade, which culminated in the conquest of Constantinople on April 1204. He was later made a marshal of the Latin Empire, a feudal Crusader state.

John of Joinville 1224–1317

John was also born in Champagne and inherited the office of seneschal at the court of the influential Count Theobald IV. In 1248, he set out with King Louis IX of France on the Seventh Crusade, a six-year campaign that took him to Egypt and the Holy Land. He became a close friend of Louis and later supported the king's canonization.

Chronicles of the Crusades 1207–1309

These eyewitness accounts of the Crusades provide fascinating insights into the mind-set behind centuries of military campaigns in the service of God. Geoffrey's account of the Conquest of Constantinople is the earliest work of historical writing in French prose. John wrote his *Life of Saint Louis* at the request of Queen Jeanne of Navarre.

2015
ed. David Carpenter
—
Published to coincide with the document's 800th anniversary, this edition includes an extensive commentary on the origins, enforcement and survival of Magna Carta.

MAGNA CARTA 1215

Magna Carta, the 'Great Charter', was forced on King John by his barons in 1215. It established the fundamental principle that a ruler is never above the law. John gave the Magna Carta to the barons in Runnymede, a meadow beside the Thames near Windsor, on 15 June.

Marco Polo 1254–1324

Marco Polo was the son of a Venetian merchant. In 1271, the 17-year-old Marco accompanied his father on a 24-year journey to the Far East. Marco learned the languages of the Mongol Empire and became a favourite of Khubilai Khan, who sent him on missions to collect detailed reports on the extremities of the realm. Marco finally returned to Venice in 1295 to find the city at war with Genoa. He was captured and imprisoned with a cellmate named Rustichello, a writer of romances. Marco described his travels to Rustichello, who transcribed the account that survives today.

The Travels 1296–9

Marco Polo's *Description of the World* was Europe's first eyewitness account of the Far East and it was exceptionally popular. It is a mixture of practical gazetteer and medieval romance, combining itineraries with colourful cultural observations and fantastical stories, from the spice forests of Sumatra to the Sea of Japan. It is populated with vast cities, pearl fishers, 'paper money' and naked warriors, and inspired Christopher Columbus (119), two centuries later, to seek a shortcut to these fantastical lands.

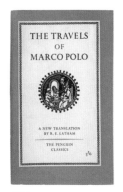

1958
• trans. R. E. Latham

MARCO POLO
The Travels

'I am glad to learn from Dr. Rieu (17) that you are prepared to entrust me with the job of turning Polo's *Description of the World* into a Penguin Classic,' wrote R. E. Latham in 1953. 'Perhaps I should warn you that it will be a very fat Penguin and will probably have to be twins.' 'We like our Penguins fat nowadays,' replied A. S. B. Glover, Penguin's general editor, 'and I don't think it will be necessary to split yours in the middle. [...] This will be a very welcome addition indeed to the Classics series.'

Jean Froissart *c.* 1337–*c.* 1405

Froissart was born in Valenciennes in the county of Hainault and came to England in 1361 to join the entourage of Philippa of Hainault, Edward III's queen. In 1368, he attended Philippa's son, Lionel of Clarence, when he travelled to be married in Milan; Chaucer (89) and Petrarch (86) were also present at the wedding. During the trip, Jean received news that Philippa had died, so he remained in Europe, under the protection of Wenceslas of Bohemia, Robert of Namur and Guy of Blois. In 1395, he returned to England and joined the court of Richard II.

Chronicles *c.* 1370–1410

Froissart charts the origins and the course of the Hundred Years War, from the deposition of Edward II in 1327 to the downfall of Richard II in 1399, as depicted memorably in the play by Shakespeare (137). He describes the battles of Sluys, Crécy, Calais and Poitiers, as well as the Peasants' Revolt and everyday scenes of medieval life. Many early manuscripts were beautifully illuminated.

1968
trans. Geoffrey Brereton
—
Brereton was a journalist, who reported on the Spanish Civil War and was press officer in General Eisenhower's North African headquarters during the Second World War.

Fiction

Between the 11th and 13th centuries, the population of Europe increased rapidly and the economy boomed. Swathes of forest and marshland were cleared, nation states began to emerge and the spires of soaring Gothic cathedrals started to dominate the landscape. The primary genre of this period was romance, a development of the military *chansons de geste* (80), infused with fantasy. Romances usually revolve around a courageous knight-errant who combines the qualities of a soldier with the chivalrous manners of courtly love, supported by a cast of damsels in distress, hermits, witches, wizards and dragons.

Poets began to write in their local vernaculars: Dante (84) wrote in Italian, Chrétien de Troyes (81) in French, Wolfram von Eschenbach (83) in German, and Chaucer (89) in English. The prose masterpiece of the Middle Ages was Boccaccio's *Decameron* (86), which is framed by the Black Death, an unprecedented bubonic plague that stole along the Silk Road in the fleas on the backs of black rats and devastated Europe between 1346 and 1353, killing up to 60 per cent of the population. It lingered until the 19th century with seasonal outbreaks, and features in the works of Chaucer, Defoe (157) and Pushkin (367). It forms a crucial plot point in Shakespeare's *Romeo and Juliet* (137).

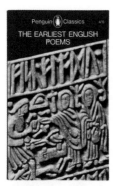

1966 *The Earliest English Poems*
2008 Reissued as *The First Poems in English*
trans. Michael Alexander
—
'It is beautiful,' ran a review in *Tribune* — 'as a clean bone, stripped of all accretions, is beautiful.' This anthology was intended to have a companion volume of *Earliest English Prose*, translated by Rowland Collins, but it never materialised.

THE FIRST POEMS IN ENGLISH
c. 680–1030

A poignant description of a ruined Roman city, a song about the death of the Venerable Bede (67), assorted gnomic proverbs, witty riddles and descriptions of heroic battles all feature in this selection of the earliest poems in Old English. *The Wanderer* and *The Seafarer* are particularly beautiful: bleak, elegiac meditations on loss and destiny.

EARLY IRISH MYTHS AND SAGAS
8th century

Although written down in Ireland in the 8th century, the stories in this anthology are remnants of the older oral traditions of the Iron Age Celts, who flourished across Europe from the 7th century BCE. Tales include 'The Destruction of Da Derga's Hostel', 'The Cattle Raid of Fróech' and 'Macc Da Thó's Pig', in which rival clans argue over a hog roast.

1981
trans. Jeffrey Gantz

1957
- trans. David Wright
—

'His view of the poem has helped to incapacitate him as its translator,' wrote Kingsley Amis in *The Spectator*, about David Wright. '[…] The naive concept of style as an ornament, lurking at the back of his mind, had led him to write far too often with the flat briskness, the explanatory paraphrasing and the all too neat syntactical subordination of a goodish sixth-former doing an unseen.'

Betty Radice (51) commissioned Michael Alexander to replace Wright's translation, following the success of his *Earliest English Poems* (78). 'Beowulf was not written to be readable but to be listened to,' Alexander writes, and in 1982 his translation was broadcast on BBC radio. His glossed edition reproduces the original Old English, with almost every word annotated on facing pages.

1973 *Beowulf: A Verse Translation*
trans. Michael Alexander

1995 *Beowulf: A Glossed Text*
ed. Michael Alexander

BEOWULF 8th – 10th centuries

The epic, anonymous *Beowulf* survives in a single, singed manuscript that was very nearly incinerated in an 18th-century house fire. It is the greatest and the longest poem that survives in Old English: Andrew Motion calls it the 'foundation stone'. Set in the Lands of the North, where the black rocks stand guard against the cold sea, it is the tale of the hero Beowulf, who engaged in three mighty duels: with Grendel, a cave-troll; Grendel's vengeful mother, whom Beowulf slays at the bottom of a lake; and a deadly, fire-breathing dragon. The poem evokes a dark world of powerful natural and supernatural forces.

A CELTIC MISCELLANY 8th – 19th centuries

This wide-ranging anthology collects stories and extracts from eleven centuries of Irish, Welsh, Scottish Gaelic, Cornish, Breton and Manx traditions, organizing them thematically. It includes tales of the ancient Irish hero Cú Chulainn, legends of magical werewolves, elegiac love songs and a celebration of the Wild Man of the Woods. 'This is quite the best anthology of the kind I have ever read,' ran the Penguin reader's report of *A Celtic Miscellany*. 'Prof Jackson has successfully blown away the "Celtic mist" so loved by cheap English romantics'.

1971
trans. Kenneth Hurlstone Jackson, 1951

THE PENGUIN BOOK OF IRISH POETRY

6th – 21st centuries

'Yeats (267) famously saw Ireland as soft wax, ready to take the imprint of his grand literary and cultural design,' writes Seamus Heaney; '[…] this anthology reveals the depth and riches of the tradition which the arch-poet's intervention helped to retrieve and which his successors have so thoroughly and variously consolidated.' It stretches from the medieval monks of the western monasteries to the 20th-century Nobel Laureates, Yeats, Beckett and Heaney himself, with dozens of Irish poets in between, including Beccán the Hermit, Fearghal Óg Mac an Bhaird, Jonathan Swift (159), Oscar Wilde (244), James Joyce, Patrick Kavanagh, Louis MacNeice, Paul Muldoon and Eiléan Ní Chuilleanáin.

1970 Penguin Poets
- ed. Brendan Kennelly

2012
ed. Patrick Crotty, 2010
pref. Seamus Heaney, 2010

1957

● trans. Dorothy L. Sayers

—

The production department suggested illustrating the cover of the 1957 edition with Roland's horn. 'I *don't* really think Roland's horn would go awfully well into a roundel, do you?' replied Sayers. 'It's not a little short curly thing like a hunting-horn, but long, with a shallow curve, like an elephant's tusk. In fact it *is* an elephant's tusk (*l'olifant*), or supposed to be. It's big enough to be quite a formidable weapon – if you remember, Roland bats a Paynim on the head with it and kills him.' Sayers suggested basing the roundel on a circular stained-glass window at Chartres Cathedral, which shows, on the right, Roland blowing his horn, and on the left, Roland trying to break his sword on a marble block.

1990
trans. Glyn Burgess

THE SONG OF ROLAND

1040–1115

Charlemagne's (73) army has finished rampaging through Saracen Spain and is returning to France, but the rearguard, led by the gallant Roland, is ambushed in the narrow Pyrenean pass of Ronceveaux. Roland blows his horn so loudly that Charlemagne hears it many miles away; unfortunately Roland's temples burst with the effort and he dies. Charlemagne returns and drives the enemy forces into the River Ebro, and goes on to conquer Saragossa, the last Muslim stronghold in Spain. The anonymous *Song of Roland* is a *chanson de geste*, a 'song of heroic deeds', a form that pre-dates verse romances. It directly inspired Ariosto's *Orlando Furioso* (128).

THE PENGUIN BOOK OF SCOTTISH VERSE

6th–21st centuries

St Columba (67) is the first poet in this collection. His 6th-century 'The Maker on High' encompasses the whole universe in Latin verses that begin with the letters A through to Z. The last poet is Don Paterson, who evokes the late-night shipping forecast:

> I sit down and turn the radio on low
> as the last girl on the planet still awake
> reads a dedication to the ships
> and puts on a recording of the ocean.

In between are Scots, Gaelic, Latin and contemporary poems from great Scottish poets, including Robert Henryson, William Dunbar, Robert Burns (193), Walter Scott (202), Robert Louis Stevenson (241), Hugh MacDiarmid, Douglas Dunn and Carol Ann Duffy.

1970 Penguin Poets
● ed. Tom Scott

2001 Penguin Books
2006 Penguin Classics
ed. Robert Crawford & Mick Imlah

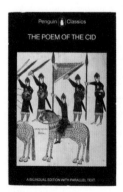

1984
trans. Rita Hamilton & Janet Perry, 1975
intro. Ian Michael, 1975

2009
● trans. Burton Raffel
intro. María Rosa Menocal

—

Raffel's parallel text edition is now out of print in the UK.

THE POEM OF THE CID 1140–1207

The Poem of the Cid is another *chanson de geste* by an unknown Spanish author. It describes the adventures of the historical Castilian warlord Rodrigo Díaz de Vivar, the Cid, who was unjustly banished from the court of King Alfonso, achieved great military victories in Valencia and saw his ill-treated daughters married to the princes of Aragon and Navarre. The honorific 'Cid' comes from the Arabic *sayyid*, meaning 'lord'. The poem is based on historical truth, although richly embellished with idealised heroism. It is the only epic poem to have survived from medieval Spain.

SELECTIONS FROM THE CARMINA BURANA

11th–13th centuries

'Songs of Beuern', *Carmina Burana*, is the name given to a manuscript containing 254 bawdy, irreverent and satirical 'vagabond songs' from France, England, Spain and the Holy Roman Empire, written in a mixture of medieval Latin, Middle High German, Old French and Provençal. They were probably compiled by a number of impudent monastic novices. The manuscript was discovered in 1803 in the monastery of Benediktbeuern in Bavaria; in 1936, Carl Orff set 24 of them to music.

1986
trans. David Parlett
—
Parlett is a board-game inventor and an expert on the history of card games; he is the author of *The Penguin Book of Patience*. Betty Radice (51) died while his translation was in proof. 'She will be missed by many,' he writes, 'as an editor who inevitably became a friend.'

Beroul

12th century

We know nothing about Beroul.

1970
trans. Alan S. Fedrick
—
Fedrick's edition also includes the short *Tale of Tristan's Madness*, an anonymous retelling of the episode in which Tristan poses as a madman to gain access to Yseult.

The Romance of Tristan

and The Tale of Tristan's Madness

The Romance of Tristan survives in just one highly illuminated manuscript in the Bibliothèque Nationale in Paris. It is one of the earliest versions of the story of Yseult, Queen of Cornwall, and Tristran, the king's nephew, who fall desperately in love with each other after accidentally sharing a powerful love potion. For a while they keep their illicit affair secret, but when the Cornish barons become suspicious and the effects of the potion begin to wear off, the lovers face unavoidable tragedy. This version of the story has been dubbed the 'vulgar' *Tristan*; whereas the fragmentary account by Thomas of Britain (83) represents the 'courtly' branch of the legend.

Chrétien de Troyes 12th century

Chrétien spent much of his career at Troyes, at the court of Marie of France, Countess of Champagne. Little else is known about his life.

Arthurian Romances

c. 1170–*c.* 1190

1991
trans. William W. Kibler & Carleton W. Carroll

Chrétien's verse romances are some of the highest achievements of medieval literature: he concentrates on the inner lives of his subjects, structuring the stories like proto-novels. *The Knight of the Cart* contains the first description of the adulterous affair between Lancelot and Guinevere. In *The Knight of the Lion*, Yvain wins back his lady's hand with the assistance of a friendly lion. *The Story of the Holy Grail* is the unfinished story of Perceval, who seeks a holy golden serving dish.

2008
trans. Ciaran Carson
—
In a review of this edition in *The Times*, John Burnside called *The Táin* 'Ireland's own *Iliad*' (16).

THE TÁIN 12th century

The *Táin Bó Cúailnge*, the 'Cattle Raid of Cooley', tells the story of the supernatural battle between the teenage hero Cú Chulainn, the Hound of Ulster and Medb of Connaught, an unscrupulous queen who craves the phenomenally fertile Bull of Cooney. It is the central text of the 'Ulster Cycle', a medieval retelling of ancient Irish legends and sagas (78).

THE MABINOGION 12th–13th centuries

Compiled in Middle Welsh in the 12th and 13th centuries, the eleven dreamlike tales that comprise the *Mabinogion* preserve far older oral traditions, which blur the border between the forested valleys of Wales and the shadowy otherworld. The four branches of the *'Mabinogi'* follow the fortunes of the heroic Pryderi and Queen Branwen; the 'native tales' recount fantastical histories; and 'Owein', 'Peredur Son of Evrawg' and 'Gereint and Enid' are Welsh versions of the Arthurian romances of Chrétien de Troyes (81).

1976
trans. Jeffrey Gantz
—
'The idea of translation the *Mabinogion* had been given to me by my twin brother, Timothy, in the fall of 1972, when I had my Harvard degree in hand but no job in sight,' wrote Gantz in 1987. '[…] I was attracted by the beauty, the colour, the mystery and the myth.'

Marie de France 12th century

Virtually nothing is known about the poet Marie de France. She seems to have been born in France but lived in England, and she was called Marie. She is considered the earliest female poet in the French language.

The Lais of Marie de France 1160–1215

Breton *lais* are short, rhyming narrative poems, usually about love, chivalry and the fairy world. Marie de France wrote twelve *lais*, which include stories of werewolves, magical boats, reunited twins, bird-humans, nightingales and emasculating thigh injuries.

1986
trans. Glyn S. Burgess & Keith Busby

EARLY FICTION IN ENGLAND
from Geoffrey of Monmouth to Chaucer
12th–14th centuries

From the doubtful histories of Geoffrey of Monmouth (76) and Geffrei Gaimar, to the Arthurian legends of Wace and Thomas of Britain (83) and the *lais* of Marie de France, this wide-ranging anthology climaxes with extracts from Chaucer's exquisitely wrought *Troilus and Criseyde* (89). It presents a portrait of the earliest verse and prose fiction to emerge in England, selecting texts that were originally written in a mixture of Latin, French and Middle English.

Early Fiction in England from Geoffrey of Monmouth to Chaucer

2015
ed. Laura Ashe

1965
trans. A. T. Hatto
—
A. T. Hatto includes a 'word of thanks' to E. V. Rieu (17), 'the veteran Editor of this series, who has given his contributors the guidance and encouragement they needed with so light and sure a touch. I am proud to have joined him here with a translation of a great heroic epic.' Rieu retired the year before Hatto's translation was published.

THE NIBELUNGENLIED
c. 1180–1210

Written by an unknown Austrian author, the *Song of the Nibelung* gathers centuries of German oral tradition into a single epic poem, comparable in scale to the *Iliad* (16). Siegfried, a Rhineland prince, wins the hand of the beautiful Kriemhild of Burgundy, having first assisted Kriemhild's brother in wooing the supernaturally powerful Queen Brünhild of Iceland. Kriemhild and Brünhild quarrel, however, and Siegfried is murdered, upon which the furious Kriemhild embarks on a bloody quest for revenge. Brünhild's magical ring is central to the plot. This epic inspired Wagner's operatic cycle *The Ring of the Nibelung* (343).

Gottfried von Strassburg

died c. 1210

Almost nothing is known about Gottfried von Strassburg; he seems to have enjoyed music, hunting and Latin literature, and to have been an admirer of the Cistercian mystic Bernard of Clairvaux (69). His *Tristan* ends abruptly; it is assumed he died while writing it.

Tristan

with the 'Tristran' of Thomas

This is the 'authentic version' of the Tristan story, according to Gottfried, based on Thomas of Britain rather than Beroul (81). It includes details of Tristan's parents, Rivalin and Blancheflor, an Irish dragon and a confusing second Isolde 'of the White Hands', who also captures Tristan's heart. Wagner (343) used this version as the basis for his *Tristan and Isolde*.

1960
trans. A. T. Hatto

The surviving fragments of *Tristran* by the Anglo-Norman poet Thomas of Britain conclude the narrative where Gottfried breaks off: Tristran marries Isolde of the White Hands, but is wounded by a poisoned spear. Only the first Isolde can cure him, but Tristan dies of grief before she can arrive, so she dies of grief too.

1971
trans. James Cable

THE DEATH OF KING ARTHUR

c. 1230–35

The anonymous *La Mort le Roi Artu* forms the fifth and final section of the 'Vulgate Cycle', a 13th-century French prose retelling of the Arthurian legends. It describes the last days of Arthur's life: the Round Table has been weakened by the debilitating Quest for the Holy Grail, Queen Guinevere's rumoured infidelity and the treachery of Arthur's son Sir Mordred. This psychologically convincing version of the legend deeply impressed Thomas Malory, who used it as the basis for his *Morte D'Arthur* (90).

Wolfram von Eschenbach

c. 1160 – c. 1220

As with most of these medieval writers, we know little about Wolfram von Eschenbach: he seems to have lived in Bavaria during the Hohenstaufen period and enjoyed the patronage of Hermann I, Landgrave of neighbouring Thuringia. As well as writing narrative verse, Wolfram was a *Minnesinger*, a composer of lyrical love poems.

1980
trans. A. T. Hatto

Parzival

Wolfram's *Parzival* is a reworking of *Perceval* by Chrétien de Troyes (81). It follows the chivalrous escapades of young Parzival, who becomes a knight of King Arthur's Round Table and finally the king of the Temple of the Grail, which Wolfram describes as a life-giving gemstone. It is a tale of love and chivalry and the quest for spiritual enlightenment, featuring the Fisher King, red knights, lost brothers and grail maidens. It was the inspiration for Wagner's (343) *Parsifal*.

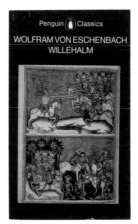

1984
trans. Marion E. Gibbs & Sidney M. Johnson

Willehalm

In *Willehalm*, Wolfram emulates the style of a chanson de geste (80). Willehalm, Margrave of Provence, falls in love with Arabel, a Saracen princess, who converts to Christianity and changes her name to Giburc. Enraged, her pagan relatives initiate a holy war, in which Willehalm must exercise both military prowess and skills in the art of courtly love, abetted by his humorous sidekick, Rennewart.

Dante 1265–1321

The love of Dante Alighieri's life was the beautiful Beatrice Portinari. After Beatrice died in 1290, he became increasingly involved in the strife between the Guelfs and the Ghibellines, and, as a Guelf, was finally exiled from his native Florence in 1302. He travelled to Verona and Paris before settling in Ravenna, where he wrote the *Divine Comedy* in his native Tuscan dialect. In Italy, Dante is known as *il Sommo Poeta* ('the Supreme Poet'). Along with Petrarch (86) and Boccaccio (86), he is considered one of the 'three fountains' of Italian literature.

Vita Nuova
(Poems of Youth) 1295

This sequence of poems and commentaries narrates Dante's love for Beatrice, from the moment they met, at the age of eight, through their exquisite but unconsummated love, to his profound grief at her premature death, after which he has a vision of her in Heaven.

1964 *The New Life*
● trans. William Anderson

1969
trans. Barbara Reynolds
—
'Five years ago Dante's *The New Life* was published in the Penguin Classics,' ran a notice in the *Times Literary Supplement* in 1969, 'a translation which in scholarship and style fell notably far below the expected standard. It is now commendably, if tacitly, superseded.'

Dante in English

Percy Bysshe Shelley (196), Elizabeth Barrett Browning (262), Dante Gabriel Rossetti (265) and Seamus Heaney have all translated Dante into English. This volume includes extracts from their translations, as well as those of many other writers. It also features works that were influenced by Dante, from Chaucer (89) and Spenser (130) to Byron (195), Beckett, Auden and more.

2005
ed. Eric Griffiths & Matthew Reynolds

The Divine Comedy *c.*1308–20

Dante called his cosmic masterwork the *Commedia*; it was Boccaccio (86) who added *Divina*. It is the greatest literary achievement of the Middle Ages, and has influenced writers such as Milton (150) and Tennyson (263).

In *Inferno*, Dante meets the ghost of Virgil (43), who guides him through the nine circles of Hell, past the lustful and the gluttonous, through the wood of suicides and the abominable sands, meeting Homer (16), the Minotaur and eventually three-headed Satan himself, frozen to the waist at the icy centre of the earth. Virgil and Dante climb through the Devil's leg-hairs and up a long tunnel, finally emerging at the foot of the antipodean Mount Purgatory.

In *Purgatorio*, Virgil leads Dante up the nine terraces of the mountain of Purgatory, which is formed from the rocks that were driven sky-high when God threw Lucifer into the bowels of the earth. Along the way they meet the envious, the wrathful, the slothful and the prodigal: only by learning from these patient sinners, awaiting admittance to Heaven, can Dante himself achieve the Earthly Paradise at the summit. Here, he is reunited with his lost love, Beatrice.

In *Paradiso*, Dante takes leave of Virgil, and ascends the planetary spheres of Heaven with Beatrice, until he finally arrives at the snow-white Rose of Paradise, beyond space and time, and he enters the dazzling presence of God himself.

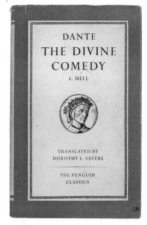

1949 *Hell*
trans. Dorothy L. Sayers

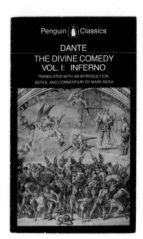

1984 *Inferno*
trans. Mark Musa, 1971

2006 *Inferno*
trans. Robin Kirkpatrick

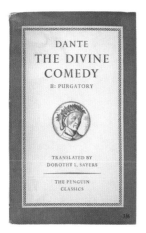

1955 *Purgatory*
trans. Dorothy L. Sayers

1962 *Paradise*
trans. Dorothy L. Sayers &
Barbara Reynolds

Sayers follows the original *terza rima* rhyme scheme, as does Musa. Kirkpatrick's translations include the original Italian on facing pages.

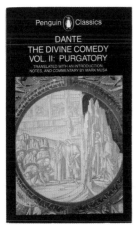

1985 *Purgatory*
trans. Mark Musa, 1981

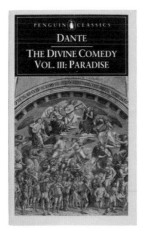

1986 *Paradise*
trans. Mark Musa, 1984

2007 *Purgatorio*
trans. Robin Kirkpatrick

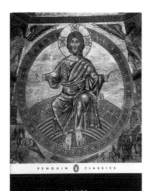

2007 *Paradiso*
trans. Robin Kirkpatrick

2012 *The Divine Comedy: Inferno, Purgatorio, Paradiso*
trans. Robin Kirkpatrick

'By one of those happy coincidences that occasionally delight the world of letters,' reads the back cover of Dorothy L. Sayers's translation of *Hell*, 'Miss Sayers's enthusiasm for Dante reached its climax just at the time when the Penguin Classics were launched.'

Sayers visited E. V. Rieu (17) in Highgate to propose her translation over lunch. She 'stayed to tea and then to dinner, still talking,' recalled Rieu, 'and just when we were about to offer her bed and breakfast, said she must go.' The collaboration was not always easy and became particularly fraught over the issue of quotation marks. 'And now I tune my brazen throat,' Sayers wrote:

> To sing in harsh, emphatic strain
> With what abhorrence, rage
> and pain
> I contemplate the Single Quote.

'I hate it,' she continued. 'For one thing the eye slips over it too easily (especially when it is combined with the beastly modern habit of insufficiently indenting the beginning of a paragraph).' She eventually got her way and double quotation marks were used, but the same issue arose with her *Purgatory*. She immediately fired off a telegram:

> URGENTLY IMPLORE DEMAND INSIST
> DOUBLE QUOTES PURGATORY
> INFERNO AS BEFORE STOP DEEPEST
> PASSIONS ROUSED WRITING

'When I die,' she wrote later, 'you will find the blessed, unambiguous, but rapidly disappearing double quote written on my heart.'

She did die in 1957, before she had completed her translation of *Paradise*. E. V. Rieu invited Barbara Reynolds, Sayers's goddaughter and a respected Dante scholar, to complete the translation. She recalled the difficult conversation: 'looking at me over his glasses in a shrewd but kindly way, he spoke one word: "Try."'

Reynolds finished the translation and later became President of the Dorothy L. Sayers Society.

Petrarch 1304–1374

Francesco Petrarca was born in Arezzo, the son of an exiled Florentine notary. He first saw the young woman he called 'Laura' in Avignon on 6 April 1327: her 'lovely hand' captured his heart and inspired the passionate sequence of love sonnets that form the *Canzoniere*, 'Song Book'. A proponent of a new wave of literary and cultural scholarship, and a key instigator of the Italian Renaissance (118), Petrarch was crowned Poet Laureate on the ancient Roman Capitol on Easter Sunday, 1341. After Laura's death he travelled around northern Italy, revising the *Canzoniere*. He died in Padua in 1374.

2002
trans. Anthony Mortimer
—
Mortimer acknowledges his 'oldest debt' to the mysterious 'girl in the white raincoat who taught me Italian'. The original text is presented in this selection of 60 poems, alongside translations on facing pages.

2005
ed. Thomas P. Roche, Jr.

Canzoniere

The poems that form the *Canzoniere* describe the many intense emotions that arise from unrequited love, ranging from joy and hope to melancholy, frustration, resignation and remorse. These introspective 'Petrarchan' sonnets would later inspire English poets, including Spenser (130) and Sidney (131).

Petrarch in English

This anthology collects translations and adaptations of Petrarch by many different writers, from Chaucer's use of his sonnet form in *Troilus and Criseyde* (89) to Ezra Pound's parody, *Silet*, with contributions from Thomas Wyatt (129); Mary Sidney (130); Queen Elizabeth I of England; Walter Raleigh; John Milton (150); John Dryden (151) and J. M. Synge (300).

Giovanni Boccaccio

1313–1375

Boccaccio was the illegitimate son of a banker. After writing his masterpiece, *The Decameron*, he became involved in Florentine politics and worked on translations of Homer (16), Euripides (22) and Aristotle (29). He left his entire library to the monastery of Santo Spirito in Florence, where it remains.

2015
trans. Peter Hainsworth
—
When Harry McWilliam was working on his monumental 1972 translation, one of his readers was Peter Hainsworth. Hainsworth has subsequently translated his own representative selection of the stories, featuring tales that were adapted by Chaucer (89), Shakespeare (141) and Keats (197).

The Decameron 1348–53

When the Black Death arrives in Florence in 1348, a group of seven young women and three young men escape to a palazzo in Fiesole. They pass the time by telling stories every day for ten days: a hundred tales of love and adventure, cuckolded husbands, lascivious priests, quick-witted women and practical jokes.

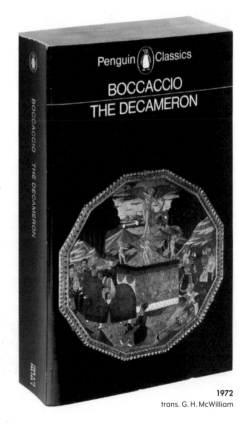

1972
trans. G. H. McWilliam

MEDIEVAL ENGLISH VERSE

13th – 14th centuries

This anthology is a gallimaufry of Middle English verse, translated into modern English. It includes the spiritual verses 'I sing of a Maiden' and 'White was his naked breast'; extracts from a bestiary; political lyrics; secular poems such as 'Tell me, broom wizard, tell me' and 'I have a noble cockerel'; religious verses; and translations of the exquisite *Patience* and *Pearl*, two of the Gawain Poet's (88) masterpieces. Cryptically, Brian Stone quotes Yeats (267) in his epigraph:

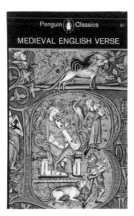

> What can a swan need but a swan?

1964
trans. Brian Stone

THE TRAVELS OF SIR JOHN MANDEVILLE

c. 1356

John Mandeville, knight, was born in St Albans and set out on Michaelmas Day 1332 to travel to Jerusalem, Egypt, India and beyond. His journey took more than 20 years and on the way he encountered tribes of dog-headed men, gold-digging ants and men with faces in their chests. He even passed close to the Earthly Paradise. Except John Mandeville did not exist. His *Travels* are an anonymous work of finely synthesized plagiarism, stitching together the best sections of Herodotus (31), Pliny the Elder (49), Jacobus de Voragine (70) and genuine medieval accounts of eastern travel. It was an extraordinarily popular book, which was used in good faith by Christopher Columbus (119) and Leonardo da Vinci, and was an inspiration for the fantasies of Swift (159), Defoe (157) and Coleridge (195).

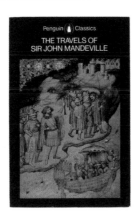

THE PENGUIN BOOK OF ENGLISH VERSE 14th – 20th centuries

This anthology is ordered chronologically according to the date of each poem's first appearance: the result is a thousand-page chronicle that treats poems 'as individuals, living in contingency', as Paul Keegan puts it – 'where the poem survives, in W. H. Auden's words, "in the valley of its saying"'. Keegan begins with anonymous 14th-century lyrics and the great poets of the Middle Ages, and aims for interesting and surprising juxtapositions throughout, concluding with Christopher Reid's 'Stones and Bones' from 1994:

> [...] we have always found
> something hard, ungracious,
> obdurate in our natures,
> a strain of the very earth
> that gave us our abrupt birth;
> but a pang too, at the back
> of the mind: a loss ... a lack ...

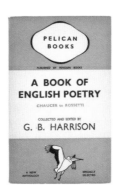

1937 Pelican Books
A Book of English Poetry
1950 Penguin Poets
● ed. G. B. Harrison
1956 Penguin Poets
● ed. John Hayward

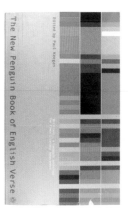

2001 Penguin Books
2004 Penguin Classics
ed. Paul Keegan

1983
trans. C. W. R. D. Moseley
—

In the early 1980s, Penguin began easing out its external editors. Betty Radice's (51) title was changed from 'Editor' to 'Advisory Editor', and some books, such as *The Travels of Sir John Mandeville*, were introduced to Penguin Classics 'over her head'.

The 'Gawain Poet' 14th century

Sir Gawain and the Green Knight survives in a single manuscript copy from about 1400, along with three other poems by the same author. His or her identity is unknown, although the vocabulary suggests northwest England, and familiarity with local geography points to either Cheshire, northwest Staffordshire or south Lancashire.

Sir Gawain and the Green Knight

A New Year's feast at Camelot is interrupted by the appearance of a gigantic green knight, riding a spectacular green horse. He challenges any of the knights present to behead him, on the condition that if he survives, he may return the blow a year later. The hot-headed Gawain leaps up and lops the green knight's head off, but this unnatural man picks up his severed head and gallops away, very much alive. The following winter, Gawain sets out glumly to find the green knight, in order to receive his own fatal blow, and on the way becomes involved in a mysterious adventure, in which his courage, courtesy and fidelity are tested. This is one of the great masterpieces of Middle English poetry.

1959
• trans. Brian Stone

1972
ed. J. A. Burrow

2006
trans. Bernard O'Donoghue

Burrow presents the original Middle English, fully glossed; O'Donoghue translates into modern English.

The Works of the Gawain Poet
Sir Gawain and the Green Knight, Pearl, Patience, Cleanness

In *Pearl*, a grieving man, mourning the loss of his 'pearl', perhaps his daughter, falls asleep and dreams of a 'Pearl-maiden' standing on the other side of a stream, who shows him an image of the Heavenly Jerusalem. *Patience* retells the story of Jonah and the whale, and *Cleanness* is a series of admonitory parables about filth.

2014
ed. Ad Putter & Myra Stokes
—
This edition presents all four works in the original Middle English.

William Langland
c. 1332–*c.* 1386

William Langland is an obscure figure. He seems to have been a jobbing cleric, who travelled around England writing poetry. He claims in his poem to have been based in London, 'idling' in a cottage on Cornhill, with a wife called Kit and a daughter called Colette. His nickname was 'Long Will'.

Piers the Ploughman *c.* 1370–90

Will, the narrator poet, sets out to travel the world 'in search of marvels'. Lying down to rest, he falls asleep and begins a wondrous cycle of dreams in which he makes a visionary, allegorical pilgrimage in search of Truth, guided by Piers, the Ploughman of Christ. Will encounters the Seven Deadly Sins, the 'spirit of the Soul' and three figures called Do-Well, Do-Better and Do-Best. He passes by the very brink of Hell before learning the meaning of life.

1959
trans. J. F. Goodridge
—
Piers the Ploughman contains one of the first literary references to Robin Hood.

1983
trans. Brian
Stone

Geoffrey Chaucer c. 1343–1400

Chaucer had a prolific career as a courtier, a lawyer, a soldier, a diplomat, a spy, a civil servant, a forester and a Justice of the Peace. He began translating the French love poem, *Roman de la Rose*, soon after he had been captured, imprisoned and ransomed during the Hundred Years War. Chaucer wrote in the evolving vernacular known today as 'Middle English', a combination of Anglo-Saxon, Anglo-Norman, French and Latin: he acquired a cult following and became known as the 'Father of English Literature'. King Edward III demonstrated his appreciation by granting Chaucer a 'gallon of wine daily' for life. As a Westminster resident, Chaucer was buried in Westminster Abbey, the first writer to be interred in what is now known as Poets' Corner.

Love Visions c. 1370–88

The Book of the Duchess; *The House of Fame*; *The Parliament of Birds*; *The Legend of Good Women*

These poems are dream stories. In *The Book of the Duchess*, the dreamer meets a knight, who has lost his Queen while playing a game of chess; *The House of Fame* is a cosmic journey to the cacophonous palace of Fame; and *The Parliament of Birds* contains the earliest known reference to St Valentine's Day as a romantic occasion.

The Canterbury Tales 1387–1400

Pilgrims from every level of society sit down together to eat at the Tabard Inn in Southwark on the south bank of the Thames, before setting out for Canterbury Cathedral. The landlord, Harry Bailey, proposes a game: those present will make the three-day journey together and pass the time by telling stories. Whoever tells their tales with 'best sentence and moost solaas' will receive a free meal on their return. This framing device allows Chaucer to assemble a diverse and ambitious collection of stories, from the Knight's tale of courtly love to the Miller's story of farts and pokers, the Wife of Bath's fairy tale and the Pardoner's fable of the three robbers who meet Death. *The Canterbury Tales* is fragmentary and unfinished, yet it still captures the entire spectrum of human experience. The pilgrims themselves are vibrant and familiar: as William Blake (192) put it, they are the 'Characters that compose all Ages & Nations'.

1971
trans. Nevill
Coghill

2003
ed. Barry Windeatt
—
Windeatt's Middle English edition forms a 'companion volume' to Jill Mann's *Canterbury Tales*.

Troilus and Criseyde

1380s

Troilus and Criseyde is Chaucer's longest complete work and one of the greatest narrative poems in English literature. Prince Troilus, an extremely marginal character in the *Iliad* (16), is woven into a tender, tragic love story, set during the siege of Troy. When Troilus falls in love with a beautiful widow, Criseyde, they are brought together by Criseyde's lascivious uncle Pandarus. It is written in *rime royale*, an Italian form, later used by Shakespeare, who also used this poem as his main source for *Troilus and Cressida* (140).

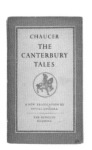

1951
trans. Nevill Coghill

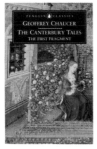

1996 *The Canterbury Tales: The First Fragment*
ed. Michael Alexander

2005
ed. Jill Mann

2008 *The Canterbury Tales: A Selection*
trans. Colin Wilcockson

2010
Retold by Peter Ackroyd

Nevill Coghill wrote a private letter to the general editor A. S. B. Glover at Penguin, pointing out that his translation of *The Miller's Tale* contains the words 'quim, arse, fart and to plumb.' 'I am a poor man,' he continued, clearly anxious about the obscenity laws, 'and cannot afford to pay a fine should one be inflicted on the suggestion of some prurient informer. I should just have to go to prison I suppose.'

THE PENGUIN BOOK OF ENGLISH SONG
14th–20th centuries

Words and music have always been intimately connected. This anthology collects a hundred different poets, from Chaucer (89) to Auden, presenting a songbook of lyric verse, all of which were written to be sung.

2018
ed. Richard Stokes, 2016

—

Stokes is the Professor of Lieder at the Royal Academy of Music. The image on the cover is a detail from William Morris's (226) *Bird and Anemone* wallpaper pattern.

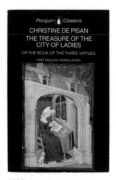

1985
trans. Sarah Lawson

Christine de Pizan 1365–c. 1430

Christine de Pizan's father was court physician and astrologer to Charles V of France. After the death of her father and husband, which left Christine a widow at 25 with three children and her own mother to support, she became one of the first professional female writers in history, producing quantities of lucrative lyric poetry, as well as moral essays and a biography of Charles V.

The Treasure of the City of Ladies
or, The Book of the Three Virtues 1405

Christine's manual provides guidance for women of all ages and at all levels of medieval society, from princesses to prostitutes. Personifications of the three Virtues – Reason, Rectitude and Justice – provide tips on running a household, dressing appropriately, bringing up children, managing the 'state of virginity' and behaving properly on all occasions.

Thomas Malory
c. 1415–1471

Sir Thomas Malory, of Newbold Revel in Warwickshire, was a shady character. Contemporary accounts accuse him of attempted murder, attempted rape and armed robbery, and he twice staged dramatic prison breaks. He may have written parts of *Le Morte D'Arthur* while incarcerated in Colchester Castle. In 1449 he was elected MP for Great Bedwyn in Wiltshire.

Le Morte D'Arthur
1468–70, pub. 1485

Malory's magnificent prose epic recounts the story of Arthur from his birth and the moment he pulled Excalibur out of the stone, to his marriage to Guenever, the treachery of Morgan le Fay, the exploits of his brave Knights of the Round Table and the last Battle of Camlann. At the tail end of the Middle Ages, Malory melds the French and the English Arthurian traditions into a nostalgic view of a faded, chivalric world.

For Renaissance poetry, turn to p.128

1969 Penguin English Library
1986 Penguin Classics
ed. Janet Cowen
intro. John Lawlor
Published in two volumes
2011 Retold by Peter Ackroyd

—

Cowen's edition is based on William Caxton's printed edition of 1485, rather than the Winchester Manuscript, discovered in 1934.

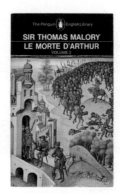

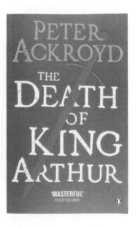

Sagas

In 870, a Swedish Viking called Garðar Svavarsson circumnavigated Iceland and stayed there over winter, building a camp at Húsavík. One of his men, Náttfari, decided to settle permanently, founding the first Icelandic community. Náttfari was followed by the Norse chieftain Ingólfr Arnarson and many other Scandinavian settlers and, within forty years, all of Iceland's arable land had been claimed. In order to regulate their new Icelandic Commonwealth, the settlers established an 'Althing', an assembly which is still the national parliament of Iceland.

The Sagas of the Icelanders were written down in the 13th and 14th centuries, but they mostly tell of historical events that took place during the 9th, 10th and early 11th centuries, a period known as the 'Saga Age'. They may have been commissioned to promote community cohesion and elevate the status of the chief dynasties on the island, and also to maintain a connection with the Icelanders' Nordic heritage.

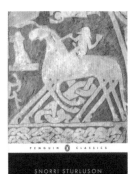

2005
trans.
Jesse L. Byock

Snorri Sturluson 1179–1241

Snorri is one of the only authors of Icelandic sagas whose name we know. He was raised in Oddi, in the south of Iceland. He was twice elected Law-Speaker of the Althing and was eventually assassinated in his own cellar.

The Prose Edda c. 1220
Norse Mythology

The word *edda* may derive from the Old Norse word for 'great-grandmother', or the word for 'poetry', or perhaps the town of Oddi. The term is applied to two collections of Norse mythology: the anonymous *Poetic* or *Elder Edda* (93) and Snorri's *Prose* or *Younger Edda*. Snorri's *Edda* is the most extensive source of Norse mythology that survives. It is a treasury of tales ranging from the creation of mankind in the armpit of a primordial giant, to the final Battle of Ragnarök, when the world will be destroyed.

1966
trans. Magnus
Magnusson &
Hermann Pálsson
—
Magnusson and
Pálsson dedicate
their translation to
the Icelandic scholar
Professor Sigurdur
Nordal 'on his eightieth
birthday, 14 September
1966', an anniversary
which 'coincides with
the ninth centenary
of King Harald's
attempted conquest
of England'.

King Harald's Saga c. 1230
Harald Hardradi of Norway

This excerpt from *Heimskringla*, Snorri's history of Norway, describes the life of Harold Hardradi, the Norwegian king who invaded England in 1066, less than two weeks before the arrival of William the Conqueror. Harald was ultimately defeated at the Battle of Stamford Bridge, but his attack weakened the English army, and left them vulnerable to the Norman conquest.

THE VINLAND SAGAS
The Norse Discovery of America
c. 1220–*c.* 1280

1965
trans. Magnus
Magnusson &
Hermann Pálsson

2008
trans. Keneva Kunz, 1997
intro. Gísli Sigurdsson,
2008

In the late 10th century, Eirik the Red discovered a harsh, glacial territory west of Iceland, which he called 'Green Land' to make it sound more attractive. He founded a colony there and before long rumours began to circulate about an even vaster, wooded continent, further to the west. Eirik's son, Leif the Lucky, sailed to this new land, and became the first European to stand on an American shore and meet its native inhabitants – 500 years before Christopher Columbus (119). Leif found grapes growing wild, so he named the new country Vinland or 'Wine Land'. There are two sagas that tell the story: *Grænlendinga Saga*, the *Saga of the Greenlanders*, and *Eirik's Saga*, the *Saga of Eric the Red*.

ORKNEYINGA SAGA
The History of the Earls of Orkney
c. 1230

This saga chronicles 400 bloody years on Orkney, starting with the Norwegian conquest in the 9th century. Portraits of mighty earls such as Sigurd the Powerful, Sigurd the Stout and St Magnus the Martyr are interspersed with tales of poisoned shirts, sorcery, pilgrimage and family feuds.

1981
trans. Hermann Pálsson &
Paul Edwards, 1978
—
Pálsson and Edwards
dedicated their translation to
George Mackay Brown, the
20th-century Orcadian poet.

EGIL'S SAGA
c. 1240

Some say that *Egil's Saga* was written by Snorri Sturluson (91). It tells the story of the historical Egil Skallagrimsson, the hideously ugly, brutally cruel warrior who was also a master of exquisite poetry. The contradictory Egil fights King Erik Bloodaxe of Norway and assists King Athelstan of England in his bloody Scottish campaigns, and all the while composes love poems and satirical pasquinades about his enemies. Several examples of his poetry are included within the saga.

1976
● trans. Hermann Pálsson &
Paul Edwards

2004
trans. Bernard Scudder, 1997
intro. Svanhildur Óskarsdóttir,
2004

THE SAGA OF THE PEOPLE OF LAXARDAL
and BOLLI BOLLASON'S TALE

c. 1245

Gudrun is the most beautiful and intelligent woman in 10th-century Iceland. A prophetic dream correctly warns that she will have four husbands, three of whom will die: the first she divorces; the others perish through witchcraft, murder and drowning; and sadly she never marries her one true love, Kjartan. This passionate tale of feuding families takes place against the backdrop of the spread of Christianity through the Nordic world. Thorstein Veblen (403) called it 'a thing of poetic beauty'. *Bolli Bollason's Tale* is a brief sequel: Gudrun's son Bolli deals out rough justice with his sword Leg-Biter and the help of his friend Arnor Crone's-Nose.

1969 *Laxdaela Saga*
• trans. Magnus Magnusson &
Hermann Pálsson

2008
trans. Keneva Kunz, 1997
intro. Bergljót S.
Kristjánsdóttir, 2008

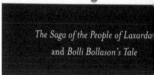

The Saga of the People of Laxarda and Bolli Bollason's Tale

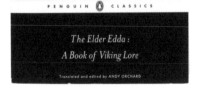

2011
trans. Andy Orchard

THE ELDER EDDA
A Book of Viking Lore
c. 1270

The *Elder* or *Poetic Edda* survives as a single brown manuscript of 45 vellum leaves in the Árni Magnússon Institute in Reykjavik. It is a trove of ancient Viking lore: tales of Thor and Grey-Beard, Loki the prankster, beautiful swan maidens, the Hel-ride of Brynhild and the treacherous Attila the Hun. Together with Snorri Sturluson's *Prose Edda* (91), it is one of the main surviving sources of Norse mythology.

THE SAGA OF THE VOLSUNGS
The Norse Epic of Sigurd the Dragon Slayer
13th century

Based on legends from the *Elder Edda*, the *Völsunga Saga* centres on the exploits of the courageous Sigurd, who kills Fefnir the dragon with a splintered sword and acquires the Helmet of Terror and the cursed ring of Andvaranaut. Other members of the Völsung clan change shape, play harps with their toes, dream of golden hawks and ignite communal funeral pyres. The story features Attila the Hun and his campaigns against the Romans, and inspired many later writers including William Morris (226) and J. R. R. Tolkien.

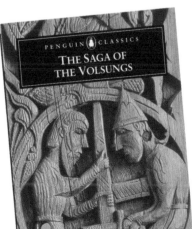

1999
trans. Jesse L. Byock
—
Jesse Byock dedicates her translation to her daughter Ashley, recalling 'the fun [they] had telling the Sigurd story on a trout fishing trip'.

1989
trans. Hermann Pálsson &
Paul Edwards, 1972

2003 *Gisli Sursson's Saga* and *The Saga of the People of Eyri*
trans. Martin S. Regal & Judy Quinn, 1997
intro. Vésteinn Ólason, 2003

—

Ólason's edition includes a prequel, *Gisli Sursson's Saga*, in which Snorri's uncle Gisli is duty-bound to murder one brother-in-law in order to avenge another. He is consequently outlawed.

EYRBYGGJA SAGA

13th century

The 'Saga of the People of Eyri' focuses on the cunning Snorri Goði, a priest who turns from worshipping Thor to advocating Christianity. Set exclusively in the Icelandic region of Snæfellsnes, it describes a land of shifting faiths, haunted by ghosts and plagued with superstition and bloodshed. Walter Scott (202) said that 'of all the various records of Icelandic history and literature, there is none more interesting than *Eyrbyggja Saga*'.

1971
trans. Hermann Pálsson

HRAFNKEL'S SAGA
and Other Icelandic Stories

13th century

These shorter sagas are portraits of unusual heroes in Iceland and abroad. Hrafnkel murders a boy for riding his prize horse; Thorstein the Staff-Struck is involved in a humiliating 'horse fight'; and Ale-Hood is a brewer who accidentally burns some valuable woodland. Hreidar travels to Norway, where the lovesick Ivar is moping; Halldor Snorrason attempts to return home from Constantinople; and Audun makes a pilgrimage to Rome.

NJAL'S SAGA

13th century

Perhaps the greatest of the Icelandic sagas, *Njal's Saga* describes a 50-year blood feud. The warrior Gunnar of Hlidarendi abhors killing, but is drawn inexorably into a cycle of murder and revenge, aided by the wise Njal but ultimately undone by the sorcery of his own beautiful wife Hallgerdur and the machinations of the villainous Mord Valgardsson. Minor slights escalate with terrible consequences, climaxing with Njal and his family being burnt alive as they attempt to defend their home.

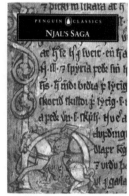

1960
● trans. Magnus Magnusson
& Hermann Pálsson
—

2001
trans. Robert Cook, 1997

'This version of *Njal* (and I believe *Njal* is the best Saga) is the best I have received,' wrote Rieu (17), about the Magnusson and Pálsson translation. 'It really does seem to me to catch exactly the curious terseness, and tenseness, of the Icelandic originals — also their subtlety and latent humour.'

COMIC SAGAS AND TALES FROM ICELAND

13th century

Icelandic sagas are frequently humorous, with stories of comical fools, farcical situations and surreal dreams. This selection of particularly amusing and peculiar stories includes the tale of Thorstein Shiver, who met a wailing demon in the garderobe, and Sarcastic Halli, who was force-fed porridge.

2013
trans. Martin S. Regal, John Tucker,
Ruth C. Ellison, Fredrik J. Heinemann,
George Clark, Robert Kellogg, Judith
Jesch & Anthony Maxwell, 1997
ed. Vidar Hreinsson, 2013

SEVEN VIKING ROMANCES

13th–14th centuries

Many of these fantastical stories are Norse interpretations of older tales: Arrow-Odd is doomed to die at the age of 300, on the spot where he was born; King Gautrek is conceived among a household of idiots; Halfdan leads military expeditions to Permia, a short-lived medieval state in the Ural mountains; Bosi and Herraud quest for a vulture's egg inscribed with golden letters and indulge in a sequence of cryptic erotic escapades; Egil and Asmund battle with Russian giants, in a tale that recalls the Polyphemus episode from Homer's *Odyssey* (17); Thorstein Mansion-Might re-enacts the adventures of the god Thor; and Helgi Thorisson becomes involved with a family of great sorcerors in a tale inspired by one of the *lais* of Marie de France (82).

1985
trans. Hermann Pálsson & Paul Edwards

2002
trans. Rory McTurk, Diana Whaley, Katrina Attwood, Alison Finlay & Marianne Kalinke, 1997
ed. Diana Whaley, 2002

SAGAS OF WARRIOR-POETS

13th–14th centuries

These sagas are the stories of the 'skalds' or poet-heroes: Kormak pursues Steingerd, the love of his life; Hallfred converts from paganism to Christianity; Gunnlaug travels the world; Bjorn, a relative of Egil (92), is accused of circulating gay pornography; and Vigland strives to marry Ketilrid, despite objections from their families. All of them compose poetry during their adventures, and the sagas are dotted with examples of their verse. 'Poets often figure among the dramatis personae of Icelandic sagas,' writes Diana Whaley. '[...] Even within this poetry-minded genre, though, the sagas of the poets are remarkable for the way in which historical skalds have been placed centre-stage'.

THE SAGA OF GRETTIR THE STRONG

14th century

After grappling with a zombie called Glam, the fiery Grettir is cursed to live as an outlaw, wandering the wilderness, fighting giants and trolls. This conflicted 11th-century warrior embodies the struggle of Iceland's transition from paganism to Christianity, from a life of marauding to a life of farming.

Grettir composes spontaneous verses after most of his violent escapades, such as this one:

The trollwoman's ugly lover
came at me from his cave,
made his long and bold
struggle with me, for certain.
I snapped his hard-edged
 pike
away from its shaft – my
 sword,
ablaze with battle, split
open his breast and black
 belly.

2005
trans. Bernard Scudder
intro. Örnólfur Thorsson

THE SAGA OF KING HROLF KRAKI

c. 1400

1998
trans. Jesse L. Byock

The 5th-century King Hrolf of Denmark rules a land of ancient magic, populated by wizards, sorceresses and 'berserkers', a warrior cult that fought in a frenzy. Snorri Sturluson (91) describes how the berserkers 'went to battle without armour and acted like mad dogs or wolves. They bit into their shields and were as strong as bears or bulls.' King Hrolf must negotiate pranks, curses, treachery and a final great battle, with the help of his champion, Bodvar Bjarki, the bear-warrior. Many of the same characters appear with Anglo-Saxon names in *Beowulf* (79).

Medieval &
Classical Asia

Night and Horses and the Desert · Robert Irwin

THE KORAN

The Thousand and One Nights · Translated by N. J. Dawood

THE BOOK OF DEDE KORKUT

Islamic Mystical Poetry · Sufi Verse from the Early Mystics to Rumi

Tales of the Marvellous and News of the Strange

IBN FADLĀN · Ibn Fadlān and the Land of Darkness · Arab Travellers in the Far North

FERDOWSI · THE LEGEND OF SEYAVASH

THE RUBA'IYAT OF OMAR KHAYYAM

USAMA IBN MUNQIDH · The Book of Contemplation · Islam and the Crusades

FARID UD-DIN ATTAR · THE CONFERENCE OF THE BIRDS

L52

1001

L298
ISBN 0 14
044.2987

PENGUIN CLASSICS

PENGUIN CLASSICS

PENGUIN CLASSICS

ISBN 0 14
044.3843

ISBN 0 14
04.4566 8

PENGUIN CLASSICS

ISBN 0 14
044.4343

Arabia

In the 7th century, the Prophet Mohammed united the self-governing tribes of the Arabian peninsula under a single, common religion and established the first Islamic nation, which expanded rapidly under the subsequent Rashidun, Umayyad and Abbasid Caliphates, ousting the ancient Sassanid Empire from Persia (101) and greatly reducing the territories held by Byzantium.

At its height in the 8th century, the Umayyad Caliphate stretched from the shores of the Atlantic Ocean to the Himalayas, the largest empire the world had ever seen. Subjects from Samarkand to Seville read the Koran and mingled on the pilgrimage to Mecca.

At the start of the 9th century, the Abbasid caliph Harun al-Rashid (98) established the 'House of Wisdom' in Baghdad, initiating a golden age during which science, art and literature flourished. Scholars translated the knowledge of the world into Arabic, including the works of Plato (26), Aristotle (29) and Hippocrates (25), and great leaps were made in scientific disciplines from alchemy and astronomy to geography, philosophy and zoology.

THE PENGUIN ANTHOLOGY OF CLASSICAL ARABIC LITERATURE

5th – 16th centuries

This expansive anthology provides a wide-ranging introduction to medieval Arabic literature, from the earliest fragments of *The Thousand and One Nights* (98) and the elegance of the Koran to the adventures of Arabian travellers (99) and the Sufis' (99) mystical pursuit of truth.

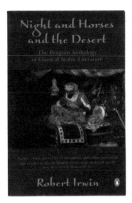

2000 Penguin Books
Night and Horses and the Desert
2006 Penguin Classics
The Penguin Anthology of Classical Arabic Literature
ed. Robert Irwin, 1999
—
Irwin is an Arabic scholar, a publisher, a novelist and a Fellow of the London College of Pataphysics. His novels include *The Arabian Nightmare, Exquisite Corpse, Dangerous Knowledge* and *Prayer-Cushions of the Flesh*.

THE KORAN 609–32

'Koran' means 'recitation'. During Ramadan, in December 609, the Prophet Mohammed was woken in the middle of the night by the archangel Gabriel, who commanded him to 'recite'. Over the next 23 years Mohammed received, through Gabriel, the actual words of Allah, and dictated them to scribes who set them down in writing. The beautifully wrought Koran provides the fundamental code of the Muslim faith, with guidance on prayer, fasting and pilgrimage, family, food, crime, punishment and warfare. As well as instruction, the 114 chapters, or *sūrahs*, contain stories of Adam, Moses, Abraham, Jesus, John the Baptist and many other prophets who preceded Mohammed. A person who has memorized the entire Koran is addressed by the honorific title *hafiz* or *hafiza*.

1956
trans. N. J. Dawood
—
Dawood's translation of *The Koran* was the result of a lifelong study of its language and style. 'Across the language barrier,' wrote *The Times*, 'Dawood captures the thunder and poetry of the original.' He revised his Penguin translation in many editions.

1990 *The Koran with Parallel Arabic Text*
trans. N. J. Dawood

2009 *The Qu'ran*
trans. Tarif Khalidi

1954 Penguin Books
1955 Penguin Classics
● trans. N. J. Dawood

1957 *Aladdin and
Other Tales*
● trans. N. J. Dawood

1973 *Tales from the
Thousand and One Nights*
trans. N. J. Dawood
—
Dawood's first selection
of *The Thousand and One
Nights* was the 1,001st Penguin Book; it joined Penguin
Classics the following year.
He produced a second
volume of tales in 1957, and
a combined edition was
published in 1973.

THE THOUSAND AND ONE NIGHTS
8th – 13th centuries

The Sassanid King Shahriyar thinks all women unfaithful: every day he marries a new bride and every morning he has her killed, so she won't cuckold him. His vizier is charged with providing this succession of virgin brides, but the supply quickly diminishes as virgins, understandably, flee the kingdom. Eventually, when the vizier can find no more girls, his own daughter, the beautiful Shahrazad, volunteers to marry the king herself. On their wedding night, Shah-razad begins telling her new husband a bedtime story about a merchant who accidentally killed a genie's son with a date stone, and how, when the genie is about to kill the merchant, he is distracted by an old man with a gazelle who tells a story about how his wife turned his son into a calf…

Shahrazad breaks off and promises to finish her story the following evening, if the king will postpone her execution. The king spares her life for one day only, but every night Shahrazad weaves a new story and breaks off before the end, so she survives from day to day. Finally, after 1,001 nights of stories, the murderous king is persuaded not to kill his queen after all.

Shahrazad's inventive tales feature genies, ghosts, apes and magicians, and range from lofty philosophical dialogues to scatological tales about notable farts. A frequent protagonist of the tales is the historical caliph Harun al-Rashid. They were popularized in Europe by Antoine Galland in the early 18th century, and inspired many subsequent works, including Voltaire's *Zadig* (176), William Beckford's *Vathek* (198) and Jan Potocki's *Manuscript found in Saragossa* (351).

2010 *The Arabian Nights: Tales of 1,001 Nights*
trans. Malcolm C. Lyons & Ursula Lyons, 2008
intro. Robert Irwin, 2008

Published in three volumes: *Volume 1* covers nights 1 to 294 and 'The Story of Ali Baba'; *Volume 2* covers nights 295 to 719; and *Volume 3* concludes with nights 719 to 1,001 and 'The Story of Aladdin'.

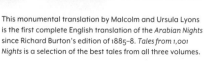

2011 *Tales from
1,001 Nights*
trans. Malcolm C.
Lyons & Ursula Lyons
intro. Robert Irwin, 2010

This monumental translation by Malcolm and Ursula Lyons is the first complete English translation of the *Arabian Nights* since Richard Burton's edition of 1885–8. *Tales from 1,001 Nights* is a selection of the best tales from all three volumes.

THE BOOK OF DEDE KORKUT

c. 8th century

'Granddaddy Korkut' was a white-bearded sage. He is said to have lived for 295 years, to have met the Prophet Mohammed and attended the election of the Great Khan. His book is a collection of twelve traditional Oghuz Turkish stories about armies of fleas, camel wrestling, the Black King of Alinja Castle and Boghazja Fatima of the Forty Lovers. The episode in which Basat defeats the cyclops Goggle-Eye was inspired by the Polyphemus episode in the *Odyssey* (17).

1974
trans. Geoffrey Lewis

TALES OF THE MARVELLOUS AND NEWS OF THE STRANGE

c. 10th century

This remarkable collection of Arabian stories exists in one ragged, incomplete manuscript, discovered in 1933 in a library in Istanbul. The stories feature monsters, jinn, jewels, living statues, twisted viziers and miraculous apes, with a cast of characters including Julnar of the Sea, Abu Disa the Bird, the White-Footed Gazelle and the Man Whose Lips Had Been Cut Off. There are libidinous mermaids and psychopathic nymphomaniacs and other raunchy high jinks, not least in the 'Tale of the Forty Girls and What Happened to Them with the Prince'.

2015
trans. Malcolm C. Lyons
intro. Robert Irwin

2009
trans. Mahmood Jamal

ISLAMIC MYSTICAL POETRY
Sufi Verse from the Early Mystics to Rumi
8th–19th centuries

A Sufi is an Islamic mystic. From Mansur Hallaj, who was executed in the 10th century for claiming 'I am the Truth', to Mian Muhammad Baksh, who died in 1907, this anthology collects the best of a millennium of Sufi verse. The centrepieces of this collection are the two greatest masters of Sufi poetry, Rumi (102) in the 13th century and Hafez (102) in the 14th.

Ibn Fadlān 10th century

All that we know about Ibn Fadlān is what he reveals in his book: he was an emissary of the Abbasid caliph Muqtadir, sent from Baghdad in 921 to the northern reaches of the Volga River, to visit the camp of the recently converted Bulga khan in order to deliver gifts and religious instruction.

Ibn Fadlān and the Land of Darkness
Arab Travellers in the Far North
921–1349

2012
trans. Paul Launde &
Caroline Stone

In medieval Arabic geography, the 'Land of Darkness' lay far to the north, inhabited by the fearsome tribes of Gog and Magog. Ibn Fadlān describes the clothes and customs of the pagan lands through which he passes, and those of the Viking Rus' traders he meets. His book contains the only eyewitness account of a Viking ship cremation, including the sacrifice of a slave girl, presided over by the sinister figure of the 'Angel of Death'. This volume also contains the 'Travels of Abū Hāmid al-Andalusī al-Gharnātī' (1130–55), an account of the 'Wonders of the West', and passages from other medieval Arabian travelogues, such as Mas'ūdī on 'the Land of the Midnight Sun', Qazwīnī on 'Gog and Magog' and Ibn Battūta.

2008
trans. Paul M. Cobb

Usama ibn Munqidh 1095–1188

Usama ibn Munquidh was a 12th-century aristocrat, who moved between prominent courts in Iraq, Syria and Egypt, travelling through a Muslim world that was reeling from the Crusades (75). He was a political strategist, adventurer, soldier, diplomat and man of letters. In 1157, his family and fortunes were destroyed in an earthquake, and he spent his last years under the patronage of Saladin, the first sultan of Egypt and Syria, who engaged with Richard the Lionheart during the Third Crusade.

The Book of Contemplation
Islam and the Crusades *c.* 1170–*c.* 1188

The Book of Contemplation was written as a gift for Saladin. It is a meditation on the nature of fate and freedom, with autobiographical episodes from Usama's life and descriptions of the European crusaders, whom he refers to as the 'Franks'. It was intended as a book of thought-provoking 'examples' (*'ibar*) from which readers could draw lessons. This volume also includes excerpts from Usama's *Book of the Staff*, an anthology of famous walking sticks, and *Kernels of Refinement*, nuggets of advice on how to live a cultured life.

Shihab al-Din al-Nuwayri 1279–1333

Shihab al-Din Ahmad ibn 'Abd al-Wahhab al-Nuwayri was an Egyptian civil servant. He held government posts in Egypt and Syria, overseeing hospitals in Cairo and the imperial chancery in Tripoli. In the 1310s, he retired from government service and devoted the rest of his life to writing a 9,000-page, 33-volume encyclopaedia.

The Ultimate Ambition in the Arts of Erudition
A Compendium of Knowledge from the Classical Islamic World
1314–33

Elias Muhanna's abridgement of Al-Nuwayri's encyclopaedia provides 'a wide and eclectic sample' of the complete work, including entries on the composition of air, the taxonomy of hair, the taste of cheese, the smell of the Egyptian mongoose, the formation of Adam and Eve, a recent Egyptian hippo-hunting trip and an account of one of al-Nuwayri's own dreams.

2016
trans. Elias Muhanna

Persia

Two centuries after the Arab conquest (97) of Persia and the fall of the Sassanid Empire in 651, the Abbasid Caliphate granted a degree of autonomy to a native Samanid state. By the end of the 9th century, the Samanid kings had thrown off Abbasid authority and achieved complete independence. They oversaw a gradual resurgence of old Persian culture, albeit within a new Islamic context: they revived the country's ancient festivals and encouraged new works of literature in the Persian language. Notable pioneers of this renaissance were the blind poet Rudaki, who wrote over a million verses, of which barely 50 survive; Avicenna, the astronomer physician, who was taught maths by an Indian greengrocer and went on to become a towering figure in the history of philosophy; and Ferdowsi, who penned the Iranian national epic.

THE RUBA'IYAT OF OMAR KHAYYAM 11th century

Omar Khayyam (1048–1131) was a Persian astronomer, mathematician and philosopher who wrote an influential book about algebra. In the west, however, he is better known for his *Ruba'iyat*, a sequence of epigrammatic stanzas (*ruba'is*) that dwell on the transience of human life and the cyclical decay of the natural world.

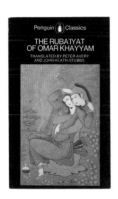

1981
trans. Peter Avery & John Heath-Stubbs, 1979
—
The *Ruba'iyat* was first translated into English by Edward FitzGerald in 1859. Avery and Heath-Stubbs describe FitzGerald's text as 'more in the nature of a fantasia than a translation', and instead they provide 'as literal an English version of the Persian originals as readability and intelligibility permit'.

Abolqasem Ferdowsi *c. 940–1020*

Ferdowsi, 'the Lord of the Word', was commissioned to write the *Shahnameh* by the Samanid prince of Khorasan, and he spent most of his adult life working on it. The Samanid dynasty was overthrown before he could finish his masterwork, but the new king, Mahmud of Ghazneh, offered him a gold piece for every further couplet he completed. There seems to have been a mix-up with the delivery of the gold pieces, however, because Ferdowsi died in poverty. He was buried in his own garden and his tomb is now a shrine.

Shahnameh
The Persian Book of Kings
c. 977–1010

The *Shahnameh* is the national epic of Iran and the world's longest poem by a single poet. It covers a vast sweep of history, from the dawn of time to the Arab conquest of Persia in the 7th century. It is divided into three sections: the 'mythical age', which covers the first king, Kayumars, who received homage from wild animals; the 'heroic age', which contains the love story of Zal and Rudaba, the seven trials of Rostam, and the wars with Afrisayab; and the 'historical age', which describes Alexander the Great and provides a chronicle of the Sassanid Empire.

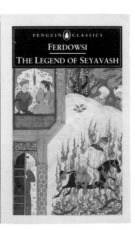

1992 *The Legend of Seyavash*
● trans. Dick Davis
1997 *Tales of Love and War from the Shahnameh*
● trans. Dick Davis

2007
trans. Dick Davis, 1997
fwd. Azar Nafisi, 2006

1984
trans. Afkham Darbandi &
Dick Davis

1999 Penguin Books
The Essential Rumi
2004 Penguin Classics
Selected Poems
trans. Coleman Banks with
John Moyne, A. J. Arberry &
Reynold Nicholson, 1995

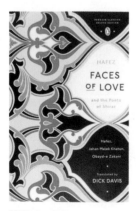

2013 Deluxe Edition
trans. Dick Davis

Farid Attar *c. 1120–c. 1220*

Farid Attar was born in Nishapur, the town where Omar Khayyam **(101) was born a hundred years earlier. As well as being a mystic poet he was also a successful pharmacist. He may have died during the Mongol Sack of Nishapur in 1229.** Rumi **said that where 'Attar has traversed the seven cities of Love, / We are still at the turn of one street'.**

The Conference of the Birds *1177*

In this allegory of the Sufi quest for truth through God, birds from around the world gather to seek their king, the mythical Simorgh bird. The journey will be long and arduous, the wise hoopoe warns, and some of the birds, who symbolise various human failings, do not last the course: only 30 birds, representing the best human qualities, achieve the dwelling place of the king. The birds look into an unruffled lake and discover the Simorgh bird in their combined reflection. In Persian, 'Simorgh' means '30 birds'.

Rumi *1207–1273*

The greatest of the mystical Sufi poets **(99), Jalaluddin Balkhi, was born in Afghanistan and grew up in Turkey. 'Rumi' means 'from Rum', the name of the territory that had been Byzantine Anatolia. He was a religious philosopher and the founder of the Whirling Dervishes. In 1244, he met a dervish named Shams of Tabriz. Their mystical conversations were so profound that when Shams disappeared mysteriously, Rumi believed their identities had merged and that he was channelling Shams whenever he wrote. He called his own collection of odes and quatrains** *The Works of Shams of Tabriz.*

Selected Poems *c. 1248–1273*

Rumi's poems are full of imagery drawn from the natural world: horses, fish, flowers, birds, rivers and stars. They touch on tolerance, the nature of goodness and the meaning of love. Their appeal is personal and universal. This anthology is organized thematically, under sections such as 'On Spring Giddiness', 'On Silence', 'On Flirtation' and 'On Howling'.

Spiritual Verses
The First Book of the Masnavi-ye Ma'navi
1258–73

Rumi spent the last years of his life working on a six-volume masterpiece: the *Masnavi* or 'spiritual couplets', the greatest work of Sufism. The text leads the reader along a spiritual path, with instructions, parables and anecdotes that reveal the way to God through divine love and a deeper understanding of the nature of reality.

2006
trans. Alan Williams

FACES OF LOVE
Hafez and the Poets of Shiraz 14th century

Hafez adopted his pen name because he learned the Koran (97) at a young age. His unrequited, poetic pursuit of the beautiful Shakh-e Nabat has been compared to Dante's (84) passion for Beatrice; he wrote lyrical ghazals about wine, women and divine love. Also featured in this anthology are Jahan Malek Khatun, a princess who wrote passionate love poetry, and Obayd-e Zakani, a bisexual satirist who wrote political fables and bawdy verses. The three poets were all writing in 14th-century Shiraz, the cultural capital of Persia.

India

Little is known about the authors of medieval India. These Sanskrit, Telugu, Kannada and Urdu texts are either anonymous or tentatively attributed to unattested authors. They all emerged during an opulent period of successive empires and dynasties, trading states and warring families. It has been estimated that India's economy in the first millennium CE accounted for one third of the world's wealth.

Nārāyana
c.800–c.950

Little is known about Nārāyana: only his name is preserved in the final line of the Hitopadeśa. He claims to have been a poet at the court of Dhavala Ćandra, an unattested king of Bengal who is said to have commissioned this work.

THE FOREST OF THIEVES AND THE MAGIC GARDEN
An Anthology of Medieval Jain Stories
7th – 15th centuries

Jainism is an ancient Indian religion: 'Jains' are 'victors' who navigate the path of multiple rebirths towards ethical and spiritual victory by advocating non-violence, non-absolutism, non-attachment and non-indulgence. Tales in this anthology include 'The Prince Who Loved Sweetmeats' and 'The Awakening of Rama'. The allegory 'Vice and Virtue' is a story of magic pills, triangular heads and the tribulations of a transmigrating soul.

2006
trans. Phyllis Granoff, 1998

The Hitopadeśa

Hitopadeśa means 'beneficial advice'. The text is a collection of fables modelled on the *Pancatantra* (9), with the same frame story about Viṣṇu Śarma and his wise counsel, although it also incorporates stories from the *Rāmāyana* (9) and the *Mahābhārata* `. Titles include 'The Monks and the Mouse', 'The Blue Jackal', 'The Foolish Tortoise', 'The Credulous Camel', 'The Short-Sighted Crane' and 'The Greedy Barber'.

1998
trans. A. N. D. Haksar

1973
trans. A. K. Ramanujan

SPEAKING OF ŚIVA 10th – 12th centuries
Basavaṇṇa; Dēvara Dāsimayya; Mahādēviyakka; Allama Prabhu

Śiva is the 'destroyer and the transformer', a supreme being who creates and manipulates the universe. He has a third eye in the middle of his forehead, a serpent around his neck and the River Ganges flows from his thickly matted hair. He is worshipped in the abstract form of the *lingam*. The Vīraśaiva religious movement is devoted to Śiva. This volume selects *vacanas*, free-verse epigrams, by four poets who all take familiar references to night and day, sex and family, and transform them into mystical insights into the nature of existence.

Śivadāsa
12th – 14th centuries

We know nothing about Śivadāsa.

The Five-and-Twenty Tales of the Genie
(Vetālapańćavinśati)

In Śivadāsa's retelling of these ancient stories, the legendary Indian king Vikramāditya's realm is under threat from a mighty necromancer so he begs help from a *vetāla*, a gruesome genie who inhabits the animated body of a corpse hanging from a tree. The cadaverous genie tells him tales, each of which ends with a riddle. If Vikramāditya can answer the riddles correctly, the genie will tell him a final tale that includes the secret to destroying his enemy.

2006
trans. Chandra Rajan, 1995
—
Rajan dedicates her translation to 'the three greatest storytellers of all times': Vyāsa, the mythical author of the *Mahābhārata* (7), Vālmīkī, who wrote the *Rāmāyana* (9) and Viṣṇu Śarma who narrates the *Pancatantra* (9).

Simhāsana Dvātriṃśikā

Though presented in orange text on the Penguin Classics cover, as if it was an author's name, *Simhāsana Dvātriṃśikā* is simply an alternative title for this anonymous work.

Thirty-Two Tales of the Throne of Vikramaditya   13th–14th centuries

The legendary King Vikramāditya once sat on a throne supported by 32 voluptuous female statuettes. When King Bhoja discovers the throne and attempts to sit on it himself, each statuette comes to life and tells a story about Vikramāditya's magnificent exploits, demonstrating his superhuman courage and Bhoja's corresponding unworthiness. The fabulous tales feature ogres, elixirs, otherworlds, occultism, magic fruit and tours of the solar system.

2006
trans.
A. N. D. Haksar, 1998
—
Haksar named his son Vikram. He dedicated this translation to his son and his daughter-in-law Annika 'with the hope that it will remind them and their progeny of the good deeds it describes'.

Mir Amman

18th – 19th centuries

Born in late 18th-century Delhi, Amman was employed as a 'munshi', a secretary, at the British East India Company's Fort William College in Calcutta.

A Tale of Four Dervishes

13th century, trans. 1801–3

When the king of Turkey spots a grey hair in the mirror, he is overwhelmed with despair because he has no heir. In disguise, he slips out of the palace to embark on a life of seclusion. In a cemetery, he comes across four wandering dervishes, one from Yemen, one from China and two from Persia. The five men tell each other stories about fairies, jinn, gardens, feasts, beautiful princesses and lost loves. Mir Amman's text is an Urdu translation of the Persian *Qissa-e-Chahār*, 'The Tale of the Four Dervishes', by the 13th-century musician Amir Khusrau.

2006
trans. Mohammed Zakir, 1994
—
Mohammed Zakir dedicates his English translation to his parents, 'who do not need to read it'.

For 19th-century India, turn to p.387

Tibet

According to Tibetan tradition, the 8th-century Buddhist master Padmasambhava and his consort Yeshe Tsogyel, the 'Wisdom Lake Queen', stashed a number of *terma* or 'hidden treasures' all over Tibet: secret texts and ritual implements in the earth, in rocks, in plants, in crystals, in lakes, in the sky and deep inside the mind. Adepts who uncover these *terma* are known as *tertöns*. The first discoveries were made in the 11th century and initiated a renaissance of Tibetan Buddhism.

2015
trans. Bryan J. Cuevas

Ra Yeshé Sengé

12th – 13th centuries

Ra Yeshé Sengé lived in the province of Tsang and is best known for this hagiography of his great-uncle, Ra Lotsawa.

The All-Pervading Melodious Drumbeat
The Life of Ra Lotsawa

Ra Lotsawa Dorjé Drak was an 11th-century saint, murderer and sorcerer, who used dark magic to slay his enemies, accumulate vast wealth and gather a cult following. He murdered thirteen learned lamas and was one of the earliest translators of Buddhist scriptures (10), from Sanskrit into Tibetan.

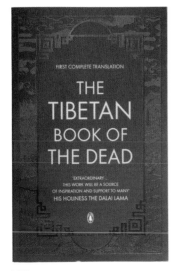

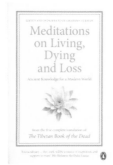

2006 Penguin Books
2008 Penguin Classics
trans. Gyurme Dorje
ed. Graham Coleman with Thuuten Jinpa
intro. His Holiness the Dalai Lama

—

This is the first unabridged English translation
of *The Tibetan Book of the Dead*, although
excerpts were included in Lopez's edition of
the *Buddhist Scriptures* (10).

2008
ed. Graham Coleman

—

*Meditations on Living, Dying
and Loss* is a selection of key
extracts in a slim introductory
volume.

THE TIBETAN BOOK OF THE DEAD
8th century

The Great Liberation by Hearing in the Intermediate States,
as it is called in Tibetan, is a text that is said to have been
composed originally in the 8th century by Padmasambhava,
the lotus-born founder of the first Buddhist monastery in
Tibet. It is a *terma*, subsequently revealed to the teacher
Karma Lingpa (1326–1386) on top of Mount Gampodar,
a geomantic 'power-place' identified as the 'head of the
ogress' by Songtsen Gampo, the first Tibetan emperor. The
text guides the reader through death and the experience of
bardo, a transitional state before consciousness is reborn.
Bardo has three stages: the moment of death, in which
one glimpses the light of truth; the experience of reality,
which takes the form of various Buddhas; and rebirth,
which involves hallucinatory visions of *yab-yum* copulating
couples.

The theosophist Walter Evans-Wentz published the first,
partial English translation in 1927 and called it *The Tibetan
Book of the Dead*, to draw a parallel with *The Egyptian Book
of the Dead* (3). It was the inspiration behind *The Psychedelic
Experience* by Leary, Metzner and Alpert, who use the text
to describe the hallucinatory effects of LSD, psilocybin and
mescaline.

2010
trans. Andrew Quintman
intro. Donald S. Lopez, Jr.

Tsangnyön Heruka
1452–1507

**Tsangnyön was a tantric
yogi, who called himself the
'Madman of Tsang' and the
'King of the Blood-Drinkers'.
He smeared his skin with
cremation ashes and tied
human fingers into his
matted hair.**

The Life of Milarepa 1488

Milarepa was an 11th-century poet and sorcerer, who could
run supernaturally fast by controlling 'internal air'. He
lived in White Horse Rock Tooth cave and subsisted on
nettle broth, which made his skin turn green and waxy.
Tsangnyön's biography is both an account of the idealized
life of contemplation and an allegorical quest for spiritual
liberation. It was one of the first Tibetan texts circulated
through woodblock printing.

Tenzin Chögyel 1701–1767

**Tenzin Chögyel was a Bhutanese monk who became Lord
Abbot, the country's highest ecclesiastical authority.**

The Life of the Buddha 1740

*The Life of the Lord Victor Shakyamuni, Ornament of One Thousand
Lamps for the Fortunate Eon* is the alternative title for this hag-
iographical account of the twelve acts of the Buddha (10). The
elegant narrative describes how Shakyamuni Buddha became
mortal, sought a solitary life and achieved enlightenment at Bodh
Gaya in India, on a spot now marked by the Diamond Throne.

2015
trans. Kurtis R. Schaeffer

China

When the T'ang dynasty reunified China in the 7th century, after three centuries of political division, it allowed a flourishing of high culture known as the 'golden age of Chinese poetry'. The greatest poets of this period were Wang Wei, Li Po and Tu Fu. Prose fiction was not traditionally a high art form, but gradually the novel established itself as a genre during the late Ming and early Qing dynasties with the 'Four Classic Novels' of pre-modern Chinese literature: *Outlaws of the Marsh*, *The Romance of the Three Kingdoms* (107), *Monkey* (107) and *The Story of the Stone* (108).

Wang Wei
699–761

1973
trans. G. W. Robinson

Wang Wei was a painter and a musician as well as a poet. He was a senior civil servant, a devout Zen Buddhist and a vegetarian. After his death, the T'ang emperor commanded Wang Jin, his younger brother, to collect and edit his poems.

Poems

Wang's poetry speaks of a deep and mystical love of nature; he was a particular master of the 'Mountains and Rivers' genre. The poet Su Shi said that 'the poems hold a painting within them. In observing his paintings you can see that, within the painting there is poetry.' Wang composed his first poem aged fifteen, an 'Inscription for a Friend's Mica Screen':

> This screen of yours unfolded
> Against that wild courtyard
> Can show you hills and springs
> Uncontrived with paint.

Li Po 701–762

Li Po was born in the far west of China. His prodigious talent was proverbial: the 'Three Wonders' were Li Po's poetry, Pei Min's swordsmanship and Zhang Xu's calligraphy. His contemporaries thought his extraordinary poetic insights must be superhuman. He is said to have died when he reached from a boat to grasp the moon's reflection in a river.

Tu Fu 712–770

Tu Fu was born into a distinguished family of statesmen. He wanted to be a civil servant himself, but failed the arduous entrance examinations and turned instead to poetry, at which he excelled. In *Tu Fu: China's Greatest Poet*, William Hung observes that Tu Fu has been described variously as 'the Chinese Virgil (43), Horace (45), Ovid (46), Shakespeare (136), Milton (150), Burns (181), Wordsworth (193), Béranger, Hugo (307), or Baudelaire (328)'.

Poems

Li Po and Tu Fu were contemporaries and friends. Their contrasting works complement each other so well that they came to be spoken of as one person, 'Li-Tu'. Li Po's poems are by turns boisterous and contemplative, featuring friends, drunken conversations, rugged journeys and vivid dreams. Titles include 'On Visiting a Taoist Master in the Tai't-ien Mountains and Not Finding Him' and 'A Song of Adieu to the Queen of the Skies, after a Dream Voyage to Her'. Tu Fu was known as 'the Poet-Historian': his poetry provides a record of his life and times, including the An Lushan Rebellion of 755, which led to years of unrest in China. Titles include 'At an Evening Picnic, with Young Bucks and Beauties on Chang-Pa Canal, It Rained!' and 'On Seeing a Painting of Horses by General Ts'ao Pa at Secretary Wei Feng's House'.

1973
trans. Arthur Cooper
ill. Shui Chein-Tung

Luo Guanzhong

14th century

Luo wrote under the pseudonym 'Huhai Sanren', the 'Wanderer of Lakes and Seas.' Little is known about his life. As well as editing *Outlaws of the Marsh* by Shi Nai'an and writing *The Romance of the Three Kingdoms* — two of the 'Four Classic Novels' — he also wrote *The Three Sui Quash the Demons' Revolt*, a supernatural fantasy story about sorceresses, fox spirits, demon armies and the burning of a magical painting.

The Romance of the Three Kingdoms

This weighty historical novel is set during the Han dynasty, between 169 and 280 CE. It traces the factions and fortunes of various feudal lords, battling for supremacy and employing every form of military strategy and skulduggery. The complete text is vast, introducing 1,000 characters over 120 chapters; this abridged edition is a seamless collection of highlights.

2018
trans. Martin Palmer

Wu Ch'eng-en

c. 1505–1580

We know very little about Wu Ch'eng-en. He is thought to have been born in Lianshui, in Jiangsu province, and may have served a term as district magistrate. He seems to have spent much of his life as a hermit and is best remembered as the author of *Journey to the West*, which he wrote in vernacular prose. He published anonymously; only the citizens of Lianshui knew the secret of the novel's authorship.

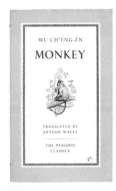

1961
trans. Arthur Waley, 1942

Monkey c. 1592

Journey to the West describes a dangerous pilgrimage made by a young Buddhist monk, Prince Tripitaka, to obtain a cache of sacred Buddhist texts from India. On his journey he has three companions: the trickster Monkey, the greedy Pigsy and Sandy the Water Buffalo. The four friends meet bandits, ogres, demons, dragons and evil wizards on their quest and must summon all their ingenuity in order to return safely. The story is rooted in Chinese folk religion and Taoist (14) and Buddhist (10) philosophy: it is an adventure story, a satire of Chinese bureaucracy and an allegory of the spiritual journey to enlightenment. Arthur Waley called his seminal translation *Monkey*, the title by which the novel is now best known in the west.

Pu Songling

1640–1715

Pu Songling was a modest private tutor, who spent most of his life in his home province of Shandong writing 'strange' stories.

Strange Tales from a Chinese Studio

c. 1679–1707, pub. 1766

Ghost cities, fox spirits, magical pear-trees and dung-beetle dumplings inhabit Pu's strange tales. He seems to have been especially drawn to love affairs between poor scholars and beautiful female ghosts. 'Of tales told I have made a book,' he writes:

> With time
> And my love of hoarding,
> The matter sent me by friends
> From the four corners
> Has grown into a pile.

He is said to have gathered tales by the roadside, offering travellers cups of tea and pipes of tobacco in exchange for their stories.

2006
trans. John Minford
—
Pu Songling collated almost 500 stories in total; John Minford selects 104 for this volume.

Cao Xueqin

c. 1715 – 1763

Cao Xueqin was born into an immensely wealthy family, which for three generations had held the office of Commissioner of Imperial Textiles. When the Kangxi Emperor died, however, the family's property was confiscated and they were reduced to poverty. Cao lived most of his life in the countryside outside Beijing, selling his paintings and poetry to make a living.

The Story of the Stone

c. 1760, pub. 1791

The Story of the Stone, also known as *The Dream of the Red Chamber*, is considered the supreme achievement of Chinese literature. The family saga is narrated by a lustrous speaking stone, the only piece of celestial masonry left over after the goddess Nü-wa repaired the sky.

In *The Golden Days* we are introduced to Bao-yu, a young boy born with a piece of jade in his mouth, and his beautiful cousins Bao-chai and Dai-yu. Bao-yu grows closer to Dai-yu in *The Crab-Flower Club*, despite the fact that his parents have selected Bao-chai to be his wife. *The Warning Voice* continues their love story, as the family fortunes start to wain. In *The Debt of Tears*, the lovers' ill-fated relationship approaches a conclusion that involves a mysterious jade pendant and Dai-yu crying the tears of a 'mortal lifetime'. The final instalment, *The Dreamer Wakes*, follows Bao-yu, who is ultimately rewarded with a vision that reveals a central understanding of Buddhism: that life is nothing but a dream, a flash of 'moonlight mirrored in the water'. At the beginning of the story, the stone gateway to the 'Land of Illusion' is revealed in a vision, with the couplet:

Truth becomes fiction when the fiction's true;
Real becomes not-real where the unreal's real.

1973
trans. David Hawkes
The Golden Days, ch. 1 – 26

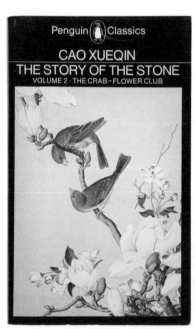

1977
trans. David Hawkes
The Crab-Flower Club, ch. 27 – 53

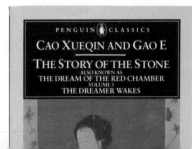

The scholar Gao E edited the last 40 chapters (volumes IV and V) when he prepared the first printed edition of *The Story of the Stone* in 1791. It is unclear to what extent Cao or Gao should be credited with their authorship.

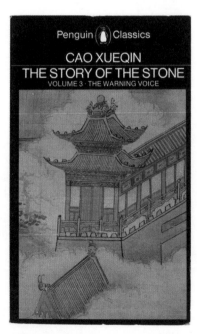

1980 trans. David Hawkes
The Warning Voice, ch. 54 – 80

1982 ed. Gao E, 1791
trans. John Minford, 1982
The Debt of Tears,
ch. 81 – 98

1986 ed. Gao E, 1791
trans. John Minford, 1986
The Dreamer Wakes,
ch. 99 – 120

Shen Fu

c. 1763 – c. 1825

Shen Fu was a Chinese government clerk from Changzhou, working under the Qing dynasty. The title of his only surviving work comes from a poem by Li Po (106), which also forms his epigraph:

> Now the heavens and earth are the hostels of creation; and time has seen a full hundred generations. Ah, this floating life, like a dream... True happiness is so rare!

Six Records of a Floating Life 1807

Shen Fu intended to present six parallel autobiographical 'layers' of his life, but only four survive: 'The Joys of the Wedding Chamber', 'The Pleasures of Leisure', 'The Sorrows of Misfortune' and 'The Delights of Roaming Afar'; the missing chapters would have been 'A History of Life at Chungshan' and 'The Way of Living'. He describes his deep passion for his childhood sweetheart, Chen Yün, who became his wife, and he mourns her untimely death. He describes travelling through China on official business and his passion for horticulture.

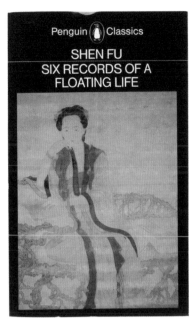

1983
trans. Leonard
Pratt & Chiang Su-hui

Korea

Before 1897, Korea was ruled for five centuries by the Joseon dynasty. Aggressive invasions from Japan and China had led the Confucian (13) kingdom of Great Joseon to adopt a strict isolationist policy and Korea became known in the west as the 'hermit kingdom'.

THE STORY OF HONG GILDONG

16th – 17th centuries

Hong Gildong is a brilliant young man with magical powers. The overlooked, illegitimate son of a government minister, he becomes the leader of a band of brave outlaws, achieving renown as a trickster and a warrior, and ultimately establishing a utopian state on a distant island. Like Robin Hood, Hong Gildong has become a folk hero. Gildong defines the national identity in both North and South Korea, explains Minsoo Kang: there is a Hong Gildong theme park in Jangseong county and a Hong Gildong festival every spring.

2016
trans. Minsoo Kang

Japan

During the Heian period (794–1185), the Japanese imperial court encouraged works of elegant literature, often produced by aristocratic ladies-in-waiting. This era is named after the capital city, Heian-kyō, modern Kyoto; the word 'Heian' means 'peace'. The greatest work of the period is *The Tale of Genji* by <u>Lady Murasaki Shikibu</u> (111). In contrast, the subsequent Kamakura period (1185–1333) was characterized by civil war, which led to the establishment of the shogunate, the samurai warrior class, and tales that focused on military prowess. The key work of this period is the epic *<u>Tale of the Heike</u>* (112). Afterwards, as the imperial court declined in the Muromachi period (1333–1603), culture became increasingly accessible to all levels of society. <u>Nō theatre</u> (112) developed as a popular form of entertainment; friends collaborated on *renga*, which developed into *<u>haiku</u>* (113); and the establishment of the first major roads in Japan prompted an enthusiasm for <u>travel literature</u> (113).

THE PENGUIN BOOK OF JAPANESE VERSE
3rd–20th centuries

The 700 poems in this volume span the last seventeen centuries, from the ancient anthologies *Kojiki* and *Manyōshū* to the contemporary poets Tanikawa Shuntarō and Itō Hiromi, embracing *tanka* and *haiku* and subjects ranging from Mount Fuji and the Mediterranean to the planet Mars.

1964 Penguin Poets
2009 Penguin Classics
trans. Geoffrey Bownas & Anthony Thwaite

THE TALES OF ISE
9th–11th centuries

One hundred and twenty-five anonymous 'chapters' celebrate Narihira, a legendary lover, from his coming of age to the approach of his death, with many amorous adventures in between. Caught among these fragments are glimpses of forbidden liaisons, loyal friendships, poems passed through fences, broken hearts and gifts of seaweed.

2016 trans. Peter MacMillan
fwd. Donald Keene

Sei Shōnagon c. 966–c. 1017

Sei Shōnagon was the daughter of a well-known *waka* poet, a form that anticipated *haiku*. She was a gentlewoman at the court of the Empress Consort Teishi.

The Pillow Book 994–1002

Shōnagon's compilation of apparently private anecdotes, observations, lists and poems reveals a rarefied world of poetry, love and fashion, as well as her views on nature, high society and romance. She relates how a minister presented the empress with a bundle of paper:

> 'What do you think we could write on this?' Her Majesty inquired. 'They are copying *Records of the Historian* over at His Majesty's court.'
> 'This should be a "pillow", then,' I suggested.
> 'Very well, it's yours,' declared Her Majesty.

The empress handed the sheaf to Shōnagon, who kept it by her pillow, and used it to record 'things I have seen and thought'.

1971
● trans. Ivan Morris

2006
trans. Meredith McKinney

Murasaki Shikibu c. 973–1031

'Murasaki Shikibu' is a courtesy title, which means 'Lady Wisteria-violet'. Lady Murasaki's real name is unknown. Her writing talent brought her to the attention of the powerful politician Michinaga, who selected her as a lady-in-waiting to attend his daughter, the Empress Consort Shoshi.

The Diary of Lady Murasaki 1008–10

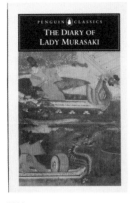

1996
trans. Richard Bowring

This intimate journal describes the author's life as a tutor and companion to the Empress Shoshi. Murasaki describes drunken courtiers, catty ladies-in-waiting and the momentous birth of a royal prince. She writes dismissively of her contemporary and rival Sei Shōnagon (110).

The Tale of Genji

c. 1021

Lady Murasaki was inspired to write her masterpiece, *The Tale of Genji*, while staying on the shores of Lake Biwa, gazing at the moon on a warm August night. It is one of the world's first novels. Genji, the 'Shining Prince', is the son of an emperor: the complex narrative follows his tempestuous love life and uncertain political fortunes as he is demoted to the status of a commoner before regaining political standing through a series of strategic affairs. The chapter 'Vanished into the Clouds' is left entirely blank, to express Genji's death without the use of words. The final section is known as 'The Bridge of Dreams'.

1980 Penguin Books
● trans. Edward G. Seidensticker

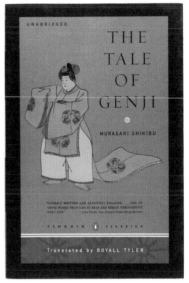

2003 Deluxe Edition
trans. Royall Tyler, 2001

AS I CROSSED A BRIDGE OF DREAMS
Recollections of a Woman in Eleventh-Century Japan

11th century

Lady Sarashina was born in 1008. We don't know her real name. Ivan Morris calls her 'Lady Sarashina' after the title she gave to her book: *Sarashina Nikki*. She was a lady-in-waiting at the Heian court, but was too melancholy and dreamy for the imperial princess's taste, so she was married off to a minor government official. Her book is an introspective diary. It describes pilgrimages through the Japanese countryside to shrines, mountain temples and palaces, and recounts her strange, mystical dreams.

1975
trans. Ivan Morris, 1971

ONE HUNDRED POETS, ONE POEM EACH
A Treasury of Classical Japanese Verse

c. 1200

2018
trans. Peter MacMillan

Uta-garuta is a traditional card game played at Japanese New Year. There are a hundred 'reading' cards with a complete *waka* poem written on each, and a hundred 'grabbing' cards spread out on the table, with just the final line of each poem. Players take it in turns to read a poem from the deck and the others race to find its concluding line on the table. Traditionally the poems are taken from this anthology of classical verse, the *Ogura Hyakunin Isshu*, compiled by the poet Fujiwara no Teika in the late 12th or early 13th centuries.

Kamo no Chōmei

c. 1115–1216

Chōmei was a prominent court poet, who became a monk at the age of 50 and retired to live as a hermit in a secluded hut in the mountains.

Yoshida Kenkō

c. 1283–*c.* 1352

Kenkō was a famous poet and calligrapher. The daughter of the prefect of Iga province broke his heart, so at a young age he became a monk and a hermit.

Hōjōki

Hōjōki means 'Record of a Ten-Foot-Square Hut'. Chōmei dwells on the Buddhist concept of impermanence while describing a series of natural disasters that have befallen Kyoto. 'On flows the river ceaselessly,' he writes, 'nor does its water ever stay the same.'

Essays in Idleness

Kenkō's 243 *Essays in Idleness* form one of the miniature classics of Japanese literature. They are the musings of his leisure hours, touching on the beauty of nature and the transience of life. His associative stream-of-consciousness style is known as *zuihitsu*, 'follow-the-brush'.

2013
trans. Meredith McKinney

2014
trans. Royall Tyler, 2012

THE TALE OF THE HEIKE

14th century

This samurai saga describes the 12th-century Genpei War and the struggle between the Taira and Genji clans for the control of Japan. It is sometimes described as Japan's *Iliad* (16). Compiled from oral traditions preserved by wandering monks, the story features such lively figures as Taira no Kiyomori, who is so consumed with fiery hatred that water boils on his dead skin; Gio, a beautiful and conscientious dancing girl; and Shigemori, Kiyomori's righteous son, who is eventually betrayed by his own brother. The central theme of the *Heike* is the Buddhist acceptance of impermanence.

JAPANESE NŌ DRAMAS

14th–15th centuries

Nō theatre is the 'perfected art': the ritualized combination of music, dance, mask, costume and the spoken word. The form flourished in the 14th and 15th centuries, pioneered by Zeami Motokiyo (*c.* 1363–*c.* 1443), a travelling actor and dramatist, who incorporated the principles of Zen Buddhism into his plays. Nō dramas examine relationships between men and gods, brothers and sisters, parents and children, and lovers. The 24 examples in this selection include *The Damask Drum*, *The Kasuga Dragon God* and *The Mountain Crone*.

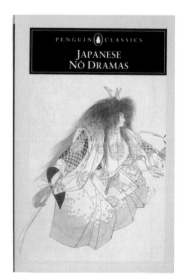

1992
trans. Royall Tyler

Matsuo Bashō

1644–1694

In his youth, Bashō was the paid companion of a local nobleman's son; together they studied *hokku*, seventeen-syllable verse. In 1667, he moved to Edo, modern Tokyo, where he continued to write. He eventually became a recluse, living in a hut on the outskirts of the city and travelling frequently, relying entirely on the munificence of temples and fellow poets. Today he is considered the greatest master of the form that has come to be called *haiku*.

The Narrow Road to the Deep North
and Other Travel Sketches

1684–94

The Records of a Weather-Exposed Skeleton; *A Visit to the Kashima Shrine*; *The Records of a Travel-Worn Satchel*; *A Visit to Sarashina Village*; *The Narrow Road to the Deep North*

In these disparate travel poems, Bashō evokes the natural world with masterful *karumi* ('lightness of touch'). He describes the changing seasons, the smell of rain and the sight of clouds drifting across the moon. He sketches those he meets, like the woman washing potatoes in the stream, farmers celebrating the mid-autumn moon festival and a party of 'snow-viewers'. In all his verses, you sense the pleasure he takes from participating in the landscape, no more so than when he enjoys a steaming bath in hot springs:

> Bathed in such comfort
> In the balmy spring of Yamanaka,
> I can do without plucking
> Life-preserving chrysanthemums.

1966
trans. Nobuyuki Yuasa
—
'Spring was very late in coming this year in Japan, but for the past few days it has been warm and plum blossoms have begun to bloom,' wrote Nobuyuki Yuasa, a Hiroshima schoolteacher, distribution agent and friend of Betty Radice (51). 'The eighty copies of Bashō I asked you to send me [. . .] arrived yesterday,' ran his letter of March 1967, 'but in a terrible, almost unreadable condition. According to the post office here, the British ship "The Benwynis" which carried them to Japan was flooded during her voyage due to a faulty draining pipe.'

1985
trans. Lucien Stryk

On Love and Barley
Haiku of Basho

Lips too chilled
for prattle —
autumn wind.

2018
trans. Adam L. Kern

The Penguin Book of Haiku

17th–19th centuries

The four classical masters of *haiku* were Bashō, the founder of the art form, who was subsequently deified by the imperial government; Bushon, who combined *haiku* with painted illustrations; Issa, who dealt with Buddhist and domestic subjects; and Shiki, who used the form to sketch realistic, secular glimpses of the natural world. All four are collected in this broad anthology, which reveals the range of what is possible with *haiku*: some are tranquilly Zen; others are mischievous, erotic and even crude.

For 19th-century Japan, turn to p.389

Medieval
Africa

African Myths of Origin

BAMBA SUSO AND BANNA KANUTE · SUNJATA

Almost all the literature of pre-colonial Africa was oral, passed down from parent to child over many generations and preserved today by professional bards known as 'griots'. The wide-ranging tradition encompasses creation myths and historical narratives, tales of animal tricksters, love songs, epigrams, proverbs and riddles.

One source of written African literature, however, is the Christian kingdom of Ethiopia, where texts written in Gəʽəz survive from as early as the 4th century CE. The most famous is the *Kəbrä Nägäśt*, the 'Glory of the Kings', which tells the biblical story (4) of the Queen of Sheba from an African perspective. Thousands of manuscripts were also produced at the University of Timbuktu between the 13th and early 20th centuries, written in Arabic and local languages such as Songhay and Tamasheq and covering astronomy, poetry, politics and philosophy and many other subjects.

AFRICAN MYTHS OF ORIGIN

From Mantis, who made the moon from a feather, to intelligent chimpanzees, monstrous crocodiles and the cripple Sunjata, who rose to found an empire, this anthology collects stories of origins from across the continent of Africa. All these ancient myths survive through an enduring oral tradition and have mostly been recorded at some point in the last 200 years.

Stephen Belcher arranges his retellings under the common themes of huntsmen, cattle-herders and trickster gods, as well as geographically, from the kingdoms of the great lakes to the forests of the Niger, the Mossi plateau, and the Sahara.

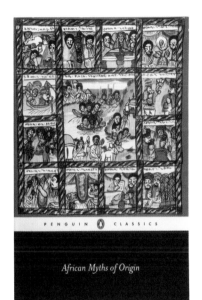

African Myths of Origin

2005
ed. Stephen Belcher

Bamba Suso

died 1974

Suso was a Gambian griot or 'jali', a bard, storyteller and repository of West African oral traditions. A jali 'has to know many traditional songs without error,' writes the historian Paul Oliver. '[…] His wit can be devastating and his knowledge of local history formidable.'

Banna Kanute

died c. 1994

Kanute was a renowned and theatrical griot as well as a virtuoso balafon player. He played with the Gambia National Troupe, a state-funded cultural ensemble drawn from all the ethnic groups of Gambia. In the 1950s, he spent time in London, making recordings for the BBC World Service.

Sunjata
Gambian Versions of the Mande Epic

c. 13th century

In the early 13th-century, there was a slow-witted, greedy child among the Malinké people of what is now eastern Guinea. He was called Sunjata Keita and, although he was the son of a hunchbacked, buffalo-woman, he grew up to be a mighty warrior with superhuman strength. With the aid of his sister, Sunjata crushed the Susu overlords and founded the Mali Empire, which lasted for four centuries.

Sunjata's story is still celebrated in West Africa as part of a vibrant oral tradition. This volume presents two versions of the myth, translated from live performances that were recorded in the early 1970s. Suso's version centres on the human and familial relationships in the story; Kanute revels in the story's violence and magic.

1999
trans. Gordon Innes & Bakari Sidibe, 1974
ed. Lucy Durán & Graham Furniss, 1999

115

Early Modern Europe

The
Renaissance

Prose

A new cultural movement emerged in 14th-century Tuscany and gradually spread throughout Europe, over a period of time that has come to be known as the 'Renaissance'. The term, first used by Giorgio Vasari (124) in 1550, means 'rebirth': the period saw both the rediscovery of classical Greek philosophy (25) and a proliferation of new ideas in the fields of art, literature, philosophy, politics and science. The basis for these new ways of thinking was the concept of 'humanism', a development of the ideas of the sophist Protagoras (25), who said that 'Man is the measure of all things'. This was the age of the polymath: figures such as Alberti, da Vinci and Michelangelo (128) demonstrated extreme skill in a variety of different fields and came to define the term 'Renaissance Man'.

Leon Battista Alberti

1404–1472

Alberti was the archetypal 'Renaissance Man'. He was an artist, a mathematician, a poet, a priest, a philosopher, a cryptographer and an athlete: he could ride wild horses and leap over a man's head. He was a close friend of the sculptor Donatello and the architect Brunelleschi, and he designed several churches including San Francesco at Rimini and the façade of Santa Maria Novella in Florence.

On Painting

1435

'Let me tell you what I do when I am painting [...] on the surface on which I am going to paint, I draw a rectangle of whatever size I want, which I regard as an open window through which the subject to be painted is seen'. Alberti's analysis of perspective captured a turning point in the history of visual art, one that was embraced in particular by artists such as Lorenzo Ghiberti, Fra Angelico and Domenico Veneziano.

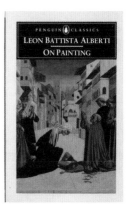

1991
trans. Cecil Grayson, 1972
intro. Martin Kemp, 1991

Christopher Columbus

1451–1506

Cristoforo Colombo was an Italian merchant sailor from Genoa. In 1492, he persuaded Ferdinand II of Aragon and Isabella I of Castile to gamble on an exploratory voyage to Japan heading west from Spain. When he touched land at San Salvador, he thought he'd discovered a new route to the eastern lands described by Marco Polo (77) and John Mandeville (87). He died without ever realizing he had travelled to an entirely new continent.

The Four Voyages of Christopher Columbus

1492–1504

Columbus made transatlantic voyages in 1492, 1493, 1498 and 1502. This volume collates a variety of sources, including extracts from his logbooks, letters and dispatches, with connecting passages from the *Life of the Admiral*, by his son, Hernando Colón. Though Columbus was not the first European to discover the Americas (92), his four voyages established the first permanent contact between Europe and the 'New World'.

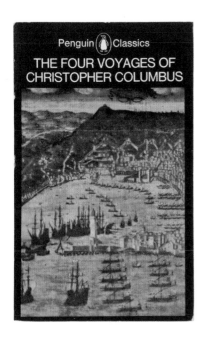

1969
trans. J. M. Cohen

Desiderius Erasmus c. 1467–1536

The Dutch 'Prince of Humanists' was a prolific man of letters who travelled widely in Europe, corresponding with princes and scholars of the Northern Renaissance. He translated the New Testament into Latin and taught at the universities of Paris and Leuven. He spent five years living in Queens' College, Cambridge, where he complained about the bad beer, bad weather and a shortage of medicinal wine for his gallstones.

Praise of Folly 1511

Moriae Encomium was written to amuse Thomas More (121); its Latin title is a pun on his name. The figure of Folly, dressed as a jester, praises herself and her companions, Self-love, Flattery, Pleasure, Drunkenness, Madness and Lust, in a satire on the pretensions and excesses of mankind, and those of the Catholic Church in particular. This volume also includes Erasmus's defensive *Letter to Maarten Van Dorp* (1515), a theologian who criticized *Praise of Folly*.

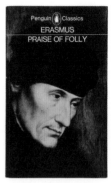

1971
trans. Betty Radice,
intro. A. H. T. Levi

—

The portrait on the cover is half of a diptych sent to Thomas More in 1517 by Erasmus and Peter Gilles, the secretary of the city of Antwerp, to whom More dedicated *Utopia* (121).

Niccolò Machiavelli 1469–1527

Machiavelli was a Florentine statesman and diplomat, until the Medici family returned to power in 1512, at which point he was accused of conspiracy, imprisoned, tortured 'with the rope' and forced to retire. He moved to his farm near San Casciano, southwest of Florence, where he spent the rest of his life writing.

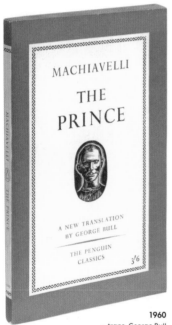

1960
• trans. George Bull
rev. Andrew Grafton, 1999

The Prince 1513, pub. 1532

This short controversial treatise appears to espouse a political strategy of deception and manipulation in pursuit of personal advantage, in which the ends famously justify the means. This unscrupulous philosophy has since been termed 'Machiavellian'. Seen by some as a scathing attack on politicians, *The Prince* has been influential for many writers including Montaigne (126), Bacon (127), Milton (150), Hume (175) and Locke (173). Machiavelli may be the reason that 'Old Nick' is a term for the Devil.

2009
trans. Tim Parks

1970 Pelican Classics
1983 Penguin Classics
trans. Leslie J. Walter, 1950
intro. Bernard Crick, 1970

—

Crick dedicates his edition of Fr. Leslie Walter's translation to the memory of Felix Raab, 'a brilliant Australian postgraduate student who, had he not by misfortune got killed in a climbing accident, a brave but imprudent action, would surely have written a truly great and sensible, sympathetic yet critical, work on Machiavelli'.

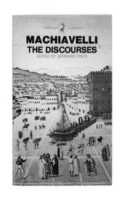

The Discourses
c. 1517, pub. 1531

The Discourses are a commentary on the first ten books of Livy's history of the Roman Republic (45). In contrast to *The Prince*, this work of historical analysis appears to promote a system of government that upholds civic freedom, encouraging citizens to put the needs of the state above selfish interests. It is considered a foundational text of republicanism.

Thomas More 1478–1535

More was a well connected and ambitious London lawyer who became a Member of Parliament, a Privy Councillor to Henry VIII, Speaker of the House of Commons and eventually Lord Chancellor of England. He later fell out with Henry VIII (144) over his split with Rome and was beheaded for treason in 1535. Four centuries later, in 1935, he was made a Catholic saint.

Utopia 1516

More began writing *Utopia* in Flanders. The first section of this 'truly golden handbook' describes his meeting with the fictional Raphael Hythlodaeus; in the second, Raphael recounts his voyage to Utopia (ou-topia), 'No-Place', an island governed along strictly rational lines: private property is banned and there is free healthcare, gender equality in the workplace and an anti-war foreign policy. Utopia (eu-topia) also means 'Perfect Place', but some qualities of Utopian life may be less attractive to modern readers: pre-marital sex is punished by a lifetime of enforced celibacy, each household comes with two complimentary slaves and the chamber pots are made of solid gold.

2012
trans. Dominic Baker-Smith
—
In an intriguing aside at the beginning of his introduction, Dominic Baker-Smith acknowledges 'the computer skills of H. C. B.-S. which prevented the whole enterprise, rather like Lucian's (57) Plato (26), from vanishing into oblivion'.

1965
● trans. Paul Turner

2017
trans. William R. Russell

Martin Luther 1483–1546

Luther was a monk and a radical professor at the University of Wittenberg. He disputed the purchasing of 'indulgences' and advocated fundamental reform of the Roman Catholic Church: in October 1517, he nailed his 'Ninety-Five Theses' to the door of All Saints' Church in Wittenberg and within two months they had circulated throughout Europe. The Catholic Church promptly excommunicated Luther and his followers, declaring him a heretic and an outlaw. He went on to translate the Bible (4) into German, marry a nun, compose a great number of hymns and instigate the epoch-defining Protestant Reformation.

The Ninety-Five Theses
and Other Writings 1517–39

1. When our Lord and Teacher Jesus Christ said, 'Repent, etc.,' he meant that the entire life of believers be a life of repentance.

27. The chant, 'When the coin in the coffer rings, the soul from purgatory springs,' is simply a human doctrine.

56. The treasures of the church, out of which the pope distributes indulgences, are not sufficiently discussed or known among the people of Christ.

Luther's explosively provocative manifesto changed the entire course of Christendom. This volume, published to mark the 500th anniversary of his 'Ninety-Five Theses', includes writings that span his career as a religious activist, from letters and sermons to catechisms and disputations.

Hans Holbein c. 1497–1543

Hans Holbein the Younger was one of the greatest portrait artists of the 16th century. He was born in Augsburg and became internationally famous after he made several portraits of Erasmus (120). He travelled to England, where he painted Thomas More (121), Thomas Cromwell, the French 'Ambassadors' (Jean de Dinteville and Georges de Selve), Henry VIII, Jane Seymour, the future Edward VI and Anne of Cleves, whose likeness Henry considered over-flattering.

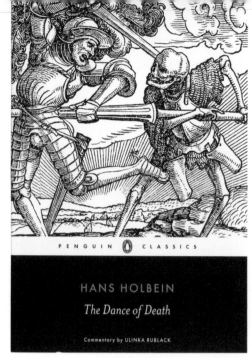

2016
ed. Ulinka Rublack

The Dance of Death 1523–6

In 41 miniature woodcuts, Holbein reinvents the medieval trope of the *danse macabre*. He depicts each rank of society in the company of grinning death's heads: a skeleton serves the king wine, snuffs the nun's candle, breaks the seaman's mast, arranges a necklace of bones around the countess's neck, whips the ploughman's horses and leads a small child away by the hand. This theatrical *memento mori* is accompanied by an extensive commentary by Ulinka Rublack.

William Tyndale 1494–1536

Tyndale translated the New Testament into English, considered heretical at the time. He fled to the city of Worms where he published his manuscript in 1526 and copies were smuggled back into England in bales of cloth. He proceeded to learn Hebrew and translated most of the Old Testament before he was finally arrested at Vilvoorde Castle near Brussels, interrogated for sixteen months and publicly strangled and burned in 1536. Seventy-five years later, his translations were incorporated, with only minor alterations, into the authorized King James Version of the Bible (4).

The Obedience of a Christian Man 1528

Tyndale sets out his religious principles in this treatise, which became one of the founding texts of the English Reformation. He argues that every Christian should have access to the Scriptures in their own language and that the Pope is an unnecessary intermediary between Christians and their God. A copy came into the hands of Henry VIII and is thought to have been a major influence in his preparations for the Act of Supremacy in 1534.

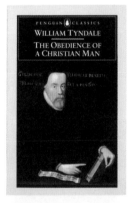

2000
trans. David Daniell

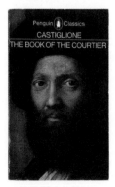

1967
trans.
George Bull

Baldesar Castiglione

1478–1529

Castiglione was a diplomat at the court of Urbino, which was renowned for its enormous library and as a centre of intellectual humanism.

The Book of the Courtier 1528

In a series of lively conversations, Castiglione presents the essential qualities required by the Renaissance courtier: discretion, decorum, nonchalance, grace, a versatile wardrobe and an acquaintance with true love.

1955
● trans. J. M. Cohen
—

'The book is full of smutty and realistic language: bollocks, roger, screw, tool, john-thomas, etc., etc., and there are plenty of passages both sexual and lavatorial,' wrote J. M. Cohen to the Penguin general editor A. S. B. Glover in 1954. 'I haven't toned it down, though I have avoided one or two very ugly words, such as that stand-by of the Public Bar, fuck.' 'I forgot to say this afternoon,' he wrote later, 'you will find my suggestion for a roundel [...] a scaled down Giant of Cerne Abbas. It may be advisable, on account of the decline in phallic worship, to scale him down in certain particulars. But I think that he is very suitable. Don't you?' Perhaps regrettably, the well-endowed Dorset chalk figure was not selected for Cohen's cover.

2006
trans. M. A. Screech

François Rabelais
c. 1488–1553

Rabelais was a monk, a lawyer and a doctor, who wrote a series of hilari-ously bawdy satirical books. He left a one-sentence will, which read: 'I have nothing, I owe a great deal, and the rest I leave to the poor.' The 'name of Rabelais is a cordial for the spirits', wrote Hazlitt (208).

Gargantua and Pantagruel 1532–64

Pantagruel was published in 1532 under the pen name 'Alcofrybas Nasier', a cunning anagram. It describes the 'dreadful deeds and prowesses' of Pantagruel, a giant of indeterminate size, who befriends a prankster called Panurge and together they defeat an army of giants with alcohol. The narrator misses a subsequent battle because he spends six months exploring the interior of Pantagruel's mouth. The prequel, *Gargantua*, is about Pantagruel's father, who has a vast codpiece and drowns the people of Paris in urine. His friend, Friar John, founds the abbey of Thélème with the motto 'do what you want'. In the *Third Book of Pantagruel*, which is dedicated to Marguerite de Navarre (125), Panurge debates whether or not to marry; and the *Fourth* and *Fifth Books* see Pantagruel and Panurge embark on a satirical odyssey.

Bartolomé de Las Casas
c. 1484–1566

Las Casas left Spain at the age of eighteen and sailed to the New World with Columbus (119). He participated in the conquest of Cuba and witnessed the brutal massacre of its native communities. He later became a Dominican priest and dedicated his life to the protection of Native Americans.

A Short Account of the Destruction of the Indies
1542, pub. 1552

Las Casas wrote this vehemently critical book to inform the Castilian crown of the atrocities being perpetrated in America. His angry documentary account of slavery, torture and genocide was instantly translated into every major European language.

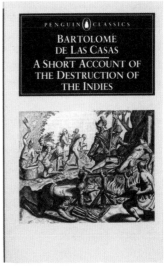

1992
trans. Nigel Griffin
intro. Anthony Pagden

The Book of Common Prayer

and Administration of the Sacraments and Other Rites and Ceremonies of the Church According to the Use of the Church of England 1549–1662

The first Book of Common Prayer was introduced by Edward VI during the English Reformation. Archbishop Thomas Cranmer drafted the new English-language liturgy that covers Morning Prayer, Evening Prayer and Holy Communion, Baptism, Confirmation, Marriage and Funeral services. It was revised several times before settling, in 1662, into the version that is still officially the prayer book of the Church of England.

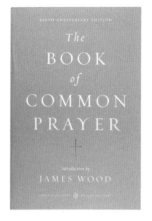

2012 Deluxe Edition intro. James Wood
—
This deluxe edition follows the 1662 text and was published to mark its 350th anniversary.

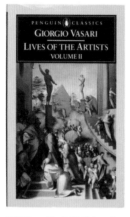

Giorgio Vasari 1511–1574

Vasari was the first person to use the term *rinascita*, 'Renaissance'. He was a painter, an architect and a friend of <u>Michelangelo</u> (128). Born in Arezzo, he worked for most of his life in Florence, painting the walls of the Palazzo Vecchio and designing the loggia of the Palazzo degli Uffizi. In 1571, he was knighted by Pope Pius V.

Lives of the Artists

1550, enlarged 1568

1965 *Lives of the Artists*
1987 Reissued as *Lives of the Artists, Volume I*
trans. George Bull

1987 *Lives of the Artists, Volume II*
trans. George Bull
—
Betty Radice (51) commissioned a second volume of Vasari's *Lives*, partly, Bull recalls, 'to satisfy her personal curiosity about some of the artists whose names were missing from the first'.

Vasari's colourful *Lives of the Most Excellent Painters, Sculptors and Architects* were instantly popular. From Cimabue and Giotto to Leonardo da Vinci and Michelangelo, he traces the development of Italian art through vivid pen portraits and gossipy anecdotes.

Lazarillo de Tormes *and* The Swindler

Two Spanish Picaresque Novels

1554, 1604

The anonymous *Lazarillo de Tormes* (1554) is considered the first 'picaresque' novel, from the Spanish *pícaro*, meaning 'rascal'. It tells the story of a roguish boy from Salamanca, initially apprenticed to a blind beggar, who has a series of corrupt clerical masters. It provided a model for Cervantes' *Don Quixote* (153).

Francisco de Quevedo (1580–1645) was a noble Spanish poet and the literary rival of <u>Luis de Góngora</u> (131). *The Swindler*, (*El Buscon*, 1604), Quevedo's only novel, describes a servant's failed attempt to become a gentleman: the miserable 'Don' Pablos is flogged, imprisoned and ends up as a thief and a cardsharp who sails for America in the hope of better fortune.

1969 *Two Spanish Picaresque Novels*
2003 Revised and reissued as *Lazarillo de Tormes and The Swindler*
trans. Michael Alpert

Nostradamus 1503–1566

Michel de Nostredame was a French apothecary, occultist and astrologer. His prophecies were greatly admired by Catherine de Médicis, the wife of Henri II of France. On the evening of 1 July 1566, he correctly predicted his own death, which occurred the following day.

The Prophecies 1555–66

> Being seated at night in secret study
> Alone upon a stool of bronze at ease:
> Slim flame issuing forth from solitude
> Fuels prophecies not futile to believe.

The gnomic quatrains of Nostradamus are thought, by some, to have predicted the Great Fire of London, the French Revolution, the rise of Adolf Hitler and the 9/11 terrorist attack.

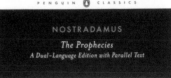

2013
trans. Richard Sieburth
intro. Stéphane Gerson
—
This is a dual-language edition, with the original French facing Sieburth's translation.

Marguerite de Navarre
1492–1549

Marguerite was the Princess of France, Queen of Navarre and Duchess of Alençon and Berry. An author herself, she was a patron of writers including Rabelais (123) and Ronsard (129) and she oversaw a celebrated intellectual salon, 'the New Parnassus' (327). At one point she came close to marrying the future Henry VIII of England.

The Heptaméron 1558

After a bridge is swept away by floodwater, five men and five women are stranded high in the Pyrenees. Over the course of the seven days it takes to repair the bridge, each member of the party tells seven stories, in emulation of Boccaccio's *Decameron* (86). The storytellers are modelled on real people, including Marguerite herself, and the stories are full of love and lust, populated by naughty friars, cunning wives, unfaithful noblemen and wise queens.

1984
trans. P. A. Chilton

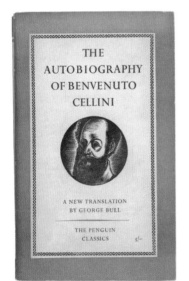

Benvenuto Cellini 1500–1571

Cellini was a Florentine sculptor and goldsmith, who worked in Rome and at the court of King François I of France. He made an elaborate gold salt cellar for the French king, which today is on display in the Kunsthistorisches Museum in Vienna.

Autobiography 1558–63

1956
trans. George Bull

Cellini describes his boyhood escapades, his amorous adventures in Rome and his artistic endeavours at Fontainebleau. He was acquainted with all the celebrated artists, politicians and prostitutes of his day. He describes mystical visions, audiences with cardinals and terms in prison, crafting a vivid picture of 16th-century Europe.

Michel de Montaigne 1533–1592

Michel Eyquem de Montaigne had an unusual upbringing, planned meticulously by his father: he spent his first three years living with a peasant family. On his return to his parents' chateau, he was addressed in Latin only, so that it became his mother tongue. Finally, he learned Greek through a system of games and solitary meditation. After his father's death in 1568, Montaigne retired to the south tower of the chateau and devoted much of the rest of his life to isolation and essay-writing. His tower 'citadel' contained a library, in which every joist was inscribed with quotations, and a study, in which every inch of wall space was filled with paintings. An inscription, still visible today, dedicates the rooms to Montaigne's personal 'freedom, tranquillity and leisure'.

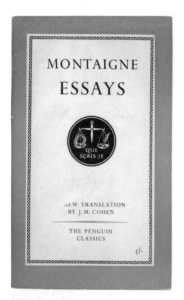

1958 Penguin Classics
1993 Penguin Books
trans. J. M. Cohen

1987 An Apology for Raymond Sebond trans. M. A. Screech

Essays c. 1570–92

Montaigne pioneered a new literary form. He assayed many diverse subjects, relying on nothing more than his own experience, judgement and reading. 'I am myself the matter of my book,' he wrote. The result was over a hundred prose 'essays' on topics ranging from cruelty to cowardice, cannibals to clothing and constancy to customs. The essays were a huge influence on contemporary and subsequent writers, including Shakespeare (134), Bacon (127), Descartes (170), Pascal (172), Rousseau (177), Hazlitt (208) and Nietzsche (348).

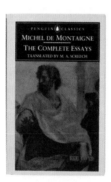

1993 The Complete Essays trans. M. A. Screech, 1991

1993 The Essays: A Selection trans. M. A. Screech

'There is no such thing as a definitive edition of the *Essays of Michel de Montaigne*,' writes Screech. 'One has to choose. The *Essays* are a prime example of the expanding book.' In 1987, he prepared an edition of *An Apology for Raymond Sebond*, the longest and perhaps greatest of Montaigne's essays. He expanded this for his monumental *Complete Essays* in 1991, from which he made a *Selection* in 1993.

Bernal Díaz

c. 1492–1584

Bernal Díaz del Castillo served under the Spanish conquistador Hernán Cortés in his campaign against the Aztecs and in the capture of Tenochtitlan, now Mexico City. He became Governor of the city of Santiago de Guatemala and began writing his account of the conquest when he was over 70; he completed it when he was 84.

The Conquest of New Spain 1576

Díaz provides a soldier's first-hand account of the overthrow of Montezuma's empire, from the overland march and the initial exploitation of the Aztec natives to the expulsion of the Spanish and their eventual capture of the capital.

1963
trans. J. M. Cohen
—
Cohen quotes the American historian W. H. Prescott, who considers Díaz 'among chroniclers what Defoe (157) is among novelists. [...] All the picturesque scenes and romantic incidents of the campaign are reflected in his page as in a mirror.'

Richard Hakluyt 1553–1616

Hakluyt was a patriotic English geographer, diplomat and part-time spy.

Voyages and Discoveries
The Principal Navigations, Voyages, Traffiques and Discoveries of the English Nation
1589–90, enlarged 1598–1600

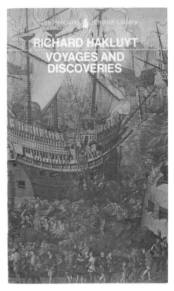

Hakluyt's *Voyages and Discoveries [...] Made by Sea or Over Land to the Most Remote and Farthest Distant Quarters of the Earth at Any Time within the Compass of These 1500 Years* is a compendium of English adventurers, from the Voyage of Ohthere in 890 'to the northeast parts' to the discovery of Guiana in 1595 by Sir Walter Raleigh. Explorers featured in this selection include Martin Frobisher, Francis Drake and Thomas Cavendish, and their destinations range from Madeira to Moscow and Malacca. Hakluyt hoped his compendium of English explorers would help to inform and inspire new generations of merchants and navigators.

1972 Penguin English Library
1985 Penguin Classics
ed. Jack Beeching

Thomas Nashe
1567–c. 1601

Nashe was a combative anti-Puritan who wrote political pamphlets, scathing essays, seditious plays and satirical fiction. He was considered by his contemporaries the 'English Juvenal' (52).

1972 Penguin English Library
1985 Penguin Classics
ed. J. B. Steane

The Unfortunate Traveller
and Other Works c. 1590–c. 1599

Nashe's works combine devout scholarship and bawdy slang. In *Pierce Penniless*, Pierce searches for the Devil, hoping to sell his soul for a thousand pounds; *Summer's Last Will and Testament* is an allegorical masque about the death of summer; *The Terrors of the Night* is a treatise on ghosts, demons and nightmares; *The Unfortunate Traveller* is a picaresque historical novella about a rogue named Jack Wilton; *Lenten Stuff* celebrates the herring fishery at Yarmouth; and *The Choice of Valentines* is an erotic poem about the disappointment of premature ejaculation and the relief supplied by a dildo, the second recorded use of that word in the *Oxford English Dictionary*.

Francis Bacon 1561–1626

Bacon was a polymathic philosopher, essayist, lawyer and statesman who held several positions of high office, including Attorney General, Lord Keeper and Lord Chancellor. In 1621, however, he was charged with bribery, dismissed from public office, imprisoned and forbidden from sitting in Parliament. He retired to the countryside and devoted the rest of his life to creating a new system of philosophy to rival that of Aristotle (29). He developed the scientific method and died of pneumonia while experimenting with the refrigeration of meat.

Essays 1597–1625

Bacon published three increasingly expanded volumes of essays: his final edition included 58 essays on subjects as various as truth, travel, goodness and gardens. He approaches his subjects scientifically, considering each from various angles before assessing different arguments. Greatly influenced by Montaigne (126), Bacon's work confirmed the essay as an enduring literary form.

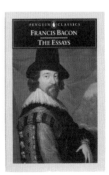

1985
ed. John Pitcher

For Enlightenment essays, turn to p.181

Poetry

The poetry of the early Italian Renaissance, especially that of Dante (84) and Petrarch (86), fuelled a renewed interest in classical authors such as Homer (16), Horace (45) and Virgil (43). As humanist ideals spread to other European countries, these interests were transmitted, and authors began to translate and imitate the Italian poets and their classical models. The familiar sonnet form, invented in Italy and perfected by Petrarch, was introduced to English literature by Thomas Wyatt (129), and Edmund Spenser's *Faerie Queene* (130) adapts the Italian metre *ottava rima*.

THE PENGUIN BOOK OF RENAISSANCE VERSE

1509–1659

This anthology of English Renaissance verse covers the period between the accession of Henry VIII and the death of Oliver Cromwell. Themed sections include 'Images of Love', 'Topographies', and 'Writer, Language and Public'. It includes poems by the familiar names Wyatt (129), Shakespeare (134), Donne (149) and Milton (150), as well as less familiar figures such as Fulke Greville, Barnabe Barnes, Anne Askew and George Wither.

1993
ed. H. R. Woudhuysen
intro. David Norbrook

Ludovico Ariosto

1474–1533

Ariosto coined the term 'humanism' (*umanesimo*) which has come to describe a school of philosophy that focuses on the strengths and qualities of humanity, rather than God. He was a courtier in the service of the dukes of Ferrara.

1975, 1977
trans. Barbara Reynolds
Published in two volumes

Orlando Furioso
(The Frenzy of Orlando) 1516, 1532

Orlando Furioso is Ariosto's continuation of the late 15th-century, unfinished epic poem *Orlando Innamorato*, 'Orlando in Love', by Matteo Maria Boiardo. Both were inspired by the people and events described in the medieval *Song of Roland* (80), but Ariosto's rambling romantic epic elaborates on the original, incorporating sorcerers, flying horses, ogres, a magic ring and a gigantic sea monster. Barbara Reynolds calls *Orlando Furioso* 'one of the most influential works in the whole of European literature'. It was the direct inspiration for Edmund Spenser's *Faerie Queene* (130) and Shakespeare's *Much Ado About Nothing* (139).

Michelangelo

1475–1564

Michelangelo Buonarroti is best known as the sculptor of *David* and the painter of the Sistine Chapel, but he was also an important lyric poet.

Poems and Letters

Michelangelo's innovative, intellectual poetry uses metaphors drawn from sculpture and painting to express his ardent love for the nobleman Tommaso de' Cavalieri and his fellow poet Vittoria Colonna. His lively letters provide a fascinating insight into his career and his fraught relationship with his family.

2007
trans. Anthony Mortimer
—
Mortimer's edition includes Vasari's (124) life of Michelangelo

Thomas Wyatt 1503–1542

Wyatt's father was Privy Councillor to both Henry VII and Henry VIII, and Thomas spent his life as a courtier and a diplomat, writing poems for private circulation. He was tall and handsome and is rumoured to have had an affair with Anne Boleyn before she married Henry; he was twice imprisoned in the Tower of London.

The Complete Poems

Wyatt was one of the first poets of the English Renaissance, self-consciously emulating the sonnets of Petrarch (86), as well as the classical poets Seneca (48) and Horace (45). He experimented with a wide variety of innovative verse forms and was one of the first poets to introduce the 'English' sonnet structure of three rhymed quatrains and a closing couplet. His poems were first published in *Tottel's Miscellany*.

1978 Penguin Poets
1997 Penguin Classics
ed. R. A. Rebholz

TOTTEL'S MISCELLANY 1557

Songs and Sonnets of Henry Howard, Earl of Surrey, Sir Thomas Wyatt and Others

Holton and MacFaul describe *Tottel's Miscellany* as the 'little book that kick-started the Golden Age of English literature': the anthology, collated by the publisher Richard Tottel, introduced English readers to the verse forms of the Renaissance with a selection of love poems, elegies, nature poems and moral odes. Henry Howard, Earl of Surrey, and Sir Thomas Wyatt were the major court poets of the reign of Henry VIII. Surrey is credited with inven-ting blank verse: unrhymed lines of iambic pentameter, which Shakespeare (134) and Milton (150) would later use to great effect.

2011
ed. Amanda Holton & Tom MacFaul

Luís Vaz de Camões

c. 1524–1580

Camões was born in Lisbon, but was banished from the Portuguese court after an illicit affair with the Princess Maria. After losing his right eye during military service he sailed to India and Macau, before returning to Lisbon where he published *Os Lusíadas*, his verse masterpiece, which has become the national epic of Portugal.

The Lusiads 1572

The 'Lusiads' are the Portuguese people, traditionally believed to be descended from Lusus, son of the Roman god Bacchus. Camões mod-elled his celebration of Portugal's seafaring prowess on Virgil's *Aeneid* (44). The *Lusiads* recounts the historic sea voyage made by the explorer Vasco da Gama around the Cape of Good Hope to India, incorporating a patriotic history of Portugal and adventurous tales of giants and sea goddesses.

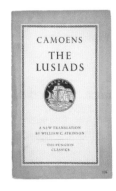

1952
trans. William C. Atkinson

Pierre de Ronsard

1524–1585

At the Collège de Coqueret in Paris, Ronsard formed the 'Pléiade', a group of poets dedicated to elevating the literary standing of the French language. He achieved widespread popularity during his lifetime, under the patronage of King Charles IX.

Selected Poems

This selection anthologizes love poems from *Les Amours de Cassandre*, written to the 15-year-old Cassandre Salviati; *Les Amours de Marie*, written for Marie Dupin; and the *Sonnets pour Helene*, which compare Helene de Surgères, a lady-in-waiting to Queen Cath-erine de Médicis, to Helen of Troy. The texts are in the original French through-out, with same-page prose translations.

2002
trans. Malcolm Quainton & Elizabeth Vinestock

Edmund Spenser c. 1552–1599

Spenser was successively the private secretary to John Young, Bishop of Rochester, Robert Dudley, Earl of Leicester, and Lord Grey de Wilton, Lord Deputy of Ireland. Sir Walter Raleigh persuaded him to present the first three books of *The Faerie Queene* to Queen Elizabeth I and as a reward she granted him a pension of fifty pounds a year. He is considered the greatest English verse stylist of the 16th century, a precursor to John Milton (150) in the following century.

EDMUND SPENSER
The Faerie Queene

1978 Penguin English Poets
1987 Penguin Classics
ed. Thomas P. Roche, Jr.
with C. Patrick O'Donnell, Jr.

1999
ed. Richard A. McCabe

The Shorter Poems 1569–96

The most significant of Spenser's shorter poems are *The Shepheardes Calender*, a series of seasonal poems in emulation of Virgil's *Eclogues* (43); *Amoretti*, a sonnet cycle celebrating his marriage to Elizabeth Boyle; and *Epithalamion*, an ode that describes a young man's anxieties on his wedding night. This volume includes all Spenser's shorter works, including 'Virgils Gnat', 'Mother Hubberds Tale' and 'Colin Clouts Come Home Again'.

The Faerie Queene 1590–99

A cross between Arthurian romance and Italian Renaissance epic, *The Faerie Queene* is Spenser's masterpiece. It consists of six books, in which knights embark on allegorical quests, and an unfinished seventh, known as the 'Mutabilitie Cantos'. King Arthur recurs throughout the cycle, madly in love with the Faerie Queene herself, a thinly veiled portrait of Elizabeth I. In a letter to Sir Walter Raleigh, included in this edition, Spenser explains that he wrote the poem in order to 'fashion a gentleman or noble person in vertuous and gentle discipline'.

Isabella Whitney

c. 1545–c. 1577

Little is known about Isabella Whitney. She may have been in domestic service in the City of London.

Mary Sidney

1561–1621

Mary Sidney, Countess of Pembroke, was the younger sister of the poet Philip Sidney (131). She oversaw the publication of his works after his death.

Aemilia Lanyer

1569–1645

Aemilia Lanyer was briefly the mistress of the Lord Chamberlain, Lord Hunsdon, but later married her first cousin, the court musician Alphonso Lanyer.

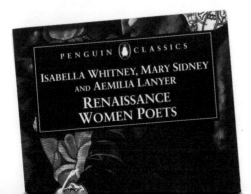

PENGUIN CLASSICS
ISABELLA WHITNEY, MARY SIDNEY
AND AEMILIA LANYER
RENAISSANCE
WOMEN POETS

Renaissance Women Poets

The three poets in this anthology come from different social and cultural backgrounds. Whitney's poems explore sexual morality in the mercantile world of 16th-century London; Sidney translates the psalms and *The Triumph of Death* by Petrarch (86); and Lanyer's proto-feminist poetry celebrates female virtues, advocating greater gender equality.

2000
ed. Danielle Clarke

Philip Sidney 1554–1586

Sir Philip Sidney was the model of the Renaissance courtier, a sensitive soldier who could as easily quill a sonnet as fillet a Spaniard. In 1586, at the age of 31, he was mortally wounded at the Battle of Zupthen. Injured and gangrenous, but gallant to the last, he offered his water to another fallen soldier, saying: 'Thy necessity is yet greater than mine.'

The Countess of Pembroke's Arcadia

1580–6, pub. 1593

Sidney began working on his ambitious prose romance while staying in Wiltshire with his sister Mary, the Countess of Pembroke (130). It tells the story of Basilius, an imprudent duke who consults an oracle about the future of his family. As a result of the oracle's doom-laden words, he retreats to the countryside with his wife and daughters to lead a secluded pastoral life. When two wandering princes turn up in disguise, however, a series of comical scrapes ensues.

1977 Penguin English Library
1987 Penguin Classics
ed. Maurice Evans

2004
ed. Gavin Alexander

SIDNEY'S 'THE DEFENCE OF POESY'
and Selected Renaissance Literary Criticism

c. 1580–1603
Philip Sidney, *Defence of Poesy*;
George Puttenham, *The Art of English Poesy*;
Samuel Daniel, *A Defence of Rhyme*

During the English Renaissance, several writers attempted to define and analyse the purpose of liter-ature. Sidney argues that poetry and fiction are beneficial because they inspire readers to 'virtuous action'; Puttenham provides an analytical guide to the art of poetry and rhetoric; and Daniel celebrates the emerging English literary tradition. This volume also includes passages from Henry Peacham, John Harington, Thomas Campion, Francis Bacon (127) and Ben Jonson (145).

Luis de Góngora
1561–1627

Góngora was a gambler, a womanizer and chaplain to King Philip III of Spain. His poems were unpublished in his lifetime, but circulated widely in manuscript and he became famous for his use of *culteranismo*, a complex, allusive poetic style. He cultivated a lifelong rivalry with Francisco de Quevedo (124). Federico García Lorca considered him 'the father of modern poetry'.

The Solitudes 1613

A shipwrecked youth stumbles up an island beach, having been spurned by his lover and alienated from society. He meets a band of goatherds and joins them on their way to a shepherd's wedding.

2012
trans. Edith Grossman
intro. Alberto Manguel
—
This novel-in-verse is presented with the original Spanish facing a parallel translation by Edith Grossman, who adheres to Góngora's philosophy that 'language itself, not its emotive referent or expressive content, is the intrinsic aesthetic component of poetry'.

For Metaphysical poetry, turn to p.148

Drama

In January 1562, a play called *The Tragedie of Gorboduc* was performed for Queen Elizabeth I at the Inner Temple in London. The play's argument summarizes the plot:

> Gorboduc, King of Britain, divided his realm in his lifetime to his sons, Ferrex and Porrex. The sons fell to division and dissension. The younger killed the elder. The mother that more dearly loved the elder, for revenge killed the younger. The people, moved with the cruelty of the fact, rose in rebellion and slew both father and mother. The nobility assembled and most terribly destroyed the rebels. And afterwards for want of issue of the prince, whereby the succession of the crown became uncertain, they fell to civil war in which both they and many of their issues were slain, and the land for a long time almost desolate and miserably wasted.

This cheerful entertainment is notable for being the first drama in the English language to employ blank verse: as such, it heralds fifty years of extraordinary literary production, the establishment of the first popular playhouses and a fizzing community of educated playwrights as well as the careers of three of the most renowned wordsmiths in the English language: Christopher Marlowe (133), William Shakespeare (134) and Ben Jonson (145).

2012
ed. Emma Smith
—
The Revenger's Tragedy also features in the *Three Revenge Tragedies* anthology (146) and Middleton's *Five Plays* (146).

FIVE REVENGE TRAGEDIES

Thomas Kyd, *The Spanish Tragedy*;
William Shakespeare, *Hamlet*;
John Marston, *Antonio's Revenge*;
Henry Chettle, *The Tragedy of Hoffmann*;
Thomas Middleton, *The Revenger's Tragedy*
1582–1606

The figure of Revenge has a walk-on role in Kyd's *Spanish Tragedy*, which includes a play-within-a-play and a ghost intent on vengeance; Shakespeare's early 'first quarto' *Hamlet* is shorter than later versions (140) and more focused on the revenge plot; Chettle's *Tragedy of Hoffmann* was originally staged in direct competition to *Hamlet* and includes many of the same themes; in Marston's *Antonio's Revenge*, a heartbroken lover murders a duke during a masque; and *The Revenger's Tragedy* by Middleton (146) is an orgy of death and debauchery at the court of a libidinous Italian duke.

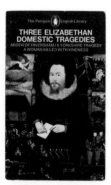

1969 Penguin English Library
1985 Penguin Classics
ed. Keith Sturgess

THREE ELIZABETHAN DOMESTIC TRAGEDIES

Arden of Faversham (anon.);
A Yorkshire Tragedy (anon.);
Thomas Heywood, *A Woman Killed with Kindness*
1592–1603

Most Elizabethan tragedies feature kings, queens and the nobility, but a few survive that have a domestic setting and plots involving ordinary people. *Arden of Faversham* tells the true story of Thomas Arden, who was murdered by his wife Alice and her lover; stylometric analysis in 2015 concluded that it may have been written by Shakespeare (134) with an unknown collaborator. *A Yorkshire Tragedy* is the true story of Walter Calverley, who murdered two of his children and stabbed his wife – scholars now attribute it to Thomas Middleton (146) – and *A Woman Killed with Kindness*, by Thomas Heywood, is the fictional tale of Master Frankford and his wife Anne, who starves herself to death after he responds to her adultery with 'kindness'.

1969 Penguin English Library
● ed. J. B. Steane

1971 Penguin Education
1979 Penguin Poets
1986 Penguin Classics
ed. Stephen Orgel

2003
ed. Frank Romany &
Robert Lindsey

Christopher Marlowe 1564 – 1593

Kit Marlowe was the son of a shoe-maker and the foremost tragedian of his generation. He may also have been a spy, a heretic, a magician, a murderer and a counterfeiter. In 1593 he was summoned to appear before the Privy Council on charges of blasphemy as a homosexual atheist, and a few days later he was stabbed in the eye during a pub brawl in Deptford, in south-east London. He died at the age of 29.

The Complete Plays

Dido, Queen of Carthage; *Tamburlaine the Great, Parts One & Two*; *The Jew of Malta*; *Doctor Faustus*; *Edward II*; *The Massacre at Paris*
c. 1586 – c. 1593

Dido dramatizes Aeneas and Dido's love affair, as described in Virgil's *Aeneid* (44); it was first performed by the Children of the Chapel, a company of boy actors. *Tamburlaine* is based on the life of the Asian warlord Timur and his savage rise to power. *The Jew of Malta* is a revenge tragedy, introduced by the ghost of Machiavelli (120). In *Doctor Faustus*, an ambitious scholar sells his soul to the Devil; *Edward II* sees the eponymous king murdered by his queen and her lover; and *The Massacre at Paris* reconstructs the St Bartholomew Day's Massacre of 1572 and includes a mysterious 'English Agent', who some have identified as Marlowe himself.

The Complete Poems and Translations

Marlowe's greatest poem is the erotic epyllion *Hero and Leander*, in which Leander swims naked across the Hellespont to greet his lover at Sestos; it was unfinished at his death and was later completed and extended by George Chapman and Henry Petowe, whose work is included in this edition. The volume also features Marlow's translations of Lucan and Ovid's *Amores* (46).

William Shakespeare

1564–1616

Soul of the age!
The applause, delight, the wonder of our stage!
My Shakespeare, rise! I will not lodge thee by
Chaucer (89), or Spenser (130), or bid Beaumont lie
A little further, to make thee a room:
Thou art a monument without a tomb,
And art alive still while thy book doth live
And we have wits to read, and praise to give.

This is part of a poem by Ben Jonson (145), which forms the preface to the 'First Folio', the first collected edition of Shakespeare's plays, published in 1623. Shakespeare wrote and contributed to at least 40 plays, 154 sonnets, two narrative poems and several other verses. He is considered by many to be the greatest writer in the English language and the greatest dramatist the world has ever seen. His work is both awe-inspiring in scope and astonishing in its detailed observation of the human condition. 'We go to Shakespeare,' writes Jeanette Winterson, 'to find out about ourselves.'

The Two Gentlemen of Verona 1590–91

The Two Gentlemen of Verona has the smallest named cast of all of Shakespeare's plays. Launce and his dog Crab provide most of the humour in a plot about one gentleman seducing another's sweetheart.

1968 New Penguin Shakespeare
2005 Penguin Shakespeare
2015 Penguin Classics
ed. Norman Sanders, 1968
intro. Russell Jackson, 2005

The Taming of the Shrew 1590–91

This controversial comedy about breaking a strong woman's spirit is framed as a play-within-a-play, staged for the benefit of a drunken tinker. In 1948, Cole Porter adapted it into the musical *Kiss Me, Kate*, and it also inspired the 1999 high school movie *10 Things I Hate About You*.

1968 New Penguin Shakespeare
2006 Penguin Shakespeare
2015 Penguin Classics
ed. G. R. Hibbard, 1968
intro. Margaret Jane Kidnie, 2006

THE PENGUIN SHAKESPEARE

1937–67

Born on Shakespeare's birthday, 23 April 1937, The Penguin Shakespeare was Penguin's first independent series, launched one month before Pelican Books (xvi). 'A sixpenny Shakespeare, edited and produced primarily for the general reader, was something new,' wrote Allen Lane in 1938. 'We were determined to treat the reader with respect and to take infinite pains over the preliminary details.'

The ethos of the series has changed little in 80 years. 'The Penguin Shakespeare series aspires to remove obstacles to understanding,' writes Professor Stanley Wells in the current General Introduction, 'and to make pleasurable the reading of the work of

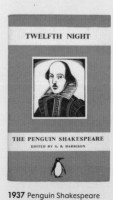

1937 Penguin Shakespeare
ed. G. B. Harrison

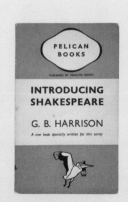

1938 Pelican Books

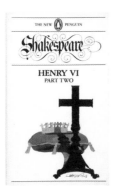
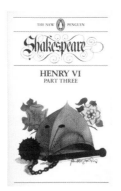

Henry VI 1591–2

Shakespeare may have collaborated with Thomas Nashe (127) or Christopher Marlowe (133) on his Henry VI plays. Together with *Richard III*, the three parts trace the causes and course of the Wars of the Roses. Memorable characters include the martyr Joan of Arc, the rebel Jack Cade and the formidable Queen Margaret. *Part Two* has the largest named cast of any Shakespeare play and *Part Three* features the longest soliloquy in any of Shakespeare's plays: 71 lines, spoken by Richard, Duke of Gloucester, later Richard III.

1981 New Penguin Shakespeare
2005 Penguin Shakespeare
2015 Penguin Classics
ed. Norman Sanders, 1981
intro. Jane Kingsley-Smith & Rebecca Brown, 2005

1981 New Penguin Shakespeare
2005 Penguin Shakespeare
2015 Penguin Classics
ed. Norman Sanders, 1981
intro. Michael Taylor & Rebecca Brown, 2005

1981 New Penguin Shakespeare
2007 Penguin Shakespeare
2015 Penguin Classics
ed. Norman Sanders, 1981
intro. Gillian Day & Rebecca Brown, 2007

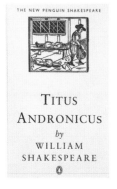

2001 New Penguin Shakespeare
2005 Penguin Shakespeare
2015 Penguin Classics
ed. Jacques Berthoud with Sonia Massai, 2001

Titus Andronicus 1592

Titus is Shakespeare's first tragedy and also his bloodiest play, with stabbings, rape, live burials, burnings, amputation and cannibalism. He probably collaborated with George Peel.

Richard III 1592–3

Richard III is the second longest of Shakespeare's plays, after *Hamlet* (140). It depicts the Machiavellian rise of Richard, Duke of Gloucester, who goes to murderous lengths to seize the throne. Shakespeare's portrayal of Richard as a 'poisonous hunchback'd toad' shaped the popular image of the monarch for centuries, until 2012, when the real king's body was discovered underneath a car park in Leicester. Analysis of his skeleton demonstrated that though he may have had slight curvature of the spine, there was no evidence of spinal kyphosis, a hunchback.

1968 New Penguin Shakespeare
2005 Penguin Shakespeare
2015 Penguin Classics
ed. E. A. J. Honigmann, 1968
intro. Michael Taylor & Gillian Day, 2005

the man who has done more than most to make us understand what it is to be human.'

Allen Lane originally approached Harley Granville-Barker, the legendary Shakespearean actor-manager, to edit the first series, but he declined, recommending instead G. B. Harrison, a reader at King's College London. Granville-Barker and Harrison discussed the project and the former's parting advice was 'Whatever you do, don't try to be consistent!'

George Bagshawe Harrison edited the Penguin Shakespeares for 23 years. He edited and wrote introductions to every play; he also wrote a Pelican in 1938 called

Introducing Shakespeare as 'a kind of General Introduction to the Penguin Shakespeares'. He aimed at pleasing the general reader, using 'the Elizabethan manner of printing a play text, with spellings conservatively modernized, but keeping most of the original peculiarities'. Over the course of preparing the series, he served in the Royal Army Service and the Intelligence Corps, became Head of the Department of English at Queen's University in Ontario and joined the Faculty of the University of Michigan in 1949.

1986 New Penguin Shakespeare
The Sonnets and *A Lover's Complaint*
1999 Penguin Classics
ed. John Kerrigan
—
Kerrigan's 1986 edition includes *A Lover's Complaint*, a narrative poem included in the 1609 publication of Shakespeare's sonnets, in which a young woman describes her betrayal by a heartless seducer. His 2015 edition is a slim, pocket volume without critical apparatus.

2015 Penguin Books
Shakespeare's Sonnets
ed. John Kerrigan

The Sonnets
1593–1603, pub. 1609

In 1593 and 1594 the London theatres closed because of the plague, so Shakespeare turned his hand to poetry. He published two narrative poems, *Venus and Adonis* and *The Rape of Lucrece*, and he began work on the 154 sonnets that were eventually published in 1609. The first 126 sonnets are romantic love poems addressed to an unnamed young man known as the 'Fair Youth'; the rest are more sexually explicit and addressed to a black-haired woman known as the 'Dark Lady'.

The Comedy of Errors
1594

Shakespeare's shortest play is a farcical comedy, in which two sets of identical twins, separated at birth, unwittingly cross paths. Hilarity ensues. Shakespeare was himself the father of a pair of twins, Hamnet and Judith, who were nine years old when he wrote *The Comedy of Errors*. The plot is taken from Plautus (37).

1972 New Penguin Shakespeare
2005 Penguin Shakespeare
2015 Penguin Classics
ed. Stanley Wells, 1972
intro. Randall Martin & Paul Edmondson, 2005

Love's Labour's Lost
1594–5

Kenneth Branagh considers *Love's Labour's Lost* the 'most beautiful of Shakespeare's comedies'. The title refers to the deferment of the four couples' weddings, after they have finally declared their love for each other. It includes the longest single word used by Shakespeare: 'honorificabilitudinitatibus'.

1982 New Penguin Shakespeare
2005 Penguin Shakespeare
2015 Penguin Classics
ed. John Kerrigan, 1982
intro. Nicholas Walton, 2005

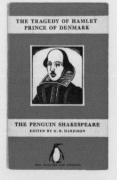

1937 Penguin Shakespeare
● ed. G. B. Harrison

The series was launched with six titles: *Twelfth Night* (140), *Hamlet* (140), *Henry V* (139), *King Lear* (142), *As You Like It* (139) and *A Midsummer Night's Dream* (137). They had red and black dust jackets and covers designed by Edward Young, with a woodcut portrait of Shakespeare by Robert Gibbings. '*Hamlet* for the price of ten Goldflake,' wrote Geoffrey Grigson in the *Morning Post*, '[...] it is pleasant to think of it on stalls at King's Cross with Dashiell Hammett and Dorothy L. Sayers (85)'.

In James Thurber's short story, 'Macbeth Murder Mystery' (1937), an American woman buys a new Penguin Shakespeare edition accidentally, thinking it's a crime novel. 'You can imagine how mad I was when I found it was Shakespeare,' she says. '[...] I don't see why the Penguin-books people had to get out Shakespeare plays in the same size and everything as the detective stories.' 'I think they have different coloured jackets,' murmurs the narrator. 'Well, I didn't notice that.' The woman proceeds to crack open the cold case of *Macbeth* (142), and deduces that Macduff did it.

Richard II 1595

Richard II is one of only four of Shakespeare's plays written entirely in verse; the others are *King John* and the first and third parts of *Henry VI* (135). It is an intricately patterned and poetic play about the nature of kingship and the responsibility of the 'hollow crown'.

1969 New Penguin Shakespeare
2008 Penguin Shakespeare
2015 Penguin Classics
ed. Stanley Wells, 1969
intro. Paul Edmondson &
Michael Taylor, 2008

Romeo and Juliet 1595

The star-crossed Romeo and Juliet are the most famous lovers in literary history. Shakespeare based his play on an Italian story, which had been translated into English in 1562 as *The Tragical History of Romeus and Juliet*. The Montagues (Montecchi) and Capulets (Capelletti) were real Italian families; Dante meets them as he climbs Mount Purgatory (84).

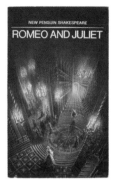

1967 New Penguin Shakespeare
2005 Penguin Shakespeare
2015 Penguin Classics
ed. T. J. B. Spencer, 1967
intro. Adrian Poole, 2005

A Midsummer Night's Dream 1595

Samuel Pepys (182) thought *A Midsummer Night's Dream* 'the most insipid ridiculous play that ever I saw in my life'. Today it is one of Shakespeare's most popular. It has four interwoven plots: the marriage of Duke Theseus and the Amazon queen Hippolyta; a love quadrangle between four young Athenians; the stormy relationship between Titania and Oberon, queen and king of the fairies; and a hilariously amateur performance of the 'Pyramus and Thisbe' episode from Ovid's *Metamorphoses* (47).

1967 New Penguin Shakespeare
2005 Penguin Shakespeare
2015 Penguin Classics
ed. Stanley Wells, 1967
intro. Helen Hackett, 2005

King John 1596

There is a lot of formal pageantry in *King John*, which made it particularly popular with Victorian audiences. The plot revolves around the weak-willed king and the many challenges he faces: war with France, would-be usurpers and his own rebellious barons.

1974 New Penguin Shakespeare
2005 Penguin Shakespeare
2015 Penguin Classics
ed. Robert Smallwood, 1974
intro. Eugene Giddens, 2005

Production paused during the Second World War, mainly due to scarcity of paper. In 1951 the series was given a new look by Jan Tschichold (xiii): the typography was reworked and the covers became black and white, with a new portrait engraving by Reynolds Stone. The series was completed in this design, from *The Taming of the Shrew* (134) to *Henry the Sixth, Parts I to III* (135) and *The Narrative Poems* in 1959. Allen

1951 Penguin Shakespeare
● ed. G. B. Harrison

Lane hoped to sell the Shakespeare series in America, but G. B. Harrison had signed a previous deal with a US publisher, so the British texts could not be distributed. The solution was to commission a parallel series in the States and the American scholar Alfred Harbage was approached to edit the Pelican Shakespeare, which began with *Macbeth* (142) in 1956. The series was refreshed in 1999 and is still going strong.

1956 Pelican Shakespeare
● ed. Alfred Harbage

1967 New Penguin Shakespeare
2005 Penguin Shakespeare
2015 Penguin Classics
ed. W. Moelwyn Merchant, 1967
intro. Peter Holland, 2005

The Merchant of Venice 1596–7

The character of Shylock, the Jewish moneylender who demands his 'pound of flesh' when a Venetian merchant defaults on a loan, continues to spark controversy. Few of Shakespeare's contemporary audience would have had first-hand experience of Judaism, as Jews had been forcibly expelled from England (69) 300 years previously.

The Merry Wives of Windsor 1596–7

There is a tradition that Queen Elizabeth 'commanded' Shakespeare to write *The Merry Wives of Windsor*, because she wanted to see Falstaff fall in love. The plot involves the blundering knight attempting to seduce two married women at once. 'It never yet had reader or spectator,' thought Samuel Johnson (183), perhaps a little generously, 'who did not think it too soon at an end'.

1973 New Penguin Shakespeare
2005 Penguin Shakespeare
2015 Penguin Classics
ed. G. R. Hibbard, 1973
intro. Catherine Richardson, 2005

Henry IV 1596–8

Henry IV has remained consistently popular with both audiences and critics. Harold Bloom calls *Part One* the 'finest, most representative instance of what Shakespeare can do' and Simon Schama describes *Part Two*, as 'the most lyrical [play] Shakespeare ever wrote'. Together they pick up after *Richard II* (137) and chart the transformation of Prince Hal from a riotous, dissolute youth into the future King Henry V (139). They also introduce one of Shakespeare's most beloved characters, the boisterous Sir John Falstaff.

1968 New Penguin Shakespeare
2005 Penguin Shakespeare
2015 Penguin Classics
ed. Peter Davison, 1968
intro. Charles Edelman, 2005

1968 New Penguin Shakespeare
2005 Penguin Shakespeare
2015 Penguin Classics
ed. Peter Davison, 1968
intro. Adrian Poole, 2005

THE NEW PENGUIN SHAKESPEARE

1967–2005

The New Penguin Shakespeare was launched in Britain exactly 30 years after the original series, with another party on Shakespeare's birthday and again with six titles: *Romeo and Juliet* (137), *A Midsummer Night's Dream* (137), *Coriolanus* (143), *Julius Caesar* (139), *Macbeth* (142) and *The Merchant of Venice*. The first titles were intended to match the recently revised Classics design by Germano Facetti (xiv), with atmospheric artwork by Pierre Clayette.

1967 New Penguin Shakespeare
ed. T. J. B. Spencer
cover Pierre Clayette

1967 New Penguin Shakespeare
ed. Stanley Wells
cover Pierre Clayette

Much Ado About Nothing 1598

'Nothing' in Shakespeare's day sounded almost identical to 'noting', which meant 'gossip' or 'rumour'. The wordplay is relevant throughout *Much Ado About Nothing*, which features multiple scenes of eavesdropping, forged letters and spying between unwilling lovers.

1968 New Penguin Shakespeare
2005 Penguin Shakespeare
2015 Penguin Classics
ed. R. A. Foakes, 1968
intro. Janette Dillon, 2005

Henry V 1598–9

Henry V, one of Shakespeare's most patriotic plays, centres on the victorious Battle of Agincourt and the Siege of Harfleur, before which Henry rouses his troops with the famous line, 'Once more unto the breach, dear friends, once more'! It briefly mentions the death of Falstaff (138).

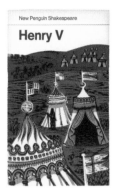

1968 New Penguin Shakespeare
2010 Penguin Shakespeare
2015 Penguin Classics
ed. A. R. Humphreys, 1968
rev. Ann Kaegi, 2010

Julius Caesar 1599

Using Plutarch (55) as his source, Shakespeare weaves a gripping political thriller around the assassination of the Roman general. Caesar (41) dies midway through the play and the second half describes the ensuing civil war between Brutus, haunted by Caesar's ghost, and Octavius, the future Emperor Augustus (43).

1967 New Penguin Shakespeare
2005 Penguin Shakespeare
2015 Penguin Classics
ed. Norman Sanders, 1967
intro. Martin Wiggins, 2005

As You Like It 1599–1600

In the most gender-bending of Shakespeare's plays, a male actor would have originally played Rosalind, a girl, who flees into the Forest of Arden disguised as a man. She meets the handsome Orlando and 'pretends' to be a woman so that he can practise his wooing skills. The melancholy Jaques famously comments that 'All the world's a stage, / And all the men and women merely players.' It is thought that Shakespeare himself played the role of Adam, Orlando's servant.

1968 New Penguin Shakespeare
2005 Penguin Shakespeare
2015 Penguin Classics
ed. H. J. Oliver, 1968
intro. Katherine Duncan-Jones, 2005

1967 New Penguin Shakespeare
ed. G. R. Hibbard
cover Pierre Clayette

1967 New Penguin Shakespeare
ed. G. K. Hunter
cover Pierre Clayette

Allen Lane appointed the scholar T. J. B. Spencer as General Editor of the series. Spencer was Professor of English and Director of the Shakespeare Institute at the University of Birmingham, a position he retained until his death in 1978. This time, rather than writing all the introductions himself, Spencer oversaw individual volume editors. Spencer also oversaw the companion Penguin Shakespeare Library series, editing *Elizabethan Love Stories* himself.

1968 Penguin Shakespeare Library
● ed. T. J. B. Spencer

1980 New Penguin Shakespeare
2005 Penguin Shakespeare
2015 Penguin Classics
ed. T. J. B. Spencer & Stanley Wells, 1980
intro. Alan Sinfield & Paul Prescott, 2005

Hamlet

1599–1601

T. S. Eliot called *Hamlet* the 'Mona Lisa of literature'. It is Shakespeare's longest and perhaps greatest play, and one of the most quoted works in the English language. The story was inspired by the legendary Amleth, Prince of Denmark, and perhaps also by the death in 1596 of Shakespeare's only son, Hamnet. Its most famous line, 'To be, or not to be', expresses deep ambivalence about the relationship between life and death, a theme that runs throughout the play.

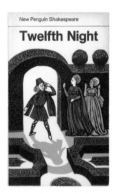

1969 New Penguin Shakespeare
2005 Penguin Shakespeare
2015 Penguin Classics
ed. M. M. Mahood, 1968
intro. Michael Dobson, 2005

Twelfth Night

1600–1601

The earliest known performance of *Twelfth Night* took place in Middle Temple Hall in London on Candlemas Night, 1602. The lawyer John Manningham described it in his diary: 'At our feast we had a play called "Twelve Night, or What you Will" [...] A good practice in it to make the steward believe his lady widow was in love him, by counterfeiting a letter as from his lady, in general terms telling what she liked best in him, prescribing his gesture in smiling, his apparel, etc., and then, when he came to practise, making him believe they took him to be mad.'

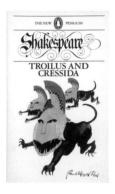

1987 New Penguin Shakespeare
2006 Penguin Shakespeare
2015 Penguin Classics
ed. R. A. Foakes, 1987
intro. Colin Burrow, 2006

Troilus and Cressida

1602

Drawing on Chaucer's *Troilus and Criseyde* (89), Shakespeare's version of the Trojan story is perhaps the most problematic of his so-called 'problem plays', which don't fit neatly into the categories of comedy, history or tragedy. The tone veers from tragic melancholy to comic bawdiness and ends with the death of the hero Hector and the dismal failure of Troilus and Cressida's relationship. 'This is tragedy of a special sort,' writes the author Joyce Carol Oates, '[...] the basis of which is the impossibility of conventional tragedy.'

Only the first six titles of the New Penguin Shakespeare series had covers by Clayette. The following 25 were issued with white covers and 'solid and chunky wood engravings' by David Gentleman (319), commissioned by the Penguin art director, Hans Schmoller.

T. J. B. Spencer died while working on his edition of *Hamlet*. Stanley Wells, a teacher at the Shakespeare Institute, took over and *Hamlet* was published in 1980. Wells also took over the general editorship of the series.

1967 New Penguin Shakespeare
ed. T. J. Spencer
cover David Gentleman, *c.* 1970

1967 New Penguin Shakespeare
ed. G. R. Hibbard
cover David Gentleman, *c.* 1970

1967 New Penguin Shakespeare
ed. Stanley Wells
cover David Gentleman, *c.* 1970

1969 New Penguin Shakespeare
2005 Penguin Shakespeare
2015 Penguin Classics
ed. J. M. Nosworthy, 1969
intro. Julia Briggs, 2005

Measure for Measure

1603

A young nun faces a stark choice: the Duke of Vienna will spare her brother's life if she will surrender her virginity. *Measure for Measure* explores the difference between legal and moral justice. The title is thought to be a reference to Matthew 7:1-2 (4):

> Judge not, that ye be not judged. For with what judgement ye judge, ye shall be judged: and with what measure ye mete, it shall be measured to you again.

1968 New Penguin Shakespeare
2005 Penguin Shakespeare
2015 Penguin Classics
ed. Kenneth Muir, 1968
intro. Tom McAlindon, 2005

Othello

1603 – 4

The character with the most lines in *Othello* is Iago, the Moorish general Othello's charismatic and unscrupulous ensign, who drips doubt into his master's ear, feeding the 'green-eyed monster' of jealousy, and ultimately destroying both Othello and his wife Desdemona. The character of Othello may have been inspired by the visit of Abd el-Ouahed ben Messaoud ben Mohammed Anoun, the Moorish ambassador from the King of Barbary, who came to London in 1600.

1970 New Penguin Shakespeare
2005 Penguin Shakespeare
2015 Penguin Classics
ed. Barbara Everett, 1970
intro. Janette Dillon, 2005

All's Well That Ends Well

1604 – 5

Based on a story from Boccaccio's *Decameron* (86), *All's Well That Ends Well* is the strange tale of a poor doctor's daughter who cures the king of France and is offered, as a reward, her choice of nobleman to marry. When she chooses Bertram, Count of Rousillon, he refuses to consummate their marriage, but Helena tricks herself into his bed. It is a 'bitter play with a bitter title', wrote George Bernard Shaw (294), although he did consider the Countess of Rousillon to be the 'most beautiful old woman's part ever written.'

At the same time, the design changed: watercolours were commissioned from Paul Hogarth, who had previously worked on the Penguin covers of Grahame Greene's novels.

In 1994, there was a further relaunch: the books became cream-coloured with small woodcuts by Louisa Hare. From 1980 until 2005, the editions carried an endorsement for the Royal Shakespeare Company on the back cover.

1967 New Penguin Shakespeare
ed. T. J. B. Spencer
cover Paul Hogarth, c. 1980

1968 New Penguin Shakespeare
ed. E. A. J. Honigmann
cover Paul Hogarth, c. 1980

1967 New Penguin Shakespeare
ed. T. J. B. Spencer
cover Louisa Hare, 1994

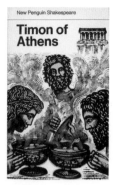

Timon of Athens

1605

Timon is a rich philanthropist who gives away all his money and is then resentful and bitter when his friends refuse to help him. Karl Marx quotes Timon in *Capital* (347) when he calls money the 'common whore of mankind'. The play was most probably written in collaboration with Thomas Middleton (146), and based in part on passages from Plutarch (54) and Lucian (57).

1970 New Penguin Shakespeare
2005 Penguin Shakespeare
2015 Penguin Classics
ed. G. R. Hibbard, 1970
intro. Nicholas Walton, 2005

Macbeth

1606

Some thespians are superstitious about 'the Scottish Play'. If someone utters the name *Macbeth*, there are several methods for dispelling the curse: the actor Michael York recommends leaving the building, walking around it three times, spitting over your left shoulder, swearing an oath and waiting to be invited back inside; alternatively, you can leave the room, knock three times, wait to be invited inside and then quote a line from *Hamlet* (140).

1967 New Penguin Shakespeare
2005 Penguin Shakespeare
2015 Penguin Classics
ed. George Hunter, 1967
intro. Carol Chillington Rutter, 2005

King Lear 1605-6

Shelley (196) thought *King Lear* was the 'most perfect specimen of the dramatic art existing in the world'. This grand masterpiece presents Lear's descent into madness, harried by his 'pelican daughters' Goneril and Regan and vainly supported by Edgar disguised as Mad Tom, Kent disguised as Caius, the Fool and his formerly estranged daughter Cordelia. Lear memorably throws off his clothes during a savage storm on the heath, revealing himself as 'a poor, bare, forked animal'.

1972 New Penguin Shakespeare
2005 Penguin Shakespeare
2015 Penguin Classics
ed. George Hunter, 1972
intro. Kiernan Ryan, 2005

Antony and Cleopatra

1606

Antony and Cleopatra acts as a sequel to *Julius Caesar* (139). It has been variously described as a history, a tragedy, a comedy, a romance and a problem play. Cleopatra is Shakespeare's most complex and fully developed female character. As Enobarbus says: 'Age cannot wither her, not custom stale / Her infinite variety.'

1977 New Penguin Shakespeare
2005 Penguin Shakespeare
2015 Penguin Classics
ed. Emrys Jones, 1977
intro. René Weis, 2005

PENGUIN SHAKESPEARE 2005-2015

In 2005, the New Penguin Shakespeare lost the 'New'. The underlying texts remained the same, but all of them were revised and supplemented by contemporary scholars. T. J. B. Spencer was listed as the Founding Editor and Stanley Wells continued as General Editor, assisted by Paul Edmondson, Head of Research and Knowledge at the Shakespeare Birthplace Trust. The Royal Shakespeare Company was replaced on the back cover: now Penguin Shakespeare editions are 'used and recommended by the National Theatre'.

The linocut prints on these covers were each designed by Clare Melinsky, who looked 'for some nugget to sum up the unique atmosphere of that particular play'.

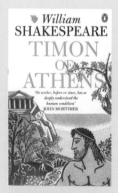

1970 New Penguin Shakespeare
2005 Penguin Shakespeare
ed. G. R. Hibbard, 1970
intro. Nicholas Walton, 2005
cover Clare Melinsky, 2005

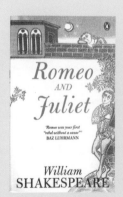

1967 New Penguin Shakespeare
2005 Penguin Shakespeare
ed. T. J. B. Spencer, 1967
intro. Adrian Poole, 2005
cover Clare Melinsky, 2005

Pericles 1607

Almost half of *Pericles* is thought to be the work of George Wilkins, a pamphleteer, innkeeper and pimp. Perhaps unsurprisingly, the play features a scene in a brothel, operated by a pander and his bawdy wife. The rest of the play is a strange, sprawling sea odyssey, narrated by the medieval poet John Gower.

1976 New Penguin Shakespeare
• ed. Philip Edwards

2008 Penguin Shakespeare
2015 Penguin Classics
ed. Eugene Giddens

Coriolanus 1608

'Coriolanus' was an honorific name granted to the Roman general Caius Martius after his suppression of the Volscian city of Corioles. Coriolanus moves into politics, but when his despotic tendencies lead to his deposition, he gathers a Volscian army and marches on Rome. Shakespeare based his account chiefly on Plutarch's *Life of Coriolanus* (55).

1967 New Penguin Shakespeare
2005 Penguin Shakespeare
2015 Penguin Classics
ed. G. R. Hibbard, 1967
intro. Paul Prescott, 2005

The Winter's Tale 1609

The Winter's Tale features Shakespeare's most famous stage direction: the courtier Antigonus is required to 'exit, pursued by a bear' whereafter he is torn apart offstage. The play has a drastic tonal shift after the first three acts, turning from an intense psychological drama into a pastoral comedy. The turning point is marked by the figure of Time, who has a speech in which he moves the action forward sixteen years.

1969 New Penguin Shakespeare
2005 Penguin Shakespeare
2015 Penguin Classics
ed. Ernest Schanzer, 1969
intro. Russ McDonald & Paul Edmondson, 2005

Finally, in 2015, Shakespeare joined the rest of the world's great authors in Penguin Classics and all the editions were rejacketed to match the series. 'Relaunched in April 2015,' reads an announcement in the printed editions, 'the books in the Penguin Shakespeare series are the most widely read editions of Shakespeare's plays available, offering accessible and authoritative versions of the plays to be enjoyed by general readers, students, theatregoers and actors alike.'

1967 New Penguin Shakespeare
2005 Penguin Shakespeare
2015 Penguin Classics
ed. T. J. B. Spencer, 1967
intro. Adrian Poole, 2005

1968 New Penguin Shakespeare
2005 Penguin Shakespeare
2015 Penguin Classics
ed. R. A. Foakes, 1968
intro. Janette Dillon, 2005

1968 New Penguin Shakespeare
2005 Penguin Shakespeare
2015 Penguin Classics
ed. George Hunter, 1972
intro. Kiernan Ryan, 2005

Cymbeline 1610

Cymbeline is inspired by the story of King Cunobeline, from Geoffrey of Monmouth's *History of the Kings of Britain* (76). Posthumus, the banished husband of Princess Imogen, flees to ancient Rome, where he ill-advisedly gambles on the fidelity of his wife. The devious Jachimo then sets about seducing her.

2005 Penguin Shakespeare
2015 Penguin Classics
ed. John Pitcher
—
There was no New Penguin Shakespeare edition of *Cymbeline*.

1968 New Penguin Shakespeare
● ed. Anne Righter

The Tempest 1611

Set on an enchanted island, the action of *The Tempest* is stage-managed by the magician Prospero, with the aid of his airy spirit Ariel. *The Tempest* is thought to be the last play written solely by Shakespeare. At one point Prospero says:

> Our revels now are ended. These our actors,
> As I foretold you, were all spirits, and
> Are melted into the air, into thin air;
> And, like the baseless fabric of this vision,
> The cloud-capped towers, the gorgeous palaces,
> The solemn temples, the great globe itself,
> Yea, all which it inherit, shall dissolve,
> And like this insubstantial pageant faded,
> Leave not a rack behind.

2007 Penguin Shakespeare
2015 Penguin Classics
ed. Martin Butler

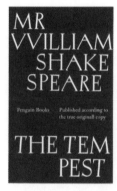

2016
—
This edition of The Tempest was brought out to commemorate the 400th anniversary of Shakespeare's death. It presents the text as it appears in the First Folio (134), with contemporary spellings set out 'According to the True Originall Copy'.

Henry VIII 1613

During a 1613 performance of *Henry VIII*, the special effects set fire to the thatched roof of the Globe theatre and the entire building burned to the ground. *Henry VIII* has more pageantry and spectacle than most other Shakespeare plays. It was co-written by Shakespeare and John Fletcher and dramatizes the king's divorce from Katherine of Aragon and England's split from the Catholic Church, events which had taken place less than a hundred years previously. It culminates with the christening of the future Queen Elizabeth I.

1971 New Penguin Shakespeare
2005 Penguin Shakespeare
2015 Penguin Classics
ed. A. R. Humphreys, 1971
intro. Catherine M. S. Alexander, 2005

The Two Noble Kinsmen 1613–14

The Two Noble Kinsmen is based on 'The Knight's Tale' from *The Canterbury Tales* (89), in which two best friends fall desperately in love with the same woman and must fight for her hand. Like *A Midsummer Night's Dream* (137) it is set in and around the court of Duke Theseus and Hippolyta. It is another collaboration with John Fletcher. Thomas de Quincey (208) thought it was 'perhaps the most superb work in the language'.

1977 New Penguin Shakespeare
2009 Penguin Shakespeare
2015 Penguin Classics
ed. N. W. Bawcutt, 1977
intro. Peter Swaab with Stanley Wells & Paul Edmondson, 2009

These compendium volumes are collections of Shakespeare's greatest plays, using the New Penguin Shakespeare editions.

1994 *Four Comedies*
ed. G. R. Hibbard, Stanley Wells, H. J. Oliver, M. M. Mahood, 1967–8

1994 *Four Histories*
ed. Stanley Wells, P. H. Davison, A. R. Humphreys, 1968–9

1994 *Four Tragedies*
ed. T. J. B Spencer, Anne Barton, Kenneth Muir, G. K. Hunter, 1967–80

1994 *Three Roman Plays*
• ed. Norman Sanders, Emrys Jones, G. R. Hubbard, 1967–77

Ben Jonson 1572–1637

Jonson was the posthumous son of a minister. He became a bricklayer, a soldier and an actor before he was a playwright and a poet. He was granted a royal pension in 1616 making him the first, unofficial Poet Laureate.

Volpone
and Other Plays

Volpone, or The Fox; *The Alchemist*; *Bartholomew Fair*
1605–14

1966 Penguin English Library
Three Comedies
1985 Penguin Classics
2004 Reissued as *Volpone and Other Plays*
ed. Michael Jamieson

Volpone is a wealthy and wily Venetian who pretends to be dying so that his venal acquaintances lavish him with gifts. In *The Alchemist*, a trio of fraudsters claim to have discovered the philosopher's stone; Coleridge (195) considered it to have one of the three most perfect plots in literature. *Bartholomew Fair* is a riotous, messy comedy set at the riotous, messy fair that took place at Smithfield in London every August for over 700 years. It features a puppet play and Ursula, a Pig-woman.

The Complete Poems

As well as a playwright, Jonson was a prolific lyric poet. He published three volumes of poetry: *Epigrams* (1612), *The Forest* (1616) and *Underwoods* (1640). This volume also includes Jonson's translation of *The Art of Poetry* by Horace (30) and 126 miscellaneous poems. 'To My Book', 'On Sir Voluptuous Beast', 'Why I Write Not of Love', 'A Satirical Shrub' and 'An Ode. To Himself' are some of his titles.

1975 Penguin Poets
1988 Penguin Classics
ed. George Parfitt

1988
ed. Bryan Loughrey
& Neil Taylor
—
The Revenger's Tragedy and
The Changeling are included
in the *Three Revenge Tragedies*
anthology; the former is also
in *Five Revenge Tragedies* (132).

Thomas Middleton

1580–1627

Middleton was the son of a wealthy member of the Bricklayer's Guild. He wrote pamphlets and plays and was appointed City Chronologer, which meant he was responsible for organizing public entertainments.

THREE REVENGE TRAGEDIES

Cyril Tourneur, *The Revenger's Tragedy*; John Webster, *The White Devil*; Thomas Middleton and William Rowley, *The Changeling*
1606–22

The Revenger's Tragedy was formerly attributed to Cyril Tourneur but is now widely recognized as the work of Thomas Middleton; Webster's *White Devil* is a dark tale of false identities, infidelity, intrigue and murder; and *The Changeling*, by Middleton and Rowley, is the tale of a ruthless woman who unwittingly engineers her own downfall.

Five Plays 1605–22

A Trick to Catch the Old One; *The Revenger's Tragedy*; *A Chaste Maid in Cheapside*; *Women Beware Women*; *The Changeling*

In *A Trick to Catch the Old One*, a mistress poses as a rich country widow in order to distract a miserly uncle and a hoard of creditors; *A Chaste Maid in Cheapside* concerns the proposed marriage between Moll Yellowhammer and Sir Walter Whorehound; and *Women Beware Women* is a tangled web of illicit love affairs which leads to one of the bloodiest denouements in Jacobean theatre.

1965 Penguin English Library
Three Jacobean Tragedies
2004 Penguin Classics
Three Revenge Tragedies
ed. Gámini Salgádo

John Webster

c. 1580 – c. 15634

Little is known for certain about John Webster. He trained as a lawyer before turning his hand to writing macabre, disturbing plays. T. S. Eliot said that Webster saw 'the skull beneath the skin'.

1972 Penguin English Library
1986 Penguin Classics
ed. D. C. Gunby

Three Plays 1612–19

The White Devil; *The Duchess of Malfi*; *The Devil's Law-Case*

Adulterous schemes result in bloody vengeance in *The White Devil*; the eponymous Duchess of Malfi marries below her social class and consequently perishes at the hands of her bloodthirsty brothers; and *The Devil's Law-Case* is a tragicomedy about a rich and arrogant Neapolitan merchant called Romelio.

The Duchess of Malfi
The White Devil
The Broken Heart
'Tis Pity She's a Whore

1612–33

As well as John Webster's masterpieces *The Duchess of Malfi* and *The White Devil*, this edition includes two plays by John Ford. Ford (1586 – c. 1639) seems to have been a depressive playwright based at the Middle Temple, one of the Inns of Court in London: 'Deep in a dump alone John Ford was gat,' runs a posthumous lyric, 'With folded arms and melancholy hat.' *The Broken Heart* is set in classical Greece and features unhappy marriages and a case of fatal anorexia; *'Tis Pity She's a Whore* is the story of incest, sororicide and a deadly birthday party.

1970 Penguin English Library
Three Plays
● ed. Keith Sturgess

2014
ed. Jane Kingsley-Smith
—
The Duchess of Malfi and *The White Devil*
also appear in Webster's *Three Plays*.

For Enlightenment drama, turn to p.166

The Enlightenment

The Metaphysical Poets

D 38

D 38

John Donne

Edited by John Hayward

D 13

DONNE · SELECTED PROSE

HERBERT · THE COMPLETE ENGLISH POEMS

ISBN 0 14
04.3239 6

ISBN 0 14
04.2348 6

Andrew Marvell: The Complete Poems

ISBN 0 14
042.213 7

JOHN MILTON

SELECTED PROSE

EL91
ISBN 0 14
043.091 1

MILTON · PARADISE LOST

ISBN 0 14
04.2363 X

Selected Poems

Milton

D 21

John Dryden

D 28

D 28

ROCHESTER · THE COMPLETE WORKS

ISBN 0 14
04.2362 1

Alexander Pope

Selected by Douglas Grant

I 14

Poetry

The Age of Enlightenment was a period in which reason and logic came to dominate the fields of philosophy (170), science, politics and literature. Over the course of the 17th and 18th centuries, Enlightenment thinkers used reasoned arguments to develop concepts of personal liberty, religious tolerance and constitutional government, which ultimately led to epoch-defining conflicts such as the English Civil War (171), the French Revolution (178) and the American War of Independence (397).

The English poetry of the earlier portion of this period has been dubbed 'metaphysical' by Samuel Johnson (183). His choice of this unusual Aristotelian (29) term was probably a sardonic reference to a previous comment made by Dryden (151), who said of John Donne (149) that he 'affects the metaphysics [...] and perplexes the minds of the fair sex with nice speculations of philosophy, when he should engage their hearts, and entertain them with the softnesses of love.'

Despite Johnson and Dryden's skepticism, 20th-century writers have championed the significance of the loose group of 17th-century poets, none more so than T. S. Eliot, who saw that

> a thought to Donne was an experience; it modified his sensibility. [...] The poets in question have, like other poets, various faults. But they were, at best, engaged in the task of trying to find the verbal equivalent for states of mind and feeling. And this means both that they are more mature, and that they wear better, than later poets of certainly not less literary ability.

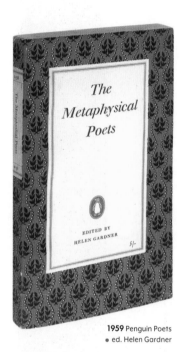

1959 Penguin Poets
● ed. Helen Gardner

METAPHYSICAL POETRY

16th – 18th centuries

Burrow's anthology showcases the most famous exponents of metaphysical poetry, such as John Donne (149), George Herbert (149), Andrew Marvell (150) and Henry Vaughan, but he also includes lesser-known poems such as Sir John Suckling's 'Love's Clock', Anne Bradstreet's 'A Letter to her Husband' and Thomas Philipot's 'On Myself Being Sick of a Fever'.

2006
ed. Colin Burrow
—
While Burrow was working on his anthology, his grandmother died at the age of a hundred. 'She was one of the first generation of students of English literature to grow up with a belief that metaphysical poetry mattered,' he writes, 'and thought that Donne was better than Shakespeare (134).'

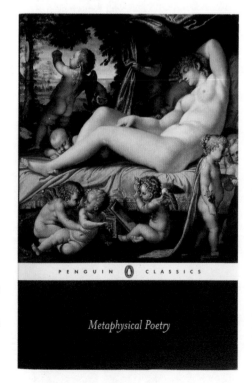

John Donne

1572–1631

Donne had a promising career in politics until he secretly married his master's niece, Anne More, upon which he was thrown into the Fleet Prison. He wrote a forlorn note to his new wife: 'John Donne, Anne Donne, Un-done'. Nonetheless, he became a Member of Parliament, a priest, a Justice of the Peace and the Dean of St Paul's Cathedral in London.

1950 Penguin Poets
● ed. John Hayward

1971 Penguin Education
The Complete English Poems
1976 Penguin Poets
1986 Penguin Classics
ed. A. J. Smith

2006 *Selected Poems*
ed. Ilona Bell

2012 *Collected Poetry*
ed. Ilona Bell

Poems

Donne's poems range from the sensual and erotic to the devout and the spiritually transcendent, in a variety of verse forms that include epigrams, epicedes, elegies, sonnets, songs and satires. He was a master of the flirtatious, preposterously reasoned argument, as when he attempts to seduce his mistress by observing that their blood has already mingled in the body of an engorged flea. 'The intricacy and subtlety of his imagination are the length and depth of the furrow made by his passion,' wrote Yeats (267).

Selected Prose

Donne was more famous in his lifetime for his sermons than for his poetry. This anthology showcases the best of his prose, from short 'paradoxes' and problems – such as 'Why Doth the Poxe so Much Affect to Undermine the Nose?' – to his *Biathanatos*, a discussion of whether suicide is ever justified. Before Donne died, he posed for a portrait sculpture in his own death shroud.

1987
ed. Neil Rhodes

George Herbert

1593–1633

Herbert was born into an aristocratic Welsh family and was initially set on an ambitious career in public office, but he had a change of heart and was ordained a deacon instead, settling in the small parish of Bemerton, near Salisbury. He died just three years later, at the age of 39. That year, his friend Nicholas Ferrar from the nearby village of Little Gidding published Herbert's English poems under the title *The Temple: Sacred Poems and Private Ejaculations*.

1992
● ed. John Tobin

2015
ed. John Drury & Victoria Moul

The Complete Poetry

Herbert wrote beautifully crafted devotional lyrics in both English and Latin. He experimented with form, as in his pattern poems 'The Altar' and 'Easter-wings', in which the lines of verse visually depict the subjects of the poems. Other examples of his experimental style include 'The Water-course' which provides alternative end-rhymes, 'Paradise', whose rhyme-words are increasingly truncated, and the self-explanatory 'Ana-[MARY / ARMY] gram'.

Andrew Marvell 1621–1678

After absconding from Cambridge, dallying with Catholicism and travelling throughout Europe, Marvell settled at Nun Appleton in Yorkshire to tutor the daughter of Lord Fairfax. Most of his poems date from this period, some of them apparently addressed to his pupil, Mary. He was a staunch republican and a supporter of Oliver Cromwell, a friend of John Milton and later Member of Parliament for Hull.

1972 Penguin Education
1976 Penguin Poets
1985 Penguin Classics
ed. Elizabeth Story Donno, 1972
intro. Jonathan Bate, 2005

The Complete Poems c. 1642–78

Marvell wrote in a variety of registers, from the erotic 'To His Coy Mistress', in which he describes the swelling of his 'vegetable love', to the politically partisan 'Horatian Ode upon Cromwell's Return from Ireland' and the environmentally astute 'The Garden'. T. S. Eliot described his style as 'more than a technical accomplishment, or the vocabulary and syntax of an epoch; it is what we have designated tentatively as wit, a tough reasonableness beneath the slight lyric grace'.

John Milton

1608–1674

Milton was the son of a scrivener. After attending St Paul's School in London and Christ's College, Cambridge, he spent six years in scholarly retirement before embarking on a political career, championing Presbyterianism and in time the new Commonwealth. Oliver Cromwell appointed him Secretary for Foreign Tongues to the Council of State and Milton worked tirelessly defending the English revolution to the rest of the world, which hastened the deterioration of his eyesight. Blind and impoverished, he lived a quiet life in London after the Restoration, working on his epic poem *Paradise Lost*, which he composed entirely through dictation.

1974 Penguin English Library
Selected Prose
● ed. C. A. Patrides

2014
ed. William Poole

Areopagitica 1642–54
and Other Writings

Milton was more famous for his polemical prose than for his poetry while he was alive. His *Areopagitica* is an impassioned attack on censorship laws and a call for a free press: he calls good books 'precious life-blood'. This volume also includes selections from his other radical pamphlets, his controversial defence of divorce and the subversive *Ready and Easy Way to Establish a Free Commonwealth*, which almost cost him his life.

1989
● ed. Christopher Ricks

2000
ed. John Leonard

Paradise Lost
1667

Milton wrote his masterpiece to 'justify the ways of God to men'. The most striking character is Satan, once the most beautiful angel in heaven, now cast down into Tartarus for leading a rebellion against God. Unrepentant, Satan presides over the infernal city of Pandæmonium, believing it 'Better to reign in Hell, than serve in Heav'n'. William Blake (192) thought the 'reason Milton wrote in fetters when he wrote of Angels & God, and at liberty when of Devils & Hell, is because he was a true Poet and of the Devil's party without knowing it'.

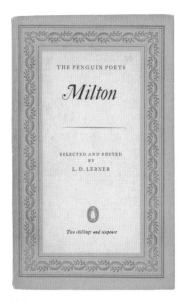

1953 Penguin Poets
● ed. L. D. Lerner

Poems

Although Milton is best remembered for *Paradise Lost*, which features in these editions, he also wrote many other poetic works, including *Lycidas*, a pastoral elegy commemorating a drowned university friend, *Paradise Regained*, a thematic sequel to *Paradise Lost* focusing on the temptation of Christ, and *Samson Agonistes*, a verse dramatization of the Samson and Delilah story from the Old Testament (4).

1998 *The Complete Poems*
ed. John Leonard

2007 *Selected Poems*
ed. John Leonard

John Dryden

1631–1700

Dryden was the foremost English writer of the late 17th century. Having processed behind Oliver Cromwell's coffin, shoulder to shoulder with Milton (150) and Marvell (150), he swiftly switched allegiance after the Restoration, and in 1668 Charles II appointed him the first official Poet Laureate. He cultivated a long and distinguished career as a professional man of letters, writing prodigious quantities of panegyrics, satires, comedies, tragedies, songs, lyric poetry, works of literary criticism and translations, including a rendering of Virgil's *Aeneid* (44). He nursed a long-standing and mutual dislike of John Wilmot, Earl of Rochester (152) and in 1679 he was attacked by thugs, probably hired by the earl. He was 'the most masculine of our poets,' wrote Gerard Manley Hopkins (266);

'his style and his rhythms lay the strongest stress of all our literature on the naked thew and sinew of the English language.'

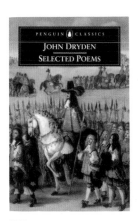

1955 Penguin Poets
● ed. Douglas Grant

2001
ed. Steven N. Zwicker &
David Bywaters

Selected Poems

Dryden established the heroic couplet as the dominant form of English verse. As Alexander Pope (152) put it,

> Dryden taught to join
> The varying pause, the full resounding line,
> The long majestic march, and energy divine.

He was the first bombast to use the phrase 'blaze of glory' and the first grammarian to outlaw 'preposition stranding' at the end of sentences. (His reasoning was that prepositions are never used in Latin to end sentences with.) He is perhaps best remembered for his satires, among which his masterpiece is *Absalom and Achitophel*, ostensibly a retelling of Absalom's rebellion against King David in the second Book of Samuel, but in reality a thinly disguised commentary on the inability of Charles II to produce an heir and the contemporary Exclusion Crisis and Popish Plot.

John Wilmot, Earl of Rochester

1647–1680

Rochester was a member of the 'merry gang' of mistresses and riotous male companions who surrounded Charles II. Marvell (150) considered him 'the only man in England that had the true veine of satyre' and he is remembered today for his scathing satires and his highly explicit poems about sex. He died at the age of 33 from venereal disease.

Selected Works

Rochester's poetry was influenced by Ronsard (129), Ovid (46) and Horace (45). His 'Satyr against Mankind' is a celebrated attack on rationalism in favour of sensual experience. Other titles include 'The Maimed Debauchee', 'Fair Cloris in a pigsty lay' and 'A Ramble in St James's Park', which includes the memorable quatrain:

> Had she picked out to rub her arse on
> Some stiff-pricked clown or well-hung
>   parson,
> Each job of whose spermatic sluice
> Had filled her cunt with wholesome juice

Some find his poetry shocking; others find much to admire. William Hazlitt (208) said his verses 'cut and sparkle like diamonds'.

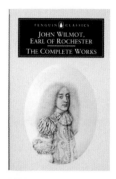

1994 *The Complete Works*
2004 Reissued as *Selected Works*
ed. Frank H. Ellis

Alexander Pope 1688–1744

Pope is said to have read an illustrated edition of Homer (16) at the age of eight, which inspired a lifelong passion for poetry. He also developed tuberculosis of the spine as a child, which gave him a hunchback and stunted his growth. The publication of *The Rape of the Lock* in 1712 confirmed him as one of the most celebrated poets of his age, but after the death of Queen Anne in 1714 he was socially sidelined, on account of his Catholicism and anti-Whig connections, and he spent the latter half of his life in his Thames-side villa at Twickenham, working on translations of Homer, a sequence of acerbic Horatian parodies (45) and his final masterpiece, *The Dunciad*, a satirical fulmination against 'hacks', 'scribblers' and 'dunces'. This poem made him so generally unpopular, he never left home without a pair of loaded pistols and his Great Dane, called Bounce.

THE PENGUIN POETS

Alexander Pope

A SELECTION BY
DOUGLAS GRANT

One shilling and sixpence

1950 Penguin Poets
● ed. Douglas Grant

2011
ed. Leo Damrosch

The Rape of the Lock
and Other Major Writings
1711–42

In the riotous *Rape of the Lock*, polite society is scandalized when the Baron snips a lock of Belinda's hair without her permission. Pope wittily dresses this 'dire offence' in the elaborate style of a Homeric epic, with ranks of attendant sylphs, ekphrastic descriptions of petticoats and a journey to the splenetic underworld. This volume also includes 'An Essay on Criticism', Pope's early poem about the rules of poetry and the virtues of a critic; his philosophical 'Essay on Man'; the auto-biographical 'Epistle to Dr Arbuthnot'; *The Dunciad*; and letters to contemporaries such as Swift (159) and Gay (169).

Fiction

The modern European novel was born at the beginning of the 17th century. Though some earlier works have been described as novels, such as the *Satyricon* by Petronius (49), *The Tale of Genji* by <u>Murasaki Shikibu</u> (111) and the picaresque *Lazarillo de Tormes* (124), Cervantes announced that he was the first to:

> set up in the square of our republic a billiard table where each one can come to amuse himself without fear of injury; I mean without hurt to soul or body

Other important early novels include Madame de Lafayette's *The Princesse de Clèves* (156) and Daniel Defoe's *Robinson Crusoe* (157).

Cervantes

1547–1616

Miguel de Cervantes Saavedra was the son of a barber-surgeon. He fought at the Battle of Lepanto, was captured by Barbary pirates, became an Algerian slave and spent several stints in prison. He is considered the greatest writer in the Spanish language.

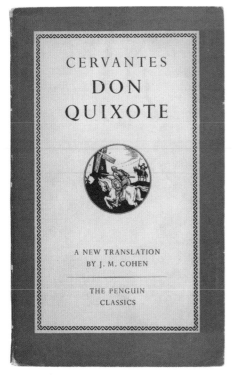

1950
● ed. J. M. Cohen
—
In 1951, H. F. Paroissien, the manager of Penguin Books Inc. in the USA, wired to say that J. M. Cohen's translation of *Don Quixote* had been adopted enthusiastically at Princeton University: although 'the boys there got a laugh out of the rendition of *castrador de puercos* as "sow-gelder" [...] and they conclude that Cohen is not much acquainted with farm animals.' Cohen retorted that the term sow-gelder had been in use since 1515, which 'suggests to me,' he said, 'that the ancients had not the same acquaintance with the facts of life as our trans-Atlantic cousins.'

Exemplary Stories 1590–1613

The six stories in this selection include *The Little Gypsy Girl*, about hidden identities and life as a gypsy; *The Glass Graduate*, about a man who eats a drugged quince and becomes convinced that he's made of glass; *The Deceitful Marriage*, about a dishonest suitor and his even wilier bride; and *The Dogs' Colloquy*, in which the bridegroom from the previous story, suffering from venereal disease, overhears a hallucin-atory night-time conversation between two dogs.

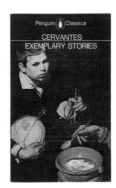

1972
trans. C. A. Jones

The Ingenious Hidalgo
Don Quixote
de la Mancha
1605–1615

Don Quixote is ostensibly a satire on 'books of chivalry': a country gentleman becomes so immersed in romantic tales of knight-errantry that he embarks on his own preposterous adventures, riding his old nag Rocinante, recruiting the simple farmer Sancho Panza as his squire and famously 'tilting at windmills', believing them to be giants with vast flailing arms. But this great book is also a tapestry of multiple plot strands and stories within stories, raising questions about the nature of reality and the implications of reading. In the second part, published ten years after the first, Don Quixote has become famous because people have read his previous adventures. <u>Fyodor Dostoyevsky</u> (371) considered it 'the ultimate and most sublime work of human thinking'. In 2002, the Nobel Institute voted *Don Quixote* 'the greatest book of all time'.

2001
trans. John Rutherford

J. M. COHEN

'I was a scholar of St Paul's School, and Exhibitioner of Queens' College, Cambridge,' wrote John Michael Cohen in 1951, 'though who would care to know that I can't guess. My greatest single achievement, of which I am still proud, was to teach myself to read Russian in the train between Maidenhead and Paddington. As you may guess, I travelled the route on more than one occasion.'

Cohen also taught himself Spanish during the Second World War, and in 1946 he was commissioned to translate *Don Quixote* (153) for Penguin Classics. Thereafter he translated Spanish, French and Russian titles for the Classics and assisted E. V. Rieu (17) in editing the modern-language translations in the series. He once described himself as 'the translation factory'. He introduced many Latin American writers to English

readers, including Jorge Luis Borges, Octavio Paz and Gabriel García Márquez. As well as translating classics, he edited *The Penguin Book of Comic and Curious Verse* (1952) and *The Penguin Dictionary of Quotations* (1960). 'He did perhaps more than anyone else in his generation,' read his obituary, 'to introduce British readers to the classics of world literature by making them available in good modern English translations.'

2016
trans. Nancy L. Canepa, 2007
fwd. Jack Zipes, 2007
ill. Carmelo Lettere, 2007

Giambattista Basile

1566–1632

Basile was a Neapolitan poet, courtier and soldier. *The Tale of Tales* was the first national collection of fairy tales published in Europe, and includes the first literary versions of the 'Sleeping Beauty', 'Cinderella', 'Hansel and Gretel' and 'Rapunzel' stories. It was published posthumously by Basile's sister Adriana.

The Tale of Tales

or, Entertainment for Little Ones

1634–6

The cursed Princess Zoza must rescue her future husband by organizing a storytelling festival: ten sharp-minded women tell one story each day for five days. The book's subtitle is 'Entertainment for Little Ones', but it's hard to imagine toddlers enjoying stories such as 'The Old Woman Who Was Skinned', 'Penta with the Chopped-Off Hands' or 'The Seven Little Pork Rinds', although 'The Two Little Pizzas' might be more appealing. These fairy tales come with a health warning: they are dark, violent and often comic, definitely written for an adult audience.

Margaret Cavendish

1623–1673

Margaret Lucas Cavendish, Duchess of Newcastle, published many volumes of poetry, fiction, romance, philosophy, drama, orations, scientific treatises and memoirs. She was a self-styled maverick who challenged patriarchal codes of femininity, championed animal welfare and vigorously defended the monarchy. She dressed eccentrically and was the first woman to attend a meeting of the Royal Society in London in 1667.

The Blazing World

and Other Writings

1656–1666

Cavendish's utopian romance *The Blazing World* is one of the earliest examples of science fiction. A young woman journeys to a parallel world, accessible via the North Pole, where animals talk and war is conducted with the aid of submarines and aerial bombardment. This anthology also includes 'The Contract', a legally harmonious romance, and 'Assaulted and Pursued Chastity', a story about the freedom a woman can achieve by dressing as a man.

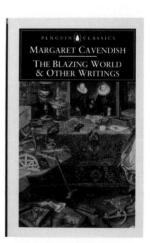

1994
ed. Kate Lilley, 1992

Hans Jakob Christoffel von Grimmelshausen

1621–1676

Grimmelshausen, the son of an innkeeper, was kidnapped at the age of ten by a passing band of Hessian soldiers and dragged around the Thirty Years War, witnessing the ravage of central Europe. He served as a musketeer in the imperial army and subsequently worked collecting taxes, selling horses and running taverns. In 1665, he became a magistrate and devoted the rest of his life to writing.

The Adventures of Simplicius Simplicissimus

1668

'Gaudy, wild, raw, amusing, rollicking and ragged, boiling with life, on intimate terms with death and evil,' said Thomas Mann, describing *Simplicius* – 'but in the end, contrite and fully tired of a world wasting itself in blood, pillage and lust.' Germany's first great novel describes the adventures of a roguish simpleton, Simplicius, as he roams through Europe during the Thirty Years War, witnessing horrors, devastating diseases and various forms of prostitution. He visits Russia, France and an alternative magical realm inhabited by mermen.

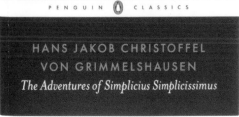

2018
trans. J. A. Underwood
intro. Kevin Cramer

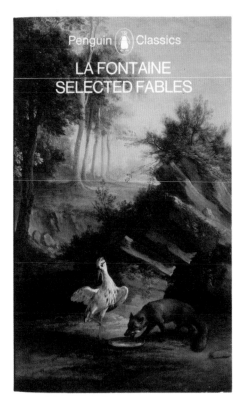

Jean de la Fontaine

1621–1695

La Fontaine had one son with his wife with whom he was later estranged, and he was wholly uninvolved in his son's upbringing. 'Ah yes,' he is said to have remarked, when he was introduced to the grown-up boy, 'I thought I had seen him somewhere.'

Selected Fables

1668–94

La Fontaine published twelve books of fables, drawn largely from Aesop (19), but also Rabelais (123), Boccaccio (86), Machiavelli (120) and the *Pańćatantra* (9). These entertaining children's tales are also sophisticated satires on human nature: titles include 'The Mountain Which Gave Birth', 'The Rat Who Retired from the World', 'The Crayfish and Her Daughter' and 'The Elephant and Jupiter's Monkey'.

1982
trans. James Michie, 1979
intro. Geoffrey Grigson, 1979

1992
trans. Robin Buss

1962 Penguin Books
• trans. Nancy Mitford

Madame de Lafayette
1634–1693

Marie-Madeleine Pioche de la Vergne married the Comte de Lafayette, but they lived largely separate lives. She ran a literary salon in Paris with her friends Madame de Sévigné (182) and La Rochefoucauld (172).

The Princesse de Clèves 1678

The Princesse de Clèves is the first French novel. Lafayette intentionally rejected the conventions of romance to create a psychologically realistic historical fiction, set at the court of Henri II, in which a beautiful young princess fosters an unrequited passion for the dashing Duc de Nemours.

Aphra Behn 1677–89

Behn visited the then-English colony of Surinam as a young woman, worked as a spy in Antwerp during the Dutch wars and belonged to the same literary circle as John Wilmot, Earl of Rochester (152). She wrote poetry, plays, stories and political propaganda. In *A Room of One's Own*, Virginia Woolf declared her the first Englishwoman to earn her living by writing: 'All women together ought to let flowers fall upon the tomb of Aphra Behn,' she writes, 'for it was she who earned them the right to speak their minds.'

Oroonoko, The Rover
and Other Works
1677–89

Oroonoko tells the tragic story of a noble and lovelorn African prince, Oroonoko, tricked into slavery in English Surinam, who spearheads a valiant but ultimately futile rebellion. It is considered one of the first English novels and an early work of anti-slavery propaganda. *The Rover* is an uproarious play about an amorous group of English revellers abroad, visiting Naples at carnival time. Other works in this edition include the erotic epistolary novel, *Love-Letters to a Gentleman*, the play *The Widow Ranter* and the poems 'On Her Loving Two Equally' and 'On Desire: A Pindaric'.

1992
ed. Janet Todd

2003 *Oroonoko*
ed. Janet Todd

In 2003, Todd edited a slim edition containing *Oroonoko* only.

Daniel Defoe

1660–1731

Daniel Foe was a hosier, brickmaker, secret agent and journalist. He wrote hundreds of books on topics ranging from politics to psychology, marriage and crime. He employed a vast array of different pen names over the course of his career and changed his own to 'Defoe'. Some consider him the first English novelist. He died hiding from his creditors and was buried in an unmarked grave in Bunhill Fields, a one-time plague cemetery in London, which now sports an obelisk in memory of Defoe.

2005
ed. Richard Hamblyn, 2003

The Storm 1704

Britain's worst storm on record began on 24 November 1703 and lasted for a week: 8,000 people died, cows were thrown into the trees and whirligig windmills spontaneously combusted. Defoe's book is a vivid, journalistic account of this devastating hurricane and its aftermath.

Robinson Crusoe 1719

Many contemporary readers believed that *Robinson Crusoe* was the genuine autobiography of a castaway, who survived for 28 years on a desert island near Trinidad, negotiating the lack of food, shelter and clothes, and his encounters with cannibals, captives and mutineers. He is famously thunderstruck when he comes across 'the print of a man's naked foot on the shore'. Defoe based his fictional story on the genuine experiences of Alexander Selkirk, a Scottish castaway who spent four years on an uninhabited island in the South Pacific with nothing but a musket, a hatchet, a knife, a cooking pot, a <u>Bible</u> (4) and some bedding.

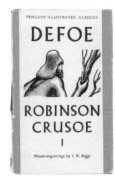 

1938 Illustrated Classics
Published in two volumes

● ill. J. R. Biggs
1966 Penguin English Library
● ed. Angus Ross

A Journal of the Plague Year
1722

Defoe's historical novel about the Great Plague of 1666 is the fictional account of a survivor, wandering the deserted, plague-ridden streets of London, watching daubed crosses appearing on doors and approaching the brink of mass burial pits.

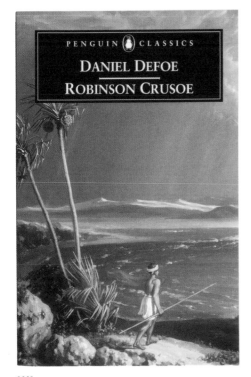

2001
ed. John Richetti

1966 Penguin English Library
● ed. Anthony Burgess

2003
ed. Cynthia Wall

'I can't describe my ties,' wrote Anthony Burgess to Jim Cochrane, an early editor of the Penguin English Library series, 'so I'll wear dark glasses. I am jowling and morose.' They met for a drink in the Café Royal in London and Burgess agreed to edit and introduce *A Journal of the Plague Year*. Wall includes Burgess's 1966 introduction in an appendix.

The Fortunes and Misfortunes of the Famous
Moll Flanders

1722

Born in Newgate Prison, Moll Flanders narrates the lively story of her picaresque life, which features incest, adultery, bigamy, prostitution and pickpocketing. She is a consummate manipulator and ultimately succeeds in enchanting the reader, despite her many transgressions.

1978 Penguin English Library
● ed. Juliet Mitchell

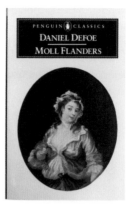

1989
ed. David Blewett

Roxana
The Fortunate Mistress

1724

When Roxana's husband leaves her destitute, with five children to support, she embarks on a career as a high-class prostitute. She moves from man to man, scaling the heights of wealth and luxury, but ends her narrative with a dark reference to unrevealed further 'calamities'.

1982 Penguin English Library
1987 Penguin Classics
ed. David Blewett

A Tour through the Whole Island of Great Britain

1724–7

Defoe describes several 'tours' throughout the length and breadth of Britain, blending research with personal observations to produce an intimate and detailed portrait of the landscapes, history, traditions and cultures of a country on the eve of the Industrial Revolution. After *Robinson Crusoe* (157), Defoe's *Tour* was his most popular and financially successful work during his lifetime.

1971 Penguin English Library
1986 Penguin Classics
ed. Pat Rogers

THE PENGUIN BOOK OF THE BRITISH SHORT STORY
from Daniel Defoe to John Buchan

18th – 20th centuries

'There are sumptuous riches in the British short story,' writes Philip Hensher, 'and the raucously exuberant piece of playfulness is only part of it. [...] the British short story can be most itself when rumbustious, violent, extravagant, fantastical; above all, when it yields to a national taste for the theatrical.' The first instalment of Hensher's anthology of British short stories stretches from a ghost story by Defoe (157) to a First World War tale by Buchan (436), with contributions from Henry Fielding (161), Mary Lamb (207), Margaret Oliphant (233), Arnold Bennett (280) and 30 others.

2016
ed. Philip Hensher

Montesquieu 1689 - 1755

Charles-Louis de Secondat was born into a French political dynasty near Bordeaux. He was a councillor at the Bordeaux Parlement, a provincial court, and *président à mortier* after he inherited the barony of Montesquieu. In 1726 he sold the post of *président* and travelled around Europe conducting love affairs. He published his most important philosophical work, *The Spirit of the Laws*, in 1748.

Persian Letters 1721

Montesquieu's epistolary novel tells the story of two Persian noblemen, Usbek and Rica, who travel around Europe in search of wisdom. In letters home to their wives and eunuchs, they comment on the contrast between west and east and on the freedom, frivolity and immodesty of Europe.

1973
trans. C. J. Betts

1938 Illustrated Classics
• ill. Theodore Nash
1967 Penguin English Library
• ed. Peter Dixon

Jonathan Swift

1667 – 1745

Swift was Dean of St Patrick's Cathedral in Dublin. He was a ferocious pacifist, who strove to improve the political situation in Ireland through satirical pamphlets and frequent, irascible visits to London. He never married, but he had intimate liaisons with Esther Johnson and Esther Vanhomrigh, which he recorded respectively in his *Journal to Stella* and the poem 'Cadenus and Vanessa'. He suffered from Ménière's disease throughout his life, a disorder of the inner ear that led to frequent fits of vertigo and giddiness.

Gulliver's Travels 1726

When Lemuel Gulliver is shipwrecked northwest of Tasmania, he wakes to find his arms, legs and hair strongly fastened to the ground with slender ligatures. Thus begins Gulliver's series of adventures to the lands of the diminutive Lilliputians and the giant Brobdingnagians, the airborne Laputians, the magical Glubbdubdribians, the immortal Struldbruggs and the Japanese. His final voyage takes him to the land of the Houyhnhnms, a breed of majestic, talking horses that rule over a grotesque humanoid race known as Yahoos. On his return, Gulliver finds the smell of his wife and child intolerable; he resorts to his stable for hours a day, talking to the horses.

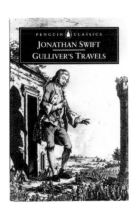

2001
ed. Robert Demaria, Jr.

A Modest Proposal
and Other Writings 1699 – c. 1738

Swift presents his 'modest proposal' as a solution to the poverty crisis in Ireland: he suggests that children, at the age of one, should be turned into 'most delicious, nourishing, and wholesome Food; whether Stewed, Roasted, Baked, or Boiled'. 'I make no doubt,' he goes on, that a baby will 'equally serve in a Fricasie, or Ragout.' This edition includes other examples of his prose pamphlets, essays and letters.

2009
ed. Carole Fabricant

1950
trans. Leonard Tancock
rev. Jean Sgard, 1991

Abbé Prévost 1697–1763

Antoine-François Prévost was a Jesuit soldier (72) who became a Benedictine monk, before abandoning the cloister for a literary career. He wrote romantic adventures and translated the voluminous novels of Samuel Richardson into French. He died of apoplexy.

Manon Lescaut 1731

The beautiful and fascinating Manon Lescaut funds a passionate love affair with the young Chevalier des Grieux by taking another wealthy lover. The doomed Chevalier cannot resist her charms and Manon cannot bring herself to give up her insalubrious income. The novel was wildly popular in France, despite or perhaps because it was immediately banned by the authorities.

Samuel Richardson

1689–1761

Richardson was a stationer and printer, who published *The True Briton* periodical and the *Journals* of the House of Commons. He was also a dedicated and talented letter writer. While compiling an anthology of model letters, he was inspired to write *Pamela*, his first, epistolary novel. Richardson's remains can be examined on request in the crypt of St Bride's Church on Fleet Street in London, where his bones are preserved in an acid-free cardboard box.

1980 Penguin English Library
1985 Penguin Classics
ed. Peter Sabor
intro. Margaret A. Doody

Pamela
or, Virtue Rewarded 1740

Pamela is the tale of 15-year-old Pamela Andrews, a maidservant who defends herself valiantly against the amorous advances of her mistress's son, Mr B., despite his increasingly violent threats and the machinations of his 'unwomanly' housekeeper. The book was extremely popular at the time, but its straitlaced portrait of a 'model woman' also provoked a flurry of ridicule, most notably in the satirical novels of Henry Fielding (161).

Clarissa
or, The History of a Young Lady 1747

Clarissa Harlowe fears the prospect of a forced marriage and so flees with the gallant Robert Lovelace. As Lovelace's sexual advances grow increasingly determined, however, Clarissa's moral standards become correspondingly scrupulous, with ultimately tragic consequences. With *Clarissa*, Richardson founded one of the most prominent, and most satirized, subgenres of the 18th century, the 'novel of sensibility', a form which foregrounded the emotional states of its main characters and aimed to evoke improving responses in its readers.

Through a printing error, Tancock's 1950 edition of *Manon Lescaut* sported the same roundel as Rieu's translation of Virgil's *Eclogues* (43). The roundel which should have been used was this one:

Before the publication of his translation of Homer's *Iliad* (16), Rieu wrote, 'I only ask that they should not print – shall we say – the medallion designed for *Manon Lescaut!* Talking of that, I have had a charming letter from Tancock, who expresses only mild surprise at the appearance of Pan on his cover.' The correct roundel was reinstated on subsequent print runs.

1985
ed. Angus Ross
—
At 1,536 pages Richardson's vast masterpiece is the longest single-volume novel published in Penguin Classics.

Henry Fielding 1707–1754

Fielding was a theatre manager, playwright and lawyer, who founded London's first police force with his blind half-brother John. He married Charlotte Cradock in 1734, the model for Sophia Western in *Tom Jones*. In his last months he travelled to Lisbon, seeking a beneficial climate for cirrhosis of the liver; he died there.

Joseph Andrews
and Shamela 1741–2

Fielding's first two novels were satirical responses to Richardson's *Pamela* (160). *Shamela* is a short parody, in which Shamela is revealed to be sexually voracious, deliberately targeting 'Squire Booby'. *Joseph Andrews* is a 'comic Epic-Poem in Prose', written in 'imitation of the Manner of Cervantes' (153). Joseph is Pamela's brother, an ingénue footman who is fired after repelling the advances of the lustful Lady Booby, Squire Booby's aunt.

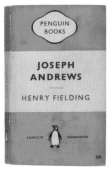

1954 Penguin Books
● —
1977 Penguin English Library
● ed. R. F. Brissenden

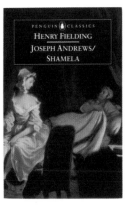

1999
ed. Judith Hawley

The History of Tom Jones
A Foundling 1749

The first six books of *Tom Jones* are set in Somerset, on the estate of the virtuous Squire Allworthy, who adopts Tom as a foundling child; the middle six follow Tom's picaresque adventures on the road to London; and the final six are set amidst the sensuous delights and dangers of the capital, as Tom and his childhood sweetheart Sophia struggle to reunite. Coleridge (195) considered it one of 'the three most perfect plots ever planned'. The others were Sophocles' *King Oedipus* (21) and Jonson's *Alchemist* (145).

1966 Penguin English Library
● ed. R. P. C. Mutter

2005
ed. Thomas Keymer &
Alice Wakely

John Cleland
1710–1789

Cleland joined the East India Company and worked in Bombay at the start of his career. He returned to London in 1741, determined to make his living as a writer, but he was not successful: he prepared *Fanny Hill* for publication while languishing in debtors' prison and it was published just before his release. When he got out he was immediately prosecuted again for having written such a scandalous book. It was officially withdrawn although it continued to circulate in illicit editions. It was not published legally in the UK until 1970.

Fanny Hill
or, Memoirs of a Woman of Pleasure
1748–9

This erotic work is one of the most notorious and widely banned novels in the history of literature. It consists of two letters, written by a respectable middle-aged woman, describing the sexual exploits of her teenage years: how she was lured into prostitution, inducted into the arts of desire and introduced to the handsome Charles, who hopes to rescue her. At one point she seduces a particularly well-endowed footman, uncovering 'not the play-thing of a boy, not the weapon of a man, but a maypole of so enormous a standard, that had proportions been observed, it must have belonged to a young giant.'

1985
ed. Peter Wagner

Tobias Smollett
1721 – 1771

Smollett was a Scottish surgeon who wrote a series of picaresque, globe-trotting novels. He founded two political periodicals, translated _Don Quixote_ (153), and kept an open table for impoverished Scottish writers in London, but he suffered from recurrent ill health and travelled in pursuit of more salutary climes. His splenetic _Travels through France and Italy_ (1766) provoked Laurence Sterne's _Sentimental Journey_ (163), in which Smollett appears, perhaps a little unfairly, as the irascible 'Smelfungus'. George Orwell considered Smollett 'Scotland's best novelist'.

Roderick Random 1748

Smollett's first, semi-autobiographical novel is narrated by its Scottish hero, a naval surgeon, who travels the world seeking his fortune and chasing the hand of the beautiful Narcissa. The story reaches its denouement in Argentina.

1995
ed. David Blewett

Humphry Clinker 1771

In Smollett's last and greatest novel, a gouty squire called Matthew Bramble travels around Britain with his nephew, niece, sister, his sister's maid Winifred and his trusty footman, Humphry Clinker, visiting fashionable resort towns and encountering pimps, drunks and con men. Most of the book is narrated through letters written by five different members of the party.

1967 Penguin English Library
• ed. Angus Ross

2008
ed. Shaun Regan
intro. Jeremy Lewis

Charlotte Lennox c. 1730 – 1804

Lennox was born in Gibraltar and brought up in New York. On her arrival in England, she entered literary society and received the patronage of Samuel Johnson (183) and Samuel Richardson (160). She wrote novels, plays and edited a periodical called _The Lady's Museum_. At the end of her life she was supported by the Royal Literary Fund.

The Female Quixote 1752

Lennox's playful novel inverts _Don Quixote_ (153). The sheltered protagonist, Arabella, reads so many French romances, she expects her life to be equally full of romantic adventure. She confidently slays lovers with smouldering looks, mistakes a transvestite prostitute for a gentlewoman in distress and cheerfully throws herself into the Thames to escape a group of 'ravishers'. _The Female Quixote_ was one of the inspirations behind Jane Austen's _Northanger Abbey_ (200).

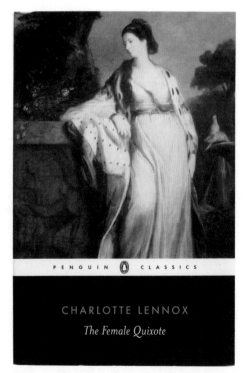

2006
ed. Amanda Gilroy & Wil Verhoven

Laurence Sterne 1713–1768

Sterne took holy orders at 23 and received the living of a series of Yorkshire parishes. He wrote, by his own admission, 'not to be fed but to be famous', at which he succeeded impressively. He became the permanent curate at Coxwold, a village in North Yorkshire, and spent the rest of his life writing there, receiving adulation in London and travelling Europe to improve his health. He named his home 'Shandy Hall' after the fictional house in *Tristram Shandy*.

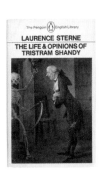

1967 Penguin English Library
ed. Graham Petrie
intro. Christopher Ricks

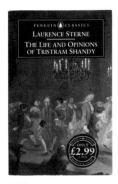

1997
intro. Christopher Ricks, 1967
ed. Melvyn & Joan New, 1978

1938 Illustrated Classics
● ill. Gwen Raverat
1967 Penguin English Library
● ed. Graham Petrie

2001
ed. Paul Goring

The Life and Opinions of Tristram Shandy, Gentleman

1759–67

'*Tristram Shandy* is the greatest shaggy-dog story in the language,' writes Christopher Ricks. The novel appears to be a fictional autobiography, but the narrator isn't born until the start of Volume III. The main events of Tristram's early life are his dysfunctional conception, his auspicious nose being crushed by forceps, his mis-baptism as Tristram (considered the worst of all names by his father) and his accidental circumcision by sash window. Sterne revels in digressions, elisions, diversions, parentheses, double entendres and soaring metafictional flights of fancy. The book includes an entirely black page, to mark the death of Parson Yorick; a marbled page of endpaper; a space for the reader to draw a portrait of the beautiful Widow Wadman; and a wiggly line to illustrate the flourish that Corporal Trim makes with his stick. Sterne inserts humorous references to Burton (181), Bacon (127), Rabelais (123) and particularly Locke (173).

A Sentimental Journey through France and Italy 1768

Parson Yorick is a marginal character in *Tristram Shandy*, but he takes centre stage as the narrator of this novel. Through wordplay, ellipses and wild digression, Sterne describes an emotional and amorous adventure through France, partly based on two of his own continental journeys. It ends *in media res* without punctuation, the final sentence running suggestively into the volume marker:

I caught hold of the Fille de Chambre's

END OF VOL. II.

THREE GOTHIC NOVELS 1764–1818

Walpole, *The Castle of Otranto*; Beckford, *Vathek*; Mary Shelley, *Frankenstein*

In the late 18th century a new genre of novel emerged, called 'tales of terror' in Britain and *romans noir* abroad. These three novellas are some of the most significant early works of what we now call Gothic literature: Walpole's *Castle of Otranto* (164) marks the first recorded use of the term 'Gothic' (in his subtitle to the second edition); Beckford's *Vathek* (198) works Walpole's Gothic style into an 'Arabian Tale' that Lord Byron (195) described as his Bible; and Shelley's *Frankenstein* (204) is the archetypal horror story of an ambitious scientist who meddles with the secrets of life itself and brings about his own downfall.

1968 Penguin English Library
1986 Penguin Classics
ed. Peter Fairclough
intro. Mario Praz

Horace Walpole 1717–1797

Horace Walpole was the son of Robert Walpole, the first Prime Minister of Britain. After his father's death, Horace built a house by the Thames in Twickenham, which he called Strawberry Hill and styled as a 'little Gothic castle', specifying turrets and battlements and filling it with a collection of highly unusual objects. Walpole encouraged visitors at Strawberry Hill and wrote his own visitor's guide. It was renovated and reopened to the public in 2010.

The Castle of Otranto 1764

Conrad, heir to the house of Otranto, is killed on his wedding day, squashed by a massive metal helmet that falls out of the sky. Conrad's scheming father Manfred resolves to marry his son's intended bride himself, but Isabella flees through an underground passage. Walpole's novel founded the Gothic genre, introducing key plot elements such as secret passages, damsels in distress, sinister trapdoors, moving pictures and ancient prophecies.

2001
ed. Michael Gamer

Oliver Goldsmith 1728–1774

Goldsmith applied for the priesthood but was rejected, so he became a private tutor, a medic, a translator, an underpaid Grub Street hack (253) and finally a recognised man of letters. He wrote periodicals, essays, poems and plays, the most famous of which is *She Stoops to Conquer* (1773).

The Vicar of Wakefield 1766

1945 Penguin Books
• —

1982 Penguin English Library
1986 Penguin Classics
ed. Stephen Coote

'The hero of this piece unites in himself the three greatest characters upon earth,' wrote Goldsmith; 'he is a priest, an husbandman, and the father of a family.' The amiable and unworldly Dr Primrose struggles in the face of failed investments, rakish squires and travelling theatricals, but his unwavering Christian faith guides him through his misadventures.

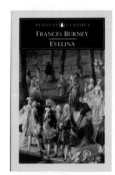

1994
ed. Margaret Anne Doody

Frances Burney
1752–1840

Frances was the daughter of the musicologist Charles Burney. She grew up in the society of her father's friends, Dr Johnson (183), Edmund Burke (178), the actor David Garrick and the artist Joshua Reynolds. She was Second Keeper of the Robes to Queen Charlotte, until she married an aristocratic French refugee, Alexandre d'Arblay, with whom she lived in France during the Napoleonic Wars.

Evelina
1778

In Burney's first novel, the beautiful and intelligent Evelina arrives in London for the first time and is amazed by the bustling, giddy city. She must circumvent the lewd advances of Sir Clement Willoughby and persuade her father to acknowledge her legitimacy, however, if she is to have any hope of happiness.

Journals and Letters

Burney's prolific journals and letters cover a 70-year period, from the diary she kept at the age of fifteen to the journal she was writing on her deathbed. She describes her youth, her father's circle of friends, the court of Queen Charlotte and the 'mad' King George III, the Napoleonic Wars and the experience of undergoing a mastectomy at the age of 59 without anaesthetic.

2001
ed. Peter Sabor & Lars E. Troide with Stewart Cooke & Victoria Kortes-Papp

Pierre Choderlos de Laclos 1741–1803

Pierre Ambroise François Choderlos de Laclos spent 20 years in the French army without once seeing battle. He wrote his only novel, *Les Liaisons Dangereuses*, while stationed on the island of Aix, off La Rochelle, in order to 'cause a stir and echo through the world after I have left it'. He was imprisoned twice during the French Revolution, but returned to Napoleon's army in 1800 as a general.

Dangerous Liaisons 1782

In this epistolary novel, the Marquise de Merteuil and the Vicomte de Valmont are former lovers and inveterate seducers. The Marquise aids the Vicomte in his relentless pursuit of a virtuous married woman, and in return challenges him to ravish an innocent convent girl, who is betrothed to a former lover of hers. Their cruel games have unexpected and perilous consequences.

1961
• trans. P. W. K. Stone

2007
trans. Helen Constantine

The Marquis de Sade

1740–1814

Donatien Alphonse François, Marquis de Sade, led a scandalous life. He was married at the age of 23, the same year that he was imprisoned for committing sacrilegious acts with a prostitute. He assaulted women, organized orgies, slept with his sister-in-law and hosted an entire winter of depravity with a household of young female servants. His penchant for punishment gave rise to the term 'sadist'. Eventually his own mother-in-law arranged his arrest and he spent the next thirteen years in prison. Napoleon later consigned him to a mental asylum, where he staged theatrical productions and seduced the 14-year-old daughter of one of the employees before dying at the age of 74. He is buried in an unmarked grave.

Philosophy in the Boudoir
1795

'You girls who have been tied down too long by the absurd and dangerous bonds of an imaginary virtue and a disgusting religion,' writes Sade in his prefatory letter, 'imitate ardent Eugénie. Destroy, trample, as swiftly as she, all the ridiculous precepts inculcated by moronic parents.' What follows is a pornographic work of philosophy, in which a teenage virgin is 'educated' in the art of libertinism over the course of seven dramatic dialogues.

2006 Deluxe Edition
trans. Joachim Neugroschel
intro. Francine du Plessix Gray

The 120 Days of Sodom 1785, pub. 1904

In this nasty novel, four wealthy libertines, a duke, a bishop, a judge and a banker, lock themselves in a remote castle in the heart of the Black Forest with 36 male and female teenagers. They engage four brothel keepers to tell stories about their sexual experiences, and then indulge in abusive, rapacious orgies inspired by the tales: they end up torturing their young victims in a carnal frenzy that grows increasingly murderous. Sade wrote the book on a continuous scroll while in prison. The manuscript was rediscovered in a copper cylinder, hidden in the wall, but remained unpublished until the 20th century. It has been widely banned and it is still an offence to display copies in the windows of French bookshops. It was tentatively admired, however, by the philosophers Gilles Deleuze and Simone de Beauvoir. The translators, McMorran and Wynn, discuss the ways in which their prize-winning translation of this work can be considered a classic. They quote Kafka who said that:

2016
trans. Will McMorran & Thomas Wynn

> If the book we are reading does not wake us, as with a fist hammering on our skull, why then do we read it? [. . .] A book must be an ice-axe to break the sea frozen inside us.

For 19th-century British fiction, turn to p.198

Drama

In the mid-17th century, French theatre was dominated by Corneille, Racine (168) and Molière (167). They adopted classical models: Corneille and Racine wrote tragedies that obeyed the three unities of place, time and action, as advocated in Aristotle's *Poetics* (30), whereas Molière reinvented the situational farces of Plautus (37) and Terence (38), creating a new 'comedy of manners'. This latter genre persisted into the 18th century; two of its finest exponents were Pierre Beaumarchais (169) and Richard Brinsley Sheridan (169).

In Britain, the theatres had reopened in 1660, after eighteen years of Civil War and the Interregnum. A wealth of sexually suggestive 'Restoration Comedies' appeared, encouraged by the recently restored monarch, Charles II. These intricately plotted, contemporary comedies played to socially diverse audiences, and women were permitted to perform on stage for the first time.

FOUR FRENCH PLAYS

1640–77

Corneille, *Cinna*; Molière, *The Misanthrope*;
Racine, *Andromache* and *Phaedra*

Cinna is set in Ancient Rome and concerns the attempted assassination of the Emperor Augustus (43), but it is also Corneille's commentary on 17th-century France and the absolute power that Cardinal Richelieu was establishing for Louis XIII. In *The Misanthrope*, Molière's anti-hero Alceste rejects the hypocrisies of French society. *Andromache*, inspired by Euripides's play (22), follows the misfortunes of Hector's widow after the Trojan War, and in *Phaedra*, Racine unravels the tragic consequences of Phaedra's incestuous attraction to her husband Theseus's son, based on Seneca's (48) version of the story.

PENGUIN CLASSICS

CORNEILLE, MOLIÈRE, RACINE

Four French Plays

Cinna, The Misanthrope, Andromache, Phaedra

2013
trans. John Edmunds
intro. Joseph Harris

Pierre Corneille

1606–1684

Corneille was a lawyer who worked as Crown Counsel in his native Rouen, writing plays for pleasure. In 1662, when he was in his late fifties, the success of his plays prompted him to move to Paris and write professionally. Voltaire (175) produced a twelve-volume annotated edition of Corneille's complete works in 1764, declaring that he had done for the French language what Homer (16) did for Ancient Greek: demonstrated it capable of producing the greatest works of art.

The Cid
Cinna
The Theatrical Illusion

1636–40

In *The Cid*, based on the Spanish legend (80), a young Spanish knight must choose between his love for the daughter of his enemy and avenging his own insulted father. It was extremely popular at the time, although it was denounced by the Académie française (305) and lost Corneille the patronage of Cardinal Richelieu. *The Theatrical Illusion* is a meta-theatrical comedy in which a magician stages a play-within-a-play about the escapades of a grieving father's long-lost son.

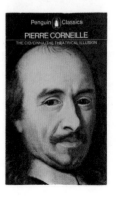

Penguin Classics
PIERRE CORNEILLE
THE CID/CINNA/THE THEATRICAL ILLUSION

1975
trans. John Cairncross
—
Cinna is also included in the
Four French Plays anthology.

Molière 1622–1673

'Molière' was the stage name of Jean-Baptiste Poquelin, the son of a wealthy Parisian upholsterer. At 21 he joined a company of provincial actors, writing scripts for them and eventually leading the troupe. On their return to Paris they secured the patronage of Louis XIV and became *la troupe du Roi*. Molière later became ill, collapsed on stage and subsequently died, while playing the eponymous lead in *The Hypochondriac*.

1959
● trans. John Wood

The Misanthrope

and Other Plays 1659–72

Such Foolish Affected Ladies; *Tartuffe*; *The Misanthrope*; *The Doctor Despite Himself*; *The Would-Be Gentleman*; *Those Learned Ladies*

Such Foolish Affected Ladies is a one-act play that satirizes the sparkling, witty gossips of polite Parisian society. *Tartuffe* sees a seemingly pious impostor inveigle his way into a gentleman's household and attempt to seduce his wife. The scrupulous protagonist of *The Misanthrope* observes faults in everyone but himself, though he cannot help loving the flirtatious Célimène. In *The Doctor Despite Himself,* a poor woodcutter is forced to pretend that he is a physician; *The Would-Be Gentleman* is a comedy-ballet about social climbing; and *Those Learned Ladies* lampoons the academic pretensions of Parisian literary salons.

The Miser

and Other Plays 1622–73

The School for Wives; The School for Wives Criticized; Don Juan; The Miser; The Hypochondriac

The School for Wives is about a middle-aged man attempting to seduce his teenage ward, and Moliére wrote *The School for Wives Criticized* as a response to the ensuing scandal. The title character of *Don Juan* is an adulterer, a womanizer, an atheist, a bankrupt and a con man; the earth finally opens up and swallows him. In *The Miser*, an avaricious old man's fortune is stolen, and *The Hypochondriac*, Molière's last play, is a scathing attack on the medical profession.

2000
trans. John Wood, 1953
rev. David Coward, 2000
—
John Wood produced a two-volume translation of Molière's plays in the 1950s, which David Coward revised, supplemented and reorganized in 2000.

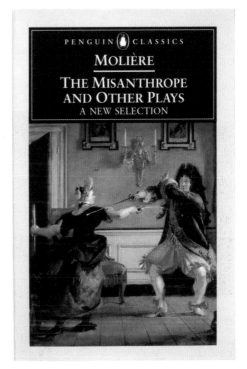

2000
trans. John Wood, 1959
rev. David Coward, 2000

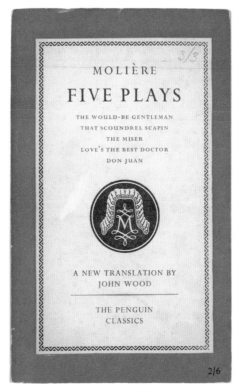

1953 *Five Plays*
● trans. John Wood

Jean Racine 1639–1699

Racine was orphaned at the age of four and raised by his grandparents. By the age of 21 he was writing plays and had been introduced at the court of Louis XIV. Despite the huge success of his tragedies, he abandoned the theatre in 1677 and accepted a series of court posts including royal historiographer, treasurer of France and ordinary gentleman of the king. At the request of the king's morganatic second wife, however, he wrote two further plays on religious subjects.

1963 *Phaedra and Other Plays*
1970 *Reissued as Iphigenia,
Phaedra, Athaliah*
trans. John Cairncross
—
John Cairncross's translation
of Racine was the first Penguin
Classic redesigned by Germano
Facetti (xiv). Rawlings's dual-
language edition of *Phèdre* is no
longer in print.

1992
● trans. Margaret Rawlings

Iphigenia, Phaedra, Athaliah
1674–91

Iphigenia is Racine's version of *Iphigenia in Aulis* by Euripides (23), in which the gods demand Agamemnon's daughter as a sacrifice before the Greeks can sail for Troy. In *Phaedra*, based on Seneca's *Phaedra* (48), Theseus's son Hippolytus is undone by the incestuous advances of his stepmother. *Athaliah*, Racine's last tragedy, retells the biblical story of the murderous, Baal-worshipping widow Athaliah in the Second Book of Kings, who is finally ousted by Jehoiada, the Jewish high priest. Flaubert (313) described it as 'the most immortal masterpiece of the French stage.'

THREE RESTORATION COMEDIES 1675–95

Etheredge, *The Man of Mode*; Wycherley, *The Country Wife*; Congreve, *Love for Love*

When Charles II was restored to the throne in 1660, dramatists were granted new freedoms and elegance and wit were prized over morality. George Etheridge's *Man of Mode, or, Sir Fopling Flutter* is a satire of contemporary London society, with recognizable portraits of the Earl of Rochester (152) and Etheredge himself. William Wycherley based his punning *Country Wife* on Molière (167): a rake claims impotence in order to seduce a series of men's wives. In *Love for Love* by William Congreve, the extravagant Valentine must choose between his own inheritance and that of his beloved Angelica.

1968 Penguin
English Library
1986 Penguin
Classics
ed. Gāmini Salgādo
—
The image on the
cover is thought to
be a portrait, by Sir
Peter Lely, of Nell
Gwyn, the orange-
seller who became
an actress and a
favourite mistress of
Charles II.

William Congreve 1670–1729

Congreve was born in Yorkshire and grew up in Ireland; he was a contemporary of Jonathan Swift (159) at Kilkenny School and Trinity College, Dublin. He never married but had several high-profile liaisons with celebrity actresses. His only tragedy, *The Mourning Bride*, includes the famous line: 'Heaven has no rage like love to hatred turned, / Nor hell a fury like a woman scorned'.

The Way of the World
and Other Plays 1693–1700
The Old Bachelor; *The Double Dealer*; *Love for Love*; *The Way of the World*

The Old Bachelor, Congreve's first play, is a comedy of manners in which a rake poses as a parson in order to pursue a married woman. *The Double Dealer* sees Lady Touchwood and her agent Maskwell attempt to spoil a budding romance between Mellefont and Cynthia. *Love for Love* is a witty farce about diverted inheritances and mistaken betrothals, and *The Way of the World* sees two young lovers attempt to trick the formidable Lady Wishfort into handing over a dowry.

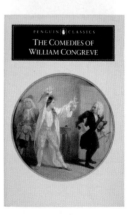

1985 *The Comedies of William
Congreve*
2006 *Reissued as The Way of the
World and Other Plays*
ed. Eric S. Rump

John Gay 1685–1732

Gay spent most of his life in the households of patrons, as secretary to the Duchess of Monmouth, the Earl of Clarendon and latterly the Duke of Queensberry. He lost most of a major investment in the South Sea Bubble disaster and wrote his own epitaph for his tomb, which is in Westminster Abbey:

> Life is a jest, and all things show it,
> I thought it once, and now I know it.

Pierre Beaumarchais 1732–1799

Pierre-Augustin Caron de Beaumarchais was the son of a Parisian clockmaker. He became a gunrunner, a secret agent and a financial speculator and described his adventurous life in a series of successful *Mémoires*. Today he is remembered for his comedies, which were adapted into operas by Rossini and Mozart (187).

1964
trans. John Wood

The Barber of Seville *and* The Marriage of Figaro

1773–8

The Beggar's Opera 1728

In 1716, Swift (159) wrote to Pope (152), asking 'what think you, of a Newgate pastoral among the thieves and whores there?' Pope passed the idea to Gay, who created a satirical 'ballad opera', woven with traditional songs and street ditties, telling the tale of the philandering highwayman

1986
ed. Bryan Loughrey & T. O. Treadwell

Macheath, his lover Polly, and the revenge of her father, the thief-catcher Peachum. It was immensely popular at the time, and remains so today. After the success of a London production, which ran to 1,463 performances in the 1920s, Bertolt Brecht and Kurt Weill adapted the story for their 1928 musical, *Die Dreigroschenoper*, 'The Threepenny Opera'.

The resourceful servant Figaro, temporarily working as a barber in Seville, assists 'the Count' to woo the beautiful Rosine, who is jealously sequestered by her elderly guardian, Dr Bartholo. In the sequel, set three years later, the Count has married Rosine and Figaro is working for them. He is on the point of marrying Suzanne, but the Count has grown bored of his own marriage and has eyes for Suzanne himself. There is a third instalment of the Figaro trilogy, *The Guilty Mother*, about marital infidelity, but it is rarely revived. 'He has everything,' wrote Voltaire (175) about Beaumarchais – 'pleasantry, seriousness, reason, vigour, pathos, eloquence of every kind.'

Richard Brinsley Sheridan

1751–1816

The hot-blooded Sheridan fought two duels over the beautiful singer Elizabeth Linley. He was borne from the second, as his biographer relates, 'with a portion of his antagonist's weapon sticking through an ear, his breast-bone touched, his whole body covered with wounds and blood, and his face nearly beaten to jelly'. Richard and Elizabeth married that same year. In 1776, Sheridan acquired David Garrick's share in the Drury Lane Theatre, which he managed until it burned down in 1809. He was Member of Parliament at various times for Stafford, Westminster and Ilchester.

The School for Scandal *and* Other Plays

The Rivals; *The Critic*; *The School for Scandal* 1775–9

1988
ed. Eric Rump

In *The Rivals*, Jack Absolute duels for the hand of the dreamy Lydia Languish; Lydia's guardian is the misspeaking Mrs Malaprop, who gives us the term 'malapropism'. In the meta-theatrical *The Critic*, Mr Puff invites a rival author, Sir Fretful Plagiary, and the critics Dangle and Sneer, to watch a rehearsal of his latest play, *The Spanish Armada*. The 'School for Scandal' refers to the coterie of gossips around Lady Sneerwell: when Sir Oliver Surface returns from the East Indies unexpectedly he disguises himself and secretly observes his two nephews, with startling results.

Philosophy

Although there were some exceptional philosophers of the Middle Ages, most notably St Augustine (62) and St Thomas Aquinas (70), many histories of western philosophy jump directly from Aristotle (29) to Descartes. The latter's radical step was to start from scratch and to base his new system of philosophy on the limits of his own knowledge, rather than on the inherited cosmological and ontological metaphysics of Aristotle or the biblical precepts that underpin Christian theology. Descartes initiated an 'enlightened' tradition that rejected the authority of received wisdom and encouraged a secular, empirical approach to knowledge, philosophy, politics and science. Enlightenment philosophy culminated with the masterwork of Immanuel Kant, the *Critique of Pure Reason* (180), in which Kant systematically reconciles the workings of the mind with the emerging disciplines of natural science and the concepts of free will and morality.

René Descartes 1596–1650

Descartes was born at La Haye, a small French town that has since been renamed 'Descartes' in his honour. In November 1619, while serving as a soldier in Germany, he experienced three hallucinatory visions that revealed to him a new system of philosophy and for the next 20 years he worked in seclusion in Holland, developing his ideas. At the age of 53, he accepted Queen Christina of Sweden's invitation to become her philosophy tutor, but the cold Stockholm weather and Christina's preference for early morning lessons led to pneumonia, from which he died. His last words were said to be 'a mon âme, il faut partier' ('my soul, it is time to depart').

Discourse on Method
and Related Writings c. 1626–39

Descartes compares mathematics and experimental science, and discusses the extent to which each can achieve certainty. He sets out a 'hypothetical method' of research, based fundamentally on doubt, which remains the bedrock method of modern scientific enquiry. He starts by doubting everything except his own existence and formulates the famous starting position, 'Je pense, donc je suis' ('I think, therefore I am').

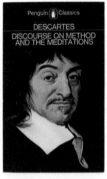

1968 *Discourse on Method and The Meditations*
trans. F. E. Sutcliffe

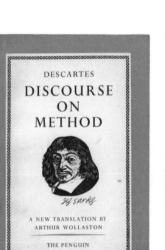

1960
● trans. Arthur Wollaston

1999
trans. Desmond M. Clarke
—
Bernard Williams reviewed Wollaston's translation in *The Spectator*: 'one stumbles over an uneven terrain,' he writes, 'tripping over obscurities, omissions and occasional downright mistranslations.' Wollaston's translation was replaced eight years later. Desmond Clarke's edition includes *Rules for Guiding One's Intelligence in Searching for the Truth* and relevant passages from *The World*.

Meditations
and Other Metaphysical Writings 1641–9

Descartes's six extended meditations take a systematic approach to the nature of existence. In the first, he discusses 'what can be called into doubt'; in the second he attempts to confirm that he himself exists; in the third that God exists; in the fourth he differentiates between truth and error; in the fifth he allows that things outside himself and God might exist; and in the sixth he confirms that they do exist. He also outlines 'Cartesian dualism', his contentious distinction between mind and body. This volume also includes 'The Principles of Human Knowledge' from *The Principles of Philosophy* and a selection of Descartes's correspondence.

1998
trans. Desmond M. Clarke

Baltasar Gracián 1601–1658

Gracián was the son of a Spanish doctor. He became a Jesuit (72) and wrote an allegorical novel, a work of poetics and several moral tracts that were later praised by Schopenhauer (348) and Nietzsche (348).

2011
trans. Jeremy Robbins

The Pocket Oracle and Art of Prudence 1647

This collection of 300 moral aphorisms inspired a French vogue for maxims (172). Gracián's words of worldly advice include 'Make people depend on you', 'Quit whilst fortune is smiling' and 'Know how to forget'. He includes commentaries alongside the aphorisms that help his reader integrate the oracle into his or her daily life.

Thomas Hobbes

1588–1679

After graduating from Oxford, Hobbes became the tutor to the Cavendish family of Hardwick Hall in Derbyshire and lived with them for much of his life. He devoted his scholarly attention to devising a 'political science', the culmination of which was the publication of *Leviathan* in 1651, two years after the execution of Charles I. He also made important contributions to history, geometry, ethics and the science of gases. He translated Thucydides (32) and later the works of Homer (16) while in his mid-eighties and died at Hardwick at the age of 91.

Leviathan 1651

Hobbes's masterpiece was written during the English Civil War. It formulates a science of morality and offers a rational basis for legitimate government. Hobbes begins by postulating a pessimistic 'state of nature', imagining the anarchy that would prevail if humans had no system of government at all: he describes the natural life of man as 'solitary, poor, nasty, brutish, and short'. From there he develops the notion of a necessary social contract between the people (the 'Common-wealth') and the central authority (the 'Leviathan'). This powerful idea has formed the basis of most subsequent political philosophy, especially that of Jean-Jacques Rousseau (177). At the time, however, the implication that mankind is fundamentally self-serving was considered appalling, and copies were burned publicly by the University of Oxford on the charge of sedition.

2017
ed. Christopher Brooke

1968 Pelican Classics
1981 Penguin English Library
1985 Penguin Classics
ed. C. B. Macpherson

François de La Rochefoucauld 1613–1680

François, Duc de La Rochefoucauld, was politically energetic until he was shot through the head in Paris during a rebellion against the crown. Thereafter he turned to the intellectual salons of the city, forming friendships with Madame de Sévigné (182) and Madame de Lafayette (156). 'When they are intelligent,' he wrote of women, 'I prefer their conversation to men's, for there is a kind of smooth ease about it that is not found in us men, and moreover it seems to me that they express themselves more clearly and give a more graceful turn to what they say.'

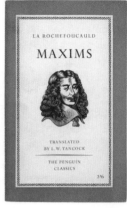

1959
trans. Leonard Tancock

Maxims 1665

In 641 pithy adages, La Rochefoucauld dissects the motives that lie behind all human behaviour. Seemingly altruistic actions are revealed as fundamental egoistical: 'What we take for virtues are often merely a collection of different acts and personal interests pieced together by chance,' he writes.

Blaise Pascal 1623–1662

Pascal was a French child genius. As a teenager he invented a mechanical calculator and made important contributions to fluid dynamics. He advanced projective geometry and probability theory and wrote an important treatise on the arithmetical triangle. He also devised and set up the first public transport system in Paris. Following a religious experience in 1654, he became a committed Jansenist, writing the *Pensées* and the anti-Jesuit *Provincial Letters*. The SI unit of pressure is named after him.

For his edition, Cohen adopted a conjectural, new arrangement of Pascal's papers, which proved unpopular. Krailsheimer's translation was brought in five years later, reverting to the traditional structure used in Pascal's executors' manuscript.

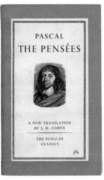

1961
• trans. J. M. Cohen

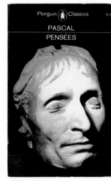

1966
trans. A. J. Krailsheimer

Pensées

Pascal's *Pensées*, 'Thoughts', were unfinished when he died and only survived as a bundle of largely unclassified scraps of paper. Nonetheless, they have become a classic of Christian philosophy. His strategy seems to have been to bamboozle unbelievers with paradoxes until they embrace God out of desperation: sections include 'Boredom', 'Beginning' and 'Perpetuity'.

John Bunyan 1628–1688

Bunyan was the son of an English tinker. After serving in the Parliamentary army during the Civil War he suffered a spiritual crisis and began publishing polemical pamphlets. He was imprisoned for heretical preaching and languished in Bedford Gaol for twelve years. On his release, he resumed preaching. He is buried in Bunhill Fields in London, the Dissenters' burial ground, near Daniel Defoe (157) and William Blake (192).

Grace Abounding to the Chief of Sinners 1666

Bunyan's spiritual autobiography recounts the inner struggle that led to his religious awakening, in which God and Satan physically vied for his soul. The title refers to Paul's epistle to the Romans (5:20): 'where sin abounded, grace did much more abound'.

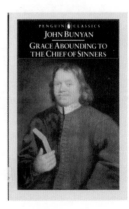

1987
ed. W. R. Owens

The Pilgrim's Progress
From This World, To That Which Is to Come
1678–84

The pilgrim Christian abandons the City of Destruction and sets out for the Celestial City. Along the way he must evade the Slough of Despond, steer clear of the Delectable Mountains and navigate the enticing Vanity Fair, before he can achieve salvation. The allegorical locations have real-life counterparts on the road between Bedford and London. In 1938, 250 years after Bunyan's death, an estimated 1,300 different editions of *Pilgrim's Progress* had been printed. This volume also includes Bunyan's sequel, published six years later, in which Christiana, Christian's wife, makes the same perilous journey accompanied by her four children, her neighbour Mercy and the guide Great-Heart.

1965 Penguin English Library
● ed. Roger Sharrock

2008
ed. Roger Pooley

Benedict de Spinoza 1632–1677

Spinoza was born in Amsterdam to Orthodox Jewish parents from Portugal. He made a living by grinding optical lenses. He was much admired by Coleridge (195), Shelley (196), Flaubert (313) and George Eliot (226), who produced an English translation of his work. The 20th-century philosopher Bertrand Russell called him the 'noblest and most lovable of the great philosophers […] ethically he is supreme'.

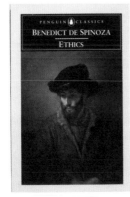

1996
trans. Edwin Curley
intro. Stuart Hampshire

Ethics 1677

The posthumously published *Ethics* form a comprehensive philosophical system. Arguments are laid out systematically, presenting an analysis of the nature of God, the mind, the emotions and the intellect. Spinoza's central philosophy is in opposition to Descartes (170): he believes that God and nature are one, body and soul indivisible.

John Locke
1632–1704

Locke was personal physician to the first Earl of Shaftesbury, an opponent of Charles II. After the Glorious Revolution of 1688, he published his masterworks: *Two Treatises on Government* and *An Essay Concerning Human Understanding*, in which he laid out his belief in human rights and a theory of knowledge based on sensory experience. He is, for John Stuart Mill (273), the 'unquestioned founder of the analytic philosophy of mind'.

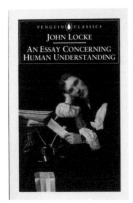

1997
ed. Roger Woolhouse

An Essay Concerning Human Understanding
1690

Locke rejects the idea that some forms of knowledge are innate. He argues that all mathematical, scientific, religious and ethical knowledge derives from external experiences, analysed by the rational mind. He then provides a taxonomy of types of knowledge, including 'Simple Ideas', 'Complex Ideas', 'Number', 'Infinity' and 'Mixed Modes', and finally describes how words relate to and express knowledge, discussing their uses, abuses and limitations.

Bernard Mandeville

1670–1733

Mandeville was a Dutch doctor who moved to London to learn English. He published several editions of *The Fable of the Bees*, which was declared a public nuisance by the Grand Jury of Middlesex on account of its cynical and immoral ideas. It provided the basis for Adam Smith's *Wealth of Nations* (179) 70 years later.

The Fable of the Bees

1705–14

In 1705, Mandeville published 'The Grumbling Hive', a short doggerel poem about a prosperous hive of selfish bees which fails disastrously after the bees become honest. Mandeville's counterintuitive point is that vice is necessary in order for a society to prosper economically. He subsequently supplemented the poem with commentaries and elaborations, which make up the rest of *The Fable of the Bees*.

1970 Pelican Classics
1989 Penguin Classics
ed. Philip Harth

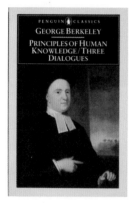

1988
ed. Roger Woolhouse

George Berkeley

1685–1753

Bishop Berkeley was an Irish philosopher who espoused the theory of immaterialism, the argument that there is no reality outside the mind: the material universe does not exist in its own right, we only think it does. He does provide a loophole, however: God is all-seeing and therefore everything does exist, because everything is held in the mind of God. Dr Johnson (183) found this theory ridiculous: 'I refute it *thus*,' he expostulated, kicking a large rock, although Bishop Berkeley would argue that Johnson only thought he'd stubbed his toe.

Principles of Human Knowledge *and* Three Dialogues 1710–13

In *Principles of Human Knowledge*, Berkeley describes a world made up exclusively of minds, the ideas inside them, and an infinite organizing spirit called God. The theory challenges John Locke's *Essay Concerning Human Understanding* (173), which assumes a tangible external universe. In response to contemporary criticism, Berkeley wrote the *Three Dialogues Between Hylas and Philonus*. These expand his theories of perceptual relativity and phenomenalism.

Giambattista Vico

1668–1744

Vico was the son of a Neapolitan bookseller, who became Professor of Rhetoric at the University of Naples. His work has since been highly influential in the fields of sociology, anthropology and the philosophy of history.

New Science

Principles of the New Science Concerning the Common Nature of Nations

1725–44

Scienza Nuova attempts to organize the humanities, literature, philosophy, history and geography, into a diagnostic science to explain the historical cycles of the rise and fall of nations. Vico's vast system covers the history, mythology and laws of the Ancient Greeks, Romans, Egyptians, Jews and Babylonians, touching on poetics, astronomy, money and monsters. It was an inspiration for Karl Marx (346) and James Joyce.

1999
trans. David Marsh
intro. Anthony Grafton

David Hume 1711–1776

Hume published *A Treatise of Human Nature* in his twenties. Now recognized as his masterwork, at the time he felt that it 'fell dead-born from the Press'. He became a tutor, librarian, diplomat and senior civil servant, building an international reputation and travelling widely, before retiring to his native Edinburgh and reworking his philosophy into the more approachable *Enquiry Concerning Human Understanding* (1748). Adam Smith (179) said of Hume, 'I have always considered him, both in his lifetime and since his death, as approaching as nearly to the idea of a perfectly wise and virtuous man, as perhaps the nature of human frailty will permit.'

A Treatise of Human Nature
1739–40

Starting from a position of good-humoured scepticism, and relying on empirical observation, Hume raises fundamental questions about what it means to be human: how do we form identity, what does it mean to be free, what is virtue, why are we driven by passions and appetites, does the soul exist? 'No man has influenced the history of philosophy to a deeper or more disturbing degree,' wrote the Russian émigré philosopher Isaiah Berlin.

1969 Pelican Classics
1985 Penguin Classics
ed. Ernest C. Mossner

Dialogues Concerning Natural Religion
1779

Published posthumously, Hume's *Dialogues* consist of twelve conversations between three fictional philosophers, Demea, Philo and Cleanthes, who debate the nature of religion. They agree that God exists, but debunk many of the orthodox arguments for his existence, notably the 'argument from design', which Darwin (269) would conclusively quash in the following century.

1990
ed. Martin Bell

Voltaire
1694–1778

François-Marie Arouet wrote a staggering quantity of books and letters under the *nom de plume* 'Voltaire'. After spending time in the Bastille for writing satirical verses, he embarked on a self-imposed exile around Europe, staying in England and the French countryside, at the Prussian court of Frederick the Great and finally near Geneva. Throughout his life he attacked the Catholic Church and advocated freedom of speech. He was one of the most influential figures of the Enlight-enment period.

Letters on England 1733

Voltaire spent three years in England in the late 1720s, where he wrote a series of enthusiastic and amusing dispatches on English culture. He describes religious sects, the workings of Parliament, smallpox inoculations, Newton's 'system of gravitation', writers including Rochester (152) and Pope (152), and in one expansive letter he covers English views of 'infinity and chronology'. Above all he holds England up as an example of tolerance, enlightenment and freedom, in contrast to the tyrannical feudal system of his French homeland.

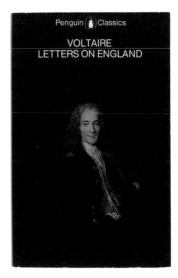

1980
trans. Leonard Tancock

1964
trans. John Butt

Zadig *and* L'Ingénu

1747, 1767

Zadig, a Babylonian philosopher, is abandoned by his fiancée, sold into slavery and sentenced to death before he finally wins a contest of strength and wisdom and reunites with his true love. He employs a form of logical detective work that influenced Edgar Allan Poe (408) and Arthur Conan Doyle (248). In *L'Ingénu*, a child raised by Huron Indians returns to Brittany and exposes engrained religious hypocrisy though simple, naïve observations.

Micromégas

and Other Short Fictions *1715–75*

Micromégas is the gigantic alien inhabitant of a planet orbiting the distant star Sirius. In this early work of science fiction, the Sirian space traveller arrives on Earth and is fascinated by the discovery of a tiny, crawling species with an adorably self-inflated sense of its intellectual achievements. Other stories in the collection include 'The One-Eyed Porter', 'Pot-Pourri', 'An Indian Incident' and 'Dialogue between a Savage and a Graduate'.

2002
trans. Theo Cuffe
intro. Haydn Mason

Candide

or, Optimism *1759*

The ingenuous Candide is raised in the German castle of Baron von Thunder-ten-tronckh and tutored in metaphysico-theologico-cosmo-nigology by Dr Pangloss, who inculcates him with the optimistic philosophy that ours is the 'best of all possible worlds'. Candide finds his optimism tested, however, by the rape, pillage, flaying, earthquakes, syphilis, murder and other misfortunes he encounters on his travels. He finally retires to a small farmstead and adopts a more pragmatic view of life: 'we must cultivate our garden,' he says. John Updike called *Candide* the 'prince of philosophical novels'.

1947
● trans. John Butt
—
'Is there going to be any difficulty in giving me a grinning (and preferably emaciated) mask on the front cover?' asked John Butt. 'A grinning mask, which I am told by the Production Department looks emaciated enough to have been feeding on Dr Edith Summerskill's mouse-trap cheese for several years, is in active preparation,' replied the Penguin editor A. S. B. Glover, a tattooed ex-convict who memorized the entire *Encyclopaedia Britannica* while in prison. Summerskill was the Undersecretary to the Ministry of Food at the time and was heavily involved in cheese rationing.

2006
trans. Theo Cuffe
intro. Michael Wood

Treatise on Toleration *1763*

Voltaire wrote this powerful demand for tolerance following the death of the Toulouse merchant Jean Calas in 1762. Calas was falsely accused of murdering his son and suffered torture and execution on the wheel, having been persecuted by 'an irrational mob'. In January 2015, after the *Charlie Hebdo* shootings in Paris, the *Treatise on Toleration* became a bestseller in France.

2016
trans. Desmond M. Clarke

Philosophical Dictionary *1764*

Voltaire worked on this dictionary throughout his life. It is an alphabetical collection of short radical essays with entries on 'Love', 'Atheism', 'Beauty', 'Equality' and 'Dreams'. It is a bitter and witty critique of Christian theology and a passionate argument for reason, justice and common sense.

1972
trans. Theodore Besterman

Jean-Jacques Rousseau 1712–1778

Rousseau was born in Geneva and led an itinerant life: he became an engraver's assistant, a footman, a Catholic, a music teacher and a tutor, travelling around Switzerland, France and Italy. He met Diderot (179) in Paris and worked with him on the *Encyclopédie*, and visited Hume (175) in London. He fell out with all his friends. He had five illegitimate children, all of whom he abandoned to a foundling home.

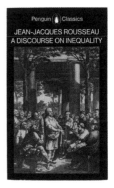

1984
trans. Maurice Cranston

A Discourse on Inequality 1754

This essay is a response to a prize question posed by the Dijon Academy: 'What is the origin of the inequality among men, and is it authorized by natural law?' Rousseau argues strongly that inequalities of wealth, power and privilege are entirely artificial and avoidable, and wholly detrimental to the happiness of mankind. Rousseau's essay didn't win the competition, although he had previously won for his *Discourse on Arts and Sciences* in 1750.

1991
trans. Allan Bloom

Émile
or, On Education 1762

In his great treatise on education and the nature of man, Rousseau imagines a moral, intellectual and political education for a fictional young boy named Émile. He begins with the line, 'Everything is good as it leaves the hands of the Author of things; everything degenerates in the hands of man.' He aims to show how it might be possible to balance the innate human goodness of youth on the one hand, and practical engagement with corrosive human society on the other. He considered this the 'best and most important' of all his writings. It was banned in Paris and Geneva and copies were publicly burned.

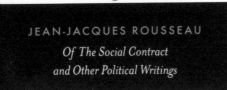

JEAN-JACQUES ROUSSEAU
*Of The Social Contract
and Other Political Writings*

The Social Contract
1762

'Man was born free, and he is everywhere in chains.' The first line of Rousseau's iconic work of political philosophy rejects the idea that authority is innate. There is always a pact between the citizens of a state and the sovereign power: citizens should be governed by laws they have chosen themselves. Some have seen this short but pivotal treatise as a blueprint for democracy, others as an excuse for totalitarian tyranny.

2012 *Of the Social Contract and Other Political Writings*
ed. Christopher Bertram
trans. Quintin Hoare
—
Bertram and Hoare's edition includes other political writings by Rousseau, such as *Principles of the Right of War* and his *Constitutional Proposal for Corsica*.

1968
trans. Maurice Cranston

The Confessions 1770, pub. 1781

'I have resolved on an enterprise which has no precedent, and which, once complete, will have no imitator. My purpose is to display to my kind a portrait in every way true to nature, and the man I shall portray will be myself.' Rousseau borrowed St Augustine's title (62) for this project, the first modern auto-biography. He paints an insightful and psychologically compelling self-portrait of the first 53 years of his life, describing the formulation of his philosophy and the events surrounding the publication of his greatest works.

1953
trans. J. M. Cohen

'On arriving back from France to this land of margarine & meatlessness, I was faced by your conundrum,' wrote J. M. Cohen (154) about the cover of his edition. 'My suggestion is a periwinkle flower. (See the lovely passage at the opening of the 6th book.) The periwinkle was for Rousseau, I believe, the flower of memory, and memory is the keynote of this book.'

Reveries of the Solitary Walker 1776–8, pub. 1782

This meditative description of walks around the streets of Paris captures Rousseau's sense of intellectual and social isolation at the end of his life. He feels alienated and resentful, but at the same time he enjoys his solitude and observing the plant life of the city. It was an inspiration for subsequent Parisian flâneurs, such as Baudelaire (328).

1979
trans. Peter France

Edmund Burke 1729–1797

Burke was an Irish politician and philosopher. He served as secretary to 'Single-Speech' Hamilton, Chief Secretary for Ireland, and subsequently to the Prime Minister, the Marquis of Rockingham. Over the course of his long political career, Burke was variously Member of Parliament for Wendover, Bristol and Malton and he championed Catholic emancipation and the relaxation of Irish trade laws. He spent much of his time wrestling with the 'problem' of India and denouncing the doctrines of the French Revolution.

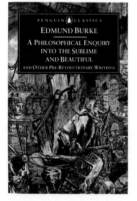

1998
ed. David Womersley
—
This edition also includes *A Vindication of Natural Society*, *Thoughts on the Cause of the Present Discontents* and *Speech on Conciliation with the Colonies*.

A Philosophical Enquiry into the Origin of our Ideas of Sublime and Beautiful
and Other Pre-Revolutionary Writings 1756–77

Burke differentiates between the sublime, which he deems a sensory experience combining 'pain and danger', and beauty, a 'social quality', which can be appreciated with rational pleasure and serenity. This treatise on aesthetics had a profound influence on later writers, including William Wordsworth (193) and Matthew Arnold (272).

Reflections on the Revolution in France
and on the Proceedings in Certain Societies
in London Relative to that Event 1790

Burke wrote his famous pamphlet in the early months of the French Revolution, predicting many of its worst excesses. This classic statement of political conservatism attacks the revolution's attitudes towards institutions, property and religion, and fears what effects it might have in England. It prompted strong rebuttals from Thomas Paine (397) and Mary Wollstonecraft (205).

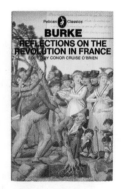

1968 Pelican Classics
1982 Penguin English Library
1986 Penguin Classics
ed. Conor Cruise O'Brien

Adam Smith 1723–1790

Smith was an absent-minded Scottish intellectual, who resigned his professorial chair at Glasgow University in 1763 in order to become the tutor to the young Duke of Buccleuch, with whom he travelled throughout Europe. He began writing *The Wealth of Nations* while in France and it was published in 1776, the same year that America declared its independence. In 1787, he succeeded his friend Edmund Burke (178) as the Lord Rector of Glasgow University and and he spent much of the rest of his life in Edinburgh.

The Theory of Moral Sentiments 1759

Smith argues that benevolence, justice and sympathy are essential elements of the human condition: 'How selfish soever man may be supposed, there are evidently some principles in his nature, which interest him in the fortune of others, and render their happiness necessary to him, though he derives nothing from it except the pleasure of seeing it.'

2009
ed. Ryan Patrick Hanley
intro. Amartya Sen
—
The economist and philosopher Amartya Sen calls this work 'one of the truly outstanding books in the intellectual history of the world'.

The Wealth of Nations 1776

In seeming contrast to *The Theory of Moral Sentiments*, Smith's magnum opus lays the foundations for modern capitalism and the free market economy. He imagines individual self-interest as innate and essential, the 'invisible hand', which ensures a fair and productive economy. He describes division of labour as a key to increased productivity, using a pin factory as an example, and delves into the philosophy of money itself, with sections on wages, profit, rent and stocks. Books I–III are mostly theoretical; Books IV and V apply Smith's economic philosophy to real-life situations.

1970 Pelican Classics
Books I–III
1982 Penguin English Library
1986 Penguin Classics
ed. Andrew Skinner

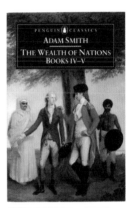

1999 *Books IV–V*
ed. Andrew Skinner

Denis Diderot 1713–1784

Diderot was the son of a master cutler. He produced the vast *Encyclopédie* with his friends Jean le Rond d'Alembert (180), Voltaire (175) and Jean-Jacques Rousseau (177). Towards the end of his life he visited St Petersburg, at the invitation of the Empress Catherine the Great. They had heated intellectual debates, during which he would slap the queen's thighs to emphasize his philosophical points. 'Your Diderot is an extraordinary man,' Catherine confided in private. 'I emerge from interviews with him with my thighs bruised and quite black. I have been obliged to put a table between us to protect myself and my members.'

The Nun c. 1760, pub. 1796

Diderot wrote *The Nun* as a joke: it is a set of seemingly genuine letters addressed to his friend the Marquis de Croismare. The letters are apparently written from a young girl, Suzanne Simonin, who has been forced into a nunnery and then persecuted by the corrupt nuns. She begs the Marquis to help her renounce her vows.

1974
trans. Leonard Tancock, 1972

Rameau's Nephew
and D'Alembert's Dream 1763, 1769

Rameau's Nephew is an uproarious and witty dialogue between
Diderot and the nephew of the composer Jean-Philippe Rameau:
it covers music, literature, education, politics and philosophy.
D'Alembert's Dream is a conversation between Diderot and the
encyclopédiste d'Alembert, broken up by a fever dream, in which
Mademoiselle de L'Espinasse and Dr Bordeau discuss d'Alembert's
state of health. It presents an atheistic view of a material universe
and includes an early formulation of the theory of evolution (270).

Jacques the Fatalist
and His Master 1771–1778

This digressive, picaresque tale follows Jacques,
a manservant, and his master as they encounter a
wide variety of comic characters and unpredictable
situations on a journey through France. Jacques
tells tales of his various love affairs, and remains
convinced that every whimsical decision he makes
has been predetermined and unavoidable. Diderot
was directly inspired by *Tristram Shandy* (163);
he even claims in the text to have 'copied' whole
paragraphs from Sterne.

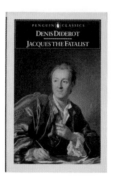

1986
trans. Michael Henry
intro. Martin Hall

1966
trans. Leonard Tancock

Immanuel Kant
1724–1804

**Kant was born in Königsberg, East Prussia, the son of a
saddler, and became the most prominent thinker of the
German Enlightenment. He was a scholar at the University
of Königsberg
throughout his
life and kept such
regular hours that
people are said
to have set their
watches by his con-
stitutional walks
around the town.**

Critique of Pure Reason 1781–7

Kant's masterwork transformed modern
philosophy: he claimed it was the equivalent
of the Copernican Revolution in astronomy,
which located the sun at the centre of our
solar system for the first time. He synthesizes
the competing philosophical schools of
rationalism, which grounds knowledge in
pure reason, and empiricism, which attributes
knowledge to external observation: he allows
that the world exists independently but considers experience as necessarily interpreted
by a framework of rational concepts. Some of
these concepts are hardwired in humans, he
believed, such as the way we perceive space
and time and cause and effect, whereas others
we develop over the course of our lives.

2007
trans. Marcus Weigelt
based on Max Müller, 1881

Essays, Letters & Memoirs

The Enlightenment saw a proliferation of different forms of literature. The essay, conceived by Montaigne (126) in the 16th century, became increasingly popular as a way to express philosophical, political and polemical points of view, especially in the many short-run pamphlets and journals that appeared during the period. Increased literacy meant that diaries and memoirs became widespread and the introduction of public postal services led to a boom in letter writing.

Sir Thomas Browne

1605–1682

Browne was a physician, knighted by default when Charles II visited Norwich: the Mayor of Norwich declined this customary honour, so Browne was suggested as a substitute. His esoteric writings have influenced many subsequent writers including Swift (159), Coleridge (195) and Melville (410), who called him a 'cracked archangel'. 'Few people love the writings of Sir Thomas Browne,' wrote Virginia Woolf, 'but those that do are the salt of the earth.'

Robert Burton 1577–1640

Burton was an Oxford librarian and churchman who suffered from severe depression throughout his life. He wrote his compendious 'anatomy' of the subject in part to ease his symptoms. He lived in Christ Church College for most of his life: 'I have lived a silent, sedentary, solitary, private life,' he wrote, '*mihi et musis* [myself and the Muses] in the University.' He meticulously calculated the date of his own death, and some say he hanged himself to prove his prediction accurate.

The Anatomy of Melancholy 1621–38

'Melancholy, the subject of our present discourse […] goes and comes upon every small occasion of sorrow, need, sickness, trouble, fear, grief, passion, or perturbation of the mind […] from these melancholy dispositions no man living is free.' Writing under the pseudonym 'Democritus' (25), Burton's pseudo-medical essay on melancholy is a sprawling reverie on the human condition, overflowing with literary references and humorous asides, and ranging across topics such as goblins, beauty, astronomy, alcohol and kisses. It was the only book, according to Boswell's *Life of Johnson* (185), that ever got Johnson 'out of bed two hours sooner than he wished to rise'. 'This is one of the indispensable books,' writes Philip Pullman (341); 'for my money, it is the best of all'.

2019
ed. Angus Gowland

The Major Works 1642–70

Religio Medici, 'The Religion of a Physician', is a psychological and spiritual self-portrait; *Pseudodoxia Epidemica* is an encyclopaedia debunking 'commonly presumed truths'; *Hydriotaphia*, or *Urne-Buriall,* is both an archaeological account of a Roman burial site and a metaphysical meditation on historical funerary customs; and *The Garden of Cyrus, or, The Quincuncial Lozenge* is an enigmatic, hermetic attempt to identify intelligent design in the quincunx pattern, the 'five' pattern on a die.

1977 Penguin English Library
2006 Penguin Classics
ed. C. A. Patrides

Madame de Sévigné 1626–1696

Marie de Rabutin Chantal, Marquise de Sévigné, was one of the world's greatest letter writers. Widowed at 25, she set about cultivating her literary and social connections, meeting everybody who was anybody in the dazzling age of Louis XIV, the Sun King. She had close friendships with Madame de Lafayette (156) and La Rochefoucauld (172).

1982
trans. Leonard Tancock

Selected Letters 1648–96

Madame de Sévigné's vivacious, witty and sensitive letters to friends and family, particularly her daughter, provide an insightful chronicle of her life and times. They feature in Marcel Proust's *In Search of Lost Time*, the favourite reading material of the narrator's grandmother.

CON MEN AND CUTPURSES
Scenes from the Hogarthian Underworld
1652–1825

This lively anthology assembles memoirs, letters, ballads and court transcripts relating to 18th-century murderers, prostitutes, thieves, pirates and highwaymen: subjects include Jack Sheppard, Blackbeard, Mother Clap, Dick Turpin and Jonathan Wild. A useful glossary of cant is appended, with definitions for terms such as 'bowse', 'cully', 'darbies', 'munge', 'rhino', 'twang' and 'wap'.

Con Men and Cutpurses: Scenes from the Hogarthian Underworld

2001 Penguin Books
2004 Penguin Classics
ed. Lucy Moore, 2000

Samuel Pepys

1633–1703

Pepys was a senior naval official and administrator and was President of the Royal Society when Newton published his *Principia Mathematica* in 1687. He left his entire library of 3,000 books, organized by size, to Magdalene College, Cambridge, with instructions that nothing should be added or taken away. It remains exactly as he left it, on the bookcases that he had made especially.

The Diary of Samuel Pepys
A Selection 1660–9

It is lucky that Pepys happened to keep a detailed diary during a particularly momentous decade in English history: his journal covers the Restoration, the Dutch War, the Great Plague and the Great Fire of London. It is also fortunate that he is such a personable companion, happy to describe his theatre trips, political opinions and amorous adventures. He wrote in shorthand and used an additional cipher for his juicier entries.

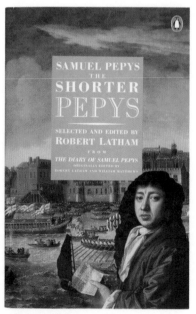

SAMUEL PEPYS
THE
SHORTER
PEPYS
SELECTED AND EDITED BY
ROBERT LATHAM
FROM
THE DIARY OF SAMUEL PEPYS
ORIGINALLY EDITED BY
ROBERT LATHAM AND WILLIAM MATTHEWS

The first complete and totally unexpurgated edition of the diary was published in eleven volumes between 1970 and 1983. This is an abridged edition of that scholarly feat.

1987 Penguin Books
The Shorter Pepys
1993 Penguin Classics
2003 *The Diary of Samuel Pepys*
ed. Robert Latham, 1985

Lady Mary Wortley Montagu

1689–1762

Lady Mary was the daughter of the Duke of Kingston. She avoided marrying an Irish aristocrat, Clotworthy Skeffington, by eloping with Edward Wortley Montagu. They married secretly in 1712 and later travelled to the Ottoman Empire, where Edward had been appointed ambassador. On her return, Lady Mary introduced inoculation against smallpox to Britain, rejected the advances of Alexander Pope (152) and fell in love with an Italian *cavaliere*. She left England in 1739 and travelled in Italy and France until she heard news of her estranged husband's death, upon which she returned to England and died later that year.

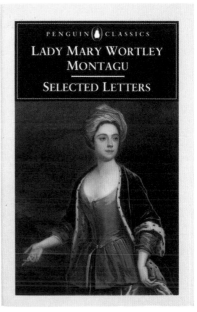

Selected Letters 1709–62

Throughout Lady Mary's remarkable life she wrote sparkling letters to her husband, sister, friends, son and her beloved daughter Mary, Countess of Bute. She discusses politics and gossip, science and literature, philosophy, the education of women, travellers' tales and various love affairs. Lady Mary is most famous for her 'Embassy Letters', which she wrote from Turkey and intended for publication, but this anthology includes intimate letters from every stage of her life.

1997
ed. Isobel Grundy

Samuel Johnson 1709–1784

Johnson was the son of a Lichfield bookseller, who moved to London to make a living by writing. He published a series of periodicals, written mostly by himself, and developed a reputation as a moral essayist before the appearance of his famous *Dictionary* (184), which secured his position as the literary giant of his age. In 1764, he founded 'The Club', an exclusive literary society at which he cultivated his virtuoso powers of witty repartee. The *Oxford Dictionary of National Biography* calls him 'arguably the most distinguished man of letters in English history'.

1968 *Selected Writings*
• ed. Patrick Cruttwell

2003
ed. David Womersley

Selected Essays

The Rambler; *The Adventurer*; *The Idler*
1750–60

Johnson began publishing twice-weekly essays under the title *The Rambler*. 'I was at a loss how to name it,' he later told his friend, the artist Joshua Reynolds. 'I sat down at night upon my bedside, and resolved that I would not go to sleep till I had fixed its title. *The Rambler* seemed the best that occurred, and I took it.' The essays were much admired by Samuel Richardson (160) and Charlotte Lennox (162). They cover subjects from sleep and solitude to marriage, mortality, time and travel. *The Rambler* was succeeded by *The Adventurer* and *The Idler*.

A Dictionary of the English Language
An Anthology
1755

After nine years 'beating the track of the alphabet with sluggish resolution', Johnson finally published his influential and idiosyncratic lexicon of the English language. He provides quotations to illustrate his definitions, frequently drawn from Shakespeare (134) and Milton (150), and includes several humorous entries, such as 'oats', which he defines as: 'A grain, which in England is generally given to horses, but in Scotland supports the people.'

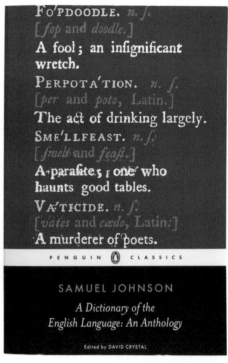

2006
ed. David Crystal

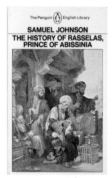

1976 Penguin English Library
• ed. D. J. Enright

2007
ed. Paul Goring

The History of Rasselas
Prince of Abissinia 1759

Johnson is said to have written this 'little story book' in the evenings of a single week, to raise money in order to visit his sick mother and settle her debts. It narrates the escape of Prince Rasselas from the Happy Valley of Abyssinia when he realizes that a life of constant pleasure is ultimately unsatisfying.

A Journey to the Western Islands of Scotland *and* The Journal of a Tour to the Hebrides
1775, 1786

In 1773, Johnson embarked on a tour of Scotland and islands with his devoted companion James Boswell (185). Both friends kept journals of the trip and this edition brings their two narratives together. Johnson's account is full of insightful observations on Scottish life, traditions, landscapes and history. Boswell focuses on Johnson. He records vignettes and details of the journey itself, including Johnson's fall from a horse and his faux pas when handling a clansman's dirk.

1984 Penguin English Library
1985 Penguin Classics
ed. Peter Levi

James Boswell 1740–1795

Boswell was born in Edinburgh and was such a rowdy student that his father packed him off to the University of Glasgow instead. Boswell then travelled to London, under the auspices of becoming a monk, but instead adopted the life of a libertine. In 1763, he met Samuel Johnson (183) at Davies's Bookshop on Russell Street in Covent Garden and formed a lasting friendship with the great man of letters, whose biography he would later write.

London Journal

1762–3, pub. 1950

Boswell kept a lively and candid diary during his time in London, in which he recorded his amorous adventures, his venereal diseases and his fateful meeting with Dr Johnson. It was only discovered in the 1920s.

1966 Penguin Books
• ed. Frederick A. Pottle

2010
ed. Gordon Turnbull

The Life of Samuel Johnson 1791

Boswell's masterpiece was his vast *Life of Johnson*. 'One would think the man had been hired to spy upon me,' remarked Johnson once, because Boswell had such an assiduous habit of keeping notes. Through a series of intimate and detailed first-hand anecdotes, Boswell sculpts what is perhaps the greatest modern biography and what he saw as a comprehensive portrait of his celebrated friend. 'Unprecedented in its time in its depth of research and its extensive use of private correspondence and recorded conversation,' writes Gordon Turnbull, 'it sought to dramatize its subject in his authorial greatness and formidable social presence, and at the same time treat him with a profound sympathy and inhabit his inner life.'

1979 Penguin English Library
• ed. Christopher Hibbert

2008
ed. David Womersley
—
Womersley's edition is majestically unabridged, with 1,312 pages weighing more than a kilo.

James Cook 1728–1779

Captain Cook was a Yorkshireman, apprenticed to a Whitby ship-owner. He joined the Royal Navy as an able seaman and rose quickly through the ranks, eventually commanding three landmark expeditions to the Pacific Ocean: to observe and record the transit of Venus, which provided the opportunity to chart the coastlines of New Zealand and Australia; to search for the hypothetical *Terra Australis*; and finally to search for the Northwest Passage. He died on this third voyage, killed by Hawaiians while attempting to kidnap their chieftain. In 1934, 'Cook's Cottage', his parents' English home, was reassembled brick for brick in Melbourne.

The Journals 1768–80

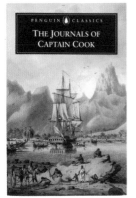

1999
ed. Philip Edwards

Cook kept detailed journals of his expeditions, describing his circumnavigation of New Zealand, his exploration of the east coast of Australia and his investigations of Antarctica, Tahiti and the west coast of North America. They evoke the dangers of sailing uncharted seas and sympathetically depict first encounters between Europeans and indigenous groups across the Pacific.

Edward Gibbon

1737–1794

Gibbon described himself as 'a puny child, neglected by my Mother, starved by my Nurse'. He was an ineffective Member of Parliament for Liskeard and Lymington, but achieved widespread renown when he published his *History of the Decline and Fall of the Roman Empire*. The historian Franco Venturi called him the 'English giant of the Enlightenment'.

 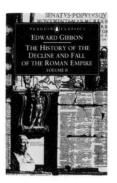 

1995
ed. David Womersley; Published in three volumes

1964 Pelican Books
● ed. D. M. Low
1982 Penguin English Library
● ed. Dero A. Saunders

The History of the Decline and Fall of the Roman Empire 1776–88

'It was at Rome, on the fifteenth of October 1764, as I sat musing amidst the ruins of the Capitol, while the barefooted fryars were singing Vespers in the temple of Jupiter,' wrote Gibbon, 'that the idea of writing the decline and fall of the City first started to my mind.' His masterwork is a hugely ambitious narrative of the history of the Roman Empire over the centuries, from the reign of the Emperor Augustus (43) to the fall of Constantinople in 1453 and Rome during the Renaissance. He describes the first Christian and last pagan emperors, Constantine and Julian, the barbarian invasions, the flourishing of Byzantium, the Crusades and the ultimate collapse of the Byzantine Empire.

2000
ed. David Womersley
Abridged edition
—
The *Times Literary Supplement* said Womersley's edition 'gives us the best text we have ever had, a vigorously intelligent introduction and an indispensable collection of ancillary documents'. His abridged edition includes complete chapters connected by bridging passages.

Memoirs of My Life 1796

Gibbons's autobiographical papers were edited posthumously by his friend Lord Sheffield. They are an intimate self-portrait of the greatest historian of the 18th century.

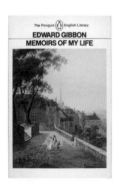

1984 Penguin English Library
2006 Penguin Classics
ed. Betty Radice

Olaudah Equiano c. 1745–1797

Equiano was born in what is now south-eastern Nigeria, enslaved at the age of eleven and transported to the West Indies.

He was brought to England by a British naval officer, who renamed him Gustavus Vassa. He eventually bought his own freedom, travelled the world and returned to London where he married an Englishwoman and became a prominent social reformer.

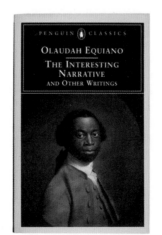

1995
ed. Vincent Carretta

The Interesting Narrative and Other Writings 1789–94

Equiano's 'interesting narrative' depicts the horrors of slavery in Africa and the West Indies. It is both a sobering autobiography and a passionate literary treatise on religion, politics and economics. It was an instant success and contributed to the passing of the the Slave Trade Act of 1807, which abolished the slave trade in the British Empire.

Gilbert White 1720–1793

Selborne is a small village in Hampshire. As a young boy, White started taking notes on the natural history of the area. He was ordained in 1749 and served as the parson of several neighbouring parishes, and simultaneously began keeping a 'Garden Kalendar'. Today his house, The Wakes, is a museum and field studies centre. The area is still good for birdwatchers, although the great bustard, observed by White, became extinct in Britain in the 19th century. (The great bustard has in fact been reintroduced on Salisbury Plain, and its population is now said to be 'close to self-sustainable'.)

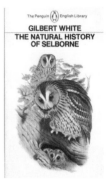

The Natural History of Selborne 1789

White's delightful, keenly observed letters to his fellow naturalists Daines Barrington and Thomas Pennant provide a fascinating overview of Selborne and of English flora and fauna in the 18th century. He includes frequent updates on the health of his tortoise Timothy, which he inherited from his aunt.

1941 Penguin Books
• ed. James Fisher

1977 Penguin English Library
1987 Penguin Classics
ed. Richard Mabey

Wolfgang Amadeus Mozart
1756–1791

Mozart wrote his first symphony when he was eight years old. He composed prolifically, producing over 600 masses, concertos, operas, serenades, chamber pieces and choral works in the course of his short life. He toured western Europe as a child, before settling in Salzburg and then Vienna.

2006
trans. Stewart Spencer
ed. Cliff Eisen

A Life in Letters

Mozart's letters, and those of his wife Constanze and father Leopold, present a multifaceted portrait of the composer, with insights into his compositions, performances, personal relationships and scatological sense of humour.

Giacomo Casanova 1725–1798

Casanova was born in Venice, the son of two actors. His parents wanted him to become a priest; instead he became a writer, adventurer, entrepreneur, soldier, con man, gambler, gourmand, violinist, librarian, necromancer, lottery director, spy and a proverbially notorious seducer. He is said to have slept with more than 200 women. He wrote novels, translated Homer (16) and may have contributed to the libretto for Mozart's *Don Giovanni*.

The Story of My Life 1791–8

Casanova began writing his autobiography in 1791 and, even at 3,600 manuscript pages, it remained unfinished when he died. He was an excellent storyteller and revels in ribald anecdotes about his youth in Venice, his escape from the prison within the Doge's Palace, his meetings with world leaders and his amorous adventures with noblewomen, nuns, and cobblers' daughters.

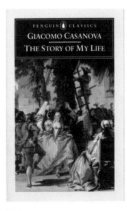

2001
trans. Stephen Sartarelli &
Sophie Hawkes
intro. Gilberto Pizzamiglio

The
Industrial
Age

Britain

The Penguin Book of English Romantic Verse

D102

CRABBE · SELECTED POEMS

ISBN 0 14 04.2365 6

William Blake

D 42

D 42

THE PENGUIN POETS

ROBERT BURNS

D 3

WILLIAM WORDSWORTH · SAMUEL TAYLOR COLERIDGE

LYRICAL BALLADS

William Wordsworth/The Prelude

ISBN 0 14 042.214 5

THE PENGUIN POETS

WORDSWORTH

2

WILLIAM WORDSWORTH   A Life in Letters

PENGUIN CLASSICS

A466

Edited by Colette Clark

Home at Grasmere

A466

S. T. Coleridge

D 35

D 35

Byron

D 26

D 26

The Romantics

A young man stands on a rocky summit, the wind ruffling his auburn hair. He leans on a stout walking stick, one foot forward, and we see what he sees: a shifting ocean of cloud and fog, swept across a vast, mountainous landscape, with great blue peaks towering in the distance. The effect is breath-taking, the view sublime (178), and though we cannot see the face of this enigmatic figure, as dark as the rocks on which he stands, we can share the powerful emotions stirring beneath his frock coat. This painting of 1818, *The Wanderer above the Sea of Fog* (350), was made by the German painter Caspar David Friedrich, who distilled the core tenet of the Romantic movement when he said: 'the artist's feeling is his law'.

Romanticism, which emerged out of the *Sturm und Drang* movement (335) in mid-18th-century Germany, was a revolt, a reaction against increasing industrialization, constricting Enlightenment rationalism (170) and a celebration of the awesome grandeur of the natural landscape and an evocation of the ungovernable inner experience of the artist. It was expressed through art, music and literature and was a profound influence throughout Europe in the first half of the 19th century.

1968 Penguin Poets
1986 Penguin Classics
ed. David Wright

POETRY

In the Romantic manifesto that forms the preface to the second edition of the *Lyrical Ballads* (193), William Wordsworth (193) describes poetry as 'the spontaneous overflow of powerful feelings [...] recollected in tranquillity'. Wordsworth and Samuel Taylor Coleridge (195), two of the first proponents of Romantic poetry in Britain, became known as the 'Lake Poets', after the Lake District of northern England where they lived along with Robert Southey and Thomas De Quincey (208). The 'second generation' of English Romantic poets was dominated by Lord Byron (195), Percy Bysshe Shelley (196) and John Keats (197).

ENGLISH ROMANTIC VERSE
1717–1848

'The Romantic Movement,' writes David Wright, 'if we are to understand what it really was about, should be viewed in its relation to the Industrial Revolution and its consequences.' His chronological selection begins with Alexander Pope (152), includes Crabbe (192), Blake (192), Burns (193), Wordsworth (193), Coleridge (195), Byron (195), Shelley (196) and Keats (197), and ends with Emily Brontë (217). He also features many lesser-known names, such as Ebenezer Elliot, James Clarence Mangan and Thomas Lovell Beddoes.

THE PENGUIN BOOK OF ROMANTIC POETRY
1773–1837

Jonathan and Jessica Wordsworth view Romanticism in relation to the French rather than the Industrial Revolution, but they agree with Wright in seeing it as an optimistic, radical movement: 'Romanticism is an aspiring, a hopefulness – an exalting, and exulting, of the imagination.' They concentrate on the two generations that followed the French Revolution, organizing their anthology thematically under headings such as 'Romantic Hallmarks', 'The Gothic and Surreal' and 'Protest and Politics'.

2003 Penguin Books
The New Penguin Book of Romantic Poetry
2005 Penguin Classics
The Penguin Book of Romantic Poetry
ed. Jonathan & Jessica Wordsworth, 2001

George Crabbe
1754–1832

Crabbe's father collected salt duties in Suffolk. Crabbe abandoned a career as an apothecary to become a writer, but he met with little success until Edmund Burke (178) befriended him, found him a publisher and enabled his second career in the Church. Crabbe became a curate at Aldeburgh and moved between various parishes before settling as rector of Trowbridge in Wiltshire.

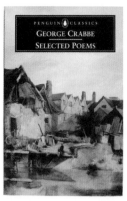

1991
ed. Gavin Edwards

Selected Poems

Crabbe's poetic career falls into two halves: in the first he wrote poems such as 'The Village' and 'Sir Eustace Gray', bleakly realistic accounts of country life, consciously reacting against the pastoral idealism of his contemporaries. After a gap of 23 years he began writing again, penning fictional verse narratives including 'Peter Grimes', 'Procrastination' and 'The Mother'. Byron (195) called him 'nature's sternest painter, yet the best'.

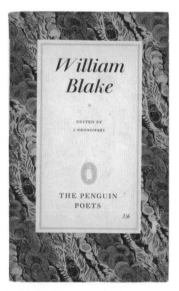

1958 Penguin Poets
• ed. J. Bronowski

William Blake 1757–1827

Blake was a fierce individualist. 'Thank God,' he wrote, 'I never was sent to School / To be Flogg'd into following the Stile of a Fool.' He trained as an engraver and taught himself to be a painter, a printmaker and a book designer. He also wrote extraordinary visionary poems, which he called 'prophecies'. He never achieved financial success in his lifetime, but today he is revered as one of the greatest and most rebellious artistic talents that Britain has ever produced. He is said to have been singing as he died. W. B. Yeats (267) called him one of the 'great artificers of God who uttered great truths to a little clan'.

Poems

Blake is most famous for his illuminated books, in which he combined text and image, individually hand-painting each relief-etched copper plate before printing. His most accessible poems are found in the *Songs of Innocence and of Experience*, which celebrate naïve virtue and condemn societal repression. He also developed a complicated personal mythology, exalting the creative imagination, which he expressed through a series of increasingly wild epic poems: the unfinished *Four Zoas*; *Milton*, in which the spirit of John Milton (150) returns to earth; and *Jerusalem*, a vast, sprawling work in which Blake dramatizes the struggle to construct a glittering city of art and science in the imagination. 'I must Create a System,' he wrote, 'or be enslav'd by another Man's.'

1977 Penguin Poets
The Complete Poems
1985 Penguin Classics
ed. Alicia Ostriker

2005 *Selected Poems*
ed. G. E. Bentley, Jr.

Robert Burns
1759–1796

Burns was the son of an Ayrshire farmer. He read voraciously alongside back-breaking farm work and he was greatly influenced by the Scots poetry of Robert Fergusson. He devoted much of his life to the collection and transcription of Scottish songs and he is now celebrated as the national poet of Scotland. Burns Night is celebrated around the world on his birthday, 25 January, with suppers that include readings of the 'Selkirk Grace' and the address 'To a Haggis', and conclude with a rendition of 'Auld Lang Syne'.

Selected Poems

'What an antithetical mind! – tenderness, roughness – delicacy, coarseness – sentiment, sensuality – soaring and grovelling, dirt and deity – all mixed up in that one compound of inspired clay!' This was Byron's (195) estimation of Burns. This selection captures the range of Burns's lyrics and poetry, from the romantic 'A Red, Red Rose' to the patriotic 'Scots Wha Hae'.

1946 Penguin Poets
ed. William Beattie

1993
ed. Carol McGuirk

William Wordsworth
1770–1850

Wordsworth was born in the Lake District and died there 80 years later. He had three brothers but was especially close to his younger sister Dorothy, with whom he lived at Dove Cottage in Grasmere from 1799. In 1802, he married Dorothy's closest friend, Mary Hutchinson. The 1815 edition of his poetry established him as the greatest poet of his age and in 1843 he was appointed Poet Laureate.

Lyrical Ballads
with A Few Other Poems 1798

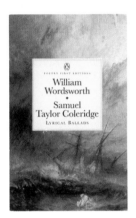

1999 Penguin Poetry First Editions
2006 Penguin Classics
ed. Michael Schmidt

Wordsworth met Samuel Taylor Coleridge (195) in 1797 and together they compiled the 23 poems that comprise the *Lyrical Ballads*, traditionally considered to be the founding text of the English Romantic movement. They explain that these poems 'are to be considered as experiments'. The volume includes many of their most famous works, including 'Tintern Abbey' and *The Rime of the Ancient Mariner*.

The Prelude
The Four Texts 1798, 1799, 1805, 1850

After Coleridge (195) encouraged him to write 'the first great philosophical poem', Wordsworth began work on a verse analysis of human consciousness, a project to which he returned throughout his career. This great poem-memoir dramatizes the 'growth of a poet's mind', recapitulating formative experiences from his childhood and his time spent as a radical student in revolutionary France. Wordsworth dedicated his masterpiece to Coleridge's memory.

 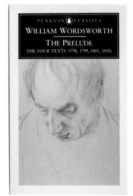

1976 Penguin Poets
ed. J. C. Maxwell

1995
ed. Jonathan Wordsworth
—
Jonathan Wordsworth is the former Chairman of the Wordsworth Trust and a descendant of the poet's youngest brother. He presents the 1805 and 1850 texts of *The Prelude* on facing pages, so they can be compared with ease.

1943 Penguin Poets
● ed. W. E. Williams
1977 Penguin Poets
The Poems
● ed. John Hayden
Published in two volumes
1994 Penguin Classics
● ed. John Hayden

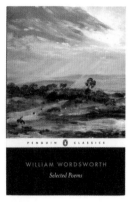

2004
ed. Stephen Gill

Selected Poems

Gill's rich selection of Wordsworth's poetry contains all his best-known verses, including 'I wandered lonely as a cloud', 'Lucy Gray' and extracts from *The Prelude* (193).

A Life in Letters

Wordsworth believed that published letters are 'a burthen to the Press, and their perusal a waste of time'. Nevertheless, the literary biographer Juliet Barker has managed to assemble a portrait of the poet's life from his own letters and those of his closest family and friends.

2007
ed. Juliet Barker, 2002

Dorothy Wordsworth 1771–1855

Dorothy lived with her brother William in Dorset, Somerset and at Dove Cottage in Grasmere. She kept a daily journal in which she captured the beauty and the grandeur of the changing Cumbrian landscape and details of life with her brother. Dorothy's biographer, Ernest de Sélincourt, called her 'probably [...] the most distinguished of English writers who never wrote a line for the general public'.

1960 Pelican Books
1978 Penguin English Library
1986 Penguin Classics
ed. Colette Clark

Home at Grasmere
Extracts from the Journal of Dorothy Wordsworth and from the Poems of William Wordsworth 1800–1803

This volume intersperses excerpts from Dorothy's journal with William's poetry, revealing the background to many of his poems and demonstrating how creatively interdependent the siblings were. For example, 'I wandered lonely as a cloud' was based on this passage from Dorothy's journal:

'When we were in the woods beyond Gowbarrow Park we saw a few daffodils close to the water-side. [...] As we went along there were more and yet more; and at last, under the boughs of the trees, we saw that there was a long belt of them along the shore, about the breadth of a country turnpike road. I never saw daffodils so beautiful. They grew among the mossy stones about and about them; some rested their heads upon these stones as on a pillow for weariness; and the rest tossed and reeled and danced, and seemed as if they verily laughed with the wind, that blew upon them over the lake; they looked so gay, ever glancing, ever changing.'

Samuel Taylor Coleridge

1772–1834

Coleridge met <u>Dorothy</u> (194) and <u>William Wordsworth</u> (193) in 1797 and wrote the drug-induced 'Kubla Khan' that same year. In 1798, he and Wordsworth published the *Lyrical Ballads* (193), which contained his nightmarish *Rime of the Ancient Mariner*. In 1800, he moved to Keswick in Cumbria and became seriously addicted to opium. His 'thoughts did not seem to come with labour and effort', wrote <u>Hazlitt</u> (208); 'but as if borne on the gusts of genius, and as if the wings of his imagination lifted him from off his feet.'

1956 Penguin Poets
• ed. Kathleen Raine

1996 Penguin Poetry Library
Selected Poetry
2000 Penguin Classics
ed. Richard Holmes

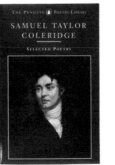

1997
The Complete Poems
ed. William Keach
—
Keach's complete edition is organized chronologically, whereas Holmes's selection is organized under headings such as 'Sonnets', 'Hill Walking Poems' and 'Visionary Fragments'.

Poems

Coleridge was the most literarily revolutionary of the Romantic poets, composing verse on a wide variety of subjects and in a number of different forms, from the medieval ballad 'Christabel' to the sombre 'Dejection: An Ode', the meditative 'Frost at Midnight' and the haunting 'Youth and Age'.

Lord Byron 1788–1824

George Gordon inherited his barony at the age of ten and in 1812 he became an overnight celebrity after the publication of the first two cantos of *Childe Harold's Pilgrimage*. He cultivated a reputation for extravagant behaviour and devastating good looks. After separation from his wife and a rumoured affair with his half-sister, Byron left England in 1816, never to return. He lived in Italy, supporting revolutionary activity there, before moving to Greece and fighting for its independence. He contracted fever and died in Missolonghi at the age of 36. <u>Goethe</u> (335) called him 'undoubtedly the greatest genius of our century'. Byron had a great fondness for animals, keeping at various times cats, dogs, horses, a fox, monkeys, an eagle, a crow, a falcon, peacocks, a badger, geese, a heron, a goat and a bear.

Don Juan 1819–24

Byron's masterpiece is an epic satire, in which a young lad romps around the world, sleeping with married women in Spain, pirates' daughters in Greece, concubines in Turkey and the Russian Empress Catherine the Great. Instead of the <u>chauvinist seducer of legend</u> (167), Byron's hero is a vulnerable *ingénue*, constantly seduced against his will by powerful women. The poem is shot through with humour, digressions and satirical attacks on western society and Byron's literary contemporaries, particularly <u>Wordsworth</u> (193) and Robert Southey. The title is pronounced to rhyme with 'true one'.

1973 Penguin Education
1977 Penguin Poets
1986 Penguin Classics
ed. T. G. Steffan, E. Steffan & W. W. Pratt
intro. Susan J. Wolfson & Peter J. Manning, 2004

Selected Poems

This selection includes the full text of *Childe Harold's Pilgrimage*, in which a young man, weary of his decadent life, travels through foreign lands seeking distraction. Harold was one of the inspirations behind the central character in Pushkin's novel-in-verse, *Eugene Onegin* (367). This volume also features the exotic eastern tales, *The Giaour*, *The Bride of Abydos* and *Mazeppa*, as well as many other poems.

1954 Penguin Poets
• ed. A. S. B. Glover

1996
ed. Susan J. Wolfson & Peter J. Manning
—
Wolfson and Manning's edition includes Byron's original notes.

Percy Bysshe Shelley

1792–1822

Shelley was the heir to a fortune and a baronetcy, but when he eloped to Scotland to marry a coffee house-owner's daughter called Harriet Westbrook, his family broke contact with him. Percy and Harriet had a daughter called Ianthe before Shelley eloped again, this time with Mary Wollstonecraft Godwin (204), whom he married after Harriet took her own life in 1816. The Shelleys lived in Italy, the 'paradise of exiles', until Percy's boat was caught in a sudden tempest in the Gulf of Spezia and he drowned. His body was cremated on the beach. 'You were all brutally mistaken about Shelley,' wrote Byron (195), 'who was, without exception, the *best* and least selfish man I ever knew.'

The boat in which Shelley foundered was called both *Don Juan* and *Ariel* after the airy spirit in Shakespeare's *Tempest* (144). The very first Penguin Book, published in July 1935, was a 'romance biography' of Shelley by André Maurois, called *Ariel*. Maurois describes Shelley as 'a demigod with flashing eyes, a shirt-collar open on a delicate throat, and hair as fine as spun silk'.

1935
Penguin
Books

1956 Penguin Poets
• ed. Isabel Quigly

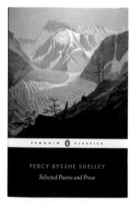

2016
ed. Jack Donovan & Cian Duffy

Selected Poems and Prose

This selection brings together all Shelley's major writings, his lyrical verses and epic poems, such as *Queen Mab*, *Prometheus Unbound*, *Adonais* and *The Mask of Anarchy*, as well as prose essays on religion, vegetarianism and the Devil. The final piece is his spirited 'Defence of Poetry', which concludes:

> Poets are [...] the mirrors of the gigantic shadows which futurity casts upon the present, the words which express what they understand not, the trumpets which sing to battle and feel not what they inspire: the influence which is moved not, but moves. Poets are the unacknowledged legislators of the World.

John Clare 1793–1864

Clare was the son of a Northamptonshire labourer. He worked as a ploughboy and a thresher and began writing poetry at the age of 13. When he was first published in 1820 he was introduced to literary London circles, but he suffered from severe bouts of melancholy and in 1837 he was admitted to an asylum on the fringes of Epping Forest. He slipped away after four years and walked home to Northborough, after which he was committed to Northampton General Lunatic Asylum, where he died 23 years later.

Selected Poems

Clare wrote from a deep knowledge and love of the fields and hedgerows of his native Northamptonshire. He was a poet of nature, but his poems are also an outcry against the enclosure of the countryside and the encroaching industrialism that threatened the landscape he loved. His expansive visionary verse is threaded with strains of madness. '[He] lived near the abyss,' wrote Seamus Heaney, 'but resolved extreme experience into something gentle.'

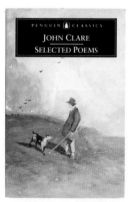

1990
ed. Geoffrey Summerfield

1973 Penguin Education
The Complete Poems

1977 Penguin Poets
1985 Penguin Classics
ed. John Barnard

John Keats

1795 – 1821

Keats trained as a surgeon at Guy's Hospital in London, before abandoning medicine for poetry. His first volume, *Poems* (1817), was a failure, as was his second, *Endymion* (1818). He was growing desperately ill from tuberculosis as he prepared his final volume for the press. He died in Rome soon after it was published, at the age of just 25.

Poems

Despite its initial lukewarm reception, Keats's poetry is now among the best-loved verse in the English language. Both these editions contain his greatest works, including 'Sleep and Poetry', 'On First Looking into Chapman's Homer', *Hyperion. A Fragment*, *The Eve of St Agnes*, 'To Autumn', 'Bright Star' and 'Ode to a Nightingale'.

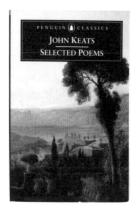

1999 *Selected Poems*
2007 Revised and reissued
ed. John Barnard, 1988

2009 *So Bright and Delicate*
intro. Jane Campion
—
So Bright and Delicate is introduced by Jane Campion, the director of *Bright Star* (2009), a romantic biopic about Keats and his beloved Fanny Brawne, starring Ben Whishaw and Abbie Cornish. The title is a reference to the poem 'Bright Star', which Keats wrote for Fanny.

Letters

Keats's letters are a literary achievement in their own right, heartbreaking, witty and sensual. 'Talking of Pleasure,' he writes to his friend Charles Dilke, 'this moment I was writing with one hand, and with the other holding to my Mouth a Nectarine – good god how fine – It went down soft pulpy, slushy, oozy – all its delicious embonpoint melted down my throat like a large beatified Strawberry.'

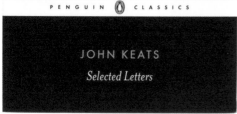

2014 *Selected Letters*
ed. John Barnard

For Victorian poetry, turn to p.262

FICTION

Sir Walter Scott's 'Waverley' novels (202) were once phenomenally popular in Britain and across Europe. They inspired artists from J. M. W. Turner to Franz Schubert and Felix Mendelssohn. Today, however, it is the novels of his contemporary Jane Austen (200) which command the equivalent international adoration. This period also saw the refinement of the Gothic novel, which emerged in the second half of the 18th century (164) and reached its peak in 1818 with the publication of Mary Shelley's *Frankenstein* (204).

William Beckford 1760–1844

Beckford was the eccentric son of a Lord Mayor of London. He fled the scandal of two rumoured affairs, with his cousin's wife and young William Courtenay, the future Earl of Devon, before returning from Europe to build a fantastical Gothic house in Wiltshire called Fonthill Abbey, where he housed Edward Gibbon's (186) library. Fonthill has since been demolished, but his ornate pink sarcophagus still lies near the folly he commissioned, Beckford's Tower, which stands on Lansdown Hill outside Bath.

Vathek and Other Stories
A William Beckford Reader c. 1781 – 1835

Vathek, Beckford's dark 'Arabian' tale of insecurity, incest and an otherworldly quest for power is his best-known work. This anthology also includes examples of his travel writing in Italy, Spain and Portugal, and the satirical, sentimental novellas *Azemia* and *The Elegant Enthusiast*.

1995
ed. Malcolm Jack, 1993
—
Vathek is also included in the *Three Gothic Novels* (163) anthology.

Elizabeth Inchbald 1753–1821

Inchbald was a Suffolk farmer's daughter with a speech impediment. She determinedly overcame her stutter, however, and ran away to London to become an actress. She became involved in radical politics and she wrote a number of successful plays: her *Lovers' Vows* (1798) features in Austen's *Mansfield Park* (201). She wrote two novels, *A Simple Story* and *Nature and Art* (1796).

A Simple Story 1791

This 'novel of passion' is a story of two halves: in the first, a Catholic priest renounces his holy orders, inherits the title Lord Elmwood and marries his young ward; the second, set seventeen years later, follows the difficult relationship between Elmwood and his daughter Matilda, whom he has avoided since his young wife had an adulterous affair and died. Maria Edgeworth (199) wrote a letter to Inchbald, saying that she had 'never read any novel that affected [her] so strongly'.

1996
ed. Pamela Clemit

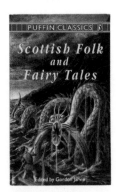

Ann Radcliffe

1764–1823

Radcliffe's novel *The Romance of the Forest* (1791) was a runaway success. She specialized in combining elements of the historical Gothic (163) with 'sublime' (178) mountainous landscapes, a style that Jane Austen would later parody in *Northanger Abbey* (200). Despite her exotic locations and sensational plots, Radcliffe and her husband lived quiet lives and she only ventured overseas once.

2000
ed. Robert Miles

The Mysteries of Udolpho

A Romance 1794

When the beautiful Emily St Aubert is orphaned, she goes to live with her aunt and her villainous Italian uncle, Signor Montoni. She must unravel the seemingly supernatural mysteries of his medieval castle of Udolpho in order to escape with her fortune and her honour intact. The novel is set in the late 16th century.

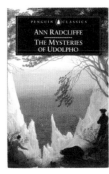

2001
ed. Jacqueline Howard

The Italian 1797

or, The Confessional of the Black Penitents

The iniquitous monk, Father Schedoni, a former leader of the Inquisition, is enlisted to murder the beautiful Ellena, with whom Vincentio is in love. Radcliffe wrote *The Italian* in response to Matthew Lewis's *The Monk*, which she saw as 'horror' Gothic as opposed to 'terror' Gothic, the style she favoured.

Matthew Lewis

1775–1818

Lewis was the son of a wealthy civil servant and became the member of parliament for Hindon in Wiltshire. On his father's death he inherited extensive slave estates in Jamaica, but he contracted yellow fever while visiting them and died on the voyage home.

The Monk

A Romance 1796

Lewis wrote *The Monk* while posted to the British embassy in The Hague. It acquired a reputation for profanity and obscenity: it is the story of Father Ambrosio, a Capuchin monk, who yields to the temptations of the flesh, engaging in increasingly depraved acts of sorcery, incest, torture and murder. Coleridge (195) was one of the novel's early reviewers: 'the author everywhere discovers an imagination rich, powerful, and fervid,' he wrote.

1998
ed. Christopher MacLachlan

Maria Edgeworth

1768–1849

Edgeworth's father was an Irish landlord who had four different wives and 22 children. She collaborated with him on a political treatise, *Practical Education* (1798), before turning her hand to writing fiction.

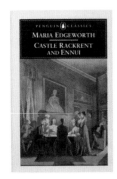

1992
ed. Marilyn Butler

Castle Rackrent
and Ennui 1800, 1809

Yeats (267) called *Castle Rackrent* 'one of the most inspired chronicles written in English'. It follows the ailing fortunes of four generations of an Anglo-Irish family as they mismanage their ruinous estate. It is narrated by the family's unreliable retainer, Thady Quirk. *Ennui* is the story of a listless Anglo-Irish earl who makes the shocking discovery that he is not in fact an aristocrat but a peasant called Christy O'Donoghoe.

The Absentee 1812

Based on an unstaged playscript, *The Absentee* is about the neglected Irish estates of Lord and Lady Clonbrony, who prefer the London high life to the management of their agents and tenants. Their son returns to Ireland incognito to assess the desperate situation.

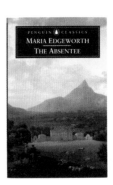

2000
ed. Heidi Thomson & Kim Walker

Jane Austen 1775–1817

Austen composed her novels with a fine brush on a 'little bit (two inches wide) of ivory'. They are scabrously witty, exquisitely observed portraits of upper-class Georgian society. The Prince Regent kept copies of her books in each of his houses and Henry James (417) ranked her alongside Shakespeare (134), Cervantes (153) and Fielding (161) as one of 'the fine painters of life'. Today she is the centre of a cult which has been growing since the 1880s: obsessive 'Janeites' host reading groups, costumed teas, literary pilgrimages and weekend retreats.

1986 *The Juvenilia of Jane Austen and Charlotte Brontë*
● ed. Frances Beer

2015
ed. Christine Alexander

1974 Penguin English Library
2003 Penguin Classics
ed. Margaret Drabble

Lady Susan
The Watsons
and Sanditon
1794–1817

Lady Susan follows the machinations of 'the most accomplished coquette in England'; *The Watsons* is a fragment of an abandoned novel, about a gifted but proud heroine called Emma (201); and *Sanditon* is Austen's last, unfinished novel, which she wrote as her health deteriorated. Set in a newly established Sussex bathing resort, it is populated with hypochondriacs and unscrupulous speculators.

Love and Freindship
and Other Youthful Writings 1787–94

Love and Freindship, as Austen misspelled it, is an anarchic parody of romantic novels, written when she was just fourteen. This collection of juvenilia also includes *The Beautifull Cassandra*, a *History of England* 'by a partial, prejudiced, and ignorant Historian', two unfinished early novels, *Evelyn* and *Catherine*, and her first complete though unpublished novella, *Lady Susan*.

Northanger Abbey 1803, pub. 1818

Young Catherine Morland's favourite novel is *The Mysteries of Udolpho* by Ann Radcliffe (199). She loves Gothic romances and imagines that life will be full of similar intrigues and adventure. She is disappointed initially by the regrettably homely Northanger Abbey, but she does eventually find love in a dramatic and romantic way.

1973 Penguin English Library
● ed. Tony Tanner

1995
ed. Ros Ballaster

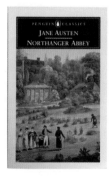

1943 Penguin Books
● —
1972 Penguin English Library
● ed. Anne Ehrenpreis

1995
ed. Marilyn Butler

Sense and Sensibility 1811

When their father dies, the Dashwood sisters find themselves in straitened circumstances. Contrasting prudence with ostentatious emotion, Elinor feels she must suppress her own affections, whereas the wild and boisterous Marianne falls disastrously in love.

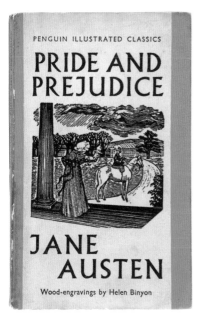

1938 Illustrated Classics
● ill. Helen Binyon
1972 Penguin English Library
● ed. Tony Tanner

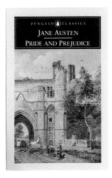

1996
ed. Vivien Jones

Pride and Prejudice 1813

'It is a truth universally acknowledged, that a single man in possession of a good fortune, must be in want of a wife.' At least, that is Mrs Bennet's view, as she determinedly sets about seeking matches for her five unmarried daughters. *Pride and Prejudice* has 'always been the most popular of Jane Austen's books', writes Claire Tomalin, Austen's biographer. It has been adapted for stage and screen numerous times, with Greer Garson, Jennifer Ehle and Keira Knightley among those playing the spirited heroine Elizabeth Bennet.

Mansfield Park

1814

Fanny Price is a poor relation, secretly enamoured of her cousin Edmund. When the charismatic Crawfords arrive from London, however, they throw life at Mansfield Park into disarray. Parts performed and games played become metaphors with real and potentially catastrophic consequences.

1973 Penguin English Library
● ed. Tony Tanner

1996
ed. Kathryn Sutherland

1973 Penguin English Library
● ed. Ronald Blythe

1996
ed. Fiona Stafford

Emma 1815

Emma is 'handsome, clever, and rich' and loves to interfere in the romantic lives of others. Austen thought she was a character 'whom no one but myself will much like', and yet many consider this Austen's masterpiece.

Persuasion 1818

Eight years ago, Anne Elliott was persuaded to break her engagement with the handsome but poor Captain Wentworth. They are given a second chance at happiness, however, when they meet again in the fashionable resorts of Lyme Regis and Bath. *Persuasion* and *Northanger Abbey* (200) were published together after Austen's death, with a biographical note from her brother.

1943 Penguin Books
● —
1973 Penguin English Library
● ed. D. W. Harding

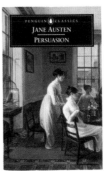

1998
ed. Gillian Beer

Walter Scott 1771–1832

Scott suffered from crippling polio as a child. He became a legal advocate and combined a day job as Sheriff-Depute of Selkirkshire with an energetic writing career, pioneering the genre of the historical novel. His works are sometimes referred to collectively as the 'Waverley Novels', because initially they were published anonymously 'by the author of *Waverley*'. Scott was made a baronet in 1820.

1972 Penguin English Library
● ed. Andrew Hook

2011
ed. P. D. Garside
intro. Ian Duncan

Waverley
or, 'Tis Sixty Years Since 1814

Scott's first novel was also the first international bestseller. Set during the Jacobite Rising of 1745, it follows a young, sensitive Englishman, Edward Waverley, who travels north to Scotland to take up an army commission. As he gets further from home, he finds his loyalties tested and his affections torn between the quiet, loyal Rose and the wild, romantic Flora. In a postscript, Scott says he aimed 'to emulate the admirable Irish portraits drawn by Miss Edgeworth' (199).

2003
ed. P. D. Garside
intro. Jane Millgate

Guy Mannering
or, The Astrologer 1815

Guy Mannering is a sceptical astrologer, who casts Harry Bertram's horoscope. Unfortunately, his prophecy comes true and Harry is kidnapped by smugglers at the age of five. Set in 18th-century Galloway and populated with scheming lairds and honest gypsies, the novel follows the fortunes of Harry and his family as he struggles to secure the inheritance of the Ellangowan estate.

Rob Roy 1817

'When I think of that novel,' wrote Robert Louis Stevenson (241) about *Rob Roy*, '[...] I am impatient with all others; they seem but shadows and imposters; they cannot satisfy the appetite which this awakened.' Rob Roy is the outlaw chieftain of the MacGregor clan, who helps young Francis Osbaldistone to pursue his dastardly and politically ambitious younger brother, Rashleigh. The book is set in 1715, on the eve of the Jacobite Uprising, and was so popular on publication in Edinburgh that an entire ship travelled from Leith to London filled with nothing but copies of the book.

1995
—
Unusually, *Rob Roy* has no critical apparatus and no named editor

1994
ed. Tony Inglis
—
As with all Scott's Scottish novels, some of *The Heart of Mid-Lothian* is written in Scots and this edition includes a glossary of terms such as 'kittle cattle' (awkward customers), 'Miss Katies' (mosquitoes) and 'cockernonie' (the gathering of a young woman's hair under the snood).

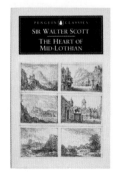

The Heart of Mid-Lothian 1818

Considered by some to be Scott's greatest novel, *The Heart of Mid-Lothian* tells the story of a dairymaid, Jeanie Deans, who walks to London to seek an audience with the Queen, to beg for a reprieve for her sister, who is due to be executed for infanticide. A different but equally implacable form of justice occurs outside the Old Tolbooth prison in Edinburgh, when Captain Porteous is lynched by a mob. This novel is thought to have inspired Eliot's *Adam Bede* (227).

PENGUIN SCOTT

The Penguin Scott editions are based on the 30-volume Edinburgh Edition of the Waverley Novels, overseen by David Hewitt and Claire Lamont between 1993 and 2012. 'This edition of Scott in Penguin offers the reader a text which is not only closer to what the author actually wrote and intended,' says Hewitt, 'but is also new in that it uses for the first time material recovered from manuscripts and proof-sheets, revealing to fuller view the flair and precision of Scott's writing.'

The Bride of Lammermoor 1819

Set in the rolling Lammermuir Hills of southeast Scotland, this is the tragic tale of young lovers Edgar Ravenswood and Lucy Ashton. Lucy's father, a devious lawyer, has previously stripped Edgar's father of his title and estate, and Lucy's mother, Lady Ashton, is hell-bent on separating the young couple.

Ivanhoe
A Romance 1820

Sir Wilfred of Ivanhoe, a Saxon noble, is banished from 12th-century England and joins Richard the Lionheart on the Third Crusade (76). On his return he is drawn into the political struggle between good King Richard and his wicked brother John. All this is set against a romanticized medieval backdrop of tournaments, witch trials, jesters, knights and Robin Hood's merry men. According to John Henry Newman (274), Ivanhoe was the book that 'first turned men's minds in the direction of the Middle Ages'.

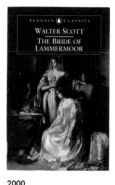

2000
ed. J. H. Alexander
intro. Kathryn Sutherland

1984 Penguin English Library
• ed. A. N. Wilson

Kenilworth
A Romance 1821

Robert Dudley, Earl of Leicester, is a favoured nobleman at the court of Queen Elizabeth I. The ambitious earl has an advantageous, flirtatious association with the Queen, but in fact he is secretly married to the beautiful Amy Robsart, whom he keeps secluded at Kenilworth Castle, his country estate, under the increasingly sinister protection of his manservant, Varney. The narrative includes walk-on parts for William Shakespeare (134) and Sir Walter Raleigh.

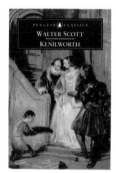

1999
ed. J. H. Alexander

Chronicles of the Canongate 1827

These three tragic stories are framed by the narrative of Chrystal Croftangry, a resident of the Canongate in Edinburgh. In 'The Highland Widow', a mother thwarts her son's ambition to join the army with fatal repercussions; 'The Two Drovers' is the tale of a violent quarrel between a Highland herdsman and an English drover; and 'The Surgeon's Daughter' is set in the streets of Madras, following the fortunes of two young Scotsmen vying for the hand of a Lowland beauty.

2003
ed. Claire Lamont

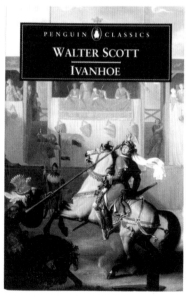

2000
ed. Graham Tulloch

Mary Shelley 1797–1851

Mary Wollstonecraft Godwin was the daughter of the radical writers Mary Wollstonecraft (205) and William Godwin (206), but she never knew her mother, who died when she was ten days old. In 1814, she eloped to Europe with Percy Bysshe Shelley (196) and they married in 1816. After Shelley drowned in 1822, Mary returned to London with their only son, Percy Florence, and worked as a professional writer for the rest of her life. Her novels include the dystopian *The Last Man* (1826), set in the 21st century, the historical *Perkin Warbeck* (1830) and *Matilda*, a novella about suicide and incest, which is published in Penguin Classics together with Wollstonecraft's *Mary* and *Maria* (205).

1985
ed. Maurice Hindle

2018
ed. Charles E. Robinson, 2008
intro. Charlotte Gordon, 2018
—
Hindle's edition is based on Shelley's 1831 single-volume edition; it includes Byron's ghost story, 'A Fragment', and Polidori's 'The Vampyre', the first modern vampire story. Gordon's volume follows the text of the first 1818 edition; it was published by Penguin to commemorate the book's 200th anniversary.

Frankenstein
or, The Modern Prometheus 1818–31

Mary and Percy spent the stormy summer of 1816 on the shores of Lake Geneva with Lord Byron (195) and his friend John Polidori. Byron suggested a ghost story competition and Mary, 18 years old at the time, based her contribution on a terrifying waking dream:

> I saw the pale student of unhallowed arts kneeling beside the thing he had put together. I saw the hideous phantasm of a man stretched out, and then, on the working of some powerful engine, show signs of life, and stir with an uneasy, half vital motion.

She worked her short story into her famous novel, which she first published anonymously in 1818. It has become the archetypal modern myth, portraying the hubris of humanity and the maker's rejection of his own creation.

Charles Maturin 1780–1824

Maturin was an Irish curate and novelist. His tragedy *Bertram* was staged at Drury Lane in London in 1816, after it was recommended by Scott (202) and Byron (195), and it proved immensely popular. Towards the end of Maturin's life, however, his works were neglected and, despite publishing volumes of his sermons, he died in poverty.

Melmoth the Wanderer 1820

The cursed Melmoth sold his soul in exchange for 150 years of extra life. Now he wanders the earth, seeking out the tortured and the helpless, offering to ease their sufferings if they will take over his satanic pact. The strange narrative is revealed through increasingly nested stories within stories that feature Jewish scholars locked inside rooms decorated with human skulls, marriages conducted by undead hermits, London lunatic asylums and the Spanish Inquisition. Influenced by the Gothic extremes of Matthew Lewis (199) and Ann Radcliffe (199), Maturin's novel is even more extravagant and macabre.

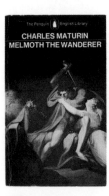

1977 Penguin English Library
• ed. Alethea Hayter

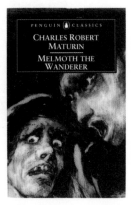

2000
ed. Victor Sage

James Hogg 1770–1835

Hogg was a Scottish Borderer who herded sheep and cattle; he became known as the 'Ettrick Shepherd'. He began conducting research for Walter Scott (202) and eventually moved to Edinburgh where he established a reputation as a narrative poet and parodist.

The Private Memoirs and Confessions of a Justified Sinner 1824

A fanatical Calvinist minister convinces a young scotsman, Robert Wringhim, that he is predestined for salvation, so he embarks on a series of escalating crimes, aided by his unnerving doppelgänger, Gil-Martin. The book is written in two halves: first the events are summarized by an 'editor', and then we read Wringhim's own account. 'It is long since I can remember being so taken hold of, so voluptuously tormented by any book,' wrote André Gide (322).

1983 Penguin English Library
● ed. John Wain

2006
ed. Karl Miller

For Victorian fiction, turn to p.210

NON-FICTION

The prose non-fiction of the Romantic period imagines optimistic utopian societies of gender equality, anarchist freedom, collective cooperation and abolished slavery, but also dark, opiate pipe-dreams, doom-laden visions of overpopulated futures and time-travelling descriptions of ancient prehistory, dwarfing humankind into insignificance.

Mary Wollstonecraft

1759–1797

Wollstonecraft was a radical and a feminist writer, in the same circle as William Blake (192) and Thomas Paine (397). After she attempted to drown herself in the Thames, her friend William Godwin (206) moved in to live with her, and they married shortly before the birth of their first child. Tragically Mary died at 38, following the birth of her daughter Mary, who later married Percy Bysshe Shelley (196) and wrote *Frankenstein* (204).

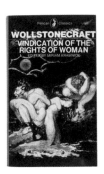

A Vindication of the Rights of Woman 1792

Published a year after Paine's *Rights of Man* (397), Wollstonecraft's pioneering treatise demands equal education for girls and boys and a society founded on fairness

1975 Pelican Classics
1982 Penguin English Library
1985 Penguin Classics
ed. Miriam Brody Kramnick

Mary *and* Maria Matilda

1788–1820

In *Mary*, a rational self-taught girl has intimate relationships with a girl and a boy, both of whom are dying of consumption. *Maria, or The Wrongs of Women* is a Gothic novel in which a woman is wrongly incarcerated in an insane asylum.

Matilda, by Wollstonecraft's daughter, Mary Shelley (204), describes a woman who is the object of her father's incestuous passion. William Godwin (206), Shelley's own father, found it 'disgusting and detestable'. It remained unpublished until 1959.

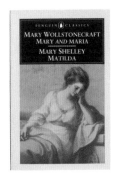

1992
ed. Janet Todd, 1991

and reason, rather than gender bias and prejudice. 'Taught from their infancy that beauty is woman's sceptre,' she writes, 'the mind shapes itself to the body, and, roaming round its gilt cage only seeks to adore its prison.' Horace Walpole (164) called Wollstonecraft 'a hyena in petticoats', but others revere her as the mother of modern feminism. 'She is alive and active,' wrote Virginia Woolf, '[…] we hear her voice and trace her influence even now.'

A Short Residence in Sweden
and Memoirs of the Author of 'The Rights of Woman'
1796, 1798

The 25 letters that form *A Short Residence in Sweden* describe a visit that Wollstonecraft made to Scandinavia in 1796: she seeks happiness through the contemplation of the sublime, comparing her quest to Rousseau's *Reveries of the Solitary Walker* (178). Wollstonecraft's biography was written by William Godwin and published after her death. The *Memoirs* are personal and candid, describing her love affairs, illegitimate children and suicide attempts. They were received with outrage by many: the poet Robert Southey accused Godwin of 'a want of all feeling in stripping his dead wife naked'.

1987
ed. Richard Holmes

William Godwin
1756–1836

Godwin trained as a Presbyterian minister in Hoxton, in East London, but subsequently lost his faith and devoted his life to polemical writing instead. He was a radical philosopher and has been described as a 'Puritanical anarchist'. He married Mary Wollstonecraft (205) and was the father of Mary Shelley (204).

Things as They Are
or, The Adventures of
Caleb Williams
1794

1988
ed. Maurice Hindle

Enquiry Concerning Political Justice
and Its Influence on Morals and
Happiness 1793

Political Justice is the founding work of anarchism, published at the height of the French Revolution. It encourages individuals to pit their inviolable liberties against the 'brute engine' of government. It calls for the abolition of rules and proposes an anarchist society based on principles of simplicity, sincerity and equality.

1976 Pelican Classics
1985 Penguin Classics
ed. Isaac Kramnick

In this 'political Gothic' novel, the honest young secretary of Squire Falkland unearths his master's terrible secret and flees, with the cruel squire in hot pursuit. It illustrates the abuses of power that Godwin observed in contemporary society, but presents his arguments as a gripping thriller. 'No one ever began *Caleb Williams* that did not read it through,' wrote William Hazlitt (208): 'no one that ever read it could possibly forget it'.

Thomas Malthus 1766–1834

Malthus was appointed Professor of History and Political Economy at the East India College in Haileybury in 1805, the first professorial appointment in economics in Britain and one he would hold for the rest of his life.

An Essay on the Principle of Population
and Other Writings 1798–1820

'The power of population is indefinitely greater than the power in the earth to produce subsistence for man.' This pioneering and prescient work of social science predicts that population growth will always outstrip food production, a view known as the 'Malthusian spectre'. His argument influenced the pioneers of evolutionary biology Charles Darwin (269) and Alfred Russel Wallace (274) and it remains highly relevant amidst today's concerns around global resources.

1971 Pelican Classics
• ed. Anthony Flew

2015
ed. Robert J. Mayhew

Charles Lamb 1775–1834

Lamb went to Christ's Hospital School in West Sussex, through the influence of Samuel Salt, his father's employer, and there he befriended Coleridge (195). Lamb joined the East India Company at seventeen as a junior clerk, and remained in the same job, at the same level, for 33 years. He took responsibility for caring for his sister Mary during her mental illness. Neither married. They lived together and adopted a child in 1823 called Emma Isola.

Selected Prose 1811–33

Lamb was a celebrated essayist, writing under the pen name 'Elia'. This selection brings together his best work, including essays on Shakespeare (134), drunkenness, witches, dreams, schoolteachers, marriage and roast pork, as well as letters to Coleridge (195), Dorothy Wordsworth (194) and other literary contemporaries.

1985
ed. Adam Phillips

2007
intro. Marina Warner

Mary Lamb 1764–1847

Mary doted on her younger brother Charles. As children, they enjoyed exploring Samuel Salt's extensive library. After Salt's death, Mary took in sewing, and cared for her invalid mother. She suffered from psychotic episodes, during one of which she murdered her mother with a kitchen knife.

Tales from Shakespeare 1807

The siblings wrote these 20 prose retellings of Shakespeare's (134) plays in collaboration. They were designed to encourage young readers to read and enjoy the plays. Mary retold the romances and comedies; Charles took the tragedies. They incorporated Shakespeare's language wherever possible: 'diligent care has been taken to select such words as might least interrupt the effect of the beautiful English tongue in which he wrote'.

The Duke of Wellington 1769–1852

'Old Nosey', Field Marshal Arthur Wellesley, 1st Duke of Wellington, fought in some 50 battles, across India and Europe, almost all of which ended in victory, and his defeat of Napoleon at the Battle of Waterloo secured his reputation as Britain's greatest military commander. After 1815, he combined civilian and military life and was twice Prime Minister of the United Kingdom, though he continued to sleep on a camp bed. He lends his name to wellington boots, a style he commissioned as more practical than the more traditional Hessian boots.

Military Dispatches

1808–15, pub. 1834–52

This selection of Wellington's dispatches traces the course of the Napoleonic Wars, from the Peninsular War in 1808 to his climactic triumph at Waterloo on 18 June 1815. They describe manoeuvres, long-term strategies, accounts of battles and losses among his men. Wellington sent the penultimate dispatch in this volume on 19 June, his official account of the Battle of Waterloo: it arrived in London on 21 June was published in full the following day in a *London Gazette Extraordinary*.

2014
ed. Charles Esdaile

—

'In some ways', writes the military historian Charles Esdaile about his edition, 'this is a very personal book.' He recalls his time as Wellington Papers Research Fellow at the University of Southampton: years that were 'some of the happiest of my whole life'.

Robert Owen 1771–1858

Owen was a successful cotton-spinner who became a pioneer of humane factory management, the eight-hour workday and universal education. He ran the New Lanark cotton mill in Scotland along these lines, but by the 1820s, he was disillusioned with capitalist economics and competitive industry, so he bought a site on the banks of the Wabash River in New Harmony, Indiana, and set up a 1,000-strong utopian community in an attempt to create a 'new moral world'.

1991
ed. Gregory Claeys

A New View of Society
and Other Writings 1813–49

Owen argues that individuals are formed by their environment, so education is essential for all levels of society. He goes on to propose a full-scale reorganization of British society into a collection of cooperative model villages. This anthology includes letters, addresses and lectures that span his career.

William Hazlitt
1778–1830

Hazlitt attended Coleridge's (195) last sermon, in 1798, where Coleridge encouraged him to pursue philosophy. Hazlitt immediately abandoned his plans to become a Unitarian minister and embarked instead on a radical literary career. Today he is best remembered for his essays, which cover philosophy and literary and social criticism, but he also refuted Malthus (206) in *A Reply to the Essay on Population* (1807) and he wrote a four-volume biography of Napoleon (1828–30).

The Fight
and Other Writings 1817–26

Hazlitt was fascinated by all kinds of performance, from theatrical productions to displays of bare-knuckle boxing, juggling and rope-dancing. This anthology includes portraits of Bentham (273), Cobbett (209), Coleridge (195), Godwin (206) and Wordsworth (193) and essays on topics such as 'Toad-Eaters', 'Hating', 'Wit' and 'Gusto'.

1970 Penguin English Library
• ed. Ronald Blythe

2000
ed. Tom Paulin &
David Chandler

Thomas de Quincey 1785–1859

De Quincey's addiction to opium began at Oxford University, at the same time that he began corresponding with his literary hero, William Wordsworth (193). He rented the Wordsworths' cottage in Grasmere for more than ten years, but the connection ended after he started publishing his candid *Recollections of the Lakes and Lake Poets* (1834–40). He had a large family and spent most of his life evading arrest for debt.

Confessions of an English Opium Eater
and Other Writtings 1821–49

In his masterpiece, De Quincey describes running away from Manchester Grammar School, wandering around Wales and London and living in poverty with a prostitute called Ann. He evokes the hallucinatory pleasures and skin-crawling pain of worshipping at the 'Church of Opium', describing nightmares, long nocturnal walks and crippling paranoia.

1971 Penguin English Library
• ed. Alethea Hayter

2003
ed. Barry Milligan
—
Milligan's edition includes two 'sequels' to the *Confessions*: the fantastical 'Suspiria de Profundis' (Sighs from the Deep) and 'The English Mail-Coach'.

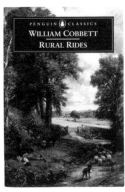

1967 Penguin English Library
• ed. George Woodcock

2001
ed. Ian Dyck

William Cobbett 1763–1835

Cobbett spent his youth as a bird-scarer and a ploughboy before enrolling in the army and serving for six years in Canada, defending the border from American incursions. He spent time in Philadelphia, writing anti-Jacobin journalism under the pseudonym 'Peter Porcupine', before returning to England and continuing to publish radical books and lectures. He ran a farm in his native Surrey and insisted that his workers were provided with the three 'Bs': bread, beer and bacon.

Rural Rides 1830

In the 1820s, Cobbett made 20 journeys around southern England on foot and horseback. This account of his trips is woven with lyrical descriptions of the changing countryside and impassioned condemnation of the deleterious conditions of agricultural workers.

Charles Lyell 1797–1875

Lyell was the son of a Scottish botanist. He studied law, but abandoned his legal practice in order to write scientific papers. He became Professor of Geology at King's College, London, President of the Geological Society and a close friend of Charles Darwin (269). He was knighted in 1848 and became a baronet in 1864.

Principles of Geology 1830–33

Lyell's revolutionary masterpiece, *Principles of Geology*, presents a world that has been shaped by vast but consistent natural forces over great aeons of time. It was controversial for placing humanity at the periphery of global history and exploring the idea of the progressive development of life. It was an important precursor of Darwinism and influenced contemporary writers including Melville (410), Emerson (399), Tennyson (263) and George Eliot (226).

1997
ed. James A. Secord

Fanny Trollope 1779–1863

Frances Milton married a London barrister called Thomas Trollope and together they leased a farm near Harrow. Their son Anthony (222) would later describe that farm as 'the grave of all my father's hopes, ambition and prosperity': the price of grain collapsed, the Trollopes spiralled into debt and Thomas sank into depression.

Domestic Manners of the Americans 1832

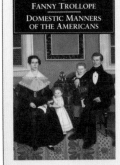

1997
ed. Pamela Neville-Sington

In an attempt to reverse the family's fortunes, Fanny took three of her five children to Tennessee to join a utopian community of emancipated slaves. The conditions were atrocious and on her return to England she published a witty and shocking account of her time in the new republic, which sold like wildfire on both sides of the Atlantic and launched her career as a bestselling author. 'If the citizens of the United States were indeed the devoted patriots they call themselves,' she concludes, 'they would surely not thus encrust themselves in the hard, dry, stubborn persuasion, that they are the first and best of the human race.'

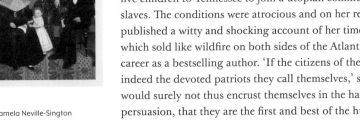

For Victorian non-fiction, turn to p.269

The Victorians

On the morning of Tuesday, 20 June 1837, just four weeks after her eighteenth birthday, a young woman was woken early in the morning. She wrote in her diary:

'I was awoke at 6 o'clock by *Mamma*, who told me the Archbishop of Canterbury and Lord Conyngham were here, and wished to see me. I got out of bed and went into my sitting-room (only in my dressing gown), and *alone*, and saw them. Lord Conyngham then acquainted me that my poor Uncle, *the King*, was no more, and had expired at 12 minutes past 2 this morning, and consequently that I am *Queen*.'

Thus began the reign of the young Queen Victoria: that morning saw the dawn of the Victorian era, a 63-year period of British history characterized by relative domestic peace, ravenous imperial expansion and the establishment of the prose novel as the pre-eminent form of literary expression in the English language.

Charles Dickens 1812–1870

Charles John Huffam Dickens had a childhood similar to the one he describes in *David Copperfield* **(213): his father was imprisoned for debt and he worked in a blacking warehouse at the age of twelve. He taught himself shorthand and became a parliamentary reporter, before writing literary sketches for periodicals.** *The Pickwick Papers* **(211) was a publishing phenomenon, which instantly elevated him and his characters to cult status, a position he maintained for the rest of his highly energetic life. He published fourteen popular novels, several novellas, hundreds of short stories and essays and he edited a weekly periodical for 20 years. When he died in 1870, there was widespread public mourning. His wish to be buried in Rochester near his country home in 'an inexpensive, unostentatious, and strictly private manner' was ignored; he was publicly interred in Poets' Corner in Westminster Abbey. Tolstoy (376) praised his social realism and he was Jules Verne's (315) favourite author. There are now Dickens Museums in London and Portsmouth, and a Dickens World theme park at Chatham.**

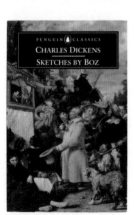

1995
ed. Dennis Walder

FICTION

The Victorian novelists are the behemoths of English literary history: a throng of men and women with large reputations and bigger bibliographies. Following the Great Reform Act of 1832, which culled rotten boroughs and expanded the conditions of suffrage, increased social awareness spawned the 'social novel', which addressed the social and economic problems associated with rapid industrialization. Dickens's *Oliver Twist* (211), Gaskell's *North and South* (221) and Trollope's *The Way We Live Now* (225) are notable examples, and this movement developed into the social realist novels of Eliot (226), Hardy (234) and Gissing (253) in the latter half of the 19th century. Other genres to emerge in this period are the fantasy stories of George MacDonald (231) and William Morris (226), the 'sensation novels' of Wilkie Collins (229) and the science fiction of H. G. Wells (255).

Sketches by Boz 1833–6

Dickens's sketches of 'every-day life and every-day people' were initially published anonymously. They are full of rich observation and a deep familiarity with the streets of London. From August 1834, he used the pen name 'Boz', taking as a pseudonym the nickname he used for his younger brother Augustus, whom he called 'Moses', after a minor character in Goldsmith's *Vicar of Wakefield* (164): Moses, 'facetiously pronounced through the nose', became 'Boses', which became 'Boz'. Dickens's identity was eventually revealed, and in 1837, a verse was published in *Bentley's Miscellany*:

Who the *dickens* 'Boz' could be
    Puzzled many a learned elf,
Till time unveil'd the mystery,
    And *Boz* appeared as Dickens' self!

1971 Penguin English Library
The Christmas Books
● ed. Michael Slater
Published in two volumes

2003
ed. Michael Slater

A Christmas Carol 1835–54
and Other Christmas Writings

A Christmas Carol is perhaps Dickens's best-loved work. It was first published on 17 December 1843 and the first edition sold out before Christmas Eve. Thackeray (219) called it 'a national benefit and to every man or woman who reads it a personal kindness'. It popularized the greeting 'Merry Christmas' and the exclamation 'Humbug!' This festive anthology also includes 'The Story of the Goblins Who Stole a Sexton', from *The Pickwick Papers*, 'The Haunted Man', 'A Christmas Tree' and other Christmas writings.

The Pickwick Papers
The Posthumous Papers of the Pickwick Club 1836–7

Dickens's first novel was an instant success. Contemporary readers loved the bumbling Samuel Pickwick, perpetual president of the 'Pickwick Club', and his fellow club members: the inept poet Augustus Snodgrass, the ineffectual lover Tracy Tupman and the incompetent sportsman Nathaniel Winkle. By far the most popular character, however, was the long-suffering, wise-cracking Sancho Panza to Pickwick's Don Quixote (153), his servant, assistant and loyal friend, Samuel Weller. Sam's popularity led to a flurry of merchandise, including a Sam Weller 'jest book' containing more than 1,000 jokes, puns, epigrams and *jeux d'esprit*.

1972 Penguin English Library
● ed. Robert Patten

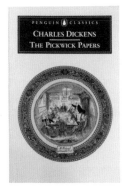

1999
ed. Mark Wormald

Oliver Twist 1837–9
or, The Parish Boy's Progress

Unlike the avuncular *Pickwick Papers*, *Oliver Twist* is set in London's criminal underworld, populated by thieves, pickpockets and murderers. 'I have yet to learn that a lesson of the purest good may not be drawn from the vilest evil,' wrote Dickens in 1841, in his preface to the third edition. '[…] I saw no reason, when I wrote this book, why the very dregs of life, so long as their speech did not offend the ear, should not serve the purpose of a moral, at least as well as its froth and cream.'

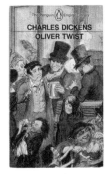

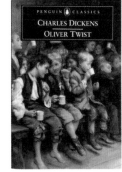

1966 Penguin English Library
● ed. Angus Wilson

2002
ed. Philip Horne

The Life and Adventures of
Nicholas Nickleby 1838–9

Dickens's third novel returns to the picaresque humour of *Pickwick*. The young Nickleby must support his mother and sister after his father dies, which he does variously by teaching at the brutal Dotheboys Hall, by acting and writing, and later by working for the benevolent Cheeryble brothers. The best passages involve the Crummles' theatre troupe, comprising panto-mimists, tragedians and an utterly untalented child known as 'the infant phenomenon'.

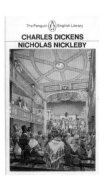

1978
Penguin English Library
● ed. Michael Slater
—
1999
ed. Mark Ford

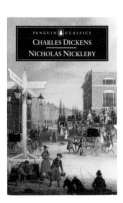

The Old Curiosity Shop 1840–41
A Tale

When the ship containing the final instalment of *The Old Curiosity Shop* was approaching the harbour in New York, desperate American readers stormed the wharf crying, 'Is Little Nell alive?' This dark novel is populated by grotesque characters: the lascivious dwarf Quilp, the feckless Dick Swiveller and Short Trotters, a travelling Punch and Judy man. It follows the picaresque fortunes of the angelic, 13-year-old Nell Trent, whom Swinburne (265) described as 'a monster as inhuman as a baby with two heads'.

 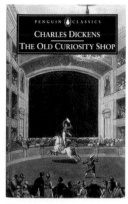

1972 Penguin English Library
● ed. Angus Easson

2000
ed. Norman Page

1973 Penguin English Library
● ed. Gordon Spence

2003
ed. John Bowen

Barnaby Rudge 1841
A Tale of the Riots of 'Eighty

The first of Dickens's two historical novels dramatizes the anti-Catholic Gordon Riots of 1780. Barnaby is a simpleton with a pet raven called Grip, an antecedent of Edgar Allan Poe's 'The Raven' (408). The most evocative descriptions are of the frenzied flaming riot itself and the destruction of Newgate Prison.

American Notes 1842
for General Circulation

Dickens visited America in 1842 with his wife and her maid. He travelled widely for five months, mobbed by avid fans wherever he went, visiting cities and institutions and preparing an account of the fascinating, post-revolutionary new country. He used his first-hand, critical observations as material in *Martin Chuzzlewit*.

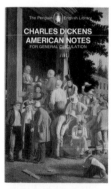 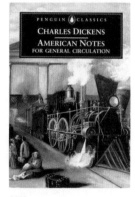

1972 Penguin English Library
● ed. John S. Whitley

2000
ed. Patricia Ingham

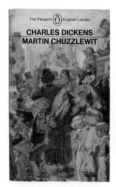 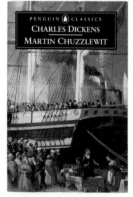

1968 Penguin English Library
● ed. P. N. Furbank

1999
ed. Patricia Ingham

The Life and Adventures of
Martin Chuzzlewit 1843–4

The first serialized instalments of *Martin Chuzzlewit* were not initially as successful as Dickens's previous publications, so he altered the plot to take Martin to the United States. The American passages are scathing: the republic is described as 'so maimed and lame, so full of sores and ulcers, foul to the eye and almost hopeless to the sense, that her best friends turn from the loathsome creature with disgust'. The *Boston Bee* ran a story about an Englishman on the voyage to America who was reading *Martin Chuzzlewit* and became so horrified at the prospect of arriving in New York that he drowned himself en route.

Pictures from Italy 1846

In July 1844, Dickens travelled to Italy and spent almost a year there. In this travelogue he presents the country, as Kate Flint puts it, 'like a chaotic magic-lantern show': he describes St Peter's in Rome, the canals of Venice and the smouldering Mount Vesuvius, and he contrasts grandiose buildings and illustrious histories with squalid poverty and disquieting social commentary.

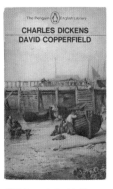

1998
ed. Kate Flint

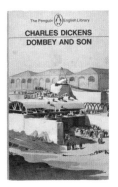

1970 Penguin English Library
• ed. Peter Fairclough

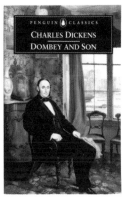

2002
ed. Andrew Sanders

Dombey and Son 1846–8

As George Gissing (253) said, the theme of *Dombey and Son* is 'Pride – pride of wealth, pride of place, personal arrogance'. Dickens unravels the consequences of pride within the dysfunctional, emotionally deprived Dombey family. The most memorable character is perhaps the piratical, hook-handed Captain Ned Cuttle, who lives in mortal fear of his landlady Mrs MacStinger, and proves to have the softest of hearts.

David Copperfield 1849–50

'Like many fond parents,' wrote Dickens, 'I have in my heart of hearts a favourite child. And his name is *David Copperfield*.' Dickens's preferred novel is a partly autobiographical *Bildungsroman*, which follows the eponymous Copperfield from his lonely Suffolk childhood to his adult vocation as a successful novelist, featuring highly memorable characters such as Mr Micawber, Uriah Heep and David's redoubtable great-aunt Betsey Trotwood.

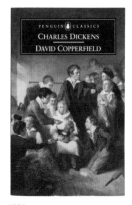

1966 Penguin English Library
• ed. Trevor Blount

1996
ed. Jeremy Tambling

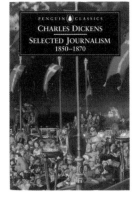

1997
ed. David Pascoe

Selected Journalism
1850–70

In 1850 Dickens founded the literary journal *Household Words*, which was succeeded in 1859 by *All the Year Round*. He took the names from Shakespeare (134): *Henry V* ('Familiar in his mouth as household words') and *Othello* ('The story of our lives, from year to year'). He serialized his own novels in these periodicals, as well as those of Elizabeth Gaskell (220) and Wilkie Collins (229) and he also contributed many standalone pieces, from which this anthology makes a selection. It includes Dickens's atmospheric account of a nocturnal ramble through the streets of London, 'Night Walks'.

1971 Penguin English Library
● ed. Norman Page
intro. J. Hillis Miller

1996
ed. Nicola Bradbury
pref. Terry Eagleton

Bleak House 1852–3

London. Michaelmas Term lately over, and the Lord Chancellor sitting in Lincoln's Inn Hall. Implacable November weather. As much mud in the streets, as if the waters had but newly retired from the face of the earth, and it would not be wonderful to meet a Megalosaurus, forty feet long or so, waddling like an elephantine lizard up Holborn Hill.

This sprawling populous novel of persistent grime, legal obfuscation, secret identities and spontaneous human combustion is summarised in its one-word opening sentence. It is Dickens's greatest evocation of the dirty labyrinthine city where he lived: London. The story is shared between the modest Esther Summerson and an omniscient narrator, who pans and zooms from gaping cityscapes to intimate scenes in garrets and graveyards. It is 'his best novel,' wrote G. K. Chesterton (293). '[…] When Dickens wrote *Bleak House* he had grown up.'

Little Dorrit

1855–7

William Dorrit has been imprisoned in the Marshalsea for so long his three children have grown up in the debtors' prison; his youngest daughter Amy, known as 'Little Dorrit', was born there. Dickens's own father did time in the Marshalsea. In this novel he shows how far its shadow stretches, touching the lives of rent-collectors, financiers and bureaucrats alike.

1970 Penguin English Library
● ed. George Woodcock

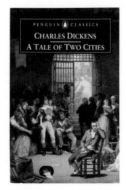

2000
ed. Richard Maxwell

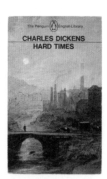

1969 Penguin English Library
● ed. David Craig

1995
ed. Kate Flint

Hard Times
For These Times 1854

Dickens's shortest novel, and the only one set entirely outside London, is based in the fictional Yorkshire mill-town of Coketown. It is fundamentally a critique of Utilitarianism (273) and a commentary on the appalling working conditions of the Industrial Revolution. George Bernard Shaw (294) called it a 'passionate revolt against the whole industrial order of the modern world'.

1967 Penguin English Library
● ed. John Holloway

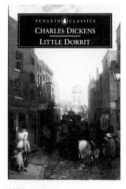

1998
ed. Stephen Wall & Helen Small

A Tale of Two Cities 1859

'It was the best of times, it was the worst of times'. Dickens's second historical novel is set during the French Revolution and the Reign of Terror and involves the disillusioned English barrister Sydney Carton, the noble Frenchman Charles Darnay, the beautiful Lucie Manette and the bloodthirsty Madame Defarge. The final line, spoken below the blade of the guillotine, is almost as famous as the first:

It is a far, far better thing that I do, than I have ever done; it is a far, far better rest that I go to, than I have ever known.

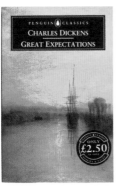

1955 Penguin Books
• –
1965 Penguin English Library
• ed. Angus Calder

1996
ed. Charlotte Mitchell
intro. David Trotter

Great Expectations 1860–61

Magwitch lurking in a marsh graveyard, Miss Havisham mouldering beside her untouched wedding cake, the haughty Estella playing cards, Jaggers washing his hands. *Great Expectations* is full of memorable images: Dickens called it a 'grotesque tragi-comic conception'. The story follows the transformation of the humble Pip into a London gentleman, with great but mysterious expectations. When the novelist Edward Bulwer-Lytton complained that the ending was too sad, Dickens rewrote it to be more ambiguous; the original ending is appended to this edition.

Our Mutual Friend 1864–5

Dickens's last complete novel opens with Gaffer Hexam and his daughter Lizzie, rifling the pockets of bloated corpses floating in the Thames. It is a novel about money and rubbish and the profits to be made from dirt and death. Dickens almost lost the manuscript of the sixteenth instalment when he was involved in a rail crash. In the novel's postscript he recalls how

> on Friday the Ninth of June in the present year, Mr. and Mrs. Boffin […] were on the South Eastern Railway with me, in a terribly destructive accident. When I had done what I could to help others, I climbed back into my carriage – nearly turned over a viaduct, and caught aslant upon the turn – to extricate the worthy couple. They were much soiled, but otherwise unhurt.

1971 Penguin English Library
• ed. Stephen Gill

1997
ed. Adrian Poole

The Mystery of Edwin Drood 1870

Edwin Drood disappears during a storm on Christmas Eve and suspicion falls on his uncle John Jasper, the respectable choirmaster and secret opium addict, who is madly in love with Drood's orphaned fiancée Rosa Bud. Tantalizingly, the mystery is never resolved, because Dickens died while writing it, but he does seem to have revealed the identity of the murderer in a letter to his friend John Forster. Many subsequent authors have contributed possible endings.

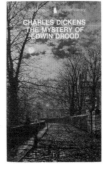
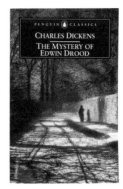

1974 Penguin English Library
• ed. Arthur J. Cox
intro. Angus Wilson

2002
ed. David Paroissien

1976 Penguin English Library
1985 Penguin Classics
ed. Deborah A. Thomas
notes Angus Calder

Selected Short Fiction 1836–66

This anthology of Dickens's shorter fiction includes 'The Signalman', 'A Christmas Tree' and 'To Be Read at Dusk' as well as lesser-known pieces such as 'The Baron of Grogzwig', 'His Brown-Paper Parcel' and 'To Be Taken Immediately'. Deborah Thomas organizes her selection under three headings: 'Tales of the Supernatural', 'Impressionistic Sketches' and 'Dramatic Monologues'.

Charlotte Brontë 1816–1855

Charlotte Brontë grew up in Haworth parsonage, on the edge of the Yorkshire moors. After her mother and two older sisters died, she was educated at home with her three surviving siblings, Emily (217), Branwell and Anne (218). She later became a teacher and a governess and encouraged her sisters to contribute to a joint poetry collection, published under the pen names 'Currer, Ellis and Acton Bell'. Her three siblings died between September 1848 and May 1849, after which she continued living alone with her father at Haworth before finally marrying her father's curate in 1854. She died herself less than a year later, along with her unborn child, a few weeks before her 39th birthday. Her father asked Elizabeth Gaskell to write her biography (221).

Tales of Angria 1838–9

Mina Laury; *Stancliffe's Hotel*; *The Duke of Zamorna*; *Henry Hastings*; *Caroline Vernon*; *The Roe Head Journal Fragments*

As children, the Brontë siblings invented an imaginary African kingdom called 'Angria'. In the 1830s, with her younger brother Branwell, Charlotte began writing several tales set in this fictional land, of which these five 'novelettes' are the last. They are narrated by Charles Townshend, who gossips about the scandalous aristocrats of Angria: the Duke of Wellington (207), the ageing roué Northangerland, his handsome son-in-law Zamorna and the young governess Elizabeth Hastings.

2006
ed. Heather Glen
—
Glen's volume replaces a 1986 edition, edited by Frances Beer, which also included the juvenilia of Jane Austen (200).

1948 Penguin Books
● —

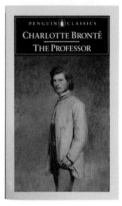

1989
ed. Heather Glen

The Professor c. 1846, pub. 1857

Charlotte's first novel was turned down by publishers, unlike Emily's *Wuthering Heights* (217) and Anne's *Agnes Grey* (218). *The Professor* was inspired by Charlotte's experience of teaching in Brussels: it follows the changeable fortunes of a young schoolmaster called William Crimsworth. *The Professor* was never published in her lifetime, but Charlotte reworked the themes and much of the content in her last novel, *Villette* (217).

Jane Eyre 1847

1953 Penguin Books
● —
1966 Penguin English Library
● ed. Q. D. Leavis
1996
● ed. Michael Mason

2006
ed. Stevie Davies

Jane Eyre is the story of an independent-spirited but lonely governess who falls in love with her Byronic employer, Mr Rochester, only to uncover a dreadful secret. Brontë blends the interiority of Romantic poetry (191) with a dramatic, Gothic (163) plot to create one of the first subjectively psychological novels. She dedicated the second edition to Thackeray (219), who thought it the 'masterwork of a great genius'. Jean Rhys wrote *Wide Sargasso Sea* as a prequel.

Shirley 1849

Shirley tells the story of a struggling Yorkshire textile mill against the backdrop of industrial unrest following the Napoleonic Wars. Shirley was a boy's name at the time: Shirley Keeldar is so-named because her father was hoping for a boy. As a result of this novel, however, Shirley is now a girl's name. Gaskell (220) reported that the character of Shirley was 'Charlotte's representation of Emily'. Charlotte was in the middle of writing the novel when her three siblings died.

1974 Penguin English Library
● ed. Andrew Hook
2006
ed. Jessica Cox
intro. Lucasta Miller

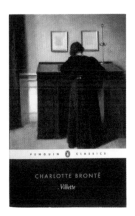

Villette 1853

Villette is a small town in Belgium, where the lonely Lucy Snowe takes a job in a girls' boarding school. She falls in love with both the school's English doctor and the fierce professor Paul Emanuel, and her unrequited desires eventually lead to a mental breakdown. *Villette* is 'a still more wonderful book than *Jane Eyre*,' (216) wrote George Eliot (226). 'There is something almost preternatural about its power.'

1979 Penguin English Library
● ed. Mark Lilly
2004
ed. Helen M. Cooper

Emily Brontë 1818–1848

Emily was two years younger than her sister Charlotte (216). She had no friendships outside the family. Her only novel, *Wuthering Heights*, was published exactly a year before she died of tuberculosis at the age of 30. Charlotte praised Emily's 'secret power and fire that might have informed the brain and kindled the veins of a hero'.

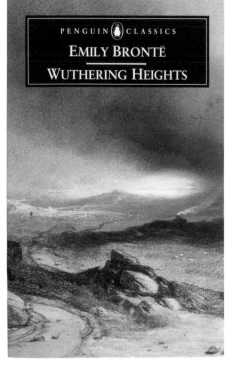

Wuthering Heights 1847

'It is a fiend of a book – an incredible monster,' wrote Dante Gabriel Rossetti (265). '[…] The action is laid in hell, – only it seems places and people have English names there.' The new tenant of Thrushcross Grange becomes lost in a snowstorm on the bleak Yorkshire moors and seeks shelter at Wuthering Heights. During his visit he starts to unravel the tumultuous events that once took place there between the brooding, swarthy Heathcliff and the passionate Catherine Earnshaw.

1946 Penguin Books
● —
1965 Penguin English Library
● ed. David Daiches

1995
ed. Pauline Nestor, 1995
pref. Lucasta Miller, 2003

Wuthering Heights was the first title in the Penguin English Library (xviii) series, which launched in 1965.

The Complete Poems

Only twenty-one of Emily Brontë's poems were published during her lifetime, in a volume with those of her sisters, but she wrote powerful verse throughout her short life. This editions collects over 200 poems: many of them describe the mythical Pacific island state of Gondal, a fantasy world she invented with her sister Anne; others are inspired by the wild Yorkshire countryside and the prospect of her own mortality.

1992
ed. Janet Gezari

Anne Brontë 1820–1849

Anne was the youngest of the Brontë family, eighteen months younger than Emily (217). Her mother died when she was just one year old. She held two positions as governess, at Blake Hall and Thorp Green Hall. She died in May 1849, five months after Emily. 'I have no horror of death,' she wrote. '[…] But I wish it would please God to spare me not only for Papa's and Charlotte's (216) sakes, but because I long to do some good in the world before I leave it.'

Agnes Grey 1847

This novel is a sobering portrait of an unmarried educated woman in Victorian society, whose only respectable option is to endure the frequently oppressive and abusive position of governess. The Irish novelist George Moore praised *Agnes Grey* as having 'all the qualities of Jane Austen (200) and other qualities'. This edition includes Charlotte Brontë's (216) biography of her two sisters, 'Biographical Notice of Ellis and Acton Bell', which she included in the 1850 reprint of the combined volume containing *Wuthering Heights* (217) and *Agnes Grey*.

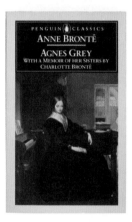

1988
ed. Angeline Goreau

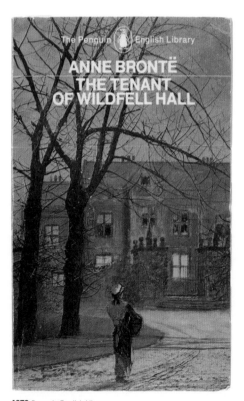

1979 Penguin English Library
● ed. G. D. Hargreaves

The Tenant of Wildfell Hall 1848

Helen Graham is the beautiful and mysterious new tenant of Wildfell Hall who soon becomes the focus of local gossip. Her neighbour, Gilbert Markham, discovers that she has escaped an abusive former marriage and is struggling for domestic independence and creative freedom as an artist. When Helen slams the door in her husband's face, wrote the novelist May Sinclair in 1914, Anne 'slammed it in the face of society and all existing moralities and conventions'.

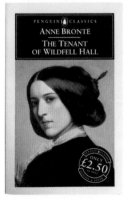

1996
ed. Stevie Davies

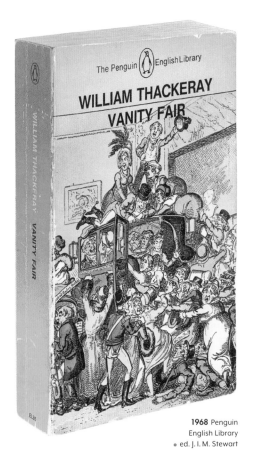

William Makepeace Thackeray 1811–1863

Thackeray was born in Calcutta but his father died when he was four and he was immediately sent home to England to be educated. On the voyage he stopped at St Helena and saw Napoleon in 1815. His works often revolve around roguish villains and are laced with social satire. He was an inveterate gourmand, addicted to spicy peppers; his favourite pastimes besides writing were 'guttling and gorging'. He died of a stroke on Christmas Eve, at the age of 52.

Vanity Fair 1847–8

Framed as a puppet play at 'Vanity Fair' (173), Thackeray's masterpiece tells the story of the enchanting and ambitious Becky Sharp, who ruthlessly scales the social ladder using every manipulative weapon in her considerable arsenal. This fiercely satirical domestic drama is set at the time of the Napoleonic Wars and John Carey compares it to the other great novel of that period, Tolstoy's *War and Peace* (378). 'You will not easily find a second Thackeray,' wrote Charlotte Brontë (216). 'How he can render, with a few black lines and dots, shades of expression, so fine, so real; traits of character so minute, so subtle, so difficult to seize and fix – I cannot tell; I can only wonder and admire'.

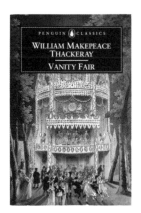

2001
ed. John Carey

The History of Pendennis 1848–50

Henry James (417) called Thackeray's later novels 'loose baggy monsters'. In a series of episodic and semi-autobiographical vignettes, *Pendennis* describes the career of the young Arthur Pendennis, 'Pen', as he moves from a brutal school to 'Oxbridge', a term invented by Thackeray, and on to the kaleidoscopic delights of London.

1972 Penguin English Library
1986 Penguin Classics
ed. Donald Hawes
intro. J. I. M. Stewart

The History of Henry Esmond 1851–2

Set during the Glorious Revolution and the reign of Queen Anne, *Henry Esmond* centres around a colonel in Marlborough's army who must learn to let go of his conservatism and Catholicism to embrace a Protestant future. Anthony Trollope (222) considered it Thackeray's greatest work, but George Eliot (226) called it 'the most uncomfortable book you can imagine [...] the hero is in love with the daughter all through the book, and marries the mother at the end.'

1970 Penguin English Library
1985 Penguin Classics
ed. John Sutherland &
Michael Greenfield

Elizabeth Gaskell 1810–1865

Elizabeth Cleghorn Gaskell was born in London but grew up in Cheshire and the north of England. In 1832 she married a Unitarian minister. They settled in Manchester, where she raised children and worked with the poor of the parish. She was a lifelong friend of Charlotte Brontë (216).

Mary Barton 1848
A Tale of Manchester Life

Gaskell's only son died in infancy in 1845 and she began writing her first novel shortly afterwards. Mary must choose between her working-class lover Jem Wilson and the well-to-do mill-owner's son Henry Carson. This bleak 'Tale of Manchester Life' is set amidst the overflowing narrow slums of that industrial city and presented contemporary readers with a stark portrait of class divisions in the 'hungry forties'. It sold thousands of copies and was highly praised by Thomas Carlyle (269) and Maria Edgeworth (199).

1970 Penguin English Library
• ed. Stephen Gill

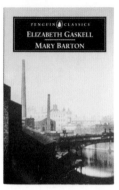

1996
ed. Macdonald Daly

Cranford 1851–3

Gaskell published the delightfully comic *Cranford* in seven irregular instalments, describing the gossipy female inhabitants of a small village, modelled on Knutsford, Cheshire, where she spent her own childhood. It is 'practically structureless', wrote the critic A. B. Hopkins; 'this is part of its charm. The successive scenes pass before the reader as easily as if he were slipping different coloured beads along a string.'

1976 Penguin English Library
Cranford and Cousin Phillis
1986 Penguin Classics
ed. Peter Keating
—
Keating's edition includes *Cousin Phillis*, a novella about a fleeting love affair between two adolescent cousins.

2005
ed. Patricia Ingham

Gothic Tales
1851–61

Gaskell wrote ghostly, gothic stories in contrast to her realist novels. The longest in this collection is 'Lois the Witch', a story about the Salem witch trials (395): the orphaned Lois Barclay, newly arrived in Massachusetts, is accused of witchcraft and blamed for the pastor's daughters' satanic convulsions. Other stories include 'The Poor Clare', about an evil doppelgänger, and 'The Grey Woman', in which a young wife attempts to escape her abusive husband.

2000
ed. Laura Kranzler

Ruth 1853

In 1850, Gaskell visited a girl called Pasley in prison. Pasley became the model for Ruth Hilton, an orphaned seamstress who is picked up by a rakish gentleman only to be deserted with an illegitimate child. Gaskell's compassionate and honest portrait of a 'fallen woman' has been compared with Hawthorne's *Scarlet Letter* (412) and Hardy's *Tess of the D'Urbervilles* (238).

1997
ed. Angus Easson

North and South 1854–5

Margaret Hale, from southern England, records her impressions of the fictional northern town of Milton. She describes the hardships of the Industrial Revolution, the clashes of mill owners with their workers and some of the first industrial strikes. The novel was serialized in Dickens' magazine *Household Words* immediately after his own *Hard Times* (214), which deals with similar subjects. Dickens described it as an 'admirable story [...] full of character and power'.

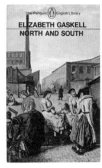 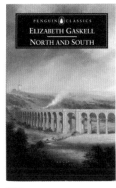

1970 Penguin English Library
● ed. Dorothy Collin

1995
ed. Patricia Ingham

 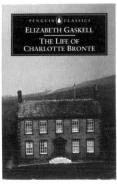

1975 Penguin English Library
● ed. Alan Shelston

1997
ed. Elisabeth Jay

The Life of Charlotte Brontë 1857

When Charlotte Brontë (216) died in 1855, Patrick Brontë asked Gaskell to write his daughter's biography. Gaskell's portrait of her friend captures the isolation of the Brontës' early childhood and describes Charlotte's intensely private life, focusing on domestic details as well as her literary genius. Patrick predicted that it would 'stand in the first rank, of Biographies, till the end of time'.

Wives and Daughters 1864–6

Gaskell's greatest novel tells the story of young Molly Gibson's relationship with her manipulative stepmother and glamorous stepsister. Set in the close-knit community of Hollingford, Molly must learn to believe in herself to save her reputation and win the man she loves. The novel was unfinished when Gaskell died of a heart attack in 1865. 'Here the story is broken off,' wrote the editor of the *Cornhill* magazine, in which *Wives and Daughters* was serialized, 'and it can never be finished. What promised to be the crowning work of a life is a memorial of death.'

Sylvia's Lovers 1863

Gaskell travelled to Whitby on the Yorkshire coast to gather material for this, her only historical novel, which she described as 'the saddest story I ever wrote'. Sylvia loves the whaler Charley, who is press-ganged into service during the Napoleonic Wars. Meanwhile, her dull Quaker cousin hopes to marry her himself. Gaskell read Eliot's *Adam Bede* (227) during her visit to Whitby.

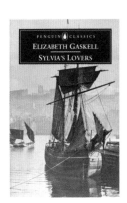

1996
ed. Shirley Foster

THE PENGUIN BOOK OF GHOST STORIES
from Elizabeth Gaskell to Ambrose Bierce 1852–1910

The nineteen tales in this collection feature phantom coaches, evil familiars, shadowy houses, sinister children and mysterious doppelgängers from the imaginations of Gaskell (220), Dickens (210), Stevenson (241), Oliphant (233) and both Jameses, Henry (417) and M.R. (283).

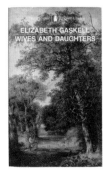 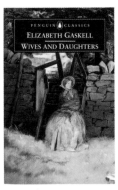

1969 Penguin English Library
● ed. Frank Smith

1996
ed. Pam Morris

1984 Penguin Books
● ed. J. A. Cuddon

2010
ed. Michael Newton

Anthony Trollope 1815–1882

Trollope was the son of an irascible, bankrupt barrister going slowly mad with mercury poisoning. His mother Fanny (209) was a bestselling author. Trollope wrote almost 50 novels while simultaneously pursuing a career as a civil servant in the General Post Office. He introduced pillar boxes to Britain and occasionally dipped into the GPO 'lost letters' box to find ideas for his novels. George Eliot (226) reportedly said that it was the Chronicles of Barsetshire that gave her the confidence to write *Middlemarch*. 'Of all novelists in any country,' wrote W. H. Auden, 'Trollope best understands the role of money. Compared with him, even Balzac (308) is too romantic.'

THE CHRONICLES OF BARSETSHIRE 1855–67

Set in the fictitious county of Barsetshire and its cathedral city of Barchester, these six novels are regarded collectively as Trollope's best-loved works. They involve the landed gentry and the clergy and their obsessive preoccupation with property. Nathaniel Hawthorne (412) praised their realism: it is 'as if some giant had hewn a great lump out of the earth and put it under a glass case,' he wrote, 'with all its inhabitants going about their daily business'.

The Warden 1855

Septimus Harding, the well-meaning elderly warden of a set of religious almshouses in Barchester, is devastated when the institution's lavish medieval bequest is called into question by his daughter's suitor, the zealous John Bold. Hiram's Hospital is modelled on the Hospital of St Cross near Winchester, where Trollope went to school. He had the idea for *The Warden* one midsummer evening while visiting Salisbury Cathedral.

1944 Penguin Books
• —

1984 Penguin English Library
1986 Penguin Classics
ed. Robin Gilmour

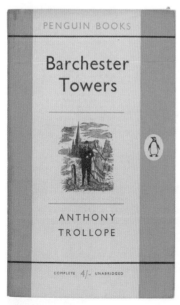

1957 Penguin Books
• —

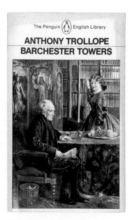

1983 Penguin English Library
1987 Penguin Classics
ed. Robin Gilmour
pref. John Kenneth Galbraith

Barchester Towers 1857

When the Bishop of Barchester dies, a struggle ensues between opposing High and Low Church factions. Finally the evangelical and ineffectual Dr Proudie is appointed, which causes deep divisions within the diocese. The formidable Mrs Proudie clashes with the disappointed Archdeacon Grantly, while the oily chaplain Obadiah Slope makes amatory advances towards the alluring, crippled widow Signora Neroni.

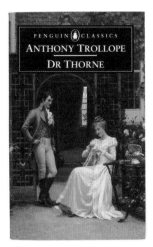

1991
ed. Ruth Rendell

Doctor Thorne 1858

Dr Thorne's illegitimate niece Mary is in love with Frank Gresham, the son of the local squire, but his mother and aunt are against the match. Only Dr Thorne knows that Mary is due to receive a great inheritance. He remains quiet because he wants her to be accepted for herself. Ruth Rendell describes Trollope as 'almost the only Victorian to bring to modern readers people with whom they can effortlessly identify'.

Framley Parsonage 1860–1

Framley Parsonage revolves around a young vicar, Mark Robarts, who agrees to guarantee a loan for a dishonourable local Member of Parliament, only to face the prospect of financial ruin. The story is 'thoroughly English', wrote Trollope. 'There was a little fox-hunting and a little tuft-hunting, some Christian virtue and some Christian cant. There was no heroism and no villainy. There was much Church, but more love-making.'

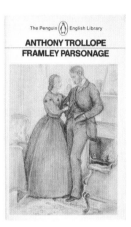

1984 Penguin English Library
1986 Penguin Classics
ed. David Skilton & Peter Miles

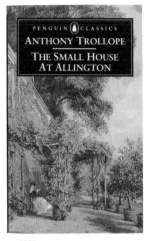

1991
ed. Julian Thompson

The Small House at Allington 1862–4

Lily Dale is a spirited, independent heroine, who nevertheless remains loyal to her erstwhile fiancé, the feckless Adolphus Crosbie, even after he jilts her for the aristocratic Lady Alexandrina. In fact her feelings blind her to a subsequent, more deserving suitor. Lily Dale was an immensely popular character: at least two ships were named after her in the 1860s. In 1992, the Prime Minister John Major selected *The Small House at Allington* as his favourite book on the BBC Radio 4 programme *Desert Island Discs*.

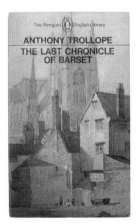

1967 Penguin English Library
• ed. Peter Fairclough

The Last Chronicle of Barset 1866–7

Trollope considered this work 'the best novel I have written'. It revolves around the impoverished Reverend Josiah Crawley, the perpetual curate of Hogglestock, who is accused of purloining a large cheque. The novel resolves narratives from across the Chronicles of Barsetshire. It features the peaceful death of Septimus Harding, who is mourned by his family and the elderly beadsmen under his charge.

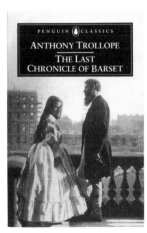

2002
ed. Sophie Gilmartin

THE PALLISER NOVELS 1864–80

Trollope's six Palliser or 'parliamentary' novels concern a political dynasty, the Pallisers, who have political influence in Barsetshire. The six novels overlap with the Chronicles of Barsetshire (222): the central character, Plantagenet Palliser, was first introduced as a minor figure in *The Small House at Allington*.

Can You Forgive Her? 1864–5

Parallel storylines follow the decisions of three strong-minded women: Alice Vavasor must choose between two contrasting suitors; her cousin Lady Glencora marries the politician Plantagenet Palliser instead of the penniless Burgo Fitzgerald; and her widowed aunt Arabella Greenow enjoys flirting with a number of attractive young beaux. An uncharitable contemporary review in *Punch* suggested the alternative title, *Can You Stand Her?*

Phineas Finn 1867–8

Phineas Finn, The Irish Member follows the fortunes of the energetic and debonair Phineas, who has recently been elected to Parliament. With the aid of influential women, he climbs the ranks of government, until he is faced with an ethical dilemma that could make or break his political career.

The Eustace Diamonds 1871–3

The dazzlingly beautiful Lizzie Eustace thinks that lies are 'more beautiful than truth'. When her wealthy husband Sir Florian dies, she finds herself in the possession of a hugely valuable diamond necklace. She claims it was a gift from her late husband, but the family lawyers insist it belongs to the Eustace estate, and Lizzie must go to increasingly desperate lengths to retain the booty.

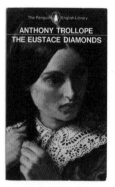

Phineas Redux 1873–4

Phineas Finn is living quietly in Dublin, resigned to the fact that his political career is over, when he receives an unexpected invitation to return to Parliament. He jumps at the opportunity, but the murder of his political adversary Mr Bonteen leaves Phineas as the prime suspect.

The Prime Minister 1875–6

Palliser Plantagenet is Prime Minister and an aristocrat of scrupulous morals. His equanimity is upset, however, by the political rise of Ferdinand Lopez, who ingratiates himself with influential ladies, including Palliser's own wife, Lady Glencora.

The Duke's Children 1879–80

The last of the Palliser novels was published as a serial in Dickens's journal *All the Year Round* (213). The former Prime Minister, Plantagenet Palliser, Duke of Omnium, has lost his beloved wife as well as his political position, and now he must support his three adult children. They disappoint him in different ways, but perhaps Palliser himself needs to change.

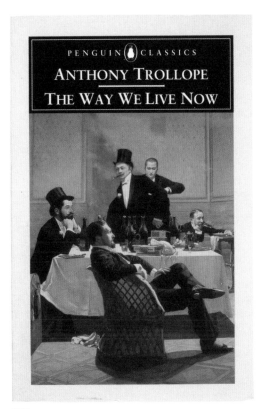

1994
ed. Frank Kermode

The Way We Live Now 1875

Many critics consider *The Way We Live Now* to be Trollope's greatest single novel. At 100 chapters, it is almost certainly his longest. This 'state of the nation' novel tells the story of Augustus Melmotte, a fraudulent financier who cons dissolute noblemen into speculating in dubious financial ventures. As his web of deceit grows wider, however, it threatens to collapse around him.

1994
ed. Frank Kermode

He Knew He Was Right
1869

Louis Trevelyan visits the remote Mandarin Islands and falls in love with Emily, the governor's daughter. They marry, but on their return to England Louis becomes increasingly and unreasonably jealous of his wife, while Emily stubbornly refuses to placate his concerns. Trollope includes references to Shakespeare's *Othello* (141) throughout.

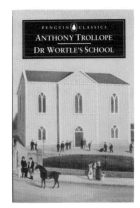

1999
ed. Mick Imlah

Dr Wortle's School 1881

Mr Peacocke, a classical scholar, arrives to teach at Dr Wortle's Christian school in Broughton-shire with his beautiful American wife. When the blackmailing brother of Mrs Peacocke's first husband appears at the school gates, however, Peacocke must rely on Dr Wortle's support to refute a dreadful revelation that threatens to scandalize the county and damage the reputation of the school.

PENGUIN TROLLOPE

In 1993, Penguin published the Penguin Trollope series: 53 volumes with matching covers, comprising all Trollope's novels, short stories and his autobiography.

1993
Penguin Trollope

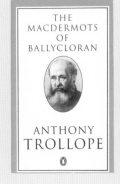
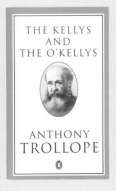
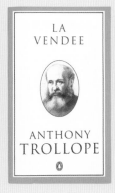
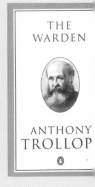

William Morris 1834–1896

Morris was a wallpaper designer, furniture craftsman, embroiderer, poet, translator of Icelandic sagas (91), businessman, socialist, conservationist and publisher. At Oxford he became lifelong friends with the painter Edward Burne-Jones and was greatly influenced by John Ruskin (271) and Dante Gabriel Rossetti (265). He resurrected medieval craft techniques, launched the design firm Morris & Co. and helped to found the Socialist League in 1884. 'Have nothing in your houses,' he said, 'that you do not know to be useful, or believe to be beautiful.'

1963 Pelican Books
Selected Writings and Designs
1984 Penguin English Library
● ed. Asa Briggs, 1963
Rev. Graeme Shankland, 1984

News from Nowhere 1856–96
and Other Writings

William Guest, the narrator of *News from Nowhere*, is swimming in the Thames after a meeting of the Socialist League, when he notices that the 'soap-works with their smoke-vomiting chimneys' are gone and Hammersmith Bridge has been transformed into a dream structure with 'gilded vanes and spirelets'. He has woken into a socialist utopia, an agrarian society with no private property, no authority, no money and no class system: he takes a boat trip up the Thames to explore this perfect, future world. Clive Wilmer's selection includes Morris's lecture 'Useful Work *versus* Useless Toil', his foreword to an edition of More's *Utopia* (121), extracts from *A Dream of John Ball*, and his essay on 'How I Became a Socialist'.

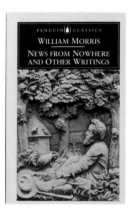

1993
ed. Clive Wilmer

George Eliot 1819–1880

'She has a low forehead, a dull grey eye, a vast pendulous nose, a huge mouth full of uneven teeth and a chin and jawbone *qui n'en finessent pas*,' wrote Henry James (417), rather ungenerously. '[...] Now in this vast ugliness resides a most powerful beauty which, in a very few minutes, steals forth and charms the mind, so that you end, as I ended, in falling in love with her.' Mary Ann Evans became her father's house-keeper at the age of sixteen, after her mother's death. They moved from Nuneaton to Coventry in 1841, where she fell in with a group of progressive intellectuals and radical publishers. For 24 years she lived in London with George Henry Lewes, a married man. Despite having published journalism under the name 'Marian Evans', she published all her fiction under the pen name 'George Eliot', to differentiate it from the 'Silly Novels by Lady Novelists' about which she wrote a scathing article (228) in 1856.

Scenes of Clerical Life 1857

These three stories are inspired by Eliot's native Warwickshire, although the place names are changed. In 'Amos Barton', a poor curate struggles to support his family; in 'Mr Gilfil's Love-Story', a chaplain falls in love with his employer's Italian ward; and in 'Janet's Repentance', the new evangelical minister divides the religious community of Milby. 'The exquisite truth and delicacy, both of the humour and the pathos of these stories, I have never seen the like of,' wrote Charles Dickens (210).

1973 Penguin English Library
● ed. David Lodge

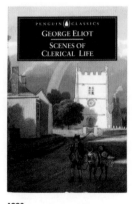

1998
ed. Jennifer Gribble

1980 Penguin English Library
● ed. Stephen Gill

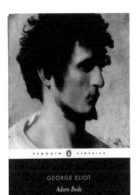

2008
ed. Margaret Reynolds

Adam Bede 1859

In 1779 in rural Hayslope, Adam Bede is an honest carpenter, besotted with the beautiful Hetty Sorrel, but Hetty is seduced by the grandson of the local squire, with tragic consequences. Eliot based the plot on a story told by her Methodist aunt, who heard a confession of child-murder while visiting a women's prison. The psychological realism and vivid landscapes of *Adam Bede* are seemingly influenced by Wordsworth and Coleridge's *Lyrical Ballads* (193), which are referred to in the novel by the feckless Donnithorne as 'twaddling stuff'.

1979 Penguin English Library
1985 Penguin Classics
ed. A. S. Byatt

The Mill on the Floss 1860

Maggie and Tom Tulliver are siblings, growing up in Dorlcote Mill on the River Floss in Lincolnshire in the lates 1820s. Maggie worships her older brother but is also fiercely independent. She is torn between love for the sensitive hunchbacked son of her family's worst enemy and illicit passion for her cousin's dangerously charismatic fiancé.

Silas Marner 1861
The Weaver of Raveloe

Silas Marner, the miserly weaver, was once wrongly accused of theft. Now he lives for his linenwork and the accumulation of money. When he comes to adopt an orphaned child, however, he learns how to change and the truth about his past begins to emerge.

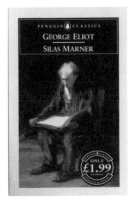

1996
ed. David Carroll

1944 Penguin Books
● —
1967 Penguin English Library
● ed. Q. D. Leavis

Romola 1862–3

In 15th-century Florence, at the time of Savonarola and the Bonfire of the Vanities, Romola is the daughter of a blind classical scholar and the wife of a mysterious and treacherous stranger called Tito Melema. As Tito's true nature is revealed, Romola must break from him and find her own path in life. Eliot spent eighteen months researching *Romola*, which she said was 'written with my best blood'.

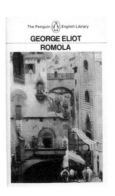

1980 Penguin English Library
● ed. Andrew Sanders

1996
ed. Dorothea Barrett

1972 Penguin English Library
● ed. Peter Coveney

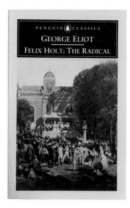

1995
ed. Lynda Mugglestone

Felix Holt
The Radical 1866

Set at the time of the <u>Reform Act of 1832</u> (210), *Felix Holt* describes a fiercely fought election in Treby Magna, in which the clash between the self-serving Radical candidate Harold Transome and the genuinely principled Felix Holt leads to dramatic scenes of romantic peril. This edition includes Eliot's 1868 article 'Address to Working Men, by Felix Holt', written in the character of Felix and responding to the Second Reform Act of 1867.

1994
ed. Rosemary Ashton

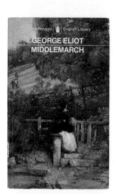

1965 Penguin English Library
● ed. W. J. Harvey

Middlemarch
A Study of Provincial Life 1871–2

Eliot weaves multiple narratives and characters into a vivid, realistic, historical portrait of Middlemarch, a fictitious provincial town in the Midlands. The resulting tapestry is at once humorous, poignant, startling and familiar, expressing all facets of human nature, from self-interest and hypocrisy to idealism and love. The self-conscious narrator compares her role with that of the Greek historian <u>Herodotus</u> (31), 'who also, in telling what had been, thought it well to take a woman's lot for his starting-point'. It was published, copying the method used for Hugo's *Les Misérables* (308), in eight two-monthly instalments. Virginia Woolf described it as 'one of the few English novels written for grown-up people'.

Selected Essays, Poems and Other Writings 1846–79

Eliot had published scholarly essays in the *Westminster Review* and elsewhere before she began writing fiction. This volume, co-edited by the novelist A. S. Byatt, presents her views on religion, art, science and the nature and purpose of fiction. It anthologizes her reviews of other writers, such as <u>Wollstonecraft</u> (205), <u>Carlyle</u> (269) and <u>Browning</u> (264), and includes samples of her poetry, her letters and her radical translation of David Friedrich Strauss's *Life of Jesus* (1835–6).

1967 Penguin English Library
● ed. Barbara Hardy

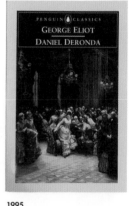

1995
ed. Terence Cave

Daniel Deronda 1876

Daniel Deronda is fascinated by two different women: the glamorous Gwendolen Harleth, who loses her fortune, and Mirah Lapidoth, whom he saves from drowning in the Thames. Deronda helps both women, and becomes drawn into Gwendolen's marital problems and fascinated by Mirah's Jewish ancestry. The novel is influenced by the tradition of the <u>Kabbalah</u> (69). 'I meant everything in the book to be related to everything else,' wrote Eliot.

1990
ed. A. S. Byatt & Nicholas Warren

Wilkie Collins 1824–1889

Wilkie was a close friend of <u>Charles Dickens</u> (210): he contributed to Dickens's magazines and they travelled and acted together. 'We saw each other every day, and were as fond of each other as men could be,' wrote Collins. He never married but established two separate households with different mistresses. He suffered from gout throughout his life and became addicted to the laudanum he took to dull the pain. The opium made him convinced that he was accompanied at all times by a doppelgänger, whom he affectionately called 'Ghost Wilkie'.

1974
Penguin English Library
● ed. Julian Symons

1999
ed. Matthew Sweet

The Woman in White 1859–60

'In one moment, every drop of blood in my body was brought to a stop [...] There, as if it had that moment sprung out of the earth [...] stood the figure of a solitary Woman, dressed from head to foot in white'. Young Walter Hartright and Marian Halcombe must unravel multiple mysteries in order to uncover the machinations of Sir Percival Glyde and his oleaginous friend Count Fosco, an obese Italian with a penchant for white mice, chocolat à la vanille bonbons and poison. *The Woman in White* established a new genre of 'sensation fiction', combining <u>Gothic</u> horror (163) with psychological realism.

No Name 1862

In eight 'scenes', *No Name* tells the story of Magdalen and Norah, two sisters who discover, after their parents' death, that they were technically illegitimate. Their expected inheritance goes to their uncle. Penniless, the stoical Norah becomes a governess, but Magdalen concocts an elaborate and thrilling plan to regain their fortune, involving disguises, false identities, strategic marriages and secret trust documents.

1994
ed. Mark Ford

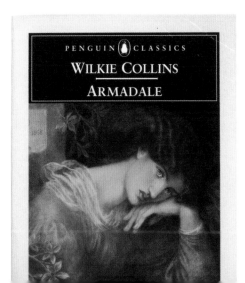

Armadale 1864–6

Readers, writes Collins in his foreword, 'will, I have some reason to suppose, be here and there disturbed – perhaps even offended – by finding that "Armadale" oversteps, in more than one direction, the narrow limits within which they are disposed to restrict the development of modern fiction.' His sensational plot revolves around the intrigues of the villainous Lydia Gwilt, a flame-haired fortune hunter, temptress, bigamist, and laudanum addict.

1995
ed. John Sutherland

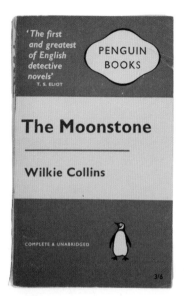

1955 Penguin Books
● –

The Moonstone 1868

The 'Moonstone' is a priceless yellow Indian diamond. Bequeathed to young Rachel Verinder, it disappears on the night of her eighteenth birthday party when a suspicious troupe of Indian jugglers has visited the house. Sergeant Cuff and Franklin Blake, a gentleman-adventurer, both attempt to unravel the drug-riddled mystery. Dorothy L. Sayers (85) called it 'probably the very finest detective story ever written'.

1966 Penguin English Library
● ed. J. I. M. Stewart
–

J. I. M. Stewart was a fellow of Christ Church, Oxford; he was also the author of popular crime novels, published by Penguin, which he wrote under the pseudonym 'Michael Innes'.

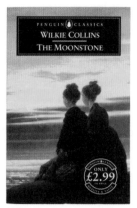

1998
ed. Sandra Kemp

The Law and the Lady 1875

Soon after her wedding, Valeria Brinton discovers that her new husband, Eustace, was previously tried for the murder of his first wife by arsenic poisoning. She sets out to prove his innocence beyond doubt and becomes entangled with a brilliant but mentally unstable paraplegic called Miserrimus Dexter.

1998
ed. David Skilton

Mary Elizabeth Braddon

1835–1915

Braddon was an actress – she once appeared as Fairy Pineapple in a pantomime – until financial support from a gentleman admirer allowed her to leave the stage and concentrate on writing. She lived with the Irish publisher John Maxwell for more than 30 years, though they weren't able to marry until 1874, when Maxwell's first wife died in an insane asylum. The phenomenal success of *Lady Audley's Secret* made Braddon rich for life. She wrote more than 80 novels.

Lady Audley's Secret

1861–2

Sir Michael Audley's nephew Robert arrives at Audley Court, with his wealthy friend George Talboys who has recently made his fortune in Australia. When George goes missing under mysterious circumstances, however, Robert begins to suspect that Lady Audley, Sir Michael's second wife, may not be as innocent as she appears.

1998
ed. Jenny Bourne Taylor & Russell Crofts

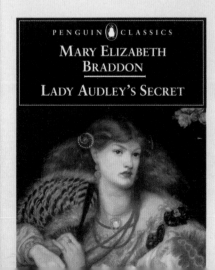

The Water Babies 1862–3
A Fairy Tale for a Land-Baby

Tom, a mistreated young chimney sweep, is miserable until he falls into a river and the fairies turn him into a water-baby. The sprite-like water-babies are supervised by three moralizing fairies called Mrs Doasyouwouldbedoneby, Mrs Bedonebyasyoudid and Mother Carey, who oversee their spiritual education. Tom has various instructive adventures: his final test is to travel to the end of the world to save Grimes, his horrendously cruel former master. Kingsley was a lifelong supporter of Darwin's *On the Origin of Species* (270) and he peppers the book with allusions to the contemporary debate around evolutionary theory.

Charles Kingsley 1819–1875

Kingsley was an Anglican minister and Regius Professor of History at Cambridge; he was also chaplain to Queen Victoria and a private tutor to the Prince of Wales, the future Edward VII. As well as children's books he wrote Christian socialist fiction and the historical novel *Westward Ho!* (1855), after which a village has been named on the north Devon coast, the only place name in Britain with an exclamation mark.

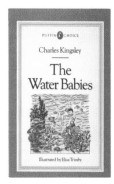

1984 Puffin Choice
● —

2008
ed. Richard D. Beards

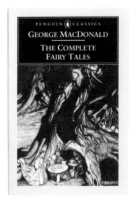

1999
ed. U. C. Knoepflmacher

George MacDonald 1824–1905

MacDonald was a Scottish Congregationalist minister who left the pulpit in 1853 and later taught English literature at King's College, London. He wrote poetry, novels and book-length 'fantasies', such as *At the Back of the North Wind* (1868). He was a friend of Lewis Carroll (232), knew Walt Whitman (413) and inspired writers from W. H. Auden and Walter de la Mare to C. S. Lewis and J. R. R. Tolkien. 'I do not write for children,' he said, 'but for the child-like, whether of five, or fifty, or seventy-five.'

The Complete Fairy Tales 1862–82

This volume collects all eleven of MacDonald's shorter fairy stories, as well as his essay on 'The Fantastic Imagination'. He spins strange tales involving wicked fairies, golden keys, unsettling dreamworlds and perilous quests.

J. Sheridan Le Fanu 1814–1873

Joseph Sheridan Le Fanu, the great-nephew of Richard Brinsley Sheridan (169), was an Irish journalist who bought and edited a series of Dublin-based magazines. He became best known for his tales of mystery and the supernatural, some of which he published in an anthology called *In a Glass Darkly* (1872). His story about the female vampire Carmilla influenced Bram Stoker's *Dracula* (260). M. R. James (283) described Le Fanu as 'absolutely in the first rank as a writer of ghost stories'.

Uncle Silas 1864
A Tale of Bartram-Haugh

When young heiress Maud Rhuthyn is orphaned, she goes to live with her sinister Uncle Silas. There she re-encounters

1942 Penguin Books
● ed. Christine Longford

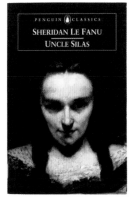

2000
ed. Victor Sage

her terrifying French governess, Madame de la Rougierre, who appears to be working in league with her uncle. She must keep her wits about her in order to avoid being the body in a locked-room murder mystery.

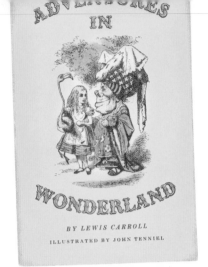

1946 Puffin
Books
• —

Lewis Carroll 1832–1898

The extremely shy Charles Lutwidge Dodgson taught mathematics at Christ Church College, Oxford. He made important advances in the fields of symbolic logic and linear algebra and he was a pioneering amateur portrait photographer, taking likenesses of Dante Gabriel Rossetti (265), George MacDonald (231), and Alfred, Lord Tennyson (263). After the publication of *Alice's Adventures in Wonderland*, he also became the most famous children's author in the world. He adopted the pen name 'Lewis Carroll', a play on the Latinized form of his two first names ('Carolus Ludovicus'). He continued living and working at Christ Church, producing volumes of nonsense verse, books of puzzles and games and a children's novel called *Sylvie and Bruno* (1889–93).

Alice's Adventures in Wonderland *and* Through the Looking Glass 1865, 1871

On a golden afternoon in July 1862, Lewis Carroll took the three Liddell sisters on a boating trip up the Thames. They stopped for a picnic near Godstow and Carroll told an impromptu story about the 10-year-old Alice Liddell falling down a rabbit hole. She persuaded him to transcribe the story, which he did, and he presented her with *Alice's Adventures Under Ground*, the text of which is included in the Penguin Classics edition along with Carroll's original illustrations. Meanwhile, Carroll adapted the manuscript and shared it with George MacDonald (231), who encouraged him to show it to a publisher. Various titles were debated, including *Alice among the Fairies* and *Alice's Golden Hour*. They settled on *Alice's Adventures in Wonderland*, with illustrations by the political cartoonist John Tenniel, and it was a huge commercial success. In 1871, Carroll published the sequel, *Through the Looking-Glass*.

1948 Puffin Books
• —

The front and back covers of this edition reproduced John Tenniel's illustrations of Alice stepping through the looking glass. On the back cover, the title and author's name are appropriately printed in mirror-writing.

1962 Puffin Books
• —

1965 Penguin Books
The Annotated Alice
ed. Martin Gardner

1998
ed. Hugh Haughton

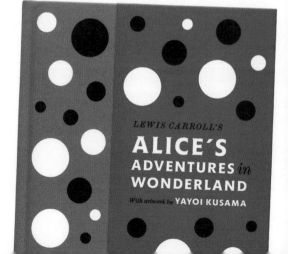

2012
ill. Yayoi Kusama

Jabberwocky and Other Nonsense
Collected Poems 1845–98

Beware the Jabberwock, my son!
The jaws that bite, the claws that catch!

Jabberwocky is a mirror-poem that Alice (232) reads after stepping through the looking-glass into a world where sense becomes nonsense. This edition collects all Carroll's poems, including the verses from the Alice books, the complete Hunting of the Snark, and poems from Phantasmagoria, Sylvie and Bruno and his childhood magazine, Mischmasch.

2013
ed. Gillian Beer

1967 Penguin Books
The Annotated Snark
1995 Penguin Classics
The Hunting of the Snark
ed. Martin Gardner, 1962
—
This edition includes the original illustrations by Henry Holiday.

The Hunting of the Snark
An Agony in Eight Fits 1876

Carroll's 'agony' is his masterpiece of non-sense verse. The quest to find a Snark is led by the Bellman, with a crew that includes a Barrister, a Broker, a Billiard-marker, a Banker, a Butcher and a Beaver. They chart a course across an entirely blank map in pursuit of the legendary Snark, which may prove to be a deadly Boojum...

Margaret Oliphant 1828–1897

Margaret Oliphant Wilson married her cousin, the artist Francis Oliphant, and became Margaret Oliphant Wilson Oliphant. After her husband's death she supported her family by writing almost a hundred novels. She is most famous for the series known as the Chronicles of Carlingford (1862–6), of which *Miss Marjoribanks* is part.

Miss Marjoribanks 1865–6

Lucilla Marjoribanks is 'a cross between Mary Poppins and Boadicea', wrote a reviewer in the *Daily Telegraph*. She comes to look after her widowed father in Carlingford, ruthlessly and hilariously determined to become 'the sunshine of his life'.

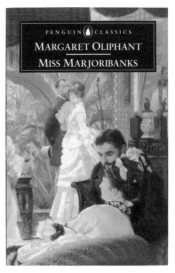

1998
ed. Elisabeth Jay

1976 Puffin Books
●—

2005
ed. R. D. Madison & Michelle Allen

R. D. Blackmore 1825–1900

Richard Doddridge Blackmore was a barrister and a classics tutor before he received an inheritance from a wealthy uncle which allowed him to become a market gardener in Teddington: for the rest of his life he concentrated exclusively on literature and vegetables. 'He is not a social man,' wrote a neighbour, 'and seems wedded to his garden in summer and his book writing in winter. That is all I know about him; except that he keeps the most vicious dogs to protect his fruit'. It was said that Blackmore would rather be remembered as the winner of first prize for swedes than as the author of *Lorna Doone*.

Lorna Doone 1869
A Romance of Exmoor

The mysterious Lorna, of the outlawed Doone family, strides across the dramatic windswept landscape of Exmoor in the 17th century. The narrator's father was murdered by one of the Doone clan, but nonetheless he falls desperately in love with Lorna. The novel was admired by Margaret Oliphant (233) and Thomas Hardy, and 'Lorna' is now cockney rhyming slang for a spoon.

Thomas Hardy 1840–1928

Hardy's novels are set in southern England, in a 'dream country' he calls Wessex, which corresponds roughly to the counties of Dorset, Wiltshire, Somerset, Devon, and parts of Hampshire, Oxfordshire and Berkshire. Though he changed the names, almost all his locations are identifiable. 'It is as if Hardy's imagination could not work unless with solid ground under its feet,' writes the novelist Susan Hill. '[…] Hardy was rarely satisfied with anything less than a one-to-one correspondence between the fictional and the real.' He was born in the parish of Stinsford (Mellstock) near Dorchester (Casterbridge). He was articled to a local architect, and met his first wife, Emma Gifford, during a work trip to Cornwall, a meeting that formed the basis for *A Pair of Blue Eyes* (235). He lived in Dorset (South Wessex) for the rest of his life. When he died, his ashes were buried in Westminster Abbey, but his heart was interred at Stinsford.

Desperate Remedies 1871
A Novel

Hardy abandoned the manuscript of his first novel, *The Poor Man and the Lady*, after George Meredith (240) deemed it too politically controversial. The first novel he published was *Desperate Remedies*, a tale of intrigue, adultery, blackmail and murder, in the style of Wilkie Collins (229). It received an excoriating review in *The Spectator*: 'the bitterness of that moment was never forgotten,' he recalled later. 'At that moment I wished I was dead.'

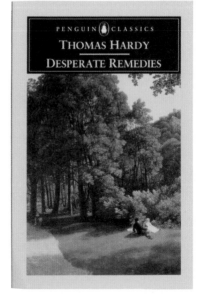

1995
●—

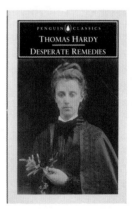

1998
ed. Mary Rimmer

Under the Greenwood Tree 1872
A Rural Painting of the Dutch School

This delightful, pastoral tale of a village 'string choir' and the impending arrival of a mechanical church organ is almost entirely set in Mellstock, modelled on Stinsford, Hardy's birthplace. 'Under the greenwood tree' is a quotation from Shakespeare's *As You Like It* (139).

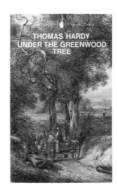 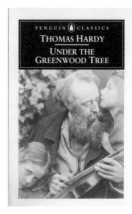

1979 Penguin English Library
● ed. David Wright

1998
ed. Tim Dolin

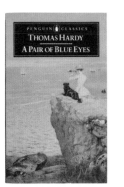 

1986
● ed. Roger Ebbatson

1998
ed. Pamela Dalziel

A Pair of Blue Eyes 1872–3

Like his protagonist Stephen Smith, Hardy visited Tintagel in north Cornwall as a young architect. He too fell for a pair of blue eyes: those of Emma Gifford, his first wife. After Emma's death in 1912, Hardy approached Edward Elgar suggesting they adapt this novel into a 'tragic Wessex opera'. It is thought to be the origin of the term 'cliffhanger', because one instalment ends with Stephen Smith's rival literally hanging from a cliff.

Far from the Madding Crowd 1874

In the first of Hardy's novels to be set explicitly in 'Wessex', Bathsheba Everdene is the independent and wilful owner of a large farm, torn between three men: the gentleman-farmer Boldwood, the seductive soldier Sergeant Troy, and her loyal friend the shepherd Gabriel Oak. 'Wonderful,' wrote Ronald Blythe, '[…] a landscape which satisfies every stir of the imagination and which ravishes the senses'.

 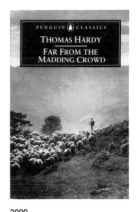

1978 Penguin English Library
● ed. Ronald Blythe

2000
ed. Rosemarie Morgan
with Shannon Russell

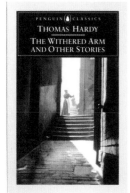

The Withered Arm
and Other Stories 1874–88

Hardy wrote these short stories as he was establishing himself as a novelist. They evoke a harsh rural world where love and suffering are intimately connected. 'Destiny and a Blue Cloak', his first published story, is about mistaken identity and a long-held grudge; and 'The Withered Arm' is a supernatural tale about a young wife whose arm mysteriously shrivels when a neighbour has a jealous dream.

1999
ed. Kristin Brady

The Hand of Ethelberta
A Comedy in Chapters 1875–6

Four persistent suitors vie for the hand of the adventuress and society poet Ethelberta Petherwin while her family act incognito as her servants. This comic tale of a strong woman with multiple identities plays with the conventions of popular romances. It was illustrated by George du Maurier (321).

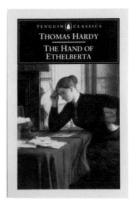

1995
● —

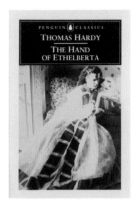

1997
ed. Tim Dolin
ill. George du Maurier

1979 Penguin English Library
● ed. George Woodcock

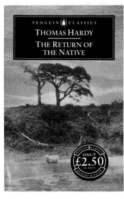

1999
ed. Tony Slade
intro. Penny Boumelha

The Return of the Native 1878

In this novel of thwarted romance, which spans exactly a year and a day, Eustacia and Clym are caught in the destructive spiral of a doomed marriage. Hardy wrote this story after moving to Sturminster Newton with his own wife. Holden Caulfield, in J. D. Salinger's *Catcher in the Rye* (1945–6), likes 'that Eustacia Vye'.

The Trumpet-Major
A Tale 1880

While England faces the prospect of imminent invasion during the Napoleonic Wars, Anne Garland must choose between three very different suitors. Hardy's only historical novel is his only full-length work for which preliminary notes survive. It is also one of the few of his novels to end without tragedy.

1984 Penguin English Library
● ed. Robert Ebbatson

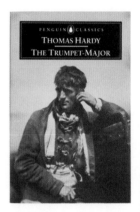

1997
ed. Linda M. Shires

1979 Penguin English Library
1987 Penguin Classics
ed. Susan Hill

The Distracted Preacher
and Other Tales
1879–97

'The whole secret of fiction,' wrote Hardy, ' […] lies in the adjustment of things unusual to things eternal and universal.' This anthology, selected by the novelist Susan Hill, spans his prose-writing career. 'The Distracted Preacher' is a comic romp about a minister who falls for his mysterious landlady and becomes entangled in an adventure involving a marauding band of cross-dressers.

1995
● —

1997
ed. John Schad

A Laodicean
or, The Castle of the De Stancys 1880–1

Laodicea was an ancient city in Asia Minor. Proverbially, a 'Laodicean' is half-hearted or lukewarm, from a reference in the *Book of Revelation* (4): 'unto the angel of the church of the Laodiceans write; […] because thou art lukewarm, and neither cold nor hot, I will spue thee out of my mouth.' In Hardy's novel, Paula Power inherits the medieval Stancy Castle from her father, a railway magnate, and then vacillates between two contrasting men: the young architect George Somerset, whom she employs to modernize the castle, and the old-fashioned Captain De Stancy, whose family once owned the building.

Two on a Tower
A Romance 1882

Lady Constantine falls in love with Swithin St Cleeve, ten years her junior and her social inferior. They woo each other at the top of an ancient tower converted into an observatory. Hardy wanted to 'set the emotional history of two infinitesimal lives against the stupendous background of the stellar universe'.

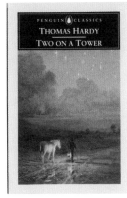

1995
● —

1999
ed. Sally Shuttleworth

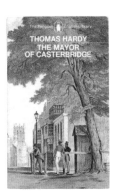

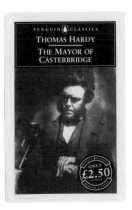

1979 Penguin English Library
● ed. Martin Seymour-Smith

1997
ed. Keith Wilson

The Mayor of Casterbridge
The Life and Death of a Man of Character 1886

After a drunken argument, Michael Henchard auctions his wife and baby daughter at a country fair, selling them both for five guineas. Many years later, he has transformed into a 'man of character', a pillar of the local community and the Mayor of Casterbridge, but he cannot forget the shameful secret from his past.

The Woodlanders 1886–7

This tragic tale of illicit affairs, disill-usionment, tooth extraction and hair transplantation is set in a woodland village. It contrasts the sophisticated but unreliable Dr Fitzpiers with the earthy and honourable woodsman Giles Winterbourne.

1981 Penguin English Library
● ed. Ian Gregor & James Gibson

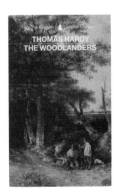

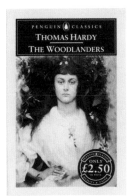

1998
ed. Patricia Ingham
—
The cover of Ingham's edition used to be this photograph of Alice Liddell, the inspiration behind *Alice's Adventures in Wonderland* (232).

2003
ed. Keith Wilson &
Kristin Brady
—
'This edition, the second in a
two-volume selection of Thomas
Hardy's short stories, was originally
to have been prepared, like the
first (235), by the late Kristin Brady,'
writes Keith Wilson. 'Professor
Brady's death in December 1998
deprived Hardy studies of one of its
most respected scholars, and her
colleagues and students of a dearly
loved friend and teacher.'

The Fiddler of the Reels
and Other Stories 1888–1900

These stories describe rash love
affairs that end in betrayal, suffering and disaster. In 'The Fiddler
of the Reels', Car'line Aspent is
swept up by the dazzling fiddler
Mop Ollamoor, but the results
prove tragic for her and the loyal
mechanic Ned Hipcroft.

Tess of the D'Urbervilles
A Pure Woman Faithfully Presented
1891–2

Tess Durbeyfield is persuaded to
claim kinship with the wealthy D'Urberville family, but meeting her libidinous 'cousin' Alec
proves to be her downfall. Tragic misunderstandings and oppressive social conventions lead
to Tess lying on the sacrificial slab at the centre of Stonehenge, where she is finally arrested
on capital charges.

1979 Penguin English Library
● ed. David Skilton
intro. A. Alvarez

1998
ed. Tim Dolin
intro. Margaret R. Higonnet

The Pursuit of the Well-Beloved
and The Well-Beloved
1892, 1897

The Pursuit of the Well-Beloved was serialized in 1892 and
then extensively reworked, and renamed *The Well-Beloved,*
for Hardy's single-volume edition of 1897. The story
describes the life of the sculptor Jocelyn Pierston, obsessed
with sculpting the perfect figure of Aphrodite, torn
between three muses: a grandmother, mother and daughter
from the same family, all called Avice Caro. The alternative
versions offer different endings and plot lines, but both
involve bigamy, suicide and seduction.

Jude the Obscure 1894–5

Jude Fawley is trapped into marrying the crude Arabella
Donn, who seduces him and pretends to be pregnant,
before abandoning him and emigrating to Australia. He
finds work as a stonemason in the town of Christminster
(Oxford), where he meets and falls in love with his free-
thinking cousin, Sue Bridehead. They live together without
marrying and are consequently shunned by society. Hardy's
novel was similarly vilified for its controversial treatment
of sex and marriage. It was sold by booksellers in brown
paper bags and the Bishop of Wakefield burned his copy.
It features the most tragic scene of all Hardy's novels,
accompanied by a note in childish handwriting: 'Done
because we are too menny'.

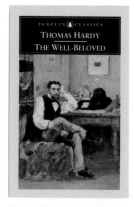

1995 *The Well-Beloved*
● —

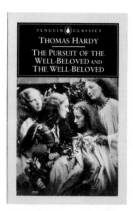

1997
ed. Patricia Ingham

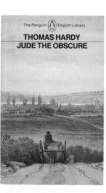

1979 Penguin English Library
● ed. C. H. Sisson

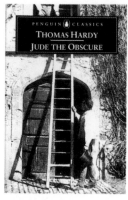

1998
ed. Dennis Taylor

Poems 1898–1928

Following the negative reception of *Tess of the D'Urbervilles* (238) and *Jude the Obscure* (238), Hardy abandoned fiction entirely and wrote only poetry in the 20th century. His first collection, *Wessex Poems*, was published in 1898, when he was nearly 60. He experimented continually, producing lyrics, folk ballads, satires and dramatic monologues. Many of his poems were written in response to wars, in particular the Boer and the First World War (433), and some of his greatest poetry is from the collection *Poems of 1912–13*, written after the death of his first wife, Emma.

1960 Penguin Poets
● ed. W. E. Williams

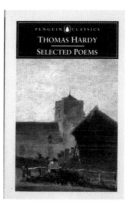

1979 Penguin Poets
Selected Poems
● ed. David Wright

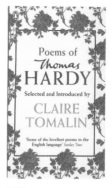

1993 *Selected Poems*
ed. Harry Thomas

2007 Red Classics
ed. Claire Tomalin
—
Thomas's selection is drawn from all Hardy's poetry collections, in chronological order. Tomalin's selection, published to coincide with her biography of Hardy, is organized thematically, with sections such as 'Marriage', 'Love in Middle Age' and 'On Himself'.

Samuel Butler 1835–1902

Butler's parents were 'brutal and stupid by nature' and he left England at the age of 23 to become a sheep farmer in New Zealand. On his return, in 1864, he took up residence at Clifford's Inn off Fleet Street in London, where he lived until his death. He composed oratorios, translated the *Odyssey* (17), which he believed to be the work of a young woman from Sicily, and his paintings were exhibited at the Royal Academy. He was greatly admired by Aldous Huxley, George Bernard Shaw (294) and E. M. Forster (284).

Erewhon
or, Over the Range 1872

'The Author wishes it to be understood that Erewhon is pronounced as a word of three syllables, all short – thus, Ĕ-rĕ-whŏn.' In *Erewhon*, or 'Nowhere' misspelled backwards, a young traveller seeks his fortune in a remote and beautiful land, populated by amazingly handsome people. They have a topsy-turvy moral code, however, which treats crime as a malady and illness as a sin and all machines have been destroyed after a prophecy predicted that artificial intelligence would evolve faster than humans and ultimately replace our species. Based on Butler's own experiences in New Zealand and Darwin's *On the Origin of Species* (270), Erewhon is a work of utopian satire, which has been compared to Swift's *Gulliver's Travels* (159) and Morris's *News from Nowhere* (226).

1935 Penguin Books
● —

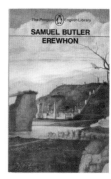

1970 Penguin English Library
1985 Penguin Classics
ed. Peter Mudford

The Way of All Flesh 1873–84, pub. 1903

This semi-autobiographical coming-of-age novel was based on Butler's own childhood and youth. It describes four generations of the Pontifex family, focusing on Ernest, the son of a tyrannical clergyman. 'It is a great book,' wrote George Orwell, 'because it gives an honest picture of the relationship between father and son, and it could do that because Butler was a truly independent observer, and above all because he was courageous. He would say things that other people knew but didn't dare to say.'

1947 Penguin Books
• —

1966 Penguin English Library
1986 Penguin Classics
ed. James Cochrane
intro. Richard Hoggart
—
The cover of Cochrane's edition is a detail from *Family Prayers*, painted by Butler himself.

Anna Sewell 1820–1878

Sewell was born in Norfolk and learned to ride there, but she slipped on her way home from school at the age of fourteen and severely injured both her ankles, and she remained disabled for the rest of her life. As she was dependent on horse-drawn carriages, her love for horses contined to grow and she was passionate about improving equine welfare. She died within five months of the publication of her only book, *Black Beauty*.

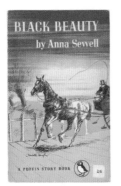

1954 Puffin Books
• —

Black Beauty 1877

Black Beauty is told from the point of view of a carefree young colt, who is forced to leave his mother, Duchess, and the idyllic English countryside for a hard life pulling hansom cabs in London. He is called at various times Darkie, Black Auster, Jack, Blackie, Old Crony and Black Beauty. Although it is often considered a children's book, Sewell intended *Black Beauty* for those working in horse husbandry and stable management. Its special aim, she wrote, was 'to induce kindness, sympathy, and an understanding treatment of horses'.

2011 Penguin Threads
fwd. Jane Smiley
cover Jillian Tamaki
—
Penguin Threads are a series of special editions with covers based on embroidered designs. The inside front and back covers reproduce the back of the actual embroidery, revealing how the design was created.

George Meredith 1828–1909

Meredith was the son of a naval outfitter from Portsmouth. In 1856, he posed for *The Death of Chatterton*, by Wallis, a painting which now hangs in the Tate Britain collection. His wife eloped with Henry Wallis two years later and Meredith wrote about the experience in *The Ordeal of Richard Feverel* (1859), his first major novel. A prolific writing career ensued, which he funded by working as a journalist and as a reader for Chapman & Hall, Dickens's (210) publishers. 'Ah, Meredith!' wrote Oscar Wilde (244), 'Who can define him? His style is chaos illumined by flashes of lightning.'

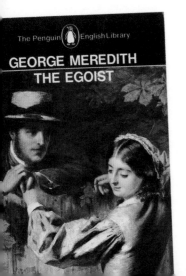

1968 Penguin English Library
1985 Penguin Classics
ed. George Woodcock

The Egoist 1879

Sir Willoughby Patterne is vain, shallow and self-interested, obsessed by fashion and imprisoned by social convention. In this comedy of social pretensions, Sir Willoughby must struggle to drop his façade and resurrect some genuine feelings. Robert Louis Stevenson (241) told an anecdote about a 'young friend of Mr. Meredith's', who 'came to him in an agony. "This is too bad of you," he cried. "Willoughby is me!" "No, my dear fellow," said the author; "he is all of us." '

Robert Louis Stevenson 1850–1894

Stevenson was born in Edinburgh, a sickly child, prone to nightmares. In 1871, he decided to become a writer, abandoning the family business of lighthouse engineering. After his father's death in 1887, Stevenson and his wife Fanny travelled the South Seas (243) and eventually settled permanently on the island of Upolu in Samoa. He was given the name Tusitala ('Teller of Tales') and became a revered wise man in the Samoan community. He died at 44, while making a batch of mayonnaise.

2004
ed. Christopher MacLachlan

Travels with a Donkey in the Cévennes *and* The Amateur Emigrant 1879, 1895

In 1878, Stevenson walked through the sparsely populated Cévennes mountains of southern France with a stubborn and manipulative donkey called Modestine. He slept outdoors, designing his own sleeping bag for the purpose. 'I travel for travel's sake,' he wrote. 'The great affair is to move; to feel the needs and hitches of our life more nearly; to come down off this feather-bed of civilisation, and find the globe granite underfoot and strewn with cutting flints.' John Steinbeck admired the travelogue and emulated its title in *Travels with Charley* (1962), the account of a road trip with his pet poodle.

Stevenson travelled to the Cévennes to distract himself from thoughts of Fanny Osbourne, a married American woman with whom he had fallen in love. In 1879, however, he received word that she was divorcing her husband and that she was also gravely ill. He set off to join her: he crossed the Atlantic in steerage and travelled by train to California. They were married in 1880. Many years later he wrote an account of the sea voyage, entitled *The Amateur Emigrant*.

Treasure Island 1881–2

The greatest of all pirate stories began with a map, drawn by Stevenson to amuse his stepson on a rainy afternoon in Aberdeenshire. This map of an imaginary island suggested an adventure story, with buccaneers and buried gold, treasure maps and tropical seas. 'No doubt the parrot once belonged to Robinson Crusoe (157),' he wrote. 'No doubt the skeleton is conveyed from Poe (408). [...] Billy Bones, his chest, the company in the parlour, the whole inner spirit and a good deal of the material detail of my first chapters – [...] all were the property of Washington Irving (407).' He based Long John Silver on his one-legged friend, the poet William Ernest Henley (266). The book was an instant success and has been adapted for the screen more than 50 times.

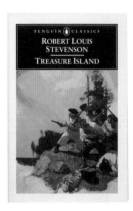

1999
ed. John Seelye

1946 Puffin Books
● intro. Eleanor Graham
–
The back cover of the 1946 Puffin edition illustrates the second map that Stevenson prepared for *Treasure Island*. This is Captain Flint's treasure map, with Billy Bones's sailing directions and a cross marking the 'bulk of the treasure'.

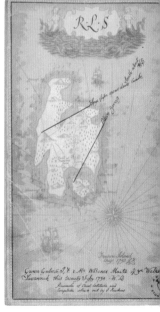

The Strange Case of Dr Jekyll and Mr Hyde
and Other Tales of Terror 1881–6

Dr Jekyll and Mr Hyde is Stevenson's 'shilling shocker', a psychological mystery in which a 'damnable young man' stalks the London fog, connected in some horrific way with the respectable Dr Jekyll and an evil chemical potion. *Olalla* is the tale of a cursed Spanish family and female vampirism; and *The Body Snatcher* fictionalizes the notorious Edinburgh 'resurrection men' Burke and Hare. This volume also includes Stevenson's 'Chapter on Dreams', in which he describes the 'Little People' inside his head, who stage-managed the 'internal theatre' of his dreams. He credits these 'Brownies' with giving him the idea for *Dr Jekyll and Mr Hyde*.

1979 Penguin English Library
● ed. Jenni Calder

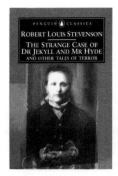

2002
ed. Robert Mighall
—
Mighall edited the Penguin Classics series between 1997 and 2000.

2007
ed. John Sutherland

Kidnapped 1886
Being Memoirs of the Adventures of David Balfour in the Year 1751

David Balfour, orphaned at seventeen, appeals to his miserly Uncle Ebenezer. Ebenezer, however, arranges for him to be kidnapped and bundled aboard a ship bound for the Carolinas to be sold into indentured servitude. After a fortunate shipwreck, Balfour joins forces with the Jacobite rebel Alan Breck, and the unlikely pair journey together across the Scottish Highlands in pursuit of justice. Balfour was Stevenson's mother's maiden name.

1946 Puffin Books
● —

The Black Arrow
A Tale of the Two Roses
1883

Set during the Wars of the Roses, *The Black Arrow* is the story of young Dick Shelton, who joins a band of forest-dwelling outlaws to avenge his father's murder and win his lady love. The outlaws are known as 'the Black Arrow' and have a poem that states their purpose:

I had four blak arrows under my belt,
Four for the greefs that I have felt,
Four for the nomber of ill menne
That have opressid me now and then.

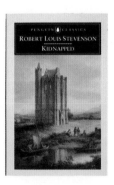

1994
ed. Donald McFarlan
fwd. Alasdair Gray, 2007
—
The Scottish artist and writer Alasdair Gray wrote a new foreword in 2007, in which he advises new readers to 'read the novel (with pauses for food, work and sleep) straight to the end. If you then want to know how Robert Louis Stevenson came to write it, return here.'

The Master of Ballantrae
A Winter's Tale 1889

James Durie, the wild Master of Ballantrae, supports the Jacobite Rising of 1745 and afterwards disappears to live a brutal life of piracy on the high seas. Meanwhile his younger brother Henry inherits the family title of Lord Durrisdeer. Many years later, however, the Master returns, and the two brothers struggle for the inheritance and their own salvation. Stevenson wrote *The Master of Ballantrae* on Tahiti and Hawaii and put into the character of the Master 'all I know of the Devil'.

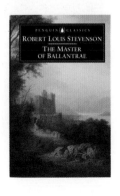

1996
ed. Adrian Poole

1998
ed. Neil Rennie

In the South Seas 1896

In June 1888, Stevenson chartered the yacht *Casco* and sailed from San Francisco with Fanny and their son Lloyd, 'across the empty deep, far from all track of commerce, far from any hand of help.' The family visited the Marquesas, the Paumotus and the Gilbert Islands. Stevenson became a close friend of King Kalaākaua of Hawaii and met the tyrant Tembinok', King of Apemama. He kept a journal and wrote letters during the voyage, which he later worked into this posthumously published collection of articles and essays. Chapters include 'Death', 'In a Cannibal Valley' and 'Graveyard Stories'.

Poems c.1882–94

Stevenson wrote poetry throughout his life. He was most famous for *A Child's Garden of Verses* (1885), which featured titles such as 'Pirate Story', 'The Land of Nod', 'Looking-Glass River' and 'Fairy-Bread'; the complete text is included in Calder's 1998 edition. Stevenson's collection *Underwoods* (1887) was written in a mixture of English and Scots and is frequently autobiographical. This selection also includes verse from *Moral Emblems* (1882) and *Songs of Travel* (1895) as well as many poems that were unpublished in Stevenson's lifetime.

1948 Puffin Books
A Child's Garden of Verses

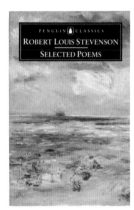

1998 *Selected Poems*
ed. Angus Calder

Olive Schreiner 1855–1920

Olive Emilie Albertina Schreiner was born in Cape Colony, South Africa, the daughter of German and English missionaries. She was named after three older brothers, all of whom died before she was born, Oliver, Albert and Emile. She worked in South Africa as a governess before travelling to England in 1881, where she campaigned for gender equality. Seven years later, she returned and later married the politically active farmer Samuel Cron Cronwright. She is buried, along with her baby, dog and husband, on top of Buffelskop mountain, near Cradock in the Eastern Cape.

1939 Penguin Books

The Story of an African Farm 1883

Two orphaned girls, gentle Em and spirited Lyndall, grow up on a remote farm in the South African veld under the harsh guardianship of their superstitious stepmother. Their lives are disrupted first by the appearance of a charismatic vagrant, Bonaparte Blenkins, and later by the charming Englishman Gregory Rose. Schreiner published her novel in England, under the pseudonym 'Ralph Iron'. It was an instant success and Lyndall, in particular, was greeted by feminists as one of the first portrayals of the 'New Woman' (252).

1971 Modern Classics
1982 Penguin English Library
1986 Penguin Classics
intro. Dan Jacobson

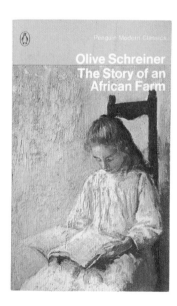

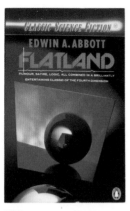

1987 Classic Science Fiction
● intro. Banesh Hoffmann

1998
intro. Alan Lightman

Edwin A. Abbott

1838– 1926

Edwin Abbott Abbott become headmaster of the City of London School, his *alma mater*, at the age of just 26, and remained there until his retirement. He taught the future Prime Minister Herbert Asquith, and introduced many new subjects to the school's curriculum, including comparative philology, chemistry and English literature.

Flatland
A Romance of Many Dimensions
1884

Narrated by A. Square, *Flatland* begins as a description of the two-dimensional Flatland, a thinly disguised satire of Victorian society. Part Two describes Square's vision of one-dimensional Lineland, the miraculous visit of A. Sphere from three-dimensional Spaceland, and Square's revelation that there may be other lands, with four, five, six or more dimensions. The novella has been described as a premonition of the fourth dimension in Einstein's general theory of relativity.

Oscar Wilde

1854– 1900

Oscar Fingal O'Flahertie Wills Wilde was the son of an eminent eye-surgeon and an Irish nationalist poet. He was a proponent of aestheticism, 'art for art's sake', and initially made a living by giving lectures on the subject. He married Constance Lloyd in 1884, with whom he had two sons, Cyril and Vyvyan, and he enjoyed literary celebrity as the author of children's stories and several popular stage <u>comedies</u> (246). In 1891, however, he fell flamboyantly in love with 'Bosie', <u>Lord Alfred Douglas</u> (266), an Oxford undergraduate. Bosie's bullish father, the Marquess of Queensberry, publicly called Wilde a 'sodomite', so Wilde brought a libel action against him. 'I don't know what the Queensberry rules are,' he said, 'but the Oscar Wilde rule is to shoot on sight.' After two trials, however, and the revelations of private investigators hired by Queensberry, Wilde was sentenced to two years' hard labour in 1895 for acts of gross indecency. 'The world was my oyster,' he quipped, 'but I used the wrong fork.' At one trial, Wilde was asked the meaning of 'the love that dare not speak its name'. 'It is that deep spiritual affection that is as pure as it is perfect,' he responded. 'It dictates and pervades great works of art, like those of <u>Shakespeare</u> (134) and <u>Michelangelo</u> (124) […] It is beautiful, it is fine, it is the noblest form of affection. There is nothing unnatural about it.'

The Soul of Man under Socialism
and Selected Critical Prose 1885– 91

'The Soul of Man under Socialism' is Wilde's only political essay: governments should promote art and individualism, he argues, to disturb 'monotony of type, slavery of custom, tyranny of habit, and the reduction of man to the level of a machine'. This selection also includes his defence of *Dorian Gray* (245) and his 'Portrait of Mr. W. H.', a blend of fact, fiction and forgery that attempts to uncover the identity of the mysterious dedicatee of Shakespeare's *Sonnets* (136).

1954 Penguin Books
Selected Essays and Poems
● ed. Hesketh Pearson & Vyvyan Holland
—
Vyvyan Holland, one of the editors of the 1954 volume, was Oscar Wilde's second son. His mother changed his surname to Holland after Wilde was convicted in 1895. Hesketh Pearson was Wilde's biographer.

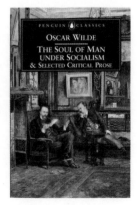

2001
ed. Linda Dowling

Complete Short Fiction 1888–94

Wilde published three volumes of short fiction, including fairy tales such as 'The Happy Prince' and 'The Selfish Giant', a humorous ghost story, 'The Canterville Ghost', and a work of inverted detective fiction, 'Lord Arthur Savile's Crime', in which Lord Arthur is convinced he is fated to commit a murder, and so sets about indentifiying a victim. This collection also includes 'The Portrait of Mr. W. H.', the complete *Poems in Prose* and a surviving fragment of the lost short story 'Elder-Tree'.

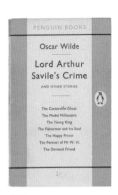

1954 Penguin Books
Lord Arthur Savile's Crime
●—

1962 Puffin Books
The Happy Prince
●—

1994
ed. Ian Small

The Picture of Dorian Gray 1890

'There is no such thing as a moral or an immoral book,' writes Wilde in the preface to his only novel. 'Books are well written, or badly written. That is all.' The beautiful Dorian Gray sells his soul in a Faustian pact in exchange for eternal youth. Inspired by his friend the hedonistic Lord Henry, he embarks on a life of decadence, debauchery and corruption. He remains physically unchanged while his portrait, painted by his friend Basil Hallward and hidden behind a curtain in an attic room, becomes increasingly and monstrously hideous. Early readers were scandalized and seduced by the Gothic plot and Gray's unspeakable sins, and the book was produced as evidence against Wilde in his trial. 'Basil Hallward is what I think I am,' he wrote: 'Lord Henry is what the world thinks of me: Dorian is what I would like to be – in other ages, perhaps.'

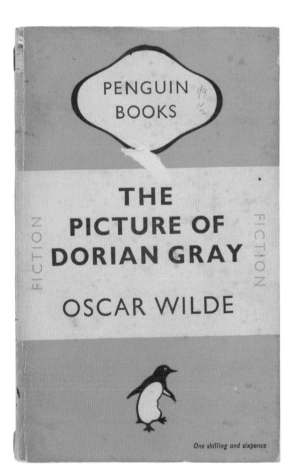

1949 Penguin Books
●—

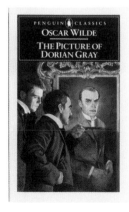

1985
● ed. Peter Ackroyd

2000
ed. Robert Mighall

1940 Penguin Books
●—

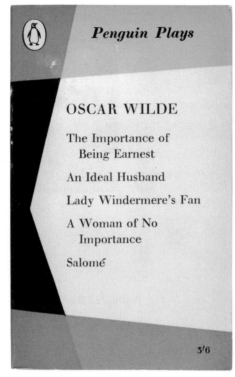

1954 Penguin Plays
●—

2000
ed. Richard Allen Cave

The Importance of Being Earnest
and Other Plays
1892–5

Wilde's theatrical masterpiece, *The Importance of Being Earnest*, is a 'trivial comedy for serious people', a sparkling social satire of mistaken identities, cucumber sandwiches and capacious handbags. Queensberry (244) planned to attend the premiere himself, to throw a bouquet of carrots, but Wilde had him barred from the theatre. This edition appends the excised 'Gribsby' scene, in which a London solicitor arrives to arrest the Bunburying 'Earnest'. Snobbish manners and hypocritical morals are similarly and hilariously exposed in *Lady Windermere's Fan*, *A Woman of No Importance* and *An Ideal Husband*. *Salomé* and *A Florentine Tragedy* use historical settings to tell stories about sex, power and death.

De Profundis
and Other Prison Writings
1895–8

Two literary works emerged from Wilde's imprisonment in Reading Gaol. The first was 'De Profundis', ('from the depths') a lengthy literary letter addressed to Bosie (244), but never delivered in Wilde's lifetime, which recounts the story of their affair and describes Wilde's conversion from a belief in pleasure and decadence to a conviction that 'the supreme vice is shallowness'. The second is 'The Ballad of Reading Gaol', written after Wilde's release, describing a hanging that he witnessed. He called it 'a sort of denial of my own philosophy of art' and it includes the famous line 'each man kills the thing he loves', which Anthony Burgess quotes in *A Clockwork Orange*. This edition presents both works, along with letters Wilde wrote while in prison.

1973 Penguin English Library
● ed. Hesketh Pearson

2013
ed. Colm Tóibín

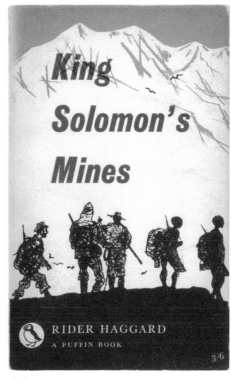

H. Rider Haggard

1856–1925

In 1875, Haggard became junior secretary to the Lieutenant-Governor of Natal in South Africa. He spent six years in Natal and was deeply affected by the landscapes, the wildlife and the myths of the indigenous tribal communities. He returned to England in 1881 to become a lawyer, but the publication of *King Solomon's Mines* was so successful he was able to return to his native Norfolk and devote most of his time to writing fabulous adventure stories set in exotic locations. He was a close friend of Rudyard Kipling (250).

1958 Puffin Books
•—

2007
ed. Robert Hampson
pref. Giles Foden
—
Ngũgĩ wa Thiong'o, the Kenyan writer, has called Haggard one of literature's great 'geniuses of racism' and, in his preface to this edition, the novelist Giles Foden discusses the cultural stereotypes behind Haggard's treatment of gender and race.

King Solomon's Mines 1885

Haggard's brother bet him five shillings he couldn't write a novel as good as Stevenson's *Treasure Island* (241). Haggard's response was *King Solomon's Mines*, the tale of the adventurer Allan Quatermain, who goes in search of the lost diamond mines of the biblical King Solomon with the aid of a map drawn in blood. When the book was published, billboards proclaimed it 'The Most Amazing Book Ever Written' and it was an instant bestseller. It provided inspiration for Conan Doyle's *The Lost World* (249), Kipling's 'The Man Who Would Be King' (250) and H. P. Lovecraft's 'At the Mountains of Madness'.

She 1886
A History of Adventure

On his 25th birthday, Leo Vincey opens a silver casket left to him by his father. It contains the 'Sherd of Amenartas' and a letter describing the legend of an African tribe ruled by a powerful white sorceress. Leo travels to Zanzibar and eventually comes face-to-face with the immortal Ayesha, '*She-who-must-be-obeyed*', the beautiful, tyrannical queen of the Amahagger tribe, who has lived below a dormant volcano for two millennia in the ruins of the lost city of Kôr. According to Haggard's daughter Lilias, '*She-who-must-be-obeyed*' was inspired by the memory of a hideous childhood rag-doll: 'This doll was something of a fetish, and Rider, as a small child, was terrified of her, a fact soon discovered by an unscrupulous nurse who made full use of it to frighten him into obedience.'

1982 Penguin Books
•—

2001
ed. Patrick Brantlinger

247

Arthur Conan Doyle 1859–1930

Doyle studied medicine at Edinburgh University and he became clerk to the surgeon Professor Joseph Bell, whose diagnostic methods of inference and observation inspired the 'science of deduction' favoured by Sherlock Holmes. After training, Doyle set up as a doctor in Southsea on the Hampshire coast, and wrote to pass the time on slow days. Before long he was an internationally famous author, which allowed him to give up medicine and take an interest in a wide variety of different subjects, from divorce law reform to the construction of a Channel tunnel, the provision of steel helmets for soldiers, the Campaign against miscarriages of justice and the veracity of spiritualism. He introduced skiing to Switzerland in 1893.

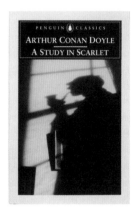

2001
ed. Ed Glinert
intro. Iain Sinclair

A Study in Scarlet 1887

Published a few months before the Jack the Ripper murders, which appeared to replicate some details of the novel, *A Study in Scarlet* was the first appearance of the retired army doctor John Watson and his flatmate, the enigmatic consulting detective Sherlock Holmes. The pair are soon wrapped up in a murder case, concerning a dead man in a grimy house in southwest London: his face is contorted into an expression of horror and 'RACHE', the German word for 'revenge', is scrawled in blood on the wall.

The Sign of Four 1890

'It is a romance!' cries Mrs Forrester in chapter nine, when Watson explains the foregoing plot of *The Sign of Four*. 'An injured lady, half a million in treasure, a black cannibal, and a wooden-legged ruffian.' This sequel to *A Study in Scarlet* is a mystery about a beautiful young woman who has been given a large lustrous pearl every year since her father mysteriously disappeared. The plot becomes increasingly complex and exotic and Watson meets his future wife during the proceedings.

2001
ed. Ed Glinert
intro. Peter Ackroyd

The Adventures of Sherlock Holmes *and* The Memoirs of Sherlock Holmes 1891–3

Doyle's two Holmes novels were so popular, he was commissioned to write a series of shorter Sherlock Holmes adventures, which were published in the *Strand* magazine between July 1891 and December 1893. These 24 stories were originally collected in two volumes: they include 'A Scandal in Bohemia', which features the opera singer Irene Adler; 'The *Gloria Scott*', Holmes's very first case; 'The Greek Interpreter', the first story to feature Holmes's brother Mycroft; 'The Speckled Band', Doyle's personal favourite; and 'The Final Problem', at the end of which Holmes plunges to his death down the Reichenbach Falls in the arms of his arch-nemesis, the 'Napoleon of crime', Professor Moriarty.

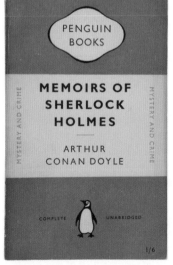

1950 Penguin Books
Memoirs of Sherlock Holmes
● —

2001
ed. Ed Glinert
intro. Iain Pears

The Hound of the Baskervilles
Another Adventure of Sherlock Holmes 1902

The public became so desperate for more Sherlock that Doyle was persuaded, nine years later, to write a new novel about the detective. *The Hound of the Baskervilles* has since become perhaps the best loved of all the Sherlock Holmes adventures.

> 'Footprints?'
> 'Footprints.'
> 'A man's or a woman's?'
> Dr Mortimer looked strangely at us for an instant, and his voice sank almost to a whisper as he answered: 'Mr Holmes, they were the footprints of a gigantic hound!'

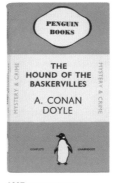

1937 Penguin Books
• —

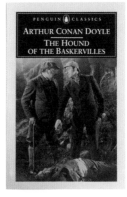

2001
ed. Christopher Frayling

The Return of Sherlock Holmes 1903–4

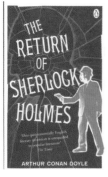

2008
Red Classics
—
Red Classics were introduced in 2006, packaged with accessible, commercial designs. Some titles were later rebranded as Pocket Classics, but both series names have been gradually phased out over the last ten years.

The Hound of the Baskervilles was so successful in its turn, that Conan Doyle finally relented and conclusively revived Holmes for another series of thirteen stories in the *Strand* magazine. In 'The Empty House', a wizened old book collector visits Dr Watson. Momentarily distracted, Watson turns away; when he looks back, 'Sherlock Holmes was standing smiling at me across my study table. I rose to my feet, stared at him for some seconds in utter amazement, and then it appears that I must have fainted for the first and the last time in my life.' 'Well, then, about that chasm,' explains Holmes, once Watson has revived. 'I had no serious difficulty in getting out of it, for the very simple reason that I never was in it.' Doyle went on to write two further collections of Sherlock Holmes stories.

The Valley of Fear 1914–15

The fourth and final Sherlock Holmes novel is set in an ancient moated manor house in Sussex, the owner of which is murdered just as Holmes deciphers a coded word of warning. The tangled plot originates in the distant 'Valley of Fear' and an old betrayal ominously resurfaces, perhaps engineered by Professor Moriarty.

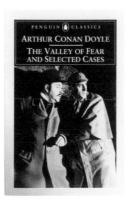

2001
• ed. Ed Glinert
intro. Charles Palliser

2014
Penguin English Library

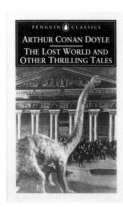

2001
• ed. Philip Gooden

2007
Red Classics

The Lost World 1912

The journalist Edward Malone travels to South America to interview Professor George Edward Challenger, an eccentric explorer. Together they trek to a vast raised plateau in the Amazon basin, where dinosaurs have survived to the present day. When their return route is destroyed, they set out into the unknown territory, facing pterodactyls, allosauruses, 50-foot snakes and a race of hostile ape-men. Doyle may have been inspired by Jules Verne's *Journey to the Centre of the Earth* (315), which also features dinosaurs surviving to the present day.

Rudyard Kipling 1865–1936

Kipling was born in Bombay and his first language was the idiomatic vernacular spoken by his parents' servants. He travelled to England at the age of six, where he lived with an abusive foster-family and attended school in Devon, but he returned to India in 1882 as a reporter and spent 'Seven Years' Hard', writing poems, sketches and stories. In 1889, he came back to London and widespread literary acclaim. He married the American Caroline Balestier in 1892 and they lived happily in Vermont for four years, where he wrote *The Jungle Books*. The family moved to England in 1896 and settled in Sussex. He refused a knighthood and the Order of Merit, but was awarded the Nobel Prize for Literature in 1907.

1971 Modern Classics
Short Stories
● —
Published in two volumes
1987 Penguin Books
Selected Stories
● ed. Andrew Rutherford

The Man Who Would Be King
Selected Stories of Rudyard Kipling
1884–1930

This selection of Kipling's best short stories follows the development of his work over fifty years. The title story is about two adventurers, who become kings of Kafiristan, a remote region of Afghanistan. Other titles include 'The Village That Voted the Earth Was Flat', 'Baa Baa, Black Sheep', 'Mary Postgate' and 'The Gardener'.

2011
ed. Jan Montefiore
—
Jan Montefiore is the series editor of the Penguin Classics Kipling editions. In her general preface, she calls him a 'virtuoso of the short story'.

Plain Tales from the Hills
1888

Many of the plain tales in Kipling's first short-story collection are set in the hill station of Simla, the 'summer capital of the British Raj'. They present a vivid and sensuous portrait of Anglo-Indian society and expose the tensions and contradictions of colonial life. Titles include 'The Rescue of Pluffles', 'A Germ-Destroyer', 'Beyond the Pale' and 'Pig'.

1987
● ed. H. R. Woudhuysen
intro. David Trotter

2011
ed. Kaori Nagai

The Jungle Books 1894–5

In *The Jungle Book* and *The Second Jungle Book*, Kipling tells the story of the man-cub Mowgli, raised by wolves in the jungle and guided by Baloo the bear, Bagheera the black panther, Chil the kite and the python Kaa. Episodes in Mowgli's story are interspersed with other tales, such as 'The White Seal', about a northern fur seal; 'Rikki-Tikki-Tavi', in which a brave mongoose defends a human family from a pair of cobras; and 'The Undertakers', about a squabble between a mugger crocodile, a jackal and an adjutant stork.

1987
● ed. Daniel Karlin

2013
ed. Kaori Nagai

1987
● ed. Edward Said

2011
ed. Harish Trivedi

Kim 1901

Kipling's masterpiece is a novel set during the 'Great Game', the struggle between Britain and Russia for imperial dominance in central Asia. Kim, short for Kimball O'Hara, is a British orphan who has grown up on the streets of Lahore. He befriends an aged Tibetan lama and together they travel along the Grand Trunk Road, scale the Himalayas and become mixed up in the uneasy world of international espionage. The lama seeks the legendary River of the Arrow in order to free himself from the wheel of life and achieve enlightenment (10).

Just So Stories

1902

Kipling told these bedtime stories to his daughter, O Best Beloved. They explain how the Camel got his hump, how the Leopard got his spots, how the Elephant got his trunk and why the Cat walked by himself. The current edition includes Kipling's original illustrations, such as this portrait of Pau Amma the Crab:

1987
● ed. Peter Levi

2011
ed. Judith Plotz

1977 Penguin Poets
Selected Verse
● ed. James Cochrane

1993 Twentieth-Century Classics
Selected Poems
2000 Penguin Classics
ed. Peter Keating

Poems

1886–1919

Arranged in chronological order, this wide-ranging selection of Kipling's poems includes his evocations of the British Empire, 'Mandalay' and 'White Man's Burden'; famous titles such as 'If – ', 'Gunga Din', 'The Smuggler's Song' and 'The Female of the Species'; less well-known poems such as 'The Undertaker's Horse', 'Christmas in India', 'Dirge of Dead Sisters'; and his deeply moving collection, 'Epitaphs of the War' (433). Kipling's son John died in 1915 at the Battle of Loos.

Jerome K. Jerome 1859–1927

Jerome Klapka Jerome left school at fourteen to become a railway clerk, a coal collector, a touring actor, a teacher and a journalist. When he married his wife Ettie in June 1888, they spent their honeymoon 'in a little boat' on the Thames, and he began writing *Three Men in a Boat* as soon as he got home. In 1892, he co-founded *The Idler*, borrowing Samuel Johnson's title (183), and published pieces by Arthur Conan Doyle (248), Robert Louis Stevenson (241), Rudyard Kipling (250) and Mark Twain (414). Like Ernest Hemingway, he served as an ambulance driver in France during the First World War (433).

1957 Penguin Books
● —

2004
ed. Jeremy Lewis, 1999

Three Men in a Boat
To Say Nothing of the Dog! 1889

Three hypochondriac friends think a boating jaunt on the Thames will suit them to a 'T'. The only one not convinced is Montmorency, J.'s opinionated fox-terrier, who tends to cause general devastation. The group's comic escapades involve unreliable barometers, bagpipes, a trout made out of plaster of Paris and the inextricable Hampton Court Maze. There is a bravura episode entitled 'Advantages of cheese as a travelling companion'. The book was a huge success: 'I pay Jerome so much in royalties,' his publisher wrote to a friend, 'I cannot imagine what becomes of all the copies of that book I issue. I often think the public must eat them.'

Three Men on the Bummel 1900

In Jerome's sequel, the three friends reunite for a cycling holiday in the German Black Forest. The title is not explained until the final paragraph: a bummel is 'a journey, long or short, without an end; the only thing regulating it being the necessity of getting back within a given time to the point from which one started. Sometimes it is through busy streets, and sometimes through the fields and lanes; sometimes we can be spared for a few hours, and sometimes for a few days. But long or short, but here or there, our thoughts are ever on the running of the sand.'

1983 Penguin Books
● —

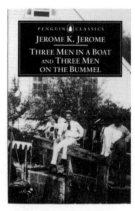

1999
ed. Jeremy Lewis

WOMEN WHO DID
Stories by Men and Women
1890–1914

'The New Woman', writes Angelique Richardson, '[...] marked a new departure in femininity: a subject, not an object, she was an icon of the 1890s. Smoking, cycling, defiant and desiring New Women were splashed across the press and entered the world of fiction with astonishing rapidity.' Richardson's anthology includes Borgia Smudgiton's 'She-Notes', Ella D'Arcy's 'The Pleasure-Pilgrim', Sarah Grand's 'When the Door Opened –', Kate Chopin's (424) 'An Egyptian Cigarette' and 'A Warrior's Daughter' by Zitkala-Ša, as well as many others.

2002 Penguin Books
2005 Penguin Classics
ed. Angelique Richardson

George Gissing 1857–1903

Gissing's brilliant academic career was cut short when he became involved with a young prostitute, and imprisoned for theft. He travelled to America, desperately poor, and almost died of starvation in Chicago. He returned to England and wrote social realist novels about the bleak conditions of the underclasses, while living in extreme poverty himself. He achieved some measure of literary acclaim and financial security towards the end of his life, when he met and befriended Henry James (417) and H. G. Wells (255). George Orwell considered him 'perhaps the best novelist England has produced'.

1968 Penguin English Library
1985 Penguin Classics
ed. Bernard Bergonzi

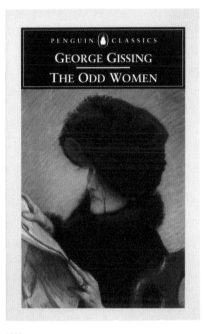

1993
ed. Elaine Showalter, 1983

2015
ed. Patrick Parrinder, 1977
intro. D. J. Taylor, 2015

New Grub Street 1891

Edwin Reardon is a careworn novelist desperate to maintain artistic integrity; his friend Jasper Milvain is a journalist willing to write anything for money. They represent the struggle between literature and hack writing, played out in shabby garrets and the British Museum Reading Room. Grub Street, now Milton Street, is a thoroughfare in London that has become proverbially associated with jobbing writers.

The Odd Women 1893

In Victorian England there were a million more women than men, so there was a contemporary notion that after the men had coupled up there would be at least a million 'odd' women left over. This work of early feminism presents two of these 'odd women', Virginia and Alice Madden, ageing sisters living in genteel poverty in a London boarding house. Their oppressive world is turned upside-down when they meet their old friend Rhoda Nunn, who rejects social conventions and pursues her own desires.

The Whirlpool 1897

Harvey Rolfe finds himself in a spiralling, faithless marriage to the restless musician Alma. 'The Whirlpool!' mutters his friend Carnaby, '[…] It's got hold of me, and I'm going down old man – and it looks black as hell.' Gissing presents late Victorian London as a cyclone, in which the old world of gentlemen's clubs and private incomes is soon to be swept away.

George Grossmith 1847–1912

George Grossmith was a legal reporter before he became an actor. He starred in Gilbert and Sullivan operas, creating the roles of the Major-General in *The Pirates of Penzance* and the lord high executioner in *The Mikado*, among many others. He toured Great Britain and the United States as a comic solo entertainer and singer and wrote two volumes of reminiscences.

Weedon Grossmith 1854–1919

Weedon Grossmith, George's younger brother, was a painter and an actor. He toured America, specializing in comic characters similar to Mr Pooter. He wrote a novel, many plays, and in his final years was a theatrical impresario in London.

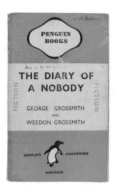

1945 Penguin Books
• —

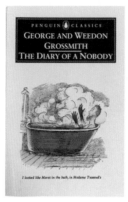

1999
ed. Ed Glinert
ill. Weedon Grossmith

The Diary of a Nobody 1892

'Why should I not publish my diary?' writes Charles Pooter. 'I have often seen reminiscences of people I have never even heard of, and I fail to see – because I do not happen to be a "Somebody" – why my diary should not be interesting. My only regret is that I did not commence it when I was a youth.' In 1888 and 1889, the Grossmith brothers collaborated on a column in *Punch*, written by 'Mr. Pooter', a self-important London clerk. The bumbling, self-aggrandizing Pooter is one of the great comic creations in the English language. The column was expanded and published in a single volume in 1892, with additional illustrations by Weedon. Evelyn Waugh thought it the 'funniest book in the world'.

Arthur Machen

1863–1947

Arthur Llewelyn Jones Machen was born in Monmouthshire. He moved from Wales to London at eighteen, where he worked as a journalist, a private tutor and a publisher's clerk during the day and he spent the nights writing. He translated the *Heptaméron* (125) and Casanova's memoirs (187) and he became obsessed by Celtic Christianity and the Quest for the Holy Grail. He believed that all literature should aspire to an ecstatic state of 'rapture, beauty, adoration, wonder, awe, mystery, sense of the unknown'.

2018 Penguin English Library

The Great God Pan 1894

Machen's first major success was *The Great God Pan*, a darkly sexual novella, in which a crazed doctor performs a scientific experiment on a young woman, which goes horrifically wrong. Stephen King calls it 'one of the best horror stories ever written. Maybe the best in the English language.'

The White People 1894–1917
and Other Weird Stories

The stories in this collection feature troglodyte monsters, mysterious potions, ancient stone axes, ghostly archers, guardian angels, the Holy Grail and a series of macabre murders. 'Machen knew that to accept our cosmic insignificance is to achieve a spiritual perspective,' writes the film director Guillermo del Toro in his foreword; '[…] no matter how wicked or how perverse we can be, somewhere in a long forgotten realm a mad God awaits, leering – and ready to embrace us all.'

1946 Penguin Books
Holy Terrors
• —

2011
ed. S. T. Joshi
fwd. Guillermo del Toro

H. G. Wells

1866–1946

Herbert George Wells was born in Bromley in southeast London. His father, a fast-bowling county cricketer, owned a small shop on the High Street selling cricket bats and chinaware. When Wells's father was declared bankrupt, however, the family broke up and the next few years were miserable for 'Bertie'. In 1884, he won a scholarship to study at the Normal School of Science, South Kensington, now Imperial College, London, after which he taught at two different schools and tutored in biology, before deciding to make his living as a professional writer. Wells had a prophetic imagination, which he channelled into pioneering works of science fiction that predicted the aeroplane, the tank, nuclear weapons and the internet; he also wrote realist novels based on his difficult childhood and novels that espoused his progressive views on sexual equality, women's rights, socialism and science. 'Some day,' he wrote, towards the end of his life, 'I shall write a book, a *real* book.'

1958 Penguin Books

2007
ed. Patrick Parrinder & Andy Sawyer
intro. Neil Gaiman

The Country of the Blind
and Other Selected Stories

1894–1915

'There was a time when life bubbled with short stories', wrote Wells. This selection presents the best of them, from 'The Cone', a sinister story of adultery amidst the blast furnaces of Stoke-on-Trent, to 'The Country of the Blind' in which a mountaineer discovers a lost civilization in the Andes. The volume also includes tales of hurtling comets, deep-sea trenches, Martian portals, plagues of ants, cavemen and a man-eating giant squid in Devon.

1946 Penguin Books

2005
ed. Patrick Parrinder &
Steven McLean
intro. Marina Warner

The Time Machine

1895

A Victorian scientist transports himself to the year 802701, when humanity has evolved into two distinct races, the pale and peaceable Eloi and the sinister chthonic Morlocks. 'The more impossible the story I had to tell, the more ordinary must be the setting,' Wells decided, so he located *The Time Machine* in Richmond, Surrey.

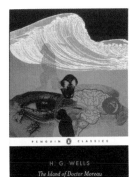

1946 Penguin Books

2005
ed. Patrick Parrinder &
Steven McLean
intro. Margaret Atwood

The Island of Doctor Moreau 1896

Edward Prendick, the sole survivor of a shipwreck, finds himself on an uncharted Pacific island, where a mad but brilliant scientist is conducting monstrous vivisectional experiments. Wells later called it an 'exercise in youthful blasphemy'.

The Invisible Man 1897

Griffin has developed a process for altering the body's refractive index, rendering himself invisible, but now he cannot find the antidote. Frustrated and increasingly deranged, he develops a taste for random and irresponsible violence. Wells may have been inspired by the 'Ring of Gyges', a mythical artefact mentioned in Plato's *Republic* (27): the ring renders the wearer invisible and Plato asks whether one would act morally if one had no fear of being caught.

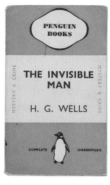

1938 Penguin Books
• —

2005
ed. Patrick Parrinder & Andy Sawyer
intro. Christopher Priest

The War of the Worlds 1898

A shooting star streaks through the sky and the next day a cylinder is discovered on Horsell Common near Woking in Surrey. Soon the tentacled Martian invaders are building killing machines, intent on destroying all humankind with their Black Smoke and Heat-Rays. In 1938, an adaptation of the novel was broadcast on American radio, narrated by Orson Welles; it was presented as a news bulletin and is said to have caused mass panic among listeners, who thought it was true.

1946 Penguin Books
• —

2005
ed. Patrick Parrinder & Andy Sawyer
intro. Brian Aldiss

The Sleeper Awakes 1899, rev. 1910

Graham falls asleep in the 1890s and doesn't wake up for 200 years. In the meantime, investments are made on his behalf and he wakes to find himself the richest and most powerful man on earth, the godhead of an oppressive, hierarchical dystopia. Wells published the short story *When the Sleeper Wakes* in 1899; he expanded and revised it in 1910 and renamed it *The Sleeper Awakes*.

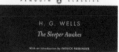

2005
ed. Patrick Parrinder &
Andy Sawyer

Love and Mr Lewisham
The Story of a Very Young Couple 1900

Mr Lewisham is a young and ambitious scientist passionately in love with his former girlfriend, Ethel Henderson. Ethel, however, assists her stepfather, a charlatan spiritualist, to cheat gullible customers with cheap trickery, which goes against all Mr Lewisham's principles. Wells considered it 'an altogether more serious undertaking than I have ever done before'.

1946 Penguin Books
• —

2005
ed. Simon J. James
intro. Gillian Beer

The First Men in the Moon 1901

Mr Cavor invents a material that 'blocks' gravity and allows him and Mr Bedford to travel to the moon. There they face roasting days, freezing nights and sinister alien life.

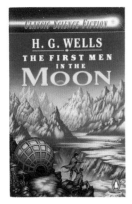

1987 Classic Science Fiction
●—

2005
ed. Patrick Parrinder &
Steve McLean
intro. China Miéville

A Modern Utopia
1905

Two Englishmen hiking in the Swiss Alps accidentally fall through a space-warp and find themselves in a parallel utopian world, similar to earth in many ways, but controlled by a single World State, with a global language, complete sexual, economic and racial equality and unanimous vegetarianism, policed by a voluntary, elite class of 'samurai'. E. M. Forster disliked the conformism of the novel, and responded with his 1909 dystopian story, 'The Machine Stops'(286). The title is a reference to *Utopia* (121) by Thomas More.

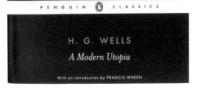

2005
ed. Gregory Claeys,
Patrick Parrinder &
Andy Sawyer
intro. Francis Wheen

1941 Penguin Books
●—

2005
ed. Simon J. James
intro. David Lodge

Kipps
The Story of a Simple Soul 1905

In this partly autobiographical novel, young Artie Kipps is apprenticed for seven years to a draper, only to discover that he is the grandson of a wealthy gentleman and heir to a large fortune. It was one of Wells's favourites among his books, and Henry James (417) called it the 'best novel in the last forty years'. It was adapted into a stage musical by David Heneker as *Half a Sixpence* (1963).

1941 Penguin Books
●—

2005
ed. Patrick Parrinder & Andy Sawyer
intro. Jay Winter

The War in the Air 1908

Bert Smallways, a 'kind of bicycle engineer of the let's-'ave-a-look-at-it and enamel-chipping variety', becomes accidentally involved in a German plot to invade America with giant floating airships. The attack prompts a devastating era of total war, in which aerial bombardment razes world civilization.

Tono-Bungay 1909

George Ponderevo is employed to market 'Tono-Bungay' as a miracle cure. In fact, Tono-Bungay is simply a pleasant-tasting liquid with no medicinal effects whatsoever, but it is extraordinarily successful and every level of British society becomes convinced of its merits, with alarming consequences. Wells was 'disposed to regard *Tono-Bungay* as the finest and most finished novel' he wrote.

1946 Penguin Books
• —

2005
ed. Patrick Parrinder
intro. Edward Mendelson

1969 Penguin Books
• —

2005
ed. Sita Schutt
intro. Margaret Drabble

Ann Veronica 1909

Ann Veronica Stanley is courageous, strong-willed and nearly two-and-twenty. She rebels against her authoritarian father and leaves her family home for London, where she studies biology at Imperial College and mixes with intellectuals, socialists and suffragettes. She falls in love with a brilliant married academic, but discovers that personal freedom comes at a price. The character of Ann was partly inspired by Amber Reeves, a feminist writer with whom Wells was having an affair at the time.

The History of Mr Polly 1910

Alfred Polly hates his life: he is facing bankruptcy and he's stuck in a loveless marriage. He decides to burn down his gentlemen's outfitting business and kill himself, but to his surprise, his failed suicide attempt makes him an accidental local hero, wins him an insurance payout that covers his debts and gives him the confidence to leave his old life behind and set out on an adventure. It is Wells's funniest novel.

1946 Penguin Books
• —

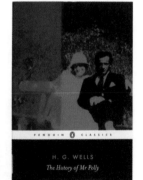

2005
ed. Simon J. James
intro. John Sutherland

1946 Penguin Books
• —

2005
ed. Simon J. James &
John S. Partington
intro. Michael Foot

The New Machiavelli 1911

Richard Remington is an author and a Member of Parliament, but underneath the veneer of success he is dissatisfied with his marriage and the politics of his party. When he meets the beautiful Isabel Rivers and embarks on a scandalous society affair, his entire life is thrown into disarray. This novel was partly inspired by Wells's relationship wih Amber Reeves, which also informed *Ann Veronica*. Joseph Conrad (277) considered it Wells's 'master-work'.

A Short History of the World 1922

In 344 pages, Wells traces the entire history of the world from the formation of the earth in space, through the ages of fish, 'coal swamps' and reptiles, to the first men, the birth of civilization, the Ancient Greeks (15) and Romans (36), the origins of Christianity (61), the 'great days of the Arabs' (97), the Mongol conquests (77), the discovery of America (119), the 'age of political experiments' (178), the Industrial Revolution (188), the First World War (433) and the Russian Revolution (385).

1936 Penguin Books
1937 Pelican Books
● —

2006
ed. Michael Sherborne
intro. Norman Stone

2005
ed. Patrick Parrinder &
John S. Partington
intro. John Clute

The Shape of Things to Come
The Ultimate Revolution 1933

The fictional Dr Philip Raven was an intellectual working for the League of Nations. When he died, he left behind an unpublished 'dream book', an account of prophetic visions he experienced that describe a 'history of the future' up to the year 2105. Wells's prescient work predicts the Second World War, the rise of chemical warfare, the instability of the Middle East and various climatic disasters. It also foresees a worldwide benevolent 'Air Dictatorship', which promotes 'Basic English' as a global language, sanctions euthanasia and eradicates all religion; this order is eventually overthrown itself to make away for a utopian society of polymaths.

In 1933, Wells's books were publicly burned by the Nazis in Berlin. That same year he was elected President of International PEN, the writers' organization campaigning for intellectual freedom. In 1940, he set out a proposal for universal human rights, published as a Penguin Special, *The Rights of Man*, which helped to bring about the Universal Declaration of Human Rights in 1948.

The Great
Science Fiction 1895–8
The Time Machine; *The Island of Doctor Moreau*; *The Invisible Man*; *The War of the Worlds*

'When one finishes one of Wells's great scientific romances or short stories,' writes Matthew Beaumont in his introduction, 'home doesn't feel quite so homely after all. His novels have a subtly disconcerting after-effect.'

1940 Penguin Special
2015 Penguin Books
–

Penguin Specials (S) were a series of topical, political books, the first 145 of which were published in the run-up to and during the Second World War. Wells's *The Rights of Man* was the second of four contributions he made to the series; it was republished in a facsimile edition in 2015.

2016
intro. Matthew Beaumont

Bram Stoker 1847–1912

Abraham Stoker was the son of an Irish civil servant. In 1878, he became the business manager of the Lyceum Theatre in London and wrote short stories and novels in his spare time, by far the most popular of which was *Dracula*.

1979 Penguin Books
•—

Richard Marsh
1857–1915

Richard Bernard Heldmann was the son of a north London lace merchant. He edited *Union Jack*, a weekly boy's magazine, until he was caught issuing forged cheques and sentenced to 18 months' hard labour. Thereafter he wrote under the pseudonym 'Richard Marsh'. *The Beetle* was his most popular novel; other titles included *The Devil's Diamond* (1893), *The Magnetic Girl* (1903) and *The Goddess: A Demon* (1900).

The Beetle 1897
A Mystery

Paul Lessingham is an upstanding British politician, pursued through the dark streets of London by 'the Beetle', a hypnotic shape-shifting creature from Egypt, hell-bent on revenge. The novel's multiple narrators touch on subjects from British imperialism to homosexuality and the '<u>New Woman</u>' (252). The story has much in common with *Dracula* and was initially more popular.

1993
ed. Maurice Hindle
pref. Christopher Frayling, 2003

Dracula 1897

After a visit to Whitby in 1890 and conversations with his Hungarian friend Ármin Vámbéry, Stoker began writing a horror novel composed of letters, journal entries, telegrams, ships' logs and newspaper clippings. His story gave form to what is now the universal myth of the blood-sucking, immortal, Transylvanian aristocrat, pitted against the redoubtable Professor Abraham Van Helsing.

Dracula's Guest 1911–4 and Other Weird Stories

This collection of Stoker's short stories was published posthumously by his widow Florence. It includes 'Dracula's Guest', which may have been the omitted first chapter of *Dracula*. The story involves an undead countess, a graveyard at night and a huge slavering wolf. Other titles include 'The Burial of the Rats' and 'A Dream of Red Hands'. This volume also features *The Lair of the White Worm*, a mythic tale of ambition, revenge and a monstrous snake with glowing green eyes.

2006
ed. Kate Hebblethwaite

2008 Red Classics
•—

2018 Penguin English Library

Elizabeth von Arnim 1866–1941

Mary Annette Beauchamp was born in Australia to British parents, and came to London when she was a young girl. She married twice, changing her name to Countess von Arnim-Schlagenthin and then Countess Russell. She was the cousin of Katherine Mansfield (393) and the philosopher Bertrand Russell's sister-in-law, she had a three-year affair with H. G. Wells (255) and her children were tutored by E. M. Forster (284). She died in South Carolina but her ashes were buried in Buckinghamshire, where her gravestone reads *parva sed apta*, 'small but sufficient'.

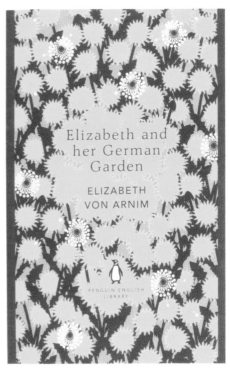

2018 Penguin English Library

Elizabeth and Her German Garden 1898

'I love my garden, I am writing in it now in the late afternoon loveliness, much interrupted by the mosquitoes and the temptation to look at all the glories of the new green leaves washed half an hour ago in a cold shower.' This humorous, poignant, autobiographical novel is based on von Arnim's unhappy marriage to the fraudulent Prussian aristocrat, Henning August, Graf von Arnim-Schlagenthin. It takes the form of a year's diary, written by 'Elizabeth' as she tends her garden and escapes her stifling household, her noisy children and her irascible husband, 'the Man of Wrath'.

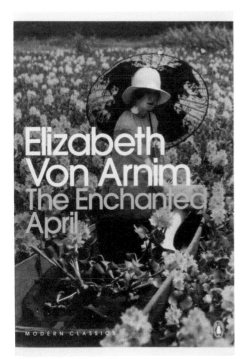

2012 Modern Classics
intro. Salley Vickers

The Enchanted April 1922

'To Those who Appreciate Wistaria and Sunshine,' runs an advert in *The Times*. 'Small mediaeval Italian Castle on the shores of the Mediterranean to be let Furnished for the month of April.' Four very different women take up the offer and escape to the Italian Riviera, abandoning rain, marriage and sad memories. Initially awkward, the four women eventually blossom in their beautiful new surroundings. Von Armin wrote the novel while staying at Castello Brown in Portofino herself. It 'sounds as if it would be an appallingly cloying cream puff of a fairy tale,' wrote a reviewer in the *Times Literary Supplement*, 'but that would be to ignore that the author habitually kept a pot of lemon juice mixed with vinegar beside her ink-pot'.

For Edwardian Fiction, turn to p.277

POETRY

'We associate the Victorian period with profusion, with outpourings of energy, with uncontrolled expansion: all this is true of its poetry,' writes Daniel Karlin in the introduction to his anthology of Victorian verse. 'More volumes of poetry appeared in the nineteenth century than in the two preceding ones combined, and the poets who published these volumes were themselves a fraction of a vast, shadowy population in the hinterland of Victorian literary culture – magazine and newspaper poets (local and regional especially), contributors to gatherings and garlands and posies and nosegays, the hundreds of fugitives from poetic justice.'

THE PENGUIN BOOK OF VICTORIAN VERSE
1837 – 1901

Karlin opens his anthology with seven poems written specifically to or about Queen Victoria, by Elizabeth Barrett Browning, Alfred Tennyson (263), A. E. Housman (268), Thomas Hardy (239) and others. He advertised in the *Times Literary Supplement* for suggestions for this anthology. As well as all the better known names like Robert Browning (264), Edward Lear (263), Emily Brontë (217), Charles Kingsley (231), Matthew Arnold (272), Christina Rossetti (265), Lewis Carroll (232), William Morris (226), Algernon Charles Swinburne (265) and W.B. Yeats (267), he includes many lesser known figures such as Ebenezer Elliott, Ebenezer Jones, Eliza Ogilvy, Emily Pfeiffer, Cosmo Monkhouse and Victor Plarr.

1969 Penguin Poets
• ed. George MacBeth

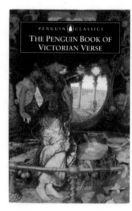

1998
ed. Daniel Karlin

1995
ed. John Robert,
Glorney Bolton &
Julia Bolton Holloway

Elizabeth Barrett Browning 1806 – 1861

Elizabeth Barrett Moulton Barrett was a crippled child and an invalid throughout her life. She wrote political poetry: 'The Cry of the Children' was read in the House of Lords and helped reform legislation around child labour. At the age of 40, she eloped to Italy with Robert Browning, her dog Flush, her maid Wilson and a heavy dependency on laudanum. They were married in secret and had a son together, nicknamed 'Pen'. Virginia Woolf later wrote a biography of Elizabeth's dog. 'Barrett Browning's ardour and abundance,' wrote Woolf, 'her brilliant descriptive powers, her shrewd and caustic humour, infect us with her own enthusiasm.'

Aurora Leigh 1826 – 62
and Other Poems

Aurora Leigh, Elizabeth's masterwork, is a semi-autobiographical novel-in-verse about a Florentine poet who struggles to reconcile the demands of social justice, artistic success and a loving relationship. Elizabeth called it 'the most mature of my works, and the one into which my highest convictions upon Life and Art have entered'. This volume also includes *The Runaway Slave at Pilgrim's Point*, written against slavery in the United States, *Sonnets from the Portuguese*, *Casa Guidi Windows* and many other poems.

Edward Lear 1812–1888

Lear was the 20th of 21 children. He began his artistic career at the age of fifteen, painting fans and selling drawings to passers-by in the street. He specialized in natural history and at nineteen created a beautiful book of birds, *Illustrations of the Family of Psittacidae, or Parrots*. On the strength of this spectacular tome, he was commissioned to illustrate the private menagerie of Lord Stanley, president of the newly founded Zoological Society of London. While working on this job, Lear amused Stanley's children with nonsense verses and drawings. In 1837, he abandoned natural history and travelled around the Mediterranean, painting landscapes and continuing to write nonsense songs. He spent his last years alone in San Remo in Italy with his beloved, tailless cat Foss, who features in many of his drawings.

The Complete Nonsense
and Other Verse 1825–88

'How pleasant to know Mr Lear!'
  Who has written such volumes of stuff!
Some think him ill-tempered and queer,
  But a few think him pleasant enough.

'Nonsense is the breath of my nostrils,' wrote Lear. This volume collects all his memorable characters and illustrations: the Dong with the luminous nose, the Pobble who has no toes, the Owl and the Pussy-cat, the Quangle Wangle and his hat, Mr and Mrs Discobbolos, The Scroobius Pip, the Akond of Swat, the fearsome Cummerbund and the tragic Jumblies.

He has many friends, laymen and clerical;
  Old Foss is the name of his cat;
His body is perfectly spherical; –
  He weareth a runcible hat.

1940 Penguin Books
A Book of Lear
● ed. R. L. Mégroz
1975 Puffin Books
A Book of Bosh
● ed. Brian Alderson
1986 Penguin Books
Edward Lear's Nonsense Omnibus
● ed. Sir Edward Strachey

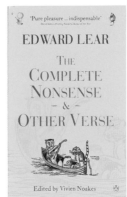

2002 Penguin Books
2006 Penguin Classics
ed. Vivien Noakes

Alfred, Lord Tennyson 1809–1892

Tennyson was the leading poet of his generation; he never had any other occupation. On Wordsworth's death (193) in 1850 he became Poet Laureate, a position he held for more than 40 years. 'He has three great qualities which are seldom found together except in the greatest poets,' wrote T. S. Eliot: 'abundance, variety and complete competence [...] He had the finest ear of any English poet since Milton (150).'

Selected Poems 1830–89

'Tis better to have loved and lost
Than never to have loved at all.

Many of Tennyson's lines have become commonplaces in English. This volume demonstrates the variety of his work, from the shorter lyrics, 'The Charge of the Light Brigade', 'The Lady of Shalott' and 'Break, Break, Break'; to tragic narratives such as *Maud*, in which the poet invites her to come into the garden, 'For the black bat, night, has flown'. One of Tennyson's greatest works is *In Memoriam A. H. H.* (1850), a profound tribute to a close friend from student days, Arthur Henry Hallam, who died of a cerebral haemorrhage at the age of 22.

1941 Penguin Poets
● ed. W. E. Williams
1991
● ed. Aidan Day

2007
ed. Christopher Ricks

Idylls of the King 1859–85

Tennyson had a lifelong interest in Arthurian legends, inspired by reading Thomas Malory (90), Geoffrey of Monmouth (76) and the *Mabinogion* (82). His early poem 'Morte d'Arthur' had been extremely popular, so he developed his retelling into a blank verse (129) cycle known as *Idylls of the King*. These twelve poems narrate the story of Arthur, from his first meeting with Guinevere to the Quest for the Holy Grail, Lancelot and Guinevere's adultery and the fateful last battle. They transpose the legend into an allegory of the morals, ideals and problems of mid-Victorian society.

ALFRED, LORD TENNYSON
IDYLLS OF THE KING

1983 Penguin Poets
1996 Penguin Classics
ed. J. M. Gray

Robert Browning 1812– 1889

As a child, Robert Browning was influenced by his father's large and eccentric library, his mother's Nonconformist religious beliefs and his early encounters with Romantic poetry (191). At seventeen, he dropped out of university and travelled around Europe for twenty years, attempting unsuccessfully to establish himself as a poet. In 1845, he began corresponding with Elizabeth Barrett (262), and in 1846 they were married in secret. After her death in Italy in 1861, Robert returned to England and, following the publication of *Dramatis Personae* (1864) and *The Ring and the Book* (1868–9), he finally earned a reputation as one of England's most popular poets; several Browning Societies were founded during his lifetime. He died in Venice.

PENGUIN ILLUSTRATED CLASSICS
ROBERT BROWNING
SELECTED POEMS
Wood-engravings by Iain Macnab

Selected Poems 1836–89

Browning is perhaps best known for his dramatic monologues, such as 'My Last Duchess' and the boisterous 'Fra Lippo Lippi'; the children's fable 'The Pied Piper of Hamelin'; 'Childe Roland to the Dark Tower Came', inspired by a line from *King Lear* (142); and 'Caliban upon Setebos', based on characters from *The Tempest* (144), which has been read as a critique of Darwin (270). This selection includes these and other poems such as 'Clive', 'Mr Sludge, The Medium' and 'An Epistle Containing the Strange Medical Experience of Karshish, the Arab Physician'. There exists a wax cylinder of Browning reciting 'How They Brought the Good News from Ghent to Aix' in 1889, one of the oldest surviving sound recordings.

1938 Illustrated Classics
● ill. Ian MacNab
1954 Penguin Poets
● ed. W. E. Williams
1981 Penguin Poets
● ed. John Pettigrew

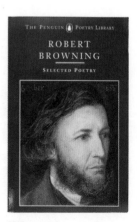

THE PENGUIN POETRY LIBRARY
ROBERT BROWNING
SELECTED POETRY

1989 Penguin Poetry Library
2000 Penguin Classics
ed. Daniel Karlin

2010
ed. Dinah Roe

THE PRE-RAPHAELITES
from Rossetti to Ruskin 1838–87

The Pre-Raphaelite Brotherhood was founded in 1848 at the house of John Everett Millais on Gower Street in London. The three original members were the artists Millais, William Holman Hunt and Dante Gabriel Rossetti. They were inspired by John Ruskin (271) to reject the 'sloshy' conventions of Victorian idealism and embrace the style of those artists who preceded Raphael and Michelangelo (128).

This anthology collects poetry by several members of the brotherhood, Dante Gabriel Rossetti, William Michael Rossetti and Thomas Woolner, as well as other figures associated with the movement: George Meredith (240), Christina Rossetti, William Morris (226) and Swinburne.

Poems and Ballads
and Atalanta in Calydon 1865, 1866

Swinburne wrote burlesques, ballads and roundels, borrowing verse forms from classical, medieval and renaissance poets. His poems are both opulent hymns to sensual love and virtuoso experiments in form and rhythm. This volume contains his first two published works: *Atalanta in Calydon*, a tragic verse drama, and *Poems and Ballads*.

Christina Rossetti 1830–1894

Christina Georgina Rossetti was the sister of Dante Gabriel Rossetti and William Michael Rossetti. Their uncle was John Polidori (204). Her maternal grandfather, an Italian poet, published a collection of her poems when she was just sixteen, after which she continued to publish poetry, sometimes under the pseudonym 'Ellen Alleyne' in her brothers' magazine *The Germ*.

Poems 1862–94

Rossetti wrote lyrical, psychologically astute poetry, interweaving the ordinary world and the magical. 'Goblin Market' and her children's verses conjure fantasy worlds, and her devotional religious poems, such as 'St Peter' and 'The Love of Christ Which Passeth Knowledge', evoke intense religious experiences. She wrote the words to the carol 'In the Bleak Midwinter', set to music by Gustav Holst.

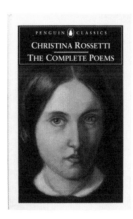

Both these volumes are based on a definitive text, edited by R. W. Crump, first published by Louisiana University Press in 1979 and revised in 1986 and 1990.

2001 *Complete Poems*
ed. Betty S. Flowers

2008 *Selected Poems*
ed. Dinah Roe

Algernon Charles Swinburne 1837–1909

Swinburne's poems feature sado-masochism, lesbianism, cannibalism, anti-theism and necrophilia. In 1866, the *Saturday Review* described him as having 'a mind all aflame with the feverish

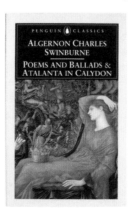

carnality of a schoolboy'. He is said to have circulated a rumour that he had had sex with and then eaten a monkey. He led a bohemian life in Europe and London, becoming increasingly dependent on alcohol, until he was eventually forced to live a teetotal existence in Putney in southwest London.

2000
ed. Kenneth Haynes

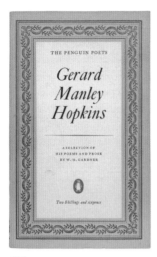

1953 Penguin Poets
1985 Penguin Classics
ed. W. H. Gardner

Gerard Manley Hopkins 1844–1889

After graduating from Oxford, Hopkins entered the Roman Catholic Church and became a member of the <u>Society of Jesus</u> (72), at which point he burned all the poems he had previously written. In 1877, he was ordained a priest. He worked in various parishes, some of which were in the slum districts of Liverpool, taught at Stonyhurst College in Lancashire and was Classics Professor at University College, Dublin.

Poems and Prose 1865–89

Hopkins is best remembered for his 'sprung rhythm' nature poems, such as 'The Windhover', which is dedicated to 'Christ our Lord' and which Hopkins considered his masterpiece. Its climactic central stanza reads:

> Brute beauty and valour and act, oh, air, pride, plume, here
>   Buckle! AND the fire that breaks from thee then, a billion
> Times told lovelier, more dangerous. O my chevalier!

This edition also includes a selection of his diaries, letters and sermons.

THE NEW PENGUIN BOOK OF ENGLISH FOLK SONGS *c.* 1870–*c.* 1980

Folk songs are an English art form, by turns amusing and poignant. This anthology presents a mixture of classic and less well-known songs, with musical scores, under thematic headings such as 'Soldiers and Sailors', 'Lust, Infidelity and Bad Living' and 'Animals and Nonsense'. It was published in cooperation with the English Folk Dance and Song Society.

1959 Penguin Books
● ed. R. Vaughan Williams & A. L. Lloyd

2014
ed. Steve Roud & Julia Bishop, 2012

DECADENT POETRY
from Wilde to Naidu
1881–1912

'Lurid, languid, perverse, amoral, immoral, impressionistic, diseased, world-weary, soul-sick, sordid, morbid, sensational, over-subtle, anti-natural, inorganic, narcissistic, blasphemous, euphuistic, fragmented, paradoxical, parodic, urbane and intensely artificial,' writes Rodensky in her introduction: 'here are the terms most often associated with the decadent poetry of the late nineteenth and early twentieth centuries; in short, not the kind of poetry you are likely to buy for your grandmother, unless you have an unusual sort of grandmother.' She anthologizes the English decadents <u>Oscar Wilde</u> (244), <u>W. B. Yeats</u> (267), <u>William Ernest Henley</u> (241), <u>Lord Alfred Douglas</u> (244), Aubrey Beardsley and many others. In 'Nini Patteen-l'Air', Arthur Symons eulogises the scarlet, pirouetting petticoats of Nini:

> The Maenad of the Decadence,
> Collectedly extravagant,
> Her learned fury wakes the sense
> That, fainting, needs for excitant
> The science of concupiscence.

2006
ed. Lisa Rodensky

W. B. Yeats 1865–1939

William Butler Yeats had a lifelong interest in the occult. He founded the Dublin Hermetic Society in 1885 and was involved in the Theosophical Society, the Hermetic Order of the Golden Dawn and the Ghost Club. As an Irish poet he sought to express himself in a distinctively Irish voice. He also became involved in Irish nationalism through his infatuation with the revolutionary Maud Gonne, to whom he proposed unsuccessfully many times throughout his life. In 1923, he was appointed a senator of the newly founded Irish Free State, and was awarded the Nobel Prize for Literature.

Writings on Irish Folklore, Legend and Myth

1888–1933

Yeats pioneered an Irish nationalism of the imagination. One of the ways in which he sought to revive Ireland's native culture was through researching and collecting Irish folk stories and legends. This is an anthology of all his essays, articles, introductions and sketches on the subject, arranged chronologically, with entries on fairies, ghosts, sorcerers, witches and the Sidhe. 'Yeats stood for enchantment,' wrote G. K. Chesterton (293). '[…] He was the real original rationalist who said the fairies stand to reason.'

1993 Twentieth-Century Classics
ed. Robert Welch

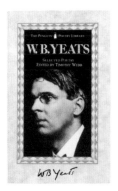

Selected Poems

1889–1938

1991 Penguin Poetry Library
2000 Modern Classics
ed. Timothy Webb

In 1917, Yeats purchased a Norman stone tower in Ballylee, County Galway, which became the focus of his 1928 collection, *The Tower*, considered by many to be his greatest poetic achievement. This selection presents the best of Yeats's poetry across his career, from part of *The Wanderings of Oisin*, based on the ancient Fenian Cycle (78) of Irish mythology, to 'The Circus Animals' Desertion' in which he decides to 'lie down where all the ladders start / In the foul rag and bone shop of the heart'.

When You Are Old

Early Poems, Plays and Fairy Tales 1892–1902
Irish Fairy Tales; *Poems*;
The Wind Among the Reeds;
The Celtic Twilight

Yeats's early writings reflect his interests in folklore, magic and the pursuit of aestheticism. This selection includes the verse dramas *The Wanderings of Oisin* and *The Countess Cathleen*; poems such as 'A Dream of Death' and 'The Valley of the Black Pig', and non-fiction pieces about ghosts, devils, enchanted woods and fairies.

2015
ed. Rob Doggett
—
The Countess Cathleen also features in the anthology *The Playboy of the Western World and Two Other Irish Plays* (300).

Selected Plays 1892–1938

As a leader of the Irish Literary Revival, Yeats co-founded the Irish Literary Theatre company in 1899 with a manifesto to 'find in Ireland […] freedom to experiment.' In 1904, the Abbey Theatre opened in Dublin, with Yeats's *Cathleen ni Houlihan* playing the opening night. He authored many plays for the Abbey, five of which portrayed the Irish epic hero Cú Chulainn (81). He was increasingly influenced by Japanese Nō plays (112). He wrote in 1916: 'my theatre must be the ancient theatre that can be made by unrolling a carpet or marking out a place with a stick, or setting a screen against the wall.' This anthology collects eighteen of his dramatic works, many of which are short, one-act pieces.

1997 Twentieth-Century Classics
ed. Richard Allen Cave

A. E. Housman 1859–1936

After studying classics at Oxford, Alfred Edward Housman spent ten years working as a clerk in the Patent Office, before becoming Professor of Latin at University College London and publishing editions of Juvenal (52) and Ovid (46). From 1911 until his death, he was Professor of Latin at Cambridge University.

A Shropshire Lad 1896–1936
and Other Poems

Throughout his career, Housman wrote poetry, but only published two volumes in his lifetime: *A Shropshire Lad* and *Last Poems*. His epigrammatic poems evoke a nostalgic rural world, tinged with sadness. Three years before his death he delivered a lecture on 'The Name and Nature of Poetry', and his unpublished poems were printed posthumously by his brother. All these texts are collected in this edition. Housman's memorial plaque in Trinity College, Cambridge, says in Latin that he:

> corrected the transmitted text of the Latin poets with so keen an intelligence and so ample a stock of learning, and chastised the sloth of editors so sharply and wittily, that he takes his place as the virtual second founder of textual studies. He was also a poet whose slim volumes of verse assured him of a secure place on the British Helicon (18).

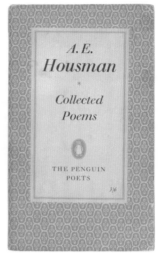

2010
ed. Archie Burnett
intro. Nick Laird

1956 Penguin Poets *Collected Poems*
• ed. John Sparrow
1989 Twentieth-Century Classics
Collected Poems and Selected Prose
• ed. Christopher Ricks

John Masefield 1878–1967

Orphaned at the age of thirteen, Masefield joined the 'school ship' HMS *Conway* and at fifteen embarked on what was to be a life at sea, sailing to Chile via Cape Horn. He saw porpoises, flying fish and a moonbow, but he was hospitalized with sunstroke in Chile and invalided back to England. On the journey home he decided to become a writer and after spending time as a vagrant, a barman and working in a carpet factory, he became a best-selling novelist and eventually Poet Laureate. His children's books *The Midnight Folk* and *The Box of Delights* were described by the *Times* as 'two of the greatest children's books ever written'.

Spunyarn 1899–1939
Sea Poetry and Prose

Inspired by sailors' yarns, sea shanties and his early life on the ocean wave, much of Masefield's writing is about stormy swells and the hardship, romance and adventure of a life at sea. This selection of short stories, poems and extracts from the novels collects the best of his sea writings, including his poems 'Sea-Fever' and 'Cargoes', which John Betjeman described as 'two lyrics which will be remembered as long as the language lasts'.

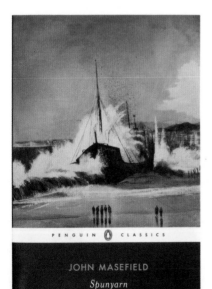

2011
ed. Philip W. Errington

For First World War poetry, turn to p.434

NON-FICTION

The Victorian period saw the first publication of two monumental reference works, the *Oxford English Dictionary* and the *Dictionary of National Biography*, as well as expanded editions of the *Encyclopaedia Britannica*. Perhaps unsurprisingly, much of the non-fiction of this era is preoccupied with classification: Thomas Carlyle sorts historical figures into 'heroes' and 'subjects'; Henry Mayhew (272) provides a taxonomy of London's impoverished street workers; Alfred Russel Wallace (274) charts the geographical distribution of species in the Malay Archipelago; John Stuart Mill (273) traces the historical struggle between liberty and authority; and, most dramatically, Charles Darwin (270) presents a vision of a single evolutionary tree of life, through which every living species on earth is related.

Thomas Carlyle 1795–1881

Carlyle was a Scottish schoolteacher before he moved to London with his wife and embarked on a literary career. He became known as 'the Sage of Chelsea', receiving visits from Ruskin (271), Morris (226) and many other celebrated artists and writers. After Carlyle's death, his house in Cheyne Walk was preserved as a literary shrine and today it is a National Trust property, maintained exactly as he left it.

Selected Writings 1829–81

Alan Shelston's selection of Carlyle's writings aims to be 'representative of all stages of his career'. It includes extracts from the fictional *Sartor Resartus* ('The Tailor Retailored'), inspired by Sterne's *Tristram Shandy* (163); extracts from *The French Revolution*, which inspired Dickens's *Tale of Two Cities* (214); Carlyle's lecture on heroes and hero-worship, 'The Hero as Man of Letters'; and many other examples of his wide-ranging interests.

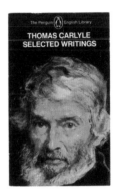

1971 Penguin English Library
1985 Penguin Classics
ed. Alan Shelston

Charles Darwin 1809–1882

In 1831, the year that Darwin completed his university degree, he joined HMS *Beagle* for a five-year scientific voyage around the world, as a self-financed naturalist. He collected a vast quantity of specimens on this voyage, including the tooth of an extinct species of giant ground sloth. On his return, he was elected a Fellow of the Royal Society in 1839 and spent the rest of his life publishing his findings from the trip and developing his theory of the 'transmutation of species'. He married his cousin Emma Wedgwood and lived with his large family at Down House in Kent, which is now open to the public. He spent his final years engaged in the close observation of earthworms. It is thought that Darwin may have died of the tropical Chagas disease, having being bitten by a 'kissing bug' in Mendoza, Argentina in 1835. After a public petition, he was buried in Westminster Abbey.

Voyage of the *Beagle* 1839
Charles Darwin's Journal of Researches

Darwin kept a detailed journal during his time on HMS *Beagle*, which was initially published as the third volume of Captain FitzRoy's account of the voyage. It was subsequently republished independently as a vivid and poetic travel memoir in its own right that describes Darwin's observations of volcanoes, gossamer spiders, coral reefs and fireflies.

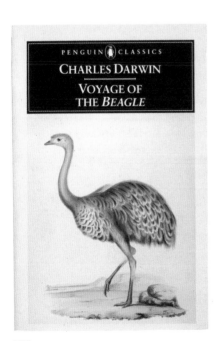

1989
ed. Janet Browne &
Michael Neve

On the Origin of Species
By Means of Natural Selection 1859

Perhaps the most controversial book of the Victorian age, *On the Origin of Species* sold out on the first day of its publication and has remained in print ever since. Its single, systematic argument transformed scientific thinking about life on earth: populations evolve over the course of generations, Darwin argues, by a process of natural selection, having descended from a single common ancestor. 'There is grandeur in this view of life, with its several powers, having been originally breathed into a few forms or into one,' he writes, in the final paragraph of the book;

> and that, whilst this planet has gone cycling on according to the fixed law of gravity, from so simple a beginning endless forms most beautiful and most wonderful have been, and are being evolved.

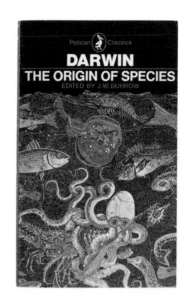

2009
ed. William Bynum

1968 Pelican Classics
1982 Penguin Classics
● ed. J. W. Burrow

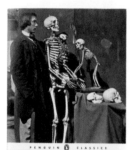

CHARLES DARWIN
The Descent of Man

The Descent of Man
and Selection in Relation to Sex 1871

Darwin refrained from discussing human evolution in *On the Origin of Species*, feeling that the subject was too 'surrounded with prejudices'. Twelve years later, however, he published *The Descent of Man*. His controversial aim was to 'consider, firstly, whether man, like every other species, is descended from some pre-existing form; secondly, the manner of his development; and thirdly, the value of the differences between the so-called races of man'. He introduces apes into the same family tree as humans and argues that racial characteristics are the result of 'sexual selection', females choosing between competing males.

2004
ed. James Moore &
Adrian Desmond

Autobiographies

1838–81, pub. 1887

Darwin wrote his 'Recollections of the Development of my Mind and Character' to amuse himself and because it 'might possibly interest my children or their children'. He modestly claims to have been 'rather below the common standard in intellect' and to have achieved his great breakthroughs by dint of luck, perseverance and a lot of hard work. This edition includes an early 'autobiographical fragment' as well as Darwin's later memoirs.

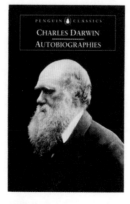

2002
ed. Michael Neve &
Sharon Messenger

The Expression of the Emotions
in Man and Animals 1872

In his last major work, Darwin asks deeper questions about the nature of humanity and the biological aspect of our humanizing emotions. He examines the ways in which we express a wide range of emotions, including anxiety, grief, joy, sulkiness, determination, contempt, guilt, patience, surprise and particularly embarrassment. He is fascinated by blushing, 'the most peculiar and the most human of all expressions'.

2009
ed. Joe Cain & Sharon Messenger

This book included many photographs and was a landmark in the history of book illustration; these are reproduced in this edition along with supplementary plates that Darwin consulted during his research.

1967 Peregrine Books
Ruskin Today
● ed. Kenneth Clark

John Ruskin 1819–1900

Ruskin's father was a wine-merchant and an art lover; his mother was a strict evangelical Christian. He became the most influential art critic of the 19th century, defending J. M. W. Turner, celebrating Gothic architecture and championing the <u>Pre-Raphaelites</u> (265). He believed that the principal role of the artist is to present 'truth to nature'. In 1848, he married Effie Gray, but the marriage was annulled after seven years on the grounds of non-consummation; it is said that Ruskin was appalled by the sight of Effie's pubic hair, which had not featured in his study of smooth classical statuary. Ruskin became passionately obsessed with a 10-year-old girl called Rose la Touche. Rose died insane in 1875, at the age of 27, and Ruskin became increasingly prone to mental disturbances himself; after seven violent breakdowns he spent the last decade of his life in quiet seclusion.

Unto This Last
and Other Writings 1841–84

This anthology of Ruskin's writings includes his essay 'The Nature of Gothic' from *The Stones of Venice*, which celebrates the craftsmen of the Middle Ages and contrasts them with unfulfilled factory workers in soul-destroying jobs. The four essays in *Unto This Last* criticize Victorian capitalism; and *The King of the Golden River*, his only work of fiction, is a fairy tale he wrote for Effie Gray when she was thirteen years old. Ruskin's writings influenced figures as disparate as <u>William Morris</u> (226) and Mahatma Gandhi.

1985
ed. Clive Wilmer

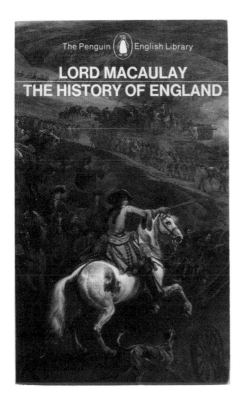

1979 Penguin English Library
1986 Penguin Classics
ed. Hugh Trevor-Roper, 1968

Lord Macaulay 1800–1859

Thomas Babington Macaulay was the son of Zachary Macaulay, a philanthropist and abolitionist. He wrote for the *Edinburgh Review* before entering Parliament in 1830. As a politician he worked on the supreme council for India, influencing the Indian educational and legal systems, and he was the Member of Parliament for Edinburgh, Secretary at War and Paymaster General. He was elevated to the peerage in 1857. His masterwork, *The History of England*, was unfinished at his death.

The History of England 1848–61

'I purpose to write the history of England from the accession of King James the Second down to a time which is within the memory of men still living,' opens Macaulay. The first two volumes of his *History of England* were published in 1848 and were immediate bestsellers, but he died before he could complete the supertask he had set himself: his five large volumes begin in 1685 and only get as far as the end of the reign of William III in 1702. This abridged edition presents the best of Macaulay's gripping narrative and demonstrates his insightful understanding of the politics behind social change.

Henry Mayhew 1812–1887

Mayhew ran away from school and went to sea, getting as far as India. On his return to England he embarked on a bumpy literary career that encompassed journalism, plays, novels, travel writing and educational material. He was one of the founders of the magazine *Punch* in 1841.

London Labour and the London Poor 1851

Mayhew is best remembered for his vast social survey, known as *London Labour and the London Poor*, which records the voices, hopes and salaries of the working classes. He meets a huge range of professionals, including costermongers, chimney sweeps, prostitutes, rat catchers, mudlarks and the unfortunate 'pure finders', who collected dog faeces and sold it to tanners. He records his conversations with unsentimental sympathy and a lively sense of humour.

1973 Pelican Classics
The Unknown Mayhew
● ed. E. P. Thompson &
Eileen Yeo

1985
ed. Victor Neuburg

Matthew Arnold 1822–1888

Arnold was the son of Dr Thomas Arnold, the influential headmaster of Rugby School. After graduating from Oxford, he spent several years travelling and writing experimental verse, before publishing three volumes of poetry that established his literary reputation. In 1851, he became an inspector of schools, a position he held throughout his life. Between 1857 and 1867, he was Professor of Poetry at Oxford.

Culture and Anarchy 1853–88
and Other Selected Prose

As well as a poet, Arnold was an education reformer, a social theorist and a passionate critic of an industrial society in 'bondage to machinery'. In *Culture and Anarchy*, he argues that the joy of art and culture, especially the 'sweetness and light' of classical civilization, are essential to human life. The other pieces in this anthology cover literary criticism, France, journalism and democracy.

1970 Penguin English Library
Selected Prose
1987 Penguin Classics
Culture and Anarchy
ed. P. J. Keating

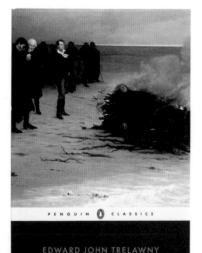

PENGUIN CLASSICS

EDWARD JOHN TRELAWNY

Records of Shelley, Byron and the Author

2013
ed. Rosemary Ashton

Edward John Trelawny 1792–1881

Trelawny was an odd character, who spent much of his long life travelling as a naval non-commissioned officer and gentleman adventurer. He had three marriages, the second of which was to the sister of the Greek warlord Odysseus Androutsos. His ashes are buried alongside Percy Bysshe Shelley's grave in Rome.

Records of Shelley, Byron and the Author 1858

Trelawny met Shelley (196) and Byron (195) in Italy, in February 1822, and seems to have become instantly infatuated with the two poets. He wrote this unauthorized memoir after their deaths, recalling his first impressions of them, Shelley's cremation on the sands and his subsequent adventures with Byron during the Greek War of Independence (359).

John Stuart Mill 1806–1873

Mill was perhaps the most influential English-speaking philosopher of the 19th century. He was educated by his father, Jeremy Bentham's assistant and propagandist: he learnt Greek at the age of three; by eight, he had read Xenophon (32) and Herodotus (31) and was proficient in maths, physics and astronomy. Perhaps unsurprisingly, he suffered a mental breakdown at the age of 20, during which he disavowed his father's teachings and read Coleridge (195), Carlyle (269) and Tocqueville (325). In later life, he established an intimate and collaborative relationship with Harriet Taylor, a married woman, who encouraged him to develop his own radical philosophy, an interpretation of Bentham's ideas. He married Harriet in 1851 after her first husband's death.

Utilitarianism
and Other Essays 1780–1861

This anthology opens with an extract by Jeremy Bentham (1747–1832). Bentham was an early proponent of the 'principle of utility', which states that the goodness of an action or law rests in how well it promotes the welfare of those affected by it, the aim being 'the greatest happiness of the greatest number'. In case it was of some practical use, Bentham left his body to be dissected after he died; today, it is preserved and dressed and sits in a glass-fronted cubicle in University College London. He has a wax head on his shoulders; his actual, desiccated head lies between his feet.

The rest of this volume is devoted to Mill's interpretations of Bentham, most importantly his 1861 essay *Utilitarianism*, in which he balances the claims of individuality with social well-being. He differentiates between qualities of happiness, separating higher and lower forms of pleasure: he determines, for example, that 'it is better to be a human being dissatisfied than a pig satisfied'.

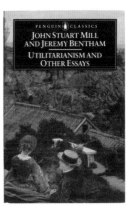

1987
ed. Alan Ryan

1974 Pelican Classics
1982 Penguin English Library
1985 Penguin Classics
ed. Gertrude Himmelfarb

2006 *On Liberty* and *The Subjection of Women*
ed. Alan Ryan
—
Ryan's edition also includes *The Subjection of Women*, written soon after his wife's death, in which Mill argues passionately for equality of the sexes. As the Member of Parliament for Westminster he was one of the first parliamentarians to call for women's suffrage, in 1866.

On Liberty 1859

On Liberty is the sacred text of liberalism: a copy is passed between successive presidents of the British Liberal Democrats as a symbol of office. It describes the historical struggle between 'authority and liberty' and warns that a democracy risks becoming a 'tyranny of the majority' if minority views are suppressed. Mill dedicates *On Liberty* to the memory of his wife Harriet. 'Were I but capable of interpreting to the world one half the great thoughts and noble feelings which are buried in her grave,' he writes, ' I should be the medium of a greater benefit to it, than is ever likely to arise from anything that I can write, unprompted and unassisted by her all but unrivalled wisdom'.

Autobiography 1873

In this moving and candid autobiography, Mill recalls his astonishingly intense education, his mental breakdown as a young man, his reading of Wordsworth (193) and Coleridge (195) and the development of his radical beliefs. It is a self-portrait of a man of deep personal integrity, who searched constantly for the truth.

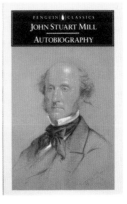

1989
ed. John M. Robson

2014
ed. Andrew Berry
—
This edition is one of the few examples of a variation on the 2003 Penguin Classics design (xv): the tail of the bird of paradise spills into what is usually a black panel. Another example of a playful tweak is *The Penguin Book of the Undead* (5).

Alfred Russel Wallace 1823–1913

Wallace was the co-discoverer of the theory of evolution by natural selection and his findings were announced along-side Darwin's in 1858, the year before Darwin published *On the Origin of Species* (270). He was the leading tropical biologist of his day having spent four years exploring the Amazon basin collecting specimens, and eight more in Southeast Asia. He was particularly interested in the geographical distribution of species: he discovered what is known as the 'Wallace Line', a boundary that divides the Malay archipelago, one side of which is populated by Asian and other by Australasian fauna. David Attenborough describes him as 'one of the most adventurous, observant and honourable scients of his time'.

The Malay Archipelago
The Land of the Orang-utan, and the Bird of Paradise 1869

Wallace travelled from Singapore to western New Guinea between 1854 and 1862. On his return to England, he wrote this lyrical and enthusiastic account of his adventures battling through jungles, enduring fevers, meeting headhunters and collecting new species. He dedicated the book to Charles Darwin (269), 'not only as a token of personal esteem and friendship but also to express my deep admiration for his genius and his works'.

John Henry Newman 1801–1890

Newman was the vicar of the University Church of St Mary the Virgin in Oxford and a leading figure of the Church of England, who caused widespread shock in 1845 when he was received into the Roman Catholic Church. He was ordained a priest and continued working as a religious leader, based in Birmingham. He was created a cardinal in 1879. His poem about the afterlife, *The Dream of Gerontius* (1865), inspired Elgar's musical masterpiece. Newman has been beatified by Pope Benedict XVI; a second miracle is required for him to become a saint.

Apologia Pro Vita Sua 1865–6

Newman wrote his theological autobiography 'A Defence of One's Life', in response to a public attack by Charles Kingsley (231). It is a description of his spiritual development from boyhood, and a candid account of his struggle to understand the nature of Christianity and its place in an industrial world. He saw it as a work of 'mental child-bearing'.

1994
ed. Ian Ker

Richard Jefferies 1848–1887

Jefferies grew up in Wiltshire, the son of a farmer. At sixteen, he and a cousin ran away to France, intending to walk to Russia. He became a journalist and wrote essays on rural life and natural history, as well as an autobiography, *The Story of My Heart* (1883), the children's book *Bevis* (1882) and the post-apocalyptic novel *After London* (1885), which influenced **William Morris** (226) and **M. P. Shiel** (432). He pioneered the modern idea of English 'nature writing'.

Landscape with Figures 1872–87
Selected Prose Writings

The nature writer Richard Mabey divides his selection into three sections: agricultural and social affairs, including pieces on 'The Amateur Poacher' and 'Events of the Village Year'; natural history, with such poetic titles as 'Rooks Returning to Roost', 'Trees about Town' and 'Haunts of the Lapwing: Winter'; and assorted essays, including 'Notes on Landscape Painting', 'Nature and Books' and 'My Old Village'.

1983 Penguin English Library
2013 Penguin Classics
ed. Richard Mabey
—
Mabey wrote a new preface for the 2013 reissue: 'I chose the selection […] in the early nineteen-eighties,' he writes, 'when interest in Jefferies reflected current political and social worries, and focused on his writings about the uneasy relations between country and city, the future of democracy, the idea of the "organic" community. I suspect that this aspect of his work is likely to come to the fore again.'

James Frazer 1854–1941

Sir James George Frazer was a fellow in classics at Trinity College, Cambridge, for 35 years. During this time, he was commissioned to write articles on 'Totemism' and 'Taboo' for the ninth edition (1875–89) of the *Encyclopaedia Britannica*, which kindled an interest in comparative anthropology. In 1890, he published the two-volume first edition of his seminal *Golden Bough*, which he revised twice, extending it to twelve volumes by 1915. It had a huge influence on subsequent anthropology and on writers including **D. H. Lawrence** (288), James Joyce and T. S. Eliot, who cited the work as a major source for *The Waste Land* (1922).

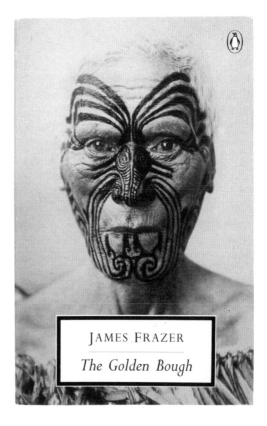

JAMES FRAZER
The Golden Bough

The Golden Bough
A Study in Magic and Religion 1890–1922

Frazer's sprawling study of magical and religious beliefs from around the globe takes its title from a reference in Virgil's *Aeneid* (44) and a painting by J. M. W. Turner. Frazer connects myths with rituals and extrapolates a universal evolutionary sequence that begins with seasonal fertility rituals and primitive magic and progresses through organized religion to modern science. Although Frazer's conclusions are not widely accepted today, his work continues to be influential for writers and artists and the detailed rituals he documents are still valuable to modern mythographers.

1996 Twentieth-Century Classics
intro. George W. Stocking, Jr.
—
This edition reissues the 1922 single-volume abridgement of Frazer's vast work, which he compiled with assistance from his wife, Lily.

Gertrude Bell 1868–1926

Gertrude Bell was born into a wealthy industrialist family. Over the course of her extraordinary career she became a traveller, a mountaineer, an archaeologist, a mapmaker, a photographer and a writer. She was the first woman to gain first-class honours in modern history at Oxford University and proceeded to conduct seven exploratory expeditions through the deserts of Arabia. During the First World War she served as an intelligence expert and advisor for the British armed forces in the Middle East. With T. E. Lawrence she played a major part in establishing the modern state of Iraq; at one time she was said to be the most powerful woman in the British Empire. She died in Baghdad two days before her 58th birthday.

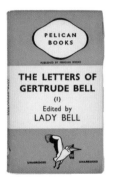
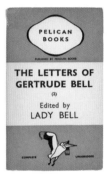

1939 Pelican Books
• ed. Gertrude Bell
Published in two volumes

A Woman in Arabia 1892–1926
The Writings of the Queen of the Desert

'It's a bore being a woman when you are in Arabia,' writes Bell in one of her letters. This anthology makes a selection from her military dispatches, personal letters, diary entries and travel writings, presenting a portrait of a forthright and spirited woman who shaped nations. 'Her letters are exactly herself,' wrote T. E. Lawrence – 'eager, interested, almost excited […]. She kept an everlasting freshness; or at least, however tired she was, she could always get up enough interest to match that of anyone who came to see her. I don't think I ever met anyone more entirely civilised.'

2015
ed. Georgina Howell

Mary Kingsley 1862–1900

Mary Kingsley was the niece of <u>Charles Kingsley</u> (231) and the daughter of a doctor who was frequently away from home. (George Kingsley spent five years accompanying General Custer's expeditions in North America.) Both her parents died in 1892, within two months of each other, which left Mary with a substantial inheritance and an untested sense of adventure. She embarked on a steamer for West Africa, intending to study native religion and collect zoological specimens. She made a second voyage in 1895 and became the first woman to climb Mount Cameroon, an active volcano that is also West Africa's highest mountain. <u>Rudyard Kipling</u> (250) called her 'the bravest woman of all my knowledge'.

Travels in West Africa 1897
Congo Français, Corisco and Cameroons

In this remarkable travelogue, a quiet Victorian woman from Cambridge describes canoeing treacherous rapids, wading through crocodile-infested swamps and encountering the fearsome Fang people. She describes an 'Odeaka cheese' recipe at one point, which is excellent 'even when made with boa constrictor, hippo or crocodile. It makes the former most palatable; but of course it does not remove the musky taste from crocodile; nothing I know of will.'

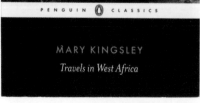

2015
ed. Lynette Turner
intro. Toby Green

For Edwardian non-fiction, turn to p.301

The Edwardians

'It was the age when crazy millionaires in curly top-hats and lavender waistcoats gave champagne parties in rococo house-boats on the Thames, the age of diabolo and hobble skirts, the age of the "knut" in his grey bowler and cut-away coat, the age of *The Merry Widow*, Saki's novels (281), *Peter Pan* (281) and *Where the Rainbow Ends*, the age when people talked about chocs and cigs and ripping and topping and heavenly, when they went for divvy week-ends at Brighton and had scrumptious teas at the Troc. From the whole decade before 1914 there seems to breathe forth a smell of the more vulgar, un-grown-up kind of luxury, a smell of brilliantine and crème-de-menthe and soft-centred chocolates – an atmosphere, as it were, of eating everlasting strawberry ices on green lawns to the tune of the Eton Boating Song. The extraordinary thing was the way in which everyone took it for granted that this oozing, bulging wealth of the English upper and upper-middle classes would last for ever, and was part of the order of things.'

from 'Such, Such Were the Joys',
an essay by George Orwell

Joseph Conrad

1857–1924

Jósef Teodor Konrad Korzeniowski was born to Polish parents in Russia, in what is now the Ukraine. Orphaned as a child, he was raised by his uncle Tadeusz Bobrowski, who allowed him to go to sea in 1874. Jósef worked on French and British merchant ships, sailing to the West Indies, the Far East and Australia. In 1886, he became a British subject and received his Masters certificate in the British merchant service. Eight years later, he left the sea, settled in Kent and devoted the rest of his life to writing in English, his third language. He published his first novel, *Almayer's Folly*, in 1895, under the anglicized pseudonym 'Joseph Conrad'. He was a friend of Henry James (417), John Galsworthy (286) and T. E. Lawrence. His gravestone is inscribed with lines from Spenser's *Faerie Queene* (130):

> Sleep after toyle, port after stormie seas,
> Ease after warre, death after life, doth greatly please

The Secret Sharer
and Other Stories 1896–1910

The Nigger of the 'Narcissus' is one of Conrad's greatest novellas, despite its problematic title. It tells the story of a stormy, mutinous voyage from Bombay to London, with a West Indian black sailor on board, dying of tuberculosis. Among the other tales in this selection, Conrad considered 'An Outpost of Progress', which bears many similarities to *Heart of Darkness* (278), to be his best story, and 'The Idiots' was his very first short story, written while he was on honeymoon, about a strained couple and their mentally handicapped children.

FICTION

The Edwardian era saw the gradual emergence of literary modernism, a style that employed increasingly experimental techniques to express subjective emotional and psychological states. Its early exponents included Henry James (417) and Joseph Conrad, though it would reach its apogee in the 1920s with the work of T. S. Eliot, Virginia Woolf and James Joyce. The other major novelists of the Edwardian period are Arnold Bennett (280), E. M. Forster (284), John Galsworthy (286), Ford Madox Ford (287) and D. H. Lawrence (288).

1943 Penguin Books
'Twixt Land and Sea
• rev. Boris Ford, 1988
1963 Modern Classics
The Nigger of the 'Narcissus'
• —

2007 *The Nigger of the 'Narcissus' and Other Stories*
2014 Reissued as *The Secret Sharer and Other Stories*
ed. J. H. Stape & Allan H. Simmons
intro. Gail Fraser

—

The General Editor of the 2007 Penguin Conrad editions was J. H. Stape, a prolific Canadian scholar, author and editor. The cover artworks by Phil Hale were commissioned for the series.

Heart of Darkness 1899

Marlow recounts his dangerous and disturbing journey into the depths of the African interior in search of the notorious ivory trader Kurtz. The reports of Kurtz's reputation and behaviour become increasingly wild the closer Marlow gets to the heart of Africa. Chinua Achebe has called Conrad a 'thoroughgoing racist'; nonetheless, this modernist masterpiece is still a horrifying and illuminating vision of the depths of human depravity.

1973 Modern Classics
● —
1983 Penguin English Library
● ed. Paul O'Prey
1995 Twentieth-Century Classics
● ed. Robert Hampson

2007
ed. Owen Knowles

—

While working for a Belgian trading company, Conrad captained a small steamer on the Congo River. Knowles's edition includes extracts from his *Congo Diary*, edited by Robert Hampson.

1943 Penguin Books
● —
1986
● ed. Cedric Watts

2007
ed. Allan H. Simmons

Lord Jim
A Tale 1900

Jim is the first mate on the *Patna* and dreams of being a hero. When the *Patna* appears to be sinking, however, Jim abandons ship. Unbearably ashamed of deserting his passengers, he retires to self-imposed exile on a remote Malay island, where he imagines himself as the benevolent ruler of an exotic land. This 'superb romance', wrote Virginia Woolf, stands 'at the head' of all Conrad's works.

Typhoon
and Other Stories
1901–2

'Typhoon' describes a captain and his mate facing a tropical cyclone in the Pacific Ocean; 'Falk' is about a grim voyage aboard a doomed ship; 'Amy Foster' explores the isolation of an eastern European immigrant in Kent, unable to speak English; and 'To-morrow' is the story of a retired coastal skipper, always expecting the return of his absent son.

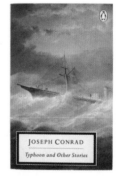

1990 Twentieth-Century Classics
● ed. Paul Kirschner

2007
ed. J. H. Stape

1963 Modern Classics
● —
1983 Penguin English Library
● ed. Martin Seymour-Smith

2007
ed. Véronique Pauly

Nostromo
A Tale of the Seaboard
1904

The San Tomé silver mine in Costaguana (a fictional version of Colombia) is a source of seemingly limitless wealth and power, but everyone connected with it eventually becomes tainted: the English mine-owner Charles Gould, the revolutionary General Montero and even the loyal stevedore Nostromo. One night, a large lighter filled with silver disappears ... 'No work of European fiction until *Nostromo*', wrote the critic Edward Said, '[...] so piercingly and unsparingly captured the imperialist project in Latin America.'

1963 Modern
Classics
● —
1984 Penguin
English Library
● ed. Martin
Seymour-Smith

The Secret Agent
A Simple Tale 1907

Adolf Verloc is a secret agent for an unnamed foreign power, operating from a seedy Soho shop that deals in pornography and bric-a-brac. When he is commissioned to commit an act of terrorism, he persuades his mentally handicapped brother-in-law Stevie to help him blow up the Greenwich Observatory.

2007
ed. Michael Newton

Under Western Eyes 1911

'In this book I am concerned with nothing but ideas,' wrote Conrad, 'to the exclusion of everything else.' Razumov is a university student in St Petersburg who becomes fatally entangled with Victor Haldin, a revolutionary terrorist, and his glamorous sister Nathalie. While Conrad was writing *Under Western Eyes*, he suffered a breakdown of several days, during which he spoke deliriously in Polish to the characters in the book.

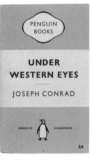

1957 Penguin Books
1969 Modern Classics
● —
1985 Penguin Classics
● ed. Boris Ford
1996 Twentieth-Century
Classics
● ed. Paul Kirschner

2007
ed. Stephen Donovan
intro. Allan H. Simmons

1974 Modern Classics
1992 Twentieth-Century
Classics

Chance 1913

Flora de Barral is a dreamy, slender girl, neglected by her bankrupt father and ignored by her governess. Reliant on her own meagre resources, she marries Captain Anthony and escapes to sea, but tragedy awaits beyond the horizon. Arnold Bennett (280) called *Chance* 'a discouraging book for a writer because he damn well knows he can't write as well as this.'

Victory 1915
An Island Tale

Axel Heyst moves to a remote island in the Malay Archipelago (274) with his Chinese assistant Wang, thinking that a life of isolation will protect him from suffering. When he accidentally rescues a young female musician from the advances of a lecherous hotel proprietor, however, his solitary paradise is threatened. A *New York Times* review compared the character of Heyst to Hamlet (144) and the ending to that of 'an Elizabethan play, where the stage is clogged with corpses'.

1963 Modern Classics
● —

1989 Twentieth-Century Classics
2000 Modern Classics
2015 Penguin Classics
ed. Robert Hampson, 1989
intro. John Gray, 2015

The Shadow-Line
A Confession 1917

The Shadow-Line tells the semi-autobiographical story of a young sea captain who finds himself becalmed in tropical seas and his crew succumbing to fever. In facing this crisis, the captain crosses the 'shadow-line' between youth and adulthood. Conrad dedicates the book to his son 'Borys and all others who like himself have crossed in early youth the shadow-line of their generation'. Borys was fighting on the Western Front (433) at the time.

1986 Penguin
Classics
1990 Twentieth-
Century Classics
ed. Jacques
Berthoud

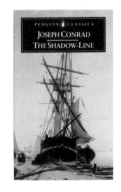

Arnold Bennett 1867–1931

Enoch Arnold Bennett was a solicitor's clerk, originally from Staffordshire, who became one of the most successful British novelists of the early 20th century. In 1902 he moved to Paris, returning to England in 1912 with a French wife, Marie. During the First World War (433) he was appointed director of propaganda for France in the Ministry of Information. He died of typhoid in 1931 after drinking tap water in a French restaurant. He lends his name to the Omelette Arnold Bennett, a speciality of the Savoy Hotel, made with smoked haddock, hollandaise sauce and cheese.

Anna of the Five Towns 1902
A Confession

Anna Tellwright lives a cramped existence, dominated by a tyrannical miserly father and hemmed in by narrow streets, tall chimneys and the small-mindedness of the Five Towns Methodist community. When she inherits a fortune and finds love, however, she is presented with the possibility of independence and escape. This was the first of Bennett's novels to be set among the towns of his childhood; he called Stoke-on-Trent 'the Five Towns' because he thought it sounded more 'euphonious' than the more accurate 'Six Towns'.

1936 Penguin Books
1973 Modern Classics

The Old Wives' Tale 1908

In 1903, Bennett sat in a Paris café watching a 'fat, shapeless, ugly and grotesque' old woman, who gave him the idea for *The Old Wives' Tale*. Constance and Sophia Baines are sisters, but their lives soon diverge: Constance remains in her mother's drapery shop, whereas Sophia elopes to Paris with an unscrupulous commercial traveller. The sisters are reunited years later and find each profoundly shaped by their different experiences. Bennett's masterpiece combines his Staffordshire roots with the influence of the French Naturalists, in particular Guy de Maupassant (318). According to Tom Wolfe, the novel was so successful that Bennett quipped, 'I don't read my reviews, I measure them.'

1954 Penguin Books
● intro. Frank Swinnerton

1983 Penguin English Library
1990 Twentieth-Century Classics
2007 Penguin Classics ed. John Wain

The Card 1911

Denry Machin is a card, a character, 'a rare 'un, no mistake', who flirts, dances and cheats his way from washerwoman's son to Mayor of Bursley. His preposterous schemes, which take place at the Welsh seaside, at civic balls, in newspaper print rooms and on the football pitch, prove to be surprisingly effective. The novel begins, 'Edward Henry Machin first saw the smoke on the 27th May 1867', Bennett's own birthday.

1975 Modern Classics

Riceyman Steps 1923

Henry Earlforward is the parsimonious owner of a gloomy second-hand bookshop in Clerkenwell, east London. When he marries Violet, the widow who runs the confectioner's nearby, his obsessive miserliness threatens to make them both wretched. Bennett was inspired by a shop in Southampton where he once bought a book about misers; the steps themselves are modelled on a real set of steps, which still exists, leading from King's Cross Road to Gwynne Place in Clerkenwell. They were originally known as the Plum-Pudding steps, before they were popularized by Bennett.

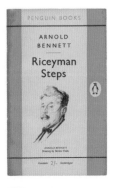

1954 Penguin Books
1991 Twentieth-Century Classics

1939 Penguin Books
Selected Short Stories
● —
1982 Penguin Books
● ed. Graham Greene

1990 Twentieth-Century Classics
The Complete Saki
2000 Modern Classics
The Complete Short Stories

Saki 1870–1916

Hector Hugh Munro was born in Burma. His father was a senior official in the Burma police; his mother died after being charged by a cow. Munro joined the Burma police himself, but was invalided out after a year's service to become a journalist, working as a foreign correspondent in the Balkans, Russia and Paris. He enlisted in the British army in 1914 and was shot dead by a German sniper in 1916, during the Battle of the Ancre. He took his pen name 'Saki' from Edward FitzGerald's translation of *The Ruba'iyat of Omar Khayyam* (101).

The Complete Short Stories 1901–16

Witty, mischievous and macabre, Saki's stories of wise children and childish adults skewer the Edwardian upper classes with a delicate and deadly blade. Two prominent characters are the debonair Clovis, exquisitely self-possessed, and the stylish but vain Reginald. Titles include 'The Byzantine Omelette', 'The Sex That Doesn't Shop', 'The Stampeding of Lady Bastable' and 'Filboid Studge, the Story of a Mouse That Helped'.

J. M. Barrie 1860–1937

When James Matthew Barrie was six years old, his older brother David died in an ice-skating accident. His mother was devastated, but Barrie believed she drew comfort from the fact that David would always remain a boy in her memory, never growing up to leave her. Barrie moved from Scotland to England in 1885. He wrote a series of books set in rural Scotland, which achieved some measure of success, but his fortunes really changed in 1897, while walking his St Bernard dog Porthos in Kensington Gardens. Barrie met the Llewellyn Davies family, including their baby Peter, and struck up a lasting friendship: Peter Llewellyn Davies inspired Barrie's most enduring and successful character, Peter Pan. Barrie was a keen cricketer and founded a team known as the Allahakbarries, which included Arthur Conan Doyle (248), G. K. Chesterton (293), Jerome K. Jerome (252), Rudyard Kipling (250) and H. G. Wells (255).

1967 Puffin Books
● —

Peter Pan 1902–11

Peter Pan began as a baby, living a magical life among birds and fairies. He first appeared as a character in *The Little White Bird*, which Barrie published in 1902. In 1904, Barrie transformed these chapters into the play *Peter Pan, or, The Boy Who Would Not Grow Up*, which premiered at Christmas. Now Peter was a flying boy from Neverland, facing Captain Hook with the assistance of Tinker Bell and Wendy Darling. The play was an immediate, spectacular success. Barrie subsequently published the original Peter Pan chapters as *Peter Pan in Kensington Gardens* and adapted the play into an equally successful novel, *Peter and Wendy*; these are the texts in this volume. Before his death, Barrie donated the rights to all the Peter Pan works to Great Ormond Street Hospital for Children.

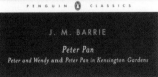

2004
ed. Jack Zipes

Erskine Childers 1870–1922

Robert Erskine Childers was born in London but raised in Ireland; both his parents had died from tuberculosis by the time he was fourteen. After graduating, he became a clerk in the House of Commons and spent his weekends boating on the Thames. In 1914, he smuggled 900 rifles and 25,000 rounds of ammunition into Howth to arm the Irish Volunteers and, after the First World War (433), he moved to Ireland and spent his last years propagandizing for Irish nationalism. Branded a rebel and a traitor by both the British and Irish authorities, he was captured in 1922 and executed by firing squad. His last words were, 'Take a step or two forward, lads, it will be easier that way.' His son, Erskine H. Childers, later became the fourth President of Ireland.

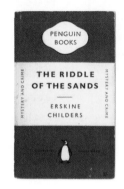

The Riddle of the Sands 1903
A Record of Secret Service

Carruthers joins his friend Davies on a duck-shooting expedition in the Baltic: their yacht is called the *Dulci-bella*, the name of one of Childers's sisters. They soon get into the treacherous waters and shifting sands of international espionage, however, as they begin to investigate mysterious activity on the Frisian island of Memmert in the North Sea. 'Vibrant, impassioned, witty, intelligent and shamelessly prejudiced in the manner of its day,' writes John le Carré, '*The Riddle of the Sands* remains one of the great foundation stones of the contemporary novel of espionage and adventure with political teeth.'

1952 Penguin Books
● –
1978 Penguin Books
● fwd. Geoffrey Household

2011
ed. Erskine C. Childers IV
–
Erskine C. Childers is the great-grandson of the author.

Frederick Baron Corvo 1860–1913

Frederick Rolfe was the son of a piano-maker and 'one of the strangest fish in the exotic aquarium of Edwardian literature' according to critic Robert McCrum. He converted to Catholicism at 26 and attempted to join the priesthood, but was ejected from the seminary. Nonetheless, he styled himself 'Fr Rolfe' and gave himself a variety of middle names, including Serafino, Lewis and Mary; he later used the pen names 'Frank English', 'Frederick Austin' and 'A. Crab Maid' and adopted the Italian aristocratic title 'Baron Corvo'. He had a penchant for painting and pederasty and relied heavily on the generosity of his publishers and friends, most of whom he insulted and ostracized. He died of a stroke in Venice, in his favourite restaurant. His unusual biography was pieced together in an equally remarkable book called *The Quest for Corvo* (1934) by A. J. A. Symons.

1964 Modern Classics
● –

Hadrian the Seventh 1904

This eccentric novel tells the story of George Arthur Rose, a Catholic convert who is first rejected from the priesthood and then unexpectedly selected for the papacy. Like Rolfe himself, Rose is a writer, an inventor and believes himself betrayed by his friends. The chain-smoking, cat-loving Pope institutes sweeping ecclesiastical and political reforms and wreaks revenge on his former enemies. 'Extraordinarily alive,' wrote D. H. Lawrence (288), '[…] a first-rate book.' He also called it 'the book of a man-demon'.

2018

1937 Penguin Books
Ghost Stories of an Antiquary
● —

1959 Penguin Books
More Ghost Stories
● —

M. R. James 1862–1936

Montague Rhodes James spent most of his life at King's College, Cambridge, as an undergraduate, a fellow and then Tutor, Dean and Provost. He was a distinguished medievalist and a scholar of biblical apocrypha (4). In 1918, he became Provost of Eton College, his old school, where he remained for the rest of his life. James penned ghost stories to be read aloud as Christmas Eve entertainments. He 'evokes fright and hideousness in their most shocking forms', wrote H. P. Lovecraft; 'and will certainly stand as one of the few really creative masters in his darksome province'.

Count Magnus and Other Ghost Stories 1904–11
The Complete Ghost Stories of M. R. James, Volume I

'Two ingredients most valuable in the concocting of a ghost story are, to me, the atmosphere and the nicely managed crescendo,' wrote James. These stories, from *Ghost Stories of an Antiquary* and *More Ghost Stories*, include a diabolical ash tree, a morphing mezzotint, dark Swedish forests and a series of sinister antiquarian books. In the chilling 'Oh, Whistle, and I'll Come to You, My Lad', James evokes the windswept Suffolk coastline he knew as a child.

2005
ed. S. T. Joshi
—
James's first ghost story, 'A Night in King's College Chapel', is included as an appendix.

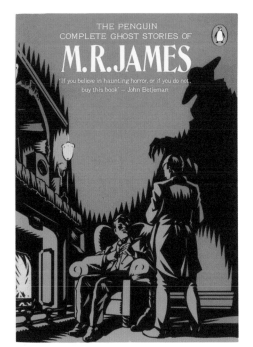

1984 Penguin Books *Complete Ghost Stories*
● —
2000 Modern Classics
● ed. Penelope Fitzgerald

The Haunted Doll's House and Other Ghost Stories 1919–31
The Complete Ghost Stories of M. R. James, Volume II

These stories are taken from *A Thin Ghost and Others* and *A Warning to the Curious and Other Ghost Stories*, as well as later editions. In 'The Haunted Dolls' House', something monstrous lies behind miniature bed curtains, and an ancient curse stalks the shoreline in 'A Warning to the Curious'. This volume also includes several less well-known stories and translations, such as 'The Fenstanton Witch' and 'Twelve Medieval Ghost-Stories'.

2006
ed. S. T. Joshi

E. M. Forster 1879–1970

Edward Morgan Forster studied at King's College, Cambridge, with which he maintained a lifelong connection. He was a peripheral member of the Bloomsbury Group and lived with his mother in Weybridge, Surrey, where he wrote all of his novels. He had a long-term relationship with Bob Buckingham, a married policeman. Interviewed by the BBC on his 80th birthday, Forster said: 'I have not written as much as I'd like [...] I am quite sure that I am not a great novelist.' Critics and readers have disagreed. In his 1943 monograph on Forster, Lionel Trilling wrote that he was 'the only living novelist who can be read again and again and who, after each reading, gives me what few writers can give us after our first days of novel-reading, the sensation of having learned something.'

Where Angels Fear to Tread 1905

Lilia Herriton, a young widow, falls in love with a dashing but unsuitable Italian man twelve years her junior. Her first husband's bourgeois family is aghast and her former brother-in-law Philip travels to Tuscany to try to persuade her to come home. Forster took his title from Pope's *Essay on Criticism* (152): 'fools rush in where angels fear to tread'.

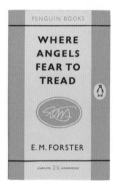

1959 Penguin Books
● —

1976 Modern Classics
1984 Penguin English Library
1986 Penguin Classics
1989 Twentieth-Century Classics
2001 Modern Classics
2007 Penguin Classics
ed. Oliver Stallybrass, 1976
intro. Ruth Padel, 2007

The Longest Journey 1907

Rickie Elliott dreams of becoming a writer, but he fails to find success. Instead he marries the beautiful but shallow Agnes Pembroke out of a sense of duty and becomes an embittered master at a second-rate school. The semi-autobiographical *Longest Journey* was Forster's favourite among his novels.

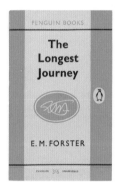

1960 Penguin Books
● —

1988 Penguin Classics
1989 Twentieth-Century Classics
2001 Modern Classics
2006 Penguin Classics
ed. Elizabeth Heine, 1984
intro. Gilbert Adair, 2006

A Room with a View 1908

In a field of violets above Florence, Lucy Honeychurch kisses the unconventional George Emerson, despite – or perhaps thanks to – the company of her prim cousin and chaperone Charlotte Bartlett. Back in England, however, Lucy becomes engaged to the repressed and supercilious Cecil Vyse and is in danger of conforming to expectations at the expense of her passionate feelings. Forster began writing *A Room with a View* in 1901, before any of his other published novels.

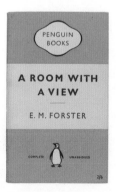

1955 Penguin Books
● —
1983 Penguin English Library
● ed. Oliver Stallybrass

2006
ed. Malcolm Bradbury, 2000

1941 Penguin Books
● —
1983 Penguin English Library
● ed. Oliver Stallybrass

2006
ed. David Lodge, 2000

Howards End 1910

The clever, cultured Schlegel sisters are based in part on Vanessa and Virginia Stephen, later Vanessa Bell and Virginia Woolf. Margaret Schlegel befriends the prosperous Mrs Wilcox, who owns the charming Howards End in the country, and Helen meets Leonard Bast, a bank clerk on the edge of poverty. They all become increasingly entwined in ways they could not have predicted. Forster's famous epigraph is 'Only connect...'

1972 Penguin Books
1985 Modern Classics
1992 Twentieth-Century Classics
2000 Modern Classics
2005 Penguin Classics
ed. P. N. Furbank, 1971
intro. David Leavitt, 2005

Maurice 1910–13, pub. 1971

Forster's tale of illicit love between two male undergraduates was published posthumously. He had written a note on the manuscript: 'Publishable, but worth it?' It is the story of Maurice Hall's emotional and sexual awakening as he becomes increasingly attracted to his friend Clive as well as Alec, a gamekeeper on Clive's country estate.

A Passage to India 1924

1936 Penguin Books
● —

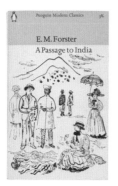

1979 Modern Classics
1985 Penguin Classics
1989 Twentieth-Century Classics
2000 Modern Classics
2005 Penguin Classics
ed. Oliver Stallybrass, 1979
intro. Pankaj Mishra, 2005

Five of Forster's novels were published before the First World War (433); fourteen years elapsed before he published his sixth, *A Passage to India*. In 1912, he had travelled to India with the classicist Goldsworthy Lowes Dickinson, and he visited again in the early 1920s as the private secretary to Tukojirao III, the Maharajah of Dewas. On the second return journey, he began to draft what is perhaps his greatest novel. When Adela Quested arrives in Chandrapore, she visits the Marabar caves with the charming Dr Aziz, but something unpleasant happens in the caves and the well-respected doctor finds himself at the centre of a scandal that explodes the tensions between the British Raj and their Indian subjects, exposing the fragility of colonial politics. The novelist Anita Desai considers *A Passage to India* Forster's 'great book [...] masterly in its prescience and its lucidity'.

Aspects of the Novel 1927

Forster developed this lucid critical analysis from lectures he delivered at Cambridge University. Writing with irreverence, wit and wisdom, he rejects a historical view of criticism (the 'demon of chronology') and imagines all writers working simultaneously in a circular room. He considers what he calls the seven universal aspects of the novel, Story, People, Plot, Fantasy, Prophecy, Pattern and Rhythm, drawing examples from James (417), Dickens (210), Thackeray (219), Eliot (216) and Dostoyevsky (371).

1962 Pelican Books
● —

1976 Pelican Books
1990 Twentieth-Century Classics
2000 Modern Classics
2005 Penguin Classics
ed. Oliver Stallybrass, 1974
intro. Frank Kermode, 2005

Selected Stories 1911–72

The stories in this anthology were first published in two separate volumes: *The Celestial Omnibus* (1911) and *The Eternal Moment and Other Stories* (1928). Forster thought of his short stories as 'fantasies', rich in myth and magic, set in Italy, Greece and India. Perhaps the most memorable are the numinous 'Story of a Panic' and the dystopian science fiction thriller, 'The Machine Stops'.

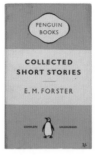

1954 Penguin Books
Collected Short Stories
● —
1975 Modern Classics
The Life to Come and Other Stories
● ed. Oliver Stallybrass

2005 *Selected Stories*
ed. David Leavitt &
Mark Mitchell, 2005

John Galsworthy 1867–1933

Galsworthy trained in marine law and in 1893 he sailed from Adelaide to Cape Town on a business trip. The first mate of the ship was an aspiring novelist called Joseph Conrad (277) and the two men became close friends. At about the same time, Galsworthy embarked on an affair with his future wife, Ada Nemesis Pearson Galsworthy, who was married to his cousin Arthur. The combined encouragement of Conrad and Ada persuaded him to publish his first collection of short stories in 1897, under the pseudonym 'John Sinjohn'. He went on to become a highly successful novelist and playwright: he was the first President of International PEN (259) and six weeks before his death in 1932 he was awarded the Nobel Prize for Literature.

1978 Penguin Books
The Forsyte Saga
1990 Twentieth-Century
Classics
2001 Modern Classics
The Forsyte Saga, Volume One

1980 Penguin Books
A Modern Comedy
1990 Twentieth-Century Classics
2001 Modern Classics
The Forsyte Saga, Volume Two

The Forsyte Saga 1906–33

The Man of Property; In Chancery; To Let; The White Monkey; The Silver Spoon; Swan Song; Maid in Waiting; Flowering Wilderness; Over the River

Spanning five decades, from the last years of fading Victorian propriety to the First World War (433) and the uncertain future of the 1930s, these three trilogies follow the fortunes of the eponymous Forsyte dynasty, a nouveau riche upper-middle-class English family, which has a snobbish talent for accruing property and suffocating its emotions. The series involves adultery, marital rape, divorce, death and war. It's 'still a terrific read', writes Susan Hill, 'a satisfying, long, absorbing family story [...] which knocks spots off its pale imitators'.

1990 Twentieth-Century Classics
The End of the Chapter
2001 Modern Classics
The Forsyte Saga, Volume Three

1951 Penguin Books
● —

1962 Modern
Classics
● —

1967 Penguin Books
● —

The Forsyte Saga novels were originally published individually by Penguin. Most of the series was published to coincide with the phenomenally popular 1967 BBC television adaptation by Donald Wilson. 'Poor old Galsworthy may in his day have won the Nobel prize for literature,' wrote the critic Sarah Crompton in the *Daily Telegraph*, 'but now he is just a footnote in televisual history – the begetter of the most popular classic serial of all time. This is no exaggeration. One hundred million people in 26 countries ended up seeing Donald Wilson's version of the saga. It was not the first literary adaptation on TV, but it was longer and more ambitious than anything screened before, and it has come to represent every value and standard to which British TV has aspired ever since.'

Ford Madox Ford 1873–1939

Ford Hermann Hueffer was born in Surrey. After writing fairy stories and collaborating with Joseph Conrad (277) on three novels, he set up the *English Review*, with contributors including Thomas Hardy (234) and H. G. Wells (255), and in which D. H. Lawrence (288) was published for the first time. He served as an infantry officer during the First World War (433) and saw action at the Somme and Ypres. Afterwards he changed his Germanic-sounding surname, inspired by that of his maternal grandfather, the painter Ford Madox Brown, whose biography he wrote. He moved to Paris where he founded the *Transatlantic Review* and took contributions from James Joyce, Ezra Pound, Ernest Hemingway, Gertrude Stein (429) and Jean Rhys, with whom he had an affair. 'Open the book to page ninety-nine and read,' was his possibly apocryphal advice on literary criticism, 'and the quality of the whole will be revealed to you.'

The Fifth Queen 1906–8

The Fifth Queen; *Privy Seal*; *The Fifth Queen Crowned*

This historical trilogy is based on the life of Katherine Howard, Henry VIII's fifth wife. Katherine is clever and beautiful and catches the ageing king's eye, but corruption and fear stalk the corridors of the Tudor court, and Katherine soon finds herself locked in a powerful fight with Thomas Cromwell, the Lord Privy Seal. Conrad (277) considered it a 'noble conception – the Swan Song of Historical Romance'.

1999 Twentieth-Century Classics intro. A. S. Byatt, 1984

The Good Soldier 1915

A Tale of Passion

Ford wrote *The Good Soldier*, which he regarded as his finest achievement, while working for the War Propaganda Bureau. Set just before the First World War (433) and told in a sequence of non-chronological flashbacks, it dissects the seemingly perfect marriage of Edward, an exemplary soldier, and Leonora Ashburnam. Despite appearances, their relationship is revealed to be a seething knot of unhappiness and lies. 'I don't know how many times in nearly forty years I have come back to this novel,' wrote Graham Greene, and Julian Barnes calls it 'a masterpiece'. After its publication, Ford left the Bureau and joined the army.

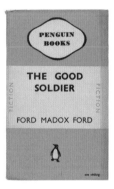

1946 Penguin Books

● —

2002 Modern Classics
2007 Penguin Classics
ed. David Bradshaw

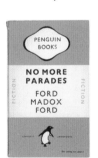

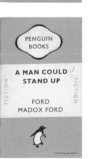

1948 Penguin Books
● —
Published in four volumes

Parade's End 1924–8

Some Do Not . . . ; *No More Parades*; *A Man Could Stand Up*; *The Last Post*

In Ford's great tetralogy about the psychological impact of war, Christopher Tietjens is a government statistician who joins the British army during the First World War (433). Increasingly distanced from his selfish, promiscuous wife Sylvia, he would like to instigate an affair with Valentine Wannop, a high-minded suffragette. It is an elegy for the war dead and a former way of life; Malcolm Bradbury considers it 'the finest English novel about the Great War'.

1982 Modern Classics
1990 Twentieth-Century Classics
2002 Modern Classics
intro. Julian Barnes, 2012

D. H. Lawrence

1885–1930

David Herbert Lawrence was born into a Nottinghamshire mining family. In 1912, he eloped to Germany with Frieda Weekley, the young German wife of his former professor. They married, after her divorce, in 1914. In the years after the First World War (433), the couple embarked on a 'savage pilgrimage', living in Italy, Sri Lanka, Australia, America and a utopian ranch in Mexico, until 1925, after which they settled in Italy and France. Lawrence died in the south of France at the age of 44. 'If ever England produced a perfect rose, he was it,' wrote Frieda, 'thorns and perfume and splendour.' He adopted the emblem of the phoenix, which features on many of his editions. E. M. Forster (284) called him 'the greatest imaginative novelist of our generation'.

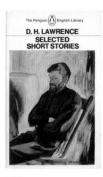

1982 Penguin English Library
● ed. Brian Finney

2007
ed. Sue Wilson
intro. Louise Welsh

Selected Stories 1907–27

This anthology of Lawrence's short stories spans his whole career, from 'The White Stocking' and 'Odour of Chrysanthemums', to 'England, my England', soaked in the horror of the First World War (433), and 'Things', in which idealism is crushed by material possessions. Sue Wilson, the editor, aims for 'diversity of place and time' in her selection.

The Prussian Officer
and Other Stories 1907–14

This was the first short story collection Lawrence published. 'The Prussian Officer', is the tale of a captain who physically abuses his orderly and prevents him from pursuing a relationship with a young woman. Other titles include 'A Fragment of Stained Glass' and 'Daughters of the Vicar'.

Sons and Lovers 1913

Anthony Burgess considered this semi-autobiographical novel to be Lawrence's masterpiece. It follows the story of Paul Morel, torn between a smothering mother's love and affairs with other women. It is set in a mining village in Nottinghamshire and includes several examples of local dialect. Lawrence wrote and rewrote the novel four times following the death of his own mother in 1910. The character of Miriam is based on Lawrence's friend Jessie Chambers; she never spoke to him again after the novel was published.

1948 Penguin Books
● —
1981 Penguin English Library
● ed. Keith Sagar

1994 Twentieth-Century Classics
2000 Modern Classics
2006 Penguin Classics
ed. Helen Baron & Carl Baron, 1994
intro. Blake Morrison, 2006

1945 Penguin Books
● —

1995 Twentieth-Century Classics
ed. John Worthen, 1983
intro. Brian Finney, 1995

Selected Poems 1913–32

Lawrence adopted a variety of styles in his poetry. This selection uses his revised versions of the poems, but they are arranged as he first published them, from the rhyming *Love Poems and Others* to the free verse of *Birds, Beasts and Flowers*, influenced by Walt Whitman (413). He made these revisions for the *Collected Poems* edition in 1928: 'A young man is afraid of his demon,' he wrote, 'and puts his hand over the demon's mouth sometimes and speaks for him.'

1949 Penguin Books
● —
1981 Penguin English Library
● ed. John Worthen

1995 Twentieth-Century Classics
2000 Modern Classics
2007 Penguin Classics
ed. Anne Fernihough, 1995
intro. James Wood, 2007

2008
ed. James Fenton
—
The cover artist Aaron Robinson chose to illustrate 'Pomegranate' because he wanted 'a really hot, intense, juicy and visceral image'. 'It is so lovely, dawn-kaleidoscopic within the crack,' wrote Lawrence, about the fruit.

1950 Penguin Poets
● ed. W. E. Williams
1972 Penguin Books
● ed. Keith Sagar
1977 Penguin Books
The Complete Poems
● ed. Vivian de Sola Pinto
& F. Warren Roberts

The Rainbow

1915

Lawrence and his wife Frieda made a home in Italy in 1913 living in a cottage in Fiascherino on the Gulf of Spezia, the bay in which Shelley drowned (196). There he began writing *The Rainbow* and *Women in Love* (290), initially conceived as a single work. They follow three generations of a Nottinghamshire farming family, the Brangwens, transitioning from a pre-industrial world into the industrial age. *The Rainbow* was prosecuted in an obscenity trial soon after publication; 1,011 copies were seized and burned and the book was unavailable in Britain for the next eleven years.

D. H. Lawrence and Italy 1916–32

Twilight in Italy; *Sea and Sardinia*; *Sketches of Etruscan Places*

During Lawrence's 1912 elopement with Frieda, they walked from Germany across the Alps to Lake Garda in Italy, a journey that he recorded in his first travel book, *Twilight in Italy*. Lawrence was drawn to the Italian countryside throughout his life. *Sea and Sardinia* describes a nine-day visit to the island of Sardinia in 1921; it is 'the most charming of all the books Lawrence ever wrote', according to Anthony Burgess. *Sketches of Etruscan Places* recounts a series of visits to archaeological sites in 1927, towards the end of Lawrence's life, the record of 'a dying man drinking from the founts of a civilisation dedicated to life'.

   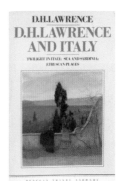

1960 Penguin Books
● —
1997 Twentieth-Century Classics
● ed. Paul Eggert

1944 Penguin Books
● —
1972 Penguin Books
● intro. Anthony Burgess
1999 Twentieth-Century Classics
ed. Mara Kalnins, 1997
intro. Jill Franks, 1997

1950 Penguin Books
● —
1999 Twentieth-Century Classics
● ed. Simonetta de Filippis

1985 Penguin Travel Library
1997 Twentieth-Century Classics
● intro. Anthony Burgess
2007 Penguin Classics
ed. Paul Eggert, Mara Kalnins & Simonetta de Filippis, 1997–9
intro. Tim Parks, 2007
notes Michael Frederick Herbert, 2007

Women in Love 1920

Women in Love continues the story of the Brangwen sisters in *The Rainbow* (289), Ursula and Gudrun, and their love affairs with Rupert Birkin, an intellectual, and Gerald Crich, an industrialist. The four characters debate their beliefs and politics and weave a complex web of attraction, passion and frustration. Ursula is based in part on Lawrence's wife Frieda, and Gudrun on Katherine Mansfield (393). Memorably, Oliver Reed and Alan Bates wrestle naked in front of a roaring fire in Ken Russell's 1969 film adaptation.

Studies in Classic American Literature 1923

'Lawrence fertilizes with fire,' wrote the author Herbert J. Seligmann. 'No living American writing in a critical sense from now on will be able to ignore him.' These essays shed fascinating light on Lawrence's view of Poe (408), Melville (410), Fenimore Cooper (407) and Whitman (413). 'The proper function of a critic', Lawrence believed, 'is to save the tale from the artist who created it.'

1971 Penguin Books
1990 Twentieth-Century Classics

1960 Penguin Books
● —
1982 Penguin English Library
● ed. Charles Ross

1995 Twentieth-Century Classics
2000 Modern Classics
2007 Penguin Classics
ed. Mark Kinkead-Weekes, 1995
intro. Amit Chaudhari, 2007

The Fox
The Captain's Doll
The Ladybird 1923

These three novellas describe the devastating effects of war on human relationships. In *The Fox*, Henry preys on two young women living alone on a small farm, while an unseen fox ravages their coop; *The Captain's Doll* depicts the complex relationship between a married Scottish soldier and a German countess; and in *The Ladybird*, an Englishwoman finds herself strongly attracted to a charismatic and wounded German prisoner of war.

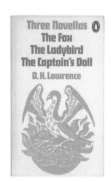

1973 Penguin Books
Three Novellas
● —
1982 Penguin Books
Complete Short Novels
● ed. Keith Sagar
Comprising *The Fox*, *The Captain's Doll*, *The Ladybird*, *The Woman Who Rode Away*, *St. Mawr* and *The Princess*

1994 Twentieth-Century Classics
2006 Penguin Classics
ed. David Ellis, 1994
intro. Helen Dunmore, 2006

The Woman Who Rode Away
St Mawr
The Princess 1928

The Woman Who Rode Away follows a woman's religious and perilous quest in Mexico; in *St Mawr*, a frustrated wife forms an intense emotional bond with her untameable bay stallion; and *The Princess* describes an increasing intimacy between an aloof woman and her male guide in the wilds of New Mexico. The feminist Kate Millett has criticized *The Woman Who Rode Away* as a work of pornographic sadism, and the author Brenda Maddox calls *St Mawr* and *The Princess* 'masterworks of misogyny'.

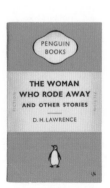

1950 Penguin Books
● ed. Richard Aldington (438)

1996 Twentieth-Century Classics
2006 Penguin Classics
ed. Brian Finney, Christa Kahnsohn & Dieter Mehl, 1983–95
intro. James Lasdun, 2006
notes Paul Poplawski, 2006

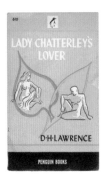

1946 Penguin Books
● —
—
A heavily censored abridgement of *Lady Chatterley's Lover* was published for the first time in the USA in 1928, and later by Penguin Books Inc. in 1946.

Lady Chatterley's Lover 1928

There has been brought to our notice within the last few weeks a book which we have no hesitation in describing as the most evil outpouring that has ever besmirched the literature of our country,

ran a notice in *John Bull* on 28 October 1928.

The sewers of French pornography would be dragged in vain to find a parallel in beastliness. The creations of muddy-minded perverts, peddled in the back-street bookstalls of Paris are prudish by comparison. The book is by one of the best known of modern English novelists, Mr D. H. Lawrence. It is entitled *Lady Chatterley's Lover*.

After a long period of travelling, Lawrence and Frieda settled in northern Italy, near Florence, where he wrote *Lady Chatterley's Lover*. It tells the story of Constance Chatterley, unfulfilled by her emotionally distant and physically paralysed husband Sir Clifford. He encourages Constance to have a liaison outside their marriage, but is aghast when she embarks on a passionate affair with his gamekeeper, Mellors. Lawrence aimed to challenge British taboos and enable both men and women 'to think sex, fully, completely, honestly, and cleanly'.

1960 Penguin Books
● —
1961
● intro. Richard Hoggart

In 1960, Penguin Books published the full unexpurgated text of *Lady Chatterley's Lover* for the first time and was immediately prosecuted under the recently passed Obscene Publications Act of 1959. Among the objections were Lawrence's use of the words 'fuck' and 'cunt'. The chief prosecutor famously asked if it were the kind of book 'you would wish your wife or servants to read'. To avoid conviction, Penguin had to demonstrate that the work was of literary merit. Witnesses were brought in to vouch for the book, including Allen Lane, E. M. Forster (284), the sociologist Richard Hoggart and the Bishop of Woolwich.

Richard Hoggart described the trial as 'the moment at which the confused mesh of British attitudes to class, to literature, to the intellectual life, and to censorship, publicly clashed as rarely before – to the confusion of more conservative attitudes. On the far side of that watershed and largely as a consequence [...] we had the Permissive Society.'

1973 Penguin Books *The First Lady Chatterley*
● —
—
The original, censored edition was republished as *The First Lady Chatterley* in 1973.

1994 Twentieth-Century Classics
2000 Modern Classics
2006 Penguin Classics
ed. Michael Squires, 1994
intro. Doris Lessing, 2006

Squires's edition includes 'A Propos of "Lady Chatterley's Lover"', an essay written by Lawrence in 1929 in defence of his most notorious novel.

PUBLISHER'S DEDICATION

For having published this book, Penguin Books were prosecuted under the Obscene Publications Act, 1959, at the Old Bailey in London from 20 October to 2 November 1960. This edition is therefore dedicated to the twelve jurors, three women and nine men, who returned a verdict of 'Not Guilty', and thus made D. H. Lawrence's last novel available for the first time to the public in the United Kingdom.

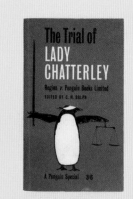

1961 Penguin Special
The Trial of Lady Chatterley
● —

In 1961, Penguin published the transcript of the *Lady Chatterley* trial. Allen Lane sent out copies instead of Christmas cards that year. This book was itself banned in Australia, but a widely circulated pirate copy eventually contributed to the relaxation of Australian censorship laws.

Apocalypse
and the Writings on Revelation
1930, pub. 1931

Lawrence's last major work is a summation of his thoughts on psychology, science, politics, art and God. Using the Book

1975 Penguin Books
● ed. Richard Aldington (438)

1995 Twentieth-Century Classics
ed. Mara Kalnins

of Revelation (4) as a starting point, he concludes that the conflict between emotion and intellect has led humans to become increasingly alienated from nature, which has in turn had a profoundly formative effect on western civilization. Nonetheless, he believes that humankind is capable of regaining its lost imaginative and spiritual values. Lawrence wrote the last words as he was approaching death:

> '[…] the magnificent here and now of life in the flesh is ours, and ours alone, and ours only for a time. We ought to dance with rapture that we should be alive and in the flesh.'

Kenneth Grahame
1859–1932

Grahame was born in Edinburgh, but his mother died when he was five years old and he and his three siblings were sent to live with their formidable maternal grandmother, 'Granny Ingles', in the Berkshire village of Cookham near the Thames. He only saw his alcoholic father once again. Grahame became a clerk in the Bank of England and published occasional essays and children's stories, including *The Reluctant Dragon*.

In 1907, he wrote a series of letters to his seven-year-old son Alistair about the exploits of a pompous character called 'Toad'.

1983 Puffin Books
● —

The Wind in the Willows 1908

In *The Wind in the Willows*, home-loving Mole, debonair Ratty and curmudgeonly Badger rally round to support their impulsive friend Toad. There are a number of chapters that stand outside the main narrative, most unusually 'The Piper at the Gates of Dawn', in which Rat and Mole meet the breathtaking demi-god Pan on a small river island fringed with willow and silver birch.

2005
ed. Gillian Avery

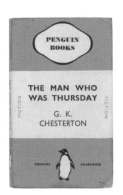

1937 Penguin Books
• —

2011
ed. Matthew Beaumont

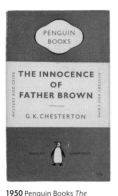

1950 Penguin Books *The Innocence of Father Brown*
• —

1981 Penguin Books
The Penguin Complete Father Brown
• —

2012
ed. Michael D. Hurley

G. K. Chesterton 1874–1936

Gilbert Keith Chesterton trained as an artist and worked as a journalist. He produced prodigious quantities of novels, essays, biographies, poetry, plays, histories, religious books and works of literary and social criticism. He was extremely portly, wore a cape, sported a cigar and carried a swordstick, and he converted to Roman Catholicism in 1922. He was known as the 'prince of paradox'.

The Man Who Was Thursday
A Nightmare 1908

Chesterton's metaphysical thriller revolves around the Central Anarchist Council, a secret society committed to destroying the world. The seven members of the council hide their identities behind codenames, the days of the week. The newly elected 'Thursday', however, is a Scotland Yard detective, but nobody is quite what they seem in this dreamlike adventure, which Kingsley Amis considered 'the most thrilling book I have ever read'.

The Complete Father Brown Stories 1911–36

Father Brown, a short, shabby, umbrella-wielding Catholic priest with a face like a Norfolk dumpling, has a peculiar talent for solving crimes. 'You see, I had murdered them all myself,' he confesses at one point, describing his technique. '[…] I had planned out each of the crimes very carefully. […] I had thought out exactly how a thing like that could be done, and in what style or state of mind a man could really do it. And when I was quite sure that I felt exactly like the murderer myself, of course I knew who he was.'

Robert Tressell 1870–1911

Robert Croker was born in Dublin. He changed his name to Noonan and moved to South Africa, where he worked as a painter and decorator for a Johannesburg construction firm. He then returned to England before deciding to emigrate to Canada. He died of pulmonary tuberculosis en route. He wrote one novel, *The Ragged Arsed Philanthropists*, under the pseudonym 'Tressell', a play on 'trestle table'. It was published posthumously, with an amended title, by his daughter.

The Ragged Trousered Philanthropists
1910, pub. 1914

A formidable construction firm exploits its workmen and their families while the shareholders grow fat on the profits. That is, until the spirited socialist Frank Owen makes a stand and strives to persuade his fellow workers to fight for a fairer society. Tressell called it 'the story of twelve months in Hell, told by one of the damned'. It is 'a book that everyone should read', said George Orwell.

1940 Penguin Books
• —
Abridged edition

2004 Modern Classics
intro. Tristram Hunt

For First World War fiction, turn to p.433

DRAMA

Initially the most popular playwright of the Edwardian era was Somerset Maugham; in 1908 he had four plays running simultaneously in London's West End. His somewhat conventional dramatic plots were increasingly usurped, however, by the 'New Drama' of George Bernard Shaw, who reacted to the late Victorian plays of the likes of Oscar Wilde (246) and became the leading dramatist of his generation with experimental plays that conveyed his sometimes unusual political, social and religious views. Two other prominent Irish dramatists of the period were W. B. Yeats (267) and J. M. Synge (300).

George Bernard Shaw

1856–1950

Shaw was born in Dublin, but he moved to London at the age of 20 and embarked on a rigorous programme of self-education in the Reading Room of the British Museum. He was an active socialist and platform speaker throughout his life, publishing essays such as *Common Sense about the War* (1914), *How to Settle the Irish Question* (1917) and *The Intelligent Woman's Guide to Socialism and Capitalism* (1928), the last of which he expanded to two volumes, that became the first two Pelican Books (xvi) in 1937. He promoted eugenics and alphabet reform and was opposed to vaccination and organized religion.

'He has no enemies,' wrote Oscar Wilde (244) tartly, 'and none of his friends like him.' Though a shy man in private life, Shaw sculpted a public persona known as 'G.B.S.', presenting himself as a wit, a showman and a satirist. In 1925, he was awarded the Nobel Prize for Literature.

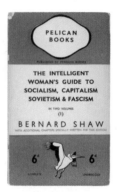 

1937 Pelican Books
• —
Published in two volumes

1946 Penguin Books
• —

1988 Penguin Bernard Shaw Library
2000 Penguin Classics
ed. Dan H. Laurence, 1988
intro. David Edgar, 2000

PENGUIN BOOKS

PLAYS UNPLEASANT

BERNARD SHAW

BERNARD SHAW

PLAYS UNPLEASANT
WIDOWERS' HOUSES
THE PHILANDERER
MRS WARREN'S PROFESSION

Plays Unpleasant 1892–3
Widowers' Houses; *The Philanderer*; *Mrs Warren's Profession*

Shaw gave these three plays this collective title, because

'their dramatic power is used to force the spectator to face unpleasant facts. [...] In *Widowers' Houses* I have shewn middle-class respectability and younger son gentility fattening on the poverty of the slum as flies fatten on filth. That is not a pleasant theme. In *The Philanderer* I have shewn the grotesque sexual compacts made between men and women under marriage laws [...]. In *Mrs Warren's Profession* I have gone straight at the fact that, as Mrs Warren puts it, "the only way for a woman to provide for herself decently is for her to be good to some man that can afford to be good to her."'

1946 Penguin Books
• —

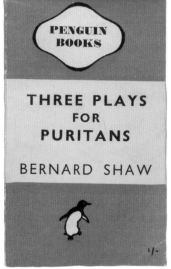

1987 Penguin Bernard Shaw Library
2003 Penguin Classics
ed. Dan H. Laurence, 1987
intro. W. J. McCormack, 2003

Plays Pleasant 1894–6

Arms and the Man; Candida; The Man of Destiny; You Never Can Tell

These plays are supposed to be gentler than those in their companion volume (294), dealing 'less with the crimes of society, and more with its romantic follies'. *Arms and The Man*, which takes its title from Virgil's *Aeneid* (44), is an 'anti-romantic comedy' about the futility of war; *Candida* is about the wife of a clergyman, wooed by an ardent poet; *The Man of Destiny* is a 'fictitious paragraph of history' about Napoleon and a mysterious Englishwoman; and *You Never Can Tell* is a comedy about a sagacious waiter and three children who can't identify their father.

Three Plays for Puritans 1896–9

The Devil's Disciple; Caesar and Cleopatra; Captain Brassbound's Conversion

'I have, I think, always been a Puritan in my attitude towards Art,' writes Shaw. 'I am as fond of fine music and handsome buildings as Milton (150) was, or Cromwell, or Bunyan (172); but if I found that they were becoming the instruments of a systematic idolatry of sensuousness, I would hold it good statesmanship to blow every cathedral in the world to pieces with dynamite, organ and all, without the least heed to the screams of the art critics and cultured voluptuaries.'

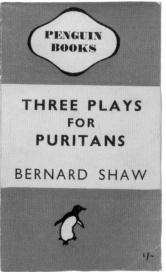

1946 Penguin Bernard Shaw
Library
• —

1988 Penguin Bernard Shaw Library
2000 Penguin Classics
ed. Dan H. Laurence, 1988
intro. Michael Billington, 2000

Man and Superman
A Comedy and a Philosophy 1902

Shaw wrote *Man and Superman* in response to a suggestion that he write 'a Don Juan (167) play'. When her father dies, Ann Whitefield becomes the joint ward of the respectable Roebuck Ramsden and the radical John Tanner, author of 'The Revolutionist's Handbook and Pocket Companion'. Ann decides to marry the reluctant Tanner and pursues him across Europe and even down into the underworld, where their alter egos (Don Juan and Doña Ana) argue with the Devil. The title comes from Nietzsche's conception of the *Übermensch* (349).

1946 Penguin Books
• —

1988 Penguin Bernard Shaw Library
2000 Penguin Classics
ed. Dan H. Laurence, 1988
intro. Stanley Weintraub, 2000
—
This edition includes the text of 'The Revolutionist's Handbook', which Shaw wrote himself and added as an appendix. 'The golden rule is that there are no golden rules,' he writes.

1984 Penguin Bernard Shaw Library
ed. Dan H. Laurence

John Bull's Other Island 1904

Written at the request of W. B. Yeats (267), this political comedy is set in Ireland and dramatizes the conflict between Britain and Ireland during the campaign for Home Rule. 'The play has some really gorgeous rhetoric,' wrote H. G. Wells (255), 'beautiful effects, much more serious Shaw than ever before and I'd rather see it again than see anyone else's new play.' King Edward VII is said to have laughed so much during a command performance that he broke the chair he was sitting on.

Major Barbara 1905

Barbara is an energetic major in the Salvation Army and the estranged daughter of the millionaire armaments manufacturer and whisky distiller Andrew Undershaft. When Andrew offers the Army a substantial donation, Barbara must examine her moral scruples and decide whether she can accept money made through 'Death and Destruction'.

1946 Penguin Books
● —

1989 Penguin Bernard Shaw Library
2000 Penguin Classics
ed. Dan H. Laurence, 1989
intro. Margery Morgan, 2000

1946 Penguin Books
● —

1988 Penguin Bernard Shaw Library
2000 Penguin Classics
ed. Dan H. Laurence

The Doctor's Dilemma
A Tragedy 1906

As usual, Shaw includes a lengthy preface, almost as long as the play itself: 'On Doctors' opens by describing contemporary medical provision as a 'murderous absurdity' and has sections about doctors' lack of conscience, reliance on superstition, obsession with vaccination and cruelty to patients. Hailed as the greatest medical satire since Molière's *Hypochondriac* (167), *The Doctor's Dilemma* is a farce in which Sir Colenso Ridgeon of Harley Street must choose between saving the life of a talented scoundrel and that of an impecunious doctor.

Misalliance *and* The Fascinating Foundling 1909

Misalliance begins as a sedate country house party, when suddenly Lina Szczepanowska crashes out of the sky in 'full acrobatic trapeze dress', thereby announcing the Theatre of the Absurd, later developed by Pirandello and Ionescu. Over the course of a single afternoon there are eight different marriage proposals. A contemporary review in the *Standard* described it as 'arrant nonsense'. This volume also includes the one-act burlesque *The Fascinating Foundling*, in which two contrasting foundlings fall in love with one another.

1984 Penguin Bernard Shaw Library
ed. Dan H. Laurence

The Shewing-Up of Blanco Posnet *and* Fanny's First Play
1909–11

Set in the American Wild West, *The Shewing-Up of Blanco Posnet* is a one-act drama about a drunken reprobate accused of stealing a horse. *Fanny's First Play* is a 'potboiler', a play-within-a-play, that had the longest stage run of any of Shaw's works.

1987 Penguin Bernard Shaw Library
ed. Dan H. Laurence

Androcles and the Lion 1912
An Old Fable Renovated

In this adaptation of a fable ascribed to Aesop (19), Androcles is a Christian tailor, walking through the woods, who helps a roaring lion remove a thorn from its paw. Later, when Androcles is thrown into the Colosseum with a group of Christians, he is saved by a remarkable coincidence … The play features a bizarre stage direction that instructs a man and a lion to 'embrace rapturously [and] waltz around the arena'. Shaw's preface, longer than the play, is an extensive examination of the four Gospels (4) and the character of Christ.

Pygmalion was reissued on Bernard Shaw's 90th birthday, 26 July 1946, along with nine other titles. 100,000 copies of each were printed, so that a million volumes of Shaw were published in a single day. The only one of the ten titles that is no longer in print was *The Black Girl in Search of God and Some Lesser Tales*. More titles were added in the 1980s, and the series was branded the Penguin Bernard Shaw Library under the editorial supervision of Dan H. Laurence. Some, but not all, have since been rejacketed as Penguin Classics. Dan H. Laurence 'devoted nearly every waking moment of his professional life to compiling the voluminous works of George Bernard Shaw', read his obituary in the *New York Times*. He edited collected volumes of Shaw's letters and plays and was literary advisor to the Shaw estate until his retirement in 1990.

1946 Penguin Books
● —

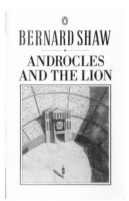

1962 Penguin Books
● —
In 1962, Penguin published *Androcles and the Lion* using the phonetic 'Shavian Alphabet' created by Shaw, the first and one of the only publications to use his invented orthography.

1987 Penguin Bernard Shaw Library
2006 Penguin Classics
ed. Dan H. Laurence

1931 Penguin Books
● —
1941 Penguin Books
● ill. Feliks Topolski

Shaw reworked his script for a 1938 film screenplay, directed by Anthony Asquith, for which he won an Academy Award. The screenplay was published by Penguin Books in 1941.

1987 Penguin Bernard Shaw Library
2000 Penguin Classics
ed. Dan H. Laurence, 1987
intro. Nicholas Grene, 2000

Pygmalion
A Romance in Five Acts 1912

Shaw's best-known play, a reworking of the Pygmalion episode from Ovid's *Metamorphoses* (47), is the tale of the phoneticist Henry Higgins who accepts a bet and sets out to transform Eliza Doolittle, a cockney flower girl, into a duchess. 'Yes, you squashed cabbage leaf,' he says, '[…] I could pass you off as the Queen of Sheba.'

1964 Penguin Plays
● —

Heartbreak House 1917
A Fantasia in the Russian Manner on English Themes

Emulating <u>Chekhov</u> (381), Shaw portrays a house party at the home of the eccentric Captain Shotover. The company argues about the correct reasons for marriage, disagreeing about money and morality, idealism and realism. The play combines high farce and bitter tragedy in an indictment of 'cultured, leisured Europe before the war'.

Back to Methuselah 1918–20
A Metabiological Pentateuch

Methuselah was a biblical patriarch who lived for almost 1,000 years, and this science fiction sequence of five plays covers the whole of time, from 4004 BCE to 31,920 CE. Shaw attacks <u>Darwinism</u> (269) in his preface and presents this dramatic cycle as the beginning of 'a Bible for Creative Evolution', a vision of evolution governed not by natural selection, but by a forward-looking 'Life Force'. *In the Beginning* features Adam and Eve and the Serpent, who whispers the secrets of sex in Eve's ear, as a method of conquering the fear of death. *As Far as Thought Can Reach* is a vision of a distant future populated by Ancients and Children: it features a scientist called Pygmalion who creates a pair of hyper-realistic androids, who turn murderous and kill him. The Ancients explain that human bodies are mere puppets: the destiny of humankind is to become a bodiless, immortal vortex of energy.

1939 Penguin Books
● —

1987 Penguin Bernard Shaw Library
ed. Dan H. Laurence

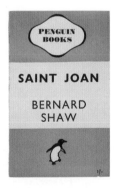

1946 Penguin Books
● —

Saint Joan 1923, pub. 1924
A Chronicle Play in Six Scenes and an Epilogue

Joan of Arc was canonized as a Catholic saint just three years before Shaw wrote this play. He based his narrative on contemporary records of her trial and execution in 1431. 'There are no villains in the piece,' he writes. 'Crime, like disease, is not interesting: [...] the tragedy of such murders is that they are not committed by murderers.'

1988 Penguin Bernard Shaw Library
2000 Penguin Classics
ed. Dan H. Laurence, 1988
intro. David Hare, 2000

1988 Penguin Bernard Shaw Library
2001 Penguin Classics
ed. Dan H. Laurence, 1988
intro. Joley Wood, 2001
—
The 2001 reissue includes 'On Playing Joan', an essay by the actress Imogen Stubbs, who took the title role in a 1994 production at the Strand Theatre in London. She describes Joan as 'a girl who has an anarchic sense of humour, who is sometimes hard, violent, hysterical, proud, serene, vulnerable, always courageous'.

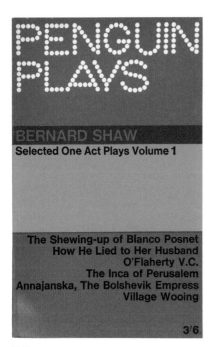

1965 Penguin Plays
● —

Plays Extravagant 1932–4
Too True to be Good; *The Simpleton of the Unexpected Isles*; *The Millionairess*

Too True to be Good opens with a soliloquy by a monster made out of a 'luminous jelly with a visible skeleton', the personification of a microbe infecting a bed-bound Patient. *The Simpleton of the Unexpected Isles* is a satire about an attempt to establish a utopian society on a Pacific island; and *The Millionairess* is about a spoilt and fabulously wealthy heiress, Epifania Ognisanti di Parerga, and her search for a suitor.

1981 Penguin Bernard Shaw Library
ed. Dan H. Laurence

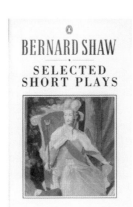

1988 Penguin Bernard Shaw Library
ed. Dan H. Laurence

Selected Short Plays
1901–36

Shaw provides admirably pithy subtitles for these fifteen short plays, which span the course of his career. The subtitles include *Constancy Unrewarded*, *A Tragedietta*, *A Piece of Utter Nonsense*, *A Recruiting Pamphlet* and *A Revolutionary Romancelet*.

Plays Political
1928–36
The Apple Cart; *On the Rocks*; *Geneva*

Shaw called *The Apple Cart* a 'political extravaganza': it has King Magnus arguing with his Prime Minister and cabinet about various political philosophies. *On the Rocks* is a 'political comedy' set entirely in the cabinet room at 10 Downing Street during the Great Depression; and *Geneva* enacts a summit meeting to discuss the containment of three dangerous dictators, Herr Battler (Hitler), Signore Bombardone (Mussolini) and General Flanco (Franco).

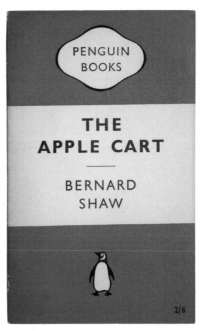

1956 Penguin Books
The Apple Cart
● —

1986 Penguin Bernard Shaw Library
1999 Penguin Classics
ed. Dan H. Laurence

Last Plays 1939–50

'In Good King Charles's Golden Days'; *Buoyant Billions*; *Farfetched Fables*; *Shakes versus Shav*; *Why She Would Not*

Set in 1680, *'In Good King Charles's Golden Days'* is a debate between Charles II, Isaac Newton, Nell Gwyn (168) and others on the true nature of power; *Buoyant Billions* is a 'comedy of no manners' about a young idealist planning how to dispose of his ailing father-in-law's wealth; *Farfetched Fables* is a collection of connected pieces about poison gas, a new Dark Age, scientific elites, the abolition of food and the introduction of asexual human reproduction; *Shakes versus Shav* is a puppet play, in which Shaw and Shakespeare (134) argue about who's the better playwright; and *Why She Would Not* is Shaw's final play, which develops his ideas around an evolutionary 'Life Force' (298).

1985 Penguin Bernard Shaw Library
2013 Penguin Classics
ed. Dan H. Laurence

J. M. Synge 1871–1909

The Irish writer John Millington Synge met Yeats (267) in Paris and promptly joined the Irish League. Soon after the foundation of the Abbey Theatre in Dublin, he became one of its directors. He was a major proponent of the Irish Literary Revival (267).

1951 Penguin Books
Collected Plays
• —

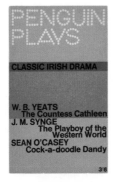

1964 Penguin Plays
Classic Irish Drama
1987 Penguin Plays
1996 Twentieth-Century
Classics
2009 Penguin Classics
The Playboy of the Western World and Two Other Irish Plays
intro. W. A. Armstrong

The Playboy of the Western World 1892–1949
and Two Other Irish Plays

Yeats, *The Countess Cathleen*; Synge, *The Playboy of the Western World*; O'Casey, *Cock-a-Doodle Dandy*

The Playboy of the Western World (1907) was suggested by an anecdote Synge heard on the Aran Islands, in which a young madcap is admired by men and adored by women for having 'murdered his own da'. The opening night at the Abbey Theatre ended in riots, and subsequent performances were pelted with eggs and potatoes. Yeats's *The Countess Cathleen* (267) is set during a famine: the countess sells her soul to the Devil in order to save her tenants from starvation; and *Cock-a-Doodle Dandy*, by Sean O'Casey, is a social satire about a magical cockerel.

The Aran Islands 1907

After Yeats suggested the idea of living with the Aran Islanders to 'express a life that has never found expression', Synge spent a few weeks every year on these remote islands off the west coast of Ireland, from 1898 to 1902. The experience inspired his plays *In the Shadow of the Glen* (1903), *Riders to the Sea* (1904), *The Well of the Saints* (1905) and *The Playboy of the Western World* (1907) and he wrote this elegiac prose portrait of their vanishing way of life, a celebration of savagely beautiful landscapes and ancestral traditions.

1992 Twentieth-Century Classics
ed. Tim Robinson

NON-FICTION

The sun never set on the British Empire during the Edwardian period, but this globe-girdling self-satisfaction was given a hideous jolt on the night of 14 April 1912, when the unsinkable symbol of imperial hubris, the RMS *Titanic* (302), foundered disastrously in the North Atlantic. The Edwardians were even less prepared for the greater catastrophe that was fast approaching in 1914 (433).

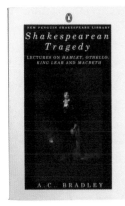

1991 New Penguin
Shakespeare Library
2005 Penguin Classics
fwd. John Bayley

A. C. Bradley

1851–1935

Andrew Cecil Bradley studied classics at Balliol College, Oxford, before teaching literature at Liverpool and Glasgow. He returned to Oxford as Professor of Poetry in 1901.

Shakespearean Tragedy

1904

These ten lectures elucidate four of Shakespeare's most famous tragedies: *Hamlet* (142), *Othello* (140), *King Lear* (141) and *Macbeth* (142). Bradley writes about the characters as if they were his acquaintances and approaches detailed readings of their speeches as a detective would approach a crime scene. This volume has been described as the most influential single work of Shakespeare criticism ever published. In 1926, the humorous poet Guy Boas wrote 'Lays of Learning':

> I dreamt last night that Shakespeare's Ghost
> Sat for a civil service post.
> The English paper for that year
> Had several questions on *King Lear*
> Which Shakespeare answered very badly
> Because he hadn't read his Bradley.

John Maynard Keynes

1883–1946

Widely considered the most influential economist of the 20th century, Keynes was a proponent of a social market economy, advocating the use of fiscal policies to mitigate the adverse effects of economic recessions and depressions. Since the Second World War, almost every nation in the world has adopted and adapted Keynes's recommendations. In 1999, *Time* magazine listed him as one of the most important people of the century, saying that 'his radical idea that governments should spend money they don't have may have saved capitalism'. He was an active member of the Bloomsbury Group and had passionate affairs with the artist Duncan Grant and the writer Lytton Strachey (303).

The Essential Keynes 1904–46

'Economics is a very dangerous science,' wrote Keynes. Robert Skidelsky, author of a three-volume biography of Keynes, divides his selected edition into five thematic sections, designed to represent the different aspects of Keynes's work: 'The Philosopher', 'The Social Philosopher', 'The Economist', 'The Policy-Maker' and 'The Essayist'. He includes complete essays, some never before published, as well as extracts from Keynes's major works, including *The Economic Consequences of the Peace* (1919), *A Treatise on Probability* (1921), *A Tract on Monetary Reform* (1923), *A Treatise on Money* (1930) and his magnum opus, *The General Theory of Employment, Interest and Money* (1936).

2015
ed. Robert Skidelsky

Edmund Gosse 1849–1928

Edmund Gosse was a poet, who worked as a librarian in the British Museum and the House of Lords and as a translator at the Board of Trade. He was also an influential art and literary critic, who encouraged the work of W. B. Yeats (276) and James Joyce, and who first introduced André Gide (322) and Henrik Ibsen (363) to English readers. He was awarded a Norwegian knighthood in 1901 and a British knighthood in 1925.

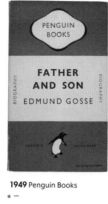

1949 Penguin Books

1983 Penguin English Library
1986 Penguin Classics
1989 Twentieth-Century Classics
ed. Peter Abbs

Father and Son 1907
A Study of Two Temperaments

Gosse's father, Philip Gosse, was an eminent naturalist who invented the term 'aquarium' and installed the first example at London Zoo in 1853. He was also a fanatical fundamentalist Christian, a member of the Plymouth Brethren, who expected his son to follow the same religious calling. At eighteen, Gosse broke dramatically from his father in order to 'fashion his inner life for himself'. This witty, psychological account of their relationship flouts the conventions of Victorian autobiography; George Bernard Shaw (294) called it 'one of the immortal pages in English literature'.

W. H. Hudson 1841–1922

William Henry Hudson was born in Argentina to New England parents and spent his youth studying the flora and fauna of the pampas. He is known as Guillermo Enrique Hudson in Argentina, where his varied writings are considered part of Argentine national literature. An ardent naturalist and ornithologist, he settled in Britain at the age of 33 and he became a founding member of the Royal Society for the Protection of Birds.

2016 Penguin Classics

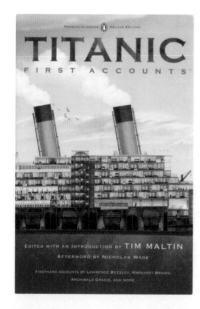

2012 Deluxe Edition
ed. Tim Maltin
aftwd. Nicholas Wade

The cover design is by Max Ellis, a precision engineer and illustrator.

A Shepherd's Life 1910
Impressions of the South Wiltshire Downs

These soaring 'impressions' revolve around the life story of Caleb Bawcombe, a shepherd of the downs for 50 years, who recounts memories of sheep-dogs, poachers, local fairs, blacksmiths and wild birds. Hudson captures a fading way of rural life in pieces entitled 'Salisbury Plain', 'Starlings and Sheep-Bells' and 'Concerning Cats'.

TITANIC 1912
First Accounts

At 11.40 p.m. on 14 April 1912, RMS *Titanic* hit an iceberg in the Atlantic Ocean, south of Newfoundland. At 2.20 a.m., less than three hours later, she broke apart and sank; more than 1,500 of the 2,224 passengers were drowned. Lawrence Beesley, a survivor of the disaster, wrote an account of his experience in 1912, extracts from which open and close this anthology; his grandson, the historian Nick Wade, provides an afterword. Also included is Archibald Gracie's *The Truth About the* Titanic, US and British official inquiries, the 'Marconi Report', first newspaper responses and extracts from Logan Marshall's *Sinking of the* Titanic *and Great Sea Disasters*.

Lytton Strachey 1880–1932

Giles Lytton Strachey was an essayist, literary critic and biographer. He was a founding member of the Bloomsbury Group and made his name with the publication of *Eminent Victorians* and the award-winning *Queen Victoria* (1921). He had a voluminous beard, which he tended with care: 'Its colour is very much admired,' he wrote in a letter to his mother, 'and it is generally considered extremely effective, though some ill-bred persons have been observed to laugh.' He was the model for the undergraduate Lord Risley in E. M. Forster's *Maurice* (285).

1948 Penguin Books
● —

—

Penguin's first paperback competitor was Pan Books, set up in June 1947. Allen Lane responded by establishing a 'group agreement' with five major hardback publishers, Chatto & Windus, Faber & Faber, Hamish Hamilton, Heinemann and Michael Joseph, who agreed to offer Penguin first refusal on the paperback rights of all their leading authors' works. Among the first additions to the Penguin list following this agreement was Lytton Strachey's *Eminent Victorians*.

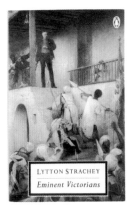

1989 Twentieth-Century Classics
intro. Michael Holroyd, 1986

Eminent Victorians 1918

Strachey pioneered a new form of biography that combined psychological insight with irreverence and wit, debunking Victorian myths of stiff upper lips and derring-do. In *Eminent Victorians*, he presents biographies of four legendary personages of the previous century: the self-serving Cardinal Manning, the unbearable Florence Nightingale, the didactic Thomas Arnold (272), and the imperialist General Gordon of Khartoum. The philosopher Bertrand Russell read the book in Brixton Prison and called it 'brilliant, delicious, exquisitely civilized. […] I often laughed out loud in my cell while I was reading the book. The warder came to my cell to remind me that prison was a place of punishment.'

W. N. P. Barbellion 1889–1919

Bruce Frederick Cummings was a young and aspiring natural historian, who achieved his ambition of becoming an entomologist at the Natural History Museum in London only to be diagnosed with disseminated sclerosis at the age of 26 and given less than five years to live. He kept a diary for most of his life, which he described as 'a study in the nude'. He published it in 1919, under the pseudonym 'W. N. P. Barbellion' with an introduction by H. G. Wells (255). He selected 'W. N. P.' as the initials of three of 'the most wretched figures in history', Kaiser Wilhelm, the Emperor Nero (52) and Pontius Pilate. Barbellion was the name of his favourite sweet shop on Bond Street.

The Journal of a Disappointed Man *and* A Last Diary 1913–19, pub. 1919–20

Barbellion's first journal spans fourteen years and transforms from a set of boyish field notes into a profound reverie on the prospect of impending death. From the first entry, written at the age of thirteen:

> Am writing an essay on the life-history of insects and have abandoned the idea of writing on 'How Cats Spend their Time'

to the last ('Self-disgust'); it is wryly philosophical and funny. Ronald Blythe called it 'among the most moving diaries ever created'. Barbellion prepared his journal for publication in 1917 and included a faked editorial note announcing his own death. In fact he was still alive and continued keeping a diary, describing his worsening physical condition and the tortuous publication process. This second journal was published posthumously as *A Last Diary* and is included in this volume, along with an afterword by his brother, A. J. Cummings.

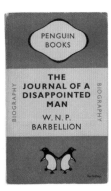

1948 Penguin Books
● —

2017
intro. H. G. Wells, 1919
aftwd. A. J. Cummings, 1920

Western Europe

BENJAMIN CONSTANT · ADOLPHE

STENDHAL · LOVE

SCARLET AND BLACK · STENDHAL

STENDHAL · THE LIFE OF HENRY BRULARD

STENDHAL · THE CHARTERHOUSE OF PARMA

HUGO · NOTRE-DAME OF PARIS

VICTOR HUGO · LES MISÉRABLES · 1

VICTOR HUGO · LES MISÉRABLES · 2

L134

L307
ISBN 0 14
044.307 X

L30

ISBN·0·14·
044.290 1

L61

ISBN 0 14
044.353 3

ISBN 0 14
044.403 3

ISBN 0 14
044.404 1

France

In 1803, Napoleon resurrected the Académie française, an institution that had been suppressed during the Revolution. Founded in the 17th century by Cardinal Richelieu (312), this council still consists of 40 French writers and scholars known as 'the Immortals'. Their task is to oversee the development of the French language and maintain the official French dictionary. Members are elected for life: it is the highest honour granted to a French writer. Prominent 19th-century Immortals include Chateaubriand (324), Alfred de Vigny (325), Alexis de Tocqueville (325), Victor Hugo (307), Alexandre Dumas *fils* (313), Alfred de Musset (311), Edmond Rostand (321) and Anatole France (323). These men helped to steward French literature between the French Revolution and the First World War, one of the most turbulent periods in the country's history, during which the monarchy came to a fitful end and a stable democracy was established.

FICTION

As elsewhere in Europe, the two major movements of 19th-century French literature were Romanticism and Realism. Literary Romanticism originated in Germany's *Sturm und Drang* movement (335) but was fuelled by the idealistic fervour that accompanied the French Revolution. The greatest French exponents were Victor Hugo (307), Alexandre Dumas (312) and Alfred de Musset (311). Towards the middle of the century, as the French state vacillated indecisively between successive empires, monarchies and republics, French Romanticism became increasingly tinged with disillusionment and ennui.

Realism emerged in France as an antidote to the Romantics: it was a systemic attempt to describe and document contemporary life and society as objectively and accurately as possible. Stendhal (306) straddles the two movements, but Realism was first fully embraced by Balzac (308) and Flaubert (313). Out of Realism grew the more polemical 'Naturalism', exemplified by Maupassant (318) and Zola (316), which focused particularly on the hardships faced by the lowest classes of an increasingly industrial French society.

Benjamin Constant

1767–1830

Henri-Benjamin Constant de Rebecque had a long and stormy love affair with Germaine de Staël, the influential woman of letters. In 1803, she was exiled by Napoleon and Constant followed her to Germany, where he published a pamphlet attacking the emperor. Nevertheless, he returned to France in 1815 to serve under Napoleon. After Waterloo (207), Constant moved to London, where he published *Adolphe*. He returned to France in 1818 and became a political journalist and the leader of the opposition in the Chamber.

1964
trans. Leonard Tancock

Adolphe

1816

The jaded young Adolphe embarks on a tempestuous love affair with a beautiful older woman, Ellenore. Having wooed her strenuously, her subsequent devotion repels him, but he cannot bring himself to leave her, and their tortured affair spirals towards tragedy. The novel is based in part on Constant's own relationship with Madame de Staël.

Stendhal

1783–1842

At seventeen, Henri Marie Beyle received a commission in Napoleon's army and took part in campaigns in Italy, Germany and Russia, where he witnessed the burning of Moscow. After Napoleon's fall in 1815, Beyle returned to Italy, settled in Milan and wrote books on Italian art under the pseudonym 'M. de Stendhal'. He chose his pen name in memory of the German town of Stendal, which was both the birthplace of the respected art historian Johann Joachim Winckelmann and the home of a beautiful blonde called Wilhelmine. In 1821, he reluctantly returned to Paris because his health was declining. In his final years, he treated his chronic syphilis with potassium and quicksilver, which resulted in swollen armpits, shrunken testicles, and terrible tremors that prevented him holding a pen. He lends his name to 'Stendhal syndrome', a psychosomatic disorder brought on by exposure to great works of art: while visiting the Basilica of Santa Croce in Florence in 1817 and looking at Giotto's (124) frescoes, he found himself in 'a sort of ecstasy [...] I had palpitations of the heart, what in Berlin they call "nerves". Life was drained from me. I walked with the fear of falling.' In *Beyond Good and Evil* (349), Nietzsche called him 'France's last great psychologist'.

1975
trans. Gilbert Sale & Suzanne Sale, 1957
intro. Jean Stewart & B. C. J. G. Knight, 1975

Love 1822

In Milan in 1818, Stendhal fell deeply in love with the beautiful Métilde, Countess Dembowska, but she rejected his advances. In despair, he wrote this quasi-scientific physiology of his unrequited emotion. He describes the seven stages of love's 'crystallization':

1. Admiration.

2. You think, 'How delightful it would be to kiss her, to be kissed by her,' and so on ...

3. Hope. [...]

4. Love is born. To love is to enjoy seeing, touching, and sensing with all the senses, as closely as possible, a lovable object which loves in return.

5. The first crystallization begins. If you are sure that a woman loves you, it is a pleasure to endow her with a thousand perfections and to count your blessings with infinite satisfaction. In the end you overrate wildly, and regard her as something fallen from Heaven [...]

6. Doubt creeps in. [...]

7. The second crystallization, which deposits diamond layers of proof that 'she loves me'.

'I agree that the combination of an ecclesiastical and a military symbol would interpret the general meaning of the title,' wrote Margaret Shaw about the cover of her translation, 'though in Stendhal's mind *Le rouge et le noir* had probably an added reference to the game of chance. The difficulty in the juxtaposition of a biretta and a soldier's cap would be that the latter at that period is not red, at any rate in Julien's imagination, but a cavalryman's helmet with black horsehair plumes. Actually the contrast is between the soldier's red coat and the priest's black cassock.' In the end, a sword and a bishop's crosier were selected for the cover illustration.

1953 *Scarlet and Black*
• trans. Margaret Shaw

2002
trans. Roger Gard

The Red and the Black 1830

Handsome, intelligent Julien Sorel is the son of a carpenter and he sets out with Machiavellian ambition to improve his social situation. Taking advantage of connections in the Church and the military world – the 'black' and the 'red' of the novel's title – he manoeuvres his way into the corrupt, glamorous heart of Parisian society, seducing the married Madame de Rênal and the aristocratic Mathilde de la Mole along the way. Everything collapses, however, when he allows his passionate feelings to derail his self-interested schemes.

The Life of Henry Brulard 1835–6, pub. 1890

In this ferociously honest, unpolished autobiography, Stendhal describes his own unhappy childhood, his attractive mother, who died when he was seven, his selfish, tyrannical father and his cruel aunt. 'His words are as fresh and as thrilling as if he were sitting by your side, talking excitedly into your ear,' writes the critic Nick Lezard, in his review of Sturrock's translation. 'It is one of the most remarkable memoirs ever composed, a *Tristram Shandy* (163) of self-disclosure: impish, rambling, outrageous, parenthetical, contradictory, obsessional, repetitive, occasionally tiresome, but shot through with wit and ferocious, lacerating honesty.'

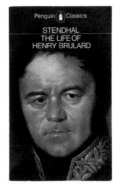

1973
● trans. Jean Stewart &
B. C. J. G. Knight

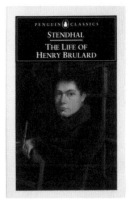

1995
trans. John Sturrock

1958
● trans. Margaret Shaw

2006
trans. John Sturrock

The Charterhouse of Parma 1839

The idealistic Italian aristocrat Fabrizio del Dongo defies his father and travels through France, hoping to fight for Napoleon. Following the emperor's defeat, Fabrizio returns to Italy and moves to the ducal court of Parma, where he lives under the protection of his devious aunt Gina and her aristocratic lover, Count Mosca. Fabrizio pursues a series of increasingly tragic love affairs until he ends up in the Charterhouse of Parma, a Carthusian monastery. Balzac (308) considered *The Charterhouse of Parma* the greatest French novel of his generation; André Gide (322) thought it the greatest French novel of all time. Stendhal's description of the chaotic Battle of Waterloo influenced Tolstoy's description of the Battle of Borodino in *War and Peace* (378).

Victor Hugo

1802–1885

Victor-Marie Hugo was conceived on one of the highest peaks in the Vosges mountains, perhaps the Storkenkopf ('Stork's Head'). His father was an officer in Napoleon's army and the young Victor moved frequently around Europe in his childhood. In 1822, he married his childhood sweetheart Adèle Foucher and he began writing poems, plays, essays and novels. Hugo abandoned France after Louis-Napoléon's 1851 *coup d'état* and lived in the Channel Islands of Jersey and Guernsey, where he wrote *Les Misérables* (308). When he died, his body lay in state under the Arc de Triomphe in Paris before being buried in the Panthéon, the mausoleum reserved for national heroes.

Notre-Dame de Paris 1831

High above 15th-century Paris in the vaulted towers of the cathedral of Notre-Dame, the hunchbacked Quasimodo rings the bells. He is devoted to the gypsy dancer Esmerelda, who has also caught the eye of Quasimodo's sinister guardian, the archdeacon Claude Frollo. When Esmerelda repels Frollo's lecherous advances, Quasimodo helps her evade the archdeacon's vengeful plans. Fanatical readers began flocking to visit the contemporary cathedral, so that the city of Paris was forced to instigate an extensive programme of restoration. The novel inspired a wave of historical preservation societies and was largely responsible for the 19th-century French vogue for Gothic revival architecture.

1978
trans. John Sturrock
—
In 1833 the first English translator, Frederic Schoberl, changed the title to *The Hunchback of Notre Dame*, because Gothic novels were more popular than romances at the time, and he considered this title to be more thrilling.

1980
trans. Norman Denny, 1976
Published in two volumes
—
Norman Denny's two-volume
translation was published in a
single volume in 1982.

Les Misérables 1862

I condemn slavery, I chase out poverty, I instruct ignorance, I treat illness, I light up the night, I hate hatred. That is what I am and that is why I have written *Les Misérables*.

'The Wretched' is the story of Jean Valjean, who served a nineteen-year sentence for stealing a loaf of bread. On his release, he is inspired by an act of Christian charity and comes to be a wealthy factory owner and the mayor of a small town, but he is doggedly pursued by the relentless policeman Javert, who won't let him forget his criminal past. The narrative opens in 1815 and features a lengthy description of the Battle of Waterloo; it culminates with the 1832 June Rebellion in Paris. 'La *misère* is not suffering; it is not merely poverty; it is a nameless thing that I have tired to define,' wrote Hugo. '[…] Suffering cannot disappear, but la *misère* must disappear. There will always be unfortunates, but it is possible that there will be no more *misérables*.' When the work was first published in Britain, Hugo sent a telegram to his English publishers that read '?' They wrote back with a single '!' It is one of the most popular novels in literary history. It is also one of the longest: in Penguin Classics, only Leopardi's *Zibaldone* (330), the Bible (4) and Richardson's *Clarissa* (160) have more pages.

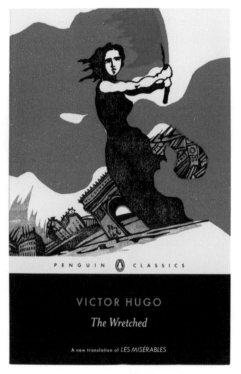

VICTOR HUGO
The Wretched
A new translation of *LES MISÉRABLES*

2013 *The Wretched*
2016 Reissued as *Les Misérables*
trans. Christine Donougher
intro. Robert Tombs

Honoré de Balzac

1799–1850

Balzac worked as a lawyer's clerk, a hack writer, a publisher, a printer and a type-founder before turning, heavily in debt, to literature at the age of 30. Over the next 20 years he produced a staggering number of interwoven novels and novellas, which form a parallel world populated with recurring and familiar characters.

This epic collection, which he called *La Comédie Humaine*, 'The Human Comedy', depicts French society under the gradually toppling, restored Bourbon Monarchy. 'What [Napoleon] was unable to finish with the sword,' Balzac wrote, 'I shall accomplish with the pen.' He died a few months after marrying Evelina Hańska, a Polish countess with whom he had been having an affair for eighteen years.

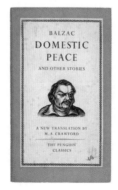

1958
trans. Marion Ayton Crawford

1977
trans. Sylvia Raphael

Selected Short Stories 1829–40

The twelve stories in this selection represent Balzac's best short fiction. They combine astute psychology and deftly handled suspense: the stories involve seductions, murders, mysteriously blocked doors, clarinet players and atheistic chief surgeons.

The Wild Ass's Skin 1831
(La Peau de Chagrin)

La Peau de Chagrin is a 'philosophical study' combining fantasy, symbolism and social history. In an old curiosity shop, the young Raphaël de Valentin discovers a magical piece of shagreen, untanned leather, which grants his every wish, but with every wish the skin shrinks and his physical energy is sapped. Through gambling dens, orgies, and royal banquets, the skin keeps shrinking until it is the size of a periwinkle leaf and finally is in danger of snuffing out altogether. The success of *La Peau de Chagrin* led to Balzac corresponding with Evelina Hańska, whom he would later marry. It was the last book that Sigmund Freud (353) was reading before he died.

1977
trans. Herbert J. Hunt

Old Man Goriot 1835

Le Père Goriot has been called the keystone of *La Comédie Humaine* and is often considered Balzac's masterpiece. It was the first of his novels in which he reintroduced recurring characters. Madame Vauquer runs a boarding house in Paris with three mysterious residents: the penniless law student Eugène de Rastignac, who appeared as an old man in *The Wild Ass's Skin*; the suspiciously jovial merchant Vautrin, who makes clandestine night-time excursions; and an elderly retired vermicelli-maker, Jean-Joachim Goriot, who bankrupted himself to see his daughters well married. Rastignac becomes increasingly involved in the lives of Goriot and Vautrin and must eventually make some terrible decisions.

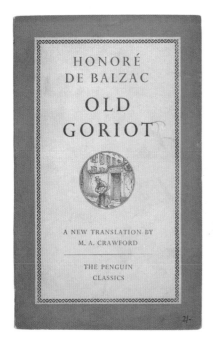

1951
● trans. Marion Ayton Crawford

2011
trans. Olivia McCannon
intro. Graham Robb

1955
trans. Marion Ayton Crawford

Eugénie Grandet
1833

Eugénie is the isolated daughter of an old miser who keeps a close watch on both her and his gold. When her handsome but indolent cousin Charles comes to visit, Eugénie falls in love with him, which brings her into conflict with her father. Dostoyevsky (371) began his literary career by translating *Eugénie Grandet* into Russian.

History of the Thirteen
1833–35

These three short novels all feature the activities of a rich sinister secret society known as 'the Thirteen'. *Ferragus* is a tragic love story about marriage destroyed by secrets, suspicion and misunderstanding; *The Duchesse de Langeais* follows the failed love affair between a society coquette and a retired war hero; and *The Girl with the Golden Eyes* is a sad tale of attempted seduction and murder.

1974
trans. Herbert J. Hunt

1971
trans. Herbert J. Hunt

Lost Illusions 1837–43

In *Illusions Perdues* Lucien Chardon is a poor but ambitious poet who has the good fortune to move to Paris with a wealthy patroness, Madame de Bargeton. Once there, however, he discovers that the *beau monde* is fickle, exclusive and potentially dangerous, and talent is less valuable than reputation and ruthlessness.

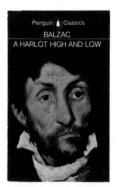

1970
trans. Rayner Heppenstall

A Harlot High and Low
(Splendeurs et Misères des Courtisanes) 1839–47

The impoverished, radiantly beautiful Esther Gobseck establishes herself as a successful society courtesan. When she meets and falls in love with the handsome poet Lucien from *Lost Illusions*, she thinks she may be able to escape her profession and lead a respectable life, but the arch-criminal Vautrin, from *Old Man Goriot* (309), draws her into a series of doomed money-making ventures.

The Black Sheep 1842
(La Rabouilleuse)

Agathe Bridau has two sons, the apparently heroic soldier Philippe and the seemingly indolent artist Joseph, but Philippe is secretly gambling away Agathe's savings and she needs to decide which of her sons is the real black sheep of the family. Meanwhile, her brother Jean-Jacques is being manipulated by his servant Flore Brazier and an ex-soldier, Max Gilet. Balzac's original title, *La Rabouilleuse*, means 'fisherwoman', a derogatory nickname for Flore.

1970
trans. Donald Adamson

Ursule Mirouët 1842

In the small town of Nemours, Dr Minoret is rumoured to be fabulously wealthy. When word gets out that he intends to leave his fortune to his orphaned niece and goddaughter Ursule, unscrupulous relatives descend on the town with a scheme to divert the inheritance.

1976
trans. Donald Adamson

Cousin Bette 1846
Part One of Poor Relations

Bette is a poor, plain spinster supported by her beautiful cousin Adeline and Adeline's husband Baron Hulot. Bette is deeply resentful of her cousin's family and becomes consumed with jealousy when she discovers that the man she loves plans to marry Adeline's daughter Hortense. Furious, Bette sets about plotting the ruin of the Hulots.

1968
trans. Herbert J. Hunt
—
The contrasting *Poor Relations* novels are considered Balzac's last great masterpieces and the culmination of *La Comédie Humaine*.

Cousin Pons 1847
Part Two of Poor Relations

This companion to *Cousin Bette* centres around Pons, a mild, harmless old musician. He shares an apartment with his friend Schmucke and has just two passions: collecting antiques and dining with his wealthy cousins. His relations view him as a tiresome parasite, until they discover the true value of his art collection, at which point they scramble to secure his affections and future inheritance.

1965
trans. Marion Ayton Crawford

Théophile Gautier 1811–1872

Pierre-Jules-Théophile Gautier was the son of a minor tax official and was a lifelong friend of Gérard de Nerval (327). Gautier was a cultural journalist for most of his life, reviewing exhibitions, books, plays and concerts. A supporter of the Second Empire, he was appointed librarian to Napoleon III's cousin Princess Mathilde, but he grew ill during the siege of Paris (1870–71) and died a year later.

Mademoiselle de Maupin 1835

1981
• trans. Joanna Richardson

2005
trans. Helen Constantine
intro. Patricia Duncker

In Gautier's reworking of Shakespeare's *As You Like It* (139), the Chevalier d'Albert fantasizes about his ideal lover, but all women fall short of his exacting standards. He is astonished, however, when he finds himself strongly attracted to Théodore, who is handsome, alluring and male. His mistress Rosette seems equally fascinated by this mysterious stranger. Perhaps there is more to Théodore than meets the eye. 'The only things that are really beautiful are those which have no use,' writes Gautier in his preface, anticipating late 19th-century aestheticism (320); 'everything that is useful is ugly.'

Alfred de Musset

1810–1857

Musset dabbled in medicine, law, art, English and piano playing before he took to writing. He wrote poems, plays and a lesbian novel called *Gamiani, or, Two Nights of Excess*. Between 1833 and 1835 he had a passionate affair with the novelist George Sand, which formed the basis of his most famous novel, *La Confession d'un Enfant du Siècle*. Sand also wrote about their affair, in *Elle et Lui* (1859).

The Confession of a Child of the Century 1836

This frank narrative describes young Octave's sexual awakening as a debauched libertine and the lover of the selfless Brigitte. He brings about his own destruction, however, when he grows insanely jealous. 'To write the story of your life, you must first have had one,' wrote Musset. '[…] Even if no one takes any notice at all, I shall at least have derived some benefit from my own words: the satisfaction of knowing that I cured myself since, like the fox caught in a snare, I did it by chewing off my trapped foot.'

2013
trans. David Coward

Eugène Sue

1804–1857

Marie-Joseph 'Eugène' Sue's father was a doctor in Napoleon's army. Sue trained as a medic himself and became a surgeon's assistant in the Navy before moving to Paris and writing nautical adventure stories. He became famous for spectacularly long-running serial novels.

2015
trans. Carolyn Betensky &
Jonathan Loesberg
fwd. Peter Brooks

The Mysteries of Paris 1842–3

When the heroic Rodolphe rescues the vulnerable prostitute Songbird from the clutches of the villainous Slasher, he sets in train a convoluted plot of audacious cliffhangers, bewildering twists and biting social commentary. Told in more than 150 chapters, this novel spawned a host of thrillers, and was the inspiration behind aspects of Hugo's *Les Misérables* (308) and Dumas's *Count of Monte Cristo* (312).

Alexandre Dumas 1802–1870

Dumas's father, the mixed-race, illegitimate son of a French marquis, was a general in the revolutionary army. He died when Alexandre was four years old and the young Dumas joined the household of the future king, Louis-Philippe, Duc d'Orléans, where he read voraciously and wrote plays and essays. In 1839, he began writing the historical novels for which he is best remembered today. He is sometimes known as '*père*' to distinguish him from his son Alexandre Dumas *fils* (313). In 2002, his ashes were reinterred in the Panthéon (307), escorted by four mounted Republican Guards dressed as Musketeers. President Chirac said: 'With you, we have been d'Artagnan, Monte Cristo, or Balsamo, riding along the highways of France, roaming fields of battle, exploring palaces and castles [...] With you, we have dreamed. With you, we dream once more'.

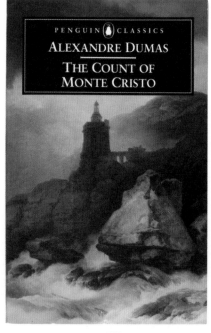

1996
trans. Robin Buss

The Three Musketeers 1844

Young d'Artagnan comes to Paris in the 17th century and falls in with Porthos, Athos and Aramis, inseparable members of the king's guard of Musketeers. D'Artagnan soon becomes entangled in the machinations of Cardinal Richelieu and a sinister world of murder, conspiracy, agents and lies. He must call on his new friends to help him escape the cardinal's clutches and win the hand of the beautiful Constance Bonacieux. In 1868, when Dumas's health was failing, his son (313) found him reading a book and asked him what it was.

> 'The *Musketeers*,' Dumas replied. 'I always promised myself that, when I was old, I'd decide if it was worth anything.'
> 'Well, where are you?' asked his son.
> 'At the end.'
> 'And what do you think?'
> 'It's good.'

The Count of Monte Cristo 1844–5

Edmond Dantès is imprisoned in the ghastly Château d'If for a crime he didn't commit. While inside, however, he learns about a hoard of hidden treasure on the Isle of Monte Cristo and sets about plotting how to escape, recover the treasure and wreak revenge on the men who had him incarcerated. Dumas based his story on the real wrongful imprisonment of Pierre Picaud, a shoemaker from Nîmes. '*Monte Cristo* is said to have been at its first appearance, and for some time subsequently, the most popular book in Europe,' writes the critic George Saintsbury. 'Perhaps no novel within a given number of years had so many readers and penetrated into so many different countries.'

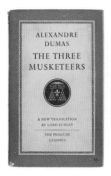

1952
• trans. Lord Sudley

2008
trans. Richard Pevear, 2006

The Women's War 1845

The Baron de Canolles, a Gascon soldier, is passionately in love with two powerful women on opposite sides of the civil war that rages in mid-17th-century France: Nanon de Lartigues, a supporter of Queen Anne of Austria, and the Viscountess de Cambes, who supports the Princess de Condé. Humorous, romantic and swashbuckling, it is Dumas's forgotten masterpiece.

2006
trans. Robin Buss

The Man in the Iron Mask 1847

The Man in the Iron Mask is the final episode in the series of sequels Dumas wrote to *The Three Musketeers* (312). Thirty-five years after their first adventure,

d'Artagnan is in the service of the corrupt King Louis XIV, but the other Musketeers have retired. 'Phillippe' is a mysterious 23-year-old prisoner languishing in the Bastille, forced to wear an iron mask to hide his identity. It is 'my favourite book', wrote Robert Louis Stevenson (241). 'No part of the world has ever seemed to me so charming as these pages, and not even my friends are quite so real, perhaps quite so dear, as d'Artagnan.'

2003
trans. Joachim Neugroschel
intro. Francine du Plessix Gray

The Black Tulip 1865

Cornelius van Baerle is a Dutch tulip-grower obsessed with cultivating the elusive black tulip, for which he would win 100,000 guilders. When his powerful godfather is assassinated, however, he is falsely accused of treason and condemned to life imprisonment, but with the aid of the gaoler's beautiful daughter Rosa, he continues his quest for the ultimate horticultural reward. This is the great novel of the tulipomania that gripped 17th-century Holland.

2003
trans. Robin Buss

Alexandre Dumas
fils 1824–1895

The illegitimate son of the famous novelist (312), Alexandre Dumas *fils* wrote novels himself, including *The Adventures of Four Women and a Parrot* (1847). A stage adaptation of *The Lady of the Camellias* drew him to playwriting, which he pursued for the rest of his career.

2013
trans. Liesl Schillinger
intro. Julie Kavanagh

The Lady of the Camellias 1848

In 1844, Dumas moved to Saint-Germain-en-Laye near Paris, to live with his father. There he met and fell for a young courtesan, Marie Duplessis, who became the model for Marguerite Gautier, the 'Lady of the Camellias', never seen without a bouquet of her favourite flowers. Gautier is beautiful and brazen, but she has never experienced true love before. Verdi's 1853 opera *La Traviata* ('The Fallen Woman') was based on the story, as was the 2001 Baz Lurhmann film, *Moulin Rouge!* In the opinion of Henry James (417), it is 'one of the greatest love stories of the world'.

Gustave Flaubert 1821–1880

Flaubert was the son of a doctor. He studied law in Paris but confessed himself 'disgusted with life' and was quite content when an unspecified nervous disease forced him to retire to Croisset, near Rouen, where he spent much of the rest of his life writing. He never married nor had any children, wishing to 'transmit to no one the aggravations and the disgrace of existence'. His novels and two plays were critically unsuccessful during his lifetime, but he is now considered one of the greatest French writers of the 19th century and a leading exponent of Realism. He saw his writing career as a continual quest for 'le mot juste'.

Flaubert in Egypt 1849–51
A Sensibility on Tour

The biographer Francis Steegmuller arranges the young Flaubert's diaries, letters and travel notes to reconstruct a trip he made to Egypt, during which he experienced bazaars and brothels that had a profound influence on his later work. 'The suggestion that such a book as this might be made was first broached to me one day by Graham Greene,' explains Steegmuller. '[…] The present compilation was subsequently undertaken, and I hope that its Onlie Begetter and a few others may enjoy it.'

1996
trans. Francis Steegmuller, 1979
—
This is Steegmller's 'most crafty and idiosyncratic book,' writes Julian Barnes, '[…] one of those books which hovers on the edge of inventing a new genre'.

313

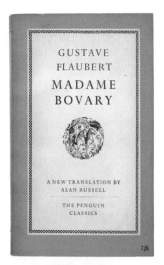

1951
• trans. Alan Russell

Madame Bovary 1857
Provincial Lives

Flaubert began work on his first published novel on his return from Egypt. The story centres on Emma Bovary, beautiful and bored, the wife of an uninspiring provincial doctor living near Rouen. She loves romantic novels and seeks to escape her stiflingly banal life through increasingly wild fantasies, reckless spending and eventually adultery. The book was attacked by public prosecutors for obscenity and the resulting trial made it notorious; after Flaubert's acquittal, it became a bestseller. '*Madame Bovary* has a perfection that not only stamps it, but that makes it stand almost alone,' wrote Henry James (417): 'it holds itself with such a supreme unapproachable assurance as both excites and defies judgment.' 'Madame Bovary,' said Flaubert, '*c'est moi*.'

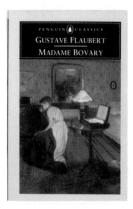

1992
trans. Geoffrey Wall, 1992
pref. Michèle Roberts, 2003

Salammbo 1862

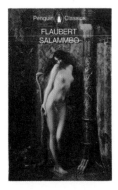

1977
trans. A. J. Krailsheimer

Set in ancient Carthage in the 3rd century BCE, this is the story of an invading barbarian army and its leader Matho, who becomes infatuated with the exotic but dangerous Salammbo, high priestess of Carthage's most sacred temple. Flaubert used Polybius (35) as his principal source on the Mercenaries' Revolt and he travelled to Carthage to gather first-hand material.

Sentimental Education 1869

Flaubert took seven years to write *L'Éducation Sentimentale*, drawing on his own youthful passion for an older woman. The novel follows Frederic Moreau, a law student who is captivated by Angèle Arnoux. Moreau befriends Angèle's husband and over the years their paths continue to cross and recross, despite other passions, ambitions and amours. Flaubert described the novel as 'the moral history of the men of my generation – or, more accurately, the history of their feelings. It's a book about love, about passion.'

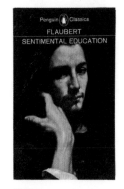

1964
trans. Robert Baldick, 1964
rev. Geoffrey Wall, 2004

1961
• trans. Robert Baldick

2005
trans. Roger Whitehouse
intro. Geoffrey Wall

Three Tales 1877

These three short stories are Flaubert's last great work. 'A Simple Heart' is the story of Félicité, a serving-woman who retains her Catholic faith and her pet parrot despite a life of desolation and loss; 'The Legend of Saint Julian Hospitator', inspired by a stained-glass window in Rouen cathedral, describes the fate of Julian, who is sadistically cruel to animals; and 'Herodias' is a reworking of the story of Salome and John the Baptist. Herodias inspired Wilde's *Salomé* (246) and 'A Simple Heart' inspired Julian Barnes's novel *Flaubert's Parrot* (1984).

Jules Verne

1828–1905

Verne was born in the seaport of Nantes and had a lifelong fascination with ships and the sea. In 1848, he moved to Paris, frequented literary salons and wrote his extremely popular series of novels, *Les Voyages Extraordinaires*. According to UNESCO, he is the world's second most translated author, after Agatha Christie and before Shakespeare (134). 'We are all, in one way or another, the children of Jules Verne,' wrote the science fiction writer Ray Bradbury.

1965
Penguin
Science Fiction
● trans. Robert
Baldick

Journey to the Centre of the Earth 1864

The eccentric Professor Otto Lidenbrock discovers, in a manuscript copy of Snorri Sturluson's *Heimskringla* (91), a mysterious cipher that describes the entrance to another world hidden beneath our own. With his reluctant nephew Axel, the professor climbs into the dormant Icelandic volcano of Snæfellsjökull and discovers layers of increasingly ancient zones inside our hollow earth, populated with dinosaurs and other extinct creatures. At one point the travellers witness a fight between an ichthyosaur and a plesiosaur. The book may have been inspired by the geological writings of Charles Lyell (209).

2009
trans. Frank Wynne
ed. Peter Cogman
intro. Jane Smiley

Twenty Thousand Leagues Under the Sea 1870

Verne's 'tour of the underwater world' is the story of the enigmatic Captain Nemo and the crew of the *Nautilus* submarine as they travel 20,000 leagues (over 40,000 nautical miles) through the ocean. On their extraordinary journey, the voyagers encounter sharks, the ruins of Atlantis (28) and a deadly giant octopus. 'Nemo' ('No One') is a reference to the pseudonym employed by Odysseus (17) to trick the cyclops Polyphemus.

2018
trans. David Coward

Around the World in Eighty Days 1873

Phileas Fogg wagers £20,000 that he can walk out of the Reform Club on Pall Mall in London and return within 80 days, having circumnavigated the globe. The Englishman sets off for Dover immediately, accompanied by his French valet Passepartout, and embarks on a wild adventure that involves trains, steamships, sailing boats, wind-powered sledges and elephants, though he draws the line at hot-air ballooning, which would have been 'very risky and, in any case, was not possible'. They arrive back, according to their calculations, one day too late, but Passepartout realizes they have travelled eastwards past the International Date Line, so they still have a day in hand. The adventurous American journalist Nellie Bly (403) recreated the feat in 1889 and described her journey in *Around the World in Seventy-Two Days*. She stopped off en route in Amiens to visit Verne.

2004
trans. Michael Glencross
intro. Brian Aldiss

Émile Zola 1840–1902

After the death of his Italian father, Zola was raised in poverty in Aix-en-Provence. He failed the *baccalauréat* twice and so could not pursue a university education and joined the new publishing house Hachette as a menial clerk instead. He showed great promise, however, and before long he was head of publicity. He left in 1865 to become a novelist himself. After the scandalous publication of *Thérèse Raquin*, Zola embarked on an ambitious series of 20 novels, which account for most of his literary output. He described the Rougon-Macquart cycle as 'the natural and social history of a family under the Second Empire'. The novels follow around 300 major characters, most of whom are related to the central interlinked families, the respectable legitimate Rougons and the disreputable illegitimate Macquarts.

1970 *L'Assommoir*
● trans. Leonard Tancock

2000 *L'Assommoir*
2003 Reissued as *The Drinking Den*
trans. Robin Buss

Thérèse Raquin 1867

Described as 'putrid' by *Le Figaro*, *Thérèse Raquin* tells the story of Thérèse, who is suffocating in a loveless marriage to her cousin Camille until she meets the dissolute Laurent, with whom she embarks on a passionate love affair. The lovers conspire to murder Camille, but are subsequently haunted by his mother, Madame Raquin, who is completely paralysed except for her eyes. In a preface, Zola explained that his purpose was to 'study temperament not character', thereby declaring himself a Naturalist (305).

The Drinking Den
(L'Assommoir) 1877

The seventh novel in the Rougon-Macquart cycle is a study of alcoholism and poverty in working-class Paris. Gervaise Macquart is abandoned by her lover and raises two children on her own. Desperate and increasingly impoverished, she accepts a marriage proposal from the teetotal roofing-working Monsieur Coupeau. The happy couple have a daughter together, Anna, whom they call 'Nana' but when Coupeau has an accident and loses his job, he descends into a spiral of drinking and debt, and threatens to pull Gervaise down with him.

Nana 1880

The ninth novel in the Rougon-Macquart cycle is the tale of Nana Coupeau, the daughter from *The Drinking Den*, who rises from the squalid Parisian slums to be the glittering star of the Théâtre des Variétés and eventually a courtesan, the idol of wealthy noblemen and the envy of great ladies. 'Nana' has entered the French language as a colloquial term for a woman with elastic morals.

1962
● trans. Leonard Tancock

2004
trans. Robin Buss

Au Bonheur des Dames
(The Ladies' Delight) 1883

The eleventh book in the Rougon-Macquart cycle is set in Au Bonheur des Dames, modelled on Le Bon Marché, the world's first department store, which is still open on the Rue de Sèvres in Paris. Zola's store is run by the philandering Octave Mouret, who exploits his young staff and intoxicates his female customers with luxurious window displays, rolls of sumptuous fabrics and extravagant advertising.

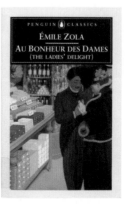

2001
trans. Robin Buss

1972
trans. George Holden

1954
● trans. Leonard Tancock
—
'If the roundel is meant to portray a scene of utter desolation I suppose it succeeds,' wrote Leonard Tancock. '[…] I have nothing to complain of in the general idea (though the slag heaps might have been larger and bolder). But the absence of cables over the pulleys and of any shaft into which the cables descend makes the thing an irritating challenge to one's sense of logic.'

2004
trans. Roger Pearson

The Earth
(La Terre) 1887

Jean Macquart arrives in the rural community of Rognes in La Beauce, where ancient farming families are fiercely territorial. Old Man Fouan decides, like King Lear (142), to divide his land between his three children: his mean-spirited daughter Fanny; his eldest son, the flatulent Hyacinthe, known as 'Jesus Christ'; and the lecherous Buteau. When Buteau declares himself unsatisfied with his lot, however, the siblings' rivalry turns nasty. This, the fifteenth book in the Rougon-Macquart cycle, was Zola's favourite.

The Beast Within
(La Bête Humaine) 1890

The seventeenth book in the Rougon-Macquart cycle is perhaps the most violent and disturbing. Jacques Lantier, the brother of Étienne from *Germinal,* is the 'human beast'. He struggles to control his desire to kill women, and finds some relief in driving his steam locomotive and meeting his cousin Flore. Meanwhile, Lantier's colleague, the stationmaster at Le Havre, discovers that his young wife Séverine has had an affair, and the plot descends into a maelstrom of jealousy, rage, murder and bestial passions.

Germinal 1885

Étienne Lantier, the son of Gervaise in *The Drinking Den* (316), takes a punishing job at the coal mine in the bleak region of Montsou and discovers that his fellow miners are sickly, starving and struggling to clothe their families with their meagre wages. As conditions deteriorate further, Étienne finds himself leading a strike that will bring either disaster or salvation. *Germinal* is the thirteenth book in the Rougon-Macquart cycle and is often regarded as Zola's masterpiece. The title refers to the 'season of germination' in the calendar of the French Revolution, which Zola alludes to in the novel's final sentence:

> New men were starting into life, a black army of vengeance slowly germinating in the furrows, growing for the harvests of the century to come; and soon this germination would tear the earth apart.

1980
trans. Douglas Parmée

The Debacle 1892

The nineteenth and penultimate book in the Rougon-Macquart cycle is a military novel about Jean Macquart, who featured in *The Earth*. He is now a middle-aged soldier in the French army. Initially suspicious of the wealthy, easy-living Maurice Levasseur, the pair forge a deep friendship during the Franco-Prussian War of 1870–71, and help each other to survive as France's Second Empire collapses around them. Zola's aim was to chronicle the events that led to the fall of Napoleon III and the establishment of the Third Republic, which he considered 'the murder of a nation'.

1972
trans. Leonard Tancock

1977
● trans. Leonard Tancock

2007
trans. Roger Whitehouse

Alphonse Daudet
1840–1897

Daudet was private secretary to the Duc de Morny, Napoleon III's half-brother. He wrote several naturalistic novels and a play, *L'Arlésienne* (1872), 'The Girl from Arles', for which Bizet composed incidental music, but he is best remembered for *Letters from My Windmill*. Daudet suffered from syphilis, which became agonizingly painful towards the end of his life; his writings on the excruciating experience of *tabes dorsalis* have been translated by Julian Barnes as *In the Land of Pain* (2002).

1978
trans. Frederick Davies
ill. Edward Ardizzone

Letters from My Windmill 1869

Daudet narrates these short stories from a ruined Provençal windmill near his native Nîmes. He describes the rural lifestyle, drawing on local folktales and day-to-day life in the south of France. These bucolic, whimsical and sometimes melancholy tales capture the beautiful light, landscape and seasonal rhythms of Provence. Titles include 'Monsieur Seguin's Goat', 'The Stars' and 'The Pope's Mule'.

Guy de Maupassant
1850–1893

When Henri-René-Albert-Guy de Maupassant was thirteen years old, his mother obtained a legal separation from his father and moved to the coastal resort of Étretat in Normandy with her two sons. At eighteen, Maupassant saved the poet Swinburne (265) from drowning in the sea. He fought briefly in the Franco-Prussian War and was a keen sportsman: he was a rower, a sailor, a swordsman and apparently a dead shot. Flaubert (313) was a friend of his mother's and encouraged his writing. In 1880, the publication of Maupassant's first short story, 'Boule de Suif', made his name overnight and he went on to write more than 300 short stories and six novels over the following decade. He disliked the new Eiffel Tower, so he frequented the restaurant at its base, the only place in Paris where it didn't dominate the view. He was a womanizer who suffered from syphilis; he spent his last years in a mental asylum after attempting to take his own life.

A Parisian Affair 1880–91
and Other Stories

Maupassant was a master of the short story. This selection of 34 stories represents a tenth of his total output but aims to present the 'finest of his oeuvre'. It includes 'Boule de Suif', the 'Ball of Fat', about a group of appalingly hypocritical Rouen residents who flee the Prussian invaders in the company of Elisabeth Rousset, a prostitute known as 'Boule de Suif'; 'The Necklace', a story of social pretension with catastrophic consequences; and 'The Horla', a horror story that inspired H. P. Lovecraft's 'The Call of Cthulhu'.

1940 *Boule de Suif and Other Stories*
● trans. Marjorie Laurie

1946
● trans. H. N. P. Sloman

1979
trans. Leonard Tancock

Bel-Ami 1885

The handsome and ambitious Georges Duroy, known to his friends as 'Bel-Ami', 'pretty friend', joins the newspaper *La Vie Française* and embarks on a successful career in investigative journalism. The more he sees of the corruption and seediness of society, however, the more cynical and manipulative he becomes, focusing his talents on blackmail, social climbing and the seduction of beautiful wealthy women.

1961
• trans. H. N. P. Sloman

1975
trans. Douglas Parmée

Pierre and Jean 1888

When an old family friend bequeaths a fortune to Pierre Roland's younger brother Jean, Pierre boils with jealousy. He roams the seaport of Le Havre, wondering why he should not have received at least half of the legacy himself. Things turn nasty when some of his wild speculations are proved correct. 'Talent is long patience,' writes Maupassant in his preface on the nature of the novel. 'It is a matter of looking at anything you want to express long enough and closely enough to discover in it some aspect that nobody has yet seen or described.'

H. N. P. Sloman's first volume of Maupassant's stories was the second Penguin Classics title to be published, after E. V. Rieu's translation of the *Odyssey* (17). The cover of Sloman's edition of *The Mountain Inn and Other Stories* was illustrated by David Gentleman. 'This was one of the first jobs that I ever was paid for by anybody and it was the first thing I did for Penguins,' Gentleman recalled. '[...] I read the stories quickly. I did a rough in my digs in Battersea at the time and posted it back to [Hans] Schmoller or John [Overton] at Penguins and they sent it back more or less instantly and I engraved it at the next weekend and I thought that – if it only would go on – this would be a good way, a nice congenial way to earn a living.'

1951
• trans. H. N. P. Sloman

1955
• trans. H. N. P. Sloman

1971
• trans. Roger Colet
2004
trans. Siân Miles

J.-K. Huysmans

1848–1907

Charles-Marie-Georges Huysmans spent most of his life working for the French civil service, in the Ministry of the Interior. His Dutch father died when he was eight years old, and he resented his mother's swift remarriage to Jules Og, a Parisian bookbinder. During the Franco-Prussian War, he spent half the time in hospital, suffering from dysentery, and the rest under fire during the siege of Paris. He began writing prose poems and novels soon after the war, which he published under the pseudonym 'Joris-Karl', or 'J.-K.' 'It takes me two years to "document" myself for a novel,' he wrote – 'two years of hard work. That is the trouble with the naturalistic novel – it requires so much documentary care. [...] When I finally get to writing it, it goes along rather fast – *assez vite*.'

Against Nature

(À Rebours)

1884

Against Nature is a novel with one character. Des Esseintes is an aristocratic aesthete who indulges in luxury and excess, vacillating between hyperactive cultural and sexual appetites and debilitating ennui. He guzzles Petronius (49) and Apuleius (53), basks in rich perfumes, soars with synaesthetic liqueurs administered through his 'mouth organ' (an instrument of his own invention) and enjoys an alluring liaison with a cherry-lipped male youth. At one point, he encrusts the shell of his pet tortoise with exotic jewels until it is crushed to death under the weight. Huysmans said the novel exploded 'like a meteorite' when it was first published. In the words of Arthur Symons (266), it became 'the breviary of the Decadence'.

1959

trans. Robert Baldick, 1956
rev. Patrick McGuinness, 2003

—

'As for the cover illustration, I have searched in vain for a suitable one,' wrote Baldick: 'even Beardsley (266) offers nothing that will fit the book. What I would suggest, therefore, is a drawing of a winged Sphinx with long talons and the face of an evil/decadent-looking woman. A Beardsley-type face, in fact, attached to a sphinx-body to produce something positively unnatural.' A. S. B. Glover, the Penguin general editor, replied: 'I think we shall be able to execute on the basis of a model that we keep on the staff.'

The Damned

(Là-Bas)

1891

Durtal, a thinly disguised self-portrait of Huysmans, is writing a biography of Gilles de Rais, the 15th-century baby-killing warlord, who inspired the legend of Bluebeard. When he investigates Gilles's involvement in satanic rituals, Durtal discovers the real world of black magic in *fin-de-siècle* Paris and is drawn in by the sensual and malevolent charms of Madame Chantelouve.

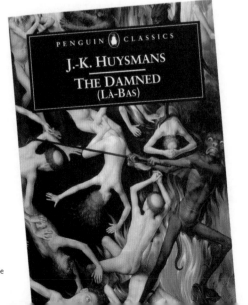

2001

trans. Terry Hale

ROBERT BALDICK

Baldick was a French scholar and the joint editor of Penguin Classics with Betty Radice (51). 'A stream of excellent translations came from his pen,' read his obituary in the *Times* in 1972. '[...] Baldick helped to raise the standard of translations into English; he also helped to raise the status of the translator. [...] As joint editor of Penguin Classics from 1964 onwards, he made sure that translators were paid a proper fee for what is a specialist job.' His first translation for Penguin Classics was *Against Nature*, on which he had written his doctorial thesis at Oxford, and he went on to publish several others. 'Amid all this,' his obituary continued, 'he retained a zest for life which was outstanding in its vigour, humanity and capacity for humour.'

George Du Maurier
1834–1896

George Louis Palmella Busson du Maurier was born in Paris, the son of an impecunious Frenchman and the English daughter of a celebrated courtesan. He trained as an artist in Paris, where he lost the sight in his left eye, and then settled in London with his wife Emma, contributing cartoons and drawings to periodicals and illustrating stories by <u>George Meredith</u> (240), <u>Thomas Hardy</u> (234), <u>Charles Dickens</u> (210) and <u>Elizabeth Gaskell</u> (220). Two of his particularly successful cartoons popularized the English expressions 'a curate's egg' and 'bedside manner'. He became a close friend of <u>Henry James</u> (417) and was the grandfather of the author Daphne du Maurier.

1994
ed. Daniel Pick

Trilby 1894

Trilby O'Ferrall is a penniless Parisian artist's model transformed into a virtuoso soprano by the hypnotist Svengali. This thrilling Gothic horror story, written in English but set on the dark streets of Paris, was sensationally popular, spawning merchandised soap, songs and toothpaste, and most famously the trilby, a style of felt hat with an indented crown, which featured in Du Maurier's original illustrations. The novel is said to have inspired Gaston Leroux's *Phantom of the Opera* (323) and it provided the name for the township of Trilby in Florida.

Edmond Rostand
1868–1918

Before he was 20, Edmond-Eugène-Alexis Rostand won the Académie de Marseille annual prize for an essay comparing 'two Provençal novelists', the 17th-century Honoré d'Urfé and <u>Gustave Flaubert</u> (313). He married at 22, had his first child at 23 and his first play was performed at the Comédie-Française theatre when he was just 26. He wrote a series of extremely successful plays, the most popular of which was *Cyrano de Bergerac*. He disliked public acclaim, however, and increasingly retreated to his home in the Pyrenees. He died in the flu pandemic after the <u>First World War</u> (433).

Cyrano de Bergerac 1897

Cyrano de Bergerac was a 17th-century French author. In Rostand's verse drama, he is a poet, a swashbuckler and an ardent lover, but he has one major handicap: his nose is extraordinarily huge. He imagines the beautiful Roxane can't see past this colossal appendage, so the gallant Cyrano retreats and assists the handsome but dim-witted Christian to woo her instead, writing beautiful, seductive love letters on his behalf. An early translation of this play introduced the figurative use of the word 'panache' into the English language.

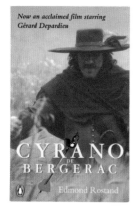

1991
• trans. Lowell Bair, 1972

2006
trans. Carol Clark

André Gide 1869–1951

'The humanist has four leading characteristics, ' wrote E. M. Forster (284) – 'curiosity, a free mind, belief in good taste, and a belief in the human race – and all four are present in Gide [...] the humanist of our age.' André-Paul-Guillaume Gide wrote essays, poetry, biographies, fiction, plays and memoirs, and he translated Conrad (277) into French. He was a proud pederast and a friend of Oscar Wilde (244), with whom he enjoyed the company of young boys in northern Africa. In 1947, he was awarded the Nobel Prize for Literature.

1960 Penguin Books
● trans. Dorothy Bussy, 1930

2000 Modern Classics
trans. David Watson
intro. Alan Sheridan

The Immoralist
1902

Michel marries the gentle Marceline out of a sense of duty to his dying father. On honeymoon in Tunisia, however, he experiences a sexual awakening as he finds himself powerfully attracted to the Arab boys, as he is subsequently drawn to the sons of his estate manager in France. He learns to follow his own unorthodox desires, but finds that his newfound moral liberation is accompanied by a sickening sense of ennui.

Strait is the Gate
1909

Jerome and Alissa are cousins who spend their childhood summers together in the idyllic Normandy countryside. They fall in love, but Alissa gradually becomes convinced that love is immoral, so she smothers her feelings with religion, leaving Jerome isolated and lovelorn. In some ways *Strait is the Gate* forms a diptych with *The Immoralist*: Alissa is cursed with morals, whereas Michel is cursed without them. 'The two subjects grew up together in my mind,' wrote Gide, 'the excess of the one finding a secret permission in the excess of the other, so that the two together form an equipoise.' It was translated into English by the novelist Dorothy Bussy, Gide's friend and Lytton Strachey's (303) sister.

1952 Penguin Books
1965 Modern Classics *Strait is the Gate* and *The Vatican Cellars*
1969 Modern Classics *Strait is the Gate*
trans. Dorothy Bussy, 1924

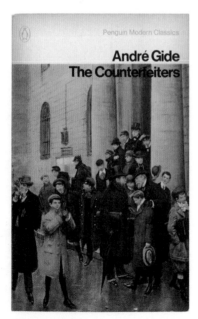

1966 Modern Classics
trans. Dorothy Bussy, 1931

The Counterfeiters
1925

Gide uses multiple characters, intersecting plot lines, a novel-within-a-novel and an inconsistent narrator to explore and contrast notions of the 'original' and the 'copy'. One plot strand concerns a gang of gold coin counterfeiters, but the novel is more concerned with homo- and heterosexual relationships, legitimate and illegitimate offspring and familial and extra-familial love.

Maurice Leblanc 1864–1941

Leblanc began his literary career emulating his heroes Flaubert (313) and Maupassant (318), but he is best remembered for the adventures of the master thief Arsène Lupin, a burglar and confidence trickster who eventually becomes a detective himself. Leblanc wrote five collections of Lupin stories, several novels and a play adaptation. This gentleman-thief was created in direct reaction to the success of the Sherlock Holmes (248) stories.

Arsène Lupin, Gentleman-Thief 1905–23

Arsène Lupin is a master of disguise. In this selection of stories, he steals jewels, woos ladies, conducts robberies while in prison, employs lookalikes and even meets an elderly Sherlock Holmes and successfully picks his pocket. Jean-Paul Sartre called Lupin 'the Cyrano of the underworld' (321).

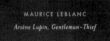

2007
trans. Michael Sims

Gaston Leroux 1868–1927

Gaston-Louis-Alfred Leroux was the son of a building contractor. He became an investigative journalist and an author of detective fiction. After covering the notorious Dreyfus Affair, he joined the prestigious *Le Matin* newspaper as an international correspondent and began writing novels in the late 1890s. His *Mystery of the Yellow Room* (1907) is a famous example of a 'locked-room' mystery.

2009 Red Classics
2012 Penguin Classics
trans. Mireille Ribière, 2009
intro. Jann Matlock, 2012

The Phantom of the Opera 1909–10

The opulent Paris Opera House is said to be haunted by a spectre that stalks its dark cellars and backstage corridors. This ghost also haunts the imagination of the young singer Christine Daaé, who seems to hear its disembodied voice coaching her to sing more and more beautifully. When Christine is courted by the handsome young Viscount Raoul de Chagny, however, the phantom becomes jealous and reveals its monstrous secret. The novel was adapted into a highly successful silent film in 1925 and has had numerous stage and film adaptions, most notably Andrew Lloyd Webber's 1986 musical.

Anatole France

1844–1924

France was born in Paris, the only son of an antiquarian bookseller who specialized in books relating to the French Revolution. He read voraciously as a child, and for 20 years worked for a publishing house reading manuscripts and writing prefaces to works of classic literature. Later he was appointed assistant librarian to the Senate, which allowed him time for his own writing. He came to dominate French literary society by the turn of the century and is thought to be the model for the writer Bergotte in Proust's *In Search of Lost Time*. He was awarded the Nobel Prize for Literature in 1921.

The Gods Will Have Blood (Les Dieux Ont Soif) 1912

The Reign of Terror is raging in Paris, and Évariste Gamelin, a fanatically idealistic young artist, has been appointed as a juror on the Revolutionary Tribunal, with the power to dispense death sentences. His conviction that 'only the guillotine' can save his country may prove to be his downfall, however.

1979
trans. Frederick Davies

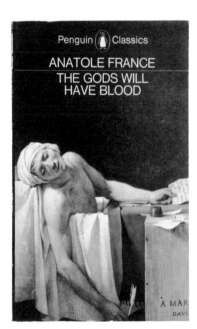

Alain-Fournier

1886–1914

Henri-Alban Fournier was the son of a country schoolmaster. In Paris, he met and fell in love with Yvonne-Marie-Elise Toussaint de Quiévrecourt. Her spirit permeates his only complete novel, *Le Grand Meaulnes,* which he published under the pseudonym 'Alain-Fournier'. He was killed in action in 1914 on the Meuse, in the first week of fighting at the start of the First World War (433). His body remained unidentified until 1991.

1966 Modern Classics
● trans. Frank Davidson

2007
trans. Robin Buss
intro. Adam Gopnik

The Lost Estate 1913

(Le Grand Meaulnes)

Augustin Meaulnes, nicknamed 'Le Grand Meaulnes', is a charismatic new boy at the local school in Sologne. He tells his new friends about a marvellous, dreamlike costume party he attended, presided over by a pale-faced pierrot and a beautiful girl called Yvonne de Galais. Now Meaulnes searches restlessly for that mysterious house and his lost love. His loyal friend François narrates the story, observing and assisting Meaulnes as they grow older, nostalgic for that border time between childhood and adulthood. The title inspired F. Scott Fitzgerald's *The Great Gatsby.*

For First World War fiction, turn to p.436

NON-FICTION

French non-fiction in the 19th century reflects the contemporary military and political upheavals at home while also looking abroad to America (325) and Russia (326), two contrasting models of government.

François-René de Chateaubriand 1768–1848

François-René, Vicomte de Chateaubriand, was a soldier, a politician and the most celebrated literary figure during the reign of Napoleon; he was an early proponent of French Romanticism. In 1797, he wrote a book of essays about the revolution and several novels, including the wildly popular *Atala, ou, Les Amours de Deux Sauvages dans le Désert* (1801), which is set in America. He was a great gourmand, and lends his name to a thick fillet beef steak. He spent the last years of his life writing his 42-volume *Memoirs from Beyond the Tomb,* which were published, as he planned, after his death. Victor Hugo (307) wrote in his notebook, 'I will be Chateaubriand or nothing'.

Memoirs from Beyond the Tomb 1811–41, pub. 1849–50

Chateaubriand lived through a tumultuous period of war and peace, monarchy and empire, hope and despair. Inspired by Rousseau's *Confessions* (178), his wide-ranging *Mémoires d'Outre-Tombe* describe adventures around the globe, heroic military battles and fierce political tussles. He decided to write his memoirs as early as 1803 and began work on them in 1811. He wrote the conclusion in 1841. The scope of the project is huge: he aims to describe not only his own life but also the major historical and political events of the period, and to convey a sense of wonder in the natural world. This edition comprises a representative selection by Robert Baldick (320).

1965
trans. Robert Baldick, 1961
intro. Philip Mansel, 2014

Jean-Anthelme Brillat-Savarin 1755–1826

Brillat-Savarin was born in eastern France, surrounded by vineyards and fine foodstuffs. His family fed his gourmet interests and he developed a love of good meat and drink that lasted throughout his life. He was a magistrate and later Mayor of Belley. During the French Revolution he worked as a violinist in a New York theatre orchestra pit, but he returned to France in 1796 and spent his days as a judge at the Supreme Court of Appeal and his evenings entertaining epicurean friends with excellent food. 'Tell me what you eat,' he famously wrote; 'I will tell you what you are.' He lends his name to a particularly rich variety of brie and a large rum baba.

The Physiology of Taste 1825

Brillat-Savarin's 'gastronomical meditations' cover topics such as appetite, 'pleasures of the table', shooting-luncheons, dreams and how to moderate obesity. He recommends approaching food with all senses alert, including the sixth sense, which he calls that 'sense of *physical desire*, which brings the two sexes together'. He includes pithy aphorisms, such as 'Dessert without cheese is like a pretty woman with only one eye.' And he inserts anecdotes, favourite recipes and tips on how to master the art of being a gourmand.

1970 Penguin Handbooks
The Philosopher in the Kitchen
1994 Penguin Classics
The Physiology of Taste
trans. Anne Drayton
—
Betty Radice (51) helped by translating a Latin recipe for stuffed dormice for Anne Drayton: 'Stuffed Dormice: Stuff the dormice with pork forcemeat and the minced flesh taken from all parts of the dormice, along with pepper, nut kernels, asafoetida and fish sauce, stitch them up and put them in a clay dish in the oven, or bake them when stuffed in a pot oven.'

Alfred de Vigny 1797–1863

Vigny came from an ancient military family. He joined the royal body-guard in 1814 and served for thirteen years, but never saw serious military action. He became a key figure in the Romantic movement, writing poems and several successful plays. After the publication of *The Warrior's Life*, he spent his remaining years caring for his ailing mother and invalid wife. The phrase 'ivory tower' was coined by the critic Charles-Augustin Sainte-Beuve to describe Vigny's seclusion.

The Warrior's Life 1835

Vigny was haunted by France's defeat in the Napoleonic Wars and disappointed that he had been too young to take part. *The Warrior's Life* is his meditation on war and the strange existence of a soldier. It is illustrated with autobiographical anecdotes and suffused with a sense of glories past. It consists of three short stories, 'Laurette, or, The Red Seal', 'An Evening at Vincennes', and 'The Malacca Cane', interspersed with essays.

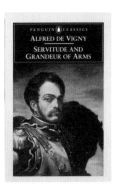

1996 *Servitude and Grandeur of Arms*
2013 Reissued as *The Warrior's Life*
trans. Roger Gard

Alexis de Tocqueville

1805–1859

Alexis-Charles-Henri Clérel, Vicomte de Tocqueville, was born into a monar-chist French family. He was a student of French and English constitutional history and had a legal career in the French civil service. In 1831, he was sent to the United States for nine months to prepare a report on the penal system there. He wrote *Democracy in America* instead, which secured his reputation as a political philosopher.

Democracy in America
and Two Essays on America 1835–40

Democracy in America is a monumental study of America's fledgling political system. Tocqueville proposed democracy as a possible model for France, on the condition that it is feasible to 'educate democracy, to reawaken, if possible, its beliefs, to purify its morals, to control its actions, gradually to substitute statecraft for its inexperience and awareness of its true interests for its blind instincts, to adapt its government to times and places, and to mould it according to circumstances and people'.

2003
trans. Gerald E. Bevan
intro. Isaac Kramnick

The Ancien Régime and the Revolution 1856

Tocqueville's powerful history book compares revolutionary France with the despotic monarchy that preceded it. He criticizes the venality and inequality of the *ancien régime* but equally condemns the tyranny and oppression of the post-revolution state. He raises questions about liberty, nationalism and justice that are still relevant today. This was supposed to be the first of a multi-volume study of the French Revolution, but he died before he could complete the project.

2008
trans. Gerald E. Bevan
intro. Hugh Brogan

Astolphe de Custine 1790–1857

Astolphe-Louis-Léonor, Marquis de Custine's father and grandfather were both executed during the Reign of Terror. He became a soldier and a diplomat and attended the Congress of Vienna (352) in 1815. He married, but his wife and young son both died soon afterwards. He then embarked on an openly gay relationship with an Englishman called Edward Saint-Barbe, which caused a public scandal that ended his diplomatic career and led to a brutal incident in which he was stripped, beaten and left unconscious in the mud outside Paris. He turned to literature after this trauma and produced a masterpiece of travel writing after a trip to Russia in 1839.

Letters from Russia 1839

Custine was encouraged by Balzac (308) to visit Russia, partly in response to Tocqueville (325), who predicted that the two 'great nations of the earth' would be America and Russia. Custine describes the court of Tsar Nicholas I

1991
trans. Robin Buss, 1991
intro. Catherine Merridale, 2014

and the frail tsarina, the streets of St Petersburg, the songs of the Cossacks and a walk by moonlight below the walls of the Kremlin in Moscow. The book is scathingly witty and was an instant bestseller around Europe; it was banned in Russia until the 20th century.

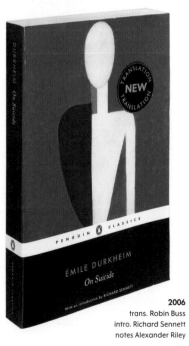

Émile Durkheim 1858–1917

Durkheim's father, grandfather and great-grandfather were rabbis. He was a pioneer of sociology and a friend of the philosopher Henri Bergson. He developed the scientific study of social phenomena and applied his ideas to religion, division of labour and suicide. He founded the first French journal of social science, *L'Année Sociologique*, and became a professor at the Sorbonne in 1906. He died of a stroke in 1917, devastated after the death of his son André, who was killed in action in 1915 in the First World War (433).

On Suicide 1897

2006
trans. Robin Buss
intro. Richard Sennett
notes Alexander Riley

Suicide was considered a personal matter before Durkheim revealed its social dimension: he observed that some social, religious and racial groups have a higher incidence of suicide and concluded that poor social integration is a major contributing factor. His ground-breaking study is organized into three sections: 'Extra-Social Factors', personal reasons why someone might take their own life; 'Social Causes and Social Types', factors that relate to society; and 'On Suicide as a Social Phenomenon in General', in which he makes practical policy suggestions for reducing the incidence of suicide.

POETRY

Inspired by Benjamin Constant's (305) doctrine of 'art for art's sake', a group of French poets emerged in the 1860s and published a journal called *Le Parnasse Contemporain*, named after Mount Parnassus, one of the supposed homes of the nine classical muses (18). The 'Parnassians' included Paul Verlaine, Lautréamont (329) and Rimbaud (329); their aim was to sculpt exquisitely wrought, emotionally detached verses about exotic subjects.

Gérard de Nerval 1808–1855

Gérard Labrunie was the son of an army doctor. He published political poetry as a teenager and translated Goethe's *Faust* (336) at the age of nineteen. He was a friend of Gautier (311), a follower of Hugo (307) and worked for a time as a ghost-writer for Dumas (312). In 1841, he suffered a breakdown and remained mentally unstable for the rest of his life. During this period, he traced his genealogy back to the Roman Emperor Nerva (59), which suggested his *nom de plume*. Confined to a sanatorium in Passy, Nerval described his madness in *Aurélia*, based on Dante's *Vita Nuova* (84). His last days were spent as a vagrant on the streets of Paris; on the morning of 26 January 1855, he was found hanged in the Rue de la Vieille-Lanterne. For Baudelaire (328), Nerval was one of the few writers who remained, even in death, 'forever lucid'.

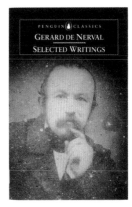

1999
trans. Richard Sieburth

Selected Writings 1839–55

Nerval blurred the boundary between dream and reality, poetry and madness, autobiography and fiction. This selection of his writings is organized into sections such as 'Shadow Selves', 'Unreal Cities' and 'Dream/Life'. It features his haunting novella *Sylvie*, which Proust considered his masterpiece; *Aurélia*; his visionary sonnets, 'The Chimeras'; and his fables 'The King of Bedlam' and 'Pandora'. When Dumas (312) read the latter, he concluded that his friend had gone completely insane.

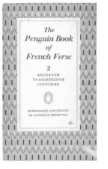

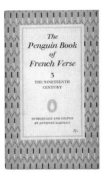

1961 Penguin Poets
● ed. Brian Woledge

1958 Penguin Poets
● ed. Geoffrey Brereton

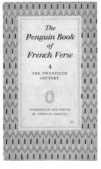

1957 Penguin Poets
● ed. Anthony Hartley
—
These four parallel text editions were published in a single volume in 1975.

1959 Penguin Poets
● ed. Anthony Hartley

1990 *French Poetry*
1992 Reissued as *The Penguin Book of French Poetry*
trans. William Rees

THE PENGUIN BOOK OF FRENCH POETRY 1820–1950

Rees organizes his anthology to reflect the major literary movements of 19th- and early 20th-century France: Romanticism, featuring Vigny (325), Hugo (307), Nerval, Musset (311), Gautier (311) and Baudelaire (328); the Parnassians, Mallarmé, Verlaine, Lautréamont (329) and Rimbaud (329); Symbolism; Lyricism; Cubism; Surrealism; and 'Négritude'. Poems are presented in the original French, with accompanying prose translations.

Charles-Pierre Baudelaire

1821–1867

Charles-Pierre Baudelaire's father died when he was six, and he hated his young mother's second husband, Lieutenant-Colonel Aupick. He rebelled at school and was expelled, despite coming second in a national Latin verse competition. He fell in with bohemian friends, so his parents sent him on a long sea voyage to Calcutta. When he came back, he set up on the Île Saint-Louis in Paris and returned to his dandyish debt-ridden artistic lifestyle. He was greatly influenced by Edgar Allan Poe (408), whom he saw as a 'twin soul'. Baudelaire suffered a stroke on a visit to Belgium in 1866 and was semi-paralysed and mute for the final year of his life.

Selected Writings on Art and Literature

1845–63

Before he published his poetry, Baudelaire was better known as a cultural critic. This selection includes reviews of Delacroix and Ingres exhibitions and essays on Poe (408), Flaubert (313) and Gautier (311).

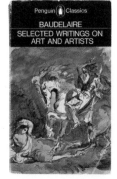

1972 *Selected Writings on Art and Artists*
1992 Reissued as *Selected Writings on Art and Literature*
● trans. P. E. Charvet

Selected Poems

1857–69

Baudelaire published his poems under the title *Les Fleurs du Mal*, 'The Flowers of Evil'. Most of his unsettling, sensuous verses are about sex and death, and he was immediately prosecuted for indecency. Six poems were removed for the next edition, and were not reinstated in France until 1942. *Les Fleurs du Mal* had a profound effect on Baudelaire's contemporaries: 'You have found a way to rejuvenate Romanticism,' wrote Flaubert (313). 'Your *fleurs du mal* shine and dazzle like stars,' wrote Victor Hugo (307).

1961 Penguin Poets
● trans. Francis Scarfe

1975 Penguin Poets
● trans. Joanna Richardson

1995
trans. Carol Clark
—
Clark's selection presents Baudelaire's verse in the original French alongside prose translations; it also includes a number of prose poems, which Baudelaire called *Le Spleen de Paris*.

THE PENGUIN BOOK OF THE PROSE POEM
from Baudelaire to Anne Carson 19th–21st centuries

'The oxymoronic name captures the complex nature of a beast bred to challenge conventional assumptions about what poetry is and what it can do,' write the poets Brian Clements and Jamey Dunham. Prose poetry has a long history, from Baudelaire, Lautréamont (329) and Rimbaud (329) to Oscar Wilde (244), Gertrude Stein (429) and Seamus Heaney; but the genre has really exploded in the third millennium, with works such as *Citizen* by Claudia Rankine, *Loop of Jade* by Sarah Howe and *Measures of Expatriation* by Vahni Capildeo. This landmark anthology traces the history of this major emerging genre.

2018
ed. Jeremy Noel-Tod

Lautréamont 1846–1870

Isidore-Lucien Ducasse was born in Montevideo in Uruguay, the son of a French diplomat. He took his *nom de plume*, 'Le Comte de Lautréamont', from one of Eugène Sue's (311) Byronic heroes. He came to France to complete his education and died during the siege of Paris at the age of 24. According to his editor A. Lacroix, he wrote 'only at night, sitting at his piano. He would declaim and work out his sentences accompanying his prosopeias by chords thumped out on the piano.'

Maldoror *and* Poems 1868–9

Les Chants de Maldoror is a surreal hallucinatory prose poem in six cantos, which Lautréamont called a 'bitter fruit'. The depraved Maldoror meets angels and gravediggers, hermaphrodites and prostitutes, lunatics and creepy children. It is delirious, erotic and blasphemous. 'May it please heaven,' writes Lautréamont, 'that the reader […] find his rugged and treacherous way across the desolate swamps of these sombre and poison-filled pages.' This edition also includes his aphoristic prose *Poesies*, for which he reworked Pascal (172), La Rochefoucauld (172), Dante (84), Kant (180) and La Fontaine (155). 'Plagiarism is necessary,' he says. 'It is implied in the idea of progress.' When *Poésies* was published privately it was not given a price; each customer chose what to pay for it.

1978
trans. Paul Knight

Arthur Rimbaud 1854–1891

Jean-Nicolas-Arthur Rimbaud began writing poems as a child. He twice ran away from his provincial home in Charleville, fleeing to Paris during the Franco-Prussian War. In 1872, he travelled to London with his lover, the poet Paul Verlaine, where they drank and argued. Rimbaud set down his bleary vision of the city in prose poems, which form his final work, *Illuminations*. At the age of 21, Rimbaud abandoned poetry: he worked as a mercenary in the Dutch East Indies, as a clerk for a travelling circus, as a quarry foreman in Cyprus and as a trader in Ethiopia. He died in his late thirties.

Selected Poems and Letters 1869–75

Rimbaud sought 'the unknown' in his poetry through the 'reasoned disordering of all the senses', chiefly by means of drugs and alcohol. The prose poems in *A Season in Hell* (*Une Saison en Enfer*) are considered his highest achievement and had a strong influence on the Symbolists, the Dadaists and the Surrealists. He was a prolific letter writer, and half this volume is devoted to his letters, many of which were written from Ethiopia.

2004
trans. Jeremy Harding &
John Sturrock

Rimbaud
SELECTED VERSE
WITH AN INTRODUCTION
AND PROSE TRANSLATIONS BY
OLIVER BERNARD

THE PENGUIN POETS

7'6

1962 Penguin Poets
• trans. Oliver Bernard

Italy

Italian literature in the 19th century was written in relation to the *Risorg-imento*, the 'Resurgence', the process by which the Italian peninsula transformed from a collection of kingdoms and city-states at the time of the Congress of Vienna (352) in 1815 to the united Kingdom of Italy in 1871. Romanticism (191) found expression through the literary journal *Conciliatore*, established in Milan in 1818. Amongst the staff was the novelist and nationalist Alessandro Manzoni, who used his increasingly political and realist novels to promote a unified Italian language and a blossoming sense of Italian nationalism.

2013
trans. Kathleen Baldwin,
Richard Dixon, David Gibbons,
Ann Goldstein, Gerard Slowey,
Martin Thom & Pamela Williams
ed. Michael Caesar & Franco
D'Intino
—
This is the first complete English translation of the *Zibaldone*, created by the Leopardi Centre at Birmingham University.

Giacomo Leopardi 1798–1837

Giacomo Taldegardo Francesco di Sales Saverio Pietro Leopardi was Italy's first and greatest modern poet. Born in the Papal States, the son of a nobleman with gambling debts, he suffered from con-genital illness throughout his life. He was a philosopher and a phi-lologist and is now considered one of the most radical and anguished thinkers of the 19th century.

Canti 1818–32

Leopardi reworked his *Canti*, 'Songs', several times: he thought of the book as a 'reliquary' for his ideas. The tone of the 41 verses varies dramatically, from personal elegies to political statements, philosophical satires and sepulchral songs.

2010
trans. Jonathan Galassi

Zibaldone
The Notebooks of Leopardi
1820–37

This sprawling, philosophical commonplace book is a *zibaldone*, a 'hodgepodge'. It is con-sidered one of the greatest books of the 19th century, a salmagundi of original aphorisms, trains of thought, shifting religious convictions and fascinating responses to the widely varied books that Leopardi read throughout his life.

Alessandro Manzoni 1785–1873

Alessandro Francesco Tommaso Antonio Manzoni was born near Lake Como. He married Henriette Blondel, a Swiss Protestant banker's daughter. They both became practising Catho-lics and moved to Milan in 1810, where Manzoni wrote poetry, historical plays and his masterpiece, *The Betrothed*. Manzoni was given a state funeral when he died and Giuseppe Verdi wrote his famous *Requiem* to honour the first anniversary of his death.

The Betrothed 1827

Set in northern Italy, during the Spanish occu-pation of the late 1620s, *I Promessi sposi* is the story of two young lovers, Renzo and Lucia, who are prevented from marrying by the tyrant Don Rodrigo, who wants Lucia for himself. They flee and are separated, facing many dangers and adventures. Along the way they are assisted by a variety of unusual characters including Gertrude, the enigmatic Nun of Monza, the irascible Padre Cristoforo and a great robber baron, sinisterly known as 'the Unnamed'. The novel was a mile-stone in establishing a unified Italian language.

1972
trans. Bruce Penman

Ippolito Nievo 1831–1861

Nievo was born in Padua in 1831, when it was still controlled by Austria. He joined Garibaldi and his Thousand in 1860 and produced prolific quantities of poetry, fiction and journalism in support of the Risorgimento (330). He died a few months before his own 30th birthday, when his ship sank in the Tyrrhenian Sea.

Confessions of an Italian 1857–8, pub. 1867

Carlo Altoviti, an old man, recalls with amused nostalgia the tumultuous events of his life, from his eccentric boyhood in the castle of Fratta in Venice to Napoleon's conquest of Italy, Carlo's passionate love for the capricious Countess Pisana and Italy's grand move towards unification. It is the 'one nineteenth-century Italian novel which has that charm and fascination so abundant in foreign literatures', wrote Italo Calvino. It is considered the most important novel of the Risorgimento.

2014
trans. Frederika Randall
intro. Lucy Riall

Giovanni Verga
1840–1922

Verga was a Sicilian author who used money intended for his university education to self-publish his first novels. He went on to develop a naturalistic style focused primarily on character and dialogue. D. H. Lawrence (288) translated several of his works into English.

Cavalleria Rusticana
and Other Stories 1874–83

'Cavalleria Rusticana', 'Rustic Chivalry', is the story that formed the basis for Mascagni's opera of the same title. It describes a young man's triumphant return home from the army, only to discover that his beloved is engaged to another man. Also included in this selection are 'Nedda', a story about the struggles of a poor olive picker, and 'The She-Wolf' and 'Black Bread', about Sicilian peasant life.

1973 *Little Novels of Sicily*
● trans. D. H. Lawrence (288)

1999
trans. G. H. McWilliam

Gabriele d'Annunzio 1863–1938

General Gabriele D'Annunzio, Prince of Montenevoso and Duke of Gallese, published his first collection of poems at the age of sixteen. As well as being the author of Decadent novels (266), poetry and plays, he was a charismatic journalist, a fighter pilot and a politician. He founded the short-lived Regency of Carnaro in the city of Fiume, with himself as duce. After he was literally defenestrated in 1922, however, he retired to the shores of Lake Garda, where he inhabited an eccentric hillside estate replete with a relic room, an amphitheatre and a full-sized decommissioned naval cruiser, which he positioned among the trees.

2013
trans. Lara Gochin Raffaelli
intro. Alexander Stille

Pleasure 1889

Andrea Sperelli is an exquisitely handsome serial seducer, who crafts his life as a work of art. He is simultaneously attracted to a beautiful young widow, Elena, and the pure, virginal Maria, and attempts to pursue both at once in a risky game of lust and deceit. D'Annunzio was inspired by Huysmans's *Against Nature* (320) and Wilde's *Picture of Dorian Gray* (245).

The Netherlands

At the end of the 18th century, the Dutch Republic was split apart by revolution, invaded by France and annexed into Napoleon's French empire. The United Kingdom of the Netherlands was formed after the French defeat at Waterloo (207), and lasted for fifteen years until fractious internal divisions led to Belgium seceding in 1830. The Dutch had established themselves as a major trading nation over the previous two centuries and, despite losing some oversees territories during this tumultuous period, they continued to exert extensive colonial control over large regions of India and southeast Asia, especially the Dutch East Indies, now Indonesia.

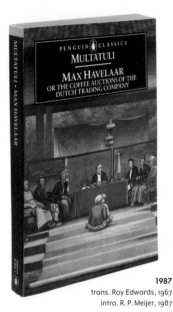

Multatuli 1820–1887

Eduard Douwes Dekker was the son of a Dutch sea captain, who left home at eighteen to join the Dutch East Indian civil service in Indonesia. He rose through the ranks, though he began to find the brutalities of colonial rule detestable. He resigned in 1856 and spent the following years wandering Europe in poverty, attempting to improve the situation for the Javanese and to earn a living by writing. His pen name 'Multatuli' comes from the Latin *multa tuli*, 'I have suffered much'.

Max Havelaar 1860
or, The Coffee Auctions of a Dutch Trading Company

Max Havelaar is a Dutch civil servant in Java who longs to release the island from the tyranny and hypocrisy of the colonial coffee trade. His idealism, however, ultimately leads to his downfall. This damning exposé caused a Europe-wide scandal when it was first published in the Netherlands. It led to welfare reforms in the Dutch colonies and continues to inspire the Fair Trade movement today. The Indonesian novelist Pramoedya Ananta Toer called it 'the book that killed colonialism'.

1987
trans. Roy Edwards, 1967
intro. R. P. Meijer, 1987

Vincent Van Gogh 1853–1890

Vincent Willem Van Gogh was born in the Netherlands, but spent much of his life in France, funded by his brother Theo. He worked in Paris, where he met Gaugin, Toulouse-Lautrec and Seurat, but many of his greatest paintings were made in the Provençal landscape around Arles. He cut off his ear after threatening Gaugin with a razor, and shot himself on 27 July 1890 at the scene of his last painting, *Wheatfield with Cows*.

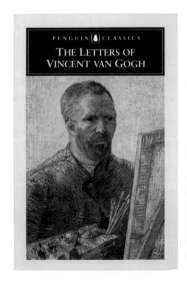

The Letters 1872–90

'Van Gogh's letters […] are one of the greatest joys of modern literature,' wrote the *Washington Post*, 'not only for the inherent beauty of the prose and the sharpness of the observations but also for their portrait of the artist as a man wholly and selflessly devoted to the work he had to set himself to.' This edition presents a selection of the letters, accompanied by Van Gogh's originally line drawings and linked by short biographical passages.

1997
trans. Arnold Pomerans
ed. Ronald de Leeuw

Spain

Spanish authors embraced the Realist movement that originated in France in the 1850s. Writers such as Benito Pérez Galdós produced lengthy objective novels that attempted to document a 'history of the present'.

1984
trans. John Rutherford

Leopoldo Alas 1852–1901

Alas was raised in Oviedo, the capital of Asturias in northern Spain. He was Professor of Roman Law at Oviedo University and Spain's most influential literary critic, writing under the pseudonym 'Clarín' (the 'Bugle').

La Regenta 1884–5

Ana Ozores is *la regenta*, 'the judge's wife', married to a retired magistrate and she is, like Madame Bovary (314) desperate to escape the stifling monotony of her life. She seeks fulfilment in religion and adultery and finds herself torn between the ministrations of a powerful cathedral canon, Don Fermín de Pas, and the advances of a dashing womanizer, Álvaro Mesía.

Emilia Pardo Bazán 1851–1921

The Countess Emilia Pardo Bazán was born into a wealthy Galician family and read voraciously as a child. At sixteen she married a law student, but the marriage was unhappy and they separated discreetly. She published her first novel in 1879 and went on to write eighteen more, as well as over 500 short stories and essays and travelogues. She became a prominent feminist and a professor of literature at Madrid University.

1990
trans. Paul O'Prey &
Lucia Graves

The House of Ulloa 1886

The Ulloa family is falling apart. Father Julián Alvarez is sent to the remote country estate to order the affairs of Don Pedro, Marquis of Ulloa, but his ineffectual attempt to reform the household's corruption and moral decadence leads eventually to tragedy.

Benito Pérez Galdós 1843–1920

Galdós was born on the Canary Islands and moved to Madrid at nineteen. He translated Dickens's *Pickwick Papers* (211) before writing a series of nationalistic novels covering the previous hundred years of Spanish history. He was also a prolific playwright and a republican politician. In his final years, he went blind and struggled financially, partly because he was supporting multiple former mistresses and his children by them.

Fortunata and Jacinta 1886–7
Two Stories of Married Women

Galdós's masterpiece revolves around a young man-about-town and the fierce jealousy between his wife Jacinta and his mistress Fortunata. The latter was based on a woman whom Galdós first met drinking a raw egg in a Madrid tenement, which is also how Juanito meets Fortunata. This sprawling novel, which embraces a huge cast of characters across all echelons of society, has been historically sidelined in the Anglophone world perhaps because of its frank descriptions of breastfeeding, sexuality, swearing and indoor urination, but many now consider it on a par with the work of Dickens (210), Balzac (308) and Tolstoy (376).

1973
• trans. Lester Clark

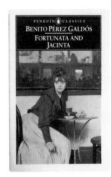

1988
trans. Agnes Moncy Gullón, 1986

Central &
Eastern Europe

GOETHE · THE SORROWS OF YOUNG WERTHER

ISBN 0 14
04.4503 X

D 74

Goethe

D 74

GOETHE · ITALIAN JOURNEY

140442332

L 12

GOETHE FAUST

L 12

GOETHE FAUST · PART TWO

L 93

GOETHE ELECTIVE AFFINITIES

140442421

GOETHE · MAXIMS AND REFLECTIONS

GOETHE · TIECK · FOUQUÉ · BRENTANO: ROMANTIC FAIRY TALES

SCHILLER THE ROBBERS & WALLENSTEIN

ISBN 0 14
044.3681

FRIEDRICH SCHILLER On the Aesthetic Education of Man

PENGUIN CLASSICS

SCHILLER · MARY STUART

ISBN 0 14
04.4711 3

D 54

Hölderlin

D 54

Germany

Germany was an association of independent states for much of the 19th century, loosely aligned under the 'German Confederation'. The kingdom of Prussia and the Austrian Empire were the two most powerful, but there were 37 others including the kingdoms of Bavaria, Saxony, Hanover and the grand duchies of Hesse and Saxe-Weimar-Eisenach. After the Franco-Prussian War of 1870–71, however, in which France was comprehensively defeated, the minister president of Prussia, Otto van Bismarck, acted decisively to unify the region. On 18 January 1871, in the Hall of Mirrors at the Palace of Versailles, princes from all the German states proclaimed Wilhelm I of Prussia the emperor of Germany, *Kaiser* of a new German Empire, albeit one that excluded Austria (352).

FICTION

On 1 April 1777, in Leipzig, a play by Maximilian Klinger was staged called *Sturm und Drang* ('Storm and Stress'). This drama about the American War of Independence (397) lent its name to a literary movement that opposed 18th-century rationalism and foregrounded emotional turmoil and subjective individuality, out of which grew Romanticism (190). The quintessential *Sturm und Drang* narrative is Goethe's *Sorrows of Young Werther*, in which the tormented protagonist is driven to violence through broiling introspection.

Johann Wolfgang von Goethe 1749–1832

Goethe studied in Leipzig, where he developed an interest in the occult, and Strasbourg, where he was first introduced to Shakespeare (134) and began writing essays and verses. His play *Götz von Berlichingen* made his name in 1773 and established him as the centre of the *Sturm und Drang* movement. He moved to live at the court of Karl August, Duke of Saxe-Weimar-Eisenach, where he held various government positions. After ten years, he made a formative journey around Italy, which influenced his plays *Iphigenie auf Tauris* (1789) and *Torquato Tasso* (1790), and on his return to Weimar he directed the state theatre, mentored Friedrich Schiller (338), married his long-standing mistress Christian Vulpius, and worked on botany and scientific theories of anatomy and colour.

The Sorrows of Young Werther 1774

Goethe wrote this international bestseller in six weeks at the age of 24. Inspired by his own infatuation with Charlotte Buff and the death of his friend Karl Wilhelm Jerusalem, he describes a sensitive, romantic young artist, Werther, who falls in love with the sweet-natured Lotte, who is betrothed to another. Increasingly tormented by his fruitless passion, Werther spirals into despair. Goethe later said that he 'shot his hero to save himself', overcoming his own suicidal obsession through the process of writing. This short epistolary novel acquired an instant cult following and could be said to have instigated the Romantic movement in Europe. Werther became the archetypal figure of the tragic tortured lover.

PENGUIN CLASSICS

JOHANN WOLFGANG VON GOETHE

THE SORROWS OF YOUNG WERTHER

1989
trans. Michael Hulse

1964
● trans. David Luke

2005
trans. David Luke, 1999

Selected Poetry 1774–1831

Goethe's autobiographical poetry reveals his interior world. It founded a movement in German poetry known as *Innerlichkeit* ('introversion'), of which a later exponent was <u>Heinrich Heine</u> (342). Goethe's intimate verses were set to music by <u>Mozart</u> (187), Beethoven, Schubert and Berlioz. Perhaps his most famous line is the opening to his poem about Italy:

> *Kennst du das Land, wo die Zitronen blühn?*
> Do you know the land where the lemons grow?

Italian Journey 1786–8, pub. 1816–7

Goethe suffered a crisis in 1786 and left Weimar abruptly, escaping the burden of administrative work and the agonies of unrequited love. He travelled south to Venice and on to Rome, Naples and Sicily, writing prolific letters and diaries. This travelogue opens with the Latin tag *Et in Arcadia ego*, 'Even in <u>Arcadia</u> (43), there am I'. It describes the people, art and history of the lands through which he travelled, as well as the plants, geology and landscape. 'Some journeys – Goethe's was one – really are quests,' write Auden and Mayer in the introduction to their translation. '*Italian Journey* is not only a description of places, persons and things, but also a psychological document of the first importance dealing with a life crisis which, in various degrees of intensity, we all experience somewhere between the ages of thirty-five and forty-five.'

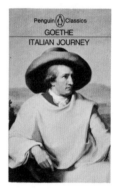

1970
trans. W. H. Auden & Elizabeth Mayer, 1962

Faust 1808, 1832

Known as *Das Drama der Deutschen* ('*the* drama of the Germans'), this two-part verse tragedy is considered Goethe's magnum opus and perhaps the greatest work of German literature. Based on the medieval myth revisited by <u>Christopher Marlowe</u> (133), the devil Mephistopheles, initially disguised as a poodle, offers to grant Dr Faust's every earthly wish, in exchange for his everlasting soul. In *Part One*, Faust strikes the deal and woos the lovely Gretchen; in *Part Two*, he scales the heights of politics and power and summons the beautiful Helen of Troy back from the dead, his arrogance and self-delusion leading inexorably towards destruction. Goethe finished *Part Two* in the year of his own death. The Serbian electrical engineer <u>Nikola Tesla</u> (357) was obsessed with Faust. He learned it off by heart and was reciting it when he had an epiphany, which led to his idea of a rotating magnetic field and ultimately his invention of alternating current.

1949 *Part One*
● trans. Philip Wayne
—

'Wayne has sent me the enclosed drawing of Goethe's head for the cover of his Faust,' wrote <u>E. V. Rieu</u> (17) to the production department: 'I hope you will like and use it. By the way, it is by Mrs Wayne, who rather expects a fee.' Dorrit Wayne was paid two guineas for her portrait on the 1949 edition. This was the first Penguin Classics cover in which <u>Jan Tschichold</u> (xiii) was involved and it is unique in that the roundel was printed on an unusual dustwrapper; the cover itself is plain brown.

1959 *Part Two*
● trans. Philip Wayne

2005 *Part I*
trans. David Constantine
pref. A. S. Byatt

2009 *Part II*
trans. David Constantine
pref. A. S. Byatt

Elective Affinities 1809

The 'principle of elective affinities' was the theory that certain chemicals are naturally drawn to one another. In this novel, the aristocratic marriage between Eduard and Charlotte is thrown into adulterous disarray when they are visited by Eduard's handsome friend, the Captain, and Charlotte's young ward Ottilie. Goethe describes the double displacement reaction that takes place:

> Imagine an *A* intimately united with a *B*, so that no force is able to sunder them; imagine a *C* likewise related to a *D*; now bring the two couples into contact: *A* will throw itself at *D*, *C* at B, without our being able to say which first deserted its partner, which first embraced the other's partner.

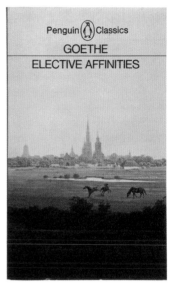

1978
trans. R. J. Hollingdale

1998
trans. Elisabeth Stopp
intro. Peter Hutchinson

Maxims and Reflections 1809–29

Goethe kept brief personal notes throughout his life on art, ethics, literature and natural science. Elisabeth Stopp assembles 1,413 of these reflective, aphoristic maxims in this collection drawn from his published and unpublished work. They include: 'The smallest hair casts its shadow' and 'One doesn't find frogs wherever there is water; but there is water where you hear frogs'.

Ludwig Tieck

1773–1853

Tieck was born in Berlin and wrote plays, including *Puss in Boots* (1797) and *Bluebeard* (1799). He also wrote a supernatural horror story, *The Rune Mountain* (1804), and worked on translations of Shakespeare (134) and *Don Quixote* (153).

2000
trans. Carol Tully

Friedrich de la Motte Fouqué 1777–1843

Fouqué was the son of a Prussian general and served as a soldier for many years. He wrote poetry and drama, but is best remembered for his prose romances based on Old French poems and Norse mythology.

Romantic Fairy Tales

1795–1817

Goethe, *The Fairy Tale*; Tieck, *Eckbert the Fair*; Fouqué, *Undine*; Brentano, *The Tale of Honest Casper and Fair Annie*

Goethe's 'Fairy Tale', sometimes called 'The Green Snake and the Beautiful Lily', is an allegory about the bridging of the conscious and the unconscious, featuring will-o'-the-wisps, a luminous snake, a cursed lady and four kings made of precious metals. Tieck's 'Eckbert the Fair' is a gruesome tale about a forest-dwelling couple who plumb the depths of incestuous and murderous depravity; in Fouqué's 'Undine', a water nymph falls in love, acquires a soul and experiences the pain of human suffering; and Brentano's 'Tale of Honest Casper' is the grimly tragic story of a young couple destroyed by a dogged sense of honour.

Clemens Brentano

1778–1842

Brentano belonged to a group of Romantic writers in Heidelberg. He later converted to Catholicism, lived in a monastery for six years and became the secretary to a visionary nun. His prose stories are considered among the finest Romantic *Märchen*, 'fairy tales'.

Friedrich Schiller 1759–1805

As a child, 'Fritz' Schiller wanted to become a priest; instead he studied medicine, served in the army and became a poet, a critic and the principal playwright of German classicism. He was a close friend of Goethe (335) and was deeply influenced by the philosophy of Kant (180). In his later years, he was the Professor of History at the University of Jena. His poem 'Ode to Joy' inspired the final movement of Beethoven's Ninth Symphony and is now the anthem of the European Union.

1979
trans. F. J. Lamport

The Robbers
and Wallenstein 1781, 1800

Schiller wrote his first play, *The Robbers*, when he was 21. It centres around two brothers, one of whom leads a band of merry forest-dwelling bandits while the other schemes to inherit their father's fortune and estate. In order to attend the first performance, Schiller left his regiment without permission and as a result was arrested, imprisoned and forbidden from writing. Nonetheless, he became an overnight literary sensation. The *Wallenstein* trilogy, written nineteen years later, is considered his masterpiece. The three plays, *Wallenstein's Camp*, *The Piccolomini* and *Wallenstein's Death*, follow the fortunes of the mercurial General Albrecht von Wallenstein after he rebels against Emperor Ferdinand II during the Thirty Years War (155).

2016
trans. Keith Tribe
intro. Alexander Schmidt

On the Aesthetic Education of Man
1795

Schiller's epistolary essay *On the Aesthetic Education of Man* sets out his idea of *Spieltrieb*, the 'playful impulse', a harmonious combination of Kant's *Sinnestrieb* ('sensual drive') and *Formtrieb* ('formal impulse'). Schiller describes a way of appreciating art, on which one could build a utopian society. He considered this essay the 'best thing that I have done in my life'. This volume also includes his letters to the Danish Prince Frederick Christian Von Augustenburg, in which he proposes that relaxed appreciation of great works of art could dispel revolutionary fever.

Mary Stuart 1800

This historical drama presents the last days of Mary, Queen of Scots. Mary is the play's tragic heroine, imprisoned while her devious cousin Queen Elizabeth of England deliberates over her death sentence. When Mary is eventually beheaded, Elizabeth banishes the courtiers who facilitated the execution, and others resign, leaving her isolated and alone on stage. In a 2016 production of *Mary Stuart*, directed by Robert Icke at the Almeida Theatre in London, the two lead actresses tossed a coin at the start of each performance to decide who would play Mary and who Elizabeth.

1969 *Five German Tragedies*
• trans. F. J. Lamport

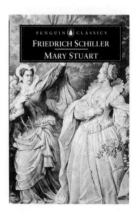

1998
trans. F. J. Lamport, 1969

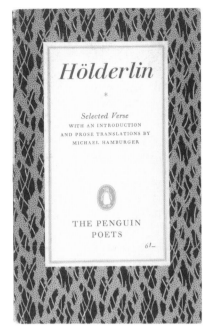

1961 Penguin Poets
1998 Penguin Classics
trans. Michael Hamburger,
1961
ed. Jeremy Adler, 1998

Friedrich Hölderlin 1770–1843

Johann Christian Friedrich Hölderlin studied at the Protestant theological seminary in Tübingen, where he became friends with the philosophers G. W. F. Hegel (345) and F. W. J. Schelling. Instead of taking holy orders he became a private tutor. He fell in love with a pupil's young mother, Susette Gontard, however, and his mind began to grow increasingly unstable. He was institutionalized briefly and was subsequently cared for by a Tübingen carpenter called Zimmer, with whom he lived for the rest of his life.

Selected Poems and Fragments
1797–1843

Hölderlin was devoted to the ideals of Classical Greece (20) and considered it his mission to instil Hellenic qualities into Germany through his writing. He wrote classical odes and epigrams addressed to Susette Gontard, hymns about cosmology and world history, and the enigmatic, fragmentary 'Canticles of Night' which anticipate the Symbolists and Surrealists.

Essays and Letters 1788–1828

Hölderlin's prose is no less intense, intelligent and perceptive than his poetry. This volume collects his complete essays, on subjects ranging from 'the concept of punishment' and 'the meaning of tragedies' to literary critiques of Homer's *Iliad* (16), Sophocles' *King Oedipus* (21) and Pindar's *Odes* (21). His letters are written to friends and family and describe his personal philosophies, ambitions, beliefs and opinions on the purpose of poetry.

2009
trans. Jeremy Adler &
Charlie Louth

Heinrich von Kleist 1777–1811

Kleist came from an old Prussian military family, but disliked the army and resigned his commission in 1799. He was extremely ambitious and also highly insecure, vacillating between frenzied enthusiasm and periods of deep melancholy. He wrote numerous plays and eight short stories. He killed his lover on the shore of the Kleiner Wannsee and took his own life at the age of 34.

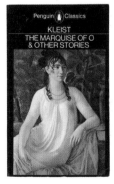

1978
trans. David Luke &
Nigel Reeves

The Marquise of O— 1810–11
and Other Stories

'The Marquise of O—' opens with the eponymous noblewoman placing an advertisement in a local newspaper, asking the unknown father of her unborn child to come forward. The plot revolves around a case of alleged rape, which happens, if it happens, during a dash: 'Then – the officer instructed the Marquise's frightened servants, who presently arrived, to send for a doctor [...]' 'Michael Kohlhaas' was much admired by Kafka; it describes an honourable man who is forced to break the law in order to see justice done. Two lovers are involved in a devastating disaster in 'The Earthquake in Chile' and 'The Beggarwoman of Locarno' is about an old woman's ghost who haunts a heartless nobleman until he goes insane.

Georg Büchner 1813–1837

Büchner was born in the grand duchy of Hesse, where he came under police investigation for his dissident activities. He fled to Strasbourg, where he studied biology, before moving to Zurich in 1836 to teach comparative anatomy at the new university. He died at the age of 23 during a typhus epidemic. Despite his short life, however, he made a profound literary impact. The writer Arnold Zweig described the short story *Lenz* as 'the beginning of modern European prose'.

Complete Plays
Lenz
and Other Writings 1831–7

Danton's Death is a fierce play about violence and the French Revolution; *Leonce and Lena* is a dark comedy about arranged marriage. The fragmentary *Woyzeck* is considered by many to be Büchner's dramatic masterpiece: a humble soldier is plagued by hellish hallucinations and murders his lover; Werner Herzog directed a film adaptation in 1979. 'Lenz' is a short story about a dramatist's descent into madness, the first literary depiction of schizophrenia; 'The Hessian Messenger' is a passionate revolutionary pamphlet, circulated clandestinely and coordinated by Büchner; and 'On Cranial Nerves' was a lecture delivered at Zurich, before his untimely death. This volume also includes his selected letters.

1993
trans. John Reddick

Johann Peter Hebel 1760–1826

Hebel was born in Basel to German parents. He was orphaned at the age of thirteen, took holy orders and spent most of his life as a teacher, eventually becoming the headmaster of his old school in Karlsruhe in southwest Germany. He wrote poems in the local dialect and stories in German for a regional almanac, which he edited himself. His work was admired by **Goethe** (335), **Tolstoy** (376) and the **Brothers Grimm** (341).

The Treasure Chest 1811

The 93 extremely short stories and snippets in *The Treasure Chest* are variously charming, humorous and sinister. Titles include 'The Mole', 'Expensive Eggs', 'The Lightest Death Sentence' and 'How a Ghastly Story was Brought to Light by a Common or Garden Butcher's Dog'. Kafka considered 'Unexpected Reunion' to be 'the most wonderful story in the world'.

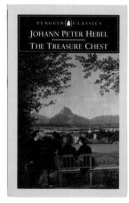

1995
trans. John Hibbard

TALES OF THE GERMAN IMAGINATION
from the Brothers Grimm to Ingeborg Bachmann
19th–20th centuries

'A streak of melancholy and depression bordering on madness unquestionably runs through the authors and tales in this book,' writes the translator Peter Wortsman. His collection of macabre, dreamlike stories covers the last 150 years of German literature. It includes the sinister 'Sandman' by E. T. A. Hoffmann (341); 'Peter Schlemiel' by Adelbert von Chamisso, in which a man sells his shadow to the Devil; 'In the Penal Colony' by Franz Kafka; the surreal 'Onion' by Kurt Schwitters; and a dark modern fairy tale, 'The Secrets of the Princess of Kagran', by Ingeborg Bachmann. All the stories express deep fears and dark truths about the human condition.

2012
trans. Peter Wortsman

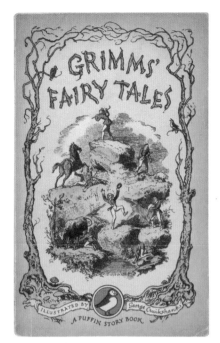

1948 *Fairy Tales*
• trans. Edgar Taylor

Jacob Grimm 1785–1863

Jacob Grimm pioneered the scientific study of the German language. With his brother he founded the multi-volume *Deutsches Wörterbuch* in 1838, the German equivalent of the *Oxford English Dictionary*, which was completed in 1961. Together they worked on studies of medieval epics and ancient German culture

Wilhelm Grimm 1786–1859

Wilhelm Grimm studied at Marburg with his brother and then they both worked as librarians in Kassel and teachers at Göttingen University. In 1837, they were dismissed by the new king of Hanover and settled in Berlin as members of the Prussian Academy of Sciences. They are best remembered for their *Kinder- und Hausmärchen*, 'Children's and Household tales', the world's most famous collection of fairy stories.

Tales 1812–58

'A fairy tale is not a text,' writes the author Philip Pullman in the introduction to his retelling of the brothers' tales. '[…] It's a transcription made on one or more occasions of the words spoken by one of many people who have told this tale. […] Like jazz, storytelling is an art of performance.' These volumes include all the most familiar tales, such as 'Rapunzel', 'Rumpelstiltskin', 'Cinderella' and 'Little Red Riding Hood', as well as many that may be less well-known, including 'The Girl with No Hands', 'Godfather Death', 'The Donkey Cabbage', 'The Boy Who Left Home to Find out about the Shivers' and the grisly 'The Mouse, the Bird and the Sausage'.

1982 *Selected Tales*
trans. David Luke

2013 *Grimm Tales*
Retold by Philip Pullman

E. T. A. Hoffmann 1776–1822

Ernst Theodor Wilhelm Hoffmann was born in Königsberg, Prussia. He swapped his middle name 'Wilhelm' for 'Amadeus', out of admiration for Mozart (187). He wanted to become a composer himself, or a painter, but instead studied law and worked in the Prussian civil service. He began writing fiction in his thirties and quickly became an influential writer of grotesque, bizarre fiction. He died of syphilis.

Tales of Hoffmann 1816–21

This selection of eight of Hoffmann's finest tales includes 'Mademoiselle de Scudery', in which Paris is plagued by a spate of jewellery robberies and gruesome deaths; 'The Sandman', beloved by Freud (353), about the sinister legend of a man who steals wakeful children's eyes; and 'The Choosing of the Bride', in which a greedy father exploits his daughter's suitors. The tales were adapted by Jacques Offenbach into an *opéra fantastique*.

1982
trans. R. J. Hollingdale
with Stella & Vernon Humphries
& Sally Hayward

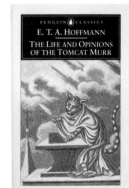

1999
trans. Anthea Bell
intro. Jeremy Adler

The Life and Opinions of the Tomcat Murr 1820–22
Together with a Fragmentary Biography of Kapellmeister Johannes Kreisler on Random Sheets of Waste Paper

Hoffmann claims to have edited the remarkable memoir of an opinionated autodidactic cat called Murr. He has also written a biography of the composer Johannes Kreisler. Unfortunately, a printer's error has allowed these two narratives to be shuffled randomly together, humorously juxtaposing the boisterous feline scholar Murr and the moody genius Kreisler. 'If the phantasmagoric *Kater Murr* were published tomorrow as the work of a young Brooklyn hipster,' wrote the critic Alex Ross in *The New Yorker*, 'it might be hailed as a tour de force of postmodern fiction.'

Heinrich Heine 1797–1856

Heine was born into a Jewish family in Düsseldorf, and was a third cousin of Karl Marx (346). He studied at the University of Berlin, where he was taught by G. W. F. Hegel (345), and in 1827 he became internationally famous for his collection of lyric verses, *Buch der Lieder*, poems from which were set to music by Robert Schumann and Franz Schubert. In 1831, he moved to Paris, inspired by the July Revolution, and he remained there for the rest of his life. His last eight years were spent bedridden and dying from lead poisoning on what he called his *Matratzengruft* ('mattress-grave'). Heine's books were burned by the Nazis in Berlin's Opernplatz in 1933; the site is now marked by a line from his play *Almansor* (1821): 'That was but a prelude; where they burn books, they will ultimately burn people as well.'

1967 Penguin Poets
1986 Penguin Classics
trans. Peter Branscombe

Selected Verse 1827–56

'The highest conception of the lyric poet was given me by Heinrich Heine,' wrote Nietzsche in *Ecce Homo* (350). Heine's poems express despair, sensuality and sweetness and often provide a commentary on contemporary political events. This selection takes poems from his *Buch der Lieder* ('Book of Songs') and *Neue Gedichte* ('New Poems') and has extracts from *Germany: A Winter's Tale* and *Atta Troll: A Midsummer Night's Dream*. The original German text is presented alongside prose translations.

The Harz Journey
and Selected Prose
1826–53

Chapter 12 of Heine's 'Ideas' reads:

> The German censors — — — — — — — —
> — — — — — — — — — — — — — — — —
> — — — — — — — — — — — — — — — —
> — — — — — — — — — — — — — — — —
> — — — — — — — — — — — — — — — —
> — — — — — — — — — — — — — — — —
> — — — — — — — — — — — — — — — —
> — — — — — — — — — — — — — — — —
> — — — — — — — — — — — — — — — —
> — — — — — — — — — — — — — — — —
> — — — — — — — — — — — — — — — —
> — — — — — — — — — — — — — — — —
> — — — — — — idiots — — — — — —
> — — — — — — — — — — — — — — — —
> — — — — — — — — — — — — — — — —
> — — — — — — — — — — — — — — — —
> — — — — — — — — — — — — — — — —
> — — — — — — — — — — — — — — — —
> — — — — — — — — — — — — — — — —
> — — — — — — — — — — — — — — — —
> — — — — — — — — — — — — — — — —

1993 *Selected Prose*
2006 Reissued as *The Harz Journey and Selected Prose*
trans. Ritchie Robertson

Richard Wagner 1813–1883

Wagner was a conductor, composer and librettist from Leipzig who believed that opera should be a *Gesamtkunstwerk*, a 'total work of art': a single magnificent artistic expression that synthesizes images, poetry, music and drama. Most of his life was spent in political exile and poverty. He has since developed a fanatical posthumous following. In *The Birth of Tragedy* (348), Nietzsche saw Wagner's music as the 'rebirth' of European culture. W. H. Auden called him 'perhaps the greatest genius that ever lived'.

The Ring of the Nibelung 1848–74

Wagner spent most of his adult life writing the libretto and composing the music for the four operas of his *Ring* cycle: *The Rhinegold*, *The Valkyrie, Siegfried* and the *Götterdämmerung* (*The Twilight of the Gods*). He drew on old myths from the *Elder Edda* (93), *The Saga of the Volsungs* (93) and the *Nibelungenlied* (82) to describe a vast mythological universe peopled with trickster gods, dwarves, Rhinemaidens, giants and the fearsome Valkyries, female deities of battle. At the centre of the cycle is an enchanted ring, created by Alberich the dwarf. The cycle takes fifteen hours to perform.

2018 Clothbound Classics
trans. John Deathridge

2003
trans. David Luke, 1997
Scots trans. Gilbert McKay, 1997

Eduard Mörike
1804–1875

Mörike was born in the electorate of Württemberg and never left. He studied theology and became a Protestant pastor. He retired in 1842 and spent the rest of his life writing and avoiding the fame his writing brought him.

Mozart's Journey to Prague
and a Selection of Poems 1824–63

Mörike's masterpiece is his novella *Mozart's Journey to Prague* (187), about the great composer and his wife Constanze travelling to Prague for the opening of *Don Giovanni* and accidentally becoming guests of honour at a wedding party. This edition also includes a selection of Mörike's poetry, some of which are written in vernacular *Knittelver*, translated here into Scots. They are presented with facing page translations.

Franz Xaver von Schönwerth
1810–1886

Schönwerth was a Bavarian lawyer and courtier, at one time the personal secretary to the Crown Prince Maximilian. In the 1850s, he travelled around the forests and mountains of northern Bavaria, recording and collecting folk tales. Some of these he published in *From the Upper Palatinate: Customs and Legends* (1857–9), but this represented a fraction of his research: the vast majority of the stories seemed to have vanished into thin air.

The Turnip Princess
and Other Newly Discovered Fairy Tales

'In 2009,' writes Erika Eichenseer, 'after searching for many years, I made the exhilarating discovery that there were about five hundred fairy tales among the Schönwerth papers stored almost like buried treasure in the municipal archive of the city of Regensburg.' Eichenseer, an expert on fairy tales, sifted 30 boxes of lost stories and compiled this selection of 70 tales. They are violent, dark and subversive; titles include 'King Goldenlocks', 'Prince Dung Beetle', 'In the Jaws of the Merman' and 'The Singing Tree'.

2015
trans. Maria Tatar
ed. Erika Eichenseer
ill. Engelbert Süsse

Theodor Fontane 1819–1898

Fontane was a Prussian pharmacist who moved to London to work as a journalist for the Prussian embassy. He was taken prisoner in 1870 during the Franco-Prussian War while working as a reporter in France. Later he settled in Berlin and published his first novel at the age of 58. He is especially remembered for his sensitive portrayal of women.

On Tangled Paths
1888

In *Irrugen, Wirrungen*, a beautiful orphaned seamstress and a handsome cavalry officer become involved in an impossible love affair across the classes in late 19th-century Berlin. Their genuine love for each leads to their undoing.

2013
trans. Peter James Bowman, 2010

2013
trans. Hugh Rorrison & Helen Chambers, 2010

No Way Back 1891

Charming Count Holk is delighted when he is summoned to the court of a Danish princess in a castle by the sea. The flirtatious Ebba von Rosenberg makes his sober home life and his marriage to the pious Countess Christine seem unbearably dull, but there may be no way back if he makes a rash decision.

Effi Briest
1894–5

Naïve Effi marries the austere Baron von Innstetten, who is twice her age. Bored and isolated in their spooky house, she finds comfort in a brief liaison with the womanizing Major Crampas. Years later, however, her half-forgotten affair resurfaces. *Effi Briest* is considered Fontane's masterpiece. 'I have been haunted by it,' writes the author Hermione Lee, '[…] as I am by those novels that seem to do more than they say, to induce strong emotions that can't quite be accounted for.'

1967
● trans. Douglas Parmée

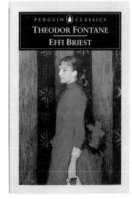

2000
trans. Hugh Rorrison & Helen Chambers, 1995

For First World War fiction, turn to p.436

NON-FICTION

The fomenting politics of 19th-century Germany produced a flurry of philosophical writing. Initially German Idealism emerged in reaction to Kant (180). Represented by G. W. F. Hegel (345), the Romantic Idealists saw inner experience as paramount: we rely on perceptions; whether external objects exist is uncertain. Arthur Schopenhauer (348) went further: he believed that our perception of the world is merely a representation of our inner will. Therefore, he argued gloomily, our emotional and sexual desires are by definition fundamentally unachievable. A group of Hegel's followers known as 'the Young Hegelians' included Karl Marx (346), who synthesized German Idealism with French socialism and set out his revolutionary economic theories in *Capital* (347). Friedrich Nietzsche (348) was an early follower of Schopenhauer, but renounced his mentor's pessimism for a more positive philosophy, developing the potent concept of 'will to power'.

Alexander von Humboldt
1769–1859

Friedrich Wilhelm Heinrich Alexander von Humboldt was born in Berlin and studied botany, literature, electromagnetism and archaeology at the universities of Frankfurt, Göttingen and Hamburg before working for the Prussian Department of Mines. A large inheritance allowed him to travel around Central and South America between 1799 and 1804 after which he settled in Paris and wrote an encyclopaedic, 30-volume account of his voyage. He was chamberlain to Friedrich Wilhelm III and councillor of state to Friedrich Wilhelm IV. Having finished his travelogue, he embarked on a comprehensive survey of creation, called *Kosmos* (1845–59).

Personal Narrative of a Journey to the Equinoctial Regions of the New Continent 1814–25

Humboldt was the first person to describe human-induced climate change, to analyze Aztec art, to observe reverse polarity in magnetism and to investigate why America is called America. 'He alone gives any notion of the feelings which are raised in the mind on first entering the Tropics,' wrote Darwin (269). Various species have been named after Humboldt, including a penguin, a squid, a hog-nosed skunk and a variety of bladderwort. This edition presents a selection from his voluminous masterwork.

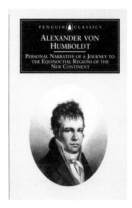

1995
trans. Jason Wilson
intro. Malcolm Nicolson

1968 Pelican Classics
1982 Penguin Classics
trans. J. J. Graham, 1908
intro. Anatol Rapoport 1968

Carl von Clausewitz 1780–1831

Carl Philipp Gottfried von Clausewitz was a Prussian soldier who served in the Rhine campaigns against the French before enrolling at the Berlin Academy and studying Kant (180). He helped to reform the Prussian army before leaving to serve in the Russian army and fighting at the Battle of Borodino (367). He was later appointed director of the military academy in Berlin.

On War 1816–30, pub. 1832

Clausewitz's landmark treatise on the art of warfare was unfinished at his death and his wife published the manuscript posthumously. He starts by asking, 'What is War?' and goes on to describe its dangers, purpose and techniques, speculating on the 'genius' required by a successful commander. He discusses the science of military theory and elements of strategy, including boldness, perseverance, surprise and geometry. He defines war as 'nothing but a continuation of political intercourse, with a mixture of other means'.

Georg Wilhelm Friedrich Hegel 1770–1831

G. W. F. Hegel was born in Stuttgart and studied at the Tübingen theological seminary, where he befriended Hölderlin (339). He finished his masterwork, *The Phenomenology of Spirit*, at the University of Jena on 14 October 1806, during the Battle of Jena, an engagement that be believed marked 'the end of history'. His Idealist philosophy was enormously influential: it inspired Marx (346) and justified 19th-century European theories of nationalism.

Introductory Lectures on Aesthetics 1823–9, pub. 1835

Hegel's lectures were delivered at the University of Berlin and his notes published posthumously by friends and former pupils. Despite living contemporaneously with Goethe (335), Mozart (187) and Schiller (338), Hegel was highly pessimistic about the state of the arts, which, in his view, have been deteriorating steadily since the high point of classical Greece. He sets out a theory of art to rival Aristotle's *Poetics* (30). Heidegger called these lectures 'the most comprehensive reflection on the essence of art that the West possesses'.

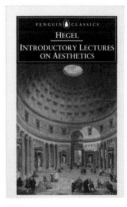

1993
trans. Bernard Bosanquet, 1886
intro. Michael Inwood, 1993

Karl Marx 1818–1883

As a student in Bonn and Berlin, Marx was strongly influenced by <u>Hegel</u> (345) but he reacted against his Idealist philosophy and developed his own theory of historical materialism. He traced the state of society to its economic foundations and held that societies move forward through class struggle: he recommended armed revolution on the part of the proletariat. In Paris, in 1844, he met <u>Friedrich Engels</u> (347) and the pair formed a lifelong partnership. After taking part in a failed democratic revolution in Germany in 1848, Marx fled to England as a refugee and remained there for the rest of his life. He wrote for the New York *Tribune* and played a leading role in the International Working Men's Association. His tomb in Highgate Cemetery in London is surmounted by a huge bust replete with his monumental beard.

1975 Pelican Marx Library
1992 Penguin Classics
trans. Rodney Livingstone & Gregor Benton
intro. Lucio Colletti
—
The design of the Pelican Marx Library editions was inspired by the bold colours and grainy, collage photography of Soviet Constructivism from the 1920s.

Early Writings 1843–4

In the years before he met Engels, the young Marx produced an astonishing number of papers and essays which reveal his early views on alienation, the state, representative government and human nature. This selection includes his critique of <u>Hegel</u> (345), his essay 'On the Jewish Question', and his early economic analysis, 'Economic and Philosophical Manuscripts'.

1967 Pelican Books
• trans. Samuel Moore, 1888
intro. A. J. P. Taylor, 1967

2002
trans. Samuel Moore, 1888
intro. Gareth Stedman Jones, 2002

The Communist Manifesto 1848

'A spectre is haunting Europe – the spectre of Communism.' After four years of collaboration with <u>Engels</u> (347), Marx condensed their ideas into this extraordinary pithy document: a summons to the working classes and a vision of a society without private property or states. The slim manifesto itself fills only 40 pages of this edition, yet those pages have formed the theoretical basis of political systems in Russia, China, Cuba and eastern Europe. In 1998, on the 150th anniversary of the manifesto's publication, the *Socialist Register* described it as 'the single most influential text written in the nineteenth century'. 'Let the ruling classes tremble at a Communistic revolution,' writes Marx. 'The proletarians have nothing to lose but their chains. They have a world to win.'

2007
ed. James Ledbetter
fwd. Francis Wheen

Dispatches for the New York *Tribune*

Selected Journalism of Karl Marx

1852–63

As well as being a great political philosopher, Marx was also a ruthless and incisive foreign correspondent. For nine years, he wrote for the New York *Tribune*, based in Britain, on topics as various as the opium trade in China, revolutionary activities around the world, British rule in India and slavery in America. The inexpensive *Tribune* was one of the most widely circulated newspapers in America at the time, with a print run of 50,000.

1973 Pelican Marx Library
1993 Penguin Classics
trans. Martin Nicolaus
notes Ben Fowkes

Grundrisse

Foundations of the Critique of Political Economy

1857–8, pub. 1939

Marx saw *Grundrisse* (literally 'ground works') as the first scientific elaboration of communist theory. These draft notebook entries develop the arguments laid out in *The Communist Manifesto* and lay the foundations for the ideas that would come to dominate his masterpiece, *Capital* (347).

1976 Pelican Marx Library
1990 Penguin Classics
trans. Ben Fowkes
intro. Ernest Mandel
—
All three volumes were published by Penguin as part of the Pelican Marx Library, in association with the *New Left Review*, before they joined Penguin Classics.

1978 Pelican Marx Library
1992 Penguin Classics
trans. David Fernbach
intro. Ernest Mandel

1981 Pelican Marx Library
1991 Penguin Classics
trans. David Fernbach
intro. Ernest Mandel

Capital
A Critique of Political Economy
1867–83, pub. 1867–94

Marx's masterwork is an incisive critique of private property and the social relations it generates. He argues that capitalism will cause ever-increasing divisions in wealth and welfare and predicts its abolition and replacement by a system involving common ownership and means of production. Engels called *Capital* 'the Bible of the working class'. Only the first volume, subtitled *The Process of Production of Capital*, was published in Marx's lifetime. It is the cornerstone of Marxian economics and has been as influential as Smith's *Wealth of Nations* (179) and Keynes's *General Theory* (301). The subsequent two volumes were edited by Engels and published posthumously.

Friedrich Engels 1820–1895

Engels was the son of a German textiles manufacturer and worked as his father's business agent in Manchester, where he became fascinated by Robert Owen (208) and the issues facing the new urban proletariat. After meeting Marx (346) in 1844, Engels spent the rest of his life collaborating with him, providing him with funds and assisting him in his research. He enjoyed poetry, fox-hunting and hosting regular late-night parties on Sunday evenings.

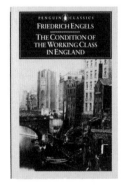

1987
trans. Florence Kelley-Wischnewetzky, 1886
ed. Victor Kiernan, 1987
intro. Tristram Hunt, 2009

The Condition of the Working Class in England 1845

Written when Engels was only 24, this powerful polemic describes the appalling conditions of the working class in Manchester and Salford. He describes overcrowded slums, abject poverty, child labour, sexual exploitation, dirt, drunkenness and death. The work was not translated into English until 1886, so it had a delayed effect on English-speaking readers.

The Origin of the Family, Private Property and the State 1884

'The modern individual family is founded upon the open or concealed domestic slavery of the wife.' Engels's provocative analysis of the family from prehistory to Victorian times argues that the monogamous household is a relatively recent societal construct, linked closely to private property ownership, in which women are forced into the roles of slave and prostitute.

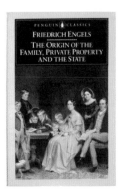

1986
trans. Alec West, 1972
● ed. Michèle Barrett, 1986

2010
trans. Alec West, 1972
intro. Tristram Hunt, 2010

Arthur Schopenhauer
1788–1860

Schopenhauer was the son of a Danzig tradesman. In 1805, his father took his own life and Arthur sold the family business and enrolled at a grammar school. He studied medicine and science at Göttingen University before switching to philosophy. After graduating, he wrote *The World as Will and Representation* (1818), an exposition of his philosophy, which has become one of the keystones of modern thought. He was greatly admired by Tolstoy (376), Nietzsche and Jorge Luis Borges.

Essays and Aphorisms 1851

In 1851, Schopenhauer published *Parerga und Paralipomena* ('Appendices and Omissions'), a collection of essays and aphorisms, from which this selection is taken. His essays cover topics such as 'The Suffering of the World', 'Affirmation and Denial of the Will to Live' and 'Suicide'. His paragraph-long aphorisms are organized thematically under subjects such as 'Ethics', 'Aesthetics' and 'Books and Writing'.

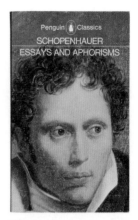

1970
trans. R. J. Hollingdale

Friedrich Nietzsche
1844–1900

'I am no man,' wrote Nietzsche in *Ecce Homo* (350), 'I am dynamite.' He studied philology at Bonn and Leipzig and became the youngest ever Professor of Classical Philology at Basel University when he was only 24. During the Franco-Prussian War of 1870–71, he volunteered as an ambulance orderly and as a result contracted diphtheria, dysentery and possibly syphilis. Ill health forced him to retire from public life and so he devoted himself to writing philosophy until, in 1889, he collapsed on the streets of Turin after attempting to protect a horse from being flogged. He spent the last decade of his life in a state of mental and physical paralysis, cared for by his mother and his sister Elisabeth. Yeats (267) saw Nietzsche as the intellectual successor to William Blake (192).

1993
trans. Shaun Whiteside
ed. Michael Tanner

The Birth of Tragedy 1872
Out of the Spirit of Music

Nietzsche's first book is a compelling argument for the necessity of art, drawing on Greek tragedy (20), the philosophy of Schopenhauer and the music of Wagner (343), to whom the book is dedicated. He describes a dialectic between Apollonian ordered beauty and Dionysian primal ecstasy: he sees all great artistic works, especially Greek tragedies, as a synthesis of these states, revealing the reality of suffering but simultaneously providing consolation for it.

Human, All Too Human 1878

'*Human, All Too Human* is the monument of a crisis,' writes Nietzsche: it was the first work to emerge after his health had declined and he abandoned his academic career. It also marks a turning point in his thinking. He rejects the German Romanticism of Wagner (343) and Schopenhauer and favours French Enlightenment thinkers such as Voltaire (175). In 638 numbered aphorisms, he ranges across subjects as diverse as art and arrogance, boredom and passion, science, vanity, women and youth.

1994
trans. Marion Faber & Stephen Lehmann, 1984

The Joyous Science 1882

Nietzsche's title comes from the traditional Provençal expression *gai saber*, the 'gay science' referring to the skill of writing poetry; and this book contains more poetry than any of his other works. Nietzsche starts to outline his theory of eternal recurrence, developed further in *Thus Spoke Zarathustra*, and he first formulates his famous pronouncement that 'God is dead'.

2018
trans. R. Kevin Hill

Beyond Good and Evil
Prelude to a Philosophy of the Future 1886

In this polemical development of *Zarathustra*, Nietzsche seeks to smash the traditional Christian notions of truth and sin, which characterize in his view a 'slave morality', and aims to move beyond the concepts of good and evil. He presents this 'prelude to a philosophy of the future' with fierce energy, urging his readers to impose their own 'will to power' on the world.

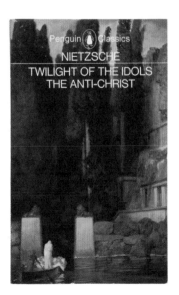

1973
trans. R. J. Hollingdale, 1973
intro. Michael Tanner, 1990

Thus Spoke Zarathustra
A Book for Everyone and No One 1883

Nietzsche conceived this book while standing next to a pyramidal block of stone on the shore of Lake Silvaplana in Switzerland; the rock is still there and is now known as the 'Nietzsche Stone'. The book describes the travels and speeches of the 'immoralist' Zarathustra, the namesake of the founder of Zoroastrianism. Zarathustra expands on ideas that Nietzsche first presented in *The Joyous Science*: that events recur eternally, that God is dead and that humans are evolving towards the *Übermensch*. I have 'given mankind the greatest gift that has ever been given it,' wrote Nietzsche about *Thus Spoke Zarathustra*.

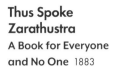
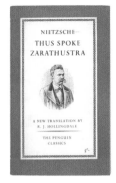

1961
trans. R. J. Hollingdale

On the Genealogy of Morals
A Polemic 1887

This work consists of three essays, which anatomize the concepts of good, bad and evil, and reveal humankind as a species that has transformed from barbarous creatures into civilized beings able to feel remorse, compassion and love. Through that process, however, we have destroyed instinct and freedom and elevated the life-denying virtues of poverty, humility and chastity.

2013
trans. Michael A. Scarpitti
intro. Robert C. Holub

Twilight of the Idols
and The Anti-Christ 1889, 1895

The subtitle of *Twilight of the Idols* is *How to Philosophize with a Hammer*. Written in a single week, this is a 'grand declaration of war' on received philosophy, psychology and theology. *The Anti-Christ* is Nietzsche's final attack on institutional Christianity, in which he identifies himself as a <u>Dionysian artist</u> (348) grappling with the Apollonian Christ.

1968
trans. R. J. Hollingdale, 1968
intro. Michael Tanner, 1990

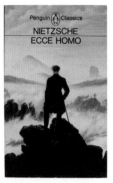

1979
trans. R. J. Hollingdale, 1979
intro Michael Tanner, 1992
—
The cover image is *The Wanderer above the Sea of Fog* by Caspar David Friedrich (191).

1977
trans. R. J. Hollingdale

Ecce Homo 1888, pub. 1908
How One Becomes What One Is

Ecce Homo ('Behold the Man') includes chapters called 'Why I Am So Wise', 'Why I Am So Clever' and 'Why I Write Such Good Books'. Nietzsche finished writing his simultaneously self-aggrandizing and self-mocking autobiography just weeks before he collapsed into insanity. He discusses his heroes, Schopenhauer (348), Wagner (343), Socrates (26) and Christ (4), defends and elaborates on each of his major works and promises a forthcoming, cataclysmic 'revolution of all values'. The last chapter is called 'Why I Am a Destiny' and he signs off, *'Dionysos against the Crucified. . .'.*

The Will to Power pub. 1901
Selections from the Notebooks of the 1880s

After Nietzsche's death, his anti-Semitic sister Elisabeth Förster-Nietzsche assembled and edited his unpublished notebooks and published them under the title *The Will to Power*. She presented the material to fit her own German nationalist ideologies and has been accused of obfuscating Nietzsche's true intentions and even creating a 'historical forgery'. On the basis of this volume, Nietzsche became associated with Fascism and Nazism, an association that Elisabeth encouraged. When she died in 1935, Hitler attended her funeral.

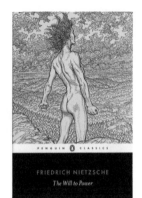

2017
trans. R. Kevin Hill &
Michael A. Scarpitti

A Nietzsche Reader 1878–88

Replicating Nietzsche's characteristic aphoristic format, R. J. Hollingdale assembles a representative selection of extracts from across Nietzsche's career, organized to express all of his key ideas: the death of God, the will to power, the *Übermensch* and eternal recurrence and he also includes sections on morality, psychology and aesthetics.

Max Weber 1864–1920

Maximilian Karl Emil Weber was a sociologist who attempted to develop a systematic methodology for cross-cultural studies. For much of his life, he lived as an independent scholar, accepting only brief professorships at the universities of Vienna and Munich. He was a member of the German delegation at the Paris Peace Conference after the First World War (433). His masterpiece, *Economy and Society*, was published posthumously.

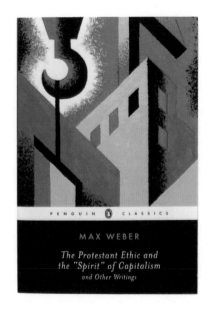

The Protestant Ethic and the 'Spirit' of Capitalism
and Other Writings 1905–10

Weber rejects Marx's (346) explanation of capitalism as an expression of historical materialism and instead draws a connection between the growth of modern capitalism and Calvinist values of hard work and duty. This volume also includes his 'rejoinders' to two of his chief critics, H. Karl Fischer and Felix Rachfahl.

2005
trans. Peter Baehr
Gordon C. Wells, 2002

Poland

Poland did not exist in the 19th century: in 1795, the Polish-Lithuanian Commonwealth, one of the largest countries in Europe, was forcibly partitioned by its three neighbours, Russia, Prussia and Austria. The country did not regain an independent identity until after the First World War (433).

The Manuscript Found in Saragossa

1805–15

This book was composed in Poland, written in French and set in Spain. It claims to be a translation of a mysterious Spanish manuscript by a Walloon named Alphonse van Worden. Alphonse is travelling to meet his regiment in Madrid, but he is detained at a roadside inn by a company of brigands, cabbalists, noblemen, coquettes, Muslim princesses and itinerant gypsies, whose interwoven stories of disguise, magic, seduction and horror he records over the course of 66 days. It is 'constructed like a Chinese box of tales', wrote Salman Rushdie. '[…] It reads like the most brilliant modern novel.'

Jan Potocki 1761–1815

Count Potocki was an aristocrat of the Polish-Lithuanian Commonwealth who was educated in Switzerland, served twice in the Polish army and spent time as a novice Knight of Malta. He spoke many languages and travelled widely throughout his life as an Egyptologist, ethnologist and occultist. He oversaw the first free press in Warsaw and became the first Polish aeronaut when he flew above the city in a hot-air balloon. His last years were plagued by depression: eventually, believing himself a werewolf, he took his own life with a silver bullet modelled on the knob of his favourite sugar-bowl.

1996
trans. Ian Maclean

Switzerland

Switzerland has four official languages, German, French, Italian and Romansch, and four corresponding branches of literature. The greatest novelist of 19th-century Switzerland was Gottfried Keller, who wrote in German and is best remembered for his autobiographical *Bildungsroman*, *Green Henry* (1850–5).

The Civilization of the Renaissance in Italy 1860

For Burckhardt, the Italian Renaissance was the crucible in which modern science, art and politics were first formed. In this landmark portrait of an era, he evokes the city-states of Florence, Venice and Rome and describes the 'development of the individual personality' in figures such as Dante (84), Alberti (119) and Michelangelo (128).

Jacob Burckhardt 1818–1897

Carl Jacob Christoph Burckhardt was a Swiss theological student before he lost his faith and devoted himself to history. He wrote an art guide to Italy and was appointed Professor of Architecture at Zurich Polytechnic. He returned to his hometown of Basel and lived there for most of his life, teaching at the university; Nietzsche (348) was one of his pupils.

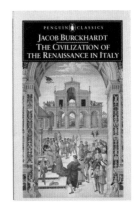

1990
trans. S. G. C. Middlemore, 1878
intro. Peter Burke, 1990
notes Peter Murray, 1990

2008
trans. Susan Bernofsky

Austria

The Empire of Austria was founded in 1804 and
emerged as one of the five great powers of Europe
during the Napoleonic Wars, alongside Britain,
France, Russia and Prussia. It hosted the Congress of Vienna in 1815 after Napoleon's defeat
at Waterloo and merged with the kingdom of Hungary to form the multicultural Austro-
Hungarian Empire in 1867. The literature of the period traditionally falls into two halves: the
pre-1848 'Biedermeier' period of heavily censored, largely apolitical works, and post-revolution
Realism, characterized by the novels of Adalbert Stifter and Marie von Ebner-Eschenbach.

Leopold von Sacher-Masoch
1836–1895

On 9 December 1869, Sacher-Masoch signed a contract with his mistress
Fanny Pistor (a.k.a. 'Baroness Bogdanoff') making him her slave for a period
of six months, with the stipulation that he should be addressed only as
'Gregor' and that she should wear fur as frequently as possible, especially
when she was feeling cruel. In 1890, Richard Freiherr von Krafft-Ebing introduced the term 'masochism' to his voluminous *Psychopathia Sexualis*.

Venus in Furs 1870

In this largely autobiographical work of philosophical
pornography, Sacher-Masoch describes a young nobleman, Severin von Kusiemski, who loves to be punished by
the merciless Wanda von Dunajew and her three African
dominatrices.

Robert Walser
1878–1956

Walser was born in Biel/Bienne in Switzerland. He left
school at fourteen and lived a precarious existence
as an inventor's assistant and a butler while writing
poems, essays, stories and three novels. After a suicide
attempt in 1929, he was committed to an asylum in
Herisau, where he remained for the rest of his life. He
spent his time gluing paper bags and sorting beans.
He told a visitor, 'I'm not here to write. I'm here to be
mad.' He died on Christmas Day after walking in the
snow. Susan Sontag described him as the literary link
between Kleist (339) and Kafka.

The Assistant
1908

Carl Tobler is an energetic but largely unsuccessful inventor who hires a poor assistant, Joseph Marti, to help him
with his ill-conceived schemes and to distract his creditors.
Marti, along with the rest of Tobler's eccentric household,
refuses to admit that Tobler is slipping towards financial
disaster. Walser wrote this brilliant semi-autobiographical
work in just six weeks as an entry for a literary competition.

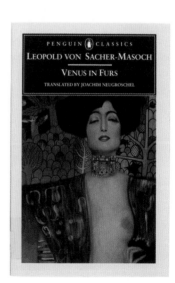

2000
trans. Joachim Neugroschel
intro. Larry Wolff

1974 Pelican Freud Library
● trans. Angela Richards

2004 Modern Classics
trans. Nicola Luckhurst
intro. Rachel Bowlby
—
Luckhurst and Bowlby's
edition includes Freud's 1908
monograph on hysteria and
bisexuality.

Sigmund Freud 1856–1939

Sigismund Schlomo Freud was born in Moravia, part of the Austrian Empire, but from the age of four he lived in Vienna, which remained his home until he was 82. His father Jakob was a Ukrainian wool merchant and a Hasidic Jew; his mother Amalia called him 'mein goldener Sigi'. Freud began his career studying the anatomy and physiology of the nervous system at the University of Vienna, but he became interested in psychology in his late twenties, and after ten years of practising clinical psychology he founded the new discipline of 'psychoanalysis'. This began as a 'talking cure' for patients but developed into a study of the human mind: Freud claimed to have identified fundamental, unconscious instincts that influence our everyday thoughts and actions and he read symbolism into dreams, objects and behaviours.

Apparently when questioned about his customary large cigar, however, he said huffily that 'a cigar is sometimes just a cigar'. In 1930, he was awarded the Goethe Prize (335) for contributions to German literary culture; in 1933, the Nazi party began burning his books. When Hitler's forces invaded Austria in 1938, Freud fled to London, where he died the following year.

Studies in Hysteria

1893–1908

The founding text of psychoanalysis was written by Freud in collaboration with his colleague Joseph Breuer. It consists of a joint introductory paper, five individual case studies of 'hysterics', an essay on theory by Breuer and one on clinical practice by Freud. For the first time, they identify hysteria with past trauma in patients' lives. Through a range of therapeutic techniques, they peel away layers of memory until, by exposing the original trauma, its pathological influence is dissipated.

Interpreting Dreams 1899

This highly influential work is Freud's masterpiece: he reveals dreams to be 'wish-fulfilments', through which our unconscious mind discloses its secret desires. Knowing this, a psychotherapist can analyse a patient's dreams and pursue their repressed memories. Freud describes many of his own dreams, as well as those of his patients, and begins to formulate his famous 'Oedipus complex' (21) and his layered theory of the mind, with its unconscious, pre-conscious and conscious realms. 'Insight such as this falls to one's lot but once in a lifetime,' he later wrote.

1976 Pelican Freud Library
● trans. Angela Richards

2006 Modern Classics
trans. J. A. Underwood
intro. John Forrester

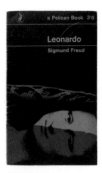

1963 Pelican Books
Leonardo
● trans. Alan Tyson
intro. Brian Farrell

1985 Pelican Freud Library
Art and Literature
● trans. Albert Dickson

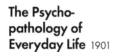

2003 Modern Classics
trans. David McLintock
intro. Hugh Haughton

The Uncanny 1899–1919

These essays all relate to the mysterious art of creativity and imagination. Freud traces artistic innovation to the intense, triangular 'family romances' of father, mother and infant. In *The Uncanny*, he uses E. T. A. Hoffmann's (341) short story 'The Sandman' to discuss the eerie feeling of confronting one's repressed impulses; *Leonardo da Vinci* is a bravura work of psycho-biography; and he draws fascinating links between literature and the art of daydreaming in an essay of 1908.

The Psycho-pathology of Everyday Life 1901

This amusing and accessible work examines 'Freudian slips', verbal mistakes that reveal our underlying anxieties. Misquoting Virgil (43), for example, may mean you're worried about your girlfriend being pregnant.

1938 Pelican Books
● trans. A. A. Brill

1975 Pelican Freud Library
● trans. James Strachey

2002 Modern Classics
trans. Anthea Bell
intro. Paul Keegan

1976 Pelican Freud Library
● trans. James Strachey

2002 Modern Classics
trans. Joyce Crick
intro. John Carey

The Joke and Its Relation to the Unconscious 1905

Why are jokes funny? Because, says Freud, like dreams (353) they satisfy our unconscious desires: they break taboos and allow us to express sexual, aggressive and playful instincts. His work doubles as a Viennese joke book, a compendium of turn-of-the-century puns, witticisms and one-liners.

The Psychology of Love 1905–31

In these essays, Freud explains how sexuality always involves semi-conscious sexual fantasies derived from 'polymorphous perverse' infantile forms of sexuality. These in turn develop into the Oedipus complex, named after the play by Sophocles (21). Feminist critics have since rejected Freud's concept of female penis envy as 'phallocentric'.

1977 Pelican Freud Library
On Sexuality
● trans. Angela Richards

2006 Modern Classics
trans. Shaun Whiteside
intro. Jeri Johnson

Mass Psychology
and Other Writings 1907–38

Freud tackles religion in these iconoclastic essays, exploring the ways in which religious identity binds a community but can also drive it towards acts of hatred. Religion is an illusion, he argues: the monotheistic God is a sublimated infantile desire for a *pater familias*, protecting us from a 'fear of nature'. Similarly, myths of the afterlife insulate us from the prospect of death.

1985 Pelican Freud Library
The Origins of Religion
• trans. Albert Dickson

2004
trans. J. A. Underwood
intro. Jacqueline Rose

The 'Wolfman'
and Other Cases
1909–18

A young Russian man had a recurring dream about wolves outside his bedroom window. After four years of therapeutic work, Freud cracked the case and completed his treatment, and the 'Wolfman' became his most famous case study. This volume also includes his other celebrated case studies of Little Hans, who was terrified of horses, and the 'Ratman', who was afraid of rats attacking his father. 'Some Character Types' draws literary comparisons from Shakespeare (134), Ibsen (363) and Nietzsche (348).

2002 Modern Classics
trans. Louise Adey Huish
intro. Gillian Beer

1977 Pelican Freud Library
Case Histories I
• trans. Angela Richards

Wild Analysis 1910–37

Freud explores the complex relationship between patient and analyst in these works, with tips on how to initiate, conduct and terminate treatment. He provides a description of patient 'transference', the projection of emotions on to the therapist, and argues compellingly that psychoanalysis is a professional, medical discipline, unsuitable for 'wild' or untrained therapists.

1962 Pelican Books
Two Short Accounts of Psycho-Analysis
• trans. James Strachey

2002 Modern Classics
trans. Alan Bance
intro. Adam Phillips

1979 Pelican Freud Library
Case Misteries III
• trans. James Strachey

2002 Modern Classics
trans. Andrew Webber
intro. Colin MacCabe

The Schreber Case 1911

In 1903, Judge Daniel Paul Schreber wrote a highly detailed memoir of his nervous illness, since diagnosed as paranoid schizophrenia: he wanted to experience sex as a woman, he thought his doctor was hypnotizing him and he believed that God was manipulating his body through supernatural 'rays'. Freud never met Schreber, but his analysis of Schreber's written narrative has become one of his most celebrated cases, revealing universal truths about psychosexual development.

The Unconscious 1911–39

These essays chart Freud's concept of the 'unconscious' mind and the mechanism by which we repress unwanted thoughts and feelings, feelings that nonetheless continue to exert a powerful influence on our behaviour and sexual proclivities.

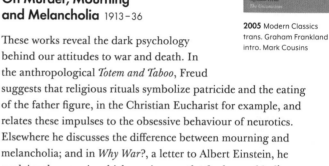

2005 Modern Classics
trans. Graham Frankland
intro. Mark Cousins

On Murder, Mourning and Melancholia 1913–36

1938 Pelican Books
Totem and Taboo
• trans. A. A. Brill

2005 Modern Classics
trans. Shaun Whiteside
intro. Maud Ellmann

These works reveal the dark psychology behind our attitudes to war and death. In the anthropological *Totem and Taboo*, Freud suggests that religious rituals symbolize patricide and the eating of the father figure, in the Christian Eucharist for example, and relates these impulses to the obsessive behaviour of neurotics. Elsewhere he discusses the difference between mourning and melancholia; and in *Why War?*, a letter to Albert Einstein, he explains the ways in which war is an outlet for humankind's essentially aggressive nature.

Beyond the Pleasure Principle
and Other Writings 1914–26

Freud identified two fundamental human drives: the desire for pleasure and the desire to avoid pain. But paradoxically, pleasure can also be a form of fear, a habit we repeat to mask a painful memory or the harshness of reality. In 'Beyond the Pleasure Principle', he explores the complex ways in which these drives express themselves. In other works in this volume, he refines his conception of the psyche and the psychodynamics between the id, ego and super-ego, the different levels of consciousness within the mind.

1979 Pelican Freud Library
On Psychopathology
• trans. Angela Richards

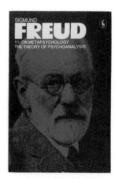

1984 Pelican Freud Library
On Metapsychology
• trans. Albert Dickson

2003 Modern Classics
trans. John Reddick
intro. Mark Edmundson

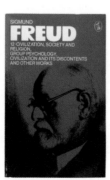

1985 Pelican Freud Library
Civilization, Society and Religion
• trans. Albert Dickson

2002 Modern Classics
trans. David McLintock
intro. Leo Bersani

Civilization and Its Discontents 1930

One of Freud's last great achievements was his diagnosis of western society in *Civilization and Its Discontents*. He argues that the hypocritical ideals of civilized society and Christian morality are impossible to uphold: they distort our natural aggressive natures into a burden of oppressive guilt and produce an innate 'death drive' that leads to war and ultimately self-destruction.

1973 Pelican Freud Library
• trans. Albert Dickson

1987 Pelican Freud Library
*Historical and Expository
Works*
• trans. James Strachey
ed. Albert Dickson

2003 Modern Classics
trans. Helen Ragg-Kirkby
intro. Malcolm Bowie

An Outline of Psychoanalysis
1933–39

In these final works, Freud looks back over his career, summarizes his revolutionary theories of the unconscious and recapitulates his therapeutic tool, psychoanalysis. *An Outline of Psychoanalysis* was his last book, which he wrote at the age of 82, as he was preparing to flee Vienna in the face of the imminent Nazi *Anschluss*, the annexation of Austria.

The Penguin Freud Reader 1899–1939

Freud wrote 'narratives that have the colour and force of fiction', said John Updike. This volume collects essential passages from across the Penguin Freud series, as well as a handful of extra translations by Shaun Whiteside, on subjects such as the 'Magic Notepad', lapses, humour and the 'Psychology of the Grammar-School Boy'. It provides an overview of the ambition and variety of Freud's writing, repositioning him as a literary phenomenon and a mind-altering reading experience.

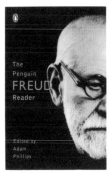

2006 Penguin Books
2008 Modern Classics
ed. Adam Phillips

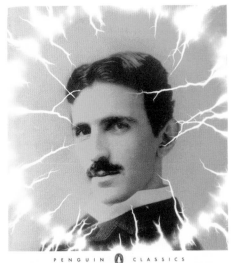

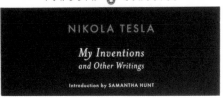

2011
intro. Samantha Hunt

Nikola Tesla 1856–1943

Tesla was born in Smiljan in the Austrian Empire, now modern Croatia. He emigrated to America when he was 28 and became a naturalized US citizen in 1891. He was a visionary electrical engineer with a photographic memory and a distaste for sleep. He invented alternating current, the magnifying transmitter, the Tesla coil and the bladeless turbine, as well as contributing the fundamental science behind the invention of the radio. He was a friend of Mark Twain (414) and nurtured a lifelong feud with Thomas Edison. He spent the last ten years of his life inside the Hotel New Yorker, wracked by phobias and spiralling obsessive-compulsive disorder. The SI unit of magnetic flux density is named in his honour, as is a leading brand of electric car.

My Inventions
and Other Writings 1893–1919

Tesla's autobiography appeared in 1919 as a series of articles in *Electrical Experimenter* magazine. It describes all his major discoveries and inventions, as well as telling the story of his Serbian upbringing, arrival in America and professional rivalries. This volume also includes articles on weaponized airships, 'the action of the eye' and harnessing the sun's energy.

Rainer Maria Rilke 1875–1926

René Karl Wilhelm Johann Josef Maria Rilke, one of the 20th century's greatest poets, was born in Prague, then part of the Austro-Hungarian Empire. He changed his name to Rainer at the suggestion of his first love, Lou Andreas-Salomé, who had trained as a psychoanalyst with Sigmund Freud (353). Rilke lived in many different places around Europe, including Russia, Spain, Germany, France and Italy; he died in Switzerland. According to one story, he was gathering roses in his garden when he pricked his finger on a thorn: the wound became infected and he never recovered.

1964 Penguin Poets
2001 Modern Classics
trans. J. B. Leishman

2012
trans. Charlie Louth
intro. Lewis Hyde

Letters to a Young Poet *and* The Letter from a Young Worker
1902–8, 1922

Between 1902 and 1908, Rilke corresponded with Franz Xaver Kappus, a young officer cadet and aspiring poet. Rilke wrote ten letters to Kappus with profound and lyrical advice on poetry, love, sex and suffering. In 1929, after Rilke's death, Kappus published the letters and they have since become a touchstone for aspiring writers and artists. This volume also includes 'The Letter from a Young Worker', Rilke's polemic against Christianity.

Selected Poems
1905–26

Rilke aimed in his poetry to express the experience of living at its most intense. This volume is a representative selection, including excerpts from his masterpieces, the mystical 'Duino Elegies', begun at Duino Castle in northern Italy and completed in 'a savage creative storm', and 'The Sonnets to Orpheus', inspired by the death of his daughter's friend Wera Knoop.

The Notebooks of Malte Laurids Brigge 1910

Rilke's semi-autobiographical and expressionist novel is about a young atheist called Malte Laurids Brigge, the last of an aristocratic dynasty, who spends his days at the library, contemplating death. Rilke's only work of fiction was inspired by the writings of Nietzsche (350) and by Jacobsen's *Niels Lyhne* (362).

2009
trans. Michael Hulse

Baroness Orczy 1865–1947

Baroness Emma Magdalena Rosalia Maria Josefa Barbara Orczy was the daughter of a Hungarian composer, and she grew up in Budapest after the formation of the Austro-Hungarian Empire in 1867. From 1880, the family lived in London, where Emma studied art, began writing short stories and married Montague MacLean Barstow, an English illustrator. In 1903, she and her husband collaborated on a play adaptation of *The Scarlet Pimpernel*, which became a long-running success and the baroness wrote a series of sequels.

The Scarlet Pimpernel c. 1900

'The Scarlet Pimpernel' is the alter ego of Sir Percy Blakeney, apparently a dull-witted English fop. In fact he is a master of disguise and a first-rate swordsman, who risks life and limb to rescue imprisoned aristocrats during the French Revolution.

1989 Puffin Classics

2018 Penguin English Library

Robert Musil 1880–1942

Musil was an Austrian mathematician, psychologist, engineer and philosopher. Having distinguished himself in the First World War (433), he devoted the rest of his life to writing. He is perhaps best known for his vast 'novel of ideas', *The Man without Qualities* (1930–43), about the decline of the Austro-Hungarian Empire seen through the eyes of a former mathematician called Ulrich. Musil was forced to emigrate from Berlin and then Vienna to escape the Nazis, who banned his books. He died, exiled and impoverished, in Switzerland.

The Confusions of Young Törless 1906

Based in part on Musil's own experiences at military school, this novella describes sadistic bullying, snobbery and homoerotic violence at an elite boy's academy. It is a dark investigation of upper-class society that foreshadows the breakdown of compassionate values in the run up to the First World War (433) and the subsequent rise of Fascism.

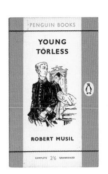

1961 Penguin Books
• trans. Eithne Wilkins & Ernst Kaiser

2001
trans. Shaun Whiteside
intro. J. M. Coetzee

Greece

After a series of revolts in the early 19th century, two civil wars and finally the decisive Battle of Navarino, Greece was liberated from almost four centuries of Ottoman Rule and the Kingdom of Greece was recognized in 1830 as an independent state. Literature of the period was written in relation to both the new spirit of Greek nationalism and the old literature of Ancient Greece (15).

C. P. Cavafy 1863–1933

Constantine Peter Cavafy was born in Alexandria, Egypt, to Greek parents. After his father's death in 1870, he moved temporarily to England, where the family business had an operation in Liverpool. He then returned to Alexandria in 1885, where he lived the rest of his life as a journalist, a civil servant and a poet. Nonetheless, E. M. Forster (284) described him as 'a Greek gentleman in a straw hat, standing absolutely motionless at a slight angle to the universe'.

1966 Penguin Poets
Four Greek Poets
• trans. Edmund Keeley & Nikos Gatsos
—
Cavafy was first published by Penguin in the 1966 anthology *Four Greek Poets*, which also featured poems by George Seferis, Odysseus Elytis and Nikos Gatsos.

Selected Poems 1897–1933

Cavafy's poems capture a rich interior world of remembered passions and imagined dialogues and often evoke historical or literary figures, such as Odysseus (17), the Emperor Nero (50) and Anna Komnene (60). They are lyrical and concise, expressing nostalgia, sensuality, morality and same-sex love through carefully chosen and enlightening metaphors.

2008
trans. Avi Sharon

Scandinavia

HANS CHRISTIAN ANDERSEN · *Fairy Tales*

KIERKEGAARD · EITHER/OR

ISBN 0 14
04.4577 3

KIERKEGAARD · FEAR AND TREMBLING

ISBN 0 14
04.4449 1

KIERKEGAARD · A LITERARY REVIEW

P44801

KIERKEGAARD · THE SICKNESS UNTO DEATH

ISBN 0 14
04.4533 1

KIERKEGAARD · PAPERS AND JOURNALS

ISBN 0 14
04.4589 7

JENS PETER JACOBSEN · *Niels Lyhne*

IBSEN · PEER GYNT

IBSEN · BRAND

ISBN 0 14
04.4676 1

IBSEN · A DOLL'S HOUSE AND OTHER PLAYS

Denmark

In 1802, the Danish philosopher Henrik Steffens gave a series of lectures describing German Romanticism (335). Thereafter Danish literature was largely inflected by the Romantic movement, until Jens Peter Jacobsen instigated Danish Naturalism with his novel *Niels Lyhne* (362).

Hans Christian Andersen 1805–1875

Andersen was the son of a shoemaker and a washer-woman, who left home at the age of fourteen to seek his fortune. He became internationally celebrated for his earthy, comic, fantastical fairy tales. Some of his stories were retellings of tales he remembered from his childhood, but many came from his own imagination, including 'The Emperor's New Clothes', 'The Little Mermaid', 'The Ugly Duckling' and 'The Snow Queen'.

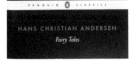

Fairy Tales

1835–72

'I seize an idea for the grown ups,' he wrote, 'and then tell the story to the little ones always remembering that Father and Mother often listen.' He wrote over 3,000 tales; this collection includes all the best known, as well as some of his later, darker stories, including 'Auntie Toothache', 'The Shadow', 'The Snowman' and 'The Ice Maiden'.

1981 Puffin Books
• trans. Naomi Lewis
1985 Penguin Books
• trans. Erik Christian Haugaard

2005
trans. Tiina Nunnally
intro. Jackie Wullschlager

Søren Kierkegaard 1813–1855

Søren Aabye Kierkegaard was born in Copenhagen, the youngest of seven children. He had a solitary and unhappy childhood before becoming a brilliant theology student and indulging in extravagant extra-curricular activities. In 1841, he broke off his engagement to the love of his life, Regine Olsen, and devoted himself instead to writing a series of major philosophical texts. His repeated attacks on the Danish Church left him scorned and isolated at the end of his life, but his reputation as an existentialist philosopher has grown steadily since.

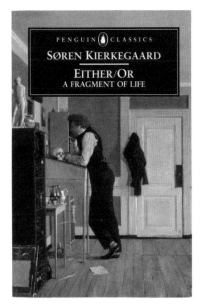

Either/Or 1843
A Fragment of Life

'Edited' by the fictional Victor Eremita, who apparently found these papers in the secret drawer of a second-hand escritoire, Kierkegaard's masterwork contrasts the writings of a fictional young man called 'A' and the letters sent to him by 'B', a moralistic judge. Through essays about Mozart (187), drama and boredom, the tussle between aestheticism and moralism reveals profound insights into the nature of Christian faith. A's contributions include the infamous 'Seducer's Diary', in which he describes the process of cynically ravishing and then rejecting a beautiful young woman.

1992
trans. Alastair Hannay

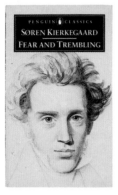

1985
trans. Alastair Hannay

Fear and Trembling 1843
Dialectical Lyric by Johannes
de silentio

This work is a discussion of the scene in Genesis (4) in which Abraham obeys God's command and prepares to sacrifice his son Isaac. It expresses Kierkegaard's deeply held belief that unreserved obedience and a fundamental 'leap of faith' are necessary in order to commit fully to one's religion.

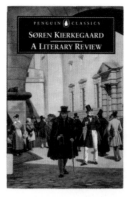

2001
trans. Alastair Hannay

A Literary Review 1846
Two Ages, a novel by the author of *A Story of Every-day Life*, published by J. L. Heiberg, Copenhagen, Reitzel, 1845

Ostensibly a lengthy appraisal of a fictional and anonymous contemporary novel, *A Literary Review* is in reality a devastating analysis of contemporary Danish society. The fictitious novel under review is called *Two Ages* and tells the story of a contemporary family in the post-revolutionary age, but Kierkegaard uses this convoluted format to present a doom-laden vision of the future, in which personal identities have been lost and ideals displaced, leaving a stark choice between empty existence and devotion to God.

The Sickness unto Death 1849
A Christian Psychological Exposition for Edification and Awakening by Anti-Climacus

Writing under the pseudonym 'Anti-Climacus', Kierkegaard presents a work of Christian existentialism which explores the concept of despair, or sin, revealing the many forms in which this bleak state can manifest itself. He recommends a way of being that eradicates despair: 'in relating to itself and in wanting to be itself', the self should be 'grounded transparently in the power that established it'.

1989
trans. Alastair Hannay

Papers and Journals 1834–55
A Selection

'Kierkegaard's journals are one of the most important sources for an understanding of his philosophy,' said Samuel Hugo Bergmann, the Israeli philosopher. Kierkegaard wrote over 7,000 pages of journal entries. This selection traces the development of his ideas and personality, freed from the mediation of his many pseudonyms and literary devices.

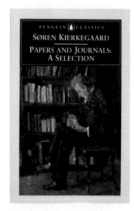

1996
trans. Alastair Hannay

Jens Peter Jacobsen 1847–1885

Jacobsen was a Danish botanist who translated Darwin's _On the Origin of Species_ and _The Descent of Man_ (270). When he was diagnosed with tuberculosis, he abandoned science and devoted his last years to literature, writing naturalistic poems, short stories and two novels.

2006
trans. Tiina Nunnally, 1990
intro. Eric O. Johannesson, 2006

Niels Lyhne 1880

Niels is an atheistic and anguished poet. Through encounters with six women, he searches for an ideal of romantic love to replace the religious faith of his childhood, but he is repeatedly disappointed and disillusioned. 'In Jacobsen,' wrote Hermann Hesse, 'we have the earliest and noblest example of an author who combines a powerful imagination and a wistfully tender nature with all the finesse of the most highly developed realism.'

Norway

1966 *Peer Gynt*
● trans. Peter Watts

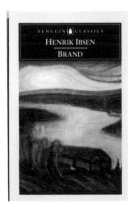

1996 *Brand*
trans. Geoffrey Hill, 1978

2016
trans. Geoffrey Hill, 1978,
rev. 2016
intro. Janet Garton, 2016

Norway began the 19th century under Danish control, before it was ceded to Sweden in 1814. Native Norwegian culture flourished, however, promoting a growing sense of a national identity, until the country finally gained its independence in 1905. The father of modern Norwegian literature is generally acknowledged to be Henrik Wergeland, a patriotic poet who became associated with the country's national day and whose grave is still decked with flowers each year. The giant of 19th-century Norwegian literature, however, was the playwright Henrik Ibsen.

Henrik Ibsen 1828–1906

Henrik Ibsen was born in the small town of Skien. Having studied medicine, he eventually became the artistic director of theatres in Bergen and Christiania, where he had a great influence on the renewal of Norwegian drama. In 1864, however, he left Norway with his wife Suzannah for a 27-year voluntary exile in Italy and Germany, during which time he wrote most of his greatest works.

Peer Gynt
and Brand 1866–7

Ibsen's reputation was established by these two verse dramas. *Brand*, which draws on Kierkegaard's *Fear and Trembling* (362), is the story of an idealistic priest who risks the lives of his wife and child in accordance with the absolute certainty of his faith. In contrast, *Peer Gynt* is the story of a semi-legendary folk hero, poet, idler and seducer, who becomes entangled in a harum-scarum plot involving kidnappings, shipwrecks and mountain trolls. Edward Grieg famously composed incidental music for the first production, which is now used as muzak at the theme park Alton Towers.

A Doll's House
and Other Plays 1877–82
Pillars of the Community; *A Doll's House*; *Ghosts*;
An Enemy of the People

After his successful verse dramas, Ibsen turned to prose
and these four plays confirmed his talent for skewer-
ing moral hypocrisy. In *A Doll's House*, Nora declares
herself 'first and foremost a human being', rejecting
definition as a wife, mother or 'doll'; in *Ghosts*, past
transgressions and scandalous secrets return to haunt
the living. The tragi-comic An *Enemy of the People* was
written in response to criticism of *Ghosts*: Ibsen shows
how community opinion can be disastrously wrong
when faced with a clear-sighted individual's inconven-
ient truth.

1965 *A Doll's House*
● trans. Peter Watts

2016
trans. Deborah Dawkin &
Erik Skuggevik
intro. Tore Rem

1950 *Three Plays*
1961 Reissued as *Hedda Gabler and Other Plays*
trans. Una Ellis-Fermor

Hedda Gabler
and Other Plays
1877–90
The Pillars of the Community; *The Wild Duck*; *Hedda Gabler*

The Pillars of the Community is the story of a corrupt ship-
owner hiding past secrets at the expense of another man's
reputation; in *The Wild Duck*,
an idealist insists on exposing truths, even though it
destroys his friend's family;
and *Hedda Gabler* is the
tragic story of a woman
trapped in a suffocating
marriage.

Ghosts
and Other Plays 1881–99
Ghosts; *A Public Enemy*;
When We Dead Wake

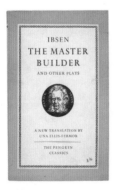

1964
trans. Peter Watts

'The plays in this book show three
very different aspects of Ibsen's work,' writes the translator
Peter Watts; 'they are a realistic drama, a comedy, and a piece
of symbolism.' Alternative translations are available in more
recent editions.

The Master Builder
and Other Plays 1892–9
The Master Builder; *Little Eyolf*; *John Gabriel Borkman*;
When We Dead Awaken

These are Ibsen's last four plays. *The Master Builde*r is a powerful but enigmatic story of overweening ambition and sexual
abuse; *Little Eyolf* is the fantastic tale of an enchanting 'Rat-
Maid' and a neglected child; in *John Gabriel Borkman*, a corrupt
bank official and his wife squabble over the future of their son;
and *When We Dead Awaken*, set in a mountain spa resort, is the
symbolic story of a sculptor who meets an old lover and subsequently rejects his own wife.

1958
● trans. Una Ellis-Fermor

2014
trans. Barbara J. Haveland &
Anne-Marie Stanton-Ife
intro. Toril Moi

Sweden

The greatest Swedish novelist of the 19th-century was Carl Jonas Love Almqvist, a defrocked priest who wrote a number of extraordinary novels, including *The Queen's Tiara* (1834) about an androgynous actor and *It Will Do* (1839) about a progressive, egalitarian marriage. Strindberg was also one of the first Swedish authors to win an international audience, as was the much-loved Selma Lagerlöf.

1958
trans. Peter Watts

August Strindberg 1849–1912

Strindberg was born in Stockholm. He wrote more than 60 plays, as well as novels, short stories, poems and political essays. He was also a painter. His novel *The Red Room* (1879) is considered the first Swedish realist novel. Always interested in ancient Scandinavian lore, Strindberg also became fascinated towards the end of his life by hypnosis, alchemy, drug-induced hallucinations and the mystic Emanuel Swedenborg. He was, in Eugene O'Neill's estimation, the 'greatest genius of all modern dramatists'.

Three Plays
1887–1900
The Father;
Miss Julia;
Easter

In *The Father*, a scientist is ruined by the paranoid suspicion that his daughter is not his child; while writing the play, Strindberg began to doubt his own children's paternity. *Miss Julia* is the story of an aristocratic woman who crosses social and moral boundaries by seducing her father's valet. Strindberg himself, the son of a servant, was married to a noblewoman, Siri von Essen. *Easter* is about a family with a criminal and mentally unstable past who come together at Easter to seek redemption.

Selma Lagerlöf 1858–1940

Lagerlöf was born in the rural Swedish region of Värmland and taught at a girl's school for ten years until she won a literary prize and became a professional author. In 1909, she was the first woman, and the first Swedish writer, to receive the Nobel Prize for Literature. Among women novelists 'of great talent and genius', wrote Marguerite Yourcenar, 'none, in my opinion, is to be placed higher than Selma Lagerlöf.'

The Saga of Gösta Berling 1891

Lagerlöf's first novel is the story of Gösta Berling, a sexually magnetic defrocked minister who comes to live on a factory estate and leads the eccentric inhabitants in a series of adventures involving wolves, snowstorms and the supernatural. A 1924 silent film adaptation of the novel launched the career of Greta Garbo, who played the Italian countess.

2009
trans. Paul Norlén
intro. George C. Schoolfield

The Wonderful Adventure of Nils Holgersson 1906–7

In 1902, Lagerlöf was commissioned to write a geography textbook for schools. She produced a wildly imaginative story of a boy, shrunk to the size of a thumb, who flies around the country on the back of a gander. His adventures incorporate various historical and geographical landmarks as well as folk stories and legends from different Swedish provinces. It is much loved in Scandinavia and the rest of Europe and has been translated into more than 30 languages.

1990 Puffin Books
• trans. Velma Swanston Howard

2017
ill. Bertil Lybeck, 1931
trans. Paul Norlén, 2016

Russia

By the beginning of the 19th century, Russia had become the largest country in the world. Peter the Great, Catherine the Great and Alexander I had expanded the empire until it stretched from Archangel on the White Sea to Azov on the Black, and from St Petersburg on the Baltic to Vladivostok on the Pacific.

With St Petersburg acting as a 'window on Europe', as Pushkin put it, Russia had become increasingly involved in European culture and politics during the 18th century, a trend that culminated in Napoleon's invasion of the country in 1812, which ultimately failed but did involve the burning of Moscow and the bloody Battle of Borodino, memorably described by Tolstoy (376).

Despite the abolition of serfdom in 1861, Russia in the 19th century was characterized by political uprisings and peasant revolts, repeatedly quashed by a series of determinedly autocratic tsars. A set of belated reforms and a 1906 constitution were too feeble, and too late, to prevent the country careering towards revolution (384).

POETRY

The 19th century is known as the 'golden age' of Russian literature, heavily influenced by European Romanticism. The greatest Russian poet was Alexander Pushkin, who inspired successive generations of poets.

Alexander Pushkin 1799–1837

The young Alexander Sergeyevich Pushkin wrote erotic poetry while working as an indolent employee of the Foreign Office in St Petersburg. In 1820, however, some of his mildly revolutionary verses were discovered and he was disgraced and exiled: he travelled through the Caucasus and the Crimea to Bessarabia, now Moldova, where his writing grew more serious and he began work on his masterpiece, *Eugene Onegin*. He was finally granted conditional freedom in 1826, after petitioning Tsar Nicholas I in person. He married the glamorous Natalya Goncharova in 1831 and died six years later, mortally wounded in a duel with his brother-in-law, one of Natalya's many admirers. He is considered the founder of modern Russian literature.

Eugene Onegin
A Novel in Verse 1825–32

Pushkin's great novel-in-verse follows the handsome, disillusioned Eugene, who abandons the glamour of St Petersburg and retreats to his country estate. There he befriends the young poet Vladimir Lensky and Lensky's fiancée Olga, whose sister Tatiana becomes infatuated with him. Eugene's cold rejection of Tatiana's affections leads them all to bitter tragedy. The verse of *Onegin* is highly complex; Vladimir Nabokov's 1964 English translation required two additional volumes to convey all the nuances of the original.

1964
● trans. Babette Deutsch
intro. Avrahm Yarmolinsky
1979
● trans. Charles Johnston
—
Charles Johnston's translation inspired Vikram Seth to write *The Golden Gate* (1986).

2008
trans. Stanley Mitchell

The Bronze Horseman 1833
and Other Poems

An equestrian statue of Peter the Great stands in Senate Square beside the River Neva in St Petersburg. In Pushkin's second great narrative poem, the lovesick Evgenii is driven mad when the Neva floods and his beloved Parasha is drowned. In his delirium he curses the bronze statue, which promptly and nightmarishly comes to life and pursues him through the streets of the city.

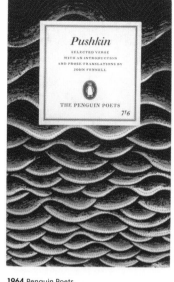

1964 Penguin Poets
Selected Verse
• trans. John Fennell

1962
trans. Rosemary Edmonds, 1958, rev. 1962

The Queen of Spades
and Other Stories
1828–41

The Negro of Peter the Great; *Dubrovsky*; *The Queen of Spades*; *The Captain's Daughter*

In 'The Queen of Spades', which has been adapted into three different operas, an officer learns of an aged countess who once won a fortune playing the 'three winning cards'. He inveigles his way into her house and demands her secret, only to be driven demented by the sinister and supernatural 'Queen of Spades'. 'The Negro of Peter the Great' is based on the life of Pushkin's own great-grandfather, a black African who was brought to Russia during the reign of Peter the Great; 'Dubrovsky' is the tale of a dispossessed young officer seeking revenge; and 'The Captain's Daughter' fictionalizes a genuine rebellion against Catherine the Great in 1773.

1982 Penguin Poets
• trans. D. M. Thomas
—
A new translation by Antony Wood is due to join Penguin Classics in 2019.

Novels, Tales, Journeys
The Complete Prose 1828–37

The works in the two other prose anthologies on this page are all included in this translation of Pushkin's complete prose, which features a number of additional fragments and sketches, including 'The Guests Were Arriving at the Dacha', 'A Novel in Letters' and 'My Fate is Decided. I Am Getting Married.'

2017
trans. Richard Pevear & Larissa Volokhonsky

Tales of Belkin
and Other Prose
Writings 1831–7

Tales of Belkin, Pushkin's first great work in prose, is a series of five interlinked stories narrated by an inscrutable Russian squire called Belkin: the best of these, 'The Shot', is about a postponed duel and ice-cold revenge. The final piece in this selection, 'A Journey to Arzrum', is Pushkin's first-hand journalistic account of the Russo-Turkish war of 1828–9.

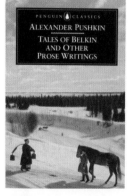

1998
trans. Ronald Wilks
intro. John Bayley

THE PENGUIN BOOK OF
RUSSIAN POETRY 18th – 21st centuries

There are such easy ways
to leave this life,
to burn to an end
without pain or thought,
but a Russian poet
has no such luck.
A bullet is more likely
to show his winged soul
the way to Heaven;
or else the shaggy paw
of voiceless terror will squeeze
the life out of his heart
as if it were a sponge.

'In Memory of Sergey Yesenin' by Anna
Akhmatova, trans. Robert Chandler

1962 Penguin Poets
• trans. Dimitri Obolensky

2015
ed. Robert Chandler, Boris
Dralyuk & Irina Mashinski
trans. Robert Chandler and
others

—

The 2015 anthology won
the English PEN Award for
Translation.

1972
trans. Ronald Wilks

FICTION

Prose fiction flourished during the Russian golden age, with virtuoso short stories and novels by the likes of Nikolay Gogol, Ivan Turgenev (374) and Nikolai Leskov (380). The three titans of 19th-century Russian fiction were Fyodor Dostoyevsky (371), Leo Tolstoy (376), both of whom are widely regarded as two of the greatest novelists of all time, and Anton Chekhov (381), internationally renowned as one of the leading dramatists of his generation. In the early 20th century, the golden age was followed by the 'silver age', populated by a new generation of writers that included Fyodor Sologub (383), Andrei Bely (384) and Ivan Bunin.

Nikolay Gogol 1809–1852

Nikolay Vasilyevich Gogol was born in the Ukraine but moved to St Petersburg and secured a minor post in an obscure government ministry. He befriended Pushkin (367) and his collections of surreal, experimental short stories soon made him famous. In 1834, he was appointed Professor of Medieval History at the University of St Petersburg, despite being totally unqualified for the position. He resigned and lived mainly abroad after 1836, claiming that distance allowed him to write about Russia with greater perspective. In 1838, he had a brief relationship with the 23-year-old Count Joseph Vielhorsky who was dying of tuberculosis. Gogol eventually died of self-starvation, complicated by typhus and severe depression.

The Diary of a Madman
The Government Inspector
and Selected Stories 1832–42

Nabokov considered *The Government Inspector* the greatest Russian play ever written: it describes the hilarious panic, obsequiousness and corruption that grips a small town when a man who claims to be a 'government inspector' arrives; Gogol is said to have got the idea from an anecdote told by Pushkin (367). 'Diary of a Madman' charts a low-ranking civil servant's descent into insanity; in 'The Nose', a bureaucrat's nose absconds from his face and begins to live a successful independent life; and the tragic 'Overcoat' is about a socially inept civil servant who devotes his life to raising the money to buy a new overcoat, only to have it stolen. 'We all come out from Gogol's "Overcoat",' wrote Dostoyevsky (371).

2005
trans. Ronald Wilks
intro. Robert A. Maguire

—

In 2005, Ronald Wilks revised and expanded his 1972 edition, adding translations of 'Nevsky Prospect', 'The Carriage' and *The Government Inspector*.

Dead Souls

A Poem 1842

In this novel, written before the abolition of serfdom in 1861, a con man arrives in a provincial town and visits the local landowners, offering to buy the names of any dead serfs who are still registered on the official census. The self-serving landowners can avoid paying tax on their dead 'souls' and Chichikov can use them to reinvent himself as a gentleman of influence. Gogol consciously emulated Dante's *Inferno* (84) and he planned to write two sequels. He worked for many years on the second instalment, burning the manuscript twice, in 1845 and again in 1852, shortly before his death.

1961
• trans. David Magarshack

2004
trans. Robert A. Maguire

Mikhail Lermontov 1814–1841

Lermontov's young mother died when he was only three years old; he was separated from his estranged father and raised on the estate of his aristocratic grandmother. After an indulgent but lonely childhood, he was made an officer in the imperial guard, but was arrested after Pushkin's death (367) for writing a satirical poem called 'Death of the Poet', and he was sent to join the army in the Caucasus. Although Lermontov was twice cited for bravery, the tsar refused to honour him with an award. In 1841, he was chal-lenged to a duel after teasing an old school friend about his dress sense and was killed on the spot. He is remembered as a Byronic (195) Romantic writer and many of his verses have been set to music. His prose inspired Dostoyevsky (371), Tolstoy (376) and Chekhov (381).

1966
• trans. Paul Foote

2009
trans. Natasha Randall
fwd. Neil LaBute

A Hero of Our Time

1840–41

This, the first major Russian novel, is a set of five loosely connected narratives about Pechorin, a young, handsome and nihilistic army officer who is bored by his life and indifferent to his many sexual conquests. It describes his adventures in the Caucasus, facing brigands, smugglers, soldiers and lovers as he feels increasingly alienated from the world. '*A Hero of Our Time* […] is indeed a portrait, but not of one person,' writes Lermontov in his preface: 'it is a portrait composed of the flaws of our whole generation in their fullest development.'

1941 Penguin Books
• ed. S. S. Koteliansky
1981 Penguin Books
• ed. David Richards

2005
trans. Robert Chandler

RUSSIAN SHORT STORIES

from Pushkin to Buida 19th–20th centuries

'The roots of literature lie in song, prayer and story,' writes Robert Chandler. 'For all its sophistication, Russian literature is relatively young and therefore closer to these roots than the literature of Western Europe.' The stories in this wide-ranging anthology include 'The Steel Flea' by Leskov (380), 'The Embroidered Towel' by Bulgakov and 'What a Pity' by Solzhenitsyn as well as examples by Gogol (369), Dostoyevsky (371), Tolstoy (376) and Chekhov (381).

Fyodor Dostoyevsky 1821–1881

Fyodor Mikhailovich Dostoyevsky was the son of a doctor. His mother died when he was fifteen and his father was murdered two years later. In 1849, he was arrested for his involvement in the 'Petrashevsky Circle', a banned-book reading group, and he was sentenced to death. At the very last minute, his sentence was commuted to hard labour in a Siberian prison camp at Omsk, where his hands and feet were kept constantly shackled. Four years later, he was forced to serve in the Russian army. He married unhappily, and in the 1860s he travelled around western Europe. He became addicted to gambling in Baden-Baden and spent his last years on the move, publishing his serial *Diary of a Writer*. Nietzsche (348) called Dostoevsky 'the only psychologist from whom I have anything to learn'.

1972
• trans. Jesse Coulson

2009
trans. Ronald Wilks
intro. Robert Louis Jackson

1988
trans. David McDuff

Poor Folk
and Other Stories 1846–8

'Poor Folk', Dostoyevsky's first literary success, is told through letters between an impoverished, elderly copy clerk and a young seamstress; their poverty eventually destroys their self-esteem and humiliates them both into misery. 'The Landlady' is about a young man who becomes obsessed with his landlady and her older husband; 'Mr Prokharchin' is a comedy about an eccentric miser; and 'Polzunkov' is a character study of an 'eternal buffoon' who hates to be laughed at.

Notes from the Underground
and The Double 1846–64

The Double is a dark fable about a timid government clerk who meets his doppelgänger. As the two men get to know each other, it becomes increasingly unclear whether the stranger is real or a facet of the narrator's splintering mind. Nabokov called it a 'perfect work of art'.

In *Notes from the Underground*, the unnamed narrator describes his tortured life as a civil servant and his refusal to perpetuate the 'anthill' of society; he has left his job and lives in a basement flat on the outskirts of St Petersburg. He painstakingly recapitulates the series of humiliations that have led to his life 'underground'.

2012
trans. Robert Chandler &
Elizabeth Chandler
with Sibelan Forrester, Anna
Gunin & Olga Meerson

RUSSIAN MAGIC TALES
from Pushkin to Platonov
19th–20th centuries

Pushkin (367) transcribed Russian folktales and prompted several subsequent collectors and the Russian folkloric tradition became a common inspiration for the literature of the next two centuries. 'Russia's vastness, and her backwardness compared with other European countries, meant that there was a much longer period during which it was possible for folklorists to study a relatively intact peasant culture,' writes Chandler. This anthology includes stories about witches, pigskins, whistling crayfish, wolves, snake-men and firebirds.

1966 *The Gambler / Bobok / A Nasty Story*
• trans. Jessie Coulson
1989 *Uncle's Dream and Other Stories*
• trans. David McDuff

2010
trans. Ronald Meyer

The Gambler
and Other Stories 1848–77

Dostoyevsky dictated 'The Gambler' in order to pay off his own roulette debts. It tells the story of Alexei Ivanovich and the destructive consequences of gambling addiction. The other stories in this volume include 'White Nights', a romance; 'A Nasty Business', about a crass civil servant; and three stories from his regular column *A Writer's Diary*: 'Bobok', about garrulous corpses; 'The Meek One', a confessional monologue; and 'The Dream of a Ridiculous Man', about a troubling dream that averts a suicide.

Netochka Nezvanova
1849

Netochka Nezvanova, 'Nameless Nobody', is a young girl dominated by her drunken stepfather, a failed musician who believes himself a genius. She is rescued by an aristocratic family, but remains an outsider, cut off from the sparkling society of St Petersburg. This was Dostoyevsky's first attempt at a novel on a grand scale, but it survives only as a fragment: it was unfinished when he was sent to Siberia (371) and he never returned to finish it. Nonetheless, it anticipates many of the themes of his later work.

1985
trans. Jane Kentish

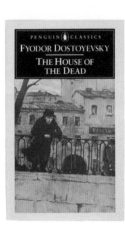

1995
trans. Ignat Avsey, 1983

The Village of Stepanchikovo
and Its Inhabitants
1859

'I have put my soul, my flesh and blood into it,' wrote Dostoyevsky to his brother Mikhail, the day before *The Village of Stepanchikovo* was published. The first novel he wrote after release from the prison camp (371) is a darkly humorous tale: when the young student Sergey is summoned to his uncle's country estate, he discovers that his uncle's household is tyrannized by a pseudo-intellectual called Opiskin. The plot takes place over 48 hours and was originally intended to be a play.

The House of the Dead 1862

The House of the Dead recreates Dostoyevsky's experiences in the Siberian labour camp (371). He describes the wooden plank beds, the cabbage soup swimming with cockroaches and the strange 'family' of desperate convicts. He incorporates his memories into the fictional story of Aleksandr Petrovich Goryanchikov, who murdered his wife and experiences a spiritual awakening during ten years at the camp.

1985
trans. David McDuff

Crime and Punishment
1866

Raskolnikov, an impoverished student, commits a hideous crime in the slums of St Petersburg. His punishment is insidious: while evading a suspicious police officer, his own conscience begins to torment him, to the point of madness. He is forced to seek redemption through the help of a compassionate prostitute, Sonya. Dostoyevsky uses the colour yellow throughout the novel to indicate moments of psychological distress.

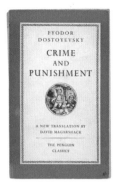

1951
● trans. David Magarshack

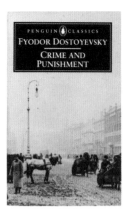

1991
trans. David McDuff

2015
trans. Oliver Ready
—
A Penguin Classics edition of *Crime and Punishment* was commissioned as early as 1946, to be translated by F. F. Seeley, but the contract was cancelled. 'Seeley is an awkward customer,' wrote Rieu (17).

1955
● trans. David Magarshack

2004
trans. David McDuff
intro. William Mills Todd III

The Idiot 1869

Dostoyevsky presents a 'positively good and beautiful man' in the gentle, Christ-like Prince Lev Nikolaevich Myshkin. He returns to Russia after several years in a Swiss sanatorium and his naïve nature wins him the nickname 'the idiot'. When he falls in love with the beautiful Nastasya Filippovna after seeing her photograph, he is unwillingly drawn into a web of blackmail, betrayal and murder. The philosopher A. C. Grayling calls it 'one of the most excoriating, compelling and remarkable books ever written; and without question one of the greatest'.

Demons
A Novel in Three Parts 1872

Inspired by a real murder case from 1869, *Demons* is the tale of a revolutionary cell run by the students Verkhovensky and Stavrogin, whose aim is to overthrow the government, disrupt society and seize power. They plan to murder a fellow conspirator in order to ensure the loyalty of the rest of the group, but their plan goes awry and has unexpected and deadly consequences. Joyce Carol Oates calls *Demons* 'Dostoyevsky's most confused and violent novel, and his most satisfactorily "tragic" work'. In the 1920s, André Gide (322) observed that it 'prophesies the revolution of which Russia is presently in the throes'.

1953 *The Devils*
● trans. David Magarshack
—
The roundel on Magarshack's edition was designed by Freda Hands. Magarshack suggested an illustration of the Gadarene swine, which for Dostoyevsky symbolized the meaning of the book, though 'I don't suppose Miss Hands will be able to get as many as 2,000 pigs into one medallion.'

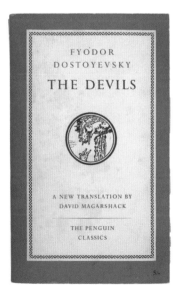

2008
trans. Robert A. Maguire
ed. Ronald Meyer
intro. Robert L. Belknap

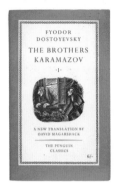

1958
● trans. David Magarshack
Published in two volumes
—
David Magarshack's
two-volume translation was
published in a single volume
in 1982.

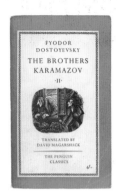

1993
trans. David McDuff

The Brothers Karamazov 1880
A Novel in Four Parts and an Epilogue

When the cruel landowner Fyodor
Karamazov is murdered, the lives of his
four sons are changed irrevocably: the
impassioned soldier Mitya is immediately
suspected of the murder; the atheist intellectual Ivan has a nervous breakdown; the
spiritual Alyosha takes it upon himself to
keep the family together; and the servant
Smerdyakov, their bastard half-brother,
suffers from epileptic fits. Everybody
is incriminated and the lines between
innocence and corruption, good and evil,
are blurred. *The Brothers Karamazov* is
considered Dostoyevsky's greatest masterpiece. Freud (353) thought it 'the most
magnificent novel ever written'. When
Tolstoy (376) died, it was the book beside
his bed.

Ivan Turgenev 1818–1883

Ivan Sergeyevich Turgenev grew up on a
country estate that was an ancestral gift
from Ivan the Terrible; he had an unhappy
childhood dominated by a tyrannical
mother. In 1843, he fell in love with Pauline
Viardot, a young Spanish singer and
they embarked on a lifelong affair: he followed her on singing tours around Europe
and lived for long periods with her and her husband. When he had an illegitimate
daughter with a seamstress, he called her Paulinette and sent the girl to be raised with
Pauline Viardot's children. After 1856, he lived mainly in Baden-Baden, where he met
Dostoyevsky (371), and Paris, where he befriended Flaubert (313).

Sketches from a Hunter's Album 1847–52

Turgenev was a keen huntsman and made his name with this collection of short stories based on
his observations and anecdotes of peasant life from his hunting trips in the forests around his
mother's country estate. He describes serfs and landowners, doctors and bailiffs, vignettes of
neglected wives, bereft mothers, love, tragedy, comedy, courage and loss. It is said to have been
the book that persuaded Tsar Alexander II to abolish serfdom in 1861; Turgenev considered it his
greatest contribution to Russian literature.

1967
trans. Richard Freeborn
—
Most of the sketches were
published in or before 1852,
but Turgenev continued
to add more stories in
subsequent editions. In 1990,
Richard Freeborn expanded
his own 1967 edition of
thirteen stories, adding a
further twelve.

Rudin 1856

Rudin is a 'superfluous man' who interferes with other people's lives
and borrows money, but he has flashes of brilliance which also inspire
love and admiration. 'Rudin is a man of genius!' insists Basistov. 'He
has enthusiasm,' admits the landowner Lezhnev; '[…] and that, believe
me – for I speak as a phlegmatic man – is a most precious quality in
our time. We have all become intolerably rational, indifferent, and
effete; we have gone to sleep, we have grown cold, and
we should be grateful to anyone who rouses us and
warms us, if only for a moment! It's time to wake up!'

1975
trans. Richard
Freeborn

1970
trans. Richard Freeborn

Home of the Gentry 1859

Lavretsky, a young nobleman, is initially dismayed when he discovers that his glamorous wife is conducting a lavish love affair. They separate acrimoniously and Lavretsky returns to his country home. There he is introduced to the quiet Liza and begins to fall in love with her, and when he reads a report of his wife's death, he begins to hope that he may have a second chance at finding happiness. But things are not all as they seem.

On the Eve 1860

On the Eve revolves around the young Elena Nikolayevna, who has three suitors: the sculptor Pavel Shubin, the philosophy student Andrei Bersyenev, and the middle-aged Kurnatovski, her father's preferred match. Elena, however, confounds them all and falls for Bersyenev's friend, the Bulgarian revolutionary Dmitri Insarov. The title is short for *On the Eve of Reform*, referring to the imminent abolition of serfdom.

1950
trans. Gilbert Gardiner

First Love 1860

The 16-year-old Vladimir Petrovich is thrilled when Princess Zasyekin moves next door with her beautiful 21-year-old daughter Zinaida. He falls deeply in love for the first time, but the capricious Zinaida has many suitors and she toys with him, rejecting his advances. His passion turns to torment when he discovers the identity of his true rival for her affections.

1977 Peacock Books
1978 Penguin Classics
trans. Isaiah Berlin, 1950
intro. V. S. Pritchett 1978

Fathers and Sons 1862

In Turgenev's most famous and enduring novel, young Arkady Petrovich returns home from college with his nihilist friend Eugene Bazarov, the first literary portrayal of a Bolshevik. Arkady's landowning father is shocked by the radical views held by his son. The novel dramatizes the universal conflict between generations and the specific social tensions of the late 1850s, the period between Russia's defeat in the <u>Crimean War</u> (431) and the Emancipation of the Serfs.

1965
• trans. Rosemary Edmonds
—
In 1955, Gilbert Gardiner was commissioned to translate *Fathers and Sons*: he wanted to call it *Fathers and Children*, a more accurate rendition of Turgenev's title. He failed to deliver his translation, however, and by 1962 Rosemary Edmonds had taken over the commission.

2009
trans. Peter Carson
intro. Rosamund Bartlett
aftwd. Tatyana Tolstaya

Spring Torrents 1872

In this semi-autobiographical novel, Dimitry Sanin stops in Frankfurt on his way home to Russia after a tour of Italy. There he falls in love with the wholesome Gemma, who works in her parents' patisserie. Besotted, he decides to sell his Russian estates and settle with Gemma in Germany, but when he meets a potential buyer, the fascinating Madame Polozov, he finds himself drawn into a darker and more dangerous infatuation.

1980 trans. Leonard Schapiro, 1972
—
The serene face on the cover is a detail from a painting of Judith by Cristofano Allori; in her left hand she holds the dripping, severed head of Holofernes.

Leo Tolstoy 1828–1910

Count Leo Nikolayevich Tolstoy led a dissipated life of gambling, drinking and womanizing before joining an artillery regiment in 1851 and fighting in the Crimean War (431). In 1856, he resigned his commission and returned to his vast family estate at Yasnaya Polyana, 125 miles south of Moscow, where he spent the rest of his life. He married Sofya Behrs in 1862 and they had thirteen children over fifteen years. He studied various theories of education and established an innovative school for peasant children on the estate. He became internationally famous for his stories, novels and political writings. At the age of 82, oppressed by his own reputation and alienated from his wife, he fled his home in the middle of the night 'in order to live out my last days in peace and solitude'. He died within a week, in the small railway station of Astapovo. He is considered by many to be the greatest of all novelists. 'When literature possesses a Tolstoy,' wrote Chekhov (381), 'it is easy and pleasant to be a writer; even when you know you have achieved nothing yourself and are still achieving nothing, this is not as terrible as it might otherwise be, because Tolstoy achieves for everyone. What he does serves to justify all the hopes and aspirations invested in literature.'

LEO TOLSTOY

Childhood, Boyhood, Youth

Childhood
Boyhood
Youth 1852–6

In his old age, Tolstoy dismissed this autobiographical trilogy as an 'awkward mixture of fact and fiction'. Nonetheless, these novellas present a charming portrait of a young man, Nikolenka, as he gradually matures and becomes aware of his position in the world, and they provide a fascinating insight into Tolstoy's own early years.

1964
● trans. Rosemary Edmonds

2012
trans. Judson Rosengrant

How Much Land Does a Man Need?
and Other Stories 1855–86

The Woodfelling; Two Hussars; How Much Land Does a Man Need?; Where Love Is, God Is; What Men Live By; Neglect a Spark and the House Burns Down; The Two Old Men; The Raid; A Prisoner of the Caucasus

'All over Europe, where the futility of war and nationalism, and Capitalism and Socialism and greed and violence, is never more in evidence,' wrote A. N. Wilson in 1993, 'men and women are continuing to ask themselves what men live by. If we can give Tolstoy's answer – Love – then we shall survive. Otherwise, we shall simply continue to destroy ourselves with all the very efficient means at our disposal.' This selection of short stories includes early tales inspired by Tolstoy's military service and later works concerned with society and spirituality. Many of these translations by Ronald Wilks have been incorporated into subsequent selections.

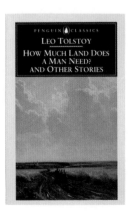

1993
trans. Ronald Wilks
intro. A. N. Wilson

The Cossacks
and Other Stories 1852–1904
The Cossacks; *Sevastopol Stories*; *Hadji Murat*

Tolstoy spent several years in the army, which had a profound effect on his writing. *The Cossacks* describes the young Olenin, who comes to despise civilized Russian life after spending time with the wild Cossack people; the *Sevastopol Stories* are a set of three pieces based on Tolstoy's first-hand experience of the siege of Sevastopol (1854–5) during the Crimean War (431); and *Hadji Murat*, one of Tolstoy's greatest short works, published posthumously, describes a mighty warlord of the Caucasus, torn by conflicted loyalties.

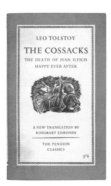

1960
• trans. Rosemary Edmonds

1986 *The Sebastopol Sketches*
trans. David McDuff

2006
trans. Paul Foote, 1977
trans. David McDuff, 1986, 2006
intro. Paul Foote, 2006

1983
• trans. David McDuff

2008
trans. Paul Foote, 1977
trans. David McDuff, 1983, 2008
intro. Donna Tussing Orwin, 2008

The Kreutzer Sonata
and Other Stories 1859–98
Family Happiness; *The Kreutzer Sonata*; *The Devil*; *Father Sergius*

All four stories in this selection describe different forms of physical desire. 'Family Happiness' follows a young couple through courtship and passion to disillusionment and finally a happily married life; 'The Kreutzer Sonata', which was banned in 1890, has strangers on a train discussing sex, suspicion and murder; in 'The Devil', published posthumously, a young man is irresistibly drawn to an attractive peasant woman, with whom he had an affair before his marriage; and 'Father Sergius' follows a desperate man who becomes a soldier, a monk, a hermit and a beggar in an attempt to quash the temptations of the flesh.

The Death of Ivan Ilyich
and Other Stories 1852–1911
The Raid; *The Woodfelling*; *Three Deaths*; *Polikushka*; *The Death of Ivan Ilyich*; *After the Ball*; *The Forged Coupon*

During Tolstoy's spiritual crisis (379), he believed he encountered Death itself, and all these stories deal with death in one way or another. *The Death of Ivan Ilyich*, perhaps Tolstoy's greatest novella, describes a high-court judge facing a terminal illness; 'Three Deaths' juxtaposes the last moments of an aristocrat, a peasant and a tree; and 'After the Ball', 'The Woodfelling' and 'The Raid' are about soldiers and the brutal violence of a military life.

2006 Red Classics
• trans. Anthony Briggs

2008
trans. David McDuff, 1983, 2004
trans. Ronald Wilks, 1993
trans. Anthony Briggs, 2006, 2008
intro. Anthony Briggs, 2008

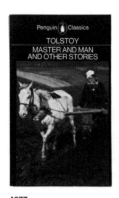

Master and Man
and Other Stories 1856–95

Two Hussars; Strider; God Sees the Truth But Waits; A Prisoner of the Caucasus; What Men Live By; Neglect a Spark and the House Burns Down; The Two Old Men; The Three Hermits; How Much Land Does a Man Need?; Master and Man

These humorous, touching and experimental stories are drawn from the full breadth of Tolstoy's career. 'What Men Live By' features an angel who descends to earth to learn the three rules of life; 'The Two Hussars' contrasts a gallant, dashing father with his mean-spirited son; and 'Master and Man' is the poignant story of a merchant battling through a blizzard with his long-suffering servant.

1977
• trans. Paul Foote

2005
trans. Paul Foote, 1977
trans. Ronald Wilks, 1993, 2005
intro. Hugh McLean, 2005

War and Peace 1863–9

War and Peace is 'not a novel, even less is it a poem, and still less an historical chronicle', wrote Tolstoy in 1868: he saw his vast masterwork as an epic in prose, a vast tapestry, describing Russia's Napoleonic Wars and incorporating 580 characters, from aristocrats to peasants, landowners, soldiers and even Napoleon himself, as well as the Russian tsar. It is one of the grandest and longest novels ever written. Tolstoy's working title was *1805*, because the book opens in that year, at a glittering party in St Petersburg, where the conversation is dominated by the prospect of war. Goncharov (380) considered *War and Peace* the Russian *Iliad* (16) and Turgenev (374) called it 'one of the most remarkable books of our age'.

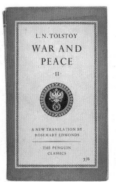

1957
• trans. Rosemary Edmonds
Published in two volumes
—
Rosemary Edmonds's
two-volume translation was
published in a single volume
in 1982.

2007
trans. Anthony Briggs, 2005
aftwd. Orlando Figes, 2005

Anna Karenina
A Novel in Eight
Parts 1873–9

'All happy families are alike; each unhappy family is unhappy in its own way.' Countess Anna Arkadyevna Karenina is beautiful, wealthy and popular, but she is married to an older government official and feels that her life is empty. Then she meets the fiery young Count Vronsky and embarks on a scandalous and self-destructive love affair which sends shockwaves rippling through Russian high society. Her story is contrasted with that of the landowner Konstantin Levin, in some ways a self-portrait of Tolstoy, who toils alongside his estate workers and pines for Anna's sister-in-law Princess Kitty. Dostoyevsky (371) called *Anna Karenina* 'flawless as a work of art'. 'We are not to take Anna Karenina as a work of art,' said Matthew Arnold (272), 'we are to take it as a piece of life. A piece of life it is.'

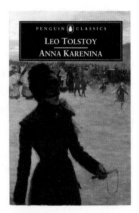

1954
• trans. Rosemary Edmonds

2001
trans. Richard Pevear & Larissa
Volokhonsky, 2000
pref. John Bayley, 2003

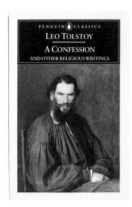

1987
trans. Jane Kentish

A Confession
and Other Religious Writings 1879–1908

A Confession; *What Is Religion and of What Does Its Essence Consist?*; *Religion and Morality*; *The Law of Love and the Law of Violence*

A Confession is a searingly honest account of the spiritual crisis Tolstoy experienced in the 1870s, during which he began to turn away from literature and aesthetics and sought instead 'a practical religion not promising future bliss but giving bliss on earth'. This same spiritual quest inspired the other three works in this volume. He became an extreme rationalist and was officially excommunicated from the Russian Orthodox Church.

What is Art? 1897

In this impassioned polemic on the purpose of the arts, Tolstoy argues that the true artist must incorporate religion and science into his or her work in order to promote the advancement of mankind. He denounces the concept of <u>art for art's sake</u> (244) and condemns writers and artists such as <u>Dante</u> (84), <u>Michelangelo</u> (128), <u>Shakespeare</u> (134), <u>Baudelaire</u> (328) and <u>Wilde</u> (244) for not constructing their works on sufficiently moral principles.

1995
trans. Richard Pevear &
Larissa Volokhonsky

1966
• trans. Rosemary Edmonds

2009
trans. Anthony Briggs

Resurrection 1899

In *Resurrection*, Tolstoy's last novel, Prince Nekhlyudov is serving on the jury at a murder trial, when he is astounded to discover that the defendant, a prostitute, is a woman he once loved, seduced and abandoned. She is sentenced to imprisonment in Siberia. Realizing that he has been the cause of her ruin, Nekhlyudov appeals for her release, gives up his callous way of life and follows her on a dark and horrifying road to his own spiritual redemption. Tolstoy wrote this book to raise funds for the pacifist Dukhober sect.

Last Steps
The Late Writings of Leo Tolstoy
1882–1910

This collection of essays, diaries and letters from Tolstoy's turbulent final years presents a comprehensive portrait of his unorthodox views on religion, art, social justice, pacifism and vegetarianism.

2009
trans. R. F. Christian, 1978, 1985
trans. Jane Kentish, 1987
trans. Constance Garnett,
Michael R. Katz, Aylmer Maude,
Jay Parini & Leo Wiener, 2009
ed. Jay Parini, 2009

Ivan Goncharov 1812–1891

Ivan Aleksandrovich Goncharov spent most of his life as a civil servant. The only events in his otherwise monotonous career were the publication of three novels and a voyage to Japan as secretary to a Russian mission. His crowning achievement was writing the masterpiece *Oblomov*. Chekhov (381) said that Goncharov was 'ten heads above me in talent'.

1954
trans. David Magarshack, 1954
intro. Milton Ehre, 2005
—
At his retirement party in 1964, E. V. Rieu (17) admitted that he had initially been uncertain whether Goncharov had written Oblomov or vice versa. 'Now, of course, I know that Oblomov was the author. Or am I wrong?'

Oblomov 1859

The apathetic, aristocratic Ilya Ilyich Oblomov is so lazy, he has abandoned his civil service job, neglected his books, alienated his friends and run himself into debt. He lives in a filthy apartment, waited on by Zakhar, his equally idle manservant, doting from afar on the love of his life, Olga. Written with humour and compassion, this great novel teeters on the edge of tragedy. 'As long as there is even one Russian alive,' wrote Turgenev (374), '*Oblomov* will be remembered.'

Nikolai Leskov 1831–1895

Nikolai Semyonovich Leskov entered the civil service at sixteen, travelling frequently within Russia. In 1860, he took up journalism and moved to St Petersburg, where he also began writing fiction. Initially politically and socially isolated, he was later admired by Tolstoy (376), Chekhov (381) and Maxim Gorky (385), who called him 'the writer most deeply rooted in the people'. According to his wish, Leskov's funeral was conducted in absolute silence.

Lady Macbeth of Mtsensk
and Other Stories 1862–1895

In Leskov's lurid masterpiece *Lady Macbeth of the Mtsensk District*, a young wife finds relief from her stifling marriage by committing adultery, casual violence and cold-blooded murder; the title is a reference to both Shakespeare's play (142) and Turgenev's story from *Sketches from a Hunter's Album* (374), 'Hamlet of the Shchigrovsky District'. *Musk-Ox* is the sad tale of an eccentric ex-seminary student; *The Sealed Angel* is about a religious group, whose icon of an angel is confiscated and sealed in wax; and *Pamphalon the Entertainer* is a satire of contemporary Russia, set in ancient Byzantium when 'the entire state was filled with vice.'

1987
trans. David McDuff

THE WAY OF A PILGRIM 1884
Candid Tales of a Wanderer to His Spiritual Father

A pilgrim makes a journey through the forests, fields and steppes of Siberia, reciting the 'Jesus Prayer' as a mantra. Along the way, he meets priests, professors, convicts, nuns and beggars, and from each he gathers wisdom. This mystical, anonymous tale of a lone wanderer was discovered in a Greek Orthodox monastery on Mount Athos in the 19th century, written in Russian, and it was first published in Kazan in 1884. As a manual of prayer, it has had a great influence around the world. It is probably the 'small pea-green cloth-bound book' that Franny keeps in her handbag in J. D. Salinger's *Franny and Zooey* (1961).

2018
trans. Anna Zaranko
intro. Andrew Louth

Anton Chekhov 1860–1904

Anton Pavlovich Chekhov was born in the port town of Taganrog on the Sea of Azov, where he paid for his own schooling by catching and selling goldfinches. He studied medicine in Moscow and, as a student, supported his family by writing humorous stories for magazines; his second volume of stories won the <u>Pushkin</u> Prize (367) in 1888. 'Medicine is my lawful wife,' he once said, 'and literature is my mistress.' He lived and worked for five years on a small country estate near Moscow before moving to Yalta in the Crimea. There he received visits from <u>Tolstoy</u> (376) and <u>Gorky</u> (385) and wrote his great late plays. In 1901, he married the actress Olga Knipper, who had played Madame Arkadina in *The Seagull*. Chekhov died from tuberculosis while drinking champagne in Germany and was borne to Moscow in a refrigerated railway carriage intended for transporting oysters.

2004
trans. Ronald Wilks
intro. John Sutherland

The Shooting Party 1884

Chekhov's only novel is a murder mystery. An enigmatic author asks a publisher to read a manuscript, a true account entitled 'The Shooting Party'. It describes the lecherous Count Alexei, whose estate is run by a middle-aged widower, Urbenin. The count also employs a crazed forester, who has a daughter called Olga. Olga marries Urbenin to escape her miserable home but is soon drawn into an open affair with the count himself. During a shooting party in the woods, Olga is murdered. Everyone assumes that her jealous husband must be the culprit, but the publisher reads between the lines and deduces the true identity of the murderer.

Plays 1887–1904
Ivanov; *The Seagull*;
Uncle Vanya; *Three Sisters*;
The Cherry Orchard

In 1887, Chekhov was commissioned to write a play, and the result was *Ivanov*, written in a fortnight. A subsequent production, in 1889, proved to be a great hit. When he returned to playwriting almost a decade later, however, *The Seagull* was a disaster: the opening night was booed, the reviews were scathing and Chekhov renounced the theatre altogether. It wasn't until Konstantin Stanislavski produced a highly acclaimed production of *The Seagull* at the Moscow Arts Theatre two years later, in which he drew out the psychological subtlety of the text, that Chekhov returned to drama and proceeded to write three more extraordinary plays, all of which reduce melodrama and reveal stark truths. His plays teeter on the boundary between laughter and tears: his last, *The Cherry Orchard*, was written as a comedy and so Chekhov was flabbergasted when Stanislavski staged it as a heart-rending tragedy.

1940
• trans. S. S. Koteliansky

1951
• trans. Elisaveta Fen
—
Elisaveta Fen's two volumes were published together in a single volume in 1959

1954
• trans. Elisaveta Fen

2002
trans. Peter Carson
intro. Richard Gilman

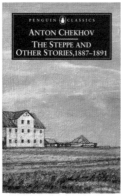

1938 Penguin Books
● trans. Constance Garnett
1985 *The Party
and Other Stories*
● trans. Ronald Wilks

2001
trans. Ronald Wilks
intro. Donald Rayfield

The Steppe
and Other Stories 1887–1891

The Steppe is the novella that helped to establish Chekhov's reputation. Inspired by a trip he made to the Ukraine, it is the story of a young boy travelling to an unknown school in Kiev, surrounded by magnificent landscapes; it has been called a 'dictionary of Chekhov's poetics'. 'Gusev' is the tale of a terrifying ocean voyage; 'The Kiss' describes a shy soldier's failed romance; and 'The Duel' is a humorous story about a fight that ends in farce.

Ward No. 6
and Other Stories 1892–1895

Set in a mental hospital, 'Ward No. 6' describes the conflict between a patient and the asylum director, a savage indictment of the medical profession. 'The Black Monk' is about strange hallucinations; 'Murder' is a story of the dangers of religious fervour; and 'The Student', Chekhov's favourite story, is about a young man's spiritual epiphany.

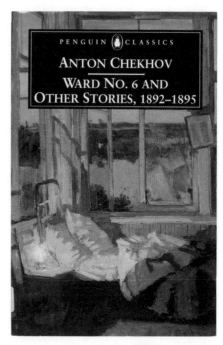

1984 *The Duel
and Other Stories*
● trans. Ronald Wilks
1986 *The Fiancée
and Other Stories*
● trans. Ronald Wilks

2002
● trans. Ronald Wilks
intro. J. Douglas Clayton

1964
● ed. David Magarshack
1982 *The Kiss and Other Stories*
● trans. Ronald Wilks

2002
trans. Ronald Wilks
intro. Paul Debreczeny

The Lady with the Little Dog
and Other Stories 1896–1904

'The Lady with the Little Dog' is the tale of a casual holiday liaison between a married man and a married woman which unexpectedly develops into a scandalous but deeply loving relationship. In 'Peasants', 'The House with the Mezzanine' and 'My Life', Chekhov presents poignant descriptions of the poor and their powerlessness in the face of hardship.

A Life in Letters 1876–1904

Chekhov wrote thousands of letters during his lifetime. This selection starts in his teenage years and charts his growing literary reputation, including discussions with publishers and theatre directors, love letters to his future wife and descriptions of his final battle with consumption. It includes the letters he sent home from Sakhalin Island, a distant penal colony north of Japan, which he visited in 1890.

2004
trans. Rosamund Bartlett &
Anthony Phillips

Sholem Aleichem 1859–1916

Solomon Naumovich Rabinovitch was born in the western Russian Empire, in modern Ukraine, and worked as a government rabbi, a clerk, a businessman and a teacher of Russian. He married the daughter of a wealthy landowner but lost her large inheritance through failed speculation on the stock market. He began writing in Yiddish in 1883, using the pen name 'Sholem Aleichem', a traditional Hebrew greeting that means 'peace be upon you'. After the 1905 pogroms in Kiev, he and his extended family fled to Italy, Denmark, Switzerland and America. In 1914, they settled in New York where he became known as the 'Jewish Mark Twain'. When Mark Twain (414) heard of this, he returned the compliment, describing himself as the 'American Sholem Aleichem'. 'Let my name be recalled with laughter,' wrote Aleichem, 'or not at all.' Accordingly, each year the Brotherhood Synagogue in New York holds a service in his memory, and one of his comic stories is read out loud.

Tevye the Dairyman *and* Motl the Cantor's Son
1894, 1916

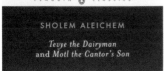

Tevye and Motl are perhaps the most celebrated characters in all Jewish fiction. Tevye, the father of seven daughters all seeking love in the shtetl, is particularly well known after the success of its 1964 musical adaptation, *Fiddler on the Roof*. Motl is a mischievous nine-year-old boy who emigrates to New York and describes the city through humorous and clear-eyed observations.

2009
trans. Aliza Shevrin
intro. Dan Miron
—
These new translations
were commissioned to
mark the 150th anniversary
of Aleichem's birth.

Fyodor Sologub 1863–1927

Fyodor Kuzmich Teternikov was a provincial schoolmaster until the success of *The Little Demon* allowed him to leave his job and devote himself to writing novels, short stories and Symbolist poems. He believed that the world is essentially evil. Love, truth and beauty are veils, behind which lurks the diabolical.

The Little Demon 1905

In *The Little Demon*, Sologub expresses the Russian concept of *poshlost*, the depressing combination of evil and banality. Peredonov is a mad, lecherous, sadistic schoolteacher who hallucinates about torturing his students and derives erotic pleasure from watching them kneel before him. He dabbles in arson, sexual perversion and murder, and yet to all appearances he is an upstanding, rather dreary member of society. In response to speculation that the novel was autobiographical, Sologub replied, 'No, my dear contemporaries, it is of you that I have written my novel about the little demon [...]. About *you*.'

1994 Twentieth-Century Classics
2013 Penguin Classics
trans. Ronald Wilks, 1994
intro. Pamela Davidson, 2013

1983 Modern Classics
● trans. R. A. Maguire

1995 Twentieth-Century Classics
2011 Penguin Classics
trans. David McDuff, 1995
intro Adam Thirlwell, 2011

Andrei Bely 1880–1934

Boris Nikolayevich Bugayev studied maths, zoology and philosophy at Moscow University before becoming a leading figure of the scandalous Symbolist movement. He used a pseudonym for his writing to avoid embarrassing his father, an eminent maths professor. In 1914, he joined a Rudolf Steiner anthroposophical community in Switzerland, but returned to Russia to support the 1917 Revolutions.

Petersburg
A Novel in Eight Chapters 1916

When Nikolai, a fervent university student, joins a revolutionary terror organization, he discovers they are planning to assassinate a senior government official with a time bomb, and the official is his father. This suspenseful story is an exhilarating synaesthetic portrait of St Petersburg in 1905, presided over by the sentient equestrian statue of Peter the Great (368). Nabokov considered it one of the four greatest novels of the 20th century, alongside Proust's *In Search of Lost Time*, Joyce's *Ulysses* and Kafka's 'Metamorphosis'.

NON-FICTION

The Industrial Revolution came late and fast to tsarist Russia. By the end of the 19th century, the competing interests of industrial capitalists, peasants and Marxist radical parties seemed irresolvable. The first rupture took place on Sunday, 22 January 1905, when soldiers opened fire on an enormous but peaceful crowd presenting a petition at the Winter Palace in St Petersburg. 'Bloody Sunday' resulted in the Revolution of 1905, with mass general strikes coordinated by 'Soviet' councils of workers. A decade later, the huge but disorganized Russian army sustained devastating casualties during the First World War (433). The people looked to their tsar, but Nicholas II failed to display decisive leadership, relying instead on bureaucratic negotiations with the new Duma assembly and the intimations of his wife's charismatic spiritual advisor, Grigori Rasputin. Soon popular opinion turned against the government again and this, combined with war-weariness and general economic breakdown, culminated in the revolutions of 1917 and the triumph of the communist Bolshevik party in October that year.

Peter Kropotkin 1842–1921

Peter Alekseyevich Kropotkin was a philosopher, a scientist and a distinguished military geographer. He conducted surveys of eastern Siberia before resigning from the army and engaging in revolutionary activities. He was arrested, but he escaped two years later and he spent most of the rest of his life in England, Switzerland and France, becoming the leading intellectual of the anarchist movement. He returned to Russia after the February Revolution of 1917, but was ultimately unimpressed by Bolshevik state socialism.

The Conquest of Bread
1892

Kropotkin's optimistic vision of an anarchist society rejects the traditional organizing principles of feudalism and capitalism and imagines instead a collective of decentralized self-sufficient communities living in non-hierarchical harmony, and supported through mutual aid. He backs up his theories with examples from the animal kingdom and contemporary human societies from around the world.

2015
trans. Peter Kropotkin, 1906
ed. David Priestland, 2015

Maxim Gorky 1868–1936

Alexei Maximovich Peshkov ran away from his home in Nizhny Novgorod at the age of twelve and scrabbled for piecemeal work in bakeries, on barges and in an icon-maker's workshop. After a failed suicide attempt, he became a pioneer of Russian social realism, writing short stories under the pen name 'Gorky', which means 'bitter'. His play, *The Lower Depths* (1902), was a huge success at the Moscow Arts Theatre. He became increasingly involved in revolutionary activity and was arrested by the tsarist government in 1905, although quickly released following a petition signed by other writers. He travelled in America and Italy before returning to Moscow in 1913, where he became a lifelong champion of the Soviet cause. He died in 1936, poisoned by political enemies.

1966
trans. Ronald Wilks

My Childhood 1913

After Gorky's father died, Maxim moved with his mother to live with his tyrannical polecat-faced grandfather and his affectionate mountainous grandmother, who told him enchanting bedtime stories. After his mother died, he ran away. This is the first and best-loved volume of Gorky's autobiographical trilogy, infused with a young boy's curiosity, dreams and fears. The translator Ronald Wilks calls it 'one of the most moving descriptions of boyhood ever written'.

Vladimir Lenin 1870–1924

After his brother's execution in 1887, Vladimir Ilyich Ulyanov became a clandestine Marxist and was exiled to Siberia for his revolutionary activism. He was the theorist and philosopher of the emerging Bolshevik faction, but lived as an émigré in western Europe until 1917, when Tsar Nicholas II abdicated, and Lenin returned dramatically to St Petersburg in a sealed train. He seized power during the October Revolution, becoming chairman of the first Soviet government. He implemented wide-ranging social and economic reforms, but also instituted a one-party communist state and a ruthless dictatorship. When he died, his body was embalmed and is still on display in Moscow.

V. I. LENIN

The State and Revolution

The State and Revolution 1918

Lenin wrote *The State and Revolution* in 1917, just weeks before he was swept to supreme power. His powerfully argued book is a rationale for a new regime, a personal interpretation of Marxism (346) and a justification of the dictatorship of the proletariat. It is a devastatingly influential political statement. 'The replacement of the bourgeois state by the proletarian state is impossible without a violent revolution', he writes.

1992 Twentieth-Century Classics
2009 Penguin Classics
trans. Robert Service

Asia

Rabindranath Tagore · Selected Poems

RABINDRANATH TAGORE *Selected Short Stories*

Rabindranath Tagore · *The Home and the World*

JOSÉ RIZAL *Noli Me Tangere (Touch Me Not)*

NATSUME SŌSEKI *Botchan*

NATSUME SŌSEKI *Kusamakura*

NATSUME SŌSEKI *Sanshirō*

NATSUME SŌSEKI *Kokoro*

The Penguin Book of Japanese Short Stories

Edited by
Jay Rubin

Introduction by
Haruki Murakami

KAKUZO OKAKURA *The Book of Tea*

PMC

PMC

PMC

ISBN 0 14
01.8425 2

ISBN 0 14
00.7961 0

ISBN 0 14
00.79385 8

PENGUIN CLASSICS

PENGUIN CLASSICS

PENGUIN CLASSICS

PENGUIN CLASSICS

PENGUIN CLASSICS

PENGUIN CLASSICS

PENGUIN CLASSICS

PENGUIN
CLASSICS

India

The British East India Company, and its private army of sepoys, became increasingly dominant in India in the first half of the 19th century. In 1857, however, rumours that gun cartridges were greased with beef and pork fat, offensive to both Hindus and Muslims, sparked a mutiny in the company army, which led to widespread violence known as the Indian Rebellion. As a result, the British government took over direct administration of the country and literature did not thrive under colonial rule. It was only towards the end of the century, as the Indian Independence Movement gathered momentum, that a new strand of nationalistic literature began to emerge.

Rabindranath Tagore 1861–1941

Tagore was the fourteenth child of the prominent Hindu reformer Debendranath Tagore. Rabindranath began composing poetry, fiction, drama, essays and songs as a child. In 1912, he travelled to Britain, where his work was praised by Yeats (267) and published by Macmillan. He was awarded the Nobel Prize for Literature in 1913, the only Indian to have received the honour to date. He spent the rest of his life as a 'peripatetic *littérateur*', making international lecture tours and campaigning against militarism and nationalism. In 1919, after the Amritsar Massacre, he returned his British knighthood. The economist and philosopher Amartya Sen, a fellow Bengali, calls Tagore a 'towering figure in the Millennium-old literature of Bengal'.

Selected Poems 1882–1941

Tagore's haunting poetry takes small miracles of nature — the eyes of a peacock, the falling rain, the flight of wild geese — and moments of human tenderness such as an old man watching his grandchild play, and turns these microcosmic details into deep reflections on the human condition and our position within the shifting political world and the harmonious universe.

1985 Modern Classics
1989 Twentieth-Century Classics
2005 Penguin Classics
trans. William Radice
—
William Radice is the son of Betty Radice (51). The editors of Penguin Classics 'bring the world together,' he wrote in a Penguin Collectors Society publication, 'to build numerous, intersecting bridges between different ages and languages and continents.'

1991 Twentieth-Century Classics
2005 Penguin Classics
trans. William Radice

Selected Short Stories 1891–1900

These 30 stories were written while Tagore was managing his family estates amidst the rivers of East Bengal. They describe the cruel realities of rural life, child marriage, official corruption and an entrenched caste system, while also offering luscious portraits of the Bengali landscape. Titles include 'Skeleton', 'Son-Sacrifice' and 'The Hungry Stones'.

The Home and the World 1916

Nikhil, an enlightened Bengali landowner, encourages his young wife Bimala to shake off the traditional female seclusion of purdah and introduces her to his charismatic friend Sandip, leader of the radical *Swadeshi* movement. Bimala becomes passionately committed to the revolutionary cause, but her struggle to resolve the conflicting demands of home life and the wider political world lead to violence and ultimately tragedy. The novel is an allegory for India's political turmoil in the early 20th century, and for Tagore's own internal conflict between embracing and rejecting the ideals of western culture.

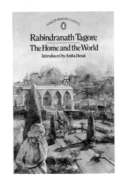

1985 Modern Classics
1990 Twentieth-Century Classics
2005 Penguin Classics
trans. Surendranath Tagore, 1919
intro. Anita Desai, 1985
pref. William Radice, 2005
—
This translation was made by Tagore's nephew Surendranath with input from the author.

Philippines

The first great author in the Filipino language was the early 19th-century poet and playwright Francisco Balagtas, whose epic poem *Florante and Laura* is considered the founding text of Filipino literature.

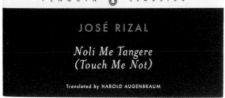

2006
trans. Harold Augenbraum

José Rizal 1861–1896

José Protasio Rizal Mercado y Alonso Realonda was born in Calamba near Manila. He studied ophthalmology in Spain and while there worked with Philippine exiles to campaign against Spanish colonial rule. On returning to the Philippines, he was suspected of treason, so he returned to Europe where he continued his anticolonial activities. When he returned to the Philippines for a second time, he was exiled to Dapitan, a town on the southern island of Mindanao, and in 1896 he was tried for treason and executed by firing squad. After his death, he became a symbol of Philippine nationalism.

Noli Me Tangere
(Touch Me Not)
1887

Rizal's first novel is considered by many to be the greatest work of Philippine literature and the text that sparked the Philippine Revolution in 1896. Initially banned by Spanish authorities in the Philippines, it is now compulsory reading for all schoolchildren. It is a love story, between Juan Crisóstomo Ibarra y Magsalin and the beautiful María Clara, set against a backdrop of religious repression and political torture. Rizal was inspired to write it after reading Harriet Beecher Stowe's *Uncle Tom's Cabin* (412). It concludes with Ibarra's friend Elías saying,

> I die without seeing dawn's light shining on my country ... You, who will see it, welcome it for me ... don't forget those who fell during the nighttime.

Noli me Tangere was a medical term for spreading, excruciating ulceration, especially of the face. Rizal set out to examine all the 'diseases' of Colonial rule in the Philippines, which other writers considered too painful to touch.

Japan

On 3 February 1867, the 14-year-old Prince Mutsuhito succeeded to the Chrysanthemum Throne and became Emperor Meiji. In November the same year, the weakening shōgun tendered his resignation, ending seven centuries of military dictatorship, and the young emperor was granted supreme power. A document was circulated around the world:

> The Emperor of Japan announces to the sovereigns of all foreign countries and to their subjects that permission has been granted to the Shōgun Tokugawa Yoshinobu to return the governing power in accordance with his own request. We shall henceforward exercise supreme authority in all the internal and external affairs of the country. Consequently, the title of Emperor must be substituted for that of Tycoon, in which the treaties have been made. Officers are being appointed by us to the conduct of foreign affairs. It is desirable that the representatives of the treaty powers recognize this announcement.
>
> *Mutsuhito*

Thus began the Meiji period, during which the feudal isolated country of Japan transitioned quickly into the Industrial Age, with drastic social, political and economic reforms. Japan opened itself to the rest of the world: there was an influx of foreign cultures and a correspondent blossoming of Japanese literature.

Natsume Sōseki

1867–1916

Sōseki was the foremost Japanese novelist of the Meiji period. He was born Natsume Kinnosuke in Edo, the year before that city was renamed Tokyo. He studied English at Tokyo University and travelled to London on a two-year government scholarship, before returning to teach English literature. He adopted the playful pen name 'Sōseki', a Chinese idiom meaning 'stubborn' and launched his writing career with *I Am a Cat* (1905–6), a novel narrated by a feline (342). As well as novels, he wrote *haiku* (113), literary criticism, essays, fairy tales and autobiographical sketches.

Botchan

1906

Botchan, 'Little Master', is the story of a young maths teacher from Tokyo who is sent to teach in the ultra-traditional Matsuyama district after the death of his parents. Naïve Botchan must learn to deal with insubordinate pupils and dangerous colleagues. In Japan, it is considered the classic evocation of adolescence.

2012
trans. J. Cohn, 2005

Kusamakura 1906

Sōseki's novel follows an unnamed artist as he makes a meandering, circular walking tour in the mountains. The title, literally 'Grass Pillow', is 'a traditional literary term for travel,' Meredith McKinney explains, 'redolent of the kind of poetic journey epitomized by Bashō's *Narrow Road to the Deep North*' (113). At a hot spring resort, the artist has a series of enigmatic encounters with the beautiful Nami, the daughter of the establishment, who reminds him of the painting of Ophelia by John Everett Millais (265). Sōseki alludes to a number of other writers, including Wang Wei (106), Laurence Sterne (163), Oscar Wilde (244) and Henrik Ibsen (368). He described *Kusamakura* as 'a haiku-style novel, that lives through beauty'.

2008
trans. Meredith McKinney

Sanshirō

A Novel 1908–9

Sanshirō Ogawa is a recent graduate from a provincial college who arrives at Tokyo University, his first time in a big city. He is amazed and exhilarated by the crowds, the scholars and especially the beautiful women. It is a story of first love and Japan's transition into the industrial world. *Sanshirō* 'is a personal favourite of mine,' writes Haruki Murakami in his introduction, 'and I suspect you will find that, no matter where in the world you are, and no matter what the particular shape and direction of your adolescence, the special fragrance of that important stage in life we all pass through is just about the same.'

2009
trans. Jay Rubin
intro. Haruki Murakami

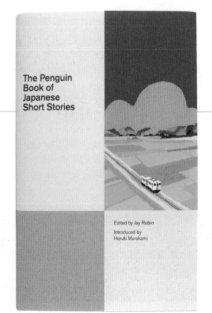

THE PENGUIN BOOK OF JAPANESE SHORT STORIES

19th – 21st centuries

Short stories are particularly popular in Japanese literature and this anthology presents a broad sweep of the best examples from the Meiji period to the present day with many well-known names including Akutagawa (391), Tanizaki, Mishima, Kawabata and Murakami, as well as lesser-known authors, such as Yuko Tsushima, Yuten Sawanishi and Banana Yoshimoto. Their stories cover life, death, love, incest, murder and motherhood.

2018
ed. Jay Rubin
intro. Haruki Murakami

Kokoro 1914

The last novel that Sōseki completed before his death is also his masterpiece. Kokoro, 'Heart', or 'the heart of things', presents an intimate friendship between two unnamed characters, a young student and a reclusive elder figure addressed as 'Sensai'. Initially secretive, the Sensai eventually reveals a series of guilt-ridden secrets from his own student days that ultimately end in tragedy and expose the generational differences that characterised early 20th-century Japan.

2010
trans.
Meredith
McKinney

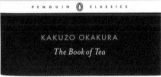

Kakuzo Okakura 1862–1913

Okakura was the son of a silk merchant and former samurai. He became an eccentric art historian and founded the Tokyo Fine Art School in 1896. He travelled to India in 1901 and to the United States, where he befriended the artist John La Farge and worked at Boston's Museum of Fine Arts as the curator of their Japanese and Chinese collections.

The Book of Tea 1906

This slim volume, written in English, is both a modern treatise on the celebrated Japanese tea ceremony and a sardonic commentary on the western view of Japan. Its sections cover the various 'Schools of Tea', the typical layout of a tearoom and tea drinking as art appreciation, and ends with a role-call of legendary 'Tea-Masters'. It is dedicated to 'John La Farge, *Sensei*'.

2010
intro. Christopher
Benfey

Ryunosuke Akutagawa

1892–1927

Akutagawa was raised in Tokyo. He was named Ryunosuke, the 'Son of the Dragon', because he was born in the Year of the Dragon, in the Month of Dragon, on the Day of the Dragon and at the Hour of the Dragon. His mother was declared insane soon after his birth and he found himself torn between his biological and his adoptive father. He studied English literature at Tokyo University before teaching English himself and writing stylistically brilliant short stories. He took his own life at the age of 35.

Rashōmon
and Seventeen Other Stories 1914–27

2006
trans. Jay
Rubin
intro. Haruki
Murakami

Akutagawa's language 'moves along like a living thing,' writes Haruki Murakami. 'His choice of words is intuitive, natural – and beautiful.' The stories in the collection include 'Rashōmon' and 'In a Bamboo Grove', famously adapted for the screen by Kurosawa, as well as the children's tale 'The Spider Thread', the humorous 'The Nose', the horrific 'Hell Screen' and the deeply introspective 'Death Register'.

Australasia

Katherine Mansfield · Bliss and Other Stories

1739

Katherine Mansfield · The Garden Party

Katherine Mansfield · In a German Pension

799

ISBN 0 14
00.2181 7

Katherine Mansfield · The Collected Short Stories

ISBN 014
00.6146 0

Although Australia and New Zealand had been written about by travellers such as Captain Cook (185) and Charles Darwin (269), and imagined by European novelists including Jonathan Swift (159) – who placed the island of Lilliput northwest of Tasmania – home-grown, written Australasian literature did not appear until the 19th century. Most early colonial fiction consisted of frontier tales of danger and excitement in the bush.

Katherine Mansfield

1888–1923

Katherine Mansfield Beauchamp was born in Wellington, New Zealand. She travelled to London as a teenager, however, and lived in Europe for most of the rest of her life. She was a consciously modernist writer, a friend of D. H. Lawrence (288) and Virginia Woolf, and an excellent cellist. She contracted tuberculosis in 1917 and died at the age of 34, but she produced a prodigious number of short stories in her short life-time. 'She was for ever pursued by her dying,' wrote Woolf, 'and had to press on through stages that should have taken years in ten minutes.'

1962 Modern Classics
Bliss and Other Stories
• —
1964 Modern Classics
In a German Pension
• —

The Collected Stories

1911–24

This volume encompasses the three story collections Mansfield published in her lifetime, *Bliss*, *The Garden Party* and *In a German Pension*, as well as two posthumously published collections and fifteen fragments of unfinished stories. Her short stories are 'near-plotless pieces of glinting brilliance', writes the novelist Ali Smith in her introduction, 'with the hint in them of light, energy, shattered glass'.

1981 Modern Classics
2007 Penguin Classics
intro. Ali Smith, 2007

1951 Penguin Books
• —
1962 Modern Classics
• —

1997 Twentieth-Century Classics
2000 Penguin Classics
ed. Lorna Sage

The Garden Party
and Other Stories 1922

Mansfield's masterwork is *The Garden Party*, a collection of short stories published the year before she died. Many are set in New Zealand, others in England and the French Riviera. The title story is based on Mansfield's childhood home in Wellington: amidst the bustling preparations for a luxurious garden party, news arrives that a poor neighbour has died. Other stories include 'At the Bay', an impressionistic evocation of the seaside; 'Mr and Mrs Dove', about a couple who seem to imitate a pair of birds; and the heart-breaking 'Miss Brill', about a lonely woman whose spirit is crushed.

The Americas

The Penguin Book of Witches

EDWARD PROCTOR HUNT · The Origin Myth of Acoma Pueblo

BENJAMIN FRANKLIN · THE AUTOBIOGRAPHY AND OTHER WRITINGS

THOMAS PAINE   COMMON SENSE

PAINE   RIGHTS OF MAN

THE THOMAS PAINE READER

MADISON, HAMILTON AND JAY · THE FEDERALIST PAPERS

OWEN CHASE AND THOMAS NICKERSON · THE LOSS OF THE SHIP ESSEX, SUNK BY A WHALE

RALPH WALDO EMERSON   SELECTED ESSAYS

PENGUIN CLASSICS

PENGUIN CLASSICS

ISBN 0 14
03.9052 9

ISBN 0 14
040.032 X

AC11

ISBN 0 14
04.4496 3

ISBN 0 14
04.4495 5

ISBN 0 14
039.013 8

The United States

European colonists began to settle along the eastern seaboard of America almost as soon as Christopher Columbus (119) touched land in 1492. By the 1770s, Britain had thirteen colonies along the Atlantic coast. When the colonists resisted a set of new British taxes, however, most memorably at the Boston Tea Party, Parliament moved to implement punitive laws, which resulted in the American Revolution. General George Washington, commander of the Continental Army, fought the British and won independence for the United States of America in 1776.

Over the course of the 19th century, the USA expanded its territory to the Pacific coast and its population multiplied thirtyfold. Much of this swift expansion in the south allowed the establishment of extensive slave plantations, producing sugar and cotton, though by 1804 slavery was abolished in all states north of the Mason-Dixon line, an 18th-century lateral surveyed by two British astronomers. When Abraham Lincoln was elected president in 1860, seven of the southern slave states seceded, forming the 'Confederacy', which prompted the American Civil War. Lincoln won the war in 1865 and legal and voting rights were eventually extended to all freed slaves.

By the beginning of the 20th century, the United States was the world's leading industrial power, fuelled by mass immigration, widespread entrepreneurship and large-scale mining and manufacturing industries in the northeast and midwest, and as the new country soared economically, a uniquely American literature flourished with it.

1981
● ed. Thomas Philbrick

The first US-originated Penguin Classic appeared in 1981: *Two Years Before the Mast* (1840) by Richard Henry Dana, Jr. was printed in Baltimore and published into the American Library series (xix) by Penguin Books USA Ltd, an increasingly autonomous division of the company. Today, many Penguin Classics titles are still published independently in America, although most titles are shared with the UK and vice versa. Today, Penguin Classics originating in America are usually identifiable by the series code 303 or 310 (446).

NON-FICTION

The major American writers of the late 18th century were Benjamin Franklin (396) and Thomas Paine (397), two of the Founding Fathers. Thereafter 19th-century non-fiction was dominated by Transcendentalism, a movement founded by Ralph Waldo Emerson (399) and developed by Henry David Thoreau (400). Transcendentalism derived from English Romanticism (191) and German Idealism (344): it postulated that people are inherently good, but that they are corrupted by society, and so the movement encouraged self-reliance and independence. In the mid-19th century, the issue of abolitionism prompted a flood of impassioned publishing, including the novel *Uncle Tom's Cabin* by Harriet Beecher Stowe (412) and several poignant 'slave narratives' written by former slaves who had escaped to the north.

THE PENGUIN BOOK OF WITCHES 16th–18th centuries

This anthology focuses on the Salem witch trials of 1692 and other cases of supposed witchcraft in New England. It presents the written warrants against the accused women, court depositions, the women's own statements and the judges' subsequent apologies, but it also reaches further back to earlier witch trials among the American colonists, and to English antecedents including an extract from *Daemonologie*, the manual for witch hunters written by James VI, King of the Scots, in 1597. It also looks forward to subsequent witch trials, horrifying tales of mob justice, and one account of a woman stoned to death in the streets of Philadelphia in 1787, even as the Continental Congress was in session nearby.

2014
ed. Katherine Howe

Edward Proctor Hunt 1861–1948

Gaire, or 'Day Break', was born in the mesa-top community of Acoma in western New Mexico. Initially he was apprenticed to a medicine man before joining the Albuquerque Indian School, where he adopted the western name Edward Proctor Hunt, after an inscription in a donated Bible (4). Returning to Acoma, Hunt trained as a sacred clown and learned the creation stories of his community. He went on to run a shop, perform as 'Big Snake' in a travelling Wild West Show and become an anthropological consultant and a professional storyteller.

The Origin Myth of Acoma Pueblo 1928

In 1928, at the age of 67, Hunt broke a strict tradition of silence and told his tribe's ancient creation myths to a pair of scholars from the Smithsonian Institution's Bureau of American Ethnology. The stories and songs were translated by Hunt's two sons, 'Wolf Robe' and 'Blue Sky Eagle'. They form an epic narrative of spiritual emergence and cosmology, of two sisters who climbed through three underworlds to establish the Acoma community on the earthly plain, with instructions to search for a permanent home at the centre of the world.

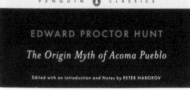

2015
trans. Henry Wayne 'Wolf Robe' Hunt & Wilbert Edward 'Blue Sky Eagle' Hunt
ed. Matthew W. Stirling, Elsie Clews Parsons, Leslie A. White & Peter Nabokov
intro. Peter Nabokov

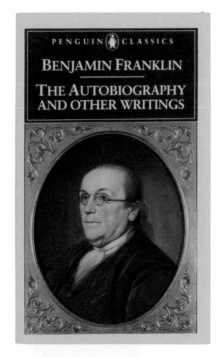

1986
ed. Kenneth Silverman

Benjamin Franklin 1706–1790

Franklin was the youngest son of a Boston soap- and candle-maker, who trained as a printer's apprentice and went on to become the only person to sign all four major documents of the founding of the United States: the Declaration of Independence, the constitution, the Treaty of Alliance with France and the treaty of peace with England. As well as being a prosperous printer and an eminent statesman, he was also an inventor: he created the Franklin stove, experimented with electricity and devised numerous philanthropic schemes and civic improvements. The American writer Walter Isaacson calls him 'the most accomplished American of his age and the most influential in inventing the type of society America would become'.

The Autobiography 1722–89
and Other Writings

Franklin began his *Autobiography* as a collection of 'little anecdotes' for his son, but with wit and insight he goes on to describe his complex and passionate career as a businessman, scientist, legislator and diplomat. This edition appends a variety of Franklin's other writings, including a description of his famous 'kite experiments' and some 'Advice to a Friend on Choosing a Mistress.'

Thomas Paine 1737–1809

Paine was born in Thetford, Norfolk, the son of
a ropemaker, but he ran away to sea. In 1774,
Franklin (396) persuaded him to emigrate to
America, where he became an American citizen
and an outspoken political theorist of the
American War of Independence. On his return to
England in 1787, his radical books were publicly
burned. He moved to France in 1792, where he
helped draft the French constitution but narrowly avoided the guillotine himself. When he
died in New York State, he had been reduced
to an impoverished social pariah. 'He had lived
long,' read his obituary, 'did some good, and
much harm.' William Cobbett (209) exhumed
his body and brought it back to England, but he
was forbidden to bury Paine in English soil, so his
plans were stymied and Paine's remains were lost.

1976 Pelican Classics
1982 Penguin American Library
1986 Penguin Classics
ed. Isaac Kramnick

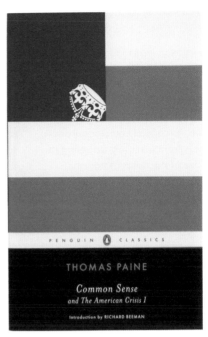

2015 *Common Sense and The
American Crisis I*
intro. Richard Beeman
—
The first edition of *Common Sense*
was published in January 1776.
Paine intended his share of the
profits to be used for purchasing
mittens for the forces fighting
in Quebec, but there were no
profits. Furious, Paine expanded
the manuscript for the second
edition in February and took it
to a different publisher; both of
the Penguin editions reproduce
the longer, second version.
Beeman's edition also includes *The
American Crisis I*, the first of Paine's
sixteen pamphlets designed to
bolster morale during the War of
Independence.

Common Sense 1776

'Without the pen of the author of *Common Sense*,' wrote
John Adams, 'the sword of Washington would have
been raised in vain.' This incendiary pamphlet was published anonymously, six months before the Declaration
of Independence. It converted millions to the cause and
persuaded the Americans to revolt against British rule.

Rights of Man 1791–2

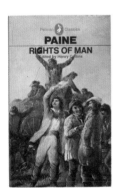

1969 Pelican Classics
1984 Penguin American Library
1985 Penguin Classics
ed. Henry Collins, 1969
intro. Eric Foner, 1984

Written as a rebuttal to Burke's *Reflections on the
Revolution in France* (178), *Rights of Man* is a passionate call for democracy, a vindication of the French
Revolution and a critique of the British government.
Paine defends popular rights, national independence
and economic growth, positions that were considered
radical, or even seditious, at the time.

The Thomas Paine Reader 1772–1805

This anthology, co-edited by the former leader of the Labour party,
contains all of Paine's key writings. It includes *Common Sense*, *Rights of
Man* and the first part of *The Age of Reason*, Paine's virulent attack on
Christianity. It also anthologizes many of his shorter pamphlets, such
as 'The American Crisis', 'Letter to George Washington' and 'Constitutional Reform'. In 1805, John Adams wrote: 'I know not whether any
man in the world has had more influence on its inhabitants or affairs for
the last thirty years than Thomas Paine.'

1987
ed. Michael Foot &
Isaac Kramnick

James Madison
1751 – 1836

Madison was the fourth President of the United States, known as 'the Father of the Constitution'. As Secretary of State under President Jefferson, he purchased Louisiana from the French in 1803, doubling the size of the nascent nation.

Alexander Hamilton 1755 – 1804

Hamilton was born in the West Indies and fought in the War of Independence. He was George Washington's aide de camp and served as the first Secretary of the Treasury. In 1801, he held the casting vote that elected Thomas Jefferson president against Aaron Burr; he subsequently fought a duel with Burr and died the following day.

John Jay
1745 – 1829

Jay was a New York attorney who became the first Chief Justice of the Supreme Court. He was Governor of New York for a time, before retiring for the last 27 years of his life to a farm in Westchester County.

The Federalist Papers 1788

'We the people …' The US Constitution, which is appended to this volume, was drafted and signed in September 1787, but its final article specified that it required the 'ratification of the conventions of nine states' in order to be adopted. Furious debates ensued across the states and New York became a centre of obstinate separatism. In response, Madison, Hamilton and Jay, under the penname 'Publius', drafted a series of clear-sighted commentaries on the constitution, known as *The Federalist Papers*. Addressed directly to the people of New York State, these papers succeeded in persuading the New York convention to accept the constitution, but their influence has transcended the context in which they written: today they are frequently cited as a cornerstone of American political theory. Thomas Jefferson called them 'the best commentary on the principles of government which ever was written'. The US Constitution was successfully ratified in June 1788 and finally came into effect in March 1789.

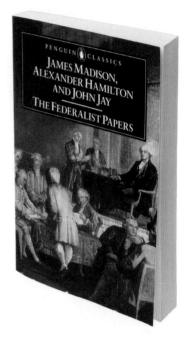

1987
ed. Isaac Kramnick

Owen Chase 1797 – 1869

Chase was first mate on the Nantucket whaleship *Essex*, which was rammed and sunk by a whale in 1820. His account of the experience and the gruelling aftermath was published the following year. He retired from the sea 20 years later in 1840.

Thomas Nickerson
1805 – 1883

Nickerson was a 15-year-old cabin boy aboard the *Essex*. He went on to have a career in whaling and the merchant service, before becoming a shipping broker in Brooklyn. He wrote an account of the ordeal in his old age, which was only discovered in 1980.

The Loss of the Ship *Essex*, Sunk by a Whale
First-Person Accounts
1821 – 76

2000
ed. Nathaniel Philbrick &
Thomas Philbrick

In November 1820, an enormous angry sperm whale repeatedly rammed the whaleship *Essex* until she broke apart and sank in the South Pacific, leaving 20 crew members drifting in leaky open boats thousands of miles from home. They resorted to cannibalism and only eight survived. The story caused a sensation and directly inspired Melville's *Moby-Dick* (410). This volume collects all the contemporary accounts, from the initial newspaper reports to Chase's narrative (including Melville's annotations), Nickerson's 'Desultory Sketches' and the account of Captain Pollard, Commander of the *Essex*.

Ralph Waldo Emerson 1803 – 1882

After graduating from Harvard, Emerson taught for five years before becoming a Unitarian minister. In 1832, he travelled to Europe, where he met Coleridge (195), Wordsworth (193) and Carlyle (269). He returned to settle in Concord, Massachusetts, where he became a public lecturer, touring annually: he delivered 1,500 public lectures over the course of his life. A group of intellectuals gathered around him, known as the 'Concord School', including Bronson Alcott (413), Henry David Thoreau (400) and Nathaniel Hawthorne (412). Emerson wrote essays, poems and philosophy and was a committed abolitionist. He was a 'Transcendentalist' and the founder of a new intellectual tradition for the newly founded nation. The American critic Harold Bloom calls him 'the most influential writer of the nineteenth century'.

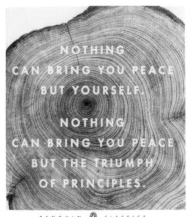

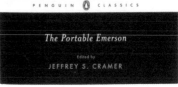

NOTHING CAN BRING YOU PEACE BUT YOURSELF. NOTHING CAN BRING YOU PEACE BUT THE TRIUMPH OF PRINCIPLES.

The Portable Emerson
Edited by
JEFFREY S. CRAMER

2014
ed. Jeffrey S. Cramer

The Portable Emerson 1832–82

'To believe your own thought, to believe that what is true for you in your private heart is true for all men,–that is genius.' All Emerson's core writings are included in this selection, organized under the headings 'Nature', 'Transcendentalism', 'Self-Reliance', 'Representative Men and Women' and 'Considerations by the Way', as well as journal entries, letters, poetry and an early sermon on 'The Last Supper'.

Nature
and Selected Essays 1836–62

1982 Penguin American Library *Selected Essays*
1985 Penguin Classics *Nature and Selected Essays*
ed. Larzer Ziff

Emerson's first published work, 'Nature', contains the essence of his Transcendentalist philosophy: that the beauty of nature provides a model for the self-reliant cultivation of the soul. This selection features all his major essays, including 'The American Scholar', 'Self-Reliance', 'The Transcendentalist' and 'Fate'.

Sarah Grimké 1792 – 1873

Sarah Grimké was born into southern aristocracy and grew up surrounded by slaves. She soon developed a strong aversion to the cruelties of slavery, however, and defied her father by teaching a slave called Hetty to read. She moved to Philadelphia in 1821, became a Quaker and started attending abolitionist meetings.

2014
intro. Mark Perry

Angelina Grimké 1805 – 1879

Angelina followed her sister to Philadelphia in 1829. In 1835, she wrote an impassioned letter to the abolitionist William Garrison, which he published, and both sisters subsequently became prominent figures in the abolitionist movement. In 1838, Angelina became one of the first women to speak before a public legislative body in America. Both sisters remained active abolitionists and women's rights campaigners throughout their lives.

On Slavery and Abolitionism
Essays and Letters 1835–8

This anthology collects Sarah's public letters to 'the Clergy of the Southern States' and on 'the Equality of the Sexes' and Angelina's letter to Garrison, her appeal to 'Christian Women of the South' and her landmark address to the Massachusetts legislature.

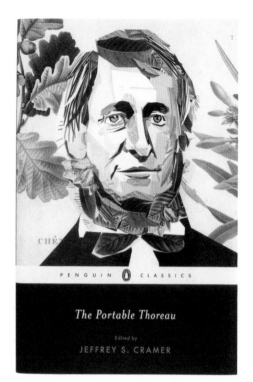

Henry David Thoreau 1817–1862

Thoreau was born in Concord, Massachusetts, the son of a pencil-maker, and he worked at the family pencil factory for most of his adult life. He described himself as a 'mystic, a transcendentalist, and a natural philosopher to boot'. He was also an essayist, poet, abolitionist, naturalist, tax resister, surveyor and historian. He is said to have become fatally ill after counting the rings of tree stumps during a rainstorm.

The Portable Thoreau 1842–62

This anthology includes all Thoreau's best-known works in full, including 'Civil Disobedience', *Walden* and his essay 'Walking', as well as other essays, extracts from his journal on 'the Art of Writing' and a selection of poems, such as 'Fog', 'Woof of the sun' and 'My life has been the poem I would have writ'.

2012 Penguin Classics
ed. Jeffrey S. Cramer

Walden and Civil Disobedience 1849–54

'I went to the woods because I wished to live deliberately, to front only the essential facts of life, and see if I could not learn what it had to teach, and not, when I came to die, discover that I had not lived.' Thoreau moved into a small hut near the shore of Walden Pond in 1845, in woods belonging to Emerson (399), and lived there for more than two years, reading, observing nature and living a simple and mostly solitary life. In 1854, he published his account of 'Life in the Woods', compressing the two years into a single cycle of the seasons and transforming his sojourn into a work of spiritual philosophy. 'In one book,' wrote the poet Robert Frost, 'he surpasses everything we have had in America.'

The other work for which Thoreau is best remembered is his essay 'Civil Disobedience', which was inspired by Shelley's political poem, *The Mask of Anarchy* (196). It encourages social activism against unjust and oppressive authority: 'That government is best which governs not at all,' he writes.

1938 Illustrated Classics
• ill. Ethelbert White

1983 Penguin American Library
1986 Penguin Classics
ed. Michael Meyer, 1983
intro. Kristen Case, 2017

Frederick Douglass 1818–1895

Frederick Augustus Washington Bailey was born into slavery in Tuckahoe, Maryland; his father may well have been his mother's owner, Captain Aaron Anthony. In 1838, he escaped to freedom in the north, changed his name, married and settled in Massachusetts, where he became an active member of a black abolitionist group. He gave impassioned public lectures across the United States and Britain, wrote several autobiographies, founded various periodicals and held a number of appointments in the United States government. He has been called the most influential African American of the 19th century.

1982 Penguin American Library
● ed. Houston A. Baker, Jr.

2014 Penguin Classics
ed. Ira Dworkin

The Narrative of the Life of Frederick Douglass
An American Slave
1845–53

Douglass's autobiography was a major influence on the abolitionist movement. It tells the story of his life as a slave, describing the daily physical and psychological brutalities. He credits literacy as his saviour: learning to read was 'the pathway from slavery to freedom'. This edition appends 'What to the Slave Is the Fourth of July?' and a short story by Douglass, 'The Heroic Slave', one of the first works of African American fiction.

The Portable Frederick Douglass 1845–94

This volume collects all Douglass's major writings. It features the full text of his *Narrative* as well as extracts from the autobiographical *My Bondage and My Freedom* (1855) and *Life and Times of Frederick Douglass* (1881). It includes his short story 'The Heroic Slave', and a representative selection of his political speeches and journalistic essays. 'His writings describe selves and societies that continually evolve, in states of constant flux,' write Stauffer and Gates, 'encouraging each new generation of readers to discover through his stories their *own* stories, to find through his words their own sources of strength and inspiration, and to seek through his imagery their own swift-winged angels that move merrily before the gentle gale.'

2016
ed. John Stauffer & Henry Louis Gates, Jr.

Solomon Northup 1807–1863

2012 Penguin Classics
ed. Ira Berlin
fwd. Steve McQueen

Northup was a free man from New York, a professional violinist, who was kidnapped into slavery in Washington, DC. After he escaped, twelve years later, he published his harrowing memoirs and brought legal action against his abductors, although they were never prosecuted. He gave a series of abolitionist lectures but little is known about his subsequent life.

Twelve Years a Slave 1853

'Solomon Northup was carried to a plantation in the Red River country – that same region where the scene of Uncle Tom's captivity was laid,' observed Harriet Beecher Stowe (412), to whom Northup dedicated this account. Considered the greatest of the 19th-century 'slave narratives', Northup's chilling memoir is the story of his kidnapping, sale, and captivity on a Louisiana cotton plantation. Steve McQueen's 2013 film adaptation won the Academy Award for Best Picture.

Harriet Jacobs 1813–1897

Harriet Ann Brent Jacobs's parents were slaves. When her mother died, she went to live with her owner, Margaret Horniblow, who taught her to read, write and sew. When Horniblow died, however, Harriet, still only twelve, was given as a slave to Horniblow's five-year-old niece, Mary Matilda, whose father attempted to force her into a sexual relationship. She ran away and hid in a crawl space in her grandmother's shack for seven years until she finally escaped to the north in 1842. Thereafter she lived and worked in New York and Boston as an abolitionist speaker and reformer.

Incidents in the Life of a Slave Girl
Written by Herself 1861

Jacobs's haunting account of life as a slave in North Carolina was one of the first narratives to address the plight of female slaves and their frequent sexual abuse. She wrote her narrative after meeting Harriet Beecher Stowe (412) and published it under the pseudonym 'Linda Brent'.

2000
ed. Nell Irvin Painter
—
This volume also includes 'A True Tale of Slavery' by Harriet's brother John S. Jacobs, which was first published in London in 1861.

Ulysses S. Grant 1822–1885

Hiram Ulysses Grant, the eighteenth President of the United States, was the son of a tanner from Ohio. In 1839, he joined the US Military Academy at West Point, where he was mistakenly registered as 'U. S. Grant', a form he adopted for the rest of his life. He served in the Mexican War and became a colonel of a militia regiment in the Civil War. Through a series of strategic and military triumphs he was promoted to general-in-chief of all the Union armies in March 1864 and he led the final campaign, which resulted in General Robert E. Lee's surrender and the end of the war. Grant was elected president in 1868.

Personal Memoirs 1885

Grant's memoirs describe his life as a soldier and his extraordinary career trajectory. The book was a huge commercial success: 350,000 copies were sold and Grant's estate received $450,000 in royalties. Mark Twain (414) called it a 'literary masterpiece', although he was somewhat biased as he was publishing it.

1999
ed. James M. McPherson

HENRY LOUIS GATES, JR.

Henry Louis Gates, Jr. has been the general editor of the Penguin Classics African American series since 2008. In his general introduction to the series, 'What Is an African American Classic?', he writes: 'I think of the Penguin Classics as the very best and most compelling in human thought, an Alexandrian library in paperback, enclosed in black and white. [. . .] Each classic black text reveals to us, uncannily, subtly, how the Black Experience is inscribed, inextricably and indelibly, in the human experience [. . .] Together, such texts also demonstrate, implicitly, that African American culture is one of the world's truly great and eternal cultures, as noble and resplendent as any.'

THE PORTABLE NINETEENTH-CENTURY AFRICAN AMERICAN WOMEN WRITERS

19th–20th centuries

This anthology collects the writings of African American women from before, during and after the Civil War. The pieces are organized thematically and include well-known names such as Mary Prince (431), Harriet Jacobs and Ida B. Wells (403), alongside many others.

2017
ed. Hollis Robbins & Henry Louis Gates, Jr.

2014
ed. Jean Marie Lutes
fwd. Maureen Corrigan

Nellie Bly 1864– 1922

Elizabeth Jane Cochran became a pioneering female journalist after she replied anonymously to a misogynist column, 'What Girls Are Good For', and the *Pittsburgh Dispatch* promptly hired her. Writing under the pseudonym 'Nellie Bly', a reference to a popular song, she became the paper's foreign correspondent, before moving to work for Joseph Pulitzer's *New York World*. She wrote investigative features on political corruption, baby-selling rings, workers' strikes and women's suffrage and became famous for travelling around the world faster than the fictional Phileas Fogg (315).

Around the World in Seventy-Two Days
and Other Writings 1885–1919

Bly was the first 'stunt girl' reporter. This anthology includes her account of committing herself to the women's lunatic asylum on Blackwell's Island in New York, going undercover as a worker in a box factory and offering to bribe a prominent political lobbyist. It also features extracts from her round-the-world stunt, inspired by Jules Verne (315), which was the subject of a nationwide competition: 900,000 people guessed how long it would take her in days, hours, minutes and seconds. She passed through France, the Suez Canal, Sri Lanka, Singapore, Hong Kong and Japan. She visited a Chinese leper colony and bought a monkey in Singapore.

Ida B. Wells 1862– 1931

Wells was born a slave in Mississippi, three years before abolition. She became a teacher and then a journalist in Memphis. Her first published piece describes being pulled off a train and arrested for not giving up her seat. When a close friend was lynched in 1892, she dedicated the rest of her life to an anti-lynching crusade, for which she received death threats. She published tirelessly on civil rights and delivered impassioned lecture tours across the northern states and in Britain. 'Brave woman!' wrote Frederick Douglass (401). 'You have done your people and mine a service which can neither be weighed nor measured.'

The Light of Truth
Writings of an Anti-Lynching Crusader 1885– 1927

This selection writings covers the scope of Wells's career, from early pieces such as 'Stick to the Race' and 'The Lynchers Wince', to the devastating, lengthy pamphlets *Southern Horrors* and *A Red Record*.

2014
ed. Mia Bay

2007
intro. Robert Lekachman, 1967

Thorstein Veblen 1857– 1929

Veblen was born in Wisconsin to Norwegian parents. He studied philosophy at Johns Hopkins and Yale universities, before becoming a fellow at the University of Chicago and associate professor at Stanford. From 1917, he worked for the US government, and edited *The Dial* magazine. He co-founded the New School in New York.

The Theory of the Leisure Class 1899

In Veblen's witty book, he describes the evolutionary development of social attitudes that lead to the misuse of wealth and the waste of resources. It introduces his concept of 'conspicuous consumption', overspending as a manifestation of social power. Veblen stylishly eviscerates our assumptions about taste and culture in what the sociologist Lewis Mumford called 'a stick of dynamite wrapped up to look like a stick of candy'. *Time* magazine called Veblen 'the most impressive American satirist of his day'.

William James
1842–1910

James was the son of a peripatetic Swedenborgian philosopher and the elder brother of the novelist Henry James (417). His godfather was Ralph Waldo Emerson (399). Having dreamt of becoming a painter, James studied chemistry, anatomy and physiology instead before moving to teach philosophy and psychology at Harvard, where he became Assistant Professor of Philosophy in 1880. He was a pragmatic empiricist who balanced materialism with post-Civil War idealism. George Santayana called him 'an impulsive poet: a master in the art of recording or divining the lyric quality of experience'.

The Varieties of Religious Experience
A Study in Human Nature 1902

In 1901 and 1902, James delivered the Gifford Lectures on natural theology at the University of Edinburgh, and subsequently worked them into this seminal work of religious pragmatism. He analyses the nature of religious experiences, from conversion and repentance to mysticism and saintliness, and concludes that spirituality exists fundamentally in the experience of individuals, not organized religions. He describes four criteria for identifying a mystical experience: it must involve passivity, the sense of being gripped by a superior power; ineffability, impossible to describe satisfactorily in words; it must be noetic, providing an insight of deep understanding; and it must be transient.

1982 Penguin American Library
1985 Penguin Classics
ed. Martin E. Marty

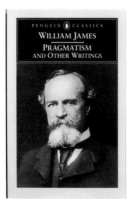

2000
ed. Giles Gunn

Pragmatism
and Other Writings 1897–1909

James developed *Pragmatism* from a set of eight lectures in which he argues for 'reasonableness of ordinary experience'. In the sixth lecture, he explains:

> Truths emerge from facts; but they dip forward into facts again and add to them; which facts again create or reveal new truth (the word is indifferent) and so on indefinitely. The 'facts' themselves meanwhile are not *true*. They simple *are*. Truth is the function of the beliefs that start and terminate among them.

This volume includes other key writings, such as 'The Stream of Consciousness', 'Is Life Worth Living?' and 'The Tigers in India'.

W. E. B. Du Bois 1868–1963

William Edward Burghardt Du Bois was a sociologist, historian, poet, novelist and one of the founders of the National Association for the Advancement of Colored People. He was the first African American to earn a doctorate from Harvard where he was mentored by William James. After a lifetime of campaigning against racial injustice, he died in Ghana at the age of 95 while working on a compendious *Encyclopedia Africana*, a project that was finally completed by Henry Louis Gates, Jr. (402) in 1999.

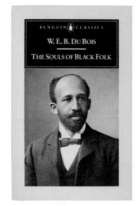

1989 Penguin Classics
1996 Twentieth-Century Classics
2001 Penguin Classics
ed. Monica M. Elbert
intro. Donald B. Gibson

The Souls of Black Folk 1903

'The problem of the Twentieth Century is the problem of the color-line,' writes Du Bois in his foreword, borrowing a phrase from Douglass (401). In his landmark collection of essays, he investigates the dual identity of African-Americans as both American and black, concluding that their goal should be neither 'assimilation nor separatism but [...] proud, enduring hyphenation.'

Ambrose Bierce 1842– c. 1914

Bierce was an acerbic newspaper columnist, known as the 'laughing devil' of San Francisco. His siblings' names were Abigail, Amelia, Ann, Addison, Aurelius, Augustus, Almeda, Andrew and Albert. Information about his life is patchy. He fought in the Civil War and at one point operated a gold mine out of the Black Hills of Dakota. In 1881 he became the editor of the *Wasp*, in which his *Devil's Dictionary* entries first appeared, and in 1887 he was hired by Randolph Hearst to work on the *Examiner*. In 1913, he travelled to Chihuahua to observe the Mexican Revolution and was never seen again.

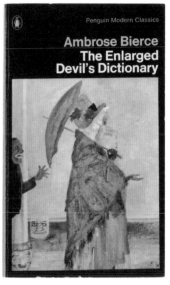

The Enlarged Devil's Dictionary 1911

Dictionary, n. A malevolent literary device for cramping the growth of a language and making it hard and inelastic. The present dictionary, however, is one of the most useful works that its author, Dr John Satan, has ever produced. It is designed to be a compendium of everything that is known up to date of its completion, and will drive a screw, repair a red wagon or apply for a divorce. It is a good substitute for measles, and will make rats come out of their holes to die. It is a dead shot for worms, and children cry for it.

This 'enlarged' edition adds 851 previously unpublished definitions including several by Harry Ellington Brook, a subsequent editor of the *Wasp*.

1971 Modern Classics
1983 Penguin American Library
1985 Penguin Classics
1989 Twentieth-Century Classics
2001 Modern Classics
ed. Ernest Jerome Hopkins, 1967
pref. John Myers Myers, 1967

Mary Antin 1881–1949

Antin was born in Russia and emigrated to the United States at the age of twelve. She wrote a long letter in Yiddish to her uncle describing the voyage. It was subsequently translated into English, and published under the title *From Plotzk to Boston* (1899), with the encouragement of the author Israel Zangwill. Antin studied at the Boston Latin School for Girls and married the geologist Amadeus William Grabau. She published short stories, essays and two enormously successful books, *The Promised Land* and *They Who Knock at Our Gates* (1914).

The Promised Land 1911–3

Antin's autobiographical masterpiece describes the experience of an eastern European Jewish immigrant arriving in America. It charts 'the processes of uprooting, transportation, replanting, acclimatization, and development [that] took place in my own soul', interweaving serious political commentary with amusing insights to form a picture of the national, religious and linguistic hurdles faced by all immigrants arriving in the Promised Land.

1997 Twentieth-Century Classics
2012 Penguin Classics
ed. Werner Sollors
—
The 2012 revised edition includes Antin's original photographs and appends two short stories, 'Malinke's Atonement' and 'The Lie'.

John Reed 1887–1920

Reed was born in Portland, Oregon, and was at one time the highest paid reporter in America. He worked as a war correspondent during the Mexican Revolution and then the First World War (433), and found himself in St Petersburg in October 1917. After returning from Russia, he toured the United States, lecturing about the October Revolution and he is one of only three Americans buried with the revolutionary martyrs beside the Kremlin's wall in Moscow.

Ten Days That Shook the World 1919

Reed was there when Lenin (385), Trotsky and the Bolsheviks seized power. This enthusiastic, eyewitness account presents the gripping events of the October revolution, capturing speeches by leaders, chance comments from bystanders, facts about the food shortages and descriptions of the fall of the Winter Palace as the proletariat, soldiers, sailors and peasants thew off the yoke of oppression. Reed calls his book 'a slice of intensified history'. 'With the greatest interest and with never-slackening attention I read John Reed's book, *Ten Days That Shook the World*,' writes Lenin in his introduction. 'Unreservedly do I recommend it to the workers of the world.'

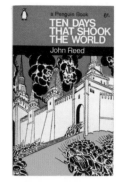

1966 Penguin Books
1977 Modern Classics
2007 Penguin Classics
intro. V. I. Lenin, 1922
intro. A. J. P. Taylor, 1977
—
A. J. P. Taylor wrote an introduction for the 1966 Penguin edition of Reed's book, but it was rejected by the Communist party of Great Britain, who owned the copyright at the time. Once the copyright expired, Taylor's original introduction was included in the 1977 reprint.

FICTION

> And the star-spangled banner in triumph shall wave
> O'er the land of the free and the home of the brave!

America fought a 'Second War of Independence' against Britain between 1812 and 1815, which resulted in a decisive victory at the Battle of New Orleans, celebrated by the 'Star-Spangled Banner', now the American national anthem. This war boosted national pride, severed any lingering attachment to the 'old country', and writers began seeking to establish a new and distinctively American literary tradition. The first authors of American fiction were Washington Irving (407), John Fenimore Cooper (407) and Edgar Allan Poe (408), and the subsequent literary giants of the age were Herman Melville (410), Walt Whitman (413), Mark Twain (414) and Henry James (417).

THE NEW PENGUIN BOOK OF AMERICAN SHORT STORIES
from Washington Irving to Lydia Davis
19th–21st centuries

Edgar Allan Poe (408) said that a collection of short stories, more than a novel or a book of poems, is able to represent a 'vast variety of modes'. The stories in this selection are extremely varied, peopled with farm labourers, artists, aunts, soldiers, sons, witches, drunks, ghosts, property developers and vacuum cleaner salesmen, as well as a dog, a frog and a caterpillar. Authors include Poe, Hawthorne (412), Twain (414) and Wharton (427) as well as more recent writers, such as John Cheever, Alice Walker, Raymond Carver and Jhumpa Lahiri.

1969 Penguin Books
● ed. James Cochrane

2011
ed. Kasia Boddy

Washington Irving 1783–1859

Irving was America's first professional writer. He was born and raised in New York and published his rollicking *History of New York* in 1809 under the pseudonym 'Diedrich Knickerbocker'. But he made his international reputation in 1819–20 with *The Sketch Book of Geoffrey Crayon, Gent.* and went on to write many more stories, novels and travelogues, as well as biographies of Columbus (119), Goldsmith (164), Mohammed (97) and others. He served as the US ambassador to Spain between 1842 and 1846 and is buried in Sleepy Hollow Cemetery in New York State.

The Legend of Sleepy Hollow
and Other Stories 1819–20

This collection features many of Irving's best-loved stories, such as 'The Legend of Sleepy Hollow', about a phantom headless horseman, and 'Rip Van Winkle', about an extremely dozy, henpecked husband. Other pieces include 'A Sunday in London', 'The Spectre Bridegroom' and 'The Mutability of Literature'. The book was originally published in segments.

1988 *The Sketch Book*
2000 Reissued as *The Legend of Sleepy Hollow*
● ed. William L. Hedges

2014
ed. Elizabeth L. Bradley

James Fenimore Cooper 1789–1851

In 1819, Cooper's wife challenged his claim that he could write a better novel than the British book he was reading. In an attempt to prove his point, Cooper wrote *Precaution* (1820), which was a flop, but his second novel, *The Spy* (1821), was a success, and he went on to become the first major American novelist. Today he is best remembered for his romantic historical novels of the frontier period, known as his 'Leatherstocking Tales'.

The Pioneers
or, The Sources of the Susquehanna 1823

Cooper presents a year in the life of a pioneer settlement on Lake Otsego, upstate New York, in the last decade of the 18th century: he describes the changing seasons, the Christmas turkey shoot, tapping maple trees, fishing for bass and marshalling the militia. As the settlement grows in complexity, it requires stricter codes of law, which puts a strain on the book's central relationship between frontiersman Natty Bumppo and his best friend, the Mohican Chingachgook.

1988
ed. Donald A. Ringe

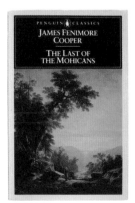

The Last of the Mohicans 1826
A Narrative of 1757

Natty Bumppo, known as 'Hawkeye', lives apart from other white men, in the company of his friend, Chingachgook. Their peaceful idyll is shattered, however, by the savage French and Indian War. Together they agree to guide two sisters in search of their missing father, amidst massacres, raids and danger from every side. This is often regarded as the first great American novel.

1986
intro. Richard Slotkin

Edgar Allan Poe 1809–1849

For <u>Tennyson</u> (263), Poe was the 'most original genius that America has produced'. He was the son of itinerant actors, but his father disappeared immediately he was born and his mother died when he was two years old; he was raised by John and Frances Allan, a Virginian merchant and his wife. Poe entered the West Point Military Academy in 1830, but was court-martialled and dishonourably discharged a year later, after which he became a newspaper editor. In 1836, he married his 13-year-old cousin, Virginia, who died eleven years later. 'I became insane,' he wrote, 'with long intervals of horrible sanity. During these fits of absolute unconsciousness, I drank.' His short and tormented life was characterized by sado-masochism, alcoholism, drug addiction, poverty and manic depression. He died after a deleterious bout of election-day drinking in October 1849. 'I do believe God gave me a spark of genius,' he said, 'but He quenched it in misery.'

PENGUIN ILLUSTRATED CLASSICS
SOME TALES OF MYSTERY & IMAGINATION
POE
Wood-engravings by Douglas Percy Bliss

1967 Penguin English Library
Selected Writings
1986 Penguin Classics
Fall of the House of Usher and Other Writings
ed. David Galloway

The Fall of the House of Usher
and Other Writings 1827–49

This anthology includes seventeen poems, nineteen stories and sixteen essays. It features all Poe's greatest works of the macabre: 'The Raven', who croaks the melancholy word, 'Nevermore'; 'The Pit and the Pendulum'; 'The Tell-Tale Heart'; 'The Black Cat'; and 'The Fall of the House of Usher', a tale about a cursed family and the destruction of their supernaturally sentient home. <u>Arthur Conan Doyle</u> (248) considered Poe the 'supreme original short-story writer of all time'.

1938 Illustrated Classics
Some Tales of Mystery and Imagination
● ill. Douglas P. Bliss
1944 Penguin Books
Some Tales of Mystery and Imagination
● —
1956 Penguin Books
Selected Tales
● ed. John Curtis

The Portable Edgar Allan Poe
1827–49

This collection features 29 stories organized thematically under the headings 'Predicaments', 'Bereavements', 'Antagonisms', 'Mysteries' and 'Grotesqueries'. It also includes 21 poems, 28 letters, nine essays on aesthetic and 'critical principles' and nineteen articles. Among the poems are the magnificent 'Eldorado', about a gallant knight's quest for the mythical city, and 'Annabel Kee', Poe's last complete poem, about a ravishingly good-looking woman who dies because the angels are jealous of her beauty. <u>Yeats</u> (267) thought Poe 'the greatest of all American poets'.

2006
ed. J. Gerald Kennedy

2009
ed. Peter Ackroyd

The Pit and the Pendulum
The Essential Poe 1831–45

This anthology is selected and introduced by the novelist and historian Peter Ackroyd. It features seven poems and fourteen stories, including the first modern detective story, 'The Murders in the Rue Morgue'; the tale of a deadly doppelgänger, 'William Wilson'; and a macabre fantasy, 'The Masque of the Red Death.'

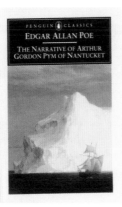

1976 Penguin English Library
1986 Penguin Classics
ed. Harold Beaver

The Science Fiction of Edgar Allan Poe

1833–49

As well as inventing detective fiction and perfecting the horror story, Poe also developed the genre of science fiction. In these sixteen stories, he draws on contemporary scientific developments to imagine time travel, resurrection of the dead and the end of the world. Also included is his sweeping cosmological prose poem *Eureka*, which sets out a comprehensive vision of the material and spiritual universe.

The Narrative of Arthur Gordon Pym of Nantucket 1838

Poe introduces his only complete novel as 'the details of a mutiny and atrocious butchery on board the American brig *Grampus*, on her way to the South Seas, in the month of June, 1827. With an account of the recapture of the vessel by the survivors; their shipwreck and subsequent horrible sufferings from famine; their deliverance by means of the British schooner *Jane Guy*; the brief cruise of this latter vessel in the Antarctic Ocean; her capture, and the massacre of her crew among the group of islands in the eighty-fourth parallel of south-ern latitude; together with the incredible adventures and discoveries STILL FURTHER SOUTH to which that distressing calamity gave rise.' Arthur Gordon Pym's extraordinary adventures include cannibalism, ghost ships, gigantic polar bears, undiscovered islands and a mysterious shrouded figure. Borges called it 'Poe's greatest work'; Poe called it 'a very silly book'.

1975 Penguin English Library
• ed. Jeffrey Meyers

1999
ed. Richard Kopley

AMERICAN SUPERNATURAL TALES

19th–20th centuries

'The true weird tale has something more than secret murder, bloody bones, or a sheeted form clanking chains according to rule,' wrote H. P. Lovecraft. 'A certain atmosphere of breathless and unexplain-able dread of outer, unknown forces must be present; and there must be a hint […] of that most terrible conception of the human brain – a malign and particular suspension or defeat of those fixed laws of Nature which are our only safeguard against the assaults of chaos and demons of unplumbed space.' This anthology deliberately assaults you with chaos and hurls you into unplumbed space, with stories by Washington Irving (407), Edgar Allan Poe (408), Shirley Jackson, Stephen King and Joyce Carol Oates.

2007
ed. S. T. Joshi

Herman Melville 1819– 1891

Melville was the son of a bankrupt New York tradesman. He joined the merchant vessel *St Lawrence* as a cabin boy, and spent the next five years at sea, initially on the whaleship *Acushnet* in the South Pacific. In 1842, he abandoned his crew on the Marquesas Islands, and made his way home via Tahiti and Honolulu. He settled in Massachusetts, living near Nathaniel Hawthorne (412), to whom he dedicated *Moby-Dick*, and he wrote a series of popular stories and novels inspired by his maritime experiences. After a trip to the Holy Land in 1857, however, he abandoned prose and spent the rest of his life working as a customs inspector in New York and writing small, privately published volumes of poetry. The manuscript of *Billy Budd, Sailor* (411) was discovered posthumously and published in 1924.

1976 Penguin English Library
1986 Penguin Classics
ed. Harold Beaver

Redburn
His First Voyage 1849

Wellington Redburn is a young New Yorker who runs away to sea as a cabin boy aboard the *Highlander*, bound for Liverpool. He is mocked by the crew and bullied by a vicious sailor called Jackson. In England, he is appalled by the destitution and endemic moral corruption. This is a largely autobiographical tale of youthful innocence beaten into bitter disillusionment.

Moby-Dick
or, The Whale 1851

'It is the horrible texture of a fabric that should be woven of ships' cables and hawsers,' wrote Melville of his masterpiece. 'A Polar wind blows through it, and birds of prey hover over it.' At 21, Melville joined the 104-foot whaleship *Acushnet*, inspired by an account he had read of a great albino sperm whale called 'Mocha Dick'. While in the South Pacific, the *Acushnet* frequently 'gammed' alongside a Nantucket whaler on which Melville met William Henry Chase, son of Owen Chase (398), who gave him a copy of his father's account of the sinking of the whaleship *Essex*, which Melville read 'upon the landless sea, & close to the very latitude of the shipwreck'.

Moby-Dick is, in part, the thrilling and eerie tale of the one-legged madman Ahab, captain of the whaleship *Pequod*, obsessively seeking a vast, dangerous creature as inscrutable and inhuman as the sea itself. It is also an encyclopaedic compendium of whaling lore, a biblical meditation on the state of America and a crucible for Melville's literary experiments: he incorporates blank verse (129), shanties, nautical terms, Homeric references (16) and stage directions into the narrative.

This great novel has had a huge and lasting influence. D. H. Lawrence (290) called it 'one of the strangest and most wonderful books in the world [...] the greatest book of the sea ever written'.

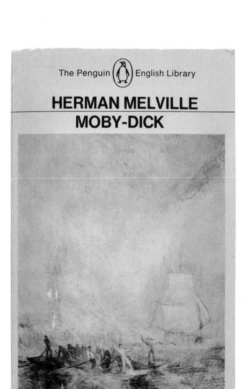

1972 Penguin English Library
● ed. Harold Beaver

1992
ed. Tom Quirk
intro. Andrew Delbanco

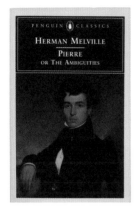

1996
ed. William C. Spengemann

Pierre
or, The Ambiguities 1852

This Gothic satire tells the story of Pierre Glendinning, engaged to the beautiful Lucy Tartan but incestuously drawn to his darkly mysterious half-sister Isabel Banford. In spiralling financial and domestic circumstances, haunted by spiritualists and visions of giants, Pierre commits a terrible crime and the narrative ends in tragedy. The New York *Herald* dismissed it as the 'dream of a distempered stomach, disordered by a hasty supper on half-cooked pork chops'; more generous critics have since praised its modernist literary techniques.

Billy Budd, Bartleby
and Other Stories 1855–c. 1891
The Piazza Tales; *The Paradise of Bachelors and the Tartarus of Maids*; *Billy Budd, Sailor*

The Piazza Tales are of six short stories, including 'Bartleby, the Scrivener', which is a fable of a Wall Street lawyer's clerk who stops working one day and refuses to make another copy or perform any task, saying, 'I would prefer not to.' *Billy Budd, Sailor*, Melville's last, unfinished novella, is the moving story of a naïve foundling from Bristol who is pressed into service on HMS *Bellipotent*. He is handsome, popular and in many ways angelic, but he stirs the envy of the master-at-arms John Claggart and the two clash fatally. It was adapted into a much-admired opera by Benjamin Britten in 1951.

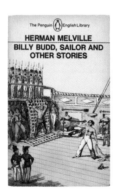

1968 Penguin English Library
● ed. Harold Beaver

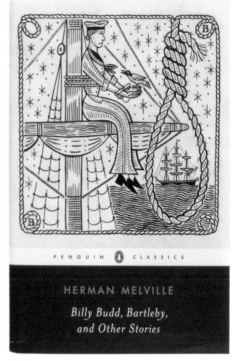

2016
ed. Peter Coviello

The Confidence-Man
His Masquerade
1857

Set on April Fool's Day aboard the Mississippi steamboat *Fidèle*, a Mephistophelean confidence trickster poses as a legless beggar, a businessman, a charity fundraiser and a cosmopolitan 'gentleman' in order to defraud the motley collection of passengers. The book includes recognizable satires of Melville's contemporaries, including Emerson (399), Thoreau (400), Hawthorne (412) and Poe (408). It was published on April Fool's Day.

1990
ed. Stephen Matterson

1945 Penguin Books
●—
1970 Penguin English Library
● ed. Thomas E. Connolly, 1970
intro. Nina Baym, 1983

2016
ed. Robert Milder
fwd. Tom Perrotta

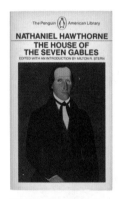

1981 Penguin American Library
1986 Penguin Classics
ed. Milton R. Stern

Nathaniel Hawthorne 1804–1864

Hawthorne was born in Salem, Massachusetts, a descendent of the only unrepentant judge who presided over the Salem witch trials of 1692 (395). Between 1839 and 1840, he worked in the Boston Custom-House, a period he recalls in his introduction to *The Scarlet Letter*. In the 1850s, he was appointed American consul in Liverpool. He returned to the Old Manse in Concord, Massachusetts, but was unable to complete a number of final projects before he died.

The Scarlet Letter 1850
A Romance

An adulterous affair in the strict Puritan community of 17th-century Massachusetts Bay leads to an illegitimate birth. The mother, Hester Prynne, is publicly ostracized and forced to wear a scarlet 'A' on her dress for the rest of her life; but she steadfastly refuses to reveal the identity of the father. The novel is an exposition on law, sin and guilt, a study of the border between private and public worlds. D. H. Lawrence (290) thought there could be no more perfect work of the American imagination.

The House of the Seven Gables 1851

The once wealthy Pyncheon family lives at the gloomy House of the Seven Gables, but their property was built on ground stolen by an ancestor and they are living under a dead wizard's curse. Through madness and murder, old family secrets are gradually revealed. It is 'a weird, wild book', wrote Henry Wadsworth Longfellow, 'like all he writes'. It had a great influence on H. P. Lovecraft, who called it 'New England's greatest contribution to weird literature'. The house is modelled on a real house that still stands in Salem, Massachussets.

Harriet Beecher Stowe 1811–1896

Beecher was born in Connecticut into a family of religious leaders and reformers. After attending the seminary run by her sister, she joined her father in Ohio and campaigned against slavery. She published *Uncle Tom's Cabin* in 1852, the first novel to criticize the institution of slavery. It was the bestselling American novel of the 19th century and caused a sensation around the world: Stowe was invited to make a lecture tour of Britain, during which she was presented to Queen Victoria. Abraham Lincoln is said to have met her at the start of the Civil War and exclaimed, 'So you're the little woman who wrote the book that made this great war!' Towards the end of her life, Stowe suffered from dementia, and at the age of 77 she began writing *Uncle Tom's Cabin* for the second time.

Uncle Tom's Cabin
or, Life Among the Lowly 1852

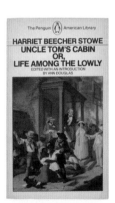

1981 Penguin American Library
1986 Penguin Classics
ed. Ann Douglas

Uncle Tom is the long-suffering good-hearted slave sold 'down the river' by his impecunious white owners. He befriends a young white girl named Eva St Clare, whose father buys him, and Tom goes to live with the St Clares in New Orleans. Almost everyone who comes into contact with Tom is either converted to Christianity or humbled and changed by his saintly nature. Despite considerable racial stereotyping, which has since proved controversial, many agree with Tolstoy (376), who called the novel 'one of the greatest productions of the human mind'.

Walt Whitman 1819– 1892

Whitman was a printer's devil, journeyman compositor, itinerant schoolteacher and newspaper editor from Long Island, New York. He was also a bisexual, a humanist, and a free-verse poet who enjoyed swimming naked. His poetry bridged the literary transition from Transcendentalism to realism. During the Civil War, he worked as a nurse in Washington, DC. He spent his last years in Camden, New Jersey, drawing international admiration from the likes of Wilde (244), Swinburne (265) and Stoker (260). Ezra Pound called him 'America's poet [...] He *is* America.' 'An individual is as superb as a nation when he has the qualities which make a superb nation,' writes Whitman in his preface to *Leaves of Grass*. '[...] The proof of a poet is that his country absorbs him as affectionately as he has absorbed it.'

WALT WHITMAN
The Complete Poems

1975 Penguin Education
1977 Penguin Poets
1986 Penguin Classics
ed. Francis Murphy

Leaves of Grass
The First Edition 1855

1986 Penguin Classics
ed. Malcolm Cowley, 1959

This is the text of Whitman's self-financed first edition of *Leaves of Grass*, the edition which prompted Emerson (399) to write to him saying, 'I greet you at the beginning of a great career.' There was no author's name on the original frontispiece, but 500 lines in he introduces himself as 'Walt Whitman, an American, one of the roughs, a kosmos, / Disorderly fleshy and sensual.' Whitman set out to write an all-American epic, using free verse and the cadences of the Bible (4). The critic Harold Bloom says that, 'if you are American, then Walt Whitman is your imaginative father and mother'; the first edition of *Leaves of Grass* is 'the secular Scripture of the United States'.

The Complete Poems 1855–91

'I believe a leaf of grass is no less than the journey-work of the stars.' Whitman expanded *Leaves of Grass* throughout his life and this complete, 900-page edition reprints his final, 'death-bed' version. It also appends earlier poems, thereby charting the complete career of the greatest American poet.

Louisa May Alcott 1832– 1888

Alcott was the second of four daughters of Abba May and Bronson Alcott, the prominent Transcendentalist thinkers and reformers. She was raised in Concord, Massachusetts, and grew up knowing Emerson (399), Hawthorne (412) and Thoreau (400), all of whom taught her at one point or another. She worked as a nurse during the Civil War before starting to write, and she later campaigned for women's suffrage and the temperance movement. She died on the day her father was buried.

Little Women 1868

Based loosely on the actual childhood of the four Alcott sisters, *Little Women* is the story of the March girls: beautiful Meg, the eldest, who marries young; tomboy Jo, based on Alcott herself, who is courted by the boy next door; shy and gentle Beth, weakened after scarlet fever; and artistic Amy, who goes on a European tour with their eccentric Aunt March. G. K. Chesterton (293) said this much-loved tale 'anticipated realism by twenty or thirty years'.

1953 Puffin Books

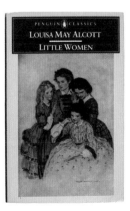

1989 Penguin Classics
ed. Elaine Showalter
notes Siobhan Kilfeather &
Vinca Showalter

Mark Twain 1835–1910

Samuel Langhorne Clemens grew up on the banks of the Mississippi River, in Hannibal, Missouri. He trained as a riverboat pilot until the outbreak of the Civil War, when all river traffic was stopped. Then he went silver prospecting in Nevada and worked as a journalist in California. He first used the pseudonym 'Mark Twain', a riverboatman's term for two fathoms on the sounding line, in 1863. His first literary success was the 1865 short story 'The Celebrated Jumping Frog of Calaveras County', which became a favourite of Charles Darwin's (269). Twain's humorous, mischievous works of astute social observation soon made him a household name and a respected public figure, famous for his white suit and thick shock of white hair. William Faulkner considered him 'the father of American literature'. Twain was born shortly after the 1835 appearance of Halley's Comet and he predicted that he would 'go out with it as well'; he died the day after the comet reappeared in 1910.

The Innocents Abroad 1867–9

In 1867, a San Francisco newspaper sent Twain on a tour of Europe and the Middle East as a roving correspondent. Later he compiled his semi-fictionalized dispatches into a single volume, a caricature of the sentimental travel books popular at the time. He includes many humorous reactions to famous European landmarks and gently satirizes the contrast between American and European manners. It is one of the bestselling travel books of all time. On this trip Twain met a fellow passenger, Charles Langdon, who showed him a photograph of his sister Olivia. Twain fell in love at first sight and married Olivia in 1870.

Roughing It 1872

In the 1860s, Mark Twain rambled around the Wild West, prospecting for gold and silver, speculating on timber and mining stocks, sailing to the kingdom of Hawaii and working as a journalist. This fictionalized and exaggerated account of those years includes hilarious tales of desperadoes, vigilantes, newspapermen and Mormons.

The Adventures of Tom Sawyer 1876

This much-loved book in modelled on Twain's own childhood in Hannibal, Missouri. Tom is a boisterous, rollicking rascal who basks on the banks of the Mississippi, whitewashes a fence, gets lost in a cave and plays all manner of pranks around the neighbourhood. Twain borrowed the name of a San Francisco fireman he had met in 1863: the real Tom Sawyer was a local hero, who rescued 90 passengers from a shipwreck. The book also introduces Tom's loyal friend Huckleberry Finn (416), who was based on Twain's own childhood friend Tom Blankenship.

1950 Puffin Books
● —
1986
● ed. John Seelye

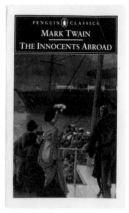

2002
ed. Guy Cardwell
intro. Tom Quirk

1981 Penguin American Library
1985 Penguin Classics
ed. Hamlin Hill

2014
ed. R. Kent Rasmussen

1997
intro. Robert Gray Bruce &
Hamlin Hill

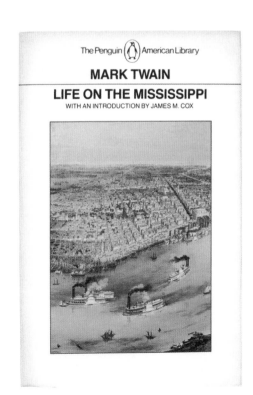

A Tramp Abroad 1880

In this sequel to *The Innocents Abroad* (414), Twain embarks on
a fictionalized walking tour of Germany, Switzerland and Italy,
accompanied by a friend called Harris. As in the previous travel
book, Twain casts himself as a humorously obtuse tourist, claiming to understand every situation, as he rafts down the Neckar,
ascends Mont Blanc 'by telescope' and studies artworks in
Venice. Twain interpolates several standalone stories, apparently
local legends, illustrates the whole book with his own primitive
sketches and appends six essays on various topics including hotel
porters, prisons and 'The Awful German Language'.

The Prince and the Pauper
1880–8

Tom Canty is a poor boy from Pudding
Lane in London, who bears a striking
resemblance to young Edward Tudor,
prince of England, the son of Henry
VIII. When the two boys meet by
chance they swap identities for a lark,
but the game backfires when they are
separated, King Henry dies and Tom
finds himself mistaken for the heir
to the throne. As well as portraying
riotous scenes of 16th-century London
this is also a commentary on social
inequality. 'My idea,' wrote Twain, 'is

1997
ed. Jerry Griswold

to afford a realizing sense of the exceeding severity of the laws
of that day by inflicting some of their penalties upon the King
himself and allowing him a chance to see the rest of them applied
to others.' This volume also includes 'A Boy's Adventure', a short
story about a whipping-boy, which Twain originally wrote as part
of *The Prince and the Pauper* but which was eventually published
separately.

Life on the Mississippi 1883

Twain's humorous tour of the Mississippi is a guide to the landscape, history and people along the banks of the river and a
nostalgic reminiscence of tall tales, anecdotes and characters from
his youth. He explains how, in his childhood, 'there was but one
permanent ambition' among his friends: to become the pilot of a
riverboat, a career that he attempted to pursue himself.

1984 Penguin American Library
1986 Penguin Classics
ed. James M. Cox

1953 Puffin Books

1966 Penguin English Library
1985 Penguin Classics
ed. Peter Coveney

2014
ed. R. Kent Rasmussen
fwd. Azar Nafisi

The Adventures of Huckleberry Finn 1884

'All modern American literature,' wrote Ernest Hemingway, 'comes from one book by Mark Twain called *Huckleberry Finn*. [...] It's the best book we've had.' Twain's acknowledged masterpiece, often regarded as 'the greatest American novel', is a sequel to *Tom Sawyer* (414). Tom's friend Huck escapes from his drunken father and the unbearably 'sivilizing' Widow Douglas and, together with the runaway slave Jim, sets out on a picaresque raft adventure down the Mississippi River.

A Connecticut Yankee at King Arthur's Court 1889

Hank Morgan is a mechanic from Connecticut. When he is knocked unconscious, he wakes up in 6th-century Camelot. With his knowledge of the future, however, he correctly predicts a solar eclipse and establishes himself as an all-powerful magician at Arthur's court, stronger than Merlin, with the power to detonate explosives and build machinery. When he tries to introduce American democratic ideals to medieval England, however, the Church publishes an interdict against him and his fortunes begin to turn. Twain wrote this burlesque romance after a dream he had in which he was a medieval knight himself, struggling to move inside a cumbersome suit of armour. He draws heavily on Malory's *Morte D'Arthur* (90).

1971 Penguin English Library
1986 Penguin Classics
intro. Justin Kaplan
ill. Dan Beard

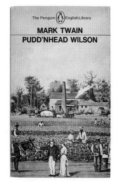

1969 Penguin
English Library
1986 Penguin
Classics
ed. Malcolm
Bradbury

Pudd'nhead Wilson
and Those Extraordinary Twins 1894

David 'Pudd'nhead' Wilson is a lawyer who becomes involved in a strange case of child-swapping. Roxy, a slave, swapped her son Tom with his playmate Chambers, her master's son, and now Tom has been to Yale and learned to drink and gamble, whereas Chambers is a subservient drudge. When a crime is committed, Pudd'nhead sets about unravelling the case, which could end disastrously for everyone concerned. This edition also includes Twain's short story 'Those Extraordinary Twins', which was the basis for the novel.

Henry James

1843–1916

James was born in Washington Place, New York, the younger brother of the philosopher William James (404). In 1875, he spent a year in Paris, where he met Flaubert (313), Daudet (318), Maupassant (374) and Turgenev (374), and in 1876 he moved to London. He remained in England for the rest of his life, settling in Rye on the Sussex coast, and he became a naturalized British citizen in 1915, one year before his death. He wrote short stories, plays, books of criticism and 20 novels. Though H. G. Wells (255) compared James's writing to 'a magnificent but painful hippopotamus' trying to pick up 'a pea which has got into a corner of its den', most readers have agreed with F. R. Leavis, who considered *The Portrait of a Lady* (419) and *The Bostonians* (420), for example, 'two of the most brilliant novels in the language'.

Daisy Miller

and Other Tales 1870–1904

The novellas and stories in this collection explore Anglo-American relations and the tension between the old world and the new. As well as *Daisy Miller* (418), it includes 'Madame de Mauves', a sad tale about a loveless marriage between an American woman and an adulterous Frenchman, and 'Europe', in which an old New England widow prevents her daughters from escaping across the Atlantic.

1963 Modern Classics
Selected Short Stories
1983 Reissued as *Daisy Miller and Other Stories*
● ed. Michael Swan

2016
ed. Stephen Fender

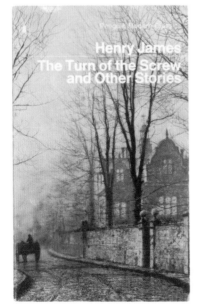

1973 Modern Classics
● ed. S. Gorley Putt
2001 *Selected Tales*
● ed. John Lyon

2017
ed. Susie Boyt

The Turn of the Screw

and Other Ghost Stories 1868–1908

'I see ghosts everywhere,' wrote Henry James. As well as *The Turn of the Screw* (421), this selection features seven other tales of the uncanny, including 'The Jolly Corner', in which a doppelgänger lives out an alternative life across the Atlantic, and 'Owen Wingrave', a tale of dark family secrets, which Benjamin Britten adapted into an opera.

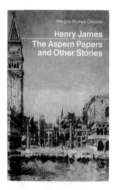

1976 Modern Classics
● ed. S. Gorley Putt

1986 *The Figure in the Carpet and Other Stories*
ed. Frank Kermode
—
Kermode's 1986 anthology has a similar selection to that in Gorra's 2014 edition.

2014
ed. Michael Gorra

The Aspern Papers
and Other Tales 1884–96

All of these elaborate, playful stories are concerned with the relationship between fiction and reality. 'The Aspern Papers' is about a fanatical critic desperate to get hold of a trove of memorabilia that once belonged to a long-dead poet, based on Shelley (196). In 'The Figure in the Carpet', an author confounds his reviewers by saying they have missed his 'secret', the 'thing for the critic to find', which he compares to a 'complex figure in a Persian carpet'.

Roderick Hudson 1875

In James's first full-length novel, Roderick Hudson is an impoverished and charismatic American sculptor. He is discovered by the wealthy patron Rowland Mallet, who brings him to Rome where he quickly establishes a reputation; but he begins to lose inspiration when he falls in love with Christina Light, a beautiful femme fatale. Christina proved such a fascinating character that James wrote another novel about her, *The Princess Casamassima* (420).

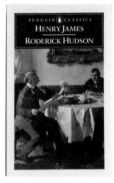

1969 Modern Classics
● ed. S. Gorley Putt

1986
ed. Geoffrey Moore
notes Patricia Crick

1981 Penguin American Library
1986 Penguin Classics
ed. William Spengemann

The American 1876–7

James wrote *The American* in response to a play by Alexandre Dumas *fils* (313) called *The Foreigner* (1876). Christopher Newman is an American millionaire in Paris. He falls in love with a beautiful aristocratic widow, Claire de Bellegarde, and proposes marriage, but her supercilious family rejects him on account of his brash American manner until he discovers a dark secret from their past.

Daisy Miller
A Study 1878

Daisy is a beautiful, independent and eccentric young American travelling in Europe with her family. Winterbourne, her fellow countryman, cannot work out

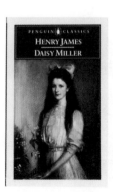

1986
● ed. Geoffrey Moore

2007
ed. David Lodge

whether she deliberately flouts social conventions or whether she is ignorant of them, especially when she becomes entangled with a smooth young Italian. This was the novella that decisively established James's reputation on both sides of the Atlantic.

The Europeans
A Sketch 1878

'This small book, written so early in James's career,' wrote F. R. Leavis, 'is a masterpiece of major quality.' The God-fearing New England world of the Wentworths is shaken by the arrival of their exotic, sophisticated cousins Eugenia Münster and Felix Young, siblings raised in Europe. Eugenia is looking for a second husband after a failed marriage to a German prince, and handsome Felix catches the eye of young Gertrude Wentworth.

Washington Square 1880

Washington Square is 'perhaps the only novel in which a man has successfully invaded the feminine field and produced a work comparable to Jane Austen's (200)', wrote Graham Greene. Plain Catherine Sloper of Washington Square, New York, is astonished when the dashing Morris Townsend asks for her hand in marriage, and correspondingly distraught when her father forbids the match on the grounds that Townsend is an insincere fortune hunter.

1964 Modern Classics
• —

2008
ed. Andrew Taylor

1963 Modern Classics
• —
1984 Penguin English Library
• ed. Brian Lee

2007
ed. Martha Banta

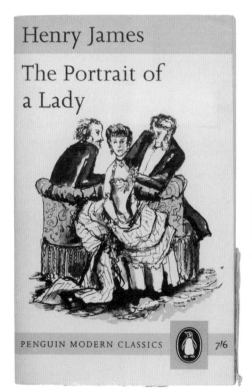

1963 Modern Classics
• —
1984 Penguin English Library
• ed. Geoffrey Moore

2011
ed. Philip Horne

The Portrait of a Lady
1881

This novel is a depiction of Isabel Archer, a spirited and wealthy American travelling in Europe with her aunt, Mrs Touchett. Determined to confront her own destiny, Isabel turns down two eligible suitors in favour of the irresistibly charming American expatriate Gilbert Osmond. One of James's most popular novels, *The Portrait of a Lady* is also considered the culmination of his 'first period' of fiction, in which he dwells mainly on the contrast between Europe and America.

1977 Modern Classics
• —

1987
ed. Derek Brewer
notes Patricia Crick

The Princess Casamassima 1886

Hyacinth Robinson is an impoverished London bookbinder, the illegitimate son of a dressmaker and a nobleman. He is acutely conscious of the social and financial inequality that surrounds him and he becomes involved in radical politics. He vows to commit an act of terrorism, but then he meets the Princess Casamassima, formerly Christina Light (418), and is introduced to her opulent world of wealth and refinement. Hyacinth is gripped by a fearful dilemma: he believes he must honour his vow but he is painfully aware of how revolution will destroy the princess's world.

The Bostonians
A Novel 1886

Basil Ransom is a handsome, conservative young lawyer from Mississippi, who visits his wealthy feminist cousin Olive in Boston. Together they attend a meeting on women's emancipation where one of the speakers is Olive's protégée Verena Tarrant. Basil is immediately enraptured by Verena and attempts to 'reform' her with his traditional views of gender roles, prompting a battle for Verena's allegiance and affection. Mark Twain (414) swore that 'he would rather be damned to John Bunyan's heaven (173) than read *The Bostonians*'. Others consider it James's comic masterpiece.

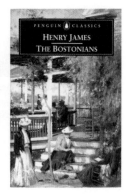

1966 Modern Classics
• —
1984 Penguin English Library
• ed. Charles R. Anderson

2000
ed. Richard Lansdown

1978 Modern Classics
• —

1995
ed. Philip Horne

The Tragic Muse 1890

Nick Dormer abandons a glittering parliamentary career in London in order to paint. He creates a portrait of the magnificently fiery actress Miriam Rooth, who poses for him as 'the Tragic Muse'. Their interwoven stories and romantic entanglements explore the border between art and reality.

What Maisie Knew 1897

Young Maisie's selfish parents have gone through a bitter divorce and now she travels between them and around the world, used by each parent as a means of irritating the other. Both her parents take lovers and remarry, and Maisie, herself growing older, becomes drawn into their web of lies and sexual betrayal. While composing this book, James began dictating to a typist, a method he used for the rest of his career. This may explain why his style shifts gradually, in favour of long sentences with multiple clauses and single paragraphs that run for page after page.

1966 Modern Classics
• —
1985
• ed. Paul Theroux

2010
ed. Christopher Ricks

The Spoils of Poynton 1897

Mrs Gereth of Poynton Park is a domineering English widow who has spent her life amassing a spectacular collection of antique treasures. She would love her son Owen to marry the sensitive Fleda Vetch, who shares her passion for beautiful things, but Owen has inconveniently proposed to the uncultured, athletic Mona Brigstock. These three women become enmeshed in a quarrel around the weak-willed Owen.

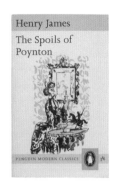

1963 Modern Classics
● —

1987
intro. David Lodge
notes Patricia Crick

1947 Penguin Books
● —
1984 Penguin English Library
● ed. Anthony Curtis
Published with 'The Aspern Papers' (418)

2011
ed. David Bromwich

The Turn of the Screw 1898

In 1877, James visited Wenlock Abbey in Shropshire, which is surrounded by gloomy monastic fishponds and is said to have inspired this celebrated ghost story. When an inexperienced young governess is sent to a country house to take charge of two orphans, Miles and Flora, she becomes conscious of an air of dark menace and is haunted by the rumours of two former employees, Peter Quint and Miss Jessel. She becomes increasingly certain that there are malevolent forces at work in the house and that the children are in desperate danger. Oscar Wilde (244) called it 'a most wonderful, lurid, poisonous little tale, like an Elizabethan tragedy (132)'. It is considered the climax of the 'second period' of James's literary career.

The Awkward Age 1899

When naïve Nanda Brookenham comes of age and makes her debut in London society, she enters her parents' superficial, corrupt circle of friends and finds herself competing with her own mother for the affections of the man she admires. Only an elderly bachelor, Mr Longdon, is immune to the scheming machinations of the marriage market; he determines to rescue Nanda, out of the love he once felt for her grandmother.

1966 Modern Classics
● —

1987
ed. Ronald Blythe
notes Patricia Crick

The Wings of the Dove 1902

Kate Croy, beautiful and ruthless, loves Merton Densher; but he is not sufficiently wealthy to secure her future, so she decides to exploit her friendship with the American heiress Milly Theale, who is gravely ill and extremely rich. Croy learns too late, however, how inconstant the human heart can be. James based the character of Milly on his much-loved cousin Minny Temple, who died of tuberculosis: he wrote *The Wings of the Dove* in order to wrap her memory in the 'beauty and dignity of art'. The loose trilogy formed by this and his next two novels, *The Ambassadors* (422) and *The Golden Bowl* (422), are considered by many to be the high point of James's career.

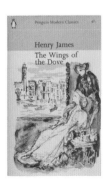

1965 Modern Classics
● —
1986
● ed. Patricia Crick
intro. John Bayley

2008
ed. Millicent Bell

The Ambassadors 1903

James thought *The Ambassadors* his greatest novel. Mrs Newsome, of Woollett Massachusetts, is concerned that her son Chad has been corrupted by a woman of dubious reputation in Paris, so she sends her fiancé Lambert Strether as an 'ambassador' to extricate him. Strether, however, falls in love with Paris himself and finds Chad refined and if anything improved by the beautiful city and the company of his charming companion Madame de Vionnet. Impatient for results, Mrs Newsome sends her daughter as a second ambassador to confront both Chad and the wayward Strether.

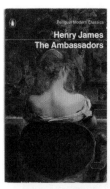

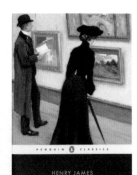

1973 Modern Classics
● —
1986
● ed. Harry Levin

2008
ed. Adrian Poole

1966 Modern Classics
● ● —
1985
● ed. Patricia Crick
intro. Gore Vidal

2009
ed. Ruth Bernard Yeazell

The Golden Bowl 1904

The young American heiress Maggie Verver lives in London with her widowed millionaire father. They are both engaged to be married, Maggie to Prince Amerigo, a penniless Italian aristocrat, and her father to the beautiful and equally impoverished Charlotte Stant, a friend of Maggie's. Little do parent and child know, however, that their affianced share a secret past which threatens to destroy their world. A. N. Wilson considers *The Golden Bowl* 'one of the greatest pieces of fiction ever written'.

Italian Hours 1909

James knew Italy well and wrote a number of essays between 1872 and 1909 about the country's art, religion, politics and culture, as well as the joy of travel itself. He collected these essays in 1909 and sculpted a single volume he called *Italian Hours*. He traces his metamorphosis from note-taking novelist to contented tourist, happy to bask in the 'luxury of loving Italy'.

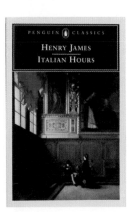

1995
ed. John Auchard, 1992

A Life in Letters 1864–1915

'Henry James was not only the greatest novelist in the English language,' says John Banville, 'but also the greatest letter writer. [His letters are] robust, funny, dignified, gossipy, informative, entertaining and, above all, beautifully written.' James corresponded with presidents and prime ministers, actresses and bishops, and many fellow writers including <u>Robert Louis Stevenson</u> (241), <u>H. G. Wells</u> (255) and <u>Edith Wharton</u> (427). James's sparkling letters form, in Philip Horne's words, his 'real and best biography.'

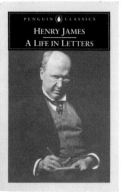

2000
ed. Philip Horne

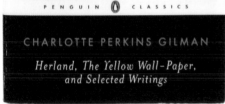

2009
ed. Denise D. Knight, 1999

Charlotte Perkins Gilman

1860–1935

Gilman was born in New England, a descendant of the prominent Beecher family; her paternal aunt was Harriet Beecher Stowe (412). In 1884, the birth of her daughter prompted a long period of depression. After attempting an exacting 'rest cure', she suffered a complete nervous breakdown, and in 1888 she left her husband and moved with her daughter to California, where she began to write. Her book *Women and Economics* (1898) was translated into seven different languages and she went on to write passionately feminist works of sociology as well as stories and poetry, which she published in her own magazine, *The Forerunner*. In 1932, she was diagnosed with inoperable breast cancer and later took her own life with an overdose of chloroform.

The Yellow Wall-Paper
Herland
and Selected Writings 1884–1916

'The Yellow Wall-Paper' is a short story about a married woman's mental breakdown during a period of enforced 'rest' overseen by her smotheringly attentive husband and sister-in-law: she becomes obsessed with the patterned yellow wallpaper in the nursery room to which she is confined. *Herland* is a novella about an idyllic land in which men have been absent for 2000 years. This edition includes other short stories and a selection of poetry.

Sarah Orne Jewett

1849–1909

Jewett was born in South Berwick, Maine, and travelled around the state assisting her father, a country doctor who specialized in obstetrics. She was a prolific writer and many of her short stories and novels are set along the southern coast of Maine. Sadly a serious road accident in 1902 left her unable to write any more and she died in 1909.

The Country of the Pointed Firs
and Other Stories 1886–1909

Jewett's masterpiece is *The Country of Pointed Firs*, a kaleidoscopic novel, made up of linked short stories, narrated by a young female writer who details her idyllic New England life, her friendships and the local community, with descriptions of the sea, the sky, the earth and the trees. Willa Cather called the chapters 'living things caught in the open, with light and freedom and air-spaces about them. They melt into the land and the life of the land until they are not stories at all, but life itself.' Henry James (417) said it was a 'beautiful little quantum of achievement'. This volume includes ten other short stories, including 'A White Heron', 'Marsh Rosemary', 'The King of Folly Island' and 'The Queen's Twin'.

1995
ed. Alison Easton

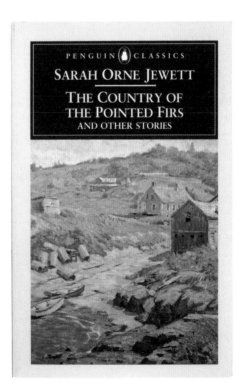

Kate Chopin 1850–1904

Kate O'Flaherty was born in St Louis, Missouri, to an Irish father and French mother. She married Oscar Chopin and moved with him to New Orleans, where they had five sons, before moving to Cloutierville, a tiny French settlement in northwest Louisiana, where they had a daughter. Oscar died three years later and Kate ran their plantations on her own, and had an affair with a married neighbour, before returning to St. Louis in 1884. Only then did she embark on a literary career, writing two novels and more than a hundred stories, poems, essays and plays.

The Awakening
and Selected Stories
1892–99

In *The Awakening*, Edna Pontellier is a young wife and mother who refuses to be constrained by marriage, maternal responsibility or social convention. Instead she seeks to sate her burgeoning feelings and desires. Condemned as sordid and immoral at the time of publication, it is now seen as Chopin's masterpiece and a landmark work of early feminism. 'The bird that would soar above the level plain of tradition and prejudice must have strong wings,' she writes. This volume also includes twelve short stories, including 'Désirée's Baby', 'The Story of an Hour', 'Emancipation' and 'The Storm'.

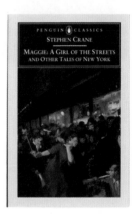

1984 Penguin American Library
1986 Penguin Classics
ed. Sandra M. Gilbert

Stephen Crane 1871–1900

Crane was the son of a Methodist minister from Newark, New Jersey, the youngest of fourteen children. The publication of *The Red Badge of Courage* in 1895 made him an overnight international celebrity, and in the next few years he travelled the world as a foreign correspondent gathering material for more works of fiction. He moved to Europe in 1899 and met Joseph Conrad (277) and H. G. Wells (255) but he died of tuberculosis in a German sanatorium at the age of just 28. Wells called him 'the best writer of our generation […] his untimely death was an irreparable loss to our literature'.

Maggie: A Girl of the Streets
and Other Tales of New York
1893–6

Maggie is raw and naturalistic but also has passages of fast-paced, vivid impressionism. It describes the denizens of the Bowery in New York, particularly the unfortunate Maggie, who 'blossomed in a mud-puddle' and descends into prostitution. This volume also includes *George's Mother*, in which Maggie makes a brief reappearance, and fourteen other stories and sketches set in New York.

2000
ed. Larzer Ziff with Theo Davis

The Red Badge of Courage
and Other Stories 1895–9

Crane's innovative masterpiece, written thirty years after the Civil War ended, is the story of the patriotic and naïve Henry Fleming, a recruit in the Union army, who hopes to earn his 'badge of courage' in combat. His heroic illusions are shattered when he faces the Confederate enemy and witnesses the ghastly death of a friend. Ernest Hemingway considered it 'one of the finest books of our literature […] as much of a piece as a great poem is'. This edition includes five other stories and a selection of Crane's poetry.

1948 Penguin Books
● —
1983 Penguin American Library
● ed. Pascal Covici

2005
ed. Gary Scharnhorst

1982 Puffin Books *The Wonderful Wizard of Oz*
• —
1985 Puffin Books *The Emerald City of Oz*
• —

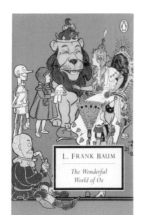

1998 Twentieth-Century Classics
2012 Penguin Threads 2012
ed. Jack Zipes
—
This edition includes the original illustrations by W. W. Denslow & John R. Neill.

L. Frank Baum 1858–1919

Lyman Frank Baum was a journalist, a horticulturalist, a chicken fancier, a fireworks salesman, a theatre manager, producer, actor and playwright, and the owner of a general store. He wrote fourteen Oz novels and several other books for children, including *The Life and Adventures of Santa Claus* (1902) and *Queen Zixi of Ix* (1905). His last words to his wife were, 'Now we can cross the shifting sands,' a reference to the Deadly Desert that surrounds the Land of Oz.

The Wizard of Oz
and Other Wonderful Books of Oz 1900–20
The Wonderful Wizard of Oz; *The Emerald City of Oz*; *Glinda of Oz*

Oz was Baum's vision of a peaceful, socialist paradise, occasionally threatened by malevolent villains. In *The Wonderful Wizard of Oz*, Dorothy Gale is blown in from Kansas and teams up with the Scarecrow, the Tin Woodman, the Cowardly Lion and a disappointing wizard to tackle the Wicked Witch of the West. In *The Emerald City of Oz*, the sixth in the series, Dorothy returns to Oz with Aunt Em and Uncle Henry to save the population from the evil Nome King; and in *Glinda of Oz*, published posthumously, Dorothy and Princess Ozma struggle to prevent a battle between the Skeezers and the Flatheads.

Theodore Dreiser 1871–1945

Dreiser was born in Indiana, the twelfth child of a German immigrant. He worked for newspapers in Chicago, St Louis and Pittsburgh before becoming a magazine writer in New York, interviewing Nathaniel Hawthorne (412) and Israel Zangwill for features. He visited Europe for the first time in 1912 and had planned to return on the *Titanic* (302); luckily his publisher persuaded him to make a cheaper crossing. The author H. L. Mencken declared that he was 'a great artist, and that no other American of his generation left so wide and handsome a mark upon the national letters'.

Sister Carrie 1900

Caroline Meeber is a poor country girl who rises to wealth and status as the mistress of a series of men in Chicago. The novel's objective style and controversial subject matter meant it was expurgated and published quietly in 1900, but nonetheless it came to the attention of many writers of the day and is now seen as marking the beginning of the naturalist movement in America. Sinclair Lewis said that 'Dreiser's great first novel […] came to housebound and airless America like a great free Western wind, and to our stuffy domesticity gave us the first fresh air since Mark Twain (414) and Whitman (413)'.

1981 Penguin American Library
1994 Twentieth-Century Classics
2004 Penguin Classics
ed. James L. W. West III
intro. Alfred Kazin

The Financier 1912

Frank Cowperwood is an ambitious businessman, the embodiment of greed, who ruthlessly pursues lucrative deals, beautiful women and power. But then his double-dealing comes back to haunt him. This scathing critique of the dog-eat-dog brutality at the heart of the American Dream is based on the life of the corrupt tycoon Charles T. Yerkes.

2008
ed. Larzer Ziff

Jack London 1876–1916

'He was an adventurer and a man of action as few writers have ever been,' wrote George Orwell. John Griffith Chaney grew up on the waterfront of San Francisco, the son of a spiritualist and an astrologer; before he was born, his father disowned him and his mother attempted to shoot herself. He left school at fourteen and worked in a cannery, as an oyster pirate, as a member of the California Fish Patrol and on a seal-hunting ship, which took him as far as Japan. On his return to the United States, he joined the gold rush to the Klondike, where he developed scurvy. He travelled to London and wrote about the slum conditions in the East End, he made voyages to the Caribbean and the South Seas, he sailed to Australia on a yacht called the _Snark_ (233) and he was a war correspondent during the Russo-Japanese War.

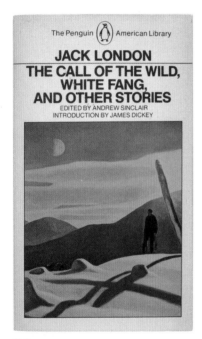

1981 Penguin American Library
1986 Penguin Classics
1993 Twentieth-Century Classics
2008 Penguin Classics
ed. Andrew Sinclair
intro. James Dickey
—
The Call of the Wild was also the first title in the Puffin Classics series, which began in 1982.

The Call of the Wild
White Fang
and Other Stories 1903–7

These are four stories of the harsh northern lands of the Yukon. In _The Call of the Wild_, a domestic dog learns how to survive in the wilderness; E. L. Doctorow considered it London's masterpiece. In contrast, _White Fang_ is the story of a wild wolf-dog who acclimatizes to the world of men. _Love of Life_ is about a lonesome trek across the Canadian tundra; and _Bâtard_ is about a fearsome dog who hates his harsh master.

Martin Eden 1909

Martin is an impoverished San Francisco seaman who dreams of education and literary fame. London wrote this semi-autobiographical novel at a time when he was dissatisfied with his own literary success, and intended the story as an attack on individual ambition. 'One of my motifs, in this book, was an attack on individualism,' he wrote to Upton Sinclair (428). '[…] I must have bungled, for not a single reviewer has discovered it.'

1967 Modern Classics

1984 Penguin American Library
1993 Twentieth-Century Classics
2008 Penguin Classics
ed. Andrew Sinclair

Tales of
the Pacific
1909–19

Always a voyager, London spent his last months writing in Hawaii, debilitated by tropical disease and exhausted after sailing across the Pacific. The twelve stories in this collection are all set in the South Seas: they feature lepers, colonial oppressors and retellings of Hawaiian myths, and are by turns funny, gruesome and tragic.

1989 Twentieth-Century Classics
ed. Andrew Sinclair

Edith Wharton 1862–1937

Edith Newbold Jones was born into a distinguished New York family, sometimes said to have inspired the phrase 'keeping up with the Joneses'. Her mother forbade her to read novels until she was married, so she started reading after she married Teddy Wharton in 1885. She published her first novel at the age of 40. She loved visiting Europe and moved permanently to France in 1910, where she lived until her death, divorcing her husband in 1913. During the First World War (433), she fed French and Belgian refugees in Paris and sheltered 600 Belgian orphans. She was awarded the *Légion d'honneur* in 1916.

The House of Mirth 1905

'The heart of the wise is in the house of mourning;
but the heart of fools is in the house of mirth.' *Ecclesiastes 7:4*

Beautiful Lily Bart glides among the sparkling New York aristocracy seeking a husband who can support her ambitious appetite for finery and social status. When malicious rumours begin to circulate, however, the glittering world starts to crumble around her. 'When I wrote *The House of Mirth* I held, without knowing it, two trumps in my hand,' declared Wharton. 'One was the fact that New York society in the nineties was a field as yet unexploited by any novelist who had grown up in that little hot-house of traditions and conventions, and the other, that as yet these traditions and conventions were unassailed, and tacitly regarded as unassailable.'

1979 Modern Classics
● —

1985 Penguin American Library
1986 Penguin Classics
intro. Cynthia Griffin Wolff

1938 Penguin Books
● —
1988
● ed. Sarah Higginson
intro. Doris Grumbach

2005
ed. Elizabeth Ammons

Ethan Frome 1911

Ethan is a long-suffering New England farmer browbeaten by his suspicious hypochondriac wife Zeena. When Zeena's cousin Mattie joins their household as a hired girl, Ethan is irresistibly drawn to her vivacious manner and good looks, with stark consequences. The climatic sledging scene was inspired by a real incident which took place in Lenox, Massachusetts, where Wharton had a house, in 1904.

The Custom of the Country 1913

Undine Spragg is a spoiled, selfish, beautiful young debutante from the midwest seeking an ambitious and lucrative match in New York. She energetically clambers up the social ladder, stepping between marriages and affairs across Europe and America. *The Custom of the Country* was an inspiration for Julian Fellowes's television series, *Downton Abbey*. 'I felt this was my book; that the novel was talking to me in a most extreme and immediate way,' said Fellowes, when he accepted the 2012 Edith Wharton Lifetime Achievement Award. '[…] Undine has no values expect ambition, greed and desire, and yet through the miracle of Wharton's writing, you are on her side.'

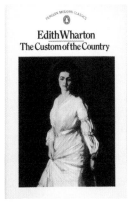

1984 Modern Classics
● ed. Anita Brookner

2006
ed. Linda Wagner-Martin

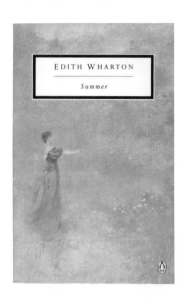

Summer 1917

Like *Ethan Frome* (427), *Summer* is set in a New England village; Wharton called it her 'hot Ethan'. Charity Royall is a young librarian, living with her alcoholic and abusive adoptive father until a handsome architect arrives in the village and awakens both her latent sexuality and her hopes of escape.

1993 Twentieth-Century Classics
2008 Penguin Classics
ed. Elizabeth Ammons

The Age of Innocence 1920

Wharton won the 1921 Pulitzer Prize for *The Age of Innocence*. 'Edith Wharton is a writer who brings glory on the name of America, and this is her best book,' wrote the *New York Times*. 'It is one of the best novels of the twentieth century [...] a permanent addition to literature.' In Gilded Age New York, Newland Archer is engaged to the glamorous and vacuous May Weller, but his world-view is upended when May's mysterious cousin, the Countess Ellen Olenska, returns from Europe, fleeing her brutish Polish husband.

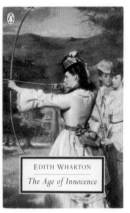

1974 Modern Classics
• —

1996 Twentieth-Century Classics
2007 Penguin Classics
ed. Laura Dluzynski Quinn
intro. Cynthia Griffin Wolff

Upton Sinclair 1878–1968

Sinclair was born in Baltimore, Maryland and began writing dime novels at fifteen in order to fund his schooling at City College in New York. He made his name with *The Jungle*, which won him literary praise and led to the passage of both the Pure Food and Drug Act and the Meat Inspection Act. Sinclair used the proceeds from the book to found a utopian community in New Jersey called Helicon Hall Colony. In 1915, he moved to California where he successfully ran for public office on four occasions, narrowly missing the governorship in 1934. After this defeat, he continued to write and won the Pulitzer Prize for Fiction in 1943. He is remembered for the adage, 'It is difficult to get a man to understand something, when his salary depends upon his not understanding it.'

The Jungle 1906

Set in the meat-packing district of Chicago, this deeply affecting novel was the result of six months Sinclair spent investigating the industry. It centres around Jurgis Rudkus, a Lithuanian immigrant working in a meat factory, his teenage wife Ona, and their mistreatment by unscrupulous, profit-driven employers. Sinclair's descriptions of the inhumane working conditions scandalized the reading public and galvanized them into action. Jack London (426) called *The Jungle* 'the *Uncle Tom's Cabin* (412) of wage slavery.' 'I aimed at the public's heart,' wrote Sinclair later, 'and by accident I hit it in the stomach.'

1936 Penguin Books
• —
1965 Modern Classics
• —

1985 Penguin American Library
1986 Penguin Classics
intro. Ronald Gottesman

O. Henry 1862–1910

William Sydney Porter was born in North Carolina and worked in his uncle's drugstore, eventually becoming a certified pharmacist. He took various jobs in Texas, before fleeing to Honduras on charges of embezzlement. On his return, he was convicted for eluding trial and began writing stories while serving three years inside Ohio State Penitentiary. After he was released, he moved to New York, remarried and kept his former identity secret, publishing 300 short stories under the pseudonym 'O. Henry'. One of his prison warders had been called Orrin Henry. He is an acknowledged master of the short story and was compared to Maupassant (318) during his lifetime. His pen name is shared with an American candy bar made of chocolate-coated caramel, peanuts and fudge.

Selected Stories 1906–17

This anthology collects 80 of O. Henry's comical, sardonic short stories set in New York and West, Central and South America. They feature con men and tricksters in tales of luck and coincidence, and all feature Henry's trademark twist endings. Titles include 'The Ransom of Red Chief', 'Proof of the Pudding', 'Dougherty's Eye-Opener' and 'Thimble, Thimble'.

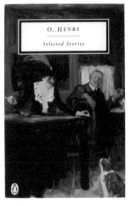

1993 Twentieth-Century Classics
2008 Penguin Classics
ed. Guy Davenport

Gertrude Stein 1874–1946

Stein was an avant-garde modernist writer and a mentor to Pablo Picasso, Henri Matisse, Ernest Hemingway, F. Scott Fitzgerald, Sinclair Lewis, Thornton Wilder, Sherwood Anderson and many others. She studied under William James (404) at Harvard before flunking out of the Johns Hopkins Medical School and settling in Paris in 1903. The Polish-American musician Alice Toklas joined her salon of artists and writers in 1907 and they became devoted life partners. Stein called Toklas 'Baby Precious' and Toklas called Stein 'Mr Cuddle-Wuddle' and they both doted on pet poodles named 'Basket' and 'Basket II'. Before undergoing surgery for stomach cancer in 1946, Stein asked Toklas, 'What is the answer?' Toklas remained silent. 'In that case,' Stein said, 'what is the question?'

1979 Modern Classics
•—

1990 Twentieth-Century Classics
2008 Penguin Classics
intro. Ann Charters

Three Lives 1909

In these three stories, Stein attempts to replicate the techniques of three visual artists: the non-linear 'The Good Anna' is inspired by Cézanne; 'Melanctha' mirrors the repeating angles of Picasso; and 'The Gentle Lena', draws on Matisse, foregrounding the psychological portrait of a woman, without plot or setting. This volume also includes the suppressed *Q.E.D.*, written in 1903, about a lesbian affair among a group of Stein's friends at Johns Hopkins University.

The Autobiography of Alice B. Toklas 1933

Stein wrote her own memoirs from the point of view of Toklas, her lover, cook, secretary, muse and life partner. It presents their years in Paris as 'a kaleidoscope slowly turning', an ever-changing roll call of extraordinary painters and writers. 'The geniuses came and spoke to Gertrude Stein and the wives sat with me,' writes Stein, as Toklas. After Stein's death, Toklas published her own book of reminiscences, *The Alice B. Toklas Cookbook*, which famously includes a recipe for hash brownies.

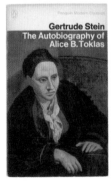

1966 Modern Classics

Canada

L. M. Montgomery 1874–1942

Lucy Maud Montgomery was born on Prince Edward Island, the smallest province of Canada, north of Nova Scotia. Her mother died before her second birthday so she was raised by her maternal grandparents. She had a lonely childhood and used to take long solitary walks, during which she experienced 'the flash', tranquil moments of ecstatic clarity. She became a prolific writer and is best remembered today for *Anne of Green Gables* and its sequels.

On 1 July, 1867, following the Quebec Conference in London, the British North America Act came into effect and the Dominion of Canada existed as a country for the first time, uniting the provinces of Canada (Quebec and Ontario), New Brunswick and Nova Scotia. Early Canadian literature reflects the hardships of survival in this rugged northern environment.

Anne of Green Gables 1908

Matthew and Marilla Cuthbert are a middle-aged brother and sister who run Green Gables Farm on Prince Edward Island. They apply for an orphan boy to help with their work, but Anne Shirley arrives instead, an eleven-year-old girl with bright red hair. The book follows Anne's adventures with the Cuthberts and at school in the nearby town of Avonlea. It is much loved around the world, especially in Japan, where there is a 'Canadian World' theme park inspired by *Anne of Green Gables*.

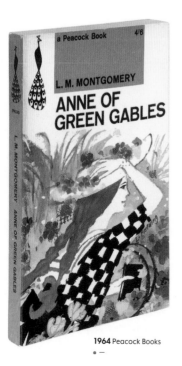

1964 Peacock Books

2017 Deluxe Edition
ed. Benjamin Lefebvre
fwd. J. Courtney Sullivan

The Caribbean

Most West Indian literature has emerged since the First World War (433), but Paula Burnett's poetry anthology reaches back to the colonial history of the region. Prince, Seacole and Shiel (432) are all West Indian authors who achieved literary recognition only after leaving their homeland.

THE PENGUIN BOOK OF CARIBBEAN VERSE IN ENGLISH

18th – 20th centuries

'I have crossed an ocean
I have lost my tongue
from the root of the old one
a new one has sprung'
Grace Nichols

This collection surveys the oral and literary traditions of Caribbean verse in English, from the 18th century to the modern age, featuring the Noble Laureate Derek Walcott, Bob Marley and Linton Kwesi Johnson.

1986 Penguin Poets
2005 Penguin Classics
ed. Paula Burnett

The History of Mary Prince 1831

Prince dictated her *History* to Susanna Strickland, an acquaintance of Thomas Pringle. It was the first account published in Britain of a black woman's life and it had a galvanizing effect on the abolitionist movement. The Slavery Abolition Act was passed in 1833, and slavery ceased in Bermuda from 1834. It is not known what happened to Prince after 1833 or whether she ever returned to her husband, Daniel James, as a free woman.

Mary Prince 1788 – after 1833

Prince was born a slave in Bermuda. She had a series of cruel masters and worked for a time in the salt ponds of Turks Island. In 1826, she married a free man, Daniel James, but she remained a slave. In 1828, she was brought to England by Mr and Mrs John Wood and appealed to the Anti-Slavery Society, demanding freedom under English law. Slavery was no longer legal in England, but it had not yet been abolished in the colonies. Prince was given a choice between remaining a free woman in England, or returning to her husband as a slave. She stayed and was employed in the household of Thomas Pringle, the secretary of the Anti-Slavery Society.

2000
ed. Sarah Salih

Mary Seacole 1805 – 1881

Mary Jane Grant was born in Kingston, Jamaica. At twelve she began helping her mother, nursing British officers. She travelled to London, New Providence, Haiti and Cuba before marrying Edwin Horatio Hamilton Seacole, Lord Nelson's godson. In her memoir, she passes over their meeting, marriage, his illness and death within a single paragraph. Newly widowed, she established a 'British Hotel' in Cruces, Panama in 1851, catering for American gold-seekers.

2005
ed. Sarah Salih

Wonderful Adventures of Mrs Seacole in Many lands 1857

When the Crimean War broke out in 1853, Seacole travelled to London to join Florence Nightingale's 'Angel Band' of military nurses, but she was rejected. Undeterred, she travelled to the Crimea anyway and established a British Hotel near the battlefront, which she described as 'a mess-table and comfortable quarters for sick and convalescent officers'. She catered for army personnel of all ranks, tending the sick and wounded herself.

M. P. Shiel 1865–1947

Matthew Phipps Shiel was born on the island of Montserrat to mixed-race parents; both his grandmothers were probably slaves. At fifteen, he was crowned 'King Felipe of Redonda', a small uninhabited rocky islet in the Caribbean. When he left his family and came to England in 1885, his father's parting advice was, 'Do not be strange.' Shiel studied medicine at St Bartholomew's Hospital in London and worked as a schoolteacher, before making his living as a writer, specializing in wildly imaginative science fiction and detective novels. He had multiple simultaneous love affairs and spent sixteen months in Wormwood Scrubs prison after assaulting the twelve-year-old daughter of one of his mistresses. Before he died in 1947, he anointed the minor poet John Gawsworth 'King Juan I', his successor to the fictional kingship of Redonda.

The Purple Cloud
1901

Adam Jeffson is the first man to reach the North Pole, but on his return journey he discovers that he is also the last person left alive on earth: an insidious, sweet-smelling cloud of poisonous gas has enveloped the world and destroyed all animal life. He wanders the empty globe, visits the empty home of Arthur Machen (254) and slowly descends into destructive madness. The poet Edward Shanks called the book 'a legend, an apocalypse, out of space, out of time'.

2012
ed. John Sutherland

South America

The literature of South America in the 19th-century was influenced by Romanticism and naturalism, and aimed at establishing a sense of national identity within the nascent states that were emerging from centuries of European, colonial rule. Nationalistic texts include Domingo Sarmiento's *Facundo* (1845) in Argentina, Jorge Isaac's *María* (1867) in Colombia, Juan León Mera's *Cumandá* (1879) in Ecuador and Euclides da Cunha's *Os Sertões* (1902), 'Rebellion in the Backlands' in Brazil. At the end of the century, a movement known as *modernismo* emerged, instigated by the Nicaraguan poet Rubén Darío, which aimed to transcend nationalism and present a purely aesthetic form of literature.

2014
trans. Mark Carlyon, 2011
intro. Lilia Moritz Schwarcz, 2014

Lima Barreto 1881–1922

Afonso Henriques de Lima Barreto was a prolific Brazilian journalist, commentator and novelist. He lived his whole life in Rio de Janeiro, struggling to support his widowed father, whose mental health was deteriorating. Barreto himself suffered from severe depression and alcoholism towards the end of his life. He is considered a major proponent of early 20th-century Brazilian literature.

The Sad End of Policarpo Quaresma 1911

Barreto's masterpiece is a satire of the First Brazilian Republic (1889–1930). A fastidious patriotic civil servant, Policarpo Quaresma is full of visionary schemes for improving his beloved Brazil, but every venture results in ridicule and disaster. He attempts to change Brazil's national language, raise the yields of Brazilian farmland and improve conditions for imprisoned revolutionary naval mutineers.

The First World War

The Penguin Book of First World War Poetry

ISBN 0 14 042.255 2

Three Poets of the First World War: Ivor Gurney, Isaac Rosenberg, Wilfred Owen

EDWARD THOMAS · SELECTED POEMS AND PROSE

PENGUIN CLASSICS

Imagist Poetry

ISBN 0 14 042.147 5

ISBN 0 14 043.144 6

John Buchan · The Thirty-Nine Steps

1130

P118705

PENGUIN CLASSICS

Henri Barbusse · Under Fire

STORM OF STEEL · ERNST JÜNGER

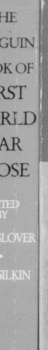

EDMUND BLUNDEN · UNDERTONES OF WAR

82

R. C. SHERRIFF · JOURNEY'S END

ISBN 0 14 048.177 X

THE PENGUIN BOOK OF FIRST WORLD WAR PROSE

EDITED BY JON GLOVER · JON SILKIN

ISBN 0 14 00.5802 8

RICHARD ALDINGTON · DEATH OF A HERO

42

FREDERIC MANNING · The Middle Parts of Fortune

ISBN 014 01.8461 9

Robert Graves · GOODBYE TO ALL THAT

1443

Penguin Biography

On the morning of 28 June 1914, a man was standing on Franz Joseph Street in Sarajevo, Bosnia. A motorcade took a wrong turning and paused in front of him. The first car had no reverse gear, so it had to be pushed back to the correct route. In that moment Gavrilo Princip stepped forward and at point blank range shot Archduke Franz Ferdinand, the heir to the Austro-Hungarian Empire (352), in the throat with a revolver. 'It's nothing,' gasped the Archduke repeatedly as he died.

Princip was a Bosnian Serb, a Yugoslav nationalist and a member of the Black Hand secret society. The assassination triggered a diplomatic crisis, in which the outraged Austro-Hungarian Empire delivered an impossible ultimatum to the kingdom of Serbia, which resulted in war. Within weeks, all the major powers in Europe were involved, the 'Allies' (Russia, France and Britain) against the 'Central Powers' (Germany and Austria-Hungary), and Italy, Japan, the United States, the Ottoman Empire and Bulgaria were all eventually drawn in.

The Great War lasted four years. It involved 70 million military personnel, of whom more than 9 million died. Seven million civilians were also killed. The 'War to End All Wars' was characterized by hellish trench warfare, gas attacks, tanks and machine guns. It was one of the deadliest conflicts in history, and it scorched the literature of the period and for many years afterwards.

THE PENGUIN BOOK OF FIRST WORLD WAR POETRY

From A. E. Housman's (268) 'steady drummer' presaging the outbreak of war, through Wilfred Owen's (435) 'stuttering rifles' rapid rattle' and Alan Seeger's 'rendezvous with Death', to Edward Blunden's (437) railway train running along the tranquil Somme valley – 'the war's over, chum' – the First World War triggered an immense outpouring of poetry, which overwhelmed contemporary periodicals and remains intensely poignant today. George Walter's anthology is arranged thematically, following the course of the war from conscription to the trenches, the action of the battlefield, the return home and the aftermath of peace. It includes well-known authors, such as Rupert Brooke, Siegfried Sassoon, Vera Brittain and the Prime Minister, Herbert Asquith, as well as less familiar names like Eleanor Farjeon, Marjorie Pickthall, Edgell Rickword and Edward Shillito, among many others. Walters also includes a 'Glossary of the Western Front'.

1979 Penguin Poets
● ed. Jon Silkin

1998 Penguin Books
Poems of the Great War

2006 Penguin Classics
ed. George Walter

Edward Thomas 1878–1917

Philip Edward Thomas published his first book before arriving at Oxford University. He became an exceptionally prolific writer, but suffered from increasingly severe depression and in 1911 had a serious breakdown. He met the American poet Robert Frost in 1913, who persuaded him to try writing poetry. In less than two years Thomas produced 142 extraordinary poems. He died at the Battle of Arras in 1917, three months after arriving on the Western Front.

1981 Penguin English Library
2013 Penguin Classics
ed. David Wright
fwd. Robert Macfarlane, 2013
—
Robert Macfarlane's foreword is an extract from his book *The Old Ways* (2012). 'Trees, birds, rocks and paths cease to be merely objects of contemplation,' he writes, describing Thomas's landscapes, 'and instead become actively and convivially present, enabling understanding that would be possible nowhere else, under no other circumstances.'

Selected Poems and Prose 1905–1917

> The flowers left thick at nightfall in the wood
> This Eastertide call into mind the men,
> Now far from home, who, with their sweethearts, should
> Have gathered them and will do never again.
> 'In Memoriam', 1915

Isaac Rosenberg 1890–1918

Rosenberg was a painter from the East End of London whose work was exhibited at the Whitechapel Art Gallery. He suffered from bronchitis and was convalescing in South Africa when war was declared; he died on 1 April 1918 near Arras.

Ivor Gurney 1890–1937

Gurney was a musician and a prolific songwriter. He was discharged from the army in 1918 suffering from gas poisoning and mental instability. He was committed to a series of asylums, during which time he believed he was Shakespeare (134) and wrote two plays in blank verse (129).

Wilfred Owen 1893–1918

Owen was teaching in France when the war began. He enlisted in the Artists' Rifles and fought on the Western Front as a commissioned officer until he was evacuated to Edinburgh, suffering from shellshock. He met Siegfried Sassoon there. He returned to the front in September 1918 and was killed on the banks of the Oise-Sambre Canal on 4 November, one week before the armistice.

Three Poets of the First World War 1912–19

This anthology celebrates three of the most distinctive poets of the First World War. Among many other poems, it includes Gurney's 'Crickley Hill', which blends details of trench life with memories of his beloved Gloucestershire countryside; Rosenberg's 'Break of Day in the Trenches', which the critic Paul Fussell called the greatest poem of the war; and Owen's famous 'Dulce et Decorum Est', his bitter twist of the patriotic line from Horace (45).

2011
ed. Jon Stallworthy &
Jane Potter

IMAGIST POETRY 1914–17

Imagism was a brief poetic movement which bucked against the late 19th-century 'doughy mess of third-hand Keats (197)', as Ezra Pound put it. Imagists sought brevity, precision and purity of meaning: 'use no superfluous word,' wrote Pound, 'no adjective, which does not reveal something.' This anthology opens with T. E. Hulme, the 'father of imagism', and includes Richard Aldington (438), D. H. Lawrence (288), William Carlos Williams and of course Pound, who defined the movement as poetry that 'does not use images as ornaments. The image itself is the speech.'

1972 Penguin Poets
1985 Modern Classics
1990 Twentieth-Century Classics
2001 Modern Classics
ed. Peter Jones

THE PENGUIN BOOK OF FIRST WORLD WAR STORIES 1914–95

Phantom archers from the Battle of Agincourt, paranoid naval officers, illicit liaisons and a Christmas truce for a game of football: these indelible stories from Arthur Machen (254), Joseph Conrad (277), Katherine Mansfield (393) and Robert Graves (439) have become part of the fabric of the First World War. Barbara Korte's anthology also features Sherlock Holmes (248), coming out of retirement to foil a spy, as well as tales of the home front from Kipling (250), Galsworthy (286) and Lawrence (288), and later reactions by Muriel Spark and Julian Barnes.

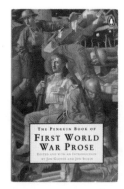

1990 Penguin Books
● ed. Jon Silkin & Jonathan Glover

2007
ed. Barbara Korte
with Ann-Marie Einhaus

John Buchan 1875–1940

John Buchan, 1st Baron Tweedsmuir, was the son of a Scottish minister. He had a varied career as a barrister, a Member of Parliament, a soldier and a publisher; he was also the Governor-General of Canada and the author of a series of extremely successful adventure thrillers, which he called 'shockers'. His chief protagonist was Richard Hannay, introduced in *The Thirty-Nine Steps* who reappeared in four sequels, two of which – *Greenmantle* (1916) and *Mr Standfast* (1918) – were set during the First World War.

The Thirty-Nine Steps 1915

Richard Hannay is bored with life in London, until a murder is committed in his flat and he goes on the run in Scotland. Over the course of summer 1914, he must keep one step ahead of the police and various foreign agents in order to warn the government about an imminent assassination plot that could trigger a world war.

1956 Penguin Books
● —

2004
ed. John Keegan

Henri Barbusse 1873–1935

Henri Barbusse was a Bolshevik, a friend of Einstein, an early publisher of Orwell, a biographer of Stalin and a leading figure of French modernism. He also fought in the First World War, during which he wrote his masterpiece, *Le Feu*.

Under Fire 1916

A ragbag squad of French '*poilus*' struggles desperately to survive. 'Will you make them speak like they really do, or will you tidy it up and make it proper?' a soldier asks the narrator. 'I'm talking about swearwords. Because, after all, […] you won't ever hear two *poilus* chat for a minute without them saying something or repeating something that the printers won't much like to print.' 'I'll put the swearwords in,' says Barbusse's narrator, 'because it's the truth.' When *Under Fire* was published, it was criticized for its harsh naturalism and anti-militarism; it is now considered the first novel to portray the truly squalid reality of conditions in the trenches.

2003 Modern Classics
trans. Robin Buss
intro. Jay Winter

Ernst Jünger 1895–1998

Jünger ran away from school to join the Foreign Legion and volunteered for the German army in 1914. He fought throughout the First World War and was decorated with the *Pour le Mérite*, the highest military decoration of the German Empire. After the war, he became a dedicated entomologist, a novelist and a habitual drug user, experimenting with ether, cocaine, hashish and mescaline. He frequently took LSD with its inventor, his friend Albert Hofmann.

Storm of Steel 1920

Jünger describes life in the chalky trenches of northern France, leading raiding parties, defending the line and enduring artillery bombardment. His memoir captures both the horror and the obsession of war. *Storm of Steel* 'is without question the finest book on war that I know,' wrote André Gide (322): 'utterly honest, truthful, in good faith.'

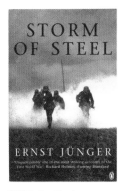

2004 Modern Classics
trans. Michael Hofmann

Edmund Blunden 1896–1974

Blunden published his first poems while serving with the Royal Sussex Regiment in the First World War. He survived nearly two years on the front line without being injured. Afterwards he studied at Oxford, where he met Robert Graves (439), and he taught in Japan and Hong Kong before returning to England to take up the Oxford Professorship of Poetry. He was a fanatical cricketer. The stone that commemorates him and others in Poets' Corner in Westminster Abbey is inscribed with words by Wilfred Owen (435): 'My subject is War, and the pity of War. The Poetry is in the pity.'

1937 Penguin Books

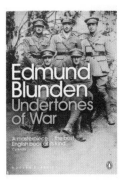

2010 Modern Classics
intro. Hew Strachan

Undertones of War 1928

Through poignant passages of prose and a sequence of poems, Blunden describes the heroic and desperate fighting in France and Flanders, the battles of the Somme, Ypres and Passchendaele. His biographer Paul Fussell calls the book an 'extended elegy in prose'.

R. C. Sherriff 1896–1975

Robert Cedric Sherriff left his father's insurance business to serve as a captain in the East Surrey Regiment; he was severely wounded at Passchendaele in 1917 and awarded the Military Cross. After the war, he returned to the insurance firm and spent ten years as a claims adjuster, with a side interest in amateur theatricals. His play *Journey's End* had one Sunday evening performance in London in 1928, with Laurence Olivier playing the lead, before it was chosen for a 1929 run at the Savoy Theatre, where it was an overnight success. The play was so wildly popular around the world that it allowed Sherriff to leave insurance and become a full-time writer.

Journey's End 1928–9

Fresh from public school, young Lieutenant Raleigh arrives in the trenches in 1918, eager to join the company of his old friend and cricketing hero Stanhope, but he finds Captain Stanhope dramatically changed. When Sherriff initially shared his manuscript, one theatre manager turned it down saying, 'How can I put on a play with no leading lady?' *No Leading Lady* became the title of Sherriff's autobiography.

1983 Penguin Plays
1992 Twentieth-Century Classics
2010 Modern Classics

Frederic Manning 1882–1935

Manning was an Australian poet from Sydney. He travelled to England at the age of sixteen and lodged with the Reverend Arthur Galton, a friend from New South Wales. After fighting in the First World War and observing the popularity of Sherriff's *Journey's End* (437), he was persuaded to publish his own novelized account of his war experiences, privately and anonymously, under the name 'Private 19022'.

The Middle Parts of Fortune
Somme and Ancre, 1916
1929

'While the following pages are a record of experience on the Somme and Ancre fronts […] and the events described in it actually happened; the characters are fictitious,' wrote Manning. Private Bourne prefers fighting in the ranks to the idea of becoming an officer: he immerses himself in the lives of his comrades and the mad war raging around them. 'Kill the buggers' he murmurs through clenched teeth during a particularly vicious engagement. 'Kill the bloody fucking swine! Kill them!'

1990 Twentieth-Century Classics
● ed. Paul Fussell

2000 Modern Classics
intro. Niall Ferguson

Richard Aldington 1892–1962

Aldington was a poet, translator and critic before the First World War, and a founding member of the Imagist movement (435) with his wife, Hilda Doolittle (H.D.). He joined the British army in 1916, fought in France and Flanders and was wounded in 1918. *Death of a Hero* was his first novel: a book, as Arnold Bennett (280) put it, 'impossible to ignore'.

Death of a Hero 1929

The artist George Winterbourne volunteers at the start of the war, and through a string of casualties finds himself promoted rapidly up the ranks. He finds the other officers cynical and inhumane, however, and during a period of home leave he cannot relate to his friends or his wife. He returns to the trenches, disillusioned and desolate. Lawrence Durrell called *Death of a Hero* 'the best war novel of the epoch'.

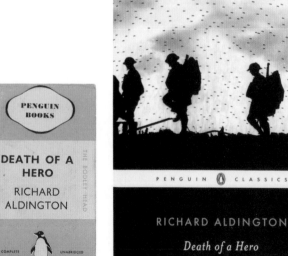

1936 Penguin Books
● —

2013
intro. James H. Meredith

Robert Graves 1895–1985

Graves went straight from the playing fields of Charterhouse School to fighting in the First World War, in which he served as a captain in the Royal Welch Fusiliers. After the war, he wrote prolifically, producing volumes of poetry, novels, works of comparative mythology and several translations for Penguin Classics including his version of the *Iliad* (16). Many of his own works are published in Modern Classics.

Goodbye to All That 1929

Graves wrote *Goodbye to All That* 'during a complicated domestic crisis, and with very little time for revision. It was my bitter leave-taking of England where I had recently broken a good many conventions; quarrelled with, or been disowned by, most of my friends; been grilled by the police on a suspicion of attempted murder; and ceased to care what anyone thought of me.' The result was, as the *Times Literary Supplement* put it, 'one of the most candid self-portraits of a poet, warts and all, ever painted'. The book describes Graves's childhood and unhappy schooldays, his increasingly fractious marriage, his encounters with writers and poets, including Siegfried Sassoon and Thomas Hardy (234), and most memorably his harrowing time as a young officer on the Western Front, a profoundly traumatic experience that stayed with him for the rest of his life. After completing this autobiography, Graves emigrated to Mallorca, vowing 'never to make England my home again'.

1960 Penguin Books

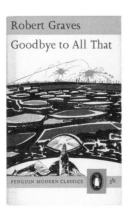

1961 Modern Classics

1967 Modern Classics

Graves is the only author in this book who does not have all of his or her works listed together. His poetry, short stories and several of his novels are published in the Modern Classics series, but they do not appear here. We have chosen to make an exception in his case, and to smuggle this title in on its own, because (a) it seemed strange for it not to be with the other First World War books, (b) Robert Graves has been involved with the Penguin Classics series from the beginning (53) and so we wanted to include one of his own titles, and (c) it seemed appropriate to end with *Goodbye to All That*. We hope to include Graves's other works in a forthcoming volume that will cover the literature of the last hundred years.

1990 Twentieth-Century Classics

2000 Modern Classics

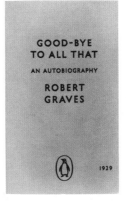

2014
ed. Fran Brearton
intro. Andrew Motion

These pages display some of the Penguin Classics titles that are no longer in print. Titles go out of print and drop off the list for the prosaic reason that low sales figures don't justify the cost of another print run, but each time one title falls away, it raises interesting questions. It implies that the way we remember literature is subject to change, that a classic may not always be a classic, that each title is required to maintain its position.

As an author's star wanes, their marginal works might be pruned; equally, a concerted cultural effort to champion or rehabilitate an author might lead to more of their works appearing or reappearing in the series. The list requires constant tending, weeding, grafting and replanting, and as editors of the series, we might conclude with Candide (176) that the most we can hope to do is 'cultivate our garden'.

All these titles below should be available through good second-hand book dealers.

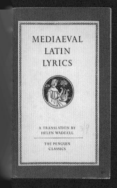

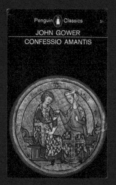
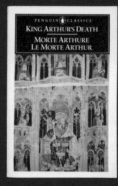

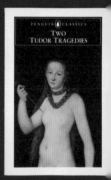

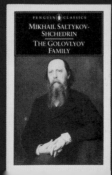

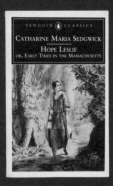

Penguin Classics

CATHARINE MARIA SEDGWICK

HOPE LESLIE
OR, EARLY TIMES IN THE MASSACHUSETTS

Penguin Classics

ANTHOLOGY OF
JAPANESE LITERATURE
TO THE NINETEENTH CENTURY

Penguin Classics

THE GREEK ANTHOLOGY

Penguin Classics

MEDIAEVAL LATIN LYRICS

Penguin Classics

WOMEN'S INDIAN
CAPTIVITY NARRATIVES

Penguin Classics

MÉRIMÉE

CARMEN / COLOMBA

Penguin Classics

SUSANNA ROWSON

CHARLOTTE TEMPLE
AND
LUCY TEMPLE

Penguin Classics

MARIVAUX
UP FROM THE COUNTRY / INFIDELITIES
THE GAME OF LOVE AND CHANCE

Penguin Classics

FOUR MORALITY PLAYS

WALTER HILTON

THE LADDER OF
PERFECTION

A NEW TRANSLATION BY
LEO SHERLEY-PRICE

THE PENGUIN
CLASSICS

DELLA CASA

GALATEO

A NEW TRANSLATION
BY R. S. PINE-COFFIN

THE PENGUIN
CLASSICS

Penguin Classics

ROLLE
THE FIRE OF LOVE

Penguin Classics

DELARIVIER MANLEY
NEW ATALANTIS

Penguin Classics

SELECTED POEMS OF
THOMAS CAMPION,
SAMUEL DANIEL AND
SIR WALTER RALEGH

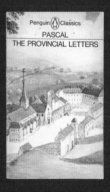

Penguin Classics

PASCAL
THE PROVINCIAL LETTERS

Penguin Classics

MAXIM GORKY
MY APPRENTICESHIP

Penguin Classics

WALTER PATER
MARIUS THE EPICUREAN

Penguin Classics

FRANK NORRIS
McTeague

Penguin Classics

THE GOLDEN CASKET
CHINESE NOVELLAS OF
TWO MILLENNIA

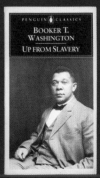

Penguin Classics

BOOKER T.
WASHINGTON
UP FROM SLAVERY

Penguin Classics — POEMS FROM THE SANSKRIT

Penguin Classics — NATHANIEL HAWTHORNE · SELECTED TALES AND SKETCHES

Penguin Classics — VIRGIL IN ENGLISH

Penguin Classics — GREEK PASTORAL POETRY

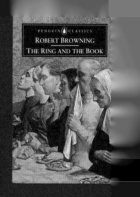

Penguin Classics — ROBERT BROWNING · THE RING AND THE BOOK

Penguin Classics — ZÁRATE · THE DISCOVERY AND CONQUEST OF PERU

Penguin Classics — THE LAST POETS OF IMPERIAL ROME

ST JOHN OF THE CROSS · POEMS · TRANSLATED BY ROY CAMPBELL · THE PENGUIN CLASSICS

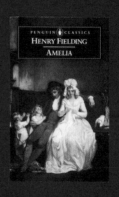

Penguin Classics — HENRY FIELDING · AMELIA

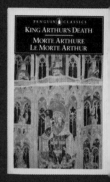

Penguin Classics — KING ARTHUR'S DEATH · MORTE ARTHURE / LE MORTE ARTHUR

Penguin Classics — AUBREY'S BRIEF LIVES

Penguin Classics — ANCRENE WISSE · GUIDE FOR ANCHORESSES

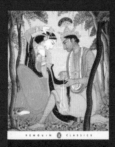

PENGUIN CLASSICS

Krishna: The Beautiful Legend of God
(Śrīmad Bhāgavata Purāṇa Book X)

Penguin Classics — LAFCADIO HEARN · WRITINGS FROM JAPAN · An Anthology

Penguin Classics — GOLDONI · THE VENETIAN TWINS · THE ARTFUL WIDOW/MIRANDOLINA · THE SUPERIOR RESIDENCE

Penguin Classics — POEMS OF HEAVEN AND HELL FROM ANCIENT MESOPOTAMIA

Penguin Classics — MATTHEW ARNOLD · SELECTED POEMS

Penguin Classics — GORKY · MY UNIVERSITIES

Penguin Classics — EXQUEMELIN · THE BUCCANEERS OF AMERICA

Penguin Classics — THE DIARY OF ALICE JAMES

Penguin Classics

ARETINO
SELECTED LETTERS

Penguin Classics

BENJAMIN DISRAELI
SYBIL

Penguin Classics

THE QUEST OF THE
HOLY GRAIL

Penguin Classics

V. I. LENIN
WHAT IS TO BE DONE?

Penguin Classics

EÇA DE QUEIRÓS
THE MAIAS

Penguin Classics

NEW SONGS FROM A
JADE TERRACE
AN ANTHOLOGY OF EARLY
CHINESE LOVE POETRY

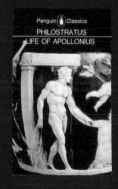

Penguin Classics

PHILOSTRATUS
LIFE OF APOLLONIUS

Penguin Classics

COLONIAL AMERICAN
TRAVEL NARRATIVES

Penguin Classics

THE JEWISH POETS
OF SPAIN

Penguin Classics

CARLO COLLODI
PINOCCHIO

Penguin Classics

The Roots of Ayurveda

Penguin Classics

BALZAC
THE CHOUANS

Penguin Classics

GUSTAVE FLAUBERT
THE TEMPTATION OF
ST ANTONY

Penguin Classics

PÉREZ GALDÓS
MIAU

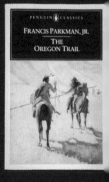

Penguin Classics

FRANCIS PARKMAN, JR.
THE
OREGON TRAIL

Penguin Classics

ROMAN POETS OF THE
EARLY EMPIRE

LUCAN
PHARSALIA
DRAMATIC
EPISODES OF THE
CIVIL WARS

A NEW TRANSLATION BY
ROBERT GRAVES

THE PENGUIN
CLASSICS

Penguin Classics

CHRISTINE DE PIZAN
THE BOOK OF
THE CITY OF LADIES

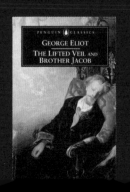

Penguin Classics

GEORGE ELIOT
THE LIFTED VEIL AND
BROTHER JACOB

Penguin Classics

THE OWL AND THE
NIGHTINGALE · CLEANNESS
ST ERKENWALD

CHARLES PERRAULT
FAIRY TALES

A NEW TRANSLATION BY
GEOFFREY BRERETON

THE PENGUIN
CLASSICS

RONALD FIRBANK
Vainglory
with *Inclinations* and *Caprice*

SIX YÜAN PLAYS

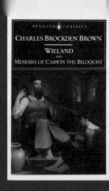

CHARLES BROCKDEN BROWN
WIELAND
AND
MEMOIRS OF CARWIN THE BILOQUIST

ALARCÓN
THE THREE-CORNERED HAT
AND OTHER STORIES

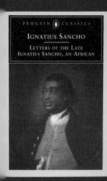

Ignatius Sancho
LETTERS OF THE LATE
IGNATIUS SANCHO, AN AFRICAN

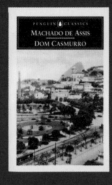

MACHADO DE ASSIS
DOM CASMURRO

THREE SANSKRIT PLAYS

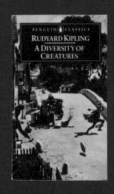

RUDYARD KIPLING
A DIVERSITY OF
CREATURES

EDMOND AND
JULES DE GONCOURT
GERMINIE LACERTEUX

E. W. HORNUNG
Raffles:
The Amateur Cracksman

FLAUBERT
BOUVARD AND PÉCUCHET

GILBERT IMLAY
THE EMIGRANTS

SELECTED POEMS OF
ROBERT HENRYSON
AND WILLIAM DUNBAR

BIRDS THROUGH
A CEILING OF ALABASTER

Fanny Fern
RUTH HALL
A Domestic Tale of the Present Time

PHILIPPE DE COMMYNES
MEMOIRS
THE REIGN OF LOUIS XI 1461–83

OVID
THE POEMS OF EXILE

THE EXETER
BOOK RIDDLES

ANTHONY HOPE
THE PRISONER OF ZENDA
AND RUPERT OF HENTZAU

IVAN TURGENEV
A MONTH IN THE COUNTRY

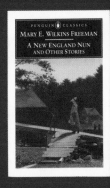

MARY E. WILKINS FREEMAN
A NEW ENGLAND NUN
AND OTHER STORIES

THREE FRENCH FARCES

THOMAS DE QUINCEY
RECOLLECTIONS OF THE
LAKES AND THE LAKE POETS

JOHN BUCHAN
The Strange Adventures of
Mr Andrew Hawthorn & Other Stories

SOR JUANA INÉS DE LA CRUZ
POEMS, PROTEST, AND A DREAM

ANTHOLOGY OF CHINESE LITERATURE

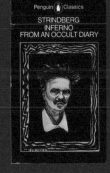

STRINDBERG
INFERNO
FROM AN OCCULT DIARY

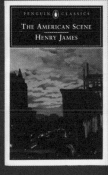

THE AMERICAN SCENE
HENRY JAMES

FRANK NORRIS
THE OCTOPUS

HORATIO ALGER, JR.
RAGGED DICK AND
STRUGGLING UPWARD

THE POEMS OF
PROPERTIUS

FOUR JACOBEAN
CITY COMEDIES

THE LITTLE
FLOWERS OF
SAINT
FRANCIS

TRANSLATED BY
L. SHERLEY-PRICE

THE PENGUIN
CLASSICS

AUGUST STRINDBERG
BY THE OPEN SEA

GEORGE FOX
THE JOURNAL

THOMAS TRAHERNE
SELECTED POEMS
AND PROSE

SOMADEVA
TALES FROM THE
KATHĀSARITSĀGARA

THE POEMS OF TIBULLUS

HAROLD FREDERIC
THE DAMNATION OF
THERON WARE

Index

In 1965, the stationers W. H. Smith began building a huge computer-controlled warehouse in Swindon. They realized their new inventory system was going to require a reliable and universal book numbering system, so they commissioned Gordon Foster, Professor of Computational Methods at the London School of Economics, to consider the problem. Foster had been a code-breaker at Bletchley Park and he devised a nine-digit system of unique 'Standard Book Numbers' (SBNs) for numbering books. Each number was made up of constituent 'parts' of variable length, including a publisher code, a book number and a check digit. His system was quickly adopted across the country. The International Organization for Standardization developed a ten-digit, international format (ISBN), which the UK adopted in 1974, and ISBNs have had thirteen digits since 2007, when they were brought in line with European Article Number (EAN) product codes. But you can still read modern ISBNs in the way that Gordon Foster intended. They break down into six sections:

978 Book Land

European Article Numbers start with a three-digit 'Country Code', indicating an object's place of manufacture, but texts transcend national boundaries, so every book in the world is allocated the arbitrary prefix 978 instead. This fictional 'country' is known affectionately as 'Book Land'. A new prefix – 979 – has recently been assigned to allow the expansion of Book Land; it is already in use in France.

0 Language

This digit usually indicates the language of a book. Penguin Classics are always English-language texts or translations, so the fourth digit of almost all Penguin Classics ISBNs is 0, the code for 'English'.

14 Publisher

Books published by Penguin have traditionally been assigned the publisher code 14, although recently 24 has been used as well.

044 Series

Penguin Books initially used these three digits to differentiate series. For example, the first Penguin Classics titles were all assigned 044, and Penguin Twentieth-Century Classics were 018. There are more examples to look out for on pp.xvi-xix. In recent years, ISBN allocation at Penguin Random House has become more random.

001 Title

These three digits identify up to a thousand unique titles for each series, and for a time Penguin series preserved their original numbering systems. The *Odyssey* (17) used to be 001, for example, and Maupassant's *Boule de Suif* (318) was 002.

0 Check Digit

The final digit is known as the 'check digit' and is generated algorithmically from the others as a precaution against manual-entry errors. A computer system can use the check digit to assess immediately whether an ISBN is genuine or not.

To calculate a check digit, number an ISBN's digits from 13 on the left to 1 on the right. Add together all the digits in even positions, and multiply the result by 3. Add to this the sum of all the digits in odd positions (except the check digit itself). Divide the result by 10. Discard the whole number, take the remainder and, if it isn't zero, subtract it from 10. The result is the check digit.

Acknowledgements

Firstly, thanks to all the former editors of the Penguin Classics series, especially E. V. Rieu (17) and Betty Radice (51), for stewarding this remarkable list over the last 70 years, and special thanks to all my colleagues at Penguin Press, who have contributed to the creation of this book in immeasurable ways. Particular thanks to my patient and insightful editors Helen Conford, Margaret Stead and Cecilia Stein, all of whom have provided calm captaincy through occasionally choppy waters, to Rebecca Lee for masterminding the Byzantine proofing process, to Rosie Glaisher, Nicola Hill, Stefan McGrath, Alice Mottram, Jon Parker, Shoaib Rokadiya, Jim Stoddart and Simon Winder for their support throughout, to Etty Eastwood, Sam Voulters, Julie Woon and Sarah Wright for publicising and marketing this book and the whole Penguin Classics list so brilliantly, and to Jessica Harrison and Bianca Bexton, teammates and friends, who provide constant advice and encouragement, and with whom it is a pleasure to be co-piloting the Penguin Classics. Thanks to the Penguin archivists, who have been exceptionally generous with their time and knowledge, especially Sue Payne and Marion Orr in Rugby, Sarah McMahon and Kirby Smith in Rushden and Hannah Lowery and Ian Coates in Bristol. Thanks to the Penguin Collectors Society for their kind support, especially James Mackay, Keith Ferguson, Tim Graham, Jim Robinson and Ross Wilson. Thanks to my friends Matt Lloyd-Rose and Ed Posnett for energizing feedback on the drafts, to my parents Simon and Olivia and sister Georgina for inspiring and fuelling my love of books, and of course to Georgie, always the very best of reading companions.

Two people require a special mention: firstly, Matthew Young, who designed this book. Matt has worked tirelessly to devise these beautiful layouts, coordinating an extraordinary team effort with assistance from Richard Carr, Tom Etherington, Theo Inglis, Richard Marston, Claire Mason, Francisca Monteiro, Mónica Oliveira and Mathieu Triay. Somehow he has remained sane amidst a whirlwind of text changes, train travel, updated bibliographic data and last-minute photography: it has been a Herculean feat of creativity and endurance and I am immensely grateful to him. Secondly, my heartfelt thanks go to the copyeditor, Kit Shepherd, who has gone far beyond the call of duty to bring passion, humour and a spectacular breadth of knowledge to this project. As well as spotting erroneous en-dashes, Kit has demonstrated a seemingly limitless familiarity with world literature, revealing errors in the text, suggesting additions and improving nuances of meaning. I am enormously grateful for his precision and enthusiasm. Needless to say, if any mistakes remain they are entirely my own.

In his essay 'On Study', Francis Bacon (127) writes that 'some books are to be tasted, others to be swallowed, and some few to be chewed and digested', and my final thanks are to all the teachers, now friends, who first set my place at the literary banquet table and showed me what delicious dishes to tuck into. Particular thanks to James Christie, Helen Cooper, Adam Crick, Anthony Dakin, Geoff Day, Michael Fontes, Bernard Holiday, Jane Hughes, Anthony Lafferty, Hester Lees-Jeffries, Lachlan Mackinnon, Charles Moseley (87), Michael Nevin, Lucia Quinault, Simon Taylor and Rob Wyke — to all of whom this book is gratefully dedicated.

2011
ed. Paulo Coelho

INSPIRATIONS
Selections from Classic Literature

'I remember having to choose from the vast collection of Penguin Classics and feeling that what lay ahead of me was of titanic proportions. Imagine: from the *Rig Veda* (7) to *Lady Chatterley* (291) — how could I possibly make any sense of the great variety of books that throughout my life have fed my imagination?'

In 2008, the Brazilian author Paulo Coelho was invited to survey the Penguin Classics list and assemble a personal anthology of texts that had inspired him and his writing. He came up with an idiosyncratic selection, arranged into four sections named after the classical elements of Water, Earth, Air and Fire. Among his chosen authors are Sun Tzu (12), Rumi (102), Niccolò Machiavelli (120), Mary Shelley (204), Lewis Carroll (232), Oscar Wilde (244), Leopold Sacher-Masoch (352) and Rabindranath Tagore (387).

'An anthology — I came to discover — comes from the Greek words meaning a flower-gathering — in other words, a bouquet of flowers,' Coelho writes. '[…] An anthology is not only a collection of texts or poems, but a gift, something we arrange, according to our sensitivities, to give to others. […] In this case, the books that I choose to present to you lie in front of me as a vast field of flowers, stretching infinitely into time's horizon.'